Understanding Contemporary Africa

UNDERSTANDING

Introductions to the States and Regions of the Contemporary World

Understanding Contemporary Africa, 6th edition
edited by Peter J. Schraeder

Understanding Contemporary Asia Pacific, 2nd edition
edited by Katherine Palmer Kaup

Understanding the Contemporary Caribbean, 2nd edition
edited by Richard S. Hillman and Thomas J. D'Agostino

Understanding Contemporary China, 5th edition
edited by Robert E. Gamer and Stanley W. Toops

Understanding Contemporary India, 3rd edition
edited by Neil DeVotta and Sumit Ganguly

Understanding Contemporary Latin America, 4th edition
edited by Richard S. Hillman and Thomas J. D'Agostino

Understanding the Contemporary Middle East, 5th edition
edited by Jillian Schwedler

Understanding Contemporary Russia, 2nd edition
edited by Michael L. Bressler

SIXTH EDITION

Understanding Contemporary Africa

edited by

Peter J. Schraeder

BOULDER
LONDON

Published in the United States of America in 2020 by
Lynne Rienner Publishers, Inc.
1800 30th Street, Suite 314, Boulder, Colorado 80301
www.rienner.com

and in the United Kingdom by
Lynne Rienner Publishers, Inc.
Gray's Inn House, 127 Clerkenwell Road, London EC1 5DB

Library of Congress Cataloging-in-Publication Data
Names: Schraeder, Peter J., editor.
Title: Understanding contemporary Africa / edited by Peter J. Schraeder.
Other titles: Understanding (Boulder, Colo.)
Description: 6th edition. | Boulder, Colorado : Lynne Rienner Publishers, Inc., 2020. | Series: Understanding | Includes bibliographical references and index. | Summary: "An unparalleled introduction to the complexities of Africa today"— Provided by publisher.
Identifiers: LCCN 2020008498 | ISBN 9781626378940 (paperback)
Subjects: LCSH: Africa—Politics and government—1960– | Africa—Social conditions—1960–
Classification: LCC DT30.5 .U536 2020 | DDC 960.32—dc23
LC record available at https://lccn.loc.gov/2020008498

British Cataloguing in Publication Data
A Cataloguing in Publication record for this book
is available from the British Library.

Printed and bound in the United States of America

The paper used in this publication meets the requirements of the American National Standard for Permanence of Paper for Printed Library Materials Z39.48-1992.

5 4 3 2

To Kate:
You still, and always will, complete me.

To Max, Marianne, and Pat:
You always inspire me to be a better father and writer.

To Rex:
Our daily walks always help me think things through.

Contents

Illustrations

Maps

Tables

Figures

Photographs

Preface

This sixth edition of *Understanding Contemporary Africa*, fully revised and expanded, documents and analyzes the most significant social, economic, and political developments taking place on the African continent. The success of all five previous editions of the book confirms our belief that—with its broad scope that covers all regions of the African continent, up-to-date and in-depth chapters on a variety of topics, and attention to readability for students and the general reader—it is not only a valuable text for undergraduate African studies courses, but it is also a vital source of cutting-edge scholarship for teachers and other professionals who wish to know more about the reality of Africa in the third decade of the twenty-first century.

The cornerstone of this book is our collective deep appreciation for interdisciplinary collaboration. The information in each chapter represents the best of the current research and thinking in various departments and disciplines of study, including anthropology, business, development studies, economics, geography, history, international studies, political science, public policy, religious studies, social justice, sociology, and urban studies. As a result, the volume combines the classic contributions of earlier volumes, such as chapters on African history, politics, and international relations, with new contributions, such as chapters on environmental challenges, public health, and the rights of Africa's lesbian, gay, bisexual, transgender, intersex, and queer (LGBTIQ) communities. Although the collaborators have produced a well-integrated volume, each chapter is designed to stand alone. This allows instructors to assign readings to meet their needs by individual topic.

We recognize that our efforts in this volume will not be perfect. We therefore look forward to receiving your impressions of our collective work as you, the reader, either begin or continue your journey to understand and appreciate the African continent.

* * *

It is an honor and a privilege to serve as the editor of the sixth edition of *Understanding Contemporary Africa*. This was truly a collective endeavor, with fifteen African studies specialists collaborating to update one of the most popular interdisciplinary introductions to contemporary Africa. We all incurred a great number of personal and professional debts along the way that are far too many to acknowledge individually, including debts to students, colleagues, family, and friends from across the globe and especially the African continent. We nonetheless wish to provide a special collective note of thanks to April A. Gordon, a sociologist, and Donald L. Gordon, a political scientist, who served as the coeditors of the first five editions of this text, beginning in 1992. They have worked tirelessly throughout their careers to advance knowledge and understanding of Africa. In so doing, they have inspired thousands of students, teachers, policymakers, and general readers—including each of us—to explore Africa from an interdisciplinary lens and to make learning about Africa a lifelong endeavor.

As the editor of the book, I wish to extend a special thanks to two additional individuals: Nora Rybarczyk, my department's senior administrative assistant, and Michael J. Schumacher, my PhD research assistant. Their invaluable support and good cheer were crucial to the successful completion of this book.

1

Introducing Africa

Peter J. Schraeder

Africa's initial wave of independence from European colo-nial rule took place during the 1950s as marked by the independence of Libya (1951), Morocco (1956), Tunisia (1956), the Sudan (1956), Ghana (1957), and Guinea (1958). Since that time, the African continent has been marked by a series of historic developments. In the early decades, notable turning points included the founding of the Organization of African Unity (OAU) in 1963 as the first pan-African organization of African countries to be headquartered on African soil (it is now known as the African Union, or AU); the establishment in 1975 of the Economic Community of West African States (ECOWAS) as one of six major African groupings designed to promote regional economic cooperation and integration;[1] and the selection in 1986 of Wole Soyinka, a Nigerian writer and political activist, as the first African to win the Nobel Prize for literature, underscoring the growing recognition of African literature within international literary circles.[2] More recently, landmark events have included South Africa's transition to black majority rule in 1994 under one of the globe's most progressive constitutions that "forbids discrimination on the basis of sex, gender or sexual orientation" (Section 9, South African Constitution); the election of Ellen Johnson Sirleaf as Africa's first female African president in 2005, thereby breaking a gender-based, political glass ceiling; and Tunisia's 2011 Dignity Revolution that ushered in democratic rule and sparked other pro-democracy movements, especially in North Africa and the neighboring Middle East.

As we progress through the third decade of the twenty-first century, the primary purpose of *Understanding Contemporary Africa* is to take stock of the socioeconomic and political-military events and challenges that continue to affect and transform the African continent. This chapter is designed to aid you in that effort by setting out some basic themes that have guided the contributors to this volume. It also includes a summary of the chapters that follow.

Understanding Contemporary Africa

Kaleidoscope of Diversity

Several themes are important to consider as we seek to understand contemporary Africa. The first is that the African continent constitutes a kaleidoscope of diversity. At the most basic level, Africa is comprised of fifty-four sovereign countries, with South Sudan emerging in 2011 as the most recent African country to gain independence (see Map 1.1). Africa's countries range in size from the small island state of Seychelles (Africa's smallest country at 174 square miles/451 square kilometers) to the medium-sized Côte d'Ivoire (Africa's twenty-eighth largest country at 124,503 square miles/322,460 square kilometers) and the geographical giant of Algeria (Africa's largest country at 905,355 square miles/2,381,741 square kilometers). To put these sizes into context: whereas the Seychelles is 43 percent *smaller* than New York City, and Côte d'Ivoire is approximately the size of the state of New Mexico, Algeria is approximately one-third the size of the continental United States. The African continent is also home to a kaleidoscope of political beliefs and orientations. African leaders have pledged their loyalties at various times and in various degrees to the global ideologies of capitalism, fascism, Islamic revivalism, Maoism, Marxism, and socialism. They subsequently have employed these beliefs to create an array of political systems, including civilian and military dictatorships; monarchies and Islamic republics; liberal and illiberal democracies; and presidential, semi-presidential, and parliamentary regimes.

The socioeconomic kaleidoscope of the African continent is equally diverse. The population size of African countries ranges from approximately 96,000 inhabitants in the Seychelles (Africa's least populous country) to nearly 191 million citizens in Nigeria (Africa's most populous country). The literacy rates of these populations range from a high of 94 percent in South Africa to a low of 15 percent in Niger. In terms of ethnic diversity, at one extreme there exist relatively homogeneous countries such as Botswana, whose Setswana people are nonetheless divided among several clan families. At the other extreme are countries such as Nigeria, which is home to nearly 250 ethnic groups. In terms of economics, oil-rich Equatorial Guinea boasts an annual gross national income (GNI) per capita of over $7,060 while economically impoverished Burundi struggles with an annual GNI per capita of less than $290. The range of trade indicators is particularly acute. When one combines an African country's imports and

Map 1.1 Contemporary Africa

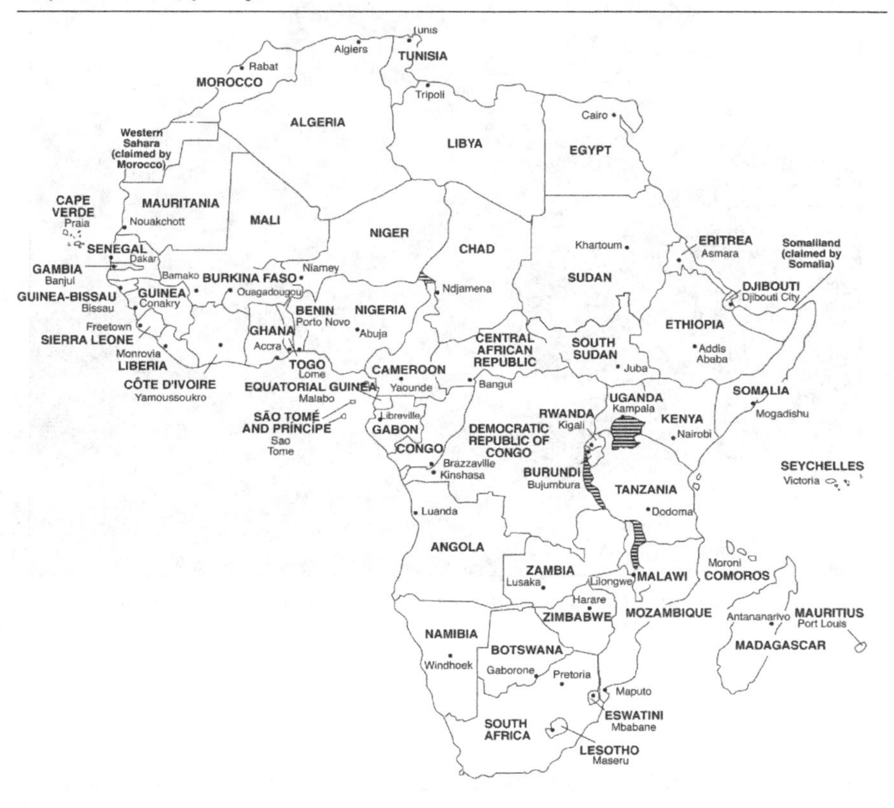

Credit: Peter J. Schraeder

exports as a percentage of the African continent's total trade output, South Africa emerges as an economic powerhouse with over $29 billion in imports/exports (19 percent of the African total). In contrast, São Tomé and Príncipe enjoys the lowest amount of roughly $13 million, or less than 1 percent of the African total. An appendix titled Basic Political Data at the end of this book provides additional socioeconomic and political data for all fifty-four African countries.

Continental Perspective

Africa's diversity does not mean that we as observers are unable to uncover and discuss general trends applicable to the entire African continent. Indeed, each of the contributing authors to this book has attempted

US Department of State

Liberian president Ellen Johnson Sirleaf is the first elected female head of state in Africa, serving from 2006 to 2018.

to explain general trends while at the same time being mindful of elements unique to a specific African region or country. Toward this end, a second theme of this book is that a comprehensive understanding of contemporary Africa requires a continental perspective inclusive of all five regions of the African continent. Specifically, one must focus on both North Africa, often referred to as Saharan Africa, as well as the four regions of Central, East, Southern, and West Africa, typically referred to as sub-Saharan Africa (see Map 1.2). Traditional studies of the African continent often focus exclusively on sub-Saharan Africa. This is due to the argument that several dimensions of contemporary North Africa, such as the greater influence of Arab culture and Islam, combine to make that region unique and, therefore, noncomparable to neighboring regions in the south. Although we recognize that specific geographical regions, countries, and even regions within countries may embody varying degrees of uniqueness, this book nonetheless seeks to examine the continental trends that transcend individual regions and thus provide us with a comprehensive understanding of contemporary Africa.

Map 1.2 Regions of Contemporary Africa

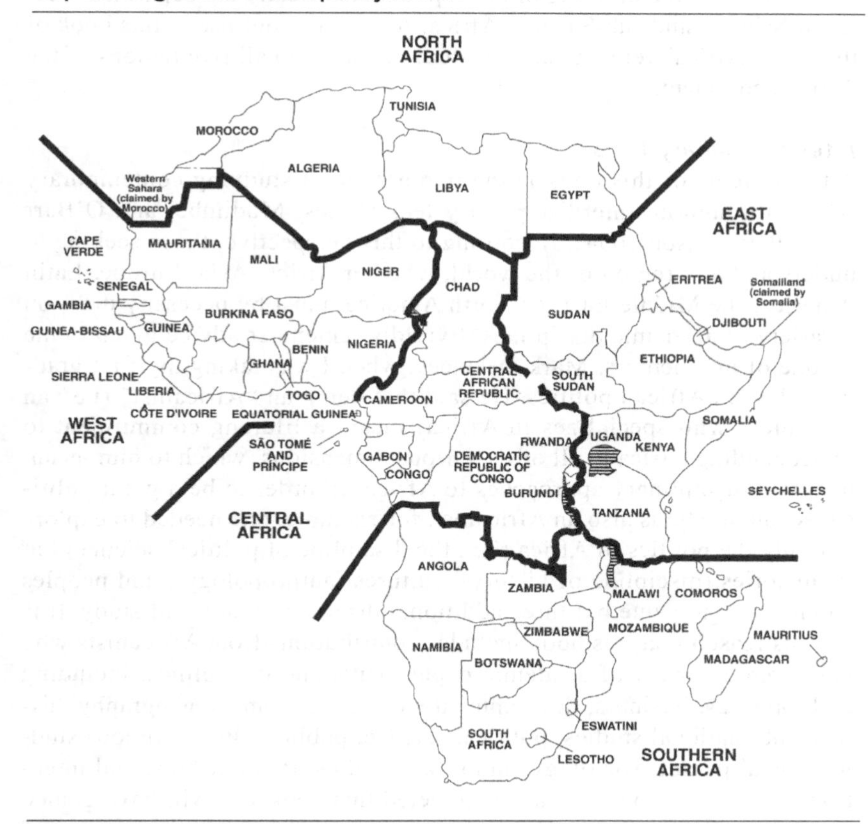

Credit: Peter J. Schraeder

Several examples demonstrate the necessity of adopting a continental perspective. From a historical viewpoint, one must focus on both North Africa and sub-Saharan Africa to have a comprehensive understanding of the trans-Saharan trade network (Austen 2010). Second, any comprehensive understanding of the rise of African nationalism and the emergence of the contemporary independence era must begin with that region—North Africa—which was part of the first wave of nationalism and independence during the 1950s. Similarly, if one wishes to understand the rise of Islamist and pan-Islamist movements, one must have a firm understanding of the predominantly Muslim countries throughout North, East, Central, and West Africa. In short, a comprehensive understanding of contemporary

Africa requires the bridging of the gap that historically has separated studies of Saharan and sub-Saharan Africa. As a result, our use in this book of the term "Africa" refers to all fifty-four countries in all five regions of the African continent.

Interdisciplinary Lens

A third theme of this book is the importance of studying contemporary Africa through an interdisciplinary lens (Bates, Mudimbe, and O'Barr 1993; P. Robinson 2004). According to this perspective, those seeking to understand any region of the world, whether Africa, Asia, Europe, Latin America, the Middle East, or North America, must by necessity draw on a variety of academic disciplines. I vividly remember advice given to me by one of my mentors, Mark Delancey, when I was taking my first graduate class in African politics. He said that being an "Africanist" (i.e., an individual who specializes in Africa) meant a lifelong commitment to understanding Africa in all of its various dimensions, which to him meant different disciplinary approaches to Africa. In order to be a great political scientist who is also an Africanist, for example, one needed to explore not only the politics of Africa (i.e., the discipline of political science) but its histories (discipline of history), cultures (anthropology), and peoples (sociology), to name but three additional disciplinary areas of study. It is for this reason that this book includes contributions from Africanists who hail from a variety of academic departments and disciplines, including anthropology, business, development studies, economics, geography, history, international studies, political science, public policy, religious studies, social justice, sociology, and urban studies. It is our hope and intention that by the time you have completed this book you will have gained an introductory understanding of how various disciplines examine and present the African continent.

The interdisciplinary field of African studies, like its counterparts in other regions of the world, has spawned a large number of academic, professional, and government institutions that subscribe to the interdisciplinary ideal. In the People's Republic of China (PRC), prominent academic institutions include the School of Asian and African Studies at both Beijing Foreign Studies University and Shanghai International Studies University. In Germany, the Institute of African Studies at the University of Leipzig is renowned for its work on Africa, as are similar German institutes at the University of Bayreuth and Humboldt University. In Russia, a leading institution is the Institute of Asian and African Studies at Moscow State University. Not surprisingly, the African continent is home to several university-based African studies centers, such as the Kwame Nkrumah Center for African Studies at the University of Ghana (Legon campus), the Centre for African Studies at the University of Cape Town in South Africa, the Institute of Africa and Diaspora Studies at the University of Lagos (Nigeria), and the University of Addis Ababa in Ethiopia.

The United States has a large network of academic institutions that promote the interdisciplinary study of Africa. The largest of these include the African Studies National Resource Centers (NRCs) at US universities that are funded with Title VI funding from the US Department of Education. For the 2019–2021 funding cycle, ten universities were NRC recipients: Boston University, Harvard University, Howard University, Indiana University, Michigan State University, University of California at Berkeley, University of Florida, University of Kansas, University of North Carolina at Chapel Hill, and University of Wisconsin at Madison. These institutions are but the tip of the iceberg of a large network of African studies degree programs and departments that exist throughout the United States, such as the African studies minor at Gustavus Adolphus College in St. Peter, Minnesota; the Alliance for Education, Science, Engineering, and Design with Africa at Pennsylvania State University; the Center for African and African American Studies at the University of Texas at Austin; and the Institute for African-American and African Studies at the University of Virginia.

Sinda Redissi

"Game Over" was one of the iconic themes of protesters who successfully overthrew the Tunisian dictatorship of Zine el-Abidine Ben Ali in 2011.

Moreover, almost all universities, colleges, and community colleges have at least one course and typically many more that focus on various aspects of contemporary Africa. It is highly likely that you are enrolled in one of these classes if you are reading this introductory chapter.

The most prominent US-based professional organization that promotes the interdisciplinary study of Africa is the African Studies Association (ASA). Originally founded in 1957 by thirty-five Africanists, the ASA is the leading US professional association for scholars and practitioners interested in promoting and sharing knowledge related to Africa. The ASA publishes one of the leading interdisciplinary African Studies journals, the *African Studies Review*, as well as another disciplinary journal, *History in Africa*. It also sponsors an annual academic meeting that is typically attended by more than 2,000 participants. The interdisciplinary nature of this conference is demonstrated by the more than twenty panel themes under which papers may fall, ranging from the classic categories of Anthropology, Education, History, Literature, and Philosophy, to more specialized categories of Extractive Industries, Health and Healing, Popular Culture and Media, Refugees and Borders, and Women, Gender, and Sexualities. Other prominent Africa-related professional associations across the globe include the African Studies Association of Australasia and the Pacific, the Canadian Association of African Studies, the Nordic Association of African Studies, the Royal African Society and the African Studies Association of the United Kingdom, and the Africa-Europe Group for Interdisciplinary Studies (AEGIS).

Governments also subscribe to the interdisciplinary ideal. The various government agencies and bureaucracies that are tasked with foreign policy typically maintain both thematically oriented offices (e.g., counterterrorism) and regional offices that focus on geographical areas of the world (e.g., Africa). In the United States, all three of the national security bureaucracies that principally deal with US foreign relations—the State Department, the Central Intelligence Agency (CIA), and the Department of Defense (Pentagon)—maintain extensive Africa-related bureaus. The State Department has maintained a Bureau of African Affairs since 1957 that largely focuses on sub-Saharan Africa; North Africa falls under the responsibility of the Bureau for Near Eastern Affairs (Anyaso 2011). The CIA's Directorate of Intelligence, which is tasked with providing the president with the most up-to-date analysis of a given topic or region, combines sub-Saharan Africa within a broader Bureau of Asian, Pacific, Latin American, and African Analysis, with North Africa falling under the responsibility of the Bureau of Near Eastern and South Asian Analysis. Only the Pentagon places the vast majority of the African continent, including North Africa, under one unified administrative structure: the United States Africa Command (AFRICOM), which is headquartered in Stuttgart, Germany. The one exception is Egypt, which falls under the responsibility of the US Central Command (CENTCOM). Regardless of how governments and their bureaucracies divide responsibilities for Africa, the common guiding principle is the importance of training area specialists who have broad knowledge that transcends individual disciplines.

Historical Periods

Finally, a note is in order regarding terminology related to different eras of African history. For the purposes of this volume, African history is divided into three broad historical periods. The first is the precolonial independence era (prior to 1884), which captures the rise and fall of hundreds of independent African political systems. This is followed by the era of colonial rule (1884–1951), in which the vast majority of previously independent African political systems were replaced by colonial states controlled by Belgium, France, Germany, Italy, Portugal, Spain, and the United Kingdom. The Berlin Conference of 1884, a gathering composed principally of the European great powers that consecrated the creation of formal empires in Africa, marks the beginning of this period. The third and most recent period, the contemporary independence era (1951–present), marks the end of colonialism and the beginning of the emergence of the fifty-four countries that currently comprise the African continent. This period began with Libya's independence in 1951 and continues today.

We have also distinguished between specific periods during the contemporary independence era. For example, the Cold War era (1947–1989) marked a period of intense ideological competition between the United States and the former Soviet Union and their respective allies that played out in all regions of the world, including the African continent. The post–Cold War era (1989–present) began with the fall of the Berlin Wall in 1989 and the breakup of the former Soviet Union into fifteen independent republics, with Russia as the largest successor country. This era has also been referred to as Africa's "second independence," Africa's "second liberation," or as the "African wave of democratization," due to the process of democratization that began in 1989 and has affected the entire continent. In Africa, this era also has been referred to as the "African renaissance" (rebirth), as witnessed by the construction of the Monument to the African Renaissance in Dakar, Senegal, that is pictured in this chapter.

Chapters That Follow

The remainder of this book is divided into thirteen chapters. The first two chapters are designed to provide important background material. Chapter 2 by Jeffrey W. Neff and Adam Hii provides a geographic preface, including perceptions of African geography throughout history, the diversity of

Monument to the African Renaissance, located in Dakar, Senegal.

Peter J. Schraeder

Africa's natural regions, and contemporary geographic challenges. Chapter 3 by Thomas O'Toole and Kirstie Lynn Dobbs provides the historical backdrop of contemporary Africa. They set out the "peopling of Africa" (including Africa's role as the "cradle of humankind"); the rise and fall of centralized and stateless polities throughout African history; the era of trade, exploration, and conquest; and the imposition of colonial rule.

Chapters 4–6 set out the basic political, economic, and international dimensions of contemporary Africa. In Chapter 4, Peter J. Schraeder examines the evolution of African politics. Among the topics discussed are the impacts of colonialism, the rise of nationalism and emergence of the contemporary independence era, the centralization of power and personal rule associated with African dictatorships, the emergence of single-party political systems and rise of military coups d'état and military governance, the African wave of democratization and various types of political transitions it has spawned, and an assessment of African politics and especially Africa's democratic experiments during the last three decades. Michael Kevane in Chapter 5 focuses on African economies and development. After setting out what economic development means for a typical African citizen, he explores the realities of African development as of 2020 and the prospects and threats to accelerated development, including civil conflict, pandemics, and climate change. In Chapter 6, Peter J. Schraeder explores the evolution of African international relations. He especially focuses on the formulation and implementation of African foreign policy, pan-Africanism and the AU, regional economic cooperation and integration, and the evolving roles of foreign powers, the United Nations, and international financial institutions in African international relations.

The next three chapters (7–9) explore challenges confronted by African citizens and policymakers. In Chapter 7, Jeffrey W. Paller explores population and urbanization. After first setting out the "contentious politics" of African urbanization, he discusses the historical legacies of urban settlement and belonging, global goals and tensions in Africa's megacities, and institutions and development in Africa's secondary cities. Amy S. Patterson in Chapter 8 focuses on public health challenges in Africa. Among the themes discussed are the roles of multiple actors and competing approaches to health governance, the impacts of communicable diseases (such as HIV/AIDS and the Ebola virus) and noncommunicable diseases (e.g., schistosomiasis and mental health disorders) on African society, and the "political prioritization" of health (i.e., when and how does health care become a priority?). In Chapter 9, Garth A. Myers discusses Africa's environmental challenges. He first sets out the political ecology perspective that forms the basis of his chapter (i.e., one cannot see environmental challenges strictly as natural phenomena). He subsequently explores six environmental challenges: impacts of global climate change; environmental challenges of economic development; African parks and wildlife; population, health, and the environment; piracy and the environment; and urban environmental challenges in Africa.

Chapters 10–13 focus on various aspects of Africa's social environments. In Chapter 10, Barbara G. Hoffman explores the relationship between family and kinship in African societies. After first setting out types and terms related to kinship, she describes the relationship between family and social organization as well as between globalization and urbanization. Gretchen Bauer in Chapter 11 explores the evolving roles of African women from the precolonial and colonial eras through the contemporary independence era. She specifically focuses on women in political transitions, women's political leadership in Africa today, and African feminism. In Chapter 12, Marc Epprecht, S. N. Nyeck, and S. M. Rodriguez examine lesbian, gay, bisexual, transgender, intersex, and queer (LGBTIQ) rights in Africa. They do so by setting out the historical and cultural context of LGBTIQ rights as well as homophobia and resistance to those rights as demonstrated by the case study of Uganda from 1999 to the present. Finally, Ambrose Moyo and Peter J. Schraeder in Chapter 13 explore the role of religion in Africa. This is accomplished by discussing the nature and trends associated with the three broad religious traditions in Africa: African traditional religions, Christianity, and Islam. This chapter also includes a discussion of the roles of minority religions in Africa, such as Hinduism and Judaism.

Chapter 14 sets out several points of reflection regarding future trends and prospects. These are intended as food for thought as you continue with your exploration of contemporary Africa.

Notes

1. The other five regional integration schemes are the East African Community (EAC); the Southern African Development Community (SADC); the Economic Community of Central African States (ECCAS); the Intergovernmental Authority on Development (IGAD); and the Arab Maghreb Union (AMU).

2. The other Africans to win the Nobel Prize for Literature include Naguib Mahfouz of Egypt (1988), Nadine Gordimer of South Africa (1991), and John M. Coetzee of South Africa (2003).

2

A Geographic Preface

Jeffrey W. Neff and Adam Hii

Africa is one of the most diverse geographical entities in the world. It is home to more than 1.2 billion people who are divided among more than 2,000 geographically distinct ethnic groups that speak more than 2,000 geographically distinct languages. It is also home to fifty-four sovereign countries that are divided among five major geographical regions—Central, East, North, Southern, and West Africa—that serve as gateways to the Western Hemisphere, Europe, the Middle East, and Asia. One, therefore, could expect that Africa would be one of the most studied regions in the world.

In the United States, however, Africa is arguably the least known and understood region for a variety of reasons. These range from the fact that the United States was not a colonial power in Africa and, therefore, has a limited historical connection to the African continent, to Africa's low standing in the US foreign policy establishment (Schraeder 1994a, 1994b). The current geographic hierarchy of US foreign policy puts Europe, including Russia, in first place; Asia and the rise of the People's Republic of China (PRC) as a global power in second place; the Middle East (most notably due to ongoing wars) in third place; and Latin America and the Caribbean in fourth place. Where is Africa in this geographical pecking order? Last—it is the region of least perceived importance (Schraeder 2018). Moreover, US citizens typically have a firmly engrained but misguided image of Africa as an untamed, unsettled continent with vast herds of wild animals, spectacular gorges and waterfalls, and trackless jungles, forests, and great deserts (Keim and Somerville 2018). Although such stereotypical images are not limited to the United States, they need revision for anyone seeking a more accurate portrayal of Africa's socioeconomic and political-military realities. For these reasons, an introduction to the geography of the vast and varied African continent is needed.

The remainder of this chapter is divided into six sections. The first section sets out how African geography has been viewed throughout history, from the ancient Greeks and Romans to the Ming Dynasty of China of the fourteenth century, to the European colonial powers of the sixteenth century. Subsequent sections explore the geographies of Africa's climate, vegetation patterns, continental drift and physical environment, and resource base. A concluding section sets out geographic realities that continue to define contemporary Africa. In so doing, this chapter is designed as a geographic preface to the various topics of contemporary Africa that are explored in greater depth in the chapters that follow.

African Geography Throughout History

Africa has a long history of contact with outside cultures. Archaeological digs indicate that North Africa, and in particular Egypt, had contact with ancient Greece from as long ago as 2000 BCE. Although there are no surviving writings from this earliest of eras, the carbon dating of cultural artifacts demonstrates that Greece engaged in trade with Egypt and the North African littoral. Several centuries later, the works of Homer, in particular *The Iliad* and *The Odyssey,* provide a glimpse of how the ancient Greeks perceived Africa. In these works, there are references to Ethiopians as living near the edges of the earth and having a privileged relationship with the gods by living near them. These writings suggest that the African continent was shrouded in mystery and intrigue as a land somewhat removed from the rest of the world.

The Phoenicians, who created a maritime empire throughout the Mediterranean region, potentially realized a remarkable, Africa-related geographical feat during the fifth century BCE, according to James Delehanty, a geographer with the African Studies Program at the University of Wisconsin at Madison. "One interesting case comes down to us from the Greek historian Herodotus, who in the fifth century BCE . . . wrote a brief but tantalizing report of a sea journey by Phoenicians, organized by King Necho II of Egypt, around the landmass we call Africa (which Herodotus called Libya), undertaken about two hundred years before Herodotus's time" (Delehanty 2014:9). Although there is no documentation from the time of the supposed voyage to prove that it actually took place, Delehanty (2014: 10) notes that it is "pleasant and plausible to believe that it occurred." The significance of this event, if corroborating evidence could be found, is that "at least one small group of Africans, probably a few Phoenician adventurers from Egypt, learned of the entirety of the African landmass as long as twenty-seven hundred years ago" (Delehanty 2014:10).

The victory and expansion of the Roman Empire after it defeated the Carthaginian Empire in the Third Punic War in 146 BCE fostered a greater international understanding of African geography. Indeed, it is noted that the term "Africa" potentially emerged from this era. "It possibly comes from 'Afer,' which in the Phoenician language was the name for the region around Carthage," explains Delehanty (2014:10–11). "According to this theory, Roman geographers, needing a word for the landmass to the south, borrowed 'Afer,' Latinized it, and broadened its application to the entire continent south of the Mediterranean (much as Herodotus had used 'Libya' in the same way, for the same purpose, a few hundred years before)" (Delehanty 2014:11).

Moving forward, the Romans had a markedly different relationship with the African continent. North Africa was divided into provinces and incorporated into the empire. The North African centerpiece of this empire was the province of Africa Proconsularis that included the western portion of present-day Libya, most of present-day Tunisia, and the eastern portion of present-day Algeria. Other North African provinces included Mauretania Caesariensis and Mauretania Tingitana to the west (including portions of present-day Algeria and Morocco) and Cyrenaica and Aegyptus to the east (incorporating portions of present-day Libya and Egypt). While there is a popular belief that the Sahara Desert made it impossible for the ancient civilizations of the Mediterranean region to interact with sub-Saharan Africa in a meaningful way, evidence of Roman artifacts along the Niger River in West Africa shows that Rome had a more detailed knowledge of the continent than its predecessors. Although the Romans were largely focused on North Africa like the Greeks and Phoenicians before them, military expeditions, commerce, and the slave trade expanded geographic knowledge of peoples and political systems in sub-Saharan Africa. Nonetheless, the process of taking resources and slaves from Africa would become a recurring trend for the region, in which outside powers viewed Africa as a land for profit and plunder.

Other, especially Asian, empires had important contact with Africa as well. One of the most fascinating examples involves the seven voyages of a fleet of Chinese ships from the Ming Dynasty led by Zheng He between 1405 and 1433. During this period, Zheng He visited the coastal areas of East Africa four times. According to Philip Snow in his classic book, *The Star Raft: China's Encounter with Africa*, Zheng He referred to his fleet as a "Star Raft" to "indicate that the fleet carried to exotic regions the star-like radiance of an ambassador from the imperial throne" (Snow 1988:xix). Chinese maps of the East African coast from the era clearly demonstrate Chinese geographical knowledge of East Africa. Additional proof of the exchange of gifts and commerce that took place as part of Zheng He's voyages was the arrival in Beijing in 1415 of a giraffe from East Africa.

Peter J. Schraeder

These Roman ruins in Dougga, Tunisia, serve as a reminder that the Roman Empire maintained an extensive network of cities and towns across North Africa.

"Its arrival was the climax of a slow growth of contact between imperial China and the scattered communities of the East Africa coast," explains Snow (1988:1). "This convergence took many centuries, and no one can be entirely sure at what point it began." These East African forays nonetheless ended soon after Zheng He's voyages as China turned inward, only to be resuscitated five hundred years later during the Cold War and especially during the last two decades. The PRC's determination to build on these early links is demonstrated by the publication in 2017 of a book, *China in Africa: In Zheng He's Footsteps*, retracing Zheng He's points of contact and travel throughout East Africa (Xinfeng 2017).

Later European expansion into Africa was marked by Prince Henry the Navigator exploring the West African coastline beginning in 1434, followed by Vasco de Gama's 1497–1499 voyage that followed the African coastline around Southern Africa's Cape of Good Hope and into the Indian Ocean. It was during this period that external, principally European, powers gained a more complete picture of African geography, as first Portugal in the sixteenth century, followed by the Netherlands in the seventeenth century and the United Kingdom during the eighteenth and nineteenth centuries, emerged as global hegemonic powers. Although the European slave trade and subsequent exploration efforts were concerned with resource exploitation and expanding European empires, it is important to note that that colonization followed geographic imperatives (Mentan 2018). In the case of the United Kingdom, for example, expansion along the Nile River was part of a quest to establish a line of colonies from Egypt in the north to South Africa at the southern tip of the continent. It was also during this period that European expansionism embraced an increasingly negative perception of Africans, perhaps to rationalize slavery and the imposition of direct European control over the continent. This perception was captured by European rationales for their Africa-related conquests, such as British pronouncements concerning the "white man's burden" and the French pronouncements of their "*mission civilisatrice*" ("civilizing mission"). European colonization that advanced from the sixteenth through the twentieth centuries was one of the major forces in shaping the geopolitical landscape seen in Africa today. It also set the stage for some of the contemporary geographic challenges discussed later in this chapter.

Geography of Climate

Nature wields a much heavier hand in Africa than in the industrialized world in directly influencing the welfare of hundreds of millions of people. In the developed world, people have been insulated to some degree from the effects of drought, flood, plagues, and other natural hazards and cycles. As a result, basic knowledge of natural phenomena and processes is required to understand contemporary Africa.

One of the most powerful environmental mechanisms affecting life and survival in Africa is a phenomenon called the Intertropical Convergence Zone (ITCZ) (see Map 2.1). The ITCZ represents a meteorological dynamic whereby large-scale airflows from generally opposite directions converge or meet, creating a relatively constant updraft of displaced air. The vertical movement is supplemented by buoyant heated air from the sun-soaked, warm surface conditions of the tropical regions. This rising air cools off rapidly, causing atmospheric water vapor to condense into droplets first, then precipitation (Strahler and Strahler 2005:258–260). At least, this is the ideal chain of events, and the ITCZ is the primary rainmaking mechanism not only in Africa but throughout the tropical world. Rainfall often occurs as daily thunderstorms and can be torrential during the rainy season.

An important geographic feature captured by Map 2.1 is that the ITCZ shifts pronouncedly from June to January. This shift is caused by changing earth-sun relationships during the year and by the inclination of the earth's axis. This motion is crucial for the delivery of rainfall to Africa and gives

Map 2.1 Natural Regions and the Intertropical Convergence Zone (ITCZ)

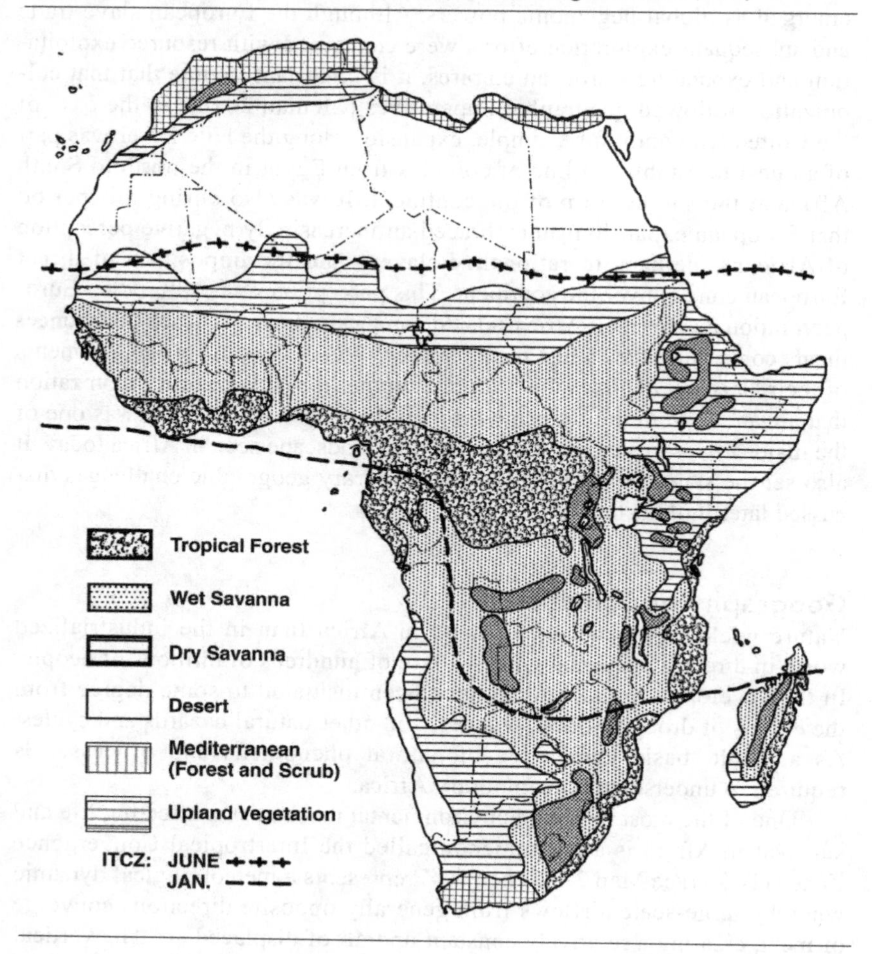

Credit: Jeffrey W. Neff

the continent its wet-and-dry seasonality. When the ITCZ is stationed at its northern June position, the rainy season is on—or should be—and Southern Africa is dry. The southward migration of the ITCZ signals rain for the south and the onset of the dry season in the north. And so it has gone, century after century. Some regions, such as the tropical forest belt, get longer rainy seasons and more rain than others, and some regions face greater unpredictability, or precipitation variation, such as the semiarid Sahel and the semiarid Kalahari. The importance of rainfall in these unpredictable regions influences not only farming and animal rearing but culture as well. For example, Botswana, which is almost exclusively in the Kalahari, has even named its currency "pula," the Setswana word for "rain." Sometimes the ITCZ misbehaves and does not shift when it is normally expected to or move where it usually should, which brings stress to the life that depends on it. Generally, though, farming societies throughout Africa continue to coordinate planting and harvesting with the ITCZ's rainmaking mechanism. Pastoralists move their cattle, and herds of wild animals migrate in similar response to seasonal moisture availability. Nature and people have adjusted to a rhythm of life tied to this slow, unending dance of the ITCZ back and forth across the length and breadth of the continent.

Vegetation Patterns

Map 2.1 also reveals the natural environments of Africa as depicted by vegetation patterns in a highly generalized rendition. The natural vegetation represents the long-term adjustment of complex plant communities to the conditions of the African climate. From a human perspective, these environmental regions possess very different capacities for life support, or "carrying capacity." Awareness of the potentials and the problems of these life zones is crucial for survival; exceeding their carrying capacities promises serious environmental penalties for the occupants, as discussed in Chapter 9.

Trouble spots abound in the drier margins. The semiarid, grassy steppe of the Sahel and the East African desert (parts of Ethiopia, Kenya, and Somalia), plagued by an unpredictable ITCZ and burgeoning populations, have been the scenes of human misery in the recent past. The specter of mass starvation brought on by drought and desertification in the semiarid regions of the dry savanna has been prominent and widely publicized, but not surprising. Tropical wet-and-dry climates have always been problematic for their human occupants. By the twenty-first century, expanding populations had seriously exceeded the carrying capacity of the more fragile, marginal zones.

Even the humid tropical forest of Africa is not immune to trouble. Here, the threats of drought and desertification are replaced by rampant deforestation, primarily from commercial logging, fuelwood gathering, and agricultural expansion. At current rates of loss, much of the easily accessible forests of coastal West Africa and East Africa will be nearly gone by the mid-twenty-first century. Probably only the relatively insulated interior forests of the eastern Congo Basin will survive. Without controls, they too could disappear by midcentury.

The more densely populated wet savanna will come under increasing pressure as population growth and the movement of environmental refugees from the deteriorating dry savanna place undue strains on its carrying capacity. But almost all of tropical Africa is marked by poor, infertile, sometimes sterile soils, and the wet savanna has only limited agricultural potential. Only temperate Southern Africa is soil rich. However, it cannot sustain more than a fraction of Africa's future food needs.

Africa's natural regions are fragile and seem destined for continuing problems. If predicted global climatic changes affect the already erratic character and behavior of the ITCZ, the human carrying capacity of these natural regions could be reduced rapidly, with tragic human consequences. The Intergovernmental Panel on Climate Change (IPCC) has identified several aspects of Africa's vulnerability. During the twentieth century, the continent warmed by 0.5 degrees Celsius or more over most of its area and experienced a rainfall decrease over large portions of the Sahel (Niang et al. 2014:1206–1211). Climate change models indicate warming trends across Africa ranging from 3 degrees Celsius (low scenario) to more than 6 degrees Celsius (high scenario) by the end of the twenty-first century, with the semiarid margins of the Sahara and central southern Africa likely to experience the greatest warming. Climate change of such magnitude will directly impact rainfall variability and seasonality, water resources supply and management, food productivity and security, biodiversity and ecosystem integrity, water-borne disease incidence and diffusion, coastal zone vulnerability to sea-level rise (especially in low-lying delta zones), and desertification rates (Boko et al. 2007:435–443).

These are not pleasant scenarios to contemplate, but every student of Africa should be aware of these possibilities. In the midst of the Sahelian drought of 1968–1974, for example, unusually large numbers of adult males in Burkina Faso and Niger left their villages to search for jobs in more favored agricultural areas to the south or in large towns such as Abidjan and Lagos in the richer coastal countries of Côte d'Ivoire and Nigeria. Such sudden movements placed heavy burdens on the meager support services and social balances of the destination areas (Caldwell 1977:95–96).

Elsewhere, human suffering caused by drought was compounded by armed conflict over the border between Ethiopia and Eritrea. The dispute, commencing in 1998, severely reduced each country's ability to respond effectively to the famine perpetuated by a lethal mix of natural and human factors. Recurring drought conditions in Somalia have uprooted tens of thousands of people and exacerbated social, political, and economic tensions in the region. In 1993, for example, massive drought—compounded by the collapse of the Somali state and fighting between clan-based guerrilla groups—put hundreds of thousands of Somalis at risk of starvation. This led to a US-led military intervention entitled Operation Restore Hope that initially opened food distribution centers to prevent a humanitarian crisis. In the end, however, US military involvement in Somalia led to increasing political-military tensions (Clarke and Herbst 1997).

Continental Drift and the Physical Environment

Until about 100 million years ago, the earth's landmasses were bound together as a supercontinent known as Pangaea. The southern landmasses constituted Gondwana, with present-day Africa the keystone. Through the phenomenon of plate tectonics, or continental drift, continent-size pieces of Gondwana began to migrate to their present positions. Specifically, the current landmasses of Antarctica, Australia, India, and North and South America all broke away from "mother" Africa, leaving it with its distinctive present-day shape and configuration. More importantly, the Africa landmass was left with relatively sharp, steep edges on all sides where the other plates tore away. In fact, the presence of deep rift valleys in East Africa suggests that this continental separation process is not yet complete. Africa may be further fractured and split along the rift zone. The Red Sea is an expanding rift, and East Africa could eventually pull away from the continent. The steep continental edge is known generally as the Great Escarpment, and it is very prominent in East and Southern Africa and somewhat less pronounced, but evident, in West Africa. It commences its sharp ascent just a few miles inland from the coast. Once topped, a high plateau-like landscape unfolds, interrupted by chains of volcanic mountains. Broad coastal lowlands are generally absent (Church 1967:23, 26).

One of the most important geographic impacts associated with this continental morphology can be referred to as "carriers and barriers," or any phenomena that influence, control, channel, restrict, or enhance human spatial processes and interactions. An examination of the patterns of Africa's railways and navigable waterways demonstrates this reality. Oddly, except for the Nile River and the lower Niger River, most river transport does not connect with the coast. Why not? It is primarily because of the barriers of waterfalls and rapids created where major rivers fall over or break through the Great Escarpment in their journeys to the sea. The most navigable stretches of water occur on interior sections of African rivers. Water access from the sea to Africa's interior is now and always has been physically restricted by the formidable barrier effect of the escarpment.

Nor does the Great Escarpment stimulate railway and road building between coast and interior. Some stretches of the escarpment tower 2,000 to 4,000 feet and more above the adjacent coastal lowland, especially in Southern Africa. An example is the Drakensberg, or the eastern portion of the Great Escarpment, which encloses the central Southern African plateau. Construction is difficult and very expensive; some rail lines were built only where access to valuable raw materials warranted the effort. Note too the dearth of natural harbors and major ports along Africa's steep, smooth, and regular coastline, highlighting the difficulty of access to the interior.

Movement within Africa has been easier. As a result, fairly lively levels of intraregional trade within and between Africa's regions developed over the centuries prior to European contact. In fact, most of the significant states and empires that evolved within Africa through the centuries did so in the interior of the continent, not along the coastal margins. By geographic edict, Africa's insular tendency was established long ago and was only slightly reoriented with the beginnings of the slave trade, first by the Arabs in East Africa and then more violently by the Europeans in the sixteenth century in the Atlantic coastal regions of West, Central, and Southern Africa. Still, for three centuries European contact and interest remained peripheral. The walls of "Fortress Africa" were violated and permanently breached by these "invaders" only in the mid- to late nineteenth century.

The Berlin Conference of 1884–1885 and the ensuing partition of Africa among the European colonial powers symbolized the inevitable geographic reorientation of Africa and Africans and a wholesale dismantling of their states, societies, and livelihoods, to be replaced by European models (Betts 1972). By the eve of World War I, a new type of fragmentation, as powerful in its own way as the Gondwana breakup 100 million years earlier, had changed the face of the "Mother Continent" forever. What became known as Europe's scramble for Africa was motivated by European competition to both expand its empires and secure raw materials that were increasingly in demand following the Industrial Revolution. The continent was divided among seven European powers (see Map 2.2). France and the United Kingdom secured the largest empires, creating colonies in all regions of the African continent. The remaining colonial powers obtained smaller numbers of colonies that were restricted to fewer regions. The partition included German colonies in East, Central, and West Africa; Portuguese colonies in West, Central, and Southern Africa; Italian colonies in North and East Africa; Spanish colonies in North and Central Africa; and Belgian colonies in Central Africa. The only African countries to escape this European partition were Ethiopia and Liberia. The historical and political dynamics of these periods are provided in greater detail in Chapters 3 and 4.

Resource Base

The huge, high block of mostly metamorphic rock that became post-Gondwana Africa is highly mineralized, ensuring that Africa is home to several categories of coveted raw materials and mineral resources. The continent is famous not only for its yield of gold—19 percent of the world's output in 2016—but also for 45 percent of global diamond output. Botswana alone comprised 22 percent of global diamond production in 2017. It is home to the world's largest producing diamond mine, De Beers Jwaneng, which produces 15 percent of the world's value of diamonds. A copper-laden zone straddling the borders of Zambia and the Democratic

Map 2.2 Colonial Partition on the Eve of World War I (with contemporary country names)

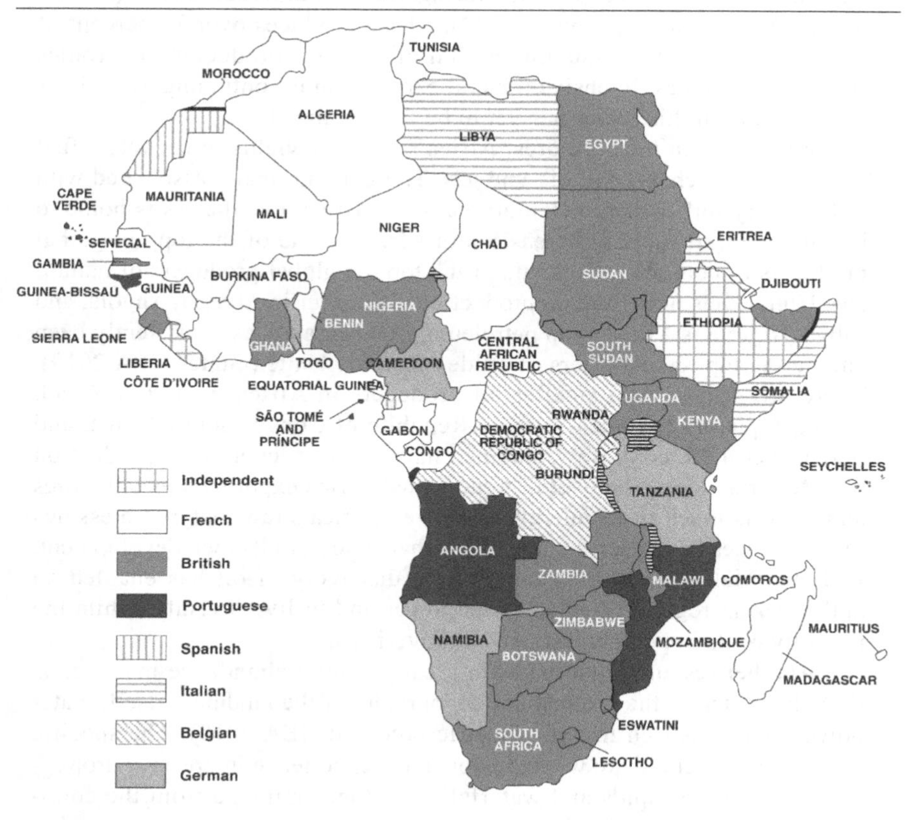

Credit: Peter J. Schraeder

Republic of Congo (DRC) and extending southward through Zimbabwe and South Africa accounted for about 9 percent of the world's production of that mineral in 2017. Africa provides about half of the world's cobalt, with mines concentrated in the DRC and a few in Zambia. Cobalt is a critical ferroalloy in the production of jet and rocket engines. In 2018, the DRC dominated production with its output of over 60 percent of the world's total of this strategic mineral (USGS 2018). Guinea ranked third in the world in 2017 in bauxite production (for aluminum) and is estimated to hold 26 percent of the world's total unmined bauxite holdings. South Africa accounts for over 40 percent of the global output of chromite, a strategic metallic mineral crucial to steel manufacturing in the industrial world (Moser, Singer, Moring, and Galloway 2012). Africa produces over 75 percent of the world's supply of tantalum, a vital mineral for producing electronics such as cell phones. Intensive mineral exploration is continuing as Africa's full potential in this sector has yet to be fully realized.

While rich in metallic ores, Africa's geology yields fewer fossil fuel occurrences, such as coal, oil, and gas. These are normally associated with sedimentary rather than metamorphic rock. Africa nonetheless is home to important fossil fuels. Whereas South Africa is one of the top ten global producers of coal, Algeria is one of the top ten global producers of natural gas. High levels of petroleum production also occur in Algeria, Angola, and Libya. Nigeria is Africa's top petroleum producer and has consistently been among the top ten exporters of crude oil to the United States (IEA 2019). There are also several smaller oil producers in Africa, including Chad, Egypt, Equatorial Guinea, Gabon, Republic of Congo, South Africa, and Sudan. Yet these countries combined have a lower level of oil production than Nigeria alone. The overall trend is that Africa exports its metallic ores and imports much of its energy. Moreover, Africa's raw material blessings in many cases have been a curse rather than a boon to its own development. In Equatorial Guinea, for example, the discovery of oil has enabled an authoritarian regime to enhance its power and to live lavishly, while the majority of its population remains impoverished.

Another resource that exists in great potential abundance in Africa is directly related to the problematic topography of the landmass itself: water power. Africa is rich in hydroelectric potential (IEA 2010). The specific sites of this potential are where major rivers experience impressive drops—thereby creating rapids and waterfalls—in their drainage from the continent's interior. Electricity generation at these sites could conceivably enhance economic development over large regions. Several noteworthy projects have been completed for just this purpose: the Nile's Aswan High Dam in Egypt; the Cahora Bassa Dam in Mozambique; the Gilgel Gibe III Dam in Ethiopia; the Inga Dams in the DRC; the Kainji Dam in Nigeria; the Tekeze Dam in Ethiopia; the Zambezi's Kariba Dam shared by Zambia and Zimbabwe; and the Volta's Akosombo Dam in Ghana.

Shared water resources have also emerged as a point of conflict. For example, the Grand Renaissance Dam in Ethiopia has been a source of increased tensions between Ethiopia and Egypt. Projections from the United Nations show that due to the decreased river flow caused by filling the dam, Egypt is set to lose 200,000 acres of farmable land along the Nile River (Leithead 2018). Recent negotiations between Ethiopia and Egypt over the impact of this project have not gone well. If progress is not made, observers fear that the dispute might escalate to armed conflict.

World Bank

Pastoralists in the unpredictable environment of the Sahel move their cattle in search of food and water.

Examples of where this has happened include conflict in Sierra Leone over the Bumbuna Dam, as well as the forced resettlement of the Tonga people as part of the construction of the Kariba Dam on the Zambian-Zimbabwean border.

While there has been an increasing push for more hydroelectric power with several new hydroelectric dams opening in the past ten years, the majority of rivers are not being harnessed for power generation to the degree that they could be. Resource abundance, large "reserves" of power, and seemingly infinite potential have not been reconfigured into actual use for a very basic economic reason: lack of markets. Africans use little electricity compared to their counterparts in the northern industrialized countries. Over 60 percent of Africans are involved in smallholder farms—and they are income poor. Over 50 percent of the global poor live in Africa. Industry, a big potential user of electrical power, is not a significant part of Africa's economic mix. Cities are also viable concentrated electricity markets, but although Africa's urban growth rates are exceptionally high, the low purchasing power of Africa's urbanites constrains electricity consumption and revenues for the time being. Huge capital investment is required to continue building dams and generating facilities, to transport the electricity great distances, and to distribute it in regional grids. Achieving a reasonable return on such an investment in Africa would be extremely difficult. As a result, this particular component of the continent's resource base remains greatly underexploited.

The long exposure of the ancient African landmass to the tropical sun, rain, and the force of gravity has also removed much of the original surface material by erosion. The poor tropical soil that remains holds little fertility. Alluvial soils (the deep, rich, stream-deposited sediments found on floodplains and deltas) and rich volcanic soils are uncommon on the high plateau surface. The fertile soils of the alluvial Inland Niger Delta between Segou and Timbuktu in Mali and the volcanically derived soils of Cameroon and the Kenya highlands constitute exceptions to this generalization. Finally, many of the more fertile coastal sites are held by large plantation operations geared to products for export, not for local or regional food supplies.

Nontropical Southern Africa is richer in soil fertility and can be considered an exception to the African rule of low soil productivity. Cooler temperatures mark this projection of the African landmass into the middle latitudes of the Southern Hemisphere. Latitudinal position and the high elevation of South Africa's Highveld combine with lower rainfall to reduce the leaching of soil nutrients while simultaneously allowing for a thicker accumulation of organic material (humus), which is a critical factor in soil fertility. The resulting greater productivity of South African soil has supported the development of a diverse agricultural economy that is relatively free of tropical disease vectors and based on grain and livestock production, including corn, wheat, sheep, and cattle. The shifting cultivation practices so typical of tropical Africa are replaced here by permanent and prosperous small family farms. For most Africans, however, agriculture continues as a subsistence endeavor, and food supply problems have increased with the growing population, an issue treated more fully in later chapters on the economy (Chapter 5) and the environment (Chapter 9).

Contemporary Geographic Realities

We conclude this chapter by setting out three geographic realities that continue to define contemporary Africa. The first involves the limited success of African governments in extending and consolidating their power over the geographic expanses of their sovereign territories. This reality was effectively set out in a book by Jeffrey Herbst, *States and Power in Africa: Comparative Lessons in Authority and Control* (2000), which adopts a "political-geography" approach. "The fundamental problem facing state-builders in Africa—be they colonial kings, colonial governors, or presidents in the independence era—has been to project authority over inhospitable territories that contain relatively low densities of people," explains Herbst (2000:11). "Relatively low population densities in Africa have automatically meant that it always has been more expensive for states to exert control over a given number of people compared to Europe and other densely settled areas." The crucial dilemma according to Herbst is that the seats of political power (the capital cities) of African countries are often physically disconnected from populations living in outlying regions, regardless of whether they contain sizable populations in provincial cities or are largely uninhabited or scarcely inhabited. In the DRC, for example, this geopolitical reality is one of the reasons why the eastern provinces of the country have been almost continuously marked by a variety of guerrilla insurgencies since independence in 1960. It also partially explains why a secessionist movement has emerged and remained active in northeastern Mali, as well as in other countries and regions of the African continent. In short, African leaders continue to grapple with how to effectively exert their control over outlying areas within their countries.

A second geographical reality involves the growing regionalization of African trade and investment. The African continent is geographically divided into six regional economic cooperation schemes: the Economic Community of West African States (ECOWAS), the Arab Maghreb Union (AMU) in North Africa, the Southern African Development Community (SADC), the Economic Community of Central African States (ECCAS), the East African Community (EAC), and the Intergovernmental Authority on Development (IGAD) in Northeast Africa. The logic of these integration schemes is that neighboring countries are natural trading partners; there is strength in numbers if one wishes to compete with global economic powers; countries that have a shared regional experience are natural trading partners; and regional cooperation with like-minded African countries is the only way to transform the ties of economic dependency inherited from the colonial era (Oyejide, Elbadawi, and Collier 1997). The impacts of regional economic cooperation schemes have been mixed. SADC and ECOWAS have achieved the greatest success, perhaps due to the willingness of an African regional power—South Africa in the case of SADC and Nigeria in the case of ECOWAS—to serve as an economic engine and leader for the other countries within the region. Economic cooperation has been stymied in other geographic regions due to the weakness of a potential regional leader amid ongoing regional instability (e.g., the DRC and ECCAS in Central Africa), state collapse and the continuation of regional conflicts (e.g., the ongoing civil war in Somalia that continues to affect IGAD partners in Northeast Africa), and political-military conflict between core members of the grouping (e.g., AMU members Algeria and Morocco in North Africa remain at loggerheads over the disposition of the former Spanish Sahara, which Morocco has annexed as part of its sovereign territory, with Algeria instead supporting independence as the Sahrawi Arab Democratic Republic [SADR]).

A final geographic reality involves the expansion of great power involvement on the African continent. As described in greater detail in Chapter 6, Africa historically has been subjected to great power politics. In addition to the "scramble for Africa" among the European great powers at the end of the nineteenth century that established the national boundaries that largely remain in force, the Cold War (1947–1989) made the African continent a battlefield for proxy wars between the United States and the former Soviet Union and their respective allies (Akindele 1985). Great power involvement was a regular characteristic of numerous African regional conflicts, such as the Congo Crisis of 1960–1965 in Central Africa, the 1974–1975 Angolan civil war in Southern Africa, and the 1977–1978 Ogaden War between Somalia and Ethiopia in East Africa. This great power rivalry has intensified in the current era. For example, the PRC has particularly focused on cultivating African leaders whose countries enjoy mineral, agricultural, or fossil fuel resources that are crucial to a rapidly expanding Chinese economy. This has ensured a Chinese foreign policy approach that targets all regions of the African continent. The United States, especially in the post-9/11 era, has focused on promoting counterterrorism initiatives along the Islamic littorals of North, Northeast, and East Africa. And, a resurgent Russia intent on regaining its superpower status was particularly active in North Africa, most notably in the Libyan civil war. Other great powers vying for regional influence in Africa include France, Germany, India, and Japan. Regional powers, such as Brazil, India, Indonesia, Iran, Saudi Arabia, and Turkey, are also increasingly active, further contributing to the mix of great power politics. In sum, geography has and continues to influence great power involvement and competition in Africa.

3

The Historical Context

Thomas O'Toole and
Kirstie Lynn Dobbs

The sheer number of sovereign African countries (fifty-four) across a landmass that is three times larger than the United States challenges historians who seek to uncover and explain continental trends. In this chapter, we present a general historical background on Africa to facilitate understanding of the issues treated in subsequent chapters. Many present-day challenges and conflicts in Africa stem from political-military and socioeconomic changes associated with the establishment of European colonial rule. However, as important as colonialism is, patterns and identities established over the millennia of precolonial African history influenced the colonial experience and continue to be a powerful force shaping postcolonial Africa. To see Africa in its historical context is to grasp the complexity of the continent and to appreciate the ingenuity and dynamism of African peoples as they respond to the challenges posed by history. Clearly, while Africans created and continue to create their own history, they did and still do under conditions that, in many cases, they do not control.

The remainder of this chapter is divided into six sections. The first section outlines the evolution of human history in Africa from 100,000 BCE up to the early twentieth century. Sections two and three examine the roles of stateless societies and centralized states, respectively, in Africa's political past. Section four outlines the impacts of trade, exploration, and external conquest on the course of African history. This is followed by an analysis of the impacts of colonialism in Africa and the eventual turn toward independence. A final section provides concluding remarks and argues that the study of African history has expanded and provides an enriched understanding of the complexity of Africa's past.

The Peopling of Africa

Cradle of Humankind

If we read a half dozen standard survey texts on African history, we could come away with multiple accounts explaining the origins of our species. We present a rather conservative and parsimonious outline of human history in Africa beginning with the first evidence of *Homo sapiens sapiens*, leaving readers to look into the many ongoing controversies regarding the evolution of our hominid ancestors to that point. In the past few decades an ever-increasing body of fossil evidence, more recent genetic studies, and even linguistics have greatly improved our understanding of human evolution. Most scholars maintain that the origins of *Homo sapiens sapiens* are found in Africa. Few scholars now doubt that the great bulk of human evolution took place in Africa and that every person alive today is descended from a population of humans anatomically indistinguishable from our African ancestors. By at least 100,000 years ago, humans occupied all of Africa. Conservatively speaking, various cultural and, perhaps even linguistic, groups had coalesced into different populations with their own foraging techniques adapted to the environments in which they were located by 50,000 BCE (Reader 2011).

Some scholars identify these different subsistence patterns with the continent's oldest language families: Afro-Asiatic, Khoisan, Niger-Congo, and Nilo-Saharan. The speakers of the oldest of these four, Khoisan, probably were the inhabitants of the southern third of Africa until sometime in the past 2,000 years. These people developed foraging and hunting strategies that were viable in the arid parts of southern Africa. People who spoke Afro-Asiatic, Niger-Congo, and Nilo-Saharan languages had each developed a distinct approach to foraging and hunting in various regions of the continent. Their unique foraging and hunting styles may also have led to different crop-raising techniques based on the unique crops derived from their foraging habits.

Niger-Congo (or Niger-Kordofanian) speakers are currently found in much of West, East, and Southern Africa. Their foraging styles emphasized the gathering of wild yams and oil palm nuts. Nilo-Saharan speakers settled in the areas across the continent that were once very wet. They developed an "aquatic tradition" based on the harvesting of the seeds of abundant wild grasses, fishing, and the hunting of crocodiles and hippopotami. Afro-Asiatic speakers occupied much of the Sahara when it was much wetter, and they relied on gathered grasses as their staple food. We should note that some scholars claim that the Afro-Asiatic languages, of which Hebrew and Arabic are the best known, originated in southwest Asia. We are not sure, though, that one can identify such subsistence/linguistic groupings with physical features as some scholars do. For instance, it was said that many Afro-Asiatic speakers were of a "slightly built Afro-Mediterranean type"; "tall and slender Nilotic people" spoke Nilo-Saharan languages; and "Negroid peoples spoke Niger-Congo languages" (Iliffe 2017:11). Given the madness of the Rwandan Tutsi/Hutu genocide in 1994, which, to some extent, was the result of confounding genetics, subsistence patterns, and linguistics as markers of human differences, we avoid projecting such phenotype-based typologies into the past.

Gathering and Hunting

In general, Africans, like all other humans, made their living by gathering and hunting for most of their history. Until about 7,000 years ago, when increasing populations—and the climatic shift that would ultimately recreate the Sahara Desert—made food cultivation and animal herding necessary, most Africans were gatherers and hunters. Archaeological evidence indicates that African gatherers and hunters adapted their tools and ways of life to three basic African environments: the tropical rainforests with hardwoods and small game; the more open savannas with a diversity of large game living in grasslands, woods, and gallery forests along the rivers; and riverbank and lakeside ecologies found along major watercourses or around lakes and ponds.

We must point out, though, that rainforest, savanna, and waterside habitats differed greatly from place to place, and the societies found in them differed more among themselves and were far more complex than this general overview might imply. For each habitat, we could easily devote a whole chapter to pointing out differences in ways and styles of life that were the products of ceaseless change over millennia. The political, social, and economic histories of each specific society, along with its history of ideas, values, and ideology, could fill whole volumes. With such diversity it is obvious that savanna dwellers, rainforest dwellers, and people in water-focused societies were not so perfectly adapted to a single environment as to be incapable of leaving one for the other. These three environmental niches are simply explanatory categories. In the real world, environments merge gradually into others, as do the societies living within them.

Despite the myriad habitats and diversity among their inhabitants, as well as the internal differences that existed within these habitats, it still makes sense to generalize about rainforest societies. A few isolated forest dwellers, even in the twenty-first century, still live in bands of thirty to fifty individuals. Their pursuit of game and harvesting of a variety of insect, stream, and plant foods keep them on the move in a rather fixed cycle as various foods come into season at different locations in their foraging areas. Consequently, they construct only temporary shelters of leaves and poles, very functional for a life in which more permanent structures are useless. Drawing upon both vegetable and animal food sources, with the men most often specializing in hunting and the women generally specializing in gathering, they have little need for contact with outsiders or for exploration beyond the confines of their regular territories. As in most gathering and hunting societies, women's economic functions, along with childbearing, are absolutely crucial. Women typically generate more food through gathering than the men who hunt animals or look for game that has already been killed. Gathering and hunting societies appear to have developed delicately balanced social relationships that permitted necessary group decisions without the need for clearly defined leaders.

Savanna-dwelling gatherers and hunters, few if any of whom exist today, led similarly mobile lives but often specialized in the collection of wild cereals that grew on the grassy plains and the occasional hunting of large grass-eating animals—giraffe, zebra, warthog, and many species of antelope. In particularly favorable circumstances, savanna dwellers might congregate in groups of 300 or more during the rainy seasons when vegetation was lush and game plentiful. They dispersed in groups of 30 to 100 during the dry months to gather and hunt, first with sticks and game pits, and later with nets, bows and arrows, and poisons. As populations grew, their contacts with other groups intensified until relatively fixed territories were established, and exotic shells, stones, feathers, and other less durable items were passed in sporadic trade over distances of hundreds of miles. Their history consisted of the gradual refinement of gathering and hunting techniques, a slow spread of new inventions from one group to another, and the very slow growth of population.

Fishing

Major fishing communities in Africa most likely predate the development of techniques for growing food crops and taming animals. Many settlements were clustered around the lakes and rivers of what are now the dry southern reaches of the Sahara. During the last great wet period in Africa's climate, about 11,000 to 5,000 years ago, Lake Chad rose to cover a huge area many times its increasingly shrinking present size and may well have overflowed southwestward into the Benue-Niger rivers, which empty into the Atlantic Ocean. This huge lake was fed by rivers from the Tibesti Plateau in the central Sahara. Lake Nakuru in present-day Kenya may have overflowed into the Great Rift Valley while Lake Turkana was eighty-five meters above its present level. The inland delta of the Niger in present-day Mali was far more vast and held enormous quantities of water in permanent lakes (Iliffe 2017).

In these lands of lakes and rivers, people lived in thriving fishing communities. They carved intricate harpoon barbs and fishhooks out of bone; fired some of the earliest pottery in Africa; probably wove baskets and nets of reeds; and hunted crocodiles, hippopotami, and waterfowl. More important, these fishing peoples supported themselves without constant movement and at much higher population densities than gathering and hunting would allow. The need to cooperate in order to fish efficiently encouraged people to settle in larger and more permanent villages. The centralized coordination required in these larger settlements led to more formalized leadership structures than were necessary for gatherers and hunters. In these riverbank and lakeside villages, experienced elders or single arbitrators may have made the decisions. Some individuals could, for the first time, gain more wealth in the form of fishing equipment and houses than others in the village. These fishing peoples may have traded dried fish for plant and animal products offered by their gatherer-hunter neighbors. Local commercial networks developed, and new ideas spread more rapidly to larger areas (Ehret 2002:68–75).

Crop Raising and Herding

Most scholars overgeneralize when they suggest that the effect of the crop-raising revolution was a great step forward for humankind. Clearly, it is only with the invention of crop cultivation that the human species could create the elaborate social and cultural patterns with which most people today would be familiar. Furthermore, it is in advanced hoe-farming and agricultural societies (those using animal traction) that the separation between rulers and ruled, inequality between men and women, and the institution of slavery evolved. Outside the Ethiopian highlands, there were no animal-drawn plows before contact with Europeans. A few very functional gathering and hunting societies continued into the present century in a variety of African natural environments. Though crop raising supports larger populations than gathering and hunting, the environmental realities of Africa limit agricultural potential in many places. (See Chapter 2 for more on this issue.) Because of the continent's location on the equator, Africa generally has very fixed wet and dry seasons. This limits agricultural production and animal pasturing during the six or seven dry months. Three-fifths of the continent is desert, much of the rest has large areas of poor soil, and the more humid areas are home to the malaria-carrying mosquito and the parasitic, infection-carrying tsetse fly. Africa's relatively light population density throughout history demonstrates the very real limits the continent's physical environment placed on the development of crop raising. In Africa, the rainfall and soils often meant that farming and herding peoples were more exposed to the dangers of famine caused by natural disasters such as drought or flood. In most African hoe-farming communities, gathering, hunting, and especially fishing have remained important sources of food and general livelihood (McCann 2009:15–19).

Following the scholarship on twentieth-century gathering and hunting of the Khoisan (Lee 1993) and Mbuti (Turnbull 1983), which led us to question why Africans ever turned to farming, we became convinced that crop production was a much more difficult and tenuous way of life than hunting and gathering. Studies on surviving gatherers and hunters, combined with archaeological evidence, seem to refute former arguments about the short, nasty, and brutish lives of gathering and hunting people. Even in the harsh environment of the Kalahari Desert ecosystems, Richard Lee (1993) claims that a larger percentage of people into the last century were older "pensioners" and children than is typical in the crop-growing areas of Africa. He points out that, even in the later part of the twentieth century, gatherers and hunters in the Kalahari knew agricultural techniques perfectly well but had no reason or desire to adopt them. Since a logical, schematic reconstruction of what happened to cause many African people to adopt crop growing seemed necessary with this generally benign view of gathering and hunting, we found the following one quite persuasive.

The fishing cultures, which evolved near the many lakes and rivers in the African savannas between the Sahara and the forests and in eastern Africa in the wet period that followed the last ice age, allowed relatively large stationary settlements to grow. At the same time, these peoples began to domesticate animals, especially cattle, using skills acquired from hunting game that gathered near watering places. Five or six thousand years ago the Sahara was drying up, pushing to its margins large populations that could not adapt to the change without moving. It was generally assumed that agricul-

April A. Gordon

Ancestors of today's San people painted beautiful rock art in many parts of Southern Africa, some dating back thousands of years.

tural innovation was forced on the populations that had grown up along the waterways to the south and east of this expanding desert (July 1998:13–17).

For us, how agriculture developed was much easier to explain than why it developed. Women, the gathering specialists, became aware of where particularly good food supplies, especially grains, grew, and they camped on sites where these foods were plentiful. Over time, the harvested seeds were planted, and larger and more firmly attached seed heads evolved. In the widespread African savanna, millets and sorghums were domesticated. In the Ethiopian highlands and the Fouta Djallon, teff and fonio, grass-like grains with tiny kernels, became the respective staples. In the marshlands of the interior delta of the Niger River in present-day Mali, a type of rice was cultivated. Many East Africans probably planted ensete, a crop related to the banana, more than 2,000 years ago (McCann 2009:45–46, 94). Root crops and the native oil palm of western Africa enabled agriculturists to penetrate the forests (McCann 2009:114–128). Yet for most gathering and hunting populations of Southern and Central Africa, there was little pressure to change from a way of life that had proven satisfactory for thousands of years. Likewise, fluctuating rainfall patterns, soils with ephemeral fertility, and relatively low populations allowed and perhaps necessitated swidden or slash-and-burn cropping techniques to persist into the present in many parts of Africa. With iron hoes and other iron tools, more efficient cropping techniques became possible. Population growth, which accompanied the slow shift to agriculture, and later the use of iron, set in motion another important process in African history.

Bantu Expansion

Early in the twentieth century, scholars were struck by the remarkable similarities in the languages and cultures of peoples living throughout the vast area stretching east from present-day Cameroon to Kenya and on south to the Republic of South Africa. All of these peoples spoke languages with the word-stem *ntu,* or something very similar to it, meaning "person." The prefix *ba* denotes the plural in many of these languages so that *ba-ntu* means, literally, "people." The source of these languages and the farming and herding cultures associated with them and how they became so widespread in Africa were major questions by the mid-twentieth century.

One plausible—though still speculative—view was based on linguistics, archaeological research (especially of pottery- and iron-making techniques), studies of plant and animal origins, and oral traditions. This view maintained that a mass migration of iron-using agriculturalists from the Benue River in today's Cameroon and Nigeria "broke through" the equatorial forest, overwhelming original populations of gatherers and hunters as they went. This kind of reasoning chimed in neatly with long-held views of physical migrations as explanations for cultural change elsewhere in the world.

Although there is abundant evidence for the spread of languages, cultures, and technologies in the Bantu case, as elsewhere, this "Bantu expansion" model is now seen as too simplistic. Rather than a sudden, massive movement of population, it is more likely to have ebbed and flowed over millennia, during which time the transfer of ideas was just as important as the movement of population. This view suggests that sometime after 5000 BCE near the Benue River in the western African savannas, fairly large-scale settlements guided by councils of lineage elders evolved based on fishing with dugout canoes, nets, fishhooks, traps, and harpoons. Cultivating yams and oil palms and raising goats, these peoples, speaking Bantu languages, were better able to survive drought and misfortune than the small pockets of cultivators that might have developed by then in and south of the tropical rainforests of central Africa. Having long mastered the art of firing pottery, these Bantu speakers were smelting iron for spears, arrows, hoes, scythes, and axes more than 2,500 years ago. Population pressures grew along the Benue as Saharan farmers slowly moved south to escape the gradually drying desert. Pushed by growing populations, the Bantu fishing peoples moved south and east. After reaching the Congo tributaries, they spread up the rivers of Central Africa to the Zambezi and south to the tip of Africa. Bantu-speaking groups intermarried with, conquered, or pushed out the Khoisan speakers and other populations they encountered. As they slowly migrated, these Bantu-speaking peoples learned to cultivate Asian yams and bananas, which had been introduced to eastern Africa by Malayo-Polynesian sailors who colonized the island of Madagascar about 1,800 years ago. In some cases, the Bantu-speaking migrants became large-scale cattle keepers. By 1,000 years ago, most of Central and Southern Africa was populated by iron-smelting, Bantu-speaking villagers who had virtually replaced all but scattered pockets of the original gathering and hunting peoples (Ehret 2002:110–119).

Stateless Societies in Africa's Political Past

Until the 1960s, most historians relied on written sources, so most history tended to be about societies with writing. Since most African societies did not develop writing, the historical record before about 500 BCE was sparse, gleaned from accounts of non-African travelers, usually Muslims, and archaeological remains. In the past sixty years, specialists in African history have learned to use historical linguistics, oral traditions, and other sources to overcome the apparent lack of evidence and develop a far better understanding of African history.

Nevertheless, many writers of world history texts continue to treat human societies without writing as "prehistoric." This is rather ironic given that even in those complex urban-centered societies called civilizations, which have had written records for more than 5,000 years, only a small minority of people were literate and most people did not live in cities. Certainly in Africa this prehistoric-historic distinction has little value. Most historians of Africa realize that a focus on written sources alone would mean virtually ignoring the histories of the vast majority of Africa's peoples, both those who were able to achieve—through kinship, ritual, and other means—relatively orderly and just societies without centralized states and those who lived in city-centered societies without writing.

In fact, until about 2,500 years ago, virtually all Africans living south of the Sahara were able to avoid relying on bureaucratic organizations or centralized "states" to carry out the political requirements of their societies. Even large groups created social systems based on lineage (kinship) with no single center of power or authority. Under the right conditions, such systems could accommodate several million people. On the local level, lineage systems depended on a balance of power to solve political problems. People in these societies controlled conflict and resolved disputes through a balance of centers of cooperation and opposition, which appear to have been almost universal in human societies. This human ethic of cooperation was especially crucial in herding and agricultural societies that existed in the often-challenging physical environments of Africa (Turnbull 1973:233–255).

Variations of lineage systems also helped Africans resist European colonial domination. For example, colonial attempts to divide Africa into districts, cantons, and even "tribes" were doomed to failure when most of the continent south of the Sahara was really a kaleidoscope of lineage fragments, scattering and regrouping as the need arose. Through marriage alliances and various forms of reciprocal exchanges, these networks could expand almost indefinitely. European officials erroneously assumed that their control of an important African authority figure ensured the "pacification" of a given territory. The Africans, not surprisingly, could simply turn to another member of a kinship linkage and continue their struggle against the outsiders. Africa's past demonstrates the truly remarkable ability of African peoples to resist incorporation into state political and economic organizations (Gilbert and Reynolds 2008:58–59). This represents one of the most interesting aspects of the history of this continent's peoples. There were many African societies that have been classified by political historians as stateless or decentralized. These terms are used to describe societies that did not have well-defined and complex or centralized systems of government. Perhaps as many as a third of the people of Africa on the eve of colonial rule lived in stateless or decentralized societies. For many years, these societies were not well studied by historians both because of a lack of sources and because of prejudice. Initially, most historians accepted a view that only societies that are centralized were worth studying. Until the past sixty years, many historians of Africa looked at African history through the lens of European history and took the existence of states as a mark of political achievement—the bigger the state, the bigger the achievement. Most authorities now agree that this view is far from accurate.

A brief case study on the Igbo-speaking peoples shows that stateless societies can be culturally and socially sophisticated. The Igbo live in the southeastern part of contemporary Nigeria. The Igbo are neighbors of the highly politically centralized Yoruba, but their political system is much different. Instead of centralized kingdoms headed by powerful "kings" and their advisers, the Igbo had no centralized system of governance. Rather they lived in politically autonomous villages. That is, each village was politically separate and was politically not directly connected to neighboring villages. Within the villages, there was not a system of hereditary chiefs. Village decisions were made by a headman and a council of elders that selected the headman. The absence of a centralized system of government did not mean that there were no systems or institutions of governance among the Igbo. In addition to village-based councils of elders, there were religious organizations, structures of kinship ties (i.e., lineage groups), and voluntary organizations that provided regulations that governed people's lives. These organizations guaranteed a system of checks and balances in which no one group or institution gained too much power. The absence of centralized rule did not hinder the economic or social development of the Igbo peoples. Indeed, just as their more centralized Yoruba neighbors, the Igbo-speaking peoples developed a specialized and diversified economy based on agriculture, textiles, and trade.

Many Africans still rely on extended family organizations and call upon kinship behavior to maintain justice and cultural and territorial integrity, not only in domestic but also in wider spheres. As in the past, some Africans still see any state without at least some symbolic lineage-based authority as inherently tyrannical. The continuing desire to seek and find order in institutions other than the state is very understandable in the African context where failed states, military dictatorships, and "presidents for life" became all too common during the initial decades of the contemporary independence era (Meredith 2005).

One important aspect of persisting kinship networks, still very important in Africa, is the degree to which people within such systems could mobilize women's labor and childbearing capacities. The formation of alliances between lineages was facilitated by marriage. This does not mean that women were simply pawns. In a good number of times and locations, women such as Queen Nzinga, the seventeenth-century Mbundu ruler (Miller 1975:201–216), or the Luso-African women in the Upper Guinea Coast (Brooks 2003) controlled many resources and could operate almost independently of their husbands' lineages. Quite often though, especially where cattle keeping was important—almost always a male-dominated activity—women had much of the crop-producing burdens as well as household and child-rearing duties. When colonial labor demands removed men even farther from household economies, this imbalance was often made worse (Coquery-Vidrovitch 1997:9–20).

For those accustomed to state forms of organization, African social organization based on kinship seems chaotic, and nonstate societies are seen as less civilized or lacking in sociopolitical sophistication. To dispel the notion that Africa lacked civilization, many dedicated Africanists have focused almost exclusively on the relatively unrepresentative centralized states when portraying Africa's past. This has sometimes obscured, however, the important role of local kinship relations in maintaining peace and harmony in most African societies. But since centralized and noncentralized state societies have a long history in Africa, we examine the significance of state societies in the history of Africa next.

Centralized States in Africa's Political Past

By the late 1960s, most scholars had rejected the essentially racial determinist views that Africans were incapable of organizing stable "civilizations" or states without external leadership. The once commonly accepted premise that the first states in Africa were the result of common patterns of "divine kingship," diffused from Egypt or elsewhere, have been gradually abandoned by most knowledgeable scholars of African history. The equally misguided view that civilization originated in sub-Saharan Africa is also unacceptable to most scholars. States came into being in different times and places for a wide variety of causes and under a large number of conditions. Likewise, the rigid distinction between state and stateless societies that continues to exist in many textbooks and other popular literature has little basis in reality. Such categories were created by social anthropologists (mostly British) in response to colonial administrators' need to classify the political structures of the peoples over whom they ruled.

Most scholars now realize that centralized African states, like such states elsewhere in the world, arose from a variety of causes and most often resulted from internal forces present in various areas of the continent (Griffiths 2005). For example, trade routes throughout Africa often impacted the formation of large African states. The largest and best known of these is the trans-Saharan trade network, which "extended throughout the Sahara Desert, an expanse of 3,320,000 square miles" (Schraeder 2004a:36). "If you traveled across the United States from Boston to San Diego, you still would not have crossed the Sahara," explain Marq de Villiers and Sheila Hirtle in a captivating history of the region, "and if you started from Paris you'd be at the Urals, deep into Russia, long before you ran out of Sahara" (de Villiers and Hirtle 2002, quoted in Schraeder 2004a:36). Various political systems in West Africa were trading with North Africa as early as 1000

BCE. Numerous "ports," such as Timbuktu in present-day Mali, that were on trans-Saharan trade networks grew into thriving cities that shaped the geography of precolonial Africa.

The North African littoral was particularly noteworthy for the development of centralized states. Indeed, one of the oldest North African city-states was Carthage, which gradually emerged as the capital of the Mediterranean-based Carthaginian Empire. Initially founded by the Phoenicians due to its natural protected port and geographical location at the center of what would become a Mediterranean seafaring trade network, Carthage was ultimately destroyed by invading Roman forces as part of the Punic Wars, only to be resuscitated as one of the most important trading centers of the Roman Empire (Melliti 2016). Carthage was not unique. In later centuries, a variety of North African cities that were part of what became known as the Barbary states, which included Algiers, Tripoli, and Tunis, would vie for regional influence (Blondy 2018).

In most cases, African states retained an element of kinship-based social organization. In fact, the process of statebuilding was usually a long one in which rulers gradually established special privileges for their own lineages and created a superlineage basis for authority. This caused some elements of reciprocity or mutual obligations between the subjects and their rulers that persisted for generations in all but the most authoritarian states. Rulers brought prosperity to their people and organized the military to protect them while the ruled supported their rulers with subsistence goods, labor, and even service in the military.

Initial Regional States

It is quite likely that the first regional states in Africa were those that united independent farming communities below the first cataract in Egypt about 5,500 years ago. It may well be that here the gradual drying of the Sahara Desert had forced together growing populations from the desert into a diminishing crop-growing area dependent upon the annual Nile floods. From this time until Egypt was conquered by the armies of Alexander the Great, the pharaohs, priests, and nobility of Egypt were able to extract surplus wealth from the cultivators of the valley. This enabled them to undertake trade and warfare and otherwise interact with the Nubians south of the cataract as well as with other peoples. The Egyptian ruling elite controlled irrigation and other public works and justified their rule through claims that the pharaoh was a god-king incarnate (Lamphear and Falola 1995:79–80).

Farther to the south, in a land called Kush by Egyptians, another independent political entity developed by about 3,800 years ago. Achieving its greatest power between 2,800 and 2,700 years ago, the history of Kush was closely linked to that of Egypt. In fact, Kushite kings ruled Egypt from about 700 to 500 BCE. Driven from Egypt about 2,500 years ago, the Kushite leaders pushed farther south into Meroe, where a vast iron industry flourished. The causes of the rise of Kush and the extent to which its political ideas and metallurgical techniques spread are still open to considerable discussion (Ehret 2002:200–221). Meroe's successor states adopted Coptic Christianity from Axum (the ancestor of today's Ethiopia) as a court religion in the first centuries of the Christian era, but this was replaced by Islam more than 1,000 years ago. Four hundred years ago, the Sennar kingdom imposed unity over much of this area, forcing peasants to pay heavy taxes to subsidize their rulers' households. A large, literate merchant class established itself in numerous towns and played a crucial role in deepening the Islamic cultural influence so important in the northern part of the present-day republic of Sudan (Hakem 1980:315–346; Leclant 1980:295–314).

Still farther south in the Ethiopian highlands, Axum, dating back more than 2,000 years, rose to challenge Kush. The founders of Axum migrated from southern Arabia as much as 2,100 years ago and later extended their authority over the northern half of what are now Ethiopia and eastern Sudan. Two thousand years ago, they controlled ports on the Red Sea and maintained trade relations with merchants from the eastern end of the Mediterranean who came to buy ivory, gold, and incense from the African interior. Four hundred years later, Axum's rulers became Christians and expanded to control other lesser-known states that had also arisen in the central and southern highlands of Ethiopia. The leaders of a state led by Amharic-speaking peoples, which arose in the north-central area of the Ethiopian highlands about 700 years ago, claimed some ties to the long-collapsed Axum. This state was based on an expanding landowning class (Shillington 2019:85). It flourished 500 to 600 years ago, broke up, and was then substantially reunited in the eighteenth century and persisted into the twentieth century.

State Formation in West and Central Africa

Until recently, scholars attributed state formation in the savannas of West Africa to the introduction of the camel into the western Sahara sometime after 1700 BCE. Camels were important in bringing the first Arab travelers to the cities and towns of West Africa—travelers who provided later historians with the earliest written documents on the existence of these cities and towns. Relying almost exclusively on such documents, scholars assumed that the cities and towns of the western Sudan had emerged in response to the needs of Arab and Berber traders. Before the appearance of rare and exotic goods supplied by the traders, scholars reasoned, rulers lacked the leverage they needed to awe their followers. According to the authors of many undergraduate texts, a succession of empires rose and fell, dominating the political landscape of the western and central Sudan from about 1,300 years ago until about 400 years ago. These were the fabled Ghana,

Mali, Songhai, and the less-mentioned Kanem and Hausa city-states. In this view, Ghana first enters the historical record about 1300 BCE via the accounts of Muslim traders, who were drawn across the desert by the lucrative trade in gold controlled by the Ghana, the rulers' title. Trans-Saharan exchange, Islamic statecraft, and literacy underpinned the process of Sudanic empire-building, giving rise to Ghana's successors and to the entrepôt cities that emerged in what Arab speakers call the Sahel (literally "shore," the southern fringe of the Sahara). These interpretations were supported by the few written sources, sympathetic colonial administrators, and pioneering African American scholars seeking to posit a golden past for precolonial Africa. For the first so-called nationalist generation of professional historians, these states were also all-important. These scholars sought to "decolonize" the African past by demonstrating that, far from being the "primitive" realm of European imperialists' mythologies, Africa had a long and noble tradition of statebuilding like other areas of the world.

Upon close examination, these interpretations fly in the face of common sense. It would have been highly unlikely that merchants would chance the arduous trip across the desert if there were not already urban markets to attract them. The assumption that military strength, trans-Saharan trade, and,

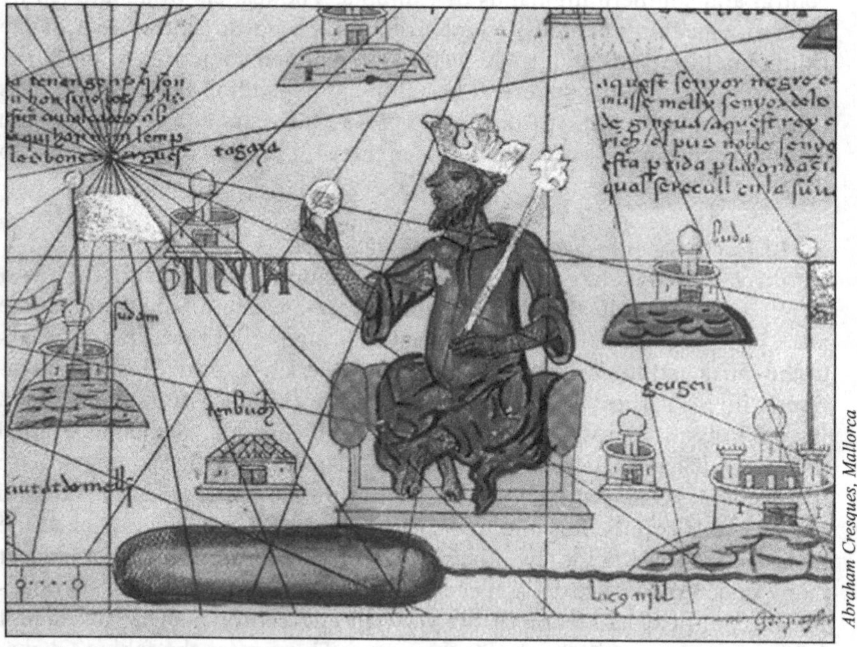

Abraham Cresques, Mallorca

Mural of Mansa Musa, who was the ruler of Mali, a large and rich empire.

later, Islam were the decisive factors in the rise and fall of these states is no longer supportable. "One [Arab] chronicler [Abu Ubayd al-Aziz al-Bakri] reported that 'the king of Ghana, when he calls up his army, can put 200,000 men into the field, more than 40,000 of them archers'" (quoted in Reader 1999:284). Ecological limits make such reports highly unlikely. Such forces could not have been assembled, fed, and deployed in this area. Figures such as these are probably tenfold, or even twentyfold, exaggerations.

Within the past thirty years, the narrative established by sympathetic colonial administrators, pioneer African American scholars, nationalist African historians, and the standard explanations of state formation here and elsewhere have been challenged. Recent archaeological research, combined with that of historians, art historians, and anthropologists, necessitates the rethinking of these established narratives. Excavations in Jenne-Jeno (old Jenne in the modern nation of Mali) have opened an entirely new paradigm of the origins of complex urban-centered societies in Africa (and by extension elsewhere in the world). The emergence of towns in the western and probably central Sudan occurred far earlier than indicated by Arab chronicles and oral traditions. It is increasingly clear that urban centers emerged from 2300 BCE onward. The lingering assumption that external forces provided the catalysts for the development of "complex societies" in Sudanic western and central Africa is no longer accepted by advanced scholars. Well before the arrival of North African Muslim traders, urban centers were parts of regional centers of trade that served to draw traders to them (McIntosh 2005).

What has also emerged from this research is that the indigenous urban cultures that did emerge in the western and central Sudan took a form that at first seemed unique but may have been foundational to civilizations in many areas of the world. The region's earliest urban landscape contains no trace of the monumental architecture that in other parts of the world has been seen as an important element of centralized political power and ritual authority. The essence of middle Niger civilization might well have been not hierarchy but pluralist "heterarchy" (i.e., where elements or portions are unranked). The real genius, in other words, may have been the ability of African peoples to organize themselves without recourse to coercive state power. It now seems that the formerly accepted, simplistic "rise of civilizations" approach may often hide heterarchical foundations for many other areas of the world (McIntosh 2005).

In any case, trans-Saharan trade lagged after the Roman defeat of the Phoenician-founded city of Carthage in present-day Tunisia. This city-state had conducted flourishing trans-Saharan trade with sub-Saharan Africans through Berber partners between 2,800 and 2,500 years ago. Another of these early urban-centered, western Sudanic African states was Tekrur on the Senegal River (mentioned by later travelers writing in Arabic). Eleven hundred years ago, Muslim traders from northern Africa also described Ghana, a state centered somewhat north and east of Tekrur. The location of Ghana's consecutive capitals, Kumbi Saleh and Walata, in what is today southern Mauritania on the northern edge of cultivation, became crucial to the rulers of these cities. Serving as staging places to assemble and equip the members of caravans carrying gold shipments north, the leaders of these cities flourished as the gold trade between peoples in northern Africa and those farther south was reestablished. Archaeological evidence suggests that Ghana was already hundreds of years old when it was visited 1,000 years ago by Arab traders searching for profits, especially this gold. The writings of these traders and other travelers about Ghana and the subsequent West African savanna kingdoms of Mali and Songhai provide little knowledge of those crucial aspects of West African society not of direct interest to commercial travelers. Ghana's decline and ultimate sacking by Berber Muslims were part of a larger shift in sub-Saharan trade centers. Trade shifted south as the spreading desert made food production around Walata much more difficult, and Muslim groups pushing into the western desert prompted a shift eastward.

Trade and power passed first to Mali, a kingdom of Mande-speaking groups on the upper Niger River. Founded according to oral traditions between 1230 and 1235 CE by Sundiata Keita, the leaders of Mali not only extracted enough grain from local farmers to maintain a standing army but also traded gold and other goods for the necessary salt from the desert and other commodities from the larger Muslim world. One of Mali's rulers, Mansa Musa, established a reputation for wealth as the result of the splendor of his pilgrimage to Mecca in 1324. From 1468 on, the power of the rulers of Mali passed to those of Songhai in a kingdom located yet farther east on the Niger, under Sonni Ali. The leaders of Songhai, who controlled the river by military canoes, were able to dominate the trading cities of Timbuktu, Jenne, and Gao until the Battle of Tondibi in April 1591 CE, when Moroccan invaders decisively defeated an empire already in decline (Bohannan and Curtin 1995:166–169).

With origins going back to a past almost as remote as that of Ghana, Kanem, a state near the desert edge in modern Chad, may have served as a trading entrepôt for centuries. Rulers of this state were in close contact with North Africa and possibly even with southwest Asia by 1,500 years ago. Arabic sources of more than 500 years ago referred to a strong successor state called Bornu, southwest of Lake Chad in what is today northern Nigeria. This southward shift probably reveals deepening control over a fixed population of cultivators. And though Bornu elites had no gold to sustain a large trade-based kingdom, they did exploit tin and copper resources (Lange 1984:238–265).

Two very interesting savanna states, which prospered as the trade north declined, were the highly centralized non-Islamic kingdoms of Mossi

(Mori-speaking) peoples in present-day Burkina Faso and the Bambara kingdoms of Segu and Kaarta in present-day Mali. Though the Mossi kingdoms date back in some form more than 500 years, the leaders of both of these clusters of states probably drew on wealth generated by the trade in enslaved people to reach the height of their power (Izard 1984:211–237).

By 400 years ago, the most dynamic political systems in the West African savanna were the Hausa city-states west of Bornu. In the area in which these states arose, a high water table and numerous river valleys permitted year-round irrigated cultivation. The resulting food supply permitted an exceptionally dense population, which established a thick network of walled settlements and an extensive, specialized, commodity production economy by about 1,000 years ago. Influenced by Islamized people from the Mali Empire, one of the cities, Kano, had become quite powerful about 500 to 600 years ago. Other Hausa cities, such as Gobir and Katsina and even Bornu, contended with Kano for dominance. Iron deposits and the availability of charcoal-producing woods, trade in kola nuts and enslaved people from the south, as well as surplus dyed textiles and leather goods supplied a substantial long-distance trade (Iliffe 2017).

Major State Clusters in East and Southern Africa

Elsewhere in Africa there were a number of major state clusters, few, if any, of which date back much more than 1,000 years. Sometime about 700 years ago, a process of formation of larger states began in the region of the Great Lakes of East Africa. Though this process was long portrayed as the creation of Kushite- and Nilotic-speaking pastoralists who imposed their rule over Bantu-speaking agriculturists, such a simplistic and essentially racist view (since the Kushite and Nilote speakers were said to have "Caucasian" features) is now largely rejected. It would appear that all of these states came into being as a conjuncture of the economic importance of salt, cattle, and iron, as well as the demographic possibilities allowed by fertile soils and crops such as bananas. Unfortunately, the persistence of beliefs by an older generation of scholars contributed much to the twentieth-century suffering in Rwanda and Burundi, where ethnic differences and animosities between so-called Tutsi and Hutu groups had been enhanced by the teaching of racist views by colonial authorities. Clearly there were peoples whose ancestors came from the south, west, and east, as well as the north into the Great Lakes regions. Descending from ancestors speaking Kushite, Nilotic, and Bantu languages, the rulers of centralized kingdoms rose to power through a variety of factors, the least of which was their genetic heritage. A state such as Buganda, which occupied the fertile plains northwest of Lake Victoria, is typical. In the eighteenth and nineteenth centuries, the *kabaka,* the ruler of the Buganda, extended his authority over much of modern Uganda by gradually taking over the prerogatives of all the Ganda lineages. Besides plentiful supplies of bananas, a very important food staple, the economic base of this state also appeared to be a lively trade in handicraft production (Lamphear and Falola 1995:91–94).

Other centralized states have existed south of the equator for centuries. Near the mouth of the river of the same name lay the Kongo kingdom. When the Portuguese first arrived more than 500 years ago, this kingdom, ruled by Nzinga Nkuwu, had already existed for several generations. In 1506, Nzinga Nkuwu's son Affonso (who had converted to Catholicism) defeated his brother to become *manicongo* (ruler) of this kingdom. His ascension to power marked the beginning of decline for the kingdom, since much of the ruler's authority depended upon local religious values (which were undermined by his conversion). The Catholic missionaries who surrounded him and the expanding Portuguese influence as slave traders further reduced his authority (Iliffe 2017). In recent years, a number of scholars have stressed the widespread influence of Christianity all along the west and west-central coast in precolonial Africa and its subsequent influence on people of African ancestry in the Americas (Thornton 1998:262–271).

Another cluster of centralized polities lay far inland east of Kongo in a basin where salt and iron deposits assisted the development of long-distance trade. In the Shaba province of the present-day Democratic Republic of Congo, a huntsman hero, Ilunga Kalala, had founded a dynasty among the Luba in the early 1400s. Other states of the southern savanna in what are now Zambia and Angola established the superiority of their ruling lineages by associating their founding legends with the Luba. The Lozi state in the upper Zambezi floodplain of western Zambia, which unified only in the nineteenth century, is one such example (Shillington 2019:296).

Great Zimbabwe (in the modern country of the same name), the center of extensive and complex archaeological remains, dates back at least 800 years. The impressive stone ruins called Zimbabwe (which literally means "great house") were built by the ancestors of modern-day Shona speakers. This complex probably served as a capital for a polity that stretched from the Zambezi to the Limpopo Rivers, had linkages with widespread Indian Ocean trade networks, and encompassed an area of rich gold works. The sophisticated stone architecture and the organization of the labor necessary to build these structures suggest the existence of a complex social, economic, and political system. Oral histories and firsthand descriptions of early Portuguese visitors to the area confirm the existence of a strong centralized polity. Though the original Shona polity probably broke up because of intergroup warfare after Indian Ocean traders found alternative African partners in the Zambezi valley, a successor polity was established by 1420 or so under a northern Shona ruler, Nyatsimba Mutota, using the title Mwene Mutapa (Iliffe 2017).

Stimuli from Outside Forces

As elsewhere in the world, some African states did derive great stimuli from outside forces. The oldest and best examples of these externally influenced states were the trading cities of the coast of eastern Africa. Evolving from previously existing coastal fishing towns linked to farming peoples in the interior, these trading entrepôts had contacts with the Greco-Roman world as early as 100 AD (Iliffe 2017). Beginning gradually in the ninth century, these cities rose and fell in concert with both the Islamized maritime cultures of the Indian Ocean and the African political systems that supplied the ivory, gold, and slaves for trade. By 1000 CE merchants in these local African towns from Mogadishu (Somalia) to Sofala (Mozambique) were deeply involved in overseas commerce. Some, like Kilwa in southern Tanzania, which drew upon the Shona-controlled goldfields of Zimbabwe, traded extensively with China, India, and the Islamic world. The peoples of these city-based, coastal trading societies were influenced by Arab and Persian immigrants and developed a unique Swahili culture derived from both African and southwest Asian sources (Connah 1987:150–182).

The kingdoms of Benin and Oyo in present-day Nigeria have historical origins dating back hundreds of years. Yet it was not until 1500, when trade with Europeans on the coast contributed to the increase in the scale of organization, that other centralized political systems developed in the forests and savannas closer to the Atlantic coast of West Africa. For example, the Asante of modern Ghana rose to power after 1680 when the *asantehene* (leader of the Asante), Osei Tutu, and his adviser and priest, Okomfo Anokye, forcefully united three smaller states into a confederation dominated by Akan-speaking peoples. The rise of the Asante polity owed much to the control of the goldfields in central Ghana (the present-day nation, not the Ghana "empire" with which it had no direct connections). The major factor in the success of the Asante leaders, though, was the growth of military activity connected with the slave trade and the imported guns that came with this trade. The Asante fought to protect the trade to the coast in much the same way that the leaders of the United States intervened in Kuwait to maintain control of the oil, which they considered a vital resource (Shillington 2019:190–191).

Four hundred years ago, the dominant polity behind the coast in western Africa was the savanna-based Yoruba state of Oyo. With far-ranging cavalry, Oyo leaders were poised to respond to the growing demand for slaves by French, English, Portuguese, and other traders at ports such as Whydah, Porto Novo, and Badagry. By 1730, Dahomey, a tributary of Oyo, became a major slave-trading power in its own right under King Agaja and dominated the major routes to the sea until the slave trade declined in the nineteenth century. Faced with the rise of the Muslim Sokoto caliphate to the north and the breaking away led by leaders of Yoruba satellite states to the south who were able to obtain guns from coastal traders, the leaders of Oyo lost power, and the empire collapsed during the first half of the nineteenth century (Shillington 2019:278).

A very different series of events, the jihads (holy wars) of western Sudan in the eighteenth and nineteenth centuries, was directly inspired by Islamic reforming movements introduced from North Africa and the Arabian peninsula and by the large-scale shift in trade and production brought about by European commercial interests pressing in from the coast. The jihads of West Africa began in the highlands of the Fouta Djallon in present-day Guinea when Fulbé (Fulani) pastoralists, supported by Muslim traders, revolted against their farming rulers and created a Fulbé-dominated Islamic state by about 1750 under the leadership of Ibrahima Sori. By 1776, the Fulbé had produced a sharia-ruled (based on Islamic law) polity on the lower Senegal River led by Abd al-Qadir. In the early nineteenth century, a similar Fulbé-inspired revolution launched by Uthman dan Fodio against the Hausa cities farther east created the Sokoto caliphate (with a population of about 10 million people) and the Ilorin emirate (Oyo's rival, in the 1830s). This jihad was extended into northern Cameroon by other Fulbé leaders. Another Fulbé jihad, inspired by that of Uthman dan Fodio, was led by Seku Ahmadu in Macina in present-day Mali. Beginning in 1852, al-Hajj Umar formed another empire on the upper Niger that united previously existing Bambara polities until it fell to the French in the 1890s (Shillington 2019:270).

Several other centralizing processes, the result of both indigenous and external forces, occurred in the past 300 years. One originated in what is now South Africa and had a large influence as far afield as Malawi. This Zulu polity-building process in South Africa set in motion the Mfecane, a period of wars and disturbances that led to migrations and the conquest of thousands of people. The Mfecane, which in the Zulu language means "the era of the crushing or breaking," may have been directly influenced by the presence of expanding white settlement in South Africa. But the conditions that made the rise of the Zulu polity possible were the result of more profound changes, such as long-distance trade in enslaved people and ivory, as well as the introduction of maize (corn) by the Portuguese centuries before, which enabled populations to expand greatly.

Until the nineteenth century, the necessities of defense, irrigation, trade, and other factors, which led to the creation of polities elsewhere in Africa, were apparently not as important farther south. Ecological pressures and perhaps the activities of Portuguese and Cape Colony slave traders caused an intensification of rivalries between small political groupings in the region between the Drakensberg Mountains and the Indian Ocean about 200 years ago. In that struggle for power, the most successful leader to emerge was Shaka. He refined and improved local warfare techniques and consolidated authority so effectively that between 1819 and 1828 he was able to create a military polity that set in motion a series of migrations and conquests resulting in the creation of many polities throughout Southern Africa. This extraordinary individual trained an army that was very effective and able to expand rapidly. He was able to do this by transforming the existing system of initiation groups (an age-grade system) into cross-lineage groups that he was able to centrally control. This revolutionary social organization allowed him to mobilize an entire generation of young men to fight for him while the women worked to produce food to support them.

The forging of this Zulu polity pushed other peoples desperate to replace cattle stolen by the Zulu into the interior grasslands of modern-day South Africa and far beyond, creating new political formations in what are now Zimbabwe, Malawi, Mozambique, Zambia, and Tanzania. The Sotho polity that was the foundation of present-day Lesotho and the Ndebele polities that were a formative element in the creation of modern Zimbabwe were among the results of the Mfecane (Omer-Cooper 1994:52–81).

Trade, Exploration, and Conquest

Slave Trade

The persistent question of whether the course of Africa's past has been determined mainly by forces internal to the continent or by those emanating from beyond its shores is certainly no more pronounced or more impassioned than with regard to the slave trade. Apologists for the slave trade in the eighteenth and nineteenth centuries argued that slavery was intrinsic in "backward societies" such as those of Africa. They also claimed that slavery in the "Christian" Americas was probably better for Africans than their situation had been in their "pagan" homelands. Abolitionists essentially agreed with these negative stereotypes about indigenous African societies. Most abolitionists supported "legitimate" trade (not based on slavery), missionary activities, and ultimately colonialism, because these intrusions would put an end to slavery and the slave trade and begin the process of redeeming this "pagan" continent. African nationalists and defenders of African culture in the twentieth century argued that African civilizations, extending back to the glories of ancient Egypt, had been deformed and barbarized by the effects of the Atlantic slave trade. It was supposed by most Africans and the supporters of Africans that the Atlantic slave trade had enriched the West at the expense of Africa and was largely responsible for Africa's relative economic backwardness (Manning 1990:8–26).

Clearly the various slave-trading patterns had economic, political, and social impacts on both African and other Atlantic societies. The profits for European merchants in the Atlantic slave trade from the mid-seventeenth century on to the early nineteenth century were immense. It should be noted, though, that these profits diminished considerably for Europeans as African traders established a dominant position in the trade. The profits from the Atlantic slave trade may well have helped lay the foundation for the Industrial Revolution and the expansion of capitalism in Europe and North America, but they also enriched many Africans and Afro-Europeans in Africa as well (see Eltis 2000; Klein 1999). The various slave trades turned African enterprise over wide geographic areas from more productive pursuits and influenced the rise of more authoritarian rulers. By the end of the eighteenth century, enslaved people were being delivered by Africans to the coast from regions as far away as the Hausa states and Katanga (Shaba) in what is now the Democratic Republic of Congo (Iliffe 2017).

It should be noted that slavery in Africa, as elsewhere, is as old as civilization. From the Egyptian dynasties through the Carthaginian and Greek trading states to the Roman Empire, a small number of black Africans were always part of trans-Saharan commerce. By the time the Arabs overran northern Africa circa 800 BCE, bondage and the slave trade were already fixtures of this part of the world as elsewhere. War prisoners from the Sudan (in Arabic *bilad al-Sudan,* "the land of the blacks") were sold north as they had been for centuries. The demand for slaves in the Mediterranean world kept a persistent and substantial movement of black humans as trade goods flowing across the desert (with many more dying on the journey) well into the twentieth century (Manning 1990:27–37, 149–164).

Furthermore, a variety of relationships, such as clientship, pawning, and the sale of individuals to pay for food in times of famine, have existed in human societies from at least the beginning of crop production. This is the case in Africa as well as elsewhere in the world. Conquered peoples were absorbed into the victors' societies, often serving in a lowly status with few rights and privileges for generations before prerogatives and status distinctions between enslaved people and free blurred. In some African states, plantation, quarry, mining, and porterage enslaved people were important parts of the economic base. Enslaved-soldiers were found in the Cayor kingdom of Senegal in the fifteenth century (Klein 1977:335–367).

While recent historical research no longer maintains, as serious scholars once did, that as many as 50 million Africans were taken from West Africa as part of the Atlantic slave trade, the economic and human loss to Africa of the 11.7 million (low estimate) to 15.4 million (high estimate) enslaved people sold throughout this network was serious enough (Manning 1990:5; Schraeder 2004b:53; Lovejoy 2011). More important to understand are the broader negative effects that the slave trade, the conflicts connected with it, and the rise of slavery within Africa associated with the trade had on African culture. At a time when European and US populations were growing rapidly, Africa's was in decline. While Europe and North America were industrializing, Africa was involved in an exploitative and unproductive system of trade in enslaved people (Bah 1993:79–84).

By 700 BCE, captives were being taken across the Sahara, over the Red Sea, and from the coast of East Africa, destined for servitude in North Africa and the Mediterranean world, in southwest Asia, and throughout the Indian Ocean. Much of this commerce was in the hands of Muslims. Although far less has been written about these trades than about the Atlantic slave trade, historians estimate that, in the course of more than 1,000 years, these slave trades involved at least as many victims as the Atlantic slave trade. The trans-Saharan slave trade was the largest of these, with about 8.4 million slaves being sold to the coastal Mediterranean regions. The Swahili coast and Red Sea slave trades were the two smaller slave networks (3.2 and 2.3 million enslaved peoples, respectively) where Africans were sold to the Indian Ocean islands, South and Southeast Asia, and the Middle East (Schraeder 2004b:53). These "Muslim" trades nonetheless differed from the Atlantic trade in one important respect: whereas the victims of the latter were bound overwhelmingly for productive labor in the plantations and mines of the Americas, most victims of the former were destined for some form of domestic servitude, including concubinage. Twice as many African men as women were transported across the Atlantic, whereas it is estimated that twice as many African women as men were taken to the Muslim world (Parker and Rathbone 2007:78–79).

Although the Indian Ocean slave trade never matched the massive numbers of the Atlantic slave trade, it did have disastrous consequences as far inland as the shores of Lake Malawi and those areas of the Congo west of Lake Tanganyika. The centuries-old, though relatively small, trade in African humans to southern and southwest Asia for plantation and mine workers, soldiers, and concubines reached substantial proportions beginning in the middle decades of the eighteenth century as demand for slaves grew on the French plantations on Mauritius and Réunion. This trade continued actively into the nineteenth century, supplying slaves for Brazil, for the clove plantations on the islands of Pemba and Zanzibar off the coast of eastern Africa, as well as for the sugar plantations on the Indian Ocean islands. The nineteenth-century Afro-Arab slavers and ivory hunters penetrated swiftly and deeply inland, causing proportionately as great a loss of life and disruption in eastern African societies as the Atlantic slave trade did at its height (Alpers 1975). The trade in enslaved people from Kilwa and the offshore island of Zanzibar reached tremendous proportions in the late eighteenth century, furnishing labor to the French plantations on the fertile and previously unpopulated islands of Mauritius and Réunion in the Indian Ocean (Shillington 2019:180–181). In Sudan, parts of West Africa (most notably Mauritania), and in various areas where "failed states" and major conflict exist in Africa, enslavement is still present.

Peter J. Schraeder

Statues portraying the inhumanity of the slave trade, situated on the path to the entrance of the National Memorial for Peace and Justice in Montgomery, Alabama.

"Legitimate" Trade

By the end of the eighteenth century, the world price of sugar was declining because of overproduction. At the same time, the price of enslaved people was rising because of stiffer competition among African suppliers in western Africa. As a result, the power and influence of plantation owners from the British West Indies were declining in the British parliament. The Industrial Revolution was spawning a new dominant class of industrialists in the United Kingdom who were finding it increasingly necessary to seek new markets abroad for the clothing, pottery, and metal goods they were producing in growing quantities. These industrialists saw that Africans in Africa could provide European producers with both necessary raw materials and new markets for their cheaply produced manufactured goods (Bohannan and Curtin 1995:213–214).

The Haitian revolution (where people of African descent overthrew European domination), the abolition movement, the French presence in the sugar industry, and perhaps some growing acceptance of the egalitarian principles of the French Revolution and the US War of Independence led the British, with the strongest navy in the world, to abandon the slave trade.

Having transported half the captives from West Africa at the end of the eighteenth century, the British government set up an antislavery squadron and began using force to stop the trade by 1807 (Manning 1990:149–157).

Beginning in the 1790s, trade in palm oil for use in soap, candles, cooking products, and lubricants for looms in return for goods produced in Europe had begun in West Africa. By the 1830s, the commercial production of peanuts for the European market was well under way in West Africa. Though slaving and the legitimate trade in these commodities, as well as gold, timber, gum arabic, skins, and spices, coexisted through midcentury, it became apparent that greater profits existed in "legitimate commerce" than in enslaved people after the markets in the United States were closed in the first decade of the nineteenth century. The Brazilian and Cuban markets dried up by the 1870s.

Large European trading firms soon squeezed out a number of smaller-scale entrepreneurs in Africa. Among those squeezed out were Afro-Europeans, groups of people of mixed European and African ancestry from the Senegambia who had promoted the peanut trade and other trades along the coast to the south, and other Eurafricans and former African slavers from Liberia to Cameroon who had become increasingly involved in palm oil commerce. Arab, subcontinent Indian, and Luso-African (of Portuguese and African ancestry) intermediaries from Angola to Somalia who had switched from trading enslaved Africans to trading ivory, gum arabic, copra, cloves, and other commodities also suffered. Some of these intermediaries were reduced to becoming agents for the European companies while others were simply driven out of business. The cloth, alcohol, tobacco, and firearms imported by the European trading houses did little to strengthen African economies. As competition grew more fierce, European trading monopolies backed by their governments fought even harder to cut out all the African intermediaries and their European competitors. This growing European trading competition played a major role in the European "scramble for Africa" in the 1880s and 1890s (Azevedo 1993:103–110).

Exploration

It is ironic that people continue to credit European explorers of the nineteenth century with the discovery of rivers, waterfalls, and such in Africa when it is obvious that Africans living there already knew these things existed. Obviously, discovery simply meant that a European had verified in writing the existence of something long known to others.

With the exception of the Portuguese and a few Afrikaans-speaking people (the language of the descendants of the mostly Dutch settlers in South Africa), the systematic exploration of Africa between the Limpopo River and the Sahara Desert by Europeans can be dated to Mungo Park's first expedition to the Niger in 1795. By 1885, crossings of the continent from east to west had been thoroughly documented, the extent of the Sahara was known to the European and North American publics, and the major rivers in Africa had been followed and mapped by Europeans. To most Africans, though, this was of little importance, and most African leaders by the latter part of the nineteenth century no longer welcomed wandering white explorers. These Africans had begun to fear the outside influence and rivalry that might weaken their control over trade or, as in the case of the African-Arab slave traders in central and eastern Africa, bring it to an end.

Mungo Park, for example, traveled up the Gambia River in 1795 to determine if it was linked to the Niger River, which appeared on some maps of the period as rising near Lake Chad and flowing west to the Atlantic. He did find the Niger and determined that it flowed eastward, not westward, thereby disproving the Gambia-Niger connection. Since he was then unable to follow the river to its mouth, he returned in 1805 bent on proving that the Niger actually was the Congo River. He died on this expedition, and only in 1830 did Richard Lander demonstrate that the Niger flows into the Gulf of Guinea.

In the first half of the nineteenth century, other explorers, like René Caillié, Hugh Clapperton, and Heinrich Barth, traversed the western parts of Africa recording information that was of interest to the governments, scientific groups, and missionary organizations that sponsored them. Not until the second half of the nineteenth century were the sporadic efforts of Portuguese and Arab explorers penetrating equatorial Africa really taken up by Europeans. One of the most famous of these explorers was David Livingstone.

Livingstone was sent to Africa by the London Missionary Society. He arrived in Cape Town, South Africa, in 1841 and then traveled north. He roamed the interior for years, reaching the Okavango swamp and delta complex in Botswana in 1849, crossing Angola to Luanda in 1854, and reaching Victoria Falls in 1855. In 1858, he traveled up the Zambezi from its mouth and then turned north up the Shire River to Lake Malawi. His death south of Lake Bangweulu in 1873 inspired a great deal of European interest in this part of Africa, especially because of the writings of Henry Morton Stanley, who had "found" the missing Livingstone in 1871.

For the majority of peoples in Europe and North America, the exploits of these explorers meant little more than excitement and drama set on an exotic stage. For small minorities, the diaries of these explorers and those of others, such as Richard Burton and John Speke, who sought the source of the Nile, did much to arouse their interest. Church groups and members of missionary societies were interested in "saving" the Africans. Also interested were the new monied classes spawned by the Industrial Revolution in Europe and North America. These entrepreneurs and investors urged their respective governments to act on their behalf to establish control of the newly found riches and regions (Shillington 2019:347–348).

Conquest and Resistance

Aided by missionaries who appealed to their home governments for various degrees of political or military protection, by explorers who touted the riches to be found in the interior of Africa if only the local inhabitants could be pacified, and by the owners of trading companies who wanted to eliminate competition, most European countries found support from their political and military authorities for the takeover of Africa by the last decades of the nineteenth century. By 1884 to 1885, at the Berlin Conference, the leaders of most European states came together and agreed on ground rules for dividing up Africa. Unfortunately, the political boundaries they drew on their largely inaccurate maps cut apart ethnic groups, kingdoms, and historically linked regions in ways that continue to cause conflicts in Africa today (Freund 2016).

The push of the seven major European powers—Belgium, France, Germany, Italy, Portugal, Spain, and the United Kingdom—into Africa in the last quarter of the nineteenth century required considerable effort. A good majority of the people of Africa, whether living in large-scale polities or small-scale lineage-based societies, opposed European occupation through force of arms or nonviolently (Freund 2016). Well-organized, if poorly armed, Muslim armies filled with a spirit of jihad resisted British advances in Sudan, and the full subjugation of the region was not completed until the late 1890s. In western Africa, Ahmadu Seku, the leader of the Tukolor state, and the Maninka leader, Samory Touré, fought the French into the 1890s. Rabih, a Muslim leader from the upper Nile, resisted French expansion until 1900 in what are today Chad and the Central African Republic (O'Toole 1986:18–20).

Dahomey, a kingdom in present-day Benin, was not conquered by Europeans until 1894—and even then the French were able to do it only with the help of Senegalese troops. Leaders of numerous groups in the forests of Côte d'Ivoire resisted the French for twenty years. The British had to invade the Asante in Ghana in 1874 and 1895–1896 and again in 1900 before they could establish the Gold Coast colony. In Nigeria, the British had to launch major offensives to defeat the various peoples. Ilorin in Yorubaland held out until 1897 as did the *oba* (leader) of Benin City; and the Sokoto caliphate was not completely overcome until 1903. In Uganda, the Bunyoro used guerrilla warfare against the British until 1898; KiSwahili speakers on the coast of Kenya successfully resisted the British for most of 1895 and 1896; and Nandi and other Kenyan peoples fought the British well into the 1900s (Shillington 2019:302).

Farther south in Nyasaland (Malawi), Yao, Chewa, and Nguni forces fought the British in the 1890s; the Gaza polity and the Barwe polity fought the Portuguese in Mozambique; and the Nama resisted the Germans in South West Africa (Namibia). South African groups, including the Afrikaner descendants of the original European settlers, resisted the imposition of British control as well.

Even after the colonial regimes seemed to have been well established, attempts to reassert independence emerged throughout Africa. In the 1890s, the Shona and Ndebele rose up against the British in Southern Rhodesia (Zimbabwe), the people of Tanganyika (Tanzania) fought the Germans in the Maji Maji resistance in 1905–1906, and the Herero and Nama peoples launched open warfare against the Germans in South West Africa in 1904–1907. Throughout colonial Africa, these and other struggles, such as those in the present-day Central African Republic (then part of French Equatorial Africa), continued as late as the 1930s (O'Toole 1984:329–344; Freund 2016).

In the end, though, the superior military technology, logistic and organizational skills, and resources of the Europeans won out. All too often, African leaders found that their inability to unite various ethnic groups and factions against their common European enemies led to defeat. Most of Africa was under European rule by 1905.

The Colonial Period

Colonial Rule

Many of the colonial powers were successful in their conquests because their armies were technologically superior to the resistance forces in Africa. For example, after Britain established a protectorate over the Asante empire in 1897, the Asante military assembled 40,000–50,000 combatants to resist imperial rule. Despite only mobilizing 2,600 men, Britain was able to defeat this resistance utilizing the latest weapons (Schraeder 2004c). Britain subsequently emerged as one of the leading colonial powers, expanding its empire throughout the African continent. The other leading colonial power was France, whose imperial empire was divided into four administrative regions. These regions included French West Africa, French Equatorial Africa, the Maghreb (Algeria, Morocco, and Tunisia), and the Overseas Departments and Territories. Indeed, the French empire extended from Algeria in North Africa and Djibouti in the Horn of Africa to Madagascar in East Africa and Senegal in West Africa.

Belgium and Portugal made far fewer advances in their colonial conquests compared to Britain and France. Although Leopold II emphasized that Belgium's presence in the Congo was occupation, not conquest, Belgium was officially recognized as the "Sovereign of the Congo Free State" in 1885 (Ryckmans 1955). One reason that Belgium was unable to obtain more power over territory in Africa is that it did not have the same military and economic power as Britain and France. Portugal colonized the five modern-day countries of Angola, Cape Verde, Guinea-Bissau, Mozambique, and São Tomé and

Príncipe, but it was also limited in its capacity to be a major imperial power given its lack of financial resources and its heavy national debt (Nowell 1947).

Spain operated as a much smaller colonial power with its imperial dominion over the Spanish Sahara (currently part of Morocco), Equatorial Guinea, and the coastal colonial enclaves of Ceuta and Melilla, the latter of which are still controlled by Spain (Amirah-Fernandez 2008). Territorial disputes remained at the heart of Spanish-Moroccan relations, and some of these disputes still exist today (Amirah-Fernandez 2008). Other smaller colonial powers, such as Germany and Italy, lost control of their territories following military defeat. The German colonies eventually became mandate territories, which transitioned to self-rule under the supervision of the Allied powers after Germany was defeated in World War I. Italy partially lost its territories following defeat in World War II, when the Italian government no longer controlled Libya and Eritrea, but still oversaw a UN-mandated trusteeship of Italian Somaliland (Hess 1966).

During much of the twentieth century, practically all of Africa was under European rule, with the exception of Liberia and Ethiopia. Each colonial power sought economic gain from its possessions, usually by facilitating the export of raw materials (minerals or crops) produced through the efforts of African labor and by selling manufactured goods to its colonial subjects. New infrastructure, notably railroads, connected wealth-producing locations in the interior. All of the colonies were run on thoroughly authoritarian (and sometimes brutal) lines and created hierarchies based on notions of European racial and cultural superiority. Yet all colonial systems depended on their subject populations, and all invoked the rhetoric of a "civilizing mission" that resulted in important changes for Africans, especially through European education.

Commonalities existed, but each European power had a somewhat different philosophy and practice, thus the experiences of Africans under colonial rule were not all the same. The British idea of indirect rule elevated certain ethnicities in importance over others and operated with a distinct mistrust of Africans who became "too British." The French, however, through their policy of assimilation, granted limited arenas for the emergence of "Black Frenchmen" (Suret-Canale 1964). The biggest difference in colonial regimes, however, depended on how many European settlers came to Africa to stay. This affected Africans in countless ways but most directly in whether they retained or lost their land.

After World War I, the limited amount of German territory in Africa was redistributed to the countries that had defeated Germany, in most cases to France or Britain, while the Belgians and Portuguese maintained smaller areas under their nominal control and the Spanish and Italians were of little consequence. Wherever and whenever colonial rule was established, it was essentially a paternalistic, bureaucratic dictatorship. Yet given the vast areas

Peter J. Schraeder

Monument in Algiers, Algeria, to Emir Abdelkader El Djezairi, a military leader who fought against French colonial rule in the nineteenth century.

occupied and the variety of African communities encountered, the colonialists were forced to recognize or create a class of intermediaries to assist them. Colonial rule from the standpoint of economic interests in different regions of Africa is discussed in Chapters 4 and 5.

Colonial policies are often divided into direct and indirect rule, with the clearest cases being indirect rule by the British and direct rule by the French (Shillington 2019:412–415). The British in particular were convinced that ruling through traditional African authorities was the most efficient way to govern and to extract whatever revenue possible. This policy, theoretically, interfered as little as possible so that Africans could advance along their own lines. In reality, even in northern Nigeria, one place where this form of colonialism came quite close to working, the African authorities could often use their positions to extort substantial incomes, though their freedom to rule was circumscribed. They often faced resistance from their own subjects, and any African ruler not acceptable to the colonial power was deposed and replaced by British appointees who were more amenable to the colonial regime.

The British tried to use indirect rule in other places—by reintroducing monarchy to Benin, restoring the Asantehene in central Ghana (Gold Coast), and attempting to reestablish the Oyo empire among the Yoruba in Nigeria. They also were instrumental in maintaining monarchies in Swaziland, Lesotho, Uganda, and Barotseland in what was then Northern Rhodesia. Overall, Britain did not seek to transform African subjects into British citizens. Instead, British administrators sought independence for their protectorates under black-majority governments (Lugard 1922) with traditional leaders at the helm, which strengthened many preexisting forms of African leadership (Gifford and Louis 1971).

The French were relatively disinterested in indirect rule, though they too utilized the old ruling classes when it seemed advantageous. The French established administrative units that cut across ethnic boundaries, created a transethnic elite, and used the French language at all levels of administration. At its extreme, French policy held that all Africans were to be completely assimilated and made equal citizens of France. More often, the highly centralized French administration maintained the necessity of creating an African elite who would accept French standards and then become associated with French rulers in the work of governing the colonies.

The authors of Belgian policy, like the French and the Portuguese, never displayed a great interest in indirect rule. Initially, the Belgians ruled through private companies whose owners were granted control of the people in their territories of interest. This was changed to direct rule by the Belgian government by the 1910s because of the gross abuses committed by those companies against the local people. The Belgians, unlike the French, deliberately limited African education to the primary levels and geared it entirely to semiskilled occupational training. Rather ironically, local political realities, coupled with a lack of finance to develop systems of bureaucratic control, meant that the French, Belgians, and Portuguese were often forced to rule through African elites in ways little different from the British. However, Belgium and Portugal were primarily concerned with the economic interests of the state and less concerned with the eventual political independence (British model) or political inclusion (French model) of the people they colonized (Young 1965).

Though the French colonies were ruled as despotically as any, they did have the anomaly of the *quatre communes,* the four towns of Senegal—Dakar, Saint Louis, Gorée, and Rufisque—where all locally born residents had the legal rights of French citizenship from the time of the French Revolution. These residents were represented, after 1848, in the French Parliament (Chamber of Deputies). Likewise, from 1910 to 1926, the Portuguese allowed a few Portuguese-speaking African Catholics from Angola, Mozambique, and Guinea-Bissau to be represented in the Portuguese parliament.

The major differences in colonial policies were based on the region of the continent rather than the particular colonial power that controlled it. In most of western Africa, both the French and British refused to allocate land to European settlers or companies because local suppliers produced enough materials for trade. By contrast, in parts of British East and Central Africa, as well as in French Equatorial Africa and the Belgian Congo, land was taken from Africans and sold to European settlers and companies to ensure sufficient production for export. This difference caused a number of grave political problems in the nationalist era (Freund 2016).

Toward Independence

Africans became increasingly involved in the world economy during the colonial period. For the seventy-plus years that countries of Europe held both political and economic control in Africa, the economies of African countries were shaped to the advantage of the colonizers. Cash crops, such as coffee, rubber, peanuts, and cocoa, were grown for the European markets. Mining also increased during colonial times. Most cash crop economies benefited the European owners of large plantations rather than African farmers, and almost all mines produced for European companies.

In both the French- and the British-ruled areas of Africa, Western-educated African elites were active participants in some form of local government from the early decades of the twentieth century. In the 1920s, reform movements developed in British West Africa, which, apart from South Africa, were probably the earliest nationalist movements in Africa (unless one includes Liberia and Ethiopia, where European colonial rule was never fully established). These movements, like those led earlier by such men as J. E. Casely Hayford and John Mensah Sarbah in the Gold Coast and Samuel Lewis in Sierra Leone, originated among urban, highly Westernized populations in the cities of the coast and were directed primarily at abuses of the rights of these elites caused by the colonial system. Nowhere before World War II did the idea of actual political independence from colonial rule gather much momentum (Bohannan and Curtin 1995:240–250).

World War II, however, helped to raise African political consciousness. Generally, African soldiers fought alongside their European masters. In cooperation with Charles de Gaulle and his "Free French," French West Africans and French Equatorial Africans joined in the fight against Nazi racialism. During the war, the Atlantic Charter was proclaimed and the United Nations created. The ideas therein contributed to the new visions of the right to freedom from colonial rule that Africans began to voice. After the war, national political parties took hold all over Africa. Initially, the strongest parties to emerge were those in West Africa, where no large European settler class blocked demands. From 1945 to 1960, African nationalist parties under men such as Kwame Nkrumah, Sékou Touré, Nnamdi Azikiwe, Leopold Senghor, and Félix Houphouët-Boigny developed mass support, won local elections, and pressured for more political rights and ultimately for independence (Freund 2016).

In 1951, Libya became the first African country to become independent in the twentieth century. Although Libya was formerly an Italian colony, the country was occupied by the British and French militaries during World War II. After World War II ended, the UN mandated that Libya become independent given that the United States, the United Kingdom, the Soviet Union, and France were unable to agree on how Libya was to be dispositioned following the Italian Peace Treaty (Lewis and Gordon 1954).

Libya's independence was part of a broader nationalist struggle for self-determination in North Africa. Tunisia's transition to self-rule first came about in April 1955, when an internal autonomy convention was established that eliminated the political rights (except at the municipal level) of French citizens living in Tunisia and ensured the transfer of police powers from France to Tunisia after two years (Perkins 2014). This convention led to the official end of the French protectorate in Tunisia in March 1956. As negotiations between France and Tunisia started to climax, France initiated Morocco's transition to self-rule and ultimately terminated its protectorate also in March 1956 (Perkins 2014). Algeria's fight for independence can be characterized by intense political violence and conflict starting with the "War of Liberation" in 1954. Despite the intense violence, Algeria joined its North African counterparts in achieving independence with the Evian Peace Accords in 1962 (Naylor 2015).

In 1957, Ghana became the first sub-Saharan African nation to become independent. From the capital, Accra, Ghana's first president, Kwame Nkrumah (1909–1972), set about creating a nation from the former British colony of Gold Coast. He was faced with a cocoa monoculture export economy and Asante nationalism dating back to the resistance against British imperialism by Asantehene Prempeh I in the nineteenth century. Nkrumah's advocacy of pan-African unity was never sufficient to overcome the influences of competing nationalisms and economic dependency that worked against unity (Shillington 2019:438).

In East Africa, the presence of European settlers made the struggle for independence even more difficult. In Kenya, colonized by the British between 1895 and 1963, a peaceful evolution to independence was ruled out by white settler opposition. Waiyaki Wa Hinga, a Gikuyu leader, initially welcomed Europeans and even entered into "blood brotherhood" with one early colonial administrator in 1890. Waiyaki was killed in 1892 by officials of the Imperial East African Company when he objected to the building of an unsanctioned fort in his area. Harry Thuku, Kenya's pioneer nationalist, also tried peaceful means to resist British colonialism. Concerned with improving the economic lot of Africans, he founded a broad-based organization known as the East African Association in 1921. Advocating civil disobedience as a political weapon, he was arrested for disturbing the peace in February 1922. His arrest led to riots and the deaths of several Africans (Freund 2016).

Independence for most settler colonies was won only through armed struggle. Like the Algerians, who fought a bitter eight-year freedom struggle against the French, Kenyans too found it necessary to resort to arms to achieve independence. The national liberation struggle in Kenya, called Mau Mau by the British, began in the late 1940s and was most strongly supported by the Gikuyu. Jomo Kenyatta, who would later emerge as the country's first postcolonial president, was imprisoned by the British between 1953 and 1961 as the alleged brains behind the movement, though the actual fighting was done by such "forest fighters" as Dedan Kimathi, who was captured and executed in 1957. During the struggle, at least 10,000 Africans (mostly Gikuyu) were killed. A growing sense of national unity against the British resulted from this conflict, and the British finally granted independence to Kenya in 1963 (Shillington 2019:455).

Among the last African nations to achieve independence north of the Limpopo were the former colonies of Portugal: Angola, Cape Verde, Guinea-Bissau, Mozambique, and São Tomé and Príncipe. After more than two decades of armed struggle, independence for these colonies came quickly when the Portuguese government was overthrown by a military coup in 1974. Faced with South African– and US-backed guerrilla opposition, the people of Angola found the goal of a peace settlement very difficult. The people of Mozambique also faced armed opposition financed by South African and ultraconservative groups from the United States well into the 1990s (Freund 2016).

Both Zimbabwe and Namibia achieved black majority rule even later. The people of African ancestry in Zimbabwe defeated the white settler government after a long liberation war, and Zimbabwe became an internationally recognized independent state in 1980. With the support of the United Nations, Namibia achieved its independence from South African control in 1990 after a long armed struggle. In 1994, Africa's "last colony," South Africa, finally attained black majority rule when Nelson Mandela was elected president in the country's first racially inclusive democratic elections (Freund 2016). It is important to remember, however, that as of this writing Spain continues to control the colonial enclaves of Ceuta and Melilla in Morocco. There are also contested cases of sovereignty, including the disposition of former Spanish Sahara, which is claimed by Morocco against the backdrop of a guerrilla insurgency that seeks independence as the Sahrawi Arab Democratic Republic.

Conclusion

African history in the third decade of the twenty-first century is quite different than what it was at the beginning of the contemporary independence era. Back in the early 1950s, African studies was rapidly expanding. As Catherine Coquery-Vidrovitch stated so well midway between then and now, "In twenty years every aspect that defines Africa today will have undergone an alteration that cannot be foretold by our present means of analysis" (1988:318).

It is no longer necessary to prove that Africans have histories. Although still reflected in much common knowledge, the racist and anti-historical synthesis that Africa was "discovered" or "saved" by Europe, or that Caucasians were the original rulers of some African polities, has been eliminated as an acceptable view by most respected scholars of Africa. Professional historians have written hundreds of works about virtually every part of the continent (for recent examples, see Austen 2010; Davenport and Saunders 2000; Fage and Tordoff 2002; Hopkins 2014; Jaffe 2017). There are specific studies of individual African nations; regional introductory histories of northern, eastern, western, central, and southern Africa; and general histories of the whole continent.

In this chapter, we followed four basic concept-centered goals that have evolved through our teaching, reading, and writing on the broad subject of African history. The first of these goals that we sought to weave into this chapter is to enhance appreciation of the long time span and wide geographical area involved in African history. The second is to increase understanding of the great diversity of Africa's past. The third is to make clear that both change and continuity have been integral parts of the human experience in Africa. Finally, we sought to foster a heightened awareness that all events of history have more than one cause and that the interwoven happenings that produce a given outcome are the result of complex chains of events.

As a student of Africa, one ought to personally pursue a fifth goal, not explicitly focused on in this chapter, while reading the other chapters in this text. That goal is to sharpen one's awareness of the role Africa has played and continues to play in world history. To deal with today's global realities, a marriage between the past and the present is needed (Ahluwalia 2012). Whereas one needs to be introduced to humanity's collective memory, a large part of which flows from Africa, one also needs to be sensitized to the current world. People must realize that what happens in Africa is linked to what happens to people everywhere, and vice versa. As was true 100,000 years ago, everyone on the earth shares a common humanity as members of one race—the human race. And while only a few of us were actually born in Africa, our destinies are still linked.

4

Politics

Peter J. Schraeder

On December 17, 2010, a twenty-six-year-old Tunisian fruit vendor, Mohamed Bouazizi, set himself on fire in the town of Sidi Bouzid to protest the harassment he was suffering at the hands of local officials. Bouazizi's actions, which led to his death on January 4, 2011, set in motion a national protest movement referred to as Tunisia's "Jasmine," or "Dignity," Revolution that led to the overthrow of the dictatorship of Zine el-Abidine Ben Ali on January 14, 2011 (Schraeder and Redissi 2011). Ben Ali's overthrow initiated a domino effect in North Africa and neighboring regions as pro-democracy demonstrators confronted dictatorships as part of broader desires for socioeconomic and political-military reforms that are commonly referred to as the Arab Spring (Schraeder 2012a, 2012b). In North Africa, protests toppled the thirty-year dictatorship of Egyptian leader Hosni Mubarak on February 11, 2011, and the forty-two-year dictatorship of Libyan leader Muammar Qaddafi on October 21, 2011. In the wider Middle East, the Arab Spring fostered the intensification of political protests and civil conflicts, most notably the Syrian civil war amid the rise of the Islamic State of Iraq and Syria (ISIS). In sub-Saharan Africa, a place often assumed to be immune to events in North Africa, the Arab Spring continues to exert an influence, especially in the predominantly Muslim countries of West, Central, and East Africa. For example, hundreds of Tuareg soldiers who fled Libya's civil war returned to the northern provinces of Mali in 2011 with

I wish to extend a special thanks to Donald L. Gordon, who wrote this chapter when he was one of the original coeditors of this volume. My new chapter was inspired by Don's writing, and I drew on some of his ideas and text.

their years of fighting experience. They served as the military bulwark of the northern region's secession in 2012 as the independent country of Azawad, an event referred to as a "perfect storm of events unleashed by the Arab Spring" that was ended only by French military intervention in support of the Malian central government (Schraeder 2011b:177–178).

Tunisia's Dignity Revolution and the wider Arab Spring that it spawned are but the latest installment within African politics of an "African wave of democratization" that began in 1989 with the fall of the Berlin Wall. The collapse of single-party regimes in Eastern Europe and the former Soviet Union set powerful precedents for African pro-democracy activists who already had begun organizing against political repression and human rights abuses. Severe economic stagnation and decline in most African economies that peaked in the 1980s served as the internal spark for political discontent, just as it had done in Tunisia. The most notable outcome of this historic turning point—often referred to as Africa's second independence or Africa's second liberation—was the discrediting of over three decades of experimentation with single-party, often military-dominated dictatorships in favor of more democratic forms of governance based on multiparty politics. The African wave of democratization is now more than three decades old and has resulted in a variety of political outcomes. These range from the emergence of Tunisia as one of the most democratic of Africa's fifty-four countries, to the collapse of the Somali state in 1991 and the emergence of civil war, which remains unresolved as of this writing.

The primary purpose of this chapter is to provide an overview of the evolution of African politics. It begins with the political impacts of colonial rule, which in many respects provided the political contours for what is unfolding on the African continent today. The chapter next explores the politics of nationalism and the emergence of the contemporary independence era, which constituted Africa's first independence or first liberation from colonial rule. The great expectations that Africans associated with this historic turning point typically remained unfulfilled or were often dashed. I then discuss how African leaders responded to independence and governing challenges from the 1950s through the 1980s by gradually replacing the political systems left behind by the former colonial powers with more authoritarian forms of governance based on the centralization of power and personal rule. The most dramatic political manifestations of this authoritarian trend involved the creation of single-party regimes as a preferred form of political governance and the rise of military coups d'état and military dictatorships. The political economy of decline and threats to African governance reached their height in the 1980s, as marked by a deepening continent-wide economic crisis, the inability of the state to provide basic social goods, the resurgence of civil society, and the intensification of domestic violence and conflict. Together these trends helped usher in an African wave of democracy that began in 1989, with Tunisia's 2011 Dignity Revolution and the wider Arab Spring that it spawned serving as the latest installment. The African wave of democratization is the next topic, including a specific focus on six sets of political transitions that have occurred. A final section provides an assessment of the status of African politics and especially Africa's democratic experiments in the three decades following the initial wave of African democratization.

Impacts of Colonialism

It is surprising to many students that the entire African continent was under direct European control for only sixty-seven years. This began with the Berlin Conference of 1884–1885, in which the continent was subdivided among seven European colonial powers (Belgium, France, Germany, Italy, Portugal, Spain, and the United Kingdom), and ended with Libya's independence in 1951, which marked the beginning of the contemporary independence era. Yet in that relatively short period (1884–1951), colonialism ushered in five political impacts that transformed the context of African politics.

The most far-reaching political impact of colonialism was the imposition of the European nation-state system onto the African political systems from the precolonial independence era. The origins of this system lie in the 1648 Treaty of Westphalia, which ended the Thirty Years' War (1618–1648) in Europe. The treaty marked the beginning of sovereign political entities that were independent of any outside authorities and exercised control over peoples residing in specific territories with officially marked boundaries. When this system was grafted onto Africa, sovereignty remained in the hands of the occupying colonial powers. The application of this system to Africa, therefore, entailed the subdivision of the entire continent into separate colonies with clearly defined boundaries and centralized political authorities. With few exceptions, the boundaries of these colonial political units became the basis for the contemporary political map of Africa (see the map of contemporary Africa in Chapter 1, and the map of colonial Africa in Chapter 2). Most important, the imposition of the European nation-state system created a series of artificial African countries that, unlike their counterparts in Europe, did not evolve gradually according to the wishes of local African peoples. They instead were constructed by European authorities with little if any concern for local conditions. In the extreme, European leaders resolved a colonial territorial issue at the Conference of Berlin by standing over a map and drawing a new line with a ruler. As a result, the artificially created colonial territories bore little resemblance to the classic definition of a nation-state: one people or ethnic group (the nation) ruled by a legitimate centralized authority (the state).

A second political impact of colonialism was the division of African ethnic groups among numerous colonial states. The division of the Somali people of the Horn of Africa is a notable example. Previously united by a common culture but lacking a centralized authority, the Somali people were subjugated and divided among four imperial powers: France, Italy, the United Kingdom, and an independent Ethiopia. The northwestern portion of the Somali population was absorbed into a French colony that achieved independence in 1977 as the Republic of Djibouti. The western Ogaden portion of the Somali population was annexed by the Ethiopian empire and remains a province of present-day Ethiopia. The southeastern portion of the Somali population became part of the British colony and subsequent independent country of Kenya. Two final portions, the British Somaliland Protectorate and Italian Somaliland, became part of the British and Italian colonial empires. These two portions achieved independence and formed a federation in 1961 that became known as the Republic of Somalia.

The primary long-term problem associated with the division of one people among many states is the potential emergence of irredentism, the political desire of nationalists to reunite their separated peoples in one unified nation-state (Chazan 1991). In Somalia, irredentism emerged as the cornerstone of a Somali nationalist movement during the 1950s that called for a redrawing of inherited colonial boundaries in the Horn of Africa. Symbolized by the five-pointed star emblazoned on the national flag of the Republic of Somalia, this irredentist quest envisioned the reunification of all five Somali territories within one pan-Somali state. The Republic of Somalia already included two of these territories (British Somaliland and Italian Somaliland) and, therefore, sought the "return" of Ethiopia's Ogaden region, the Somali portion of Djibouti, and the Northern Frontier District of Kenya (Laitin and Samatar 1987; Touval 1963). Somali leaders of this irredentist movement opted to seek reunification by force of arms. As a result, Somali leaders funded guerrilla insurgencies in Djibouti, Ethiopia, and Kenya during the 1960s that led to the deterioration of relations between the Republic of Somalia and its neighbors. The Republic of Somalia and Ethiopia also fought a war (1977–1978) over the Ogaden region that became internationalized due to the superpower involvement of the United States and the former Soviet Union (Patman 1990; Zartman 1985). Regardless of whether one is sympathetic to past Somali demands to redraw the inherited colonial boundaries of the Horn of Africa, there is no question that the roots of this and other irredentist conflicts are at least partially the result of illogically drawn European colonial boundaries.

The third political impact of European colonialism was the incorporation of previously separate and independent African peoples within one colonial state. The United Kingdom's creation of Nigeria as first a colony and subsequently as an independent country is illustrative. Nigeria is comprised of over

250 different ethnic groups, although three ethnic groups comprise roughly 66 percent of the total population and primarily reside in three geographical regions: the Igbo in the southeast, the Yoruba in the southwest, and the Hausa/Fulani in the north. Over the course of colonial rule, political identity became fragmented by the imposition of "Nigeria," a concept that initially meant nothing to the diverse ethnic members of the new colonial state. How would individuals describe themselves over time? Am I British? Am I Nigerian? Am I Igbo? Or am I some combination of these?

A number of practical challenges are associated with the creation and maintenance of such a nation-state. For example, how does one communicate effectively across the entire territory? The British imposed English as the national language of administration, but only a minority of the population was fluent in the language at the time of independence. As a result, after independence a series of Nigerian governments included Igbo, Yoruba, and Hausa as official languages of administration and recognized the importance of adopting less-widely spoken languages in local education. Indeed, thirteen additional "state" languages are each spoken by more than 500,000 people, and another fifty-four "local" languages are each spoken by at least 100,000 people (Brann 1993). The practical issues and financial costs associated with such a multilingual effort are enormous. Should all government documents be published in the four major languages or expanded to include the thirteen state languages or the fifty-four local languages? What language should be used for political debate in the parliament? Does television and radio broadcasting need to be transmitted in different languages? What should be the language of the nation's armed forces? Are some languages favored over others, providing an unfair advantage to a particular linguistic group?

The most notable challenge associated with the creation of these artificial colonial states was the potential clash between highly diverse political cultures. In the case of Nigeria, the hierarchical political culture of the Hausa/Fulani clashed with the egalitarian political culture of the Igbo. The Hausa/Fulani political culture demanded deference of its subjects to the proclamations of the emir (king), whereas the Igbo political culture considered it the citizen's duty to publicly challenge and criticize the errors of his or her leaders. A Hausa/Fulani subject was expected to bow facedown, his or her nose touching the ground, as a sign of deference. An Igbo would never bow. The political ramifications of these differences, especially when one multiplies them by the over 250 ethnic groups that comprise Nigeria, were enormous, even under the best of circumstances. The worst-case scenario emerged on May 30, 1967, when the Igbo attempted to secede from Nigeria and announced an independent Igbo nation-state known as Biafra. A brutal three-year civil war followed (1967–1970) in which an ultimately victorious Nigerian military government led by Lieutenant Colonel Yakubu

Peter J. Schraeder

The tomb of King Hassan II, who ruled Morocco from 1961 to 1999, is a reminder of the much more prominent role that monarchies played in African politics during the precolonial independence era. Morocco and Eswatini are the only remaining monarchies in which the king is the country's supreme leader.

Gowon undertook a devastating policy of starvation designed to bring the secessionist Igbos to their knees.

A fourth political impact of colonialism was the dismantling of the traditional checks and balances that regulated political systems during the precolonial independence era. Whereas traditional leaders answered to the political norms and customs of their individual societies and/or ethnic groups during the precolonial independence era, the creation of the colonial state meant that the ultimate source of power became the European colonial administrator. In most cases, the European administrators would appoint only Africans who pledged unswerving allegiance to the colonial power. Even under the British model of indirect rule, popular traditional rulers kept in power by British colonial administrators often saw their traditional power base deteriorate. Tensions arose when the demands of British colonialism ran counter to the interests of the local population, and the local ruler had to choose between siding with his people and risking removal from office or siding with the colonial authorities and maintaining favor with the Europeans. In many cases, even authoritarian African leaders could count on remaining in power as long as they served the interests of the European colonial power.

A final political impact of colonialism was an authoritarian legacy that permeated all aspects of political life. In a normal functioning democracy, the relationship between the nation and the state is based on legitimacy. The primary objective of the colonial nation-state, however, was to achieve and maintain European domination. This authoritarian model of state-society relations became known as "Bula Matari" (he who breaks all rocks). As explained by Crawford Young, this title was bestowed on the famous explorer, Henry Stanley, after he successfully forced a caravan of African porters to dismantle and hand carry several steamships up the Congo River. In the context of state-society relations, Bula Matari embodied the vision of a state "which crushes all resistance" (Young 1994:1).

A coercive apparatus of police and military forces was created in every colony with the intention of ensuring local compliance with colonial rules and regulations. Success was achieved through a conscious policy of divide and rule. Drawing upon the multiethnic and sometimes multiracial nature of their empires, the European powers would station troops from other ethnic or racial groups within a given colony. The cornerstone of this practice was the expectation that troops with little or no ethnic attachment to the subjugated population would have few reservations about taking military action against that population. The same divide-and-rule logic was employed when creating local police forces. The coercive nature of colonial police and military forces contributed to the creation of an authoritarian environment that carried over into the contemporary independence era.

Colonialism also had significant economic impacts, which continue to affect Africa's economies in the contemporary independence era (see Chapter 5). One of the most influential impacts was the transformation of individual colonies into export-oriented economies that, in the extreme, produced one primary product desired by the European colonial power. These so-called monocrop or monomineral economies were designed to serve as convenient and cheap sources of raw materials for European industry. Once developed, the colonies were also expected to serve as markets for the sale of manufactured goods produced in Europe and other regions of the widely scattered European empires.

One example of the promotion of a monocrop colonial economy was the French effort during the nineteenth century to expand the cultivation of peanuts in Senegal. Peanuts, the oil of which was used for a variety of cooking and industrial purposes in Africa and Europe, historically had been grown on a limited scale in Senegal even prior to the imposition of direct colonial rule. The dramatic surge in peanut production that took place under the colonial state resulted from an alliance between French colonial administrators and local Muslim religious leaders (*marabouts*), both of whom jointly recognized the financial profits to be gained from making Senegal a center for peanut production within the French colonial empire. The willingness of local *marabouts* to promote peanut production through the mobilization of their disciples (*talibés*) achieved remarkable results. From 1885 to the eve of World War I, annual peanut production increased sevenfold from 45,000 to 300,000 metric tons (Gellar 1995:12–13). On the eve of independence from colonial rule in 1960, roughly two-thirds of Senegal's rural population was involved in peanut production, and the peanut crop accounted for at least two-thirds of the total value of all Senegalese exports (Gellar 1995:13, 60). In short, the prosperity of Senegal's colonial economy had become "inextricably linked" to peanut production (Gellar 1995:12).

The promotion of monocrop or monomineral colonial economies during the colonial era constituted at best a mixed blessing and at worst a severe hindrance to the long-term economic development of the African continent (Gellar 1995:13). The basic economic reasons are twofold. First, an economy geared toward the production of a primary product is vulnerable to the unreliability of international prices paid for that product. The economic history of the second half of the twentieth century demonstrated that the prices for primary products fluctuate dramatically and in general have declined relative to the costs of manufactured products. As a result, estimating government revenues from taxes in order to ensure a variety of government services becomes difficult if not impossible. How can a government dependent on revenues from one product maintain its domestic and international financial commitments if a significant portion of the crop is decimated by poor weather? Moreover, how does the government respond when, as in the case of Senegal, the peanut crops upon which its colonial economy was based suffer a sharp decrease in international demand due to replacement by a cheaper and more effective substitute like petroleum oil from the Middle East?

A second, equally nefarious, impact of monocrop and monomineral economies is the negative relationship between the promotion of primary products and food production. Specifically, the creation of monocrop and monomineral colonial economies was directly associated with a dramatic decline in the production of traditional foodstuffs. This agricultural shortcoming carried over into the contemporary independence era, as levels of food production declined relative to the needs of growing populations, contributing to malnutrition and chronic famine conditions in various regions. One troubling consequence of this trend is that Africa was the only region of the world that suffered from a per capita decline in food production from the 1960s to the 1980s.

The bottom line is that African economies were designed to be subordinate to European colonial needs. In no case, even after World War II, when the pressures of world opinion and decolonization were heavy, did European colonizers invest in cogent, rational programs of development designed to make African states self-sufficient. Without joining the debate whether Europe actually "underdeveloped" Africa (Rodney 1972), it is obvious that colonial policies worked to handicap independent Africa's economic future. Indeed, on departure, colonial administrations left Africa with weak, poorly integrated, severely distorted economies, placing most of Africa into a multifaceted and tenacious dependency relationship with more economically advanced European states. The decisions, strategies, and even sovereignty of emergent African countries would be contingent on *foreign* markets, industry, finance, and expertise.

Nationalism and the Politics of Independence

The emergence of African nationalism and African demands for national self-determination (i.e., independence for the colonies) followed a different pattern than its classic European counterparts of earlier centuries (Neuberger 1986). The emergence of European "nations" (i.e., a cohesive group identity) generally preceded and contributed to the creation of European "states" (the structures of governance). The net result was the creation of viable nation-states that enjoyed the legitimacy of their peoples. This process was reversed in Africa. In most cases, the colonial state was created prior to the existence of any sense of nation. As a result, the creation and strengthening of a nationalist attachment to what in essence constituted artificially created African states became one of the supreme challenges of colonial administrators and the African leaders who replaced them during the contemporary independence era. African nationalism was also different than its European counterparts due to its inherently anticolonial character. African nationalist movements were sharply divided on political agendas, ideological orientation, and economic programs. Regardless of their differences, the leaders of these movements did agree on one point: the necessity and desirability of independence from foreign control. Anticolonial sentiment served as the rallying point of African nationalist movements to such a degree that African nationalism was equivalent to African anticolonialism.

African nationalism was driven by a series of factors, some of which were internal to the colonies, while others emerged from the broader international arena. The creation of the colony itself, most notably the designation of regional administrative centers and a capital city, played an important initial role in providing the basis for the emergence of nationalism (Hodgkin

1957:63–83). The urban areas served as magnets for Africans seeking employment and education, contributing to a process of urbanization in which Africans moved in increasing numbers from the countryside to the capital cities and towns. The "lure of the town," notes Kenneth Little (1970:7–23), was due to the role of the urban areas as centers of politics, economics, and education.

The new towns served as the focal points of emerging national identities. In contrast to the relatively homogeneous nature of life in the villages, the colonial towns functioned as meeting grounds for the numerous ethnic groups that inhabited individual colonies. The towns acted as melting pots in the sense that diverse ethnic cultures were gradually overshadowed by a sense of belonging to a larger political unit. Yet the promotion of nationalist sentiment did not necessarily mean a weakening of ethnic identity or the breaking of socioeconomic and political ties between the urbanized migrant and his or her village of birth. Simply put, the colonial towns fostered the emergence of an overarching national culture and language while at the same time individuals maintained their specific cultural attachments.

The promotion of educational training for select groups of Africans served as a second pattern of social change that contributed to the rise of nationalism. The practical problem confronted by colonial administrators was that the small number of Europeans posted in each colony were incapable of managing all aspects of the colonial economic and political systems. In order to ensure effective rule, colonial administrators oversaw a series of educational programs specifically designed to train the local peoples in the language and philosophy of the colonial power; create an auxiliary "technical" staff capable of performing a variety of technical tasks, such as accounting, plumbing, and electrical work; and train a select elite to collaborate with the colonial powers (Ake 1981:72–73). Each colony, therefore, went beyond the traditional literacy programs of missionaries by creating grade schools, high schools, and technical training institutes.

Rather than creating a subservient population and a collaborationist elite, colonial education served as one of the seeds of nationalism that contributed to colonialism's ultimate demise. Small numbers of secondary schools for the most part located in the capital city meant that students selected by colonial administrators would arrive from all regions of the colony. As a result, a student who had most likely never traveled outside of his or her village and who had rarely if ever met students their own age from other ethnic groups suddenly found himself or herself in new surroundings with students from all over the colony. As time went by, friendships were created that transcended ethnic lines.

Students began seeing themselves as part of a larger nation (the colony) that was multiethnic in nature. In the British colony of Nigeria, for example, the vast majority of colonial civil servants were trained in the capital city at King's College, the standard name for such institutions throughout the British colonies. The formative years spent at this institution prompted students from various ethnic backgrounds, such as Yoruba, Igbo, and Hausa-Fulani, to think of themselves as belonging to a greater Nigerian nation that, in turn, formed part of the greater British Empire.

The sense of belonging to something larger than a particular ethnic group developed further when students were sent to study at regional colonial schools. Prior to the beginning of World War II, the only postsecondary school throughout Afrique Occidentale Française (AOF, or French West Africa) was the École Normale William Ponty (William Ponty School) in Dakar, Senegal. The school was renowned as the "most important center" for elite training in francophone West Africa (Ajayi, Goma, and Johnson 1996:39). For the first time in their lives, students were able to interact with their counterparts from other colonies, realizing that they often shared much more in common with each other as colonized peoples than they did with their colonial educators, who in any case rarely accepted them as either political or intellectual equals. Furthermore, these institutions served as the training centers for individuals who often emerged as the founding leaders of the newly independent African countries. One of the most influential leaders to graduate from the William Ponty School was Félix Houphouët-Boigny, one of the founding leaders of Côte d'Ivoire who served as president from 1960 to 1993.

African students sent to Paris, London, and the capitals of other colonizing powers to pursue advanced education and training had the greatest impact on nationalist demands for independence. The sharing of ideas and the nurturing of lifelong friendships became possible not only with students from colonies in other regions of the world but with citizens from the host country itself. The close personal relationship between Léopold Sédar Senghor, the first president of Senegal (1960–1981), and Georges Pompidou, president of France from 1969 to 1974, was due to the fact that they were classmates during the same era at Lycée Louis-le-Grand (Louis-le-Grand High School), a prestigious school in Paris (Vaillant 1990:64–86).

An equally important impact of studying abroad was direct exposure to the inherent contradictions between the colonizer's democratic heritage and traditions and the reality of authoritarian colonial rule at home. As any student who has studied in Paris can attest, the French curriculum has always underscored the importance of French democracy, with special emphasis being placed on the universal democratic ideal of the French Revolution: "Liberté, Égalité, Fraternité" ("Liberty, Equality, Fraternity"). However, even the most enamored African student of French civilization and French culture was hard pressed to rationalize the realities of undemocratic rule throughout the French colonies. Regardless of whether they studied in Berlin, Brussels, Lisbon, London, Madrid, Paris, or Rome, African students inevitably were confronted by the chasm that existed between the practice of democracy in Europe and the undemocratic realities of day-to-day life in the colonies. African students, once trained to serve as the colonial administrators of their respective colonies, more often than not returned home intent on doing everything in their power to achieve independence for their peoples.

African nationalism was also driven by factors within the broader international system. One factor revolved around the emergence of pan-African linkages and organizations (Esedebe 1982). Inspired by the anticolonial and antiracist activities of peoples of African descent living in North America, the West Indies, and Europe during the nineteenth and twentieth centuries, African leaders sought to promote a unified African front against colonial rule. Fascist Italy's 1935 invasion of Abyssinia (present-day Ethiopia) and defeat of Emperor Haile Selassie's 250,000-strong Ethiopian army marked a turning point in the emergence of pan-African sentiment. Ali A. Mazrui, the Kenyan historian, notes that foreign occupation of a country that served as a "proud symbol of African independence and black achievement" had a "resounding impact" on Africans and members of the African diaspora (Mazrui and Tidy 1984:7). An example is found in the autobiography of Kwame Nkrumah, the first president of Ghana. At the time of Ethiopia's invasion, Nkrumah had just arrived in London to pursue his university studies. Nkrumah captures the moral outrage he felt when he first learned of the invasion while walking down a London street: "At that moment it was almost as if the whole of London had declared war on me personally," explained Nkrumah. "For the next few minutes I could do nothing but glare at each impassive face wondering if those people could possibly realize the wickedness of colonialism, and praying that the day might come when I could play my part in bringing about the downfall of such a system. My nationalism surged to the fore; I was ready and willing to go through hell itself, if need be, in order to achieve my object" (Nkrumah 1957:27).

What subsequently became known as the pan-African ideal was enunciated for the first time at the 1945 meeting of the Pan-African Congress (PAC) held in Manchester, England. Participants adopted a resolution, "Declaration to the Colonial Peoples," that affirmed the rights of all colonized peoples to be "free from foreign imperialist control" and "to elect their own governments, without restrictions from foreign powers" (Ajala 1988:36). In a separate resolution, "Declaration to the Colonial Powers," participants further underscored that if the colonial powers were "still determined to rule mankind by force, then Africans, as a last resort, may have to appeal to force in the effort to achieve freedom" (Ajala 1988:39).

The outbreak of two world wars in Europe served as a second international factor that affected the rise of African demands for decolonization. Each of the colonial powers maintained standing armies comprised of African recruits, several of which clashed during skirmishes on the African continent during World War I (Farwell 1986). During World War II, African conscripts played a greater combat role in the European theater, especially in the case of France. By the beginning of 1939, seven African divisions of the Tirailleurs Sénégalais (Senegalese Riflemen), a fighting force comprised of African recruits from francophone West Africa, constituted 7 percent of all French military forces stationed in Europe, with 20,000–25,000 soldiers losing their lives during the course of World War II (Echenberg 1991).

The most decisive impact of African soldiers' fighting in Europe was the shattering of colonially inspired images of whites as invincible and all-powerful. The rank and file of the Senegalese Riflemen were direct participants in numerous battles in which French military forces were overrun by other white (Nazi German) and nonwhite (Imperial Japanese) military forces. The pace of Japanese victories was especially significant because Africans saw that European militaries could in fact be defeated by non-European armies. Many African soldiers concluded that Africans were militarily superior to Europeans in terms of both courage and valor. Laqui Condé, a Senegalese Rifleman recruited from Côte d'Ivoire, summarized a belief among African soldiers: "We were stronger than the whites. That bullet that hit my tooth would have killed a white. When the shooting came, the whites ran. They knew the area and we did not, so we stayed. Our officers? They were behind us" (quoted in Echenberg 1991:92).

A turning point in the development of nationalist sentiment for many soldiers occurred upon demobilization. Unlike their white French counterparts who were usually quickly demobilized, given "tumultuous welcomes," and provided with back pay and demobilization premiums, the African soldiers, many of whom spent several years in prisoner of war (POW) camps, "languished" in demobilization centers in southern France and West Africa (Echenberg 1991:98). African soldiers became disenchanted when French authorities sought to deny them the same financial benefits accorded white soldiers, resulting in a series of protests and uprisings, the most notable of which occurred at a military camp in Thiaroye, Senegal. A heavy-handed French military response resulted in at least thirty-five deaths and hundreds of casualties among the Senegalese Riflemen, and further inflamed the sense of betrayal felt by soldiers who perceived themselves as having made sacrifices for France (Echenberg 1991:96–104). The events of Thiaroye were captured in a 1988 film, *Le Camp de Thiaroye* (*The Thiaroye Military Camp*), by the celebrated novelist and filmmaker Ousmane Sembène. Soldiers responded to the events of Thiaroye and other shortcomings of demobilization, such as the lack of jobs, by forming and joining veterans' associations. Collectively, veterans asserted that equal sacrifices required equal benefits (Echenberg

1991:104). The veterans' associations not only fought for equal treatment for African veterans, but they also played an integral role in the nationalist movements seeking independence.

Independence and the Centralization of State Power Around Individual Leaders

The process of decolonization unfolded gradually in a series of waves of independence. The first wave took place during the 1950s and was led by the North African countries of Libya, Morocco, and Tunisia, as well as Ghana, Guinea, and Sudan. The second and largest wave of independence took place during the 1960s, when more than thirty African countries achieved independence. The majority of these countries were former British and French colonies in East, Central, and West Africa. A third wave in the 1970s was dominated by the independence of the former Portuguese colonies of Angola, Cape Verde, Guinea-Bissau, Mozambique, and São Tomé and Príncipe (MacQueen 1997), although Comoros, Djibouti, and Seychelles also became independent during this period. A final wave of independence in the 1980s and the 1990s led to the emergence of black majority–ruled regimes in Zimbabwe (1980), Namibia (1990), and South Africa (1994). Except for the minor coastal enclaves of Ceuta and Melilla in present-day Morocco, which remain under Spanish control, Nelson Mandela's emergence in 1994 as the first democratically elected leader of South Africa signaled the end of the decolonization process during the contemporary independence era.

The early days of freedom from colonial rule—especially during the 1950s and 1960s when the majority of countries gained independence—were charged with excitement and full of hope. The immediately obvious burdens of racist imperial rule were gone. New flags flew over government offices, Africans rather than Europeans held political control, and the world recognized the new states as sovereign.

African leaders nonetheless were confronted with two paradoxes at the beginning of the contemporary independence era. First, they had to respond to what can be called the "great expectations–minimal capabilities paradox." The newly elected leaders had to contend with popular expectations that the fruits of independence, most notably higher wages and better living conditions, would be quickly and widely shared after the departure of the former colonial powers. While Africans did not necessarily identify with the new state or its leadership, their expectations about what should come from the end of colonialism were high. They wanted education for their children, higher wages, hospitals and health care, better living conditions, drinkable water, farm-to-market roads, and better prices for their crops. In short, they wanted an instantly better life, and they wanted it yesterday! In almost every case, however, the newly independent African countries simply did not have the capabilities to satisfy public demands. In addition to being heavily dependent on the former colonial power for trade, investment, and even personnel to staff key governmental ministries, African leaders and their countries were constrained by export-oriented monocrop and monomineral economies, low levels of education among the general population, and economies that favored the maintenance of external links with the European powers at the expense of national development priorities and regional cooperation with other African countries.

Second, the political frameworks bequeathed to the African continent at the beginning of the contemporary independence era embodied what can be called an "authoritarian-democratic paradox," in which newly elected African leaders, educated in authoritarianism during the colonial era, were expected to perform like seasoned experts in democracy. Despite their almost complete disregard for the promotion of democratic values during the colonial era, departing colonial administrators hastily constructed political arrangements that purported to embody Western democratic ideals, such as systems of checks and balances in which offices of the president, legislatures, and judiciaries would balance each other's power and prevent the emergence of authoritarianism. The relatively decentralized Westminster model of parliamentary governance was grafted onto the authoritarian structures of colonial rule in the former British colonies, and the more centralized Elysée model was similarly introduced into France's former colonies (Munslow 1983; Rothchild 1960). For the most part, however, the so-called democracies left behind by the departing colonial powers represented largely untested and ill-suited political practices and procedures that were not grounded in African traditions or political cultures.

The vast majority of African leaders resolved these paradoxes of independence by gradually replacing the political systems left behind by the former colonial powers with more authoritarian forms of governance based on the centralization of power and personal rule. One set of tactics involved the Africanization of state institutions. This included the immediate replacement of departing senior colonial administrators with African politicians, followed by the dramatic expansion of the number of African civil servants working in the various bureaucracies of the executive branch. According to one study, African civil services grew at such a rapid rate during the 1960s—an annual average of 6 percent—that by 1970 approximately 60 percent of all African wage earners were employed by their respective governments (Markovitz 1970:183–200). Such positions were coveted due to the popular perception of the state as the most lucrative source of wage employment and privileges, including government-provided cars, chauffeurs, and housing. From the leader's perspective, the doling out of ever-increasing numbers of jobs was an important form of political patronage. Indeed, these positions more often than not were provided to the leader's ethnic or clan group, as well as their principal ethnic or clan allies.

African leaders also expanded the number of state-owned or state-controlled corporations known as parastatals (Ake 1981). The state, when in this mode, attempts to bring under its control all economic activity, especially economic decisionmaking. The purpose, generally speaking, is obtaining power. But equally important is the economic power that derives from the revenues of all these activities. One of the most common forms of parastatals is the marketing board, a state agency that sets the prices and maintains monopolistic control over the buying and selling of primary products. Originally derivative of the colonial era, this particular form of parastatal expanded in both size and scope to include almost all forms of primary products, including both natural resources, such as oil, gas, and mineral wealth, and agricultural products, such as cotton, peanuts, and coffee.

Another set of tactics designed to centralize power involved the suppression and dismantling of other centers of political power capable of challenging the supremacy of the presidential mansion. Actions undertaken by authoritarian presidents included the suspension of constitutions, the banning of opposition political parties and the jailing of political opponents, the marginalization or even dismantling of independent judiciaries and parliaments so that they became at best rubber-stamp institutions, and the suppression of a free press. These actions not surprisingly conflicted with the increasingly vocal demands of "civil society," or the vast array of voluntary associations throughout African societies that seek access to state power (Rothchild and Chazan 1988). Numerous components of African civil society, including but not limited to political parties, labor unions, student organizations, and religious groups, had played important roles in the ultimate downfall of colonialism and the transition to independence during the 1950s. After independence these groups expected to wield equal if not greater levels of influence in their newly independent countries. These expectations proved ill-founded, as African leaders consistently employed two sets of policies—co-optation and repression—to silence the demands of civil society as part of a growing trend toward "predatory rule" (Fatton 1992). Indeed, one scholar even went so far as to underscore the emergence of a "vampire state" (Frimpong-Ansah 1992).

The movement toward the suppression of other state actors and civil society meant that authoritarian leaders had to depend on a loyal security apparatus that was both willing and able to enforce presidential directives. As a result, the creation and rapid expansion of a coercive apparatus comprising a wide variety of security forces served as a critical component of the concentration of state power. These typically included a national police force, a presidential guard devoted to protecting the leader, intelligence services, and a military. According to one study, military spending as a percentage of gross national product (GNP) nearly doubled throughout the African continent from 1.8 percent in 1963 to 3.4 percent in 1971 (US Arms Control and Disarmament Agency 1975:16). This was at a time when African military forces were principally focused on assuring domestic control and stability as opposed to protecting the country from an external threat.

A final trend associated with the concentration of state power revolved around the creation of "personal rule networks," or a "neopatrimonial" system of governance in which power is ultimately vested in an individual leader as opposed to legally based institutions (Jackson and Rosberg 1982; see also Cohen 2015; Medard 1992). The system is based on a series of concentric circles of patron-client relationships in which the leader is at the center of the system. The leader selects senior advisers based on personal ties, those advisers subsequently do the exact same thing, and so on and so forth. This results in a cascading series of patron-client ties that penetrate all levels of the political system. The leader is exalted in this system and seeks to instill loyalty through a delicate combination of charisma and the provision of economic and political patronage. In extreme cases, the inherently personal nature of patron-client systems ensures that they often do not survive the death of the leader. However, as long as the leader is capable of maintaining and increasing the level of political and economic resources provided through the patronage network, he or she can at least ensure their continued domination of the political system.

The degree to which personal rule increasingly dominated African politics during the early decades of the contemporary independence era is demonstrated by drawing on the Polity IV data project (Marshall, Gurr, and Jaggers 2019). This data project documents an array of political attributes for all countries in the world, including an annual assessment of institutional constraints on executive power that can be recast in terms of personal rule. Specifically, the dataset allows us to assess the degree of personal rule of African regimes on a scale of 1 to 7, with 1 being the highest level of personal rule (i.e., the lowest degree of institutional constraints on the executive) and 7 being the lowest level of personal rule (i.e., the highest degree of institutional constraints on the executive).

Table 4.1 sets out the extent of personal rule in 1988, the year preceding the beginning of Africa's wave of democratization. In that year, 54 percent or twenty-seven countries of the African continent's fifty independent countries at the time exhibited an extremely high degree of personal rule by their leaders. This figure increases to an extraordinary 88 percent, or forty-four countries, if we also include countries with high or very high degrees of personal rule. Personal rule dominated African governance, regardless of whether one focuses on large regional powers such as Algeria under Chadli Bendjedid; mini-states such as Djibouti under Hassan Gouled Aptidon; oil-rich countries such as Gabon under Omar Bongo; economically

Table 4.1 Degree of Personal Rule in Africa, 1988

Extremely High Degree of Personal Rule	Very High Degree of Personal Rule	High Degree of Personal Rule	Moderate Degree of Personal Rule	Low Degree of Personal Rule	Very Low Degree of Personal Rule	Extremely Low Degree of Personal Rule
54% (27/50)	12% (6/50)	22% (11/50)	0% (0/50)	2% (1/50)	2% (1/50)	4% (2/50)
Algeria	Cameroon	Angola		Gambia	Botswana	Mauritius
Benin	Cape Verde	Egypt				Sudan
Burkina Faso	Congo Brazzaville	Kenya				
Burundi	Djibouti	Madagascar				
Central African Republic	Guinea-Bissau	Mauritania				
Chad	Morocco	Mozambique				
Comoros		Niger				
Côte d'Ivoire		Sierra Leone				
Democratic Republic of Congo		Tanzania				
Equatorial Guinea		Tunisia				
Eswatini		Zimbabwe				
Ethiopia						
Gabon						
Ghana						
Guinea						
Lesotho						
Liberia						
Libya						
Malawi						
Mali						
Nigeria						
Rwanda						
Senegal						
Somalia						
Togo						
Uganda						
Zambia						

Source: Adapted from Polity IV data set (1988 data). See Marshall, Gurr, and Jaggers (2019).

Notes: Polity uses a 7-point scale of "institutional constraints on executive power" that is recast in terms of personal rule and foreign policy as follows: 1 = extremely high degree of personal rule (extremely low degree of institutional constraints); 2 = very high degree of personal rule (very low degree of institutional constraints); 3 = high degree of personal rule (low degree of institutional constraints); 4 = moderate degree of personal rule (moderate degree of institutional constraints); 5 = low degree of personal rule (high degree of institutional constraints); 6 = very low degree of personal rule (very high degree of institutional constraints); 7 = extremely low degree of personal rule (extremely high degree of institutional constraints).

Regimes unclassified by Polity IV in 1988 (4% or 2/50) were São Tomé and Príncipe and Seychelles. South Africa is not included because it was under apartheid rule until 1994. Eritrea, Namibia, and South Sudan are not included because they had yet to obtain independence.

impoverished countries such as Mozambique under Joasquim Chissano; or any number of ideologically inspired regimes, whether the African Marxism of Ethiopia's Mengistu Haile Mariam, the African socialism of Zambia's Kenneth D. Kaunda, or the African capitalism of Kenya's Daniel arap Moi. In contrast, only four countries (8 percent) occupied the low to extremely low categories of the personal rule spectrum: the democracies of Botswana under Quett Masire, Gambia under Dawda Jawara, and Mauritius under Anerood Jugnauth, as well as the Sudanese military dictatorship under Ahmed al-Mirghani. No country in 1988 occupied the middle category of having a moderate degree of personal rule. In short, the vast majority of African leaders from the 1950s through the 1980s had created authoritarian forms of governance based on the centralization of power and personal rule.

Single-Party Systems as the Dominant Form of Political Governance

The creation of single-party political systems constituted one of the most significant political acts undertaken by African leaders during the contemporary independence era (Collier 1982). These parties ranged from Chama Cha Mapinduzi (CCM), a mass mobilizing party created by Julius Nyerere (the former socialist leader of Tanzania), to the Workers' Party of Ethiopia (WPE), a vanguard party created by Mengistu Haile Mariam (the former Marxist leader of Ethiopia), and the Kenya African National Union (KANU), the sole ruling party of capitalist-oriented Kenya that was created by former President Jomo Kenyatta. In short, regardless of their political ideology, nearly all African leaders exhibited authoritarian tendencies that inevitably resulted in the creation of single-party political systems (Kilson 1963; Sylla 1977).

African leaders offered numerous rationales to justify the establishment of political monopolies over their respective political systems (Liebenow 1986:225–229). The first justification was that single-party systems were reflective of traditional African political systems as they existed prior to the imposition of direct colonial rule (Lonsdale 1989). According to this argument, the single-party system was not to be perceived as a "temporary aberration" from a universal norm of multiparty democracy but rather as a "modern adaptation of traditional African political behavior" (Lonsdale 1989:226). Unlike the divisive nature of Western multiparty systems in which one party emerges dominant and the others are marginalized, the concept of single-party democracy was heralded as conducive to promoting the traditional African norm of seeking consensus in which every participant has the right to voice an opinion and decisions are made only when agreed upon by all present. It is for this reason that Tanzanian President Nyerere chose the Kiswahili term *ujamaa* (brotherhood) as the symbolic guiding principle of the CCM and his country's "return" to traditional African socialism (Nyerere 1968).

A second rationale for creating single-party systems was the imperative of responding to existing and potential crises. African leaders argued against "wasting" scarce resources on competitive politics when their countries were confronted with crises of development ("How can we quickly develop our society?"), crises of administration ("How do we quickly educate the required leaders?"), and, most important, crises of governance ("How do we quickly satisfy rising popular demands for the fruits of independence?") (Liebenow 1986:225). Unity was crucial to the attainment of independence, argued those who led the nationalist struggles during the 1950s, but it was equally crucial once that independence had been achieved. African leaders feared that multiparty systems would foster the fragmentation of ethnically diverse African societies and, therefore, perceived the single-party system as one of the most important tools for transforming colonially inspired, artificial states into true nations.

A third rationale, especially offered by African leaders from the Marxist tradition, underscored the vanguard role that single parties were expected to play. Drawing upon the Leninist concept that the "masses" of individual African societies needed to be led by an "enlightened elite," the single party was envisioned as serving to protect and promote Marxist revolutions on the African continent (Liebenow 1986:228–229). The single party was particularly oriented toward the future evolution of African societies, especially in terms of ensuring industrial development and the promotion of basic human needs such as guaranteed access to adequate food, shelter, and health care.

The nearly thirty-year experiment with single-party rule achieved few positive results (Decalo 1992; Nyong'o 1992). Even in the most benevolent of examples, such as Nyerere's *ujamaa* experiment in Tanzania, the country made significant strides in promoting mass literacy and the provision of basic human needs only at the expense of a failed overall economy that witnessed an annual average decline of 7 percent in agricultural output. One of the primary reasons for this failure was that an initially voluntary villagization program—the centerpiece of the *ujamaa* ideology in which peasants were grouped together in new communal villages—ultimately became coercive in nature. Many peasants were forced to move from their traditional lands to village projects that were either poorly conceived or simply inappropriate for farming practices. If the state inevitably became coercive and, therefore, counterproductive to the goal of development in the most benevolent of single-party systems, one only has to imagine its impact on the development of the most authoritarian single-party systems such as the Marxist-inspired tyranny created in Mengistu's Ethiopia.

The most notable problem associated with the single-party experiment of Tanzania and its contemporaries was that it led to a stagnation of ideas. For example, although Tanzanian legislative candidates were allowed to run against each other under the unified banner of the CCM, they were not permitted to question either the socialist domestic ideology or the foreign policy of the Nyerere regime. Candidates could debate the instrumental aspects of carrying out party-approved policies but were unable to offer alternatives to misguided policies. In this and other cases, African leaders who felt they knew best restricted the range of political debate to such a degree that the single party ultimately became a means for maintaining control rather than a dynamic tool for promoting change and development.

The growing stagnation of single-party rule from the 1950s to the end of the 1980s was matched by the growing power and influence of African

Peter J. Schraeder

A contemporary example of a de facto single-party regime is Uganda's National Resistance Movement headed by Yoweri Museveni, who has served as president from 1986 to the present. The campaign poster is from the 2016 legislative and presidential elections.

militaries and African military leaders. The sharp increase in military coups d'état led to the replacement of entrenched civilian leaders with their military counterparts and became one of the most important forms of regime change in African politics during the initial decades of the contemporary independence era. Most important, the emergence of military leaders as power brokers within African presidential mansions and parliaments did not usher in a new period of democracy and prosperity, but instead led to new forms of military-led authoritarianism as bad as, if not worse than, their civilian counterparts.

Military Coups d'État and Military Dictatorships

African militaries emerged from the shadows of obscurity during the 1950s to become one of the most important institutional actors in African politics and society. The primary means for African military personnel to achieve power and influence over their respective political systems was the military coup d'état, or the sudden and illegal overthrow of an existing government by a portion of the state's armed forces. By the end of the 1960s, military leaders had launched over twenty-nine successful coups, ushering in a period of militarization that soon left more than 50 percent of all African countries governed by military regimes. Even in cases where they led their troops back to the barracks after turning over power to elected civilian regimes, military leaders maintained, and often enhanced, their newfound levels of political influence. Once having enjoyed the fruits of power, military leaders, often referred to as the "men on horseback" or "leaders in khaki," were prone to return to presidential mansions in later coups, leading foreign observers to characterize African militaries as the primary forces for change throughout the African continent from the 1950s to the 1980s.

Scholars initially overlooked the role of the military in African politics during the immediate postcolonial era. At the time of independence, the militaries inherited by newly elected African leaders were usually very small and lacked sophisticated weapons, such as armored vehicles, combat aircraft, and guided missile systems (Thom 1984). African militaries were, therefore, more symbols of sovereignty and independence than independent actors capable of influencing their respective political systems. Moreover, most African militaries played little if any role in the largely peaceful decolonization process during the initial independence decade of the 1950s. Even after a series of coups overthrew five civilian governments from 1958 to 1965, scholars perceived these events as mere aberrations from the expected consolidation of multiparty democracies (Liebenow 1985:127).

A growing sense that the so-called aberrations were becoming the norm of African politics occurred in 1966 when military coups overthrew civilian regimes in seven countries, ranging from the traditional monarchy of King Ntare V of Burundi to the multiparty democracy of Prime Minister Abubakar Tafawa Balewa of Nigeria. From this point forward, scholars and analysts took note of the explosion of military involvement (Decalo 1976). According to a dataset that was created by drawing on Powell and Thyne (2020) and McGowan (2003; see also McGowan and Johnson 1986, 1984), the first thirty-nine years (1951–1989) of the contemporary independence era witnessed 161 attempted military coups in which 75 (47 percent) were successful. Only five African countries—Botswana, Cape Verde, Eritrea, Namibia, and South Africa—have never faced armed challenges from their military, police, or other security personnel.

The majority of coups share several characteristics. First, military leaders have been able to intervene successfully within their respective political systems due to the weak nature of the African state in the immediate post-independence era. Weak state power was often exacerbated by the rise to power of illegitimate leaders whose corrupt and authoritarian practices led to widening gaps between the self-interested policies of incumbent regimes and the needs and demands of their respective populations. Regardless of regime type (e.g., democratic or authoritarian) or ideology (e.g., capitalist, socialist, or Marxist), African states increasingly incapable of responding to their citizens fell prey to military leaders who professed a special capability to undertake political-military reforms and socioeconomic development.

African coups are also similar in the sense that they are usually carried out by members of African armies as opposed to other branches of the armed services, such as the air force or the navy. The primary reason for this similarity is that African navies and air forces are usually the smallest and most poorly equipped branches of African militaries, lacking both the capability and the prestige to carry out a coup that can garner the support of officers within the army. The only exceptions to this general rule are the successful coups in Ghana in 1979 and 1981 that were led by Air Force Flight Lieutenant Jerry Rawlings, and the unsuccessful military bid for power in Kenya in 1982 that was led by the air force. No African country has ever experienced a coup led by naval personnel.

Another similarity revolves around what can be termed "coups of descending order." The first coup that occurs within a country is usually led by the most senior members of the military establishment, most notably generals, who command the respect of lower ranking military officers. Once they assume control of the political system, however, their refusal to relinquish power in favor of enjoying the perks of their newfound political power often leads to grumbling within the lower ranks. The lower ranking officers often regard their commanders as pursuing a lifestyle as bad as, if not worse than, their deposed civilian counterparts. The response is a "palace coup" in which the senior commanders are overthrown by junior officers who, after assuming power, can fall prey to yet another coup by even lower ranking officers. In Burkina Faso, President Maurice Yaméogo was overthrown in 1966 by Lieutenant Colonel Sangoulé Lamizana, who in turn was overthrown by Colonel Sayé Zerbo in 1980. Zerbo was overthrown by noncommissioned officers in 1982, followed by three further coups led by Major General Jean Baptiste Ouedraogo (1983), Captain Thomas Sankara (1983), and Captain Blaise Compaoré (1987). In each of these cases, senior officers were overthrown by officers of lower or equal rank.

The contagion effect constitutes another common characteristic of military coups (Li and Thompson 1975). The underlying principle of this phenomenon is that once a coup occurs in one country, there exists a greater possibility that a coup will take place in a neighboring country. As in the case of a contagious illness, military leaders are affected by the activities of their neighbors, and perhaps become emboldened by the thought that, "If *they* can do it, so can we!" This trend also holds true in terms of successive coups within a single country. Once the military intervenes against civilian leaders, military leaders become much more confident and willing to pursue similar actions in the future.

Not surprisingly, African military leaders seek to justify their seizure of power and the imposition of military rule. Most often these rationales are at best a misinterpretation of political and social realities, at worst a thinly disguised attempt at obtaining and maintaining control over the reins of power. Indeed, the common assumption of African military leaders that they, as opposed to their civilian counterparts, have governed more effectively during the contemporary independence era is based on a variety of myths that have been strongly challenged by several decades of military governance (Liebenow 1986:255–264).

One of the most noteworthy myths often posited by military leaders is that the very nature of military organization makes military rule more efficient than its civilian counterparts (Liebenow 1986:254–255). The core of this argument is that military personnel are members of a hierarchical chain of command and trained in discipline. Lower ranking military personnel are expected to follow orders without question. This hierarchical structure theoretically allows military leaders to avoid the inefficient political compromises of civilian governance. Even if one accepts the basic premise of the argument that military rule is efficient rule, most African militaries are incapable of staffing all civilian positions with adequately trained personnel. As a result, civil-military coalitions become the norm, and the presumably inefficient civilian politicians remain at various levels of governance. Even the most extreme form of military involvement within the political system requires some level of civilian participation.

The most serious contradiction associated with the efficiency argument is that the military's direct entry into the political system via military coup invariably politicizes the military and makes it subject to the same political demands and challenges confronted by civilian politicians. In the simplest sense, the newfound access to the privileges associated with leadership, such as luxury housing and access to state wealth, almost invariably "creates a gulf between senior and junior grade officers as well as between officers and the rank and file" (Liebenow 1986:255). It is for this reason that one often witnesses coups of descending order, as more junior members of the military chain of command seek access to the privileges enjoyed by their superiors.

The corruption associated with the long series of coups and military regimes in Nigeria is but one counterpoint to military claims of greater efficiency (Diamond 1995:442–464). In the aftermath of Major General Ibrahim Babangida's seizure of power in August 1985, official promises to prosecute the corrupt civilian officials of the Second Republic "quietly evaporated" as military-dominated patterns of corruption steadily emerged (Diamond 1995:444). According to Larry Diamond, Babangida acquired the status of the "most massively corrupt ruler" in Nigerian political history (Diamond 1995:449). "Numerous recipients and one-time insiders confirmed the pattern of largesse, and one former top-ranking officer and longtime associate of Babangida's claimed he entered the presidency with a net worth in the tens of millions of dollars from previous corruption in weapons purchases and other transactions," explains Diamond. "As in the Second Republic, foreign business leaders privately estimated the personal wealth of top [military] officials in the hundreds of millions, and objective evidence pointed to annual leakages of revenue in the billions of dollars, approximating 10 percent of the country's total annual output of goods and services!" (Diamond 1995:449–450). As is the case in both civilian and military regimes alike, the extreme corruption of Babangida's regime was a double-edged sword. "It oiled the wheels of a constantly whirring political machine, buying support, compliance, and alliances within and outside the military," explains Diamond. "But it also greatly intensified public alienation and revulsion toward the regime, the sense of acute injustice, the readiness to protest, and the need for [government] repression to suppress that protest (as well as any concrete exposure of what was happening)" (Diamond 1995:450).

The combination of the spread of single-party regimes discussed in the previous section and the rise of military coups d'état and military governance meant that dictatorship would steadily become the dominant form of political governance from the 1950s to the 1980s. This is demonstrated by drawing on the Comparative Survey on Freedom data project published by Freedom House, which provides an annual assessment for every country's level of freedom that can be recast in terms of democracy and authoritarianism (Freedom House 2019). Specifically, the dataset allows us to assess an

African country's level of democracy on a scale of 1 to 7, with 1 being the highest level of democracy and 7 being the highest level of authoritarianism.

Table 4.2 sets out the range of democracy and dictatorship in Africa in 1988, the year preceding the beginning of Africa's wave of democratization. In that year, 30 percent (fifteen countries) of the African continent's fifty independent countries at the time embodied highly authoritarian political systems. An additional 44 percent (twenty-two countries) were very authoritarian and 18 percent (nine countries) were leaning authoritarian. This means that an extraordinary forty-six countries (92 percent) occupied the authoritarian side of the spectrum. In contrast, only two countries (4 percent) occupied the category of leaning democratic (Gambia and Senegal) and two countries (4 percent) occupied the category of very democratic (Botswana and Mauritius). Not one African country could be characterized as highly democratic. Nor did any country fall under the middle category of partially authoritarian/partially democratic. In short, dictatorship had become the norm in African politics by the end of the 1980s.

Political Economy of Decline and Challenges to African Dictators

For ordinary Africans, the political economy of development is seen in personal terms. It means additional money for children's schoolbooks so that their sons and daughters can excel in school, usable roads that allow farmers to get their produce to market, electric lights in the village, affordable basic foodstuffs such as rice and flour, or a health clinic within walking distance. Development is also measured by access to land, jobs, and better housing (Bates 1981). However, most Africans experienced little real economic progress during the initial decades of the contemporary independence era. Resources needed for effective, broad-scale development were drained away to support the consolidation of power around presidents, among other reasons. As already discussed, these efforts included providing patronage resources to regime supporters and funding an extensive security apparatus to suppress those who opposed the regime. Moreover, the average African was unable to speak his or her mind without the threat of being persecuted by the government, nor was he or she able to change the political and economic direction of the country. For the most part, free and fair electoral processes did not exist.

It was against this backdrop that authoritarian leaders in the 1980s were confronted by economic, political, and military developments often referred to as the "crisis of the African state" (Villalón and Huxtable 1998; see also Wunsch and Olowu 1990). Hobbled by decades of corruption and economic mismanagement, many African states had become "lame Leviathans" (i.e.,

Table 4.2 Range of Democracy in Africa, 1988

Highly Authoritarian	Very Authoritarian	Leaning Authoritarian	Authoritarian/ Democratic	Leaning Democratic	Very Democratic	Highly Democratic
30% (15/50)	44% (22/50)	18% (9/50)	0% (0/50)	4% (2/50)	4% (2/50)	0% (0/50)
Angola	Algeria	Egypt		Gambia	Botswana	
Benin	Cameroon	Liberia		Senegal	Mauritius	
Burkina Faso	Cape Verde	Madagascar				
Burundi	Central African Republic	Morocco				
Chad	Comoros	Nigeria				
Congo Brazzaville	Côte d'Ivoire	Sierra Leone				
Democratic Republic of Congo	Djibouti	Sudan				
Equatorial Guinea	Eswatini	Tunisia				
Ethiopia	Gabon	Uganda				
Guinea	Ghana					
Guinea-Bissau	Kenya					
Malawi	Lesotho					
Mozambique	Libya					
São Tomé & Príncipe	Mali					
Somalia	Mauritania					
	Niger					
	Rwanda					
	Seychelles					
	Tanzania					
	Togo					
	Zambia					
	Zimbabwe					

Source: Freedom House data for 1988, which actually cover the period November 1987–November 1988. See Freedom House (2019).

Notes: Highly authoritarian = 6.5–7.0 (13–14 combined score) on Freedom House scale; very authoritarian = 5.5–6.0 (11–12 combined score) on Freedom House scale; leaning authoritarian = 4.5–5.0 (9–10 combined score) on Freedom House scale; partially authoritarian/partially democratic = 4.0 (8 combined score) on Freedom House scale; leaning democratic = 3–3.5 (6–7 combined score) on Freedom House scale; very democratic = 2–2.5 (4–5 combined score) on Freedom House scale; highly democratic = 1–1.5 average score (2–3 combined score) on Freedom House scale.

South Africa is not included because it was under apartheid rule until 1994. Eritrea, Namibia, and South Sudan are not included because they had yet to obtain independence.

relatively impotent states) (Callaghy 1987) or "shadow states" (i.e., those in which large areas of the national territory were no longer effectively governed by central authorities) (Reno 1995). Four patterns in particular captured the process of state decline that peaked in the 1980s, and that set the stage for the African wave of democratization discussed in the next section of this chapter.

First, a severe continent-wide economic crisis threatened the economic foundations of the African state. The initial symptom of this crisis, which appeared during the latter half of the 1970s as weak economic growth, was followed by sharp economic decline during the 1980s. One economic indicator, per capita income, captured the economic dilemma confronted by African policymakers. From 1975 to 1979, per capita income for the African continent registered a less than 1 percent annual growth rate. During the decade of the 1980s, this meager growth rate turned into a 2.2 percent annual *decline* in per capita income (Ravenhill 1993:18). The problem was that African leaders had expanded the scope of state power without also increasing the state's capacity to use that power to create wealth. As a result, African leaders were increasingly incapable of mustering the resources to maintain the African state's unparalleled control of the economic and political systems. The growing indebtedness of the African continent further compounded the problem. From 1980 to 1989, Africa's debt burden nearly tripled in size from $55 billion to $160 billion (Ravenhill 1993:18). In fact, nearly every economic indicator compiled by the World Bank and the International Monetary Fund (IMF) suggested an emerging economic crisis of epic proportions.

Mounting debt opened the door for the growing influence of international financial institutions in the restructuring of African economies and political systems in the image of the northern industrialized democracies (Lofchie 1989). African leaders, sometimes desperate for solutions, increasingly accepted externally imposed reform measures known as structural adjustment programs (SAPs) to obtain much-needed IMF and World Bank loans. As noted by Thomas M. Callaghy, African leaders were "caught between a rock and a hard place" (Callaghy 2000). At least four types of private sector reforms are characteristic of SAPs, including those that were imposed during the 1980s: (1) the termination of food subsidies that kept food prices artificially low, effectively discouraging farmers from planting food crops; (2) the devaluation of national currencies to stimulate exports and the domestic production of manufactured products; (3) the trimming of government bureaucracies; and (4) the privatization of parastatals (state-owned corporations). As discussed in Chapter 6, the SAPs embodied the liberal economic consensus of the northern industrialized democracies that Africa's future economic success depended on the pursuit of an export-oriented strategy of economic growth that dismantled all forms of governmental intervention in national economies. For the average citizen who depended on low food prices, or for the employee working in a government bureaucracy or parastatal, such policies were a disaster (van de Walle 2001; Widner 1994).

A second pattern of state decline involved the growing inability of the state to provide a wide variety of social goods expected by civil society. From the 1950s to the 1980s, roads and rail systems deteriorated. Services to agriculture were abandoned. School systems, which needed to teach growing populations that were under fifteen years of age, had little money available for school construction or teacher salaries. As explained by John F. Clark, after conducting field research in the DRC during 1994, an expansive and effective road network that had crisscrossed the country in the early 1960s had deteriorated to such a degree as to become virtually nonexistent (Clark 1998:109–125). Something seemingly as simple as traveling sixty miles by car between the capital of Kinshasa and a neighboring town had become a "grueling, four-hour journey" due to the extremely poor condition of the road system (Clark 1998:116). The telephone system had also deteriorated to the point that the only effective means of telephone communication was through a variety of cell phone systems offered by private companies. To make matters worse, power and water service outages became so frequent as to constitute the norm, and most public hospitals had declined to the point that local residents found "little use in going to them" (Clark 1998:116). Even the most essential government tasks, such as tax collection, became problematic in weakened states such as the DRC (Hyden 1983:60–63; see also Callaghy 1984). The mounting economic problems led some to wonder whether the children of the 1980s would become a *génération sacrifiée* (sacrificed generation), permanently discouraged by the fact that a poor job market offered them nothing more than positions as street vendors, maids, and cooks.

As African states weakened, Africans turned to the informal economy—webs of economic activities that are "unmeasured, unrecorded and, in varying degrees, illegal" (MacGaffey 1991:12). These activities formed the majority of income for many people across the continent. They might entail, for example, an African cocoa farmer deciding to sell his or her cocoa crop on the black market for twice the government price as opposed to selling that crop through the government-sponsored marketing board or agency. It could also entail the hoarding and exchanging of scarce goods above both official and justified market prices; smuggling lucrative cash crops, precious metals, or manufactured foods either into or out of the country; or engaging in illegal currency transactions to avoid monetary exchange controls or exchange rates. These and other activities that avoided regulations and especially taxes ensured that African states lost huge amounts of money, further weakening the already precarious fiscal basis of the state (Lemarchand 1988:160–166; MacGaffey 1988:177–185; Sandbrook 1985:139–149).

As the administrative capacity of states decreased, decay within regimes increased. In many states, corrupt practices among strategically placed politicians and bureaucrats became so habitual as to be institutionalized. Under these circumstances, citizens expected to pay bribes, and they viewed politicians raiding government treasuries as simply the way things are done. The term "kleptocracy" has been applied to especially corrupt states such as the former DRC under the Mobutu dictatorship, where corruption was systematically practiced at all levels (Young and Turner 1985:183). Yet even in countries with a professional civil service, the economic crisis created conditions or "structured" incentives for corruption. In Ghana, "where hyper-inflation rapidly outran increases in salaries, demanding a bribe (or a higher one than previously) was an understandable reaction of junior or middle-ranking government officials to the problem of feeding their families" (Jeffries 1989:80).

A third pattern associated with the crisis of the African state involved the resurgence of increasingly vocal African civil societies that were intent on opening up the political space within their respective countries (Harbeson, Rothchild, and Chazan 1994). Civil society encompasses voluntary organizations, such as student groups, women's organizations, labor unions, human rights organizations, religious groups, and political organizations. They seek access to the formal institutions of state power, such as the presidency, the policymaking bureaucracies of the executive, and the parliament, with the objective of influencing both domestic and foreign policies. A vibrant civil society is arguably a central component of the democratization process, playing a central role in opening up authoritarian regimes (Stepan 1986; see also Cavatorta and Durac 2011; O'Donnell, Schmitter, and Whitehead 1986). The assumption is that civil society can pressure authoritarian regimes to cede power and control over public life, thereby further allowing civil society to flourish and organize (Cavatorta and Durac 2011).

The combination of declining African economies and foreign-imposed austerity measures fueled the growing activism of civil society. Civil society groups that were deeply rooted in society, such as self-help organizations, cooperatives, and professional organizations, and that had economic livelihoods affected by economic crisis and structural adjustment, formed the basis of popular dissent toward the regime. Civil servants and trade union members, whose living standards and incomes were perhaps most threatened by the economic crisis and austerity measures, also began demanding political reforms. Additional voices included women's organizations that were seeking greater rights for women (see Chapter 11), religious groups that were speaking out in favor of religious freedom (see Chapter 13), and human rights organizations that were calling for greater adherence to international human rights conventions. Even university students and professors facing cutbacks and poor job prospects actively worked against their respective regimes. Indeed, throughout the 1980s, civil society groups were on the front lines of making demands and taking part in protests. This trend peaked in 1991 when a total of eighty-six popular protests were recorded in thirty African countries (Bratton and van de Walle 1997:3; see also Mueller 2018). In short, many of the organizations that had played a role in the independence struggle beginning in the 1950s were regaining their voices as they coordinated against authoritarian regimes.

A fourth and final pattern of the crisis of the African state was a growing inability to contain domestic conflict by violent nonstate actors, most notably African insurgent groups and terrorist organizations (e.g., see Varin and Abubakar 2017). The emergence of these actors was partially fueled by the geographical dilemma of porous national borders and expanses of ungoverned territory that are common to all African countries. "The fundamental problem facing state-builders in Africa—be they colonial kings, colonial governors, or presidents in the independence era," explains Herbst (2000:11), "has been to project authority over inhospitable territories that contain relatively low densities of people." Additional explanations for the rise of violent nonstate actors range from socioeconomic factors, such as poverty and unemployment, to identity-based explanations, including the roles of race, ethnicity, and religion, and those focusing on the weak nature of African states (Mentan 2004; Varin and Abubakar 2017; Weigert 1996). A broad literature focuses especially on regime type (i.e., democracy versus dictatorship), arguing that political systems governed by authoritarian regimes breed political radicalization. This is due to the simple fact that authoritarian regimes, such as those that existed during the 1980s, favor stability over freedom, democracy, and accountability. Individuals from these types of political systems are more likely to be dissatisfied and will not have legitimate domestic outlets to relay their dissatisfaction. They, therefore, are more prone to join radical organizations, such as insurgent groups and terrorist organizations that pledge to change the existing political order.

The classic violent nonstate actor is an insurgent group that undertakes military action against the central government (Bøås and Dunn 2007, 2017). Africa historically has experienced at least four different types of guerrilla insurgencies, each of which intensified in the 1980s (Clapham 1998:5–9). First, "liberation insurgencies" have been directed against African colonial empires maintained by Belgium, France, Germany, Italy, Portugal, Spain, and the United Kingdom. The Algerian war of independence against French colonial rule is a classic example, in which success meant the emergence of a new foreign policy elite and the restructuring of foreign policy ties away from France. The 1980s witnessed the intensification of this form of guerrilla insurgency, but against the white minority–ruled dictatorships in southern Africa (Namibia, Rhodesia, and South Africa). Southern Africa embodied one of the most extensive sets of interlocking liberation insurgencies that, with the coordinated support of the Front-Line States (the African countries on the borders of the white minority–ruled countries), was intent on ending white minority rule in Africa.

A second type of insurgent group has sought greater rights for specific regions of already independent African countries. In the extreme, such "separatist insurgencies" have sought the secession and recognition of their territories as independent countries. An example is the Polisario Front, which started as an anticolonial insurgency but seeks to create an independent Sahrawi Arab Democratic Republic from territory still claimed and controlled by Morocco. A unique foreign policy element of these separatist insurgencies is that they sometimes maintain embassy networks abroad in countries that recognize their quest for independence. In the 1980s, the SADR was recognized by over forty countries, several of which hosted SADR embassies.

A third set of guerrilla insurgents, that are best described as "reform insurgencies," have sought to maintain the territorial integrity of existing countries. They nonetheless are committed to overthrowing existing regimes and reordering both foreign policy institutions and foreign policy ties. An example is the Tigray People's Liberation Front (TPLF), which initially began as a guerrilla insurgency intent on seeking greater autonomy within its region of Tigray in Ethiopia. The TPLF subsequently became one of the leaders in the larger guerrilla struggle of the 1980s against the Ethiopian dictatorship of Mengistu Haile Mariam. It also emerged as the leader of a coalition of ethnically based guerrilla movements, the Ethiopian People's Revolutionary Democratic Front (EPRDF), that defeated the Mengistu regime and assumed power in 1991 (Young 1998).

Finally, "warlord insurgencies" typically "arise in cases where the insurgency is directed towards a change in leadership which does not entail the creation of a state any different from that which it seeks to overthrow, and which may involve the creation of a personal territorial fiefdom separate from existing state structures and boundaries" (Clapham 1998:7; see also Reno 1998). Typically lacking a coherent, future policy vision beyond the more immediate goal of overthrowing the regime in power, such insurgencies in the extreme are unable to reestablish centralized states after achieving victory, often leading to the continuation of conflict among competing insurgent leaders and their respective armies. An extreme variant of warlord insurgencies—successful regime overthrow but with rival insurgent factions unable to recreate a functioning centralized state—was realized in the case of Somalia after the overthrow in 1991 of the dictatorship of Mohamed Siad Barre.

African Wave of Democratization

The downfall of single-party communist systems throughout Eastern Europe and the former Soviet Union beginning in 1989 sent shock waves throughout the African continent (Anglin 1990). The rejection of single-party rule in its intellectual heartland ensured that African leaders could no longer justify the continuation of this model on the African continent. "If the owners of socialism have withdrawn from the one-party system," proclaimed Frederick Chiluba, the leader of the Zambian pro-democracy movement and future president of Zambia, "who are the Africans to continue with it?" (quoted in Bratton and van de Walle 1997:105–106). Severe economic stagnation and decline in most African economies that peaked in the 1980s served as the internal spark for political discontent. A wide swath of African civil society, including average African citizens, were unhappy with their economic and political lots in life, and were willing to make their demands heard, including through political protests. Twenty-two years later in 2011, Tunisia's Dignity Revolution served as a powerful example of what is now variously referred to as Africa's second independence, Africa's second liberation, or the African wave of democratization. This chapter emphasizes the latter term, which places the African experience within the broader global context of what Samuel Huntington referred to as the "third wave of democratization" (Huntington 1991).

There is no question that the African wave of democratization has resulted in a period of political experimentation previously unknown in African history. Whereas many of these experiments resulted in the replacement of single-party systems with more inclusive forms of multiparty politics, several potential transitions to democracy have either stalled, are being co-opted, or have been completely derailed by authoritarian leaders intent upon maintaining power. The range of political change that has occurred in Africa since 1989 is best characterized as a spectrum of political transition, ranging from the peaceful replacement of incumbent leaders via multiparty elections, at one extreme, to a complete breakdown in the transition process and the unfolding of civil war, at the other. At least six types of political transition have unfolded on the African continent during the post-1989 era (Martin 1993).

The first type of political transition involves the creation of multiparty political systems and the holding of "founding elections" in which "the office of the head of government is openly contested following a period during which multiparty political competition was denied" (Bratton and van de Walle 1997:198). A comparison of the periods immediately preceding and following the beginning of the African wave of democratization demonstrates the role of multiparty elections. During the preceding five-year period (1985–1989), truly competitive elections were held in only five African countries: Botswana, Gambia, Mauritius, Senegal, and Zimbabwe. From 1990 to 1994, more than thirty-eight countries held competitive elections. Most important, twenty-nine of the multiparty contests of the 1990–1994 era constituted founding elections. Multiparty democracy had made an impressive start, with scholars subsequently assessing the evolution of these systems over time (e.g., see Bleck and van de Walle 2019; Van Ham and Lindberg 2018; Riedl 2018).

South Africa's founding election of April 26–29, 1994, serves as one of the most heralded examples of African democratic transition. For the first time, voters of all races cast ballots in free and fair elections that ushered in South Africa's first multiracial, multiethnic, and multiparty democracy. Nelson Mandela, who had spent nearly twenty-eight years in prison under the previous apartheid system, was elected president, and the party he represented, the African National Congress (ANC), won 63 percent of the popular vote, 252 of 400 seats in the National Assembly, and a majority of seats in seven of the nine provincial legislatures. F. W. de Klerk, the last president of the apartheid era, and his Afrikaner-based National Party (NP) that dominated South African politics from 1948 to 1994, won only 21 percent of the popular vote (eighty-two National Assembly seats), but majority control of the legislature in the Western Cape province, which is predominantly inhabited by Afrikaners. The third most influential presidential candidate was Chief Mangosuthu Buthelezi, a prominent Zulu leader. His predominantly Zulu political party, the Inkatha Freedom Party (IFP), won 10 percent of the popular vote, ensuring forty seats in the National Assembly as well as a majority victory in the KwaZulu-Natal province, which is largely inhabited by the Zulu ethnic group. The fact that both the NP and the IFP won at least 10 percent each of the popular vote ensured their inclusion in a constitutionally mandated government of national unity. "From the moment the results were in and it was apparent that the ANC was to form the government, I saw my mission as one of preaching reconciliation, of binding the wounds of the country, of engendering trust and confidence," explains Nelson Mandela in his autobiography, *Long Walk to Freedom: The Autobiography of Nelson Mandela*. "At every opportunity, I said all South Africans must now unite and join hands and say we are one country, one nation, one people, marching together into the future" (Mandela 1995:619–620).

A second type of political transition that became particularly influential in francophone Africa is the "national conference" (Clark and Gardinier 1997; Robinson 1994). In this scenario, a broad coalition of leaders from all sectors of society, including elders and the heads of women's organizations, ethnic and religious leaders, labor and student activists, and ruling and opposition political leaders, holds an extended national gathering that serves as the basis for debating the outlines of a new democratic political order. In its ideal form, such a conference builds upon the traditional African concept of consensus building, in which every participant has the right to voice his or her opinion, and decisions are made only when agreed upon by all members present (unlike the Western concept of majority rule).

The democratization process under the guidance of the national conference generally follows five major steps (Martin 1993:6). First, a broad coalition of leaders responds to a growing crisis of governance in the country by convening a national conference in the capital city. The guiding principle of this body is its self-appointed sovereignty (i.e., independence) from either the existing constitutional framework or any interference on the part of the ruling regime. Second, the national conference appoints a transitional government that initially seeks a dialogue with the ruling regime. Third, over time, a weakened president is either gradually robbed of his executive powers or is simply declared an illegitimate authority who no longer has the authority to lead. In either case, the president is usually reduced to a figurehead. Fourth, the national conference transforms itself into a transitional legislative body (often referred to as the High Council) that, in turn, formally elects a prime minister who manages the transition process. Finally, the transitional government adopts a new constitution and holds legislative and presidential elections, subsequently dissolving itself upon the inauguration of the newly elected democratic regime.

The strong appeal of the national conference model—demanded in some shape or form by pro-democracy movements in almost every nondemocratic African country—was primarily due to the extraordinary success achieved in Benin (Heilbrunn 1993; Nzouankeu 1993; see also Wing 2008). More than eighteen years of authoritarian rule under the Marxist dictatorship of Mathieu Kérékou were peacefully overcome by a 488-member national conference that lasted ten days. During February 19–28, 1990, the national conference declared its sovereignty, provided Kérékou with political amnesty while at the same time stripping him of his official powers, and drafted a timetable that led to the holding of multiparty elections in 1991. The critical element that contributed to the success of this democratization process was Kérékou's peaceful acceptance of the national conference's self-declared right to take control of the political process. As observed by Jacques Mariel Nzouankeu, Kérékou still enjoyed the loyalty of the Beninois Armed Forces, and presumably could have crushed the opposition with military force (Nzouankeu 1993:45). Moreover, the military elite constituted a potential threat to the national conference in that the transition to a civilian regime inevitably ensured a reduction in the political power of the military. Nonetheless, both Kérékou and his military officers eventually accepted the popular legitimacy of the national conference and embraced its timetable for the introduction of multiparty politics to Benin (Nzouankeu 1993:45).

A third form of political transition is "guided democratization." This occurs when an authoritarian, typically military, regime is committed to democratization but maintains tight control over the transition process. The hallmark of this model is an extremely powerful and usually charismatic leader who, due to the lack of any major competing centers of power, can slowly institute "democratization from above" according to his or her own timetable and preferences.

The Ghanaian military regime of Flt. Lt. Jerry Rawlings provides a clear-cut example of the process of guided democratization (Chazan 1989). Assuming power in a military coup d'état in June 1979, Rawlings led the Ghanaian Armed Forces back to the barracks in September 1979 after Dr.

Hilla Limann was elected president in democratic elections. However, political corruption, economic stagnation, and popular discontent with the Limann regime prompted Rawlings to once again assume the leadership of Ghana in a coup in December 1981. Rather than returning to the barracks for a second time, Rawlings remained in power as the head of the Provisional National Defense Council (PNDC), a military-based revolutionary organ that outlawed opposition political parties and implemented its vision to economically restructure the country. The unchallenged status of the PNDC would be altered only in 1992—nearly eleven years after assuming power—when Rawlings decided that Ghana was ready for another attempt at multiparty democracy.

Rawlings oversaw a deliberately slow and measured liberalization of the Ghanaian political system that included the writing of a new constitution, the legalization of opposition political parties, the emergence of a private press, and the creation of independent national human rights organizations (Ofori 1993:33–35). In multiparty presidential elections held in November 1992, a combination of popular support within the rural areas, careful planning, and strong control exerted by the ruling PNDC led to a Rawlings victory with 58.3 percent of the popular vote. Claiming that Rawlings and the PNDC had exerted "excessive control" over an inherently flawed election process, opposition leaders boycotted the legislative elections held one month later, thereby ensuring a sweep of the National Legislature by pro-Rawlings parties (Joseph 1993:45–46). Despite the fact that electoral irregularities, most notably flawed voter registration lists reportedly favoring the incumbent government, marred the democratization process, Rawlings nonetheless emerged from the 1992 elections firmly in control of the Ghanaian political system. As was the case with other military leaders intent on promoting guided democracy from above, however, Rawlings's "toughest test" was that of "shedding the image of the radical military dictator and becoming a democratic constitutional ruler able to create a climate of tolerance" (Ofori 1993:35).

A fourth form of political transition involves "co-opted transitions." This occurs when leaders are able to co-opt the transition process and maintain themselves in power despite the holding of relatively free and fair elections. The co-optation of the democratic process usually follows three major steps. First, unlike the successful cases of transition by national conference, the president under this scenario is acutely aware of the precarious nature of his or her political rule and acts in a quick, albeit relatively peaceful manner to preempt the democratization forces. The usual course of action is to quickly accede to opposition demands to dismantle the single-party system, and to legalize all opposition parties within a new multiparty framework. Second, rather than giving the new opposition parties time to organize and, therefore, present a viable and competitive alternative to the voters, snap

Peter J. Schraeder

The Tunisian military briefly assumed power during the Tunisian Revolution of 2011 after facilitating President Zine el-Abidine Ben Ali's departure from the country. It established military checkpoints at key areas, such as the pictured intersection in La Marsa (a suburb of Tunis), but swiftly returned power in 2011 to civilian leaders who launched Tunisia's democracy.

elections (often to be held within months) are announced by the ruling party. In this case, the ruling party, which usually still commands a formidable organizational structure and supporters within every region of the country, advocates for the proliferation of numerous new parties so as to divide the opposition vote. Finally, during the period immediately preceding the elections, the ruling party uses its monopoly of the government-controlled print, radio, and television media to dominate the political debate. The net result is a peaceful, albeit tainted, victory by the ruling president and party.

Multiparty elections held in Côte d'Ivoire in October 1990 offer a classic example of a ruling party's ability to peacefully co-opt the democratization process (Faure 1993; Widner 1991). Considered by many analysts as a "master-tactician," President Félix Houphouët-Boigny "completely outmaneuvered" his country's pro-democracy movement by "promptly legalizing all political parties, and acceding to their fullest demands—open presidential and legislative elections—rushing the democratic transformation before opposition leaders could expand or redefine their demands, sharpen their tactics, or properly organize for electoral contests" (Decalo 1992:27).

"When some requested a delay (so they could get organized) this was rejected on the grounds of *their own* recent demonstrations for instant national elections," explains Samuel Decalo. "Election funds were allocated to all parties so they could not claim being at a disadvantage (some parties took the funds and withdrew from the elections!), and the outcome was never in doubt" (Decalo 1992:27). Deep divisions within an unprepared opposition, and government control of all the major media outlets, not only ensured Houphouët-Boigny's victory in presidential elections with approximately 81 percent of the popular vote, but also helped his ruling party, the Democratic Party of Côte d'Ivoire–African Democratic Assembly (PDCI-RDA), win 163 out of a total of 175 seats in the National Assembly. In short, Houphouët-Boigny's foresight and ability to act quickly and decisively enabled him to peacefully co-opt the democratization process under the guise of free but ultimately unfair multiparty elections that left the opposition forces with little alternative but to accept the results and set their sights on future electoral contests.

In contrast to the previous examples of democratization, the fifth form of political transition is "authoritarian reaction." It entails high levels of state-sponsored violence against proponents of democracy designed to preserve the existing (authoritarian) status quo. Under this scenario, the incumbent leader conducts elections that are neither free nor fair, with the intent of stealing votes. The promotion of ethnic fighting in order to divide the opposition and intimidate the general population is often one of the hallmarks of this model. After "winning" the election, the leader subsequently seeks to silence the opposition through such varied means as imprisonment, exile, and, in extreme cases, execution.

Cameroon demonstrates the lengths to which incumbent leaders are willing to go to maintain themselves in office through the use of authoritarian tactics (Hubbard 1993). In October 1992, President Paul Biya and his ruling Cameroon People's Democratic Movement (CPDM) declared victory in the country's first multiparty presidential elections with 39.9 percent of the popular vote. During the two years preceding the elections, human rights groups estimate that at least 400 people associated with the democratization movement were killed by the Biya regime, and the elections were fraught with gross violations of human rights and electoral procedures. "Widespread irregularities during the election period, on election day, and in the tabulation of results seriously calls into question, for any fair observer, the validity of the outcome," explained a report from the US National Democratic Institute for International Affairs (NDI), one of the foreign groups that monitored the elections. "It would not be an exaggeration to suggest that this election system was designed to fail" (quoted in Hubbard 1993:42).

Biya's self-proclaimed victory in the elections was followed by a wave of repression and arrests directed against opposition elites. John Fru Ndi, the leader of the Social Democratic Front (SDF) who took second place in the presidential elections with 35.9 percent of the popular vote, was placed under house arrest with 135 of his supporters. Another 200 opposition figures were also jailed, and a state of emergency was declared in the province of western Cameroon. "The brutality of the forces of law and order, particularly during arrests, is very alarming," explains Solomon Nfor Gwei, the chairman of Cameroon's National Commission for Human Rights and Freedom. "Many detainees are continuously being subjected to psychological and physical torture, some of whom we saw in great pain, with swollen limbs and genitals, blisters and deep wounds and cracks on skulls" (quoted in Hubbard 1993:42). In this and other cases, the facade of victory actually encourages authoritarian leaders to unleash waves of repression designed to maintain the status quo at any cost.

A final form of political transition is "civil war and contested sovereignty." Under this scenario, the authoritarian response of the incumbent leader can lead to civil war and the complete breakdown of the state (Zartman 1995a). The result is a state of contested sovereignty in which no one group is capable of asserting its authority over the entire territory or constructing a government considered to be legitimate either domestically or internationally.

This extreme scenario was characteristic of the bloody clan warfare that erupted in Somalia after Somali dictator Mohamed Siad Barre was overthrown by a coalition of guerrilla forces in January 1991. Rather than abide by an October 2, 1990, accord in which the major guerrilla groups agreed to decide the shape of a post-Siad political system, the United Somali Congress (USC), by virtue of its control of the capital, unilaterally named a Hawiye clan member, Ali Mahdi Mohammed, president of the country. This move heightened the already tense relations between the Isaak-dominated Somali National Movement (SNM), the Hawiye-dominated USC, and the Ogadeni-dominated Somali Patriotic Movement (SPM), as well as among scores of other, less organized, clan groupings (Compagnon 1990).

Based on a strongly held Isaak belief that the north would continue to be victimized by a southern-dominated government, the SNM announced on May 17, 1991, that the former British Somaliland territory was seceding from the 1960 union to become the Somaliland Republic. This event was followed by the intensification of clan conflict in the southern portion of the country between the USC and the SPM, which, in turn, was exacerbated by regrouping Siad's Darod clan under the military banner of the Somali National Front (SNF). Moreover, a brutal intraclan power struggle erupted in Mogadishu between USC forces loyal to interim president Mahdi, a member of the Abgal subclan of the Hawiye, and those led by General Mohamed Farah Aidid, a member of the Habar Gedir subclan of the Hawiye. In short, once the common political enemy no longer existed, traditional clan differences, worsened by the dictatorial divide-and-rule practices of the Siad years, led to an intensification of clan conflict and famine throughout southern and central Somalia.

As it became increasingly clear that the United Nations Security Council was incapable of managing intensifying levels of clan conflict and famine, President George H. W. Bush announced in a live television address to the American public on December 4, 1992, that US troops would be deployed in Somalia to "create a secure environment" for the distribution of famine-relief aid. Five days later the first contingent of US troops led by three teams of Navy SEALs (Sea, Air, Land forces) landed on the beaches of Mogadishu and secured the airport and the port. The US military landing, designated Operation Restore Hope, was carried out under the auspices of a UN Security Council resolution sanctioning foreign intervention. In the weeks that followed, 38,000 troops from twenty countries (including approximately 24,000 US military personnel) occupied various cities and towns throughout central and southern Somalia and began the task of opening food supply routes, as well as creating distribution networks (Clarke and Herbst 1997; Hirsch and Oakley 1995).

Despite the withdrawal of US troops in May 1994, and a series of UN-sponsored diplomatic initiatives and interventions, a permanent political solution to the Somali crisis as of 2020 has yet to be found. Southern clans refuse to accept the self-proclaimed independence of the northern-based Somaliland Republic, which has yet to be officially recognized by any other country in the world. In the southern and central portions of the country, civil war continues between a radical Islamist insurgency, al-Shabaab ("The Youth"), which seeks to impose a theocratic form of governance, and the UN-backed government in Mogadishu, which is kept in power by an African Union–authorized military intervention known as AMISOM (African Union Mission in Somalia). Meanwhile, tens of thousands of Somalis have died during the periodic intensification of clan-based conflict. The primary challenge remains the lack of a centralized Somali state capable of exerting authority over the entire Somali nation. Conflict is sure to continue as long as the Somali nation remains divided among dozens of clan-dominated fiefdoms.

Assessing African Politics and the African Wave of Democratization

The African wave of democratization is now more than three decades old, leading to both optimistic and pessimistic interpretations of its impact on contemporary African politics (see Gyimah-Boadi 2019; Lewis 2019; Radelet 2010). Optimism has been generated by a host of successes, ranging from the South African "miracle" (Bratton 1998) of Nelson Mandela's emerging in 1994 as the first democratically elected leader of South Africa, to the more recent emergence of Tunisia as one of the most democratic of Africa's fifty-four countries in the aftermath of the Dignity Revolution in 2011. Pessimism has been generated by the political transitions that have resulted in democratic decay, such as the complete breakdown of the Somali state in 1991 and the country's descent into civil war—including the secession of the northern portion of the country as the Somaliland Republic—both of which remain unresolved as of this writing. More recently, a much heralded transition to democracy in Egypt in 2011 under President Mohamed Morsi and a moderate Islamist party, the Freedom and Justice Party, was ended in 2013 by a military coup and a return to military rule. In a throwback to an earlier era of authoritarian rule and highly questionable democratic practices, the Egyptian army chief who led the coup, General Abdel Fattah el-Sisi, announced that there would be multiparty elections in 2014, presented himself as one of the "civilian" candidates for president, and subsequently won an inherently flawed electoral contest.

Yet even in those cases marked by a successful transition to more democratic forms of governance, newly elected leaders are confronted with the long-term challenge of ensuring the consolidation (institutionalization) of democratic practices in political systems still marked by democratic fragility (Sandbrook 1996). "The frequency of democratic breakdowns in this century—and the difficulties of consolidating new democracies—must give serious pause to those who would argue . . . for the inevitability of global democracy," explains Larry Diamond (1989:142). "As a result, those concerned about how countries can move 'beyond authoritarianism and totalitarianism' must also ponder the conditions that permit such movement to endure. . . . To rid a country of an authoritarian regime or dictator is not necessarily to move it fundamentally beyond authoritarianism."

The primary purpose of this section is to provide an assessment of the status of African politics and, particularly, Africa's democratic experiments in the three decades following the beginning of the African wave of democratization (e.g., see Bleck and van de Walle 2019; Buijtenhuijs and Thiriot 1995; Cheeseman 2015; see also Dunn and Englebert 2019). A useful starting point involves setting out the broad strokes of African democracy versus African dictatorship as they currently exist. This can be achieved by once again drawing on the Comparative Survey on Freedom data project published by Freedom House that was used earlier in this chapter to establish the range of democracy in Africa as of 1988 (see Table 4.2). As a reminder, the dataset allows us to assess an African country's level of democracy on a scale of 1 to 7, with 1 being the highest level of democracy and 7 being the highest level of authoritarianism.

Table 4.3 sets out the range of democracy and dictatorship in contemporary Africa, according to data published in 2019. One of the most striking results is that seventeen (31 percent) of Africa's fifty-four countries now occupy the democratic side of the spectrum of democracy and authoritarianism. The diversity of democracies includes seven leaning democratic countries (Burkina Faso, Lesotho, Liberia, Madagascar, Malawi, Seychelles, and Sierra Leone), seven very democratic countries (Benin, Botswana, Namibia, São Tomé and Príncipe, Senegal, South Africa, and Tunisia), and three highly democratic countries (Cape Verde, Ghana, and Mauritius). This represents an important advancement over 1988, when only four African countries occupied these three categories. It also highlights that important differences exist among African democracies, such as between the longer-term democracy of Ghana, which is more consolidated than the more recent democracy of Tunisia.

Table 4.3 also serves as a reminder that twenty-nine countries, or 53 percent of the African continent, continue to occupy the authoritarian side of the spectrum. This includes seven countries that can be labeled as leaning authoritarian (Gambia, Guinea, Guinea-Bissau, Morocco, Tanzania, Togo, and Zimbabwe), eleven countries that are very authoritarian (Algeria, Angola, Cameroon, Congo Brazzaville, Djibouti, Egypt, Ethiopia, Gabon, Mauritania,

Table 4.3 Range of Democracy in Africa, 2018

Highly Authoritarian	Very Authoritarian	Leaning Authoritarian	Authoritarian/ Democratic	Leaning Democratic	Very Democratic	Highly Democratic
20% (11/54)	20% (11/54)	13% (7/54)	15% (8/54)	13% (7/54)	13% (7/54)	5% (3/54)
Burundi	Algeria	Gambia	Comoros	Burkina Faso	Benin	Cape Verde
Central African Republic	Angola	Guinea	Côte d'Ivoire	Lesotho	Botswana	Ghana
Chad	Cameroon	Guinea-Bissau	Kenya	Liberia	Namibia	Mauritius
Democratic Republic of Congo	Congo Brazzaville	Morocco	Mali	Madagascar	São Tomé & Príncipe	
Equatorial Guinea	Djibouti	Tanzania	Mozambique	Malawi	Senegal	
Eritrea	Egypt	Togo	Niger	Seychelles	South Africa	
Eswatini	Ethiopia	Zimbabwe	Nigeria	Sierra Leone	Tunisia	
Libya	Gabon		Zambia			
Somalia	Mauritania					
South Sudan	Rwanda					
Sudan	Uganda					

Source: Freedom House data for 2018 (which were published in spring 2019 but cover 2018). See Freedom House (2019).

Notes: Highly authoritarian = 6.5–7.0 (13–14 combined score) on Freedom House scale; very authoritarian = 5.5–6.0 (11–12 combined score) on Freedom House scale; leaning authoritarian = 4.5–5.0 (9–10 combined score) on Freedom House scale; partially authoritarian/partially democratic = 4.0 (8 combined score) on Freedom House scale; leaning democratic = 3–3.5 (6–7 combined score) on Freedom House scale; very democratic = 2–2.5 (4–5 combined score) on Freedom House scale; highly democratic = 1–1.5 average score (2–3 combined score) on Freedom House scale.

Rwanda, and Uganda), and eleven countries that are highly authoritarian (Burundi, Central African Republic, Chad, the DRC, Equatorial Guinea, Eritrea, Eswatini, Libya, Somalia, South Sudan, and Sudan). As underscored by a growing literature on "competitive authoritarianism," this breakdown indicates the importance of understanding differences between types of authoritarian regimes, which use varying electoral strategies to maintain power (Levitsky and Way 2002, 2010; Svolik 2012; see also Carothers 2018). Finally, eight countries (15 percent of the African total) occupy a middle ground status of being partially authoritarian and partially democratic (Comoros, Côte d'Ivoire, Kenya, Mali, Mozambique, Niger, Nigeria, and Zambia). Although one may disagree over the specific placement of countries in individual categories, there is no question regarding the broader trend captured by this table: in comparison to the African political universe that existed in 1988, Africa's wave of democratization from 1989 to the present has fostered the rise of a greater diversity of African democracies and African dictatorships, as well as an overall growth in the number of countries that now fall on the democratic side of the political spectrum.

A case in point is Tunisia, which in 1988 fell under the category of "leaning authoritarian." This was due to the fact that the country's dictator, Ben Ali, had just taken power in 1987, and he was still holding out an olive branch to members of civil society who believed that he was going to establish some form of democracy. As the years progressed, Ben Ali created a dictatorial regime that some considered impervious to change owing to the "force of obedience" (Hibou 2006) or an "authoritarian syndrome" in Tunisian society (Camau and Geisser 2003). Ben Ali's hold over power was in part due to the creation of a police state that was locally referred to as the *mukhabarat*. Aside from a military establishment totaling 35,000 troops, the key to the state's control was a set of security forces commonly assumed to number as high as 130,000—enough to saddle Tunisia and its 10.5 million people with a police presence as large as that of France, a country almost six times Tunisia's population (Entelis 2005:537–558). Security formations included the Presidential Guard (roughly 8,000 members) with headquarters in Carthage (a suburb of Tunis where the presidential mansion is located), the National Guard (roughly 20,000) based next to the Tunis-Carthage International Airport, and a variety of other security forces such as the political police, the tourism police, and the university police (Schraeder and Redissi 2011).

Ben Ali's dictatorship was upended in 2011 as a result of the self-immolation of a twenty-six-year-old fruit vendor, Mohamed Bouazizi. His act of protest against the local police and government in his southern town of Sidi Bouzid not only sparked the protests that led to Tunisia's Dignity Revolution but ushered in a wider series of protests in other countries and regions of the world that are now commonly referred to as the Arab Spring.

A series of electoral turning points have assured Tunisia's place as one of the most democratic countries on the African continent: elections in 2011 for a Constituent Assembly that would govern while writing the country's new democratic constitution, which was adopted in 2014; the holding in 2014 of the country's first democratic presidential and legislative elections; the adoption of a decentralization program designed to give more authority to local leaders, followed by local elections in 2018; and the acceleration of the country's 2019 presidential and legislative elections by two months, due to the fact that incumbent president Beji Caid Essebsi died while in office. The elected president as of 2020 is Kais Saied, a former university professor who shares power with a prime minister in Tunisia's semipresidential system. The country enjoys a vibrant political party system, including a moderate Islamist party, Ennahda, which has the largest number of seats (52) in the 217-seat parliament.

Another measure for assessing Africa's contemporary political landscape is to examine the evolution of political rights enjoyed by African populations (see Figure 4.1). These include the ability to form political organizations free from government intrusion; the meaningful representation of ethnic, racial, religious, and other minority groups in the political process; and the right to choose national and local political leaders through free and fair competitive elections. Although individual countries will vary, the African continent as a whole has experienced an increase in political rights since 1989.

It is important to note, however, that the establishment of a multiparty, democratic political system does not necessarily lead to competitive elections in which the party in power is replaced. Botswana serves as an example. Although the country is rightfully heralded as Africa's oldest surviving multiparty democracy in which free and fair elections have been held on a regular basis since independence in 1966 (Holm and Molutsi 1989; Wiseman 1977), an examination of its parliamentary elections underscores the existence of a de facto single-party system (Charlton 1993). Specifically, the ruling Botswana Democratic Party (BDP) has consistently won majorities in all parliamentary elections since 1965. In the 2019 parliamentary elections, for example, the BDP won thirty-eight seats (67 percent) of the fifty-seven-seat parliament. The BDP has been able to maintain its political monopoly in large part due to a political system that heavily favors the incumbent president and his ruling party (Molutsi and Holm 1990; Zaffiro 1989). Other democracies that embody de facto single-party systems include South Africa under the ANC and Namibia under SWAPO.

It is for this reason that a more rigorous bar for assessing Africa's newest democracies might involve their ability to foster and survive the "alternation of power" between rival political movements and political parties. Benin serves as an example of the alternation of power between presidents who rep-

Figure 4.1 Protection of Political Rights

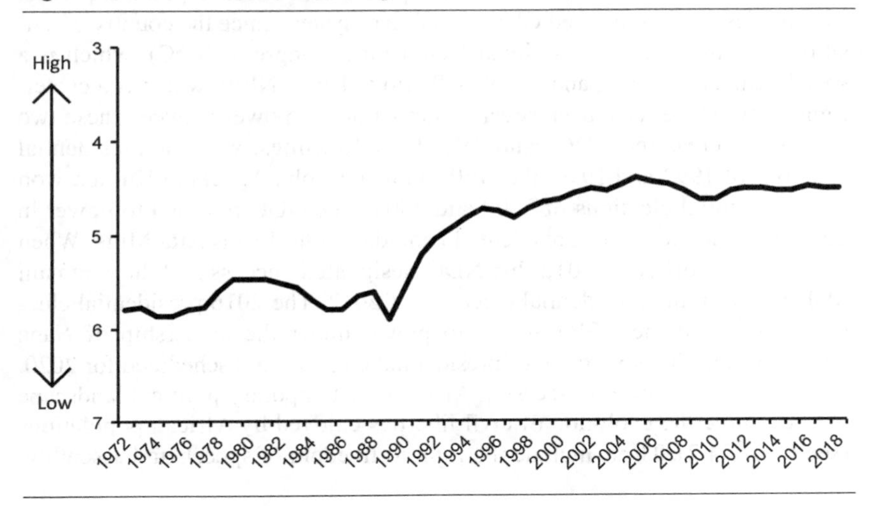

Source: Freedom House (2019).
Notes: 1 = highest level of protection of political rights and 7 = lowest level of protection of political rights.

resent different political movements or ideological orientations (Magnusson 2005). In the founding elections of 1991 that followed the 1990 national conference and Benin's transition to democracy, a pro-West technocrat, Nicéphore Soglo, was elected president. Mathieu Kérékou, the former Marxist dictator who had been previously elected under the banner of the People's Revolutionary Party of Benin (PRPB), accepted defeat and retired from the political system, only to return five years later as the leading opposition candidate in the 1996 presidential elections. With Soglo's reelection campaign hampered by the poor performance of the national economy and public perceptions of his disregard for the average citizen, Kérékou overcame the political odds and emerged victorious in the presidential elections. Dubbed the "chameleon" by friends and enemies alike, Kérékou's return to office for two terms (1996–2006) served as a powerful example of how democratic practices were being consolidated on the African continent. Soglo, as was the case with his predecessor, graciously accepted defeat, and joined the ranks of the "loyal opposition." Subsequent elected presidents, both of whom have run as independents (i.e., no party affiliation), have included Thomas Boni Yayi, who served two terms of office (2006–2016), and Patrice Talon, who was elected to a five-year term beginning in 2016.

Ghana, which is one of the three most democratic countries on the African continent, is an example of a multiparty democracy that has successfully weathered the alternation of power between rival political parties. Two parties have dominated Ghana's political system since the country's transition to democracy: the National Democratic Congress (NDC), which is a social democratic party, and the New Patriotic Party (NPP), which is a center-right party. There have been several alternations of power between these two parties. Whereas the NDC candidate, Jerry Rawlings, won the presidential elections of 1992 and 1996, the NPP candidate, John Agyekum Kufuor, won the presidential elections of 2000 and 2004. The NDC returned to power in 2008 with the victory of presidential candidate John Evans Atta Mills. When Mills died in office in 2012, his NDC-designated successor, John Dramani Mahama, won the presidential elections of 2012. The 2016 presidential elections witnessed the NPP's return to power under the leadership of Nana Akufo-Addo. The next round of presidential elections are scheduled for 2020.

A third measure for assessing Africa's contemporary political landscape is to examine the evolution of civil liberties enjoyed by African populations (see Figure 4.2). These include the right to freedom of speech and assembly;

Gretchen Bauer

Poster published by the Electoral Commission of Ghana asking Ghanaian citizens to check their names on voter registration lists in preparation for the 2016 presidential and legislative elections.

access to vigorous, independent media; constitutional guarantees of due process by independent judiciaries; freedom of religion and worship; and the general protection of individual rights regardless of one's ethnicity, race, religious creed, or gender. Although individual cases will vary, the African continent as a whole has experienced an increase in civil liberties since 1989. Figure 4.2 nonetheless demonstrates a slight degree of backsliding after 2004, as authoritarian regimes learned the lessons of transition and sought to restrict the maneuverability of civil society actors. Such actions were minor against the backdrop of a deepening democratic culture supportive of civil society activity that was crucial to the unfolding of the Arab Spring and especially Tunisia's transition to democracy. As we are reminded by Schaffer's (2000) insightful book on Senegalese democracy, *Democracy in Translation: Understanding Politics in an Unfamiliar Culture*, the concept of democracy means different things in different cultures, with important implications for how we understand democratic consolidation.

The caution one must exercise when assessing the consolidation of newly formed democracies is demonstrated by events in Zambia. In 1991, the country transitioned from a single-party system, headed by President Kenneth Kaunda, to a multiparty political system under the leadership of President Frederick Chiluba and his Movement for Multiparty Democracy (MMD) party (Bjornlund, Bratton, and Gibson 1992; Simon 2005). As a

Figure 4.2 Protection of Civil Liberties

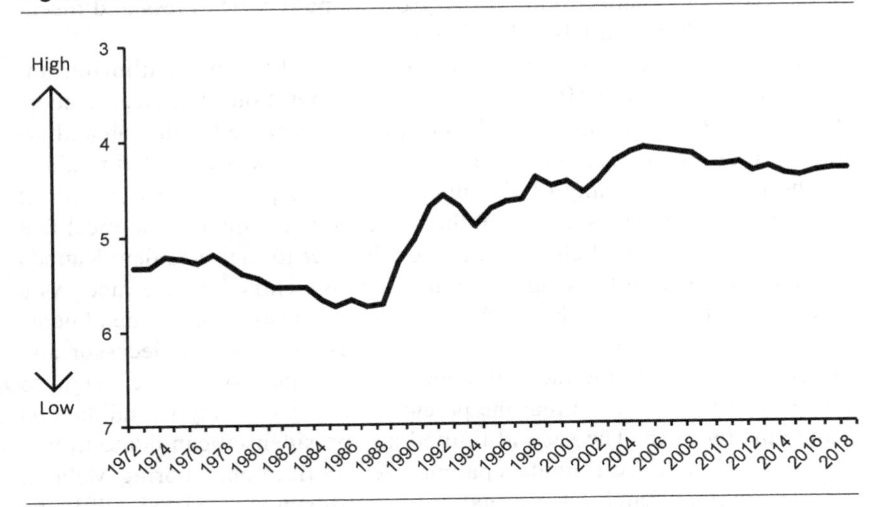

Source: Freedom House (2019).
Notes: 1 = highest level of protection of civil liberties and 7 = lowest level of protection of civil liberties.

labor leader from civil society, Chiluba seemingly represented a new generation of political leaders intent on opening the political spaces in their political systems. Eighteen months after achieving victory, Chiluba reinstated a state of emergency that had existed throughout Kaunda's rule and arrested and detained without charges fourteen members of the opposition, the United National Independence Party (UNIP). Critics of the government's actions drew parallels between Kaunda's use of states of emergency during the 1970s and the 1980s to silence political opponents and Chiluba's desire to curb rising criticism of his regime's inability to resolve Zambia's pressing economic problems. Most important, critics noted that the domination of Zambia's parliament by Chiluba's ruling MMD party (125 out of 150 seats) called into question the independence of the legislature from the executive, especially after Chiluba was successful in acquiring legislative approval for his harsh measures (Ham 1993).

An important aspect of Chiluba's political predicament was the economic dimension of the democratization process. Like leaders who took office beginning in the 1950s, Chiluba confronted unrealistic popular expectations that the fruits of democratization—especially higher wages and better living conditions—would be widely and quickly shared after multiparty elections. Indeed, a significant portion of the Zambian people believed a multiparty system would serve as a panacea for the country's economic problems. However, the combination of the overall weakness of the Zambian state and the constraints imposed on executive action by even the minimal checks and balances of the democratic system have led to little success in the economic realm, followed by growing public weariness and disenchantment with the Chiluba administration.

Chiluba's declining popularity presented the same authoritarian-democratic paradox confronted by the first generation of African leaders during the 1950s. Although largely socialized and trained within an authoritarian tradition, as were his predecessors, Chiluba was expected to abide by the rules of the game of Zambia's multiparty political system. Strict adherence to those rules, however, threatened to seal Chiluba's political fate in the 1996 presidential elections, especially after former president Kaunda accepted opposition backing and announced his entry into the race. As a result, Chiluba oversaw the ratification of two constitutional amendments that harkened back to the authoritarian excesses of his predecessor and threatened to undermine the very democratic political system he sought to create. The first required that the parents of any presidential candidate be Zambians by birth. The second limited any presidential candidate to two terms of office. Since Kaunda's parents were born in neighboring Malawi, and he had ruled Zambia for a total of twenty-seven years (1964–1991), he was forced to withdraw from the race. Chiluba's political maneuvering removed the only serious challenge to his rule and ensured his reelection (Bratton and van de Walle 1997:233, 260).

A fourth measure for assessing Africa's contemporary political landscape is to examine the degree to which personal rule and neopatrimonial forms of governance still dominate African political systems. This can be achieved by once again drawing on the Polity IV data project (Marshall, Gurr, and Jaggers 2019) that was used in section three of this chapter to assess the degree of personal rule of African regimes as of 1988 (see Table 4.1). As a reminder, the dataset allows us to assess the degree of personal rule on a scale of 1 to 7, with 1 being the highest level of personal rule (i.e., the lowest degree of institutional constraints on the executive) and 7 being the lowest level of personal rule (i.e., the highest degree of institutional constraints on the executive).

Table 4.4 sets out the personal rule enjoyed by African leaders in 2019. One of the most striking results is that twenty-nine (54 percent) of Africa's fifty-four countries now occupy the side of the spectrum indicative of lower degrees of personal rule. The breakdown includes eleven countries with a low degree of personal rule (Algeria, Benin, Côte d'Ivoire, Gambia, Mali, Mozambique, Namibia, Niger, Senegal, Zambia, and Zimbabwe), ten countries with a very low degree of personal rule (Burkina Faso, Ghana, Guinea-Bissau, Liberia, Madagascar, Malawi, Nigeria, Sierra Leone, Somalia, and Tunisia), and eight countries with an extremely low degree of personal rule (Botswana, Cape Verde, Central African Republic, Comoros, Kenya, Lesotho, Mauritius, and South Africa). This changing reality of African governance holds regardless of whether one focuses on large regional powers such as South Africa under Cyril Ramaphosa, mini-states such as Cape Verde under Jorge Carlos Fonseca, oil-rich countries such as Nigeria under Muhammadu Buhari, or economically impoverished countries such as Burkina Faso under Roch Marc Christian Kabore. This represents an advancement over 1988, when only four African countries occupied these three categories.

Table 4.4 also serves as a reminder that fifteen countries, or 28 percent of the African continent, still occupy the high to extremely high categories of the personal rule spectrum. The breakdown includes seven countries with a high degree of personal rule (Angola, the DRC, Egypt, Ethiopia, Rwanda, Togo, and Uganda) and seven countries with a very high degree of personal rule (Cameroon, Chad, Congo Brazzaville, Eritrea, Eswatini, Mauritania, and Sudan). Only one country, the petroleum-rich dictatorship of Equatorial Guinea under Teodoro Obiang Nguema Mbasongo, exhibited an extremely high degree of personal rule. Finally, six countries (11 percent of the African total) occupy the middle category of having a moderate degree of personal rule (Burundi, Djibouti, Gabon, Guinea, Morocco, and Tanzania). Although one may disagree over the specific placement of countries in individual categories, there is no question regarding the broader trend captured by this table: In comparison to the African political universe that existed in 1988, Africa's wave of democratization from 1989 to the present has contributed to a decrease in the role of personal rule on the African continent.

Table 4.4 Degree of Personal Rule in Africa, 2019

Extremely High Degree of Personal Rule	Very High Degree of Personal Rule	High Degree of Personal Rule	Moderate Degree of Personal Rule	Low Degree of Personal Rule	Very Low Degree of Personal Rule	Extremely Low Degree of Personal Rule
2% (1/54)	13% (7/54)	13% (7/54)	11% (6/54)	20% (11/54)	19% (10/54)	15% (8/54)
Equatorial Guinea	Cameroon Chad Congo Brazzaville Eritrea Eswatini Mauritania Sudan	Angola Democratic Republic of Congo Egypt Ethiopia Rwanda Togo Uganda	Burundi Djibouti Gabon Guinea Morocco Tanzania	Algeria Benin Côte d'Ivoire Gambia Mali Mozambique Namibia Niger Senegal Zambia Zimbabwe	Burkina Faso Ghana Guinea-Bissau Liberia Madagascar Malawi Nigeria Sierra Leone Somalia Tunisia	Botswana Cape Verde Central African Republic Comoros Kenya Lesotho Mauritius South Africa

Source: Adapted from Polity IV dataset (2019 data). See Marshall, Gurr, and Jaggers (2019).

Notes: Polity uses a 7-point scale of "institutional constraints on executive power" that is recast in terms of personal rule and foreign policy as follows: 1 = extremely high degree of personal rule (extremely low degree of institutional constraints); 2 = very high degree of personal rule (very low degree of institutional constraints); 3 = high degree of personal rule (low degree of institutional constraints); 4 = moderate degree of personal rule (moderate degree of institutional constraints); 5 = low degree of personal rule (high degree of institutional constraints); 6 = very low degree of personal rule (very high degree of institutional constraints); 7 = extremely low degree of personal rule (extremely high degree of institutional constraints).

Regimes unclassified by Polity IV in 2019 (7% or 4/54) were Libya, São Tomé and Príncipe, Seychelles, and South Sudan.

Stated another way, the African wave of democratization has contributed to growing institutional constraints on African leaders. This is due to the rising influence of both state actors (the parliament, the judiciary, and government bureaucracies and agencies) and nonstate actors (public opinion, political parties, and civil society [e.g., see Cheeseman 2018; Collord 2018; Ndulo 2018; Pitcher and Teodoro 2018; VonDoepp 2018; Bratton, Mattes, and Gyimah-Boadi 2005]).

Tunisia once again offers an example. Prior to the country's democratic transition, Tunisia embodied a neopatrimonial form of governance that exalted Ben Ali's personal rule. The key to personal rule was not achievement in a given field, but links to the extended family of the ubiquitously photographed president. Regional specialists like to joke that you can tell how bad a dictatorship is by the number of presidential portraits on display everywhere. Ben Ali was known for posting large and ostentatious images of himself—sporting suspiciously jet-black hair for a man in his seventies—on countless billboards and buildings. One multistory portrait loomed over the busy port of La Goulette, where the smiling strongman seemed to be reminding cruise-ship passengers and other travelers that he and his *mukhabarat* were always watching and listening. Another consisted of a massive and supremely tacky mosaic that Ben Ali had positioned within the ruins of the magnificent Roman amphitheater at El Djem. Such ostentatiousness is a thing of the past in Tunisia's new democratic system. It is important to remember, however, that personal rule is not an either-or scenario (i.e., all African countries maintain a mixture of personal rule and institutional constraints), but rather one of degree. In this regard, Beck's (2008) outstanding book on clientelism in Senegal demonstrates that patron-client relationships serve as important parts of African democracies.

A final measure for assessing Africa's contemporary political landscape is to examine the degree to which political change occurs peacefully or through extralegal means, most notably military coups d'état. African public opinion assumes that civilian-dominated political systems should constitute the proper norm of civil-military relations. Even military leaders intent on maintaining themselves in power are forced to offer, at minimum, rhetorical support for an eventual return to civilian rule, usually accompanied by some sort of specific timetable. The notion of demilitarization, sometimes referred to as promoting the civilianization of military regimes, became increasingly important in the post-1989 era as African policymakers and pro-democracy movements sought to consolidate transitions to democracy (Chege 1995; Luckham 1994). The greatest threat of the demilitarization process, of course, is that previously powerful militaries return to their barracks but remain poised for reintervention. This is what happened in the case of Egypt and the military's 2013 coup against the democratically elected Morsi government, less than two years after the military returned to the barracks (i.e., stepped down from power).

Table 4.5 provides some insight into the evolving role of military coups during the contemporary independence era, broken down by decade. It is striking that the percentage of successful coups peaked in the 1960s (58 percent, or twenty-six of the forty-five attempted coups), and that the overall number of attempted coups (fifty-nine) peaked in the 1970s. Moreover, the overall success rate for the 1951–1989 era was 47 percent (75 of the 161 attempted coups). These numbers have declined in the post-1989 era, indicating that the African wave of democratization is strengthening peaceful avenues for change. For example, the number of attempted coups went down from fifty-one during the 1990s to twenty-five during the 2000s and eighteen during the 2010s. The number of successful coups also declined from seventeen in the 1990s to nine in the 2000s and eight in the 2010s. As noted by Clark (2007:153), "the bulk of evidence suggests that democratic legitimacy makes African states much less vulnerable to military intervention than they otherwise would be." He nevertheless cautions that "economic

Table 4.5 Military Coups d'État in Africa

	Coup Attempts	Successful Coups	Success Rate (%)
Total 1951–1989	161	75	47
1951–1959	7	3	43
1960–1969	45	26	58
1970–1979	59	23	39
1980–1989	50	23	46
Total 1990–2019	94	34	36
1990–1999	51	17	33
2000–2009	25	9	36
2010–2019	18	8	44
Total 1951–2019	255	109	43

Sources: Powell and Thyne (2020); McGowan (2003).

progress and public order are as important to state legitimacy as are democratic credentials, and woe betide the government—no matter how democratic—that cannot provide the former two" (Clark 2007:154). This statement harkens back to our discussion earlier in this chapter of the great expectations–minimal capabilities paradox that existed at the beginning of the contemporary independence era. Then, as now, the average African citizen expected to receive immediately the fruits of their struggles for independence and more recently democratization. As long as Africa's democratizing states are able to effectively deliver the public goods expected by their populations, African militaries can be expected to remain in their barracks. In the absence of such success, the role of African militaries and military governance could once again increase.

Whether Africa's wave of democratization will result in further democratic consolidation or democratic decay will also depend on how the new generation of democratically elected African leaders responds to the democratic-authoritarian paradox. Will they accept defeat and join the ranks of the loyal opposition, as was the case in Kérékou's defeat in the 1992 elections and Soglo's defeat in the 1996 Beninois presidential elections, or will they increasingly turn to a variety of authoritarian tactics to maintain power, as Chiluba's manipulation of the 1996 Zambian presidential elections illustrates? Indeed, the response of African leaders to this democratic-authoritarian paradox in the 1950s ushered in nearly four decades of single-party, often military-dominated, dictatorships. The ways in which Africa's democratically elected leaders resolve this paradox during the decade of the 2020s and beyond potentially portend the strengthening and increasing spread of democracy, destined to last well into the twenty-first century. In this sense, the African wave of democratization, more than three decades after its beginning, remains a "work in progress" (Widner 2005), as is the case with democracy and politics in all regions of the world.

5

Economies and Development

Michael Kevane

Social scientists and ordinary people say that an economy is "developing" when average well-being is expanding, incomes are rising, poverty is falling, people are increasingly earning their livings from specialized activities, and greater investments are being made in the capabilities of individuals to discern and cultivate their talents and interests. Development means more freedom for people to realize their aspirations and thus have a fulfilling life. In the Anthropocene era (i.e., the period marking the impact of humans on the Earth's ecosystems), it is important to add the qualifier of "sustainable" to development, since regional ecological degradation and global climate change threaten to undermine the freedoms enabled by development for future generations.

Development has always been a relative concept in terms of geographic relevance and time scales. The term emerged during the 1950s, as it became clear that the new economy that had evolved in Europe and a few other regions was spreading throughout the world. This new economy, which at its root involved the systematic application of energy-intensive technology to production, was a different economic process than anything prior in human history. The term "development" became ubiquitous as many countries developed rapidly (e.g., Indonesia, Japan, Malaysia, South Korea, and, since the 1980s, China and India), and citizens in other countries aspired to emulate them. Social scientists and political leaders promoted the idea that the right mix of social institutions and government policies might enable any country or region to enjoy rapid development.

With this sense of development in mind, the available record suggests that African economies developed relatively slowly and unevenly during the colonial era (1884–1951). Huge swathes of the continent experienced little change, relative to what they could have experienced, as colonial administrations stifled indigenous innovation and investment. The end of colonial rule enabled leaders of newly independent countries to focus more attention on development. There was a burst of investment, especially in schooling and infrastructure, that in turn accelerated migration to cities, as people were freer to move. Consequently, the pace of development accelerated.

The twin legacies of 300 years of slave trade and 100 years of imperialism, however, proved nefarious, and by the 1970s governments almost everywhere turned into military and civilian dictatorships that quite often sent some components of the development process—especially income growth and poverty alleviation—into reverse. As late as the 1980s, it was common to find villages with virtually no energy-intensive technologies utilized. Men, women, and children tended to fields by hand or with animal-drawn plows; women crushed grain in mortars and ground flour between rocks, carried water from wells on their heads, and washed clothes by hand.

The pace of African development turned strongly positive in the late 1990s, though perhaps not sustainably so. Much recent economic growth has been due to oil, mineral, and primary commodity exports, and also to domestic urban service sectors. Little economic growth has been attributable to the production of industrial goods or exports of services. The agricultural sector remains the principal source of livelihood for about half of the African population and is increasingly vulnerable to regional ecological degradation and global climate change. However, well-being has steadily improved as mortality and morbidity have fallen dramatically. Schooling has spread rapidly, as has access to information. African countries have been among the fastest adopters of smartphone technologies. Energy-intensive technologies, including automobiles and motorcycles, tractors, grain mills, oil presses, food processing, leather tanning, and beverage bottling, are rapidly becoming ubiquitous.

This chapter summarizes the consensus of social science research on the many factors that explain the mixed and uneven development trajectory of most African countries. The chapter also draws attention to controversies and lacunae in knowledge. The first section provides a narrative description of an African economy as experienced by a typical person. The second section presents the aggregate statistics for the present state of development in Africa. Section three addresses prospects for accelerating development in African countries, focusing on the policy and institutional environment that promotes entrepreneurialism and investor confidence, prospects for productivity improvements through technology adoption, the extension of financial systems, and the provision of infrastructure, especially transport and power. A final section explores some of the threats to accelerated development, and steps that might be taken to prevent development disasters.

Overall, an optimistic forecast for African economic development is reasonable. Market-based development can be rapid, equitable, and sustainable. Alternatives are riskier, with greater likelihood of disasters rather than continued development. This forecast should not be grounds for complacency, however. Social justice requires attention to and prioritization of accelerating development in Africa and mitigating likely setbacks and disasters.

Economic Development for a Typical Person

More than 1 billion people live in Africa. Some are rich, and some are poor. Men and women earn their living by farming, manufacturing commodities in factories, and serving the public in restaurants, gas stations, laundries, and hair salons. There are bankers, newspaper editors, railway engineers, fashion designers, data scientists, and YouTube influencers. African economies are largely market economies. In a market economy, individuals and social groups such as families, ethnic groups, community associations, and private companies exchange goods and services using money as a medium of exchange. The assets owned by an individual or social group significantly influence the entitlements of that individual or group, in the sense that assets, including a person's own labor, are valued by prices in the market, and goods and services are obtained through purchase at market prices.

There is much variety between and within African economies. But one often wants to have an idea of a typical economy. What does it look like? At the risk of simplification, the following is a portrait of part of a typical African economy, told from the perspective of a somewhat packed day of a woman, whom we shall call Fati, who lives in a village close to a town. About 60 percent of people in Africa still live in rural areas, although as discussed in Chapter 7 they are increasingly connected to regional towns, and cities are growing rapidly.

Fati wakes in the morning in her new mud brick home. She and her family purchased the mud bricks from a neighbor who molds and sun-bakes the bricks in a field where the soil is especially clay-rich. Fati purchased the corrugated steel for the roof from a merchant in a neighboring town who operates a hardware and construction goods store. They also purchased several bags of cement, produced in a government-owned cement factory in the capital city and transported to the town by private truckers. Fati makes her family some tea with powdered milk and sugar, all purchased from a small shopkeeper in the village. The tea is imported from India; the sugar is made domestically in the south where plantations grow cane for a large sugar refinery operated under a contract by a multinational agribusiness corporation. The family dresses in secondhand clothing that a young man sells every Friday in the open-air market. The children go to a new private school in the village, which has a better reputation than the run-down government school.

Fati checks the balance in her money account on her mobile phone. She has the equivalent of $200. This money is her working capital. She takes the village bus, a small minivan, into town. The trip takes an hour because the driver stops at every village on the way to load passengers and merchandise. In town, Fati goes to several cloth wholesalers and uses her mobile money to purchase bolts of cloth that she will resell in her village. She gets a call from a sister in the city whose child is sick and needs medicine. Fati transfers money using her phone.

After spending two hours in the market, Fati goes to a funeral. The town imam has passed away. He had complained of fever and muscle aches and cramps. By the time he was taken to the government hospital in the city, it was too late for treatment. No one in the family seemed to know what the illness had been. Only a nurse had examined the imam before he died. All the influential people of town are at the funeral, and Fati spends two hours consoling family and talking with friends. At first the women attendees are directed to a separate area to sit and eat. As the hours go by, though, men and women start to cross the "line" and engage in quiet conversation. Fati meets a nephew of the imam, who works in the capital for one of the three mobile phone service providers. He has been working with a team building a new app that provides hourly meteorological forecasts based on the phone location. The company hopes to initially provide the service free of charge, gradually adding more functionality and then charging a subscription fee for enhanced services. The nephew talks excitedly about how farmers want to know what other neighboring farmers are doing. "No farmer wants to be the last to plow, or the last to apply herbicide. They can use our app to be more informed," he says excitedly. Fati agrees. "Yes! The new apps are so useful. I have been using an app that places a dress of my material over the picture of a woman so she can see what it might look like, and what style might suit her." Before leaving, Fati presses the equivalent of $10 into the hands of one of the musicians performing the funerary songs. She knows they work only for gifts, never for a fee. One of the musicians touts a display of CDs and flash drives with MP3 versions of their music, processed in a neighboring country known for its music industry.

Fati negotiates with a motorized-tricycle driver to load and transport her cloth. Donkey carts have disappeared since importers started bringing in Chinese and Indian tricycles. And even though everyone complains about the noise and pollution from the exhaust of the two-stroke engines, they are everywhere. The tricycles are especially ridden by young men working in the informal gold mines that dot the area, who use them to load the bags of rock they feed into diesel-powered crushers. They use cyanide to extract the gold from the resulting watery slurry. Fati shudders to think of the residues of the previous cargoes that her cloth now sits on.

Back in the village, dusk falls. The girls have gone into the countryside, ten kilometers away, to fetch wood for cooking over the three-stone fire. Fati's daughters draw water at the village hand pump and carry it back to the house to be stored in an old plastic barrel. The boys watch television at the neighbor's house, the only one nearby that has been hooked up to electricity. Fati's house has a small solar panel with three light bulbs. The family sleeps under mosquito nets. Fati often remarks how much malaria has declined since the bed nets began to be distributed by the government health clinic. It is a pleasant thought to drift off to sleep knowing that her children are less likely to wake with a fever.

The portrait of Fati's life is intended to reinforce several themes about African economies. The days of subsistence, where a village resident made everything needed—food, shelter, clothing, and transport—using local materials, are over. Specialization is increasingly the norm. Machinery and imports are ubiquitous, even though not everyone works with or consumes them. New electronic technologies, such as internet-connected smartphones and solar-powered lighting, are in every village. Transport to towns and cities is now measured in hours rather than in days. Practically everything is transacted in markets. Everyone uses money, and increasingly money is electronic. Finally, African economies have few large organizations. Only a

Brian Lance

Local repair shops, such as that portrayed in Houndé, Burkina Faso, are a staple of African urban and rural settings.

small share of people work in factories or large retail or service organizations. Economic activity remains at a small scale.

Development as of 2020

At the beginning of the twenty-first century, most African countries were at the bottom of the global distribution of well-being, even though several African economies were among the fastest growing countries in the world in terms of real gross national income per capita (hereinafter GNI per capita). For the fifty-four countries and approximately 1.25 billion people of Africa, the population-weighted GNI per capita in 2018 was about $1,800 when using the World Bank's Atlas method for converting local currency into the US dollar, a common reference currency. This was the lowest for any world region. Of the twenty-two countries with the lowest GNI per capita in the world (under $900), twenty were in Africa (the two exceptions were Afghanistan and Haiti). Of the forty-five countries with GNI per capita below $2,000, thirty-four were in Africa. By comparison, high-income countries enjoyed an average GNI per capita of about $45,000, while middle-income countries had a GNI per capita of about $5,300.

GNI is a reasonable broad indicator of development because it is strongly correlated with many other indicators of well-being, including infant, child, and maternal mortality; schooling attainment; access to clean water; life expectancy; and urbanization. These correlations are by no means deterministic or indicative of causality (i.e., that GNI causes well-being or that well-being causes GNI). Much of the reduction in mortality and fertility around the world has been due to advances in medical knowledge and technology, such as treatment and prevention of infectious diseases and contraception devices, rather than growth of GNI. And some societies with low GNI per capita levels have good childhood nutrition, decent access to primary and basic health care, low mortality, and high education levels.

Unfortunately, the evidence that African populations are disadvantaged, on average, on most dimensions of well-being is consistent with the low GNI numbers. Figures 5.1 through 5.5 compare Africa to China and India (each line represents the average experience of more than 1 billion people). Figures 5.1 and 5.2 show that infant and child mortality has declined in all three regions, but for Africa, mortality remains high at about 50 death per 1,000 live births for infants (compared with 32 for India and 8 for China), and around 75 deaths per 1,000 for children under five (compared with 39 for India and 9 for China). Maternal mortality (not shown) is about 500 per 100,000 live births in Africa, compared with about 150 for India and only 25 for China. Overall, life expectancy in Africa was about sixty-one years in 2017, while it was sixty-nine years in India and seventy-six years in China, as seen in Figure 5.3.

Figure 5.1 Infant Mortality (ages 0 to 1 year, per 1,000 people), 1975–2018

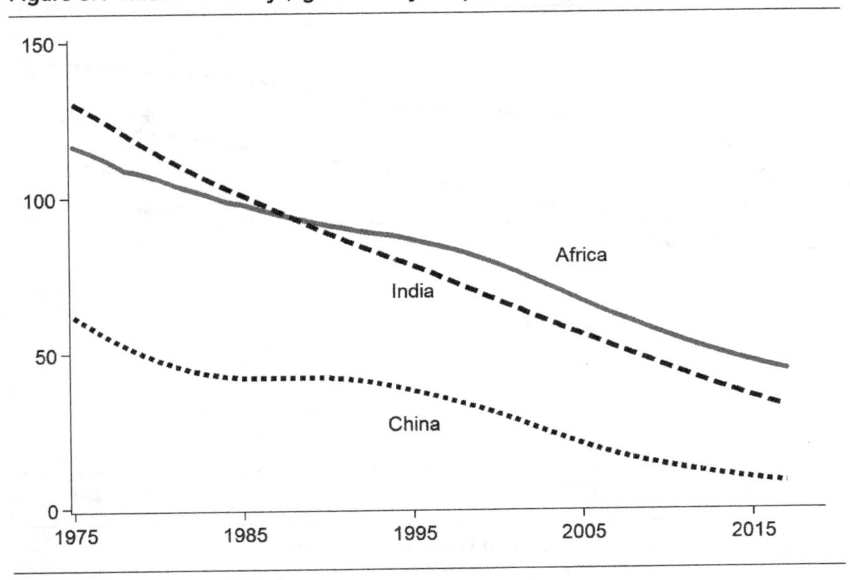

Source: World Bank (2019), World Development Indicators.

Figure 5.2 Child Mortality (ages 0 to 5 years, per 1,000 people), 1975–2018

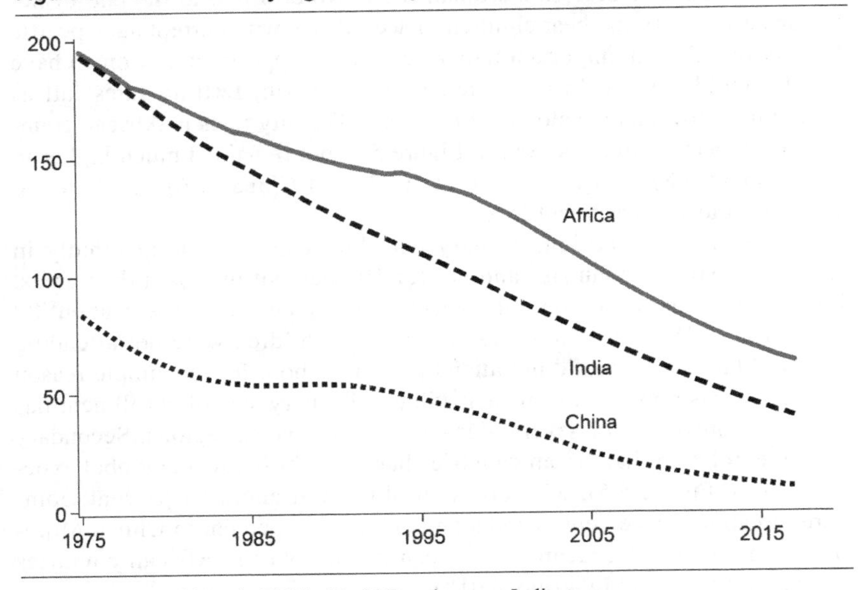

Source: World Bank (2019), World Development Indicators.

Figure 5.3 Life Expectancy, 1975–2017

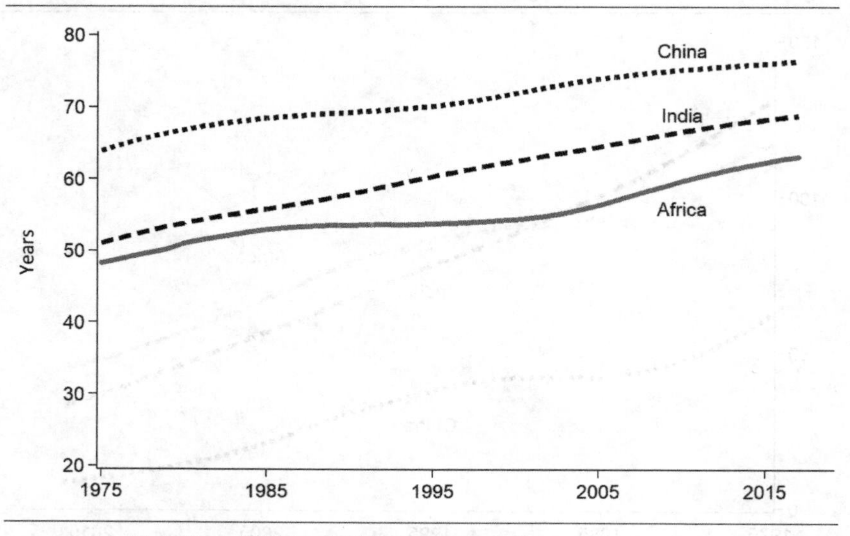

Source: World Bank (2019), World Development Indicators.

Total fertility rate, defined by the World Bank as "the number of children that would be born to a woman if she were to live to the end of her childbearing years and bear children in accordance with current age-specific fertility rates," is an important indicator of other opportunities women have besides child-rearing. In all societies of the world, fertility rates fall as economies grow and development increases. Fertility rates in African countries have been falling, as seen in Figure 5.4, but remained much higher in 2018 (about 4.8) than those of India (2.3) and China (1.6), the latter of which is below replacement level.

In terms of schooling, primary enrollment has increased rapidly in almost all African countries and is near 100 percent in most urban areas. For the continent as a whole, however, primary enrollment was about 80 percent in 2018; about 40 million school-age children were not attending school. Many children did not attend primary school for the simple reason that there was no school near their village. Primary school enrollment has been near universal for several decades in other world regions. Secondary school enrollment in African countries has been far below the global experience (see Figure 5.5), with gross enrollment at about 55 percent, compared to about 75 percent in India and close to 95 percent in China. Moreover, the quality of education has been much lower in African countries (Altinok, Angrist, and Patrinos 2018).

Figure 5.4 Fertility Rate, 1975–2018

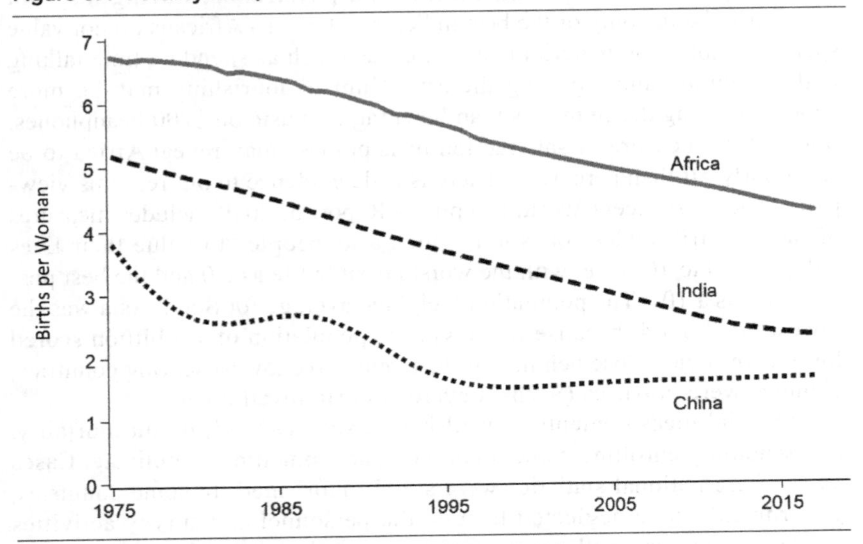

Source: World Bank (2019), World Development Indicators.

Figure 5.5 Enrollment in Secondary School, 1975–2015

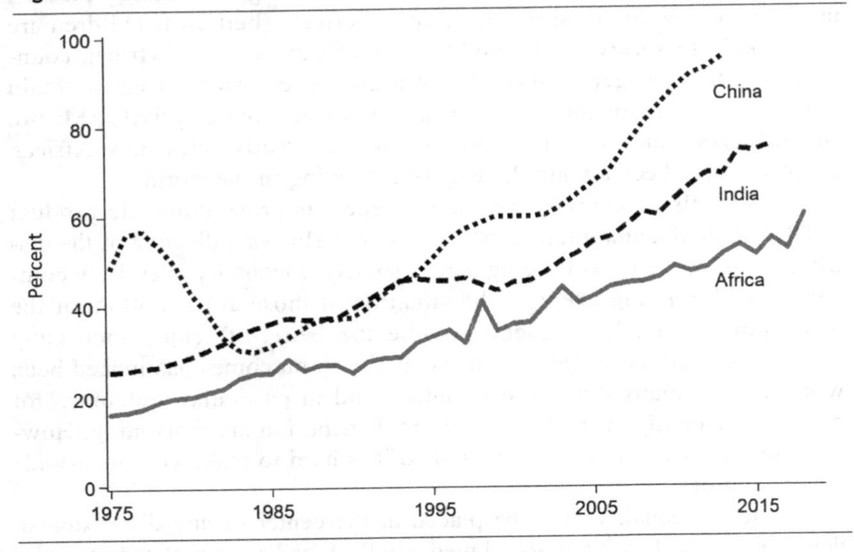

Source: World Bank (2019), World Development Indicators.
Note: Enrollment in secondary school as a percentage of the population corresponding to official ages for secondary school.

To measure development, income and physical well-being may not necessarily be the only or the best indicators. Perhaps Africans do not value spending money on material possessions as much as spending time talking with neighbors and enjoying the arts. Human flourishing may be more about mastering dance moves than listening to music on $200 headphones. Some other measure of satisfaction or happiness may reveal Africa to be less poorly off than perceived. There is little evidence to buttress this viewpoint. The most recent World Happiness Report of 2019 includes measures of the "Cantril ladder" question, which asks people "to value their lives today on a 0 to 10 scale, with the worst possible life as a 0 and the best possible life as a 10." The population-weighted average for South Asia was the lowest (at about 4, because India with its population of 1.3 billion scored low), with Africa close behind. Of the twenty-five lowest scoring countries, eighteen were in Africa (Sachs, Layard, and Helliwell 2019).

Official measurements of well-being, such as GNI, infant mortality, and schooling enrollment and attainment, are sometimes unreliable. Cases exist where national statistics were simply fabricated. In some countries, governments have neglected to fund the personnel and survey activities needed to measure well-being, despite the modest expenditures involved. Social scientists thus often turn to alternative measures such as the Demographic and Health Surveys (DHS) that are carried out by international agencies. Anthropometric measures of young people, such as height for age, are sometimes proxies for nutritional well-being, though they must be used cautiously due to survivor selection effects (better-off children are more likely to survive) that might be significant in many African countries. Satellite imagery, especially of night lights, can be used to obtain objective and reasonable proxy measures of economic activity (Mamo, Bhattacharyya, and Moradi 2019). On these alternative measures, African countries have been among the worst-performing in the world.

The levels of average well-being, such as gross domestic product (GDP) per capita and infant mortality, are not always indicative of the distribution or range of well-being across society. Inequality is entirely compatible with a rising average; the situation of those at the bottom of the distribution could be worsening while the better-off enjoy increasing plenty. Some studies suggest that inequality in outcomes has indeed been worsening in many African economies, and in particular, outcomes for people perennially at the bottom of the distribution are worsening. However, the picture is not uniform, and so it is hard to make continent-wide generalizations.

Gender inequality must be placed at the center of any discussion of development. In July 2019, social media in Burkina Faso circulated an urgent appeal from a schoolteacher in the province of Bazèga. A fourteen-year-old girl who was the top student at her school was being married off by her family and would be forced to leave school. Her situation was emblematic of the lost opportunities for more than one-third of young women throughout Africa. Early marriage interrupts schooling and reduces the autonomy of women throughout their lives (Delprato, Akyeampong, and Dunne 2017; Efevbera et al. 2017; Maswikwa et al. 2015). The high fertility associated with early marriage exacerbates health problems that undermine well-being. The risk of death in childbirth remains high, and complications associated with pregnancy may include anemia, infection, postpartum depression, and fistula (Ellis, Elledge, and de Chesnay 2019).

Early marriage has been but one manifestation of pervasive gender inequality unfavorable to women (see Chapter 11 for further discussion). It is true that all societies of the world have significant gender inequality, and some African societies were characterized by greater gender equality than the global average. Nevertheless, in the early twenty-first century, African economies were characterized by considerable gender inequality compared to the rest of the world (Doss et al. 2015; Kevane 2014; Nyambura 2018). Gender inequality is a drag on development in its own right. There is less investment in the capabilities of women and children, inefficiency in household production, and worse outcomes in terms of public services. Moving to gender equality is likely to enhance well-being and accelerate development.

Prospects for Accelerating Development in Africa

For a longer-term perspective on development, the World Bank's World Development Indicators (WDI) and other datasets report real GDP per capita. GDP is closely correlated with GNI, but diverges especially for oil- and mineral-exporting economies where a fraction of domestic product is income for foreign-owned firms rather than domestic firms. Figure 5.6 shows the path of population-weighted GDP per capita for African countries and compares that change to India and China. As of 2018, African countries generally have not had the transformational change in economic activity that has characterized China, and they do not yet appear to be on a steady growth path like that of India since 1985.

Three populous African countries saw GDP grow above a 4.5 percent annual rate over the years 1995–2018. These were Ethiopia (with a population of approximately 100 million), Rwanda (12 million), and Mozambique (28 million). A 4.5 percent growth rate implied a doubling time of approximately fifteen years, so the next generation entered an economy with incomes that were twice as high as the previous generation's. Another eleven countries had real GDP per capita growth above 3 percent, ten others had growth above 2 percent, and ten moderate performers had growth in the 1–2 percent range. Fourteen countries had negative growth or growth below 1 percent over the period. The growth disasters were Central African

Figure 5.6 Real GDP per Capita, 1960–2018

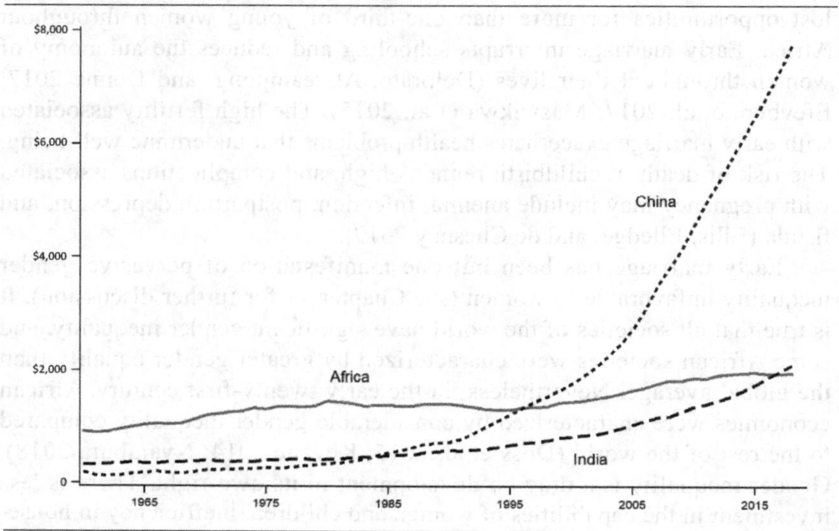

Source: World Bank (2019), World Development Indicators.
Note: Figures are in constant 2005 $US dollars.

Republic, Gabon, Libya, and Zimbabwe, with negative annualized growth rates of about 1 percent, so that by the end of the twenty-five-year period they were only about two-thirds as well off as they had been at the beginning of the period. The paradox of measuring development by GDP growth rates, and the reason GDP measures need to be complemented with other indicators, is that Equatorial Guinea was the fastest growing economy in terms of GDP, but most of the oil wealth from exports went to regime leaders while the quality of life for most of the population remained quite low by global standards.

Although the development indicators discussed above remain among the lowest in the world, they have been steadily improving, often at a pace faster than income growth. The years of 1995–2018 demonstrated that rapid development was possible. There is room for optimism about future prospects, and for discussion of how to accelerate the speed of development.

In market economies, development happens because people and organizations invest. A decision to make an investment depends on knowledge about investment opportunities and expectations about the future. These include expectations about prices of output, costs of producing output, technologies for production and distribution, enforcement of property rights and contracts, and tax rates. Knowledge and opportunities enable someone who is making an investment decision to calculate the expected profitability, or return, on the investment. We imagine that people rank investment projects according to expected returns and the riskiness of those returns. They invest in projects with higher risk-return profiles. In general, the more people invest, the more productive they will be in subsequent years, with greater possibilities for improvement in well-being.

While investment depends on expectations, the level of investment also depends on the ability of an entrepreneur (someone making an investment) to obtain funds to finance the investment. The nature of investments is that people work in the present and materials must be purchased in the present, while the returns of the investment accrue in the future. The gap between present expenditures and future returns must be bridged through a grant or loan. Loans typically come in the form of bank loans or from selling shares in the profits of the future investment (i.e., selling equity or stock). The financial system then becomes a critical factor in affecting the level of investment. Around the world, there is considerable variation in the performance of financial systems. Many countries have repressed their financial systems—that is, they have so many barriers to impede the functioning of the financial system that few investments are able to be financed through the system. Instead, entrepreneurs must patiently save assets until they have enough to self-finance the investment.

Investment activity also depends on mechanisms that coordinate expectations, enable collective decisionmaking, and mitigate monopoly. The profitability of many investments depends on the level of infrastructure provided by larger social entities and the prices they charge. Governments, for example, often provide a large array of public goods. These goods are non-rival and non-excludable; their capacity to provide services to individual users changes little as the volume of users rises, and it is difficult to prevent users from accessing the services. Some public goods are non-rival but excludable, and so are natural monopolies. For example, only one firm will supply electricity or water to a town because the cost of adding additional users once a network of wires or pipes has been laid is negligible.

In summary, investment depends on knowledge and expectations of investment opportunities, the financial system, and reasonable coordination or collective decisionmaking mechanisms. When people have low expectations about the profitability of investments at home, financial systems encourage financial capital to be transferred and invested abroad, and social institutions permit government officials to loot public resources rather than to manage collective services, then development might be very slow, or even negative.

Improved Prospects for the Profitability of Investments

There are many reasons why African investors and entrepreneurs think that the future will likely be favorable to those who make investments in the present. One reason is increased certainty about the broad direction of economic policy by future governments. In 1776, Adam Smith remarked in *The Wealth of Nations* that increasing the wealth of a nation was a matter of establishing peace, rule of law, and a reasonable rate of taxation. Smith believed that in these circumstances, a virtuous circle was possible: specialization and investment led to higher productivity, which increased the size of the market for producers, which induced them to invest and specialize more. An emerging consensus across African economies favors the Smithian program. Governments are increasingly committed to the peaceful resolution of conflicts, to stronger rule of law, to sound macroeconomic policies (the contemporary version of Smith's "easy taxes"), and to investment in basic infrastructure to promote trade. Economic policy is more eclectic, strategic, and pragmatic, informed by the apparent lackluster performance of doctrinaire policymaking of both the "Washington consensus" (neoliberal privatization) variety and the "African socialism" variety (Asongu and Nwachukwu 2017; Barrett et al. 2017; Monga and Lin 2015; Noman and Stiglitz 2015).

This is not to say that there are no relevant big debates over economic policy. Indeed, economists have been sharply divided over whether interventionist industrial policy is needed to perennialize economic growth. Some assert that industrialization, where a large fraction of the labor force moves from informal economy service work into factory work, is the only path to long-term development, and so government should undertake many policies and programs to develop the manufacturing sector (Behuria and Goodfellow 2019; Haraguchi, Cheng, and Smeets 2017; Hauge and Chang 2019). Others are more sanguine, arguing that economic growth and development have been brisk for almost two decades, and there seems to be no reason an agriculture and service-led development path could not continue for several more decades. In this view, government should be investing in human capital so future generations can be effective knowledge workers in the global economy and make their own investment decisions.

There are other reasons why development is likely to continue as long as economic policy is not actively detrimental. Demographic trends are likely to boost growth in per capita income and well-being. Fertility rates are declining throughout the continent, from about 6.5 in 1975 to 4.8 in 2018. There is, moreover, considerable variation in fertility across the continent, with rates quite high in the Sahelian countries (close to 6.0) and quite low in many countries of southern Africa (close to 3.0). This is not to say that fertility rates are not relatively high, even when comparing African countries to other regions at similar stages of development. Consider Burkina Faso. With an overall fertility rate of 5.7, the population of about 20 million in 2020 is likely to double to 40 million by 2040, and possibly even double again before stabilizing in 2060. Burkina Faso has a similar size and climate to the states of Arizona, Utah, and Nevada in the United States, which have populations of about 5 million each. Overall, the United Nations has projected that Africa's population might rise to almost 4 billion in 2100, even if fertility rates decline from 5.0 to 3.0 by 2050 and to 2.0 by 2090.

Fertility can decline more rapidly, hence the grounds for more optimism. Bangladesh went from a fertility rate of 6.9 in 1970 to 2.2 in 2010, even though the country is poor and rural. Reductions in fertility, in Africa as elsewhere in the world, are closely correlated with indicators of greater female autonomy, especially with greater schooling. Access to secondary schooling for girls is one of the largest factors leading to declines in fertility. Urbanization is another important correlate of declining fertility. The pace of both education and urbanization has been increasing in most countries. As a result, around 2030, there will likely begin a period of sustained decline in children per working adult. This demographic transition strongly favors development, as women shift into activities that are more productive than child-rearing and as working adults have more resources to invest in their skills. It also favors the growth of more complex economies, as the patterns of consumer purchases become more varied and less concentrated on the labor-intensive services of raising children.

Urbanization will likely enhance the profitability of investments for two other reasons. In rural societies, the extent of the market is small and limited by the costs of carrying goods using donkey or ox carts or, increasingly, small motorized vehicles. In urban societies, however, the extent of the market becomes very large. A producer of goods or services might imagine a market consisting of tens or hundreds of thousands of customers. Moreover, the administration and planning of city functions have become increasingly professionalized and routinized. While rural villages are subject to the thousand whims of a thousand village chiefs, an urban planning department in a city of 5 million people becomes quite predictable and can be counted on to ensure that the city operates reasonably effectively. Entrepreneurs are thus more willing to invest. This virtuous circle of widespread investment in both private productivity and public infrastructure accelerates growth.

Expanded Investment Opportunities

One of the surest kinds of profitable investment is the deployment of a new technology or innovation that enables fewer people and less material to produce the same, or more, output. Most African countries have a sizable backlog of technological innovations that have not yet been adopted, and entrepreneurs are rapidly closing the gap by importing capital goods that embody that technology. Signs of this are everywhere (Aker and Blumenstock 2015; Chen et al. 2016). Consider the motorized tricycle mentioned in the story of Fati. This transport technology, and motorcycles generally, are more efficient than a donkey or ox cart, in the sense that at current prices, the cost per kilogram per kilometer of transporting goods is considerably lower (and the speed is also much faster). Thus, investing in a motorized tricycle or motorcycle for transport services is profitable (Ehebrecht, Heinrichs, and Lenz 2018; Ntewusu and Nanbigne 2015). We note, of course, the caveat about environmental consequences, which are not straightforward since animals also produce greenhouse gases as a by-product of digestion.

There are many profitable technologies that have recently been and may continue to be adopted by relatively poor people in African economies: metal detectors for identifying promising sites for artisanal gold mining, solar lanterns, ATM machines, gig economy coordination platforms such as AirBnb, and wind-powered electrical generation. Many of these adoptions have beneficial implications for equity (poor people might be less poor).

Medical and public health technologies continue to be widely adopted. Technologies to prevent and treat infectious diseases have not only an immediate direct effect in improving development (well-being goes up) but also longer-term effects by raising the productivity of people who are sick less often and thus more free to either work or enjoy leisure. One significant effect has come from the control and treatment of malaria, a debilitating pandemic disease that diverts enormous amounts of people's time and value away from productive uses. Twenty years ago it was common for adults to be debilitated for up to one month per year, both for recovering from their own malarial fevers and caring for (and often burying) their children who suffered from the disease. Another case is the distribution of deworming pills. Intestinal worms are a significant drag on schooling outcomes for students, who are often rendered anemic. Despite the evidence of sizable returns, many governments remain reluctant to spend even modest amounts on deworming. Similar such failures have been seen in other areas where externalities are sizable: antimalarial bed nets, vaccines, and antiretroviral HIV therapies. There is much room for growth-enhancing distribution of medical technologies. (See Chapter 8 for further discussions.)

African agriculture has benefited and will continue to benefit from technology adoption (Otsuka and Muraoka 2017). Some crop and agricultural technologies that have only begun to be adopted include soybeans, pineapple, cut flowers, small edible-oil presses, fortification of many foods, and germplasm upgrading of livestock breeds through artificial insemination (Moseley, Schnurr, and Bezner-Kerr 2017). Fertilizer adoption remains quite low throughout the continent and has substantial potential to greatly increase crop profitability.

An example of how technology can accelerate development is the shift to adopt herbicides in agricultural production. A sharp acceleration of herbicide use occurred in the mid-2000s and appeared to be due to expiring patents and introduction of generic herbicides, rapid expansion of Chinese and Indian chemical firms into African markets, and quick proliferation of wholesale and retail supply chains throughout rural areas (Haggblade et al. 2017). Agricultural economists have observed that herbicides quickly became more cost-effective than manual labor and possibly also animal traction, hitherto used for weeding (Rodenburg et al. 2019). The profitability of herbicide use quickly became evident as millions of farmers adopted this technology throughout the continent.

The caveat for herbicide use is that while there is clear profitability for farmers in the short term, there are negative externalities and market issues that governments should be monitoring closely (Korres, Burgos, and Duke 2018). Herbicides can be dangerous to human health if not handled properly. Some studies have found that the costs of managing ill health that resulted from herbicides can exceed the profits saved on labor costs. Uncoordinated and excessive use of herbicides can accelerate ecosystem changes in weeds and pests that ultimately render a farm ecosystem less productive than it was originally. Invasive plants that may be resistant to herbicides occupy the niche opened up by the absence of possibly less noxious weeds. As the new invasive species builds up a seed or root base in the soil, it may become more costly to control.

An important problem in maximizing the benefits of herbicide use for weed control is that farmers have difficulty verifying the quality of herbicides sold in marketplaces. Chemical analyses find that many herbicides have much lower concentrations of active ingredients than stated on labels. The absence of trustworthy brands places the burden of discovery of quality on individual farmers. Quality is a public good. A brand that is known to have high quality does not need to be investigated by every individual farmer. Governments have been slow, however, to regulate and enforce quality assurance in the herbicide market (Ashour et al. 2019).

The speed and appropriateness of technology adoption depends on the social institutions that facilitate and hinder the process. Some of the social institutions include government policy frameworks. It is reasonable for governments to assess the ecological sustainability and downside risks of many innovations, whether herbicides or genetically altered mosquitoes. Governments and aid organizations may also design "nudges" that encourage or discourage certain kinds of technology adoption. A technology that is profitable, both privately and socially, may not be adopted because people are unsure about benefits, unforeseen costs, durability, and other properties of the technology. They may also be unable to borrow at reasonable interest rates to finance the investment in the technology. Many randomized control trials have found that different marketing arrangements generate quite different adoption patterns. One study in Uganda in 2010, for example, found that a package of marketing techniques increased adoption of improved cookstoves that cost the equivalent of $10 from about 5 percent to almost 50 percent of customers (Levine et al. 2018).

Technology adoption also commonly exhibits network externalities. When some firms adopt certain technologies, other firms are more likely to adopt them as well. This arises partly from learning by doing, and from a growing supply of human capital able to effectively adapt a technology to a particular market or production environment. These insights have prompted research on generalizable lessons for encouraging industrial clusters, where firms agglomerate and technology and productivity advance more rapidly (Newman and Page 2017; Page and Tarp 2017; Sonobe 2016; Sonobe, Otsuka, and Hashino 2016).

Enhanced Access to Financial Systems

Financial systems channel purchasing power from savers to investors, enabling greater investment in the present. The colonial regimes maintained repressed financial systems, and many Africans were only able to access finance from the rotating savings and credit associations that were inefficient at financing for investment. Several financial innovations and reforms have enabled rapid expansion of financial systems in the twenty-first century, and this expansion seems likely to continue.

One innovation has been labeled the microfinance revolution (MkNelly and Kevane 2002; Steinert et al. 2018). In the 1980s, nonprofit organizations started to experiment with more effective delivery mechanisms for credit, using joint liability, female empowerment and solidarity, frequent repayment schedules, and small loan amounts to make loans and savings mechanisms more accessible. Microfinance spread rapidly throughout the continent, with a much better track record than the credit cooperatives of the prior decades that usually ended with mass default and bailouts. It is important, however, not to overstate the effects of microfinance. At one time, policymakers and donors were convinced that massive expansion of small-scale credit programs primarily targeting micro-entrepreneurs would unleash a wave of investment and enterprise growth that would accelerate general economic growth. Numerous studies and meta-analyses, however, have suggested that the impact of these microfinance programs has been positive but rather modest (Van Rooyen, Stewart, and De Wet 2012).

A part of the financial system that remains promising but still needs innovation involves agricultural insurance. Some researchers thought that farmers across the continent were underinvesting in farm inputs because of the riskiness of farming. Risk comes both from the ecosystem (rainfall, pests) and from the market (price fluctuations). More easily accessible and reliable ecosystem and market data have made the pricing of insurance products more reliable. Numerous experiments, however, have found that farmers are very reluctant to purchase insurance products (Marr et al. 2016; Tadesse, Shiferaw, and Erenstein 2015). There has been considerable interest in new strategies to encourage the adoption of insurance.

Another innovation enabling the financing of investments has been the growth of cash transfer programs implemented by governments and nonprofit organizations (Parker and Todd 2017). Distributing monthly stipends to poor families became an important component of development strategies of countries around the world during the 2000s. Numerous reviews of the impact of cash transfer programs, including some in African countries, whether conditional or unconditional and using a variety of econometric strategies to credibly identify effects, found that they were generally pro-investment and effective antipoverty programs (Bastagli et al. 2016; Davis et al. 2016; Handa et al. 2018; Haushofer and Shapiro 2016). That is, the transfers typically led to investments in human capital and in business capital that raised productivity. In that sense, cash transfers have been both equitable and efficient. The funds distributed have gone toward those most in need, and the tax revenue generated in the future is likely to be of the same order of magnitude as the transfers.

African countries, on the whole, have been relatively slow to adopt cash transfer programs, with the exceptions of South Africa and Namibia (Barrientos and Villa 2015; Simpson 2018). Most programs have been small and of limited duration. Governments seem not to want to publicize or extend them. The idea that every poor citizen should be entitled to a basic cash transfer as a matter of rights appears to be viewed by most political leaders as dangerous.

In addition to government-provided cash transfers, another large change in the financial system has been the growth of financial remittances. The remittances that come from increasingly numerous and wealthy expatriate communities of Africans in Europe, North America, and more recently in countries such as Turkey and China, are a major contributor to enabling the financing of investment (Ajefu 2018; Hines and Simpson 2014; Jena 2018).

A private sector innovation that has improved financial systems is the growth of mobile banking. In many African countries, a mobile phone owner can take cash to a kiosk store and have the agent transfer the cash into an electronic account available on the phone. The person can then easily transfer the electronic money to other phone account holders. They can store the money or go to a kiosk and have the funds debited from the electronic account and received as cash. Numerous studies have found that mobile money has become an important financial mechanism in many countries (Asongu 2013; Mbiti and Weil 2015; Ouma, Odongo, and Were 2017; Riley 2018). Aker et al. (2016), reporting on a randomized control trial, found that diet diversity and calorie intake were higher where transfers were available through mobile phones, partly because of time savings and possibly also because of shifts in intrahousehold bargaining power favoring women. Munyegera and Matsumoto (2016) similarly found a positive effect of mobile money access on real per capita consumption, with mobile phone users more likely to receive remittances, receive them more frequently, and receive larger transfers.

There is room for even more innovation. African economies are underdeveloped in terms of quantity and quality of residential finance. This sector seems likely to grow rapidly as the urban sector grows and stimulates the capacity of governments or the private sector to deliver greater assurance of property title (Asabere, McGowan, and Lee 2016; Feather and Meme 2018; Nkechi, Samuel, and Ifurueze 2018).

Extended Infrastructure

The consensus of social scientists about infrastructure spending is that it is difficult to make generalizations, partly because infrastructure projects are often opportunities for corruption and wasteful extravagance. At the aggregate level, some studies find strong correlations between public infrastructure and growth (Kodongo and Ojah 2016). Torero and Chowd-

Peter J. Schraeder

An important part of African infrastructure where roads are poor involves water transport, such as the small boats and ferries that link the towns of Goma and Bukavu on Lake Kivu in the eastern province of the Democratic Republic of Congo.

hury (2005) asserted that capital-intensive infrastructure generated significant benefits in excess of costs. Calderón and Servén (2004) analyzed a large sample of countries over the period 1960–2000 and concluded that infrastructure investment had substantial antipoverty effects. Other studies have been skeptical. Devarajan, Easterly, and Pack (2003) advocated against significant infrastructure investment for Africa. They suggested that the productivity of infrastructure investment generally was extremely low and might even be declining over time, because of governance and macroeconomic failures.

There is a very long list of potential public infrastructure projects, including roads, railroads (Luiu, Torbaghan, and Burrow 2018), dams (Awojobi and Jenkins 2015), energy, electrification, health facilities, airports and air travel (Hovhannisyan and Keller 2015), radio spectrum management, and broadband. Some of these infrastructure investments will likely have sizable long-term growth effects. Consider the internet backbone that a country needs (underwater cables and access points to link to local internet service providers). African countries have lagged in investing in the infrastructure required to provide internet access. The lag has been an unintended blessing for researchers, because cables and national networks have been adopted by different countries at different times. Hjort and Poulsen (2019) exploited these differences and estimated that employment increased by perhaps 10 percent and that incomes (proxied by night light luminescence) may have increased by about 2 percent. It is not known whether these onetime effects will be seen again as countries move from 3G to 4G and eventually 5G networks, and as other innovations in internet technology are disseminated, but it is possible.

In contrast to internet backbone investment, discussions about building roads are more illustrative of perennial debates regarding infrastructure trade-offs. The extended question about road infrastructure is: How much public money should be spent building road and rail networks, considering that due to limited government capacity the monitoring of construction quality may be poor and the construction programs may exacerbate a culture of corruption in the government and private sector? Citizens and their representatives around the world often disagree on this question. One side typically holds up an illustration of an empty four-lane highway to the hometown of the transport minister, and links excessive public spending to graft and favoritism. The other side holds up a photo of a large truck stuck in the mud, holding up dozens of vehicles behind it, and likewise links the lack of public spending to graft and favoritism. When John Garang, then the leader of the Sudan People's Liberation Army, was asked in the early 2000s about his priorities for the south, he said, "Roads, roads, and more roads." At the time, there were no paved roads in South Sudan outside of the capital, Juba, and most unimproved roads were in poor condition.

Certainly there were abundant possibilities for road building to improve incomes and reduce poverty.

But the same may have been said of any antipoverty program in South Sudan. The crucial job of economists is to weigh costs against benefits. Roads are generally expensive propositions, with considerable variation in cost across quality. Obviously every road is different (which is why corruption is always present in road-building ventures). But it is possible to gauge an approximate cost from various sources, and one might reasonably estimate that a typical paved two-lane highway connecting towns through rural regions costs about $250,000 per mile. Moreover, roads deteriorate quickly without maintenance, and politicians are often favorable to new road construction while being unfavorable to allocating public spending to maintenance. The benefits of roads depend crucially on their locations. So, the cost-benefit exercise is substantial and difficult. There are now a number of good econometric exercises that attempt to control for the endogenous placement of roads and thus estimate the impact of roads on household outcomes in Africa (Ali et al. 2015; Berg, Blankespoor, and Selod 2018; Gebresilasse 2018; Hine et al. 2019; Stifel, Minten, and Koru 2016). These studies find that road investment generally has positive and often substantial effects on local income and well-being.

Threats to Accelerated Development and Averting Development Disasters

Though the prospects for more rapid growth are good, due to greater consensus around more pragmatic policymaking, the expanding adoption of productive technology, the broadening and deepening of financial institutions, and greater attention to infrastructure, several threats loom over the likely acceleration of improvement in well-being in African countries. Civil conflict is probably the most important threat. Two other threats—pandemics and climate change—are global in scale, and so much of the effort toward prevention and mitigation is the responsibility of multinational institutions such as the World Health Organization (WHO) and the various frameworks for addressing global climate change. Still, much can be done to prevent and mitigate negative effects. Political actors often neglect the unrewarding work of investing to prepare for events that have only small probabilities of occurring. Citizens must become more engaged and mobilize to affect policies and programs that will counter the significant threats.

Civil Conflict

Violent civil conflict remains the most likely threat to African economic development. War not only slows development, it destroys existing infrastructure and creates a burden on survivors who must care for the wounded and displaced. Riots and protests also can have significant negative effects on economic activity by destroying investments, dissuading future investors, and reducing economic activity in the short term.

Risks of conflict are elevated in most African countries, where institutions for the peaceful resolution of conflict are weak. The foremost institution for resolving conflict is the national political order, institutionalized in democratic societies by constitutions, parliaments, independent judiciaries, open media, and regular elections. Most African countries have robust national institutions, but some have been in periods of extended political disorder (Somalia since 1991, and Libya since 2011), and others have significant regions no longer participating in the national political order because of endemic violence (Central African Republic, Democratic Republic of Congo, and Mali).

Some countries have also fostered other institutions as guarantors of peaceful transitions of power. Many countries have rehabilitated institutions of traditional chieftaincy (and kingships) and given traditional leaders prominence in intercommunal dialogue. Burkina Faso, Mali, and other Sahelian countries promote traditional "joking relationships" where members of different ethnic groups ritually insult each other as a way to defuse social tensions. Sudan, in its better days, encouraged local gatherings to manage conflicts between herders and farmers as they competed for access to water.

Unfortunately, civil conflict has not been diminishing in Africa over the past decades. Figures 5.7 through 5.10 use data from the Armed Conflict Location and Event Data Project (ACLED), a comprehensive database of violence, riots, and protests over the 1997–2019 period (Raleigh et al. 2010). Figure 5.7 shows that the number of violent incidents has been rising since 2010. Figure 5.8 likewise traces a dramatic increase in the number of protests and riots across the continent. Figure 5.9 lists the fifteen countries with the largest number of fatalities over the 1997–2019 period. Angola far exceeded the other countries, with the most intense years of the civil war accounting for 150,000 fatalities. Figure 5.10 traces the annual total fatalities since 2000 (the Angola war; the earlier genocide in Rwanda with an estimated 600,000 dead; and the civil wars of Sudan, Ethiopia, and Somalia that ended in the 1990s would swamp the totals for the 2000–2019 period). The levels of fatalities have been high, and the intensity of violence appears to have mostly risen throughout the 2005–2019 period, averaging almost 30,000 deaths per year.

Mali is one country that has been trapped in a downward spiral of conflict (Benjaminsen and Ba 2019; Wing 2013). The country of almost 20 million people had been considered an increasingly strong democracy where political power was contested through peaceful elections. A low-level

Figure 5.7 Number of Violent Incidents in Africa, 1997–2019

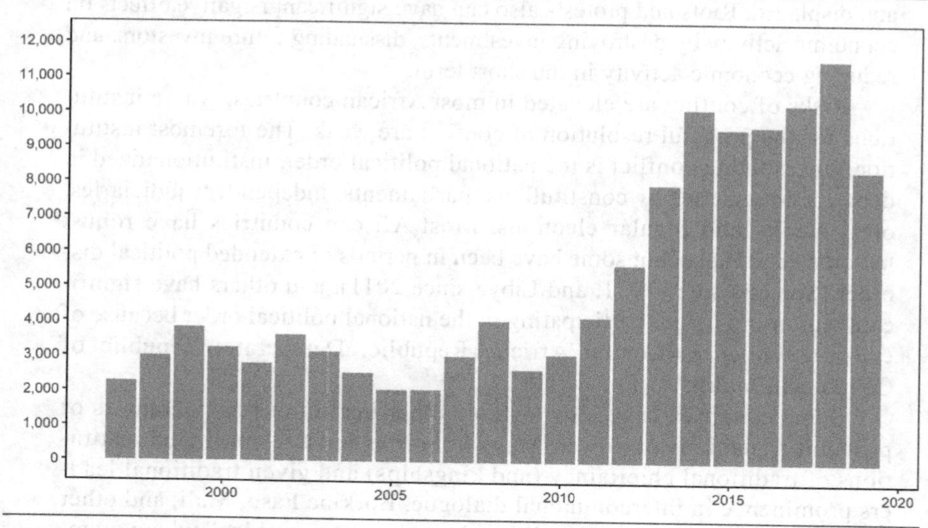

Source: ACLED (2019).

Figure 5.8 Number of Protests and Riots in Africa, 1997–2019

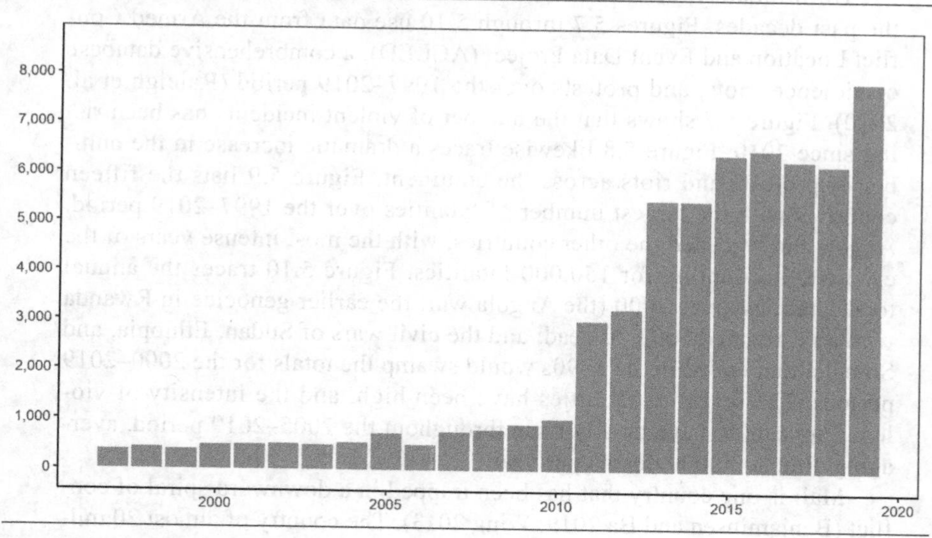

Source: ACLED (2019).

Figure 5.9 African Countries with Highest Number of Fatalities Due to Violent Incidents, 1997–2019

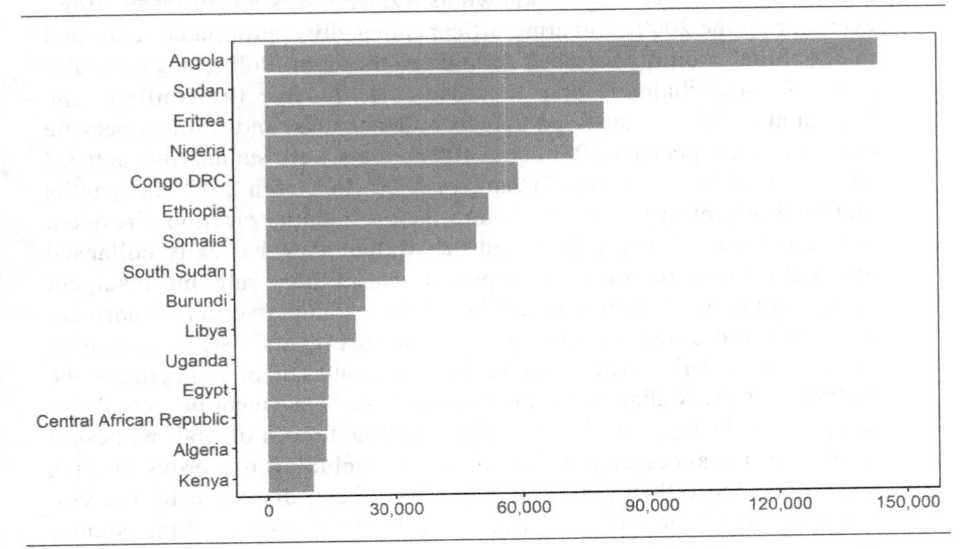

Source: ACLED (2019).

Figure 5.10 Fatalities Due to Violent Incidents in Africa, 2000–2019

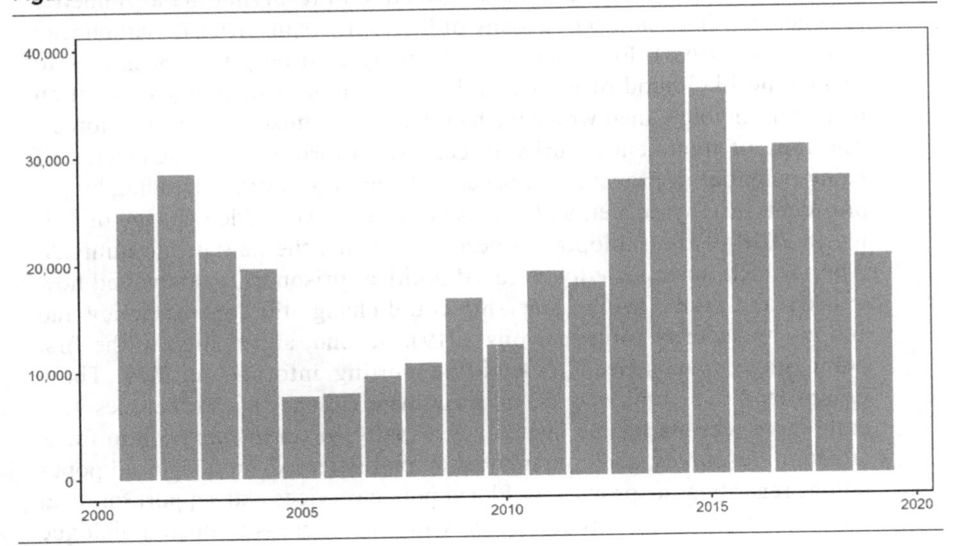

Source: ACLED (2019).

separatist insurgency seeking greater autonomy, and at times independence, for the northern region known as Azawad, was left to fester. However, during the 2000s, top army officers allegedly appropriated funds and matériel that should have been devoted to the fight. Politicians cynically avoided using dialogue and concessions to resolve the conflict. The Malian armed forces suffered defeats and setbacks, and soldiers became demoralized, especially after about 100 soldiers were summarily captured and executed by insurgents in January 2012. In March 2012, army units mutinied in protest just weeks before the presidential election. President Amadou Toumani Touré fled, and the Malian state basically collapsed overnight. Low-ranking soldiers proclaimed military rule, but insurgent groups in the northern region quickly mobilized and overran all northern territories and cities. In January 2013 the insurgents were approaching Mali's center region when French forces defeated them and restored the authority of the Malian army and government. Subsequent peacebuilding has proven elusive, and by 2019, the center and north of Mali witnessed near daily instances of political violence, including numerous civilian massacres. More than 200,000 people have been displaced by the violence. Economic activity and investment in large swathes of the country have ground to a halt.

Conflicts like those in Mali sometimes appear intractable. Yet, in semidemocratic societies where there is a modicum of accountability, citizens can encourage governments to prevent conflict and to mitigate its effects. Three steps appear to be especially effective in resolving the asymmetric insurgencies that characterize many of the conflicts in Africa (Charbonneau 2019; Keita 1998). First, security forces need to be given incentives to reduce the likelihood of human-rights violations. Insurgent groups often recruit from young men who have had family victimized by security forces. The tone of treatment security forces use toward civilians suspected of being potential insurgent allies is set at the highest levels, including by the president, prime minister, and defense minister. The sudden change of policy in 2018 of the Ethiopian government, when the new prime minister, Abiy Ahmed, unexpectedly released political prisoners, exemplified how quickly and dramatically leadership could change the tone of policy and actions by security forces (Lyons 2019). Second, and related to the first point, governments need to avoid supporting informal militias. These groups tend to commit acts of indiscriminate violence and sometimes generate more recruits for the insurgency. Finally, governments need to focus attention, resources, and communication on distressed and displaced populations regarding the provision of local public services and support for local administration. These actions, along with a willingness to open a dialogue with insurgents to broker reasonable peace deals, seem to lead to better long-term outcomes than other alternative strategies.

Pandemics

Elechi Amadi closes his masterpiece, *The Great Ponds*, with a chilling image of Nigerian villages, so vibrant and alive throughout the novel but emptied by the great influenza pandemic of 1918. It can happen again. HIV/AIDS, Ebola, avian bird influenza, and other epidemics of the twenty-first century have confirmed that humanity remains vulnerable to infectious diseases. The HIV epidemic has been one of the world's worst recent experiences with a deadly virus. By some estimates, more than 30 million people have died from it in Africa, especially in the countries of southern Africa. The epidemic has persisted for decades. In 2017, about 26 million people were still carrying the virus. Unknown pandemics are increasingly likely. The list of potential sources of new or mutated diseases continues to grow, such as widespread encroachment on natural habitats, melting permafrost, inexpensive genetic modifications, and enhanced capabilities for developing and deploying biological agents for warfare. Moreover, drug discoveries to treat new viruses and other organisms are becoming increasingly costly. The initial discoveries of important broad antibiotics and vaccines are unlikely to be repeated.

But pandemics are often manageable through public health approaches, as discussed in Chapter 8. The experiences with the Ebola epidemics in West Africa in 2016 and in Congo in 2019 are indicative that effective action is possible. The costs of basic research to detect new biological threats and craft prevention strategies to benefit public health are often lower by orders of magnitude than the direct and indirect costs of epidemics (Bartsch, Gorham, and Lee 2015; Jamieson and Kellerman 2016; McCloskey et al. 2014). Castillo-Chavez et al. (2015) suggest a variety of high-level strategies—to be directed by international decisionmakers—that include promoting more research on cataloging and modeling currently unknown viruses in animal populations along the human-wild borderlands. African governments can likely increase the efficacy of this research program and the suitability of interventions by ensuring that local research centers are adequately resourced to work in tandem with international efforts.

Health technologies and practices present social science researchers with new challenges that can inform policy. A hard truth is that many health interventions prolong the lives of the sick, and thus possibly increase the extent of an epidemic. Measuring the magnitude of that feedback effect is vital. Friedman (2018) examined such complex behavior in a study of the provision effects of antiretroviral (ARV) therapy on the spread of the HIV epidemic in Kenya. She found, using Demographic and Health Surveys data, that ARV recipients apparently were more likely to engage in risky sex than comparable persons infected with HIV who did not have access to ARV. But ARV treatment also reduced the likelihood of transmission. Friedman then conducted calibrated simulations, under various assumptions, and concluded that, on the whole, the ARV treatment was unlikely to have exacerbated the epidemic.

As this book went to press, the COVID-19 virus was spreading rapidly throughout African countries. It was difficult in May 2020 to know the true extent of spread and mortality rates, since health systems had limited testing capability. African populations are much younger than the rest of the world, and so it was likely that the pandemic would lead to large numbers of asymptomatic carriers. Older and immune-compromised persons might be less vulnerable in Africa despite difficulties in enforcing social distancing, simply because many reside in rural villages with family rather than in nursing homes and other concentrated population settings. It was becoming clear in May 2020 that the lockdown and other preventative measures taken by African health authorities, and more importantly the near total global shutdown of economic activity and international trade, would have severe and unpredictable negative economic and possibly destabilizing political effects.

Climate Change

As early as 1995, researchers were warning that the costs of sea-level rise might be tragic for Nigeria, where much of the population lives in coastal areas that are only a few feet above current sea levels (Brown, Kebede, and Nicholls 2009; Danladi, Kore, and Gül 2017). Development is of little value if a city of 10 million people finds itself under three feet of water. Similarly, the average temperature of Sahelian regions is likely to rise several degrees, and peak temperatures possibly much more (Engelbrecht et al. 2015). Development is of little value if a region's population finds that the temperature regularly soars to 140 degrees Fahrenheit during the hot season. Both sea-level rise and temperature rise are likely to lead to significant population movement, eroding the value of public infrastructure and private investment. Global climate change represents a significant threat to development for these and other reasons (Odey et al. 2018; Yalew et al. 2018).

As with pandemics, citizens can lobby their governments to invest more in preventing and mitigating the likely effects of climate change. For example, decisions about public infrastructure investment should consider longer-term climate change projections and redirect spending to regions less likely to be adversely affected. While developing infrastructure for seaside resorts may enable short-term development through jobs, tax revenues, and skill formation, the opportunity cost is that infrastructure is not established in regions that will be vital population centers in 2060 (Kantamaneni 2016).

Climate change produces multipart feedback effects, with one of the most important being that people move. Henderson, Storeygard, and Deichmann (2017) estimate that rising temperatures prompted rural residents to migrate to cities where they were likely to obtain jobs in industrial zones. The "industrial" is important. People did not move to cities, apparently, where the occupations would be perhaps just as vulnerable to rising temperatures and a declining agricultural economy. Interestingly, the receiving cities seemed to have more rapid income growth (as measured by night lights, which means there is no per person measure available) than they might have had without the migrants. The research underscores the importance of planning for urban growth when climate-dependent activities such as farming are likely to decline.

Conclusion

African economies have lagged relative to the rest of the world on most indicators of development. The slow development prior to the contemporary independence era and over the 1975–1995 period was most likely a legacy of 300 years of the slave trade and then 100 years of colonial conquest and rule by European powers (Nunn and Wantchekon 2011; Rodney 1972). African economies are poised, however, to continue the reasonably rapid rate of development enjoyed since the mid-1990s. Countries will experience demographic transitions to lower fertility rates. Educational attainment has risen high enough to be largely self-sustaining. Those who have completed basic primary school now constitute a majority of the population in almost all countries, and a high priority for them is to pass on the skills to their children. An educated population is more likely to adapt technology for productive uses. Technological change is likely to improve the productivity and well-being of hundreds of millions of people in Africa, thus primarily benefiting the bottom of the income distribution. Governments throughout the continent are increasingly capable, and urbanization creates a virtuous circle of self-sustaining accountability. Managing large cities demands competence. There nonetheless are threats to sustained growth: civil conflict is ubiquitous; pandemic diseases have appeared; and global climate change is expected to lead to temperature rise, sea-level rise, and the disruption of rainfall patterns. Citizens need to educate themselves about these threats. They also need to engage with government in order to pursue policies and programs that will reduce the likelihood of occurrence and mitigate the effects of these threats.

6

International Relations

Peter J. Schraeder

Libya's independence in 1951 marked the beginning of the end of formal colonial rule as well as the emergence of the "dependency-decolonization" debate over the degree to which Africa's newly independent countries truly control their international relations (see Shaw and Newbury 1979). According to a group of observers belonging to the dependency school of thought, the granting of legal independence to the fifty-four African countries that comprise the African nation-state system did little to alter the constraining web of economic, political, military, and cultural ties that continued to bind African countries to the former colonial powers (Amin 1973). This conceptualization of African international relations, often called neocolonialism (Nkrumah 1965), is especially prominent in writings about the relationship between France and its former colonies, primarily due to policies designed to maintain what French policymakers often referred to as their *chasse gardée* (literally "exclusive hunting ground") in francophone Africa (Suret-Canale 1975). Even in those former colonies where the European power was either too weak (e.g., Spain) or uninterested (e.g., United Kingdom) to preserve privileged ties, the contemporary independence era witnessed the gradual replacement of European neocolonial relationships with a new set of ties dominated by other great powers, such as the People's Republic of China (PRC), the United States, and the former Soviet Union and its successor state, Russia (Laïdi 1990). In short, dependency theorists argue that direct colonial rule has been replaced by a series of neocolonial relationships that perpetuate external domination of African international relations.

Scholars of the decolonization school of thought argue instead that legal independence beginning in the 1950s was but the first step of an evolutionary process permitting African leaders to assume greater control over the international relations of their countries (Zartman 1976; see also Bayart 2000). According to this perspective, although external influences were extremely powerful in the immediate post-independence era, layer upon layer of this foreign control is slowly being peeled away with the passage of time. While carefully underscoring that individual African countries can follow different pathways, proponents of the decolonization school argue that the most common pattern begins with legal independence, followed by efforts to assure national sovereignty in the military, economic, and cultural realms. "In this view, each layer of colonial influence is supported by the others, and as each is removed, it uncovers and exposes the next underlying one, rendering it vulnerable, untenable, and unnecessary," explains I. William Zartman (1976:326–327), a prominent proponent of the decolonization school. "Thus, there is a natural progression to the removal of colonial influence: its speed can be varied by policy and effort, but the direction and evolution are inherent in the process and become extremely difficult to reverse."

The durability of the dependency-decolonization debate is demonstrated by how both sides interpret the end of the Cold War in 1989 and the subsequent spread to the African continent of the "third wave" of democratization in global history (Huntington 1991). According to decolonization theorists, Africa since 1989 has been undergoing a second independence or a second national liberation in which a new generation of African leaders is assuming greater control over the international relations of their respective countries. One example of this trend is Tunisia's Jasmine Revolution in 2011 that overthrew the dictatorship of Zine el-Abidine Ben Ali, ushered in a multiparty democracy, and sparked other pro-democracy movements, especially in North Africa and the neighboring Middle East (Schraeder and Redissi 2011). In sharp contrast, dependency theorists equate the end of the Cold War and the third wave of democratization with the rising marginalization of African countries in international relations. They argue that African leaders enjoy fewer, rather than more, options in a post–Cold War international system marked by an increasingly intrusive UN system, international financial institutions such as the International Monetary Fund (IMF) and the World Bank, and exploitative great powers and regional powers (e.g., Shaw 1991). Focusing on aggressive foreign efforts to promote democratization and economic reform, some observers have even suggested that a "recolonization" or "new scramble" for Africa is occurring (Ake 1995; Carmody 2011; Southall and Melber 2009).

Although the dependency-decolonization debate is far from being resolved, 2018 marked a symbolic turning point as Africa's contemporary independence era (1951–2018) had lasted as long as the core colonial era (1884–1951). This chapter is designed to provide food for thought for the dependency-decolonization debate through the exploration of five topics within the broad arena of African international relations: the formulation and conduct of African foreign policies; pan-Africanism and the African Union (AU); regional economic cooperation and integration; the role of foreign powers in African international relations; and the United Nations and international financial institutions.

African Foreign Policy in a Changing International Environment

African countries have a rich foreign policy history dating back to the precolonial independence era, when diplomacy was key to the relationships between literally hundreds if not thousands of independent political systems and kingdoms. The case study of West Africa, as described in the work of Robert S. Smith (1976) and Joseph K. Adjaye (1996), demonstrates the existence of sophisticated diplomatic practices that in many respects are similar to those of the twenty-first century. For example, the dispatch of diplomats to neighboring political systems was common. Often called "messengers," "linguists," or "heralds," these individuals sometimes lived as resident diplomats in neighboring political systems. Unlike contemporary diplomats who work at elaborate embassies that may employ hundreds of workers, the resident diplomats usually served as the sole representatives of their peoples.

African diplomats also carried diplomatic credentials or "badges of office." Whereas all contemporary diplomats carry special diplomatic passports, their precolonial African counterparts carried various culturally significant credentials that included canes, staffs, whistles, fans, batons, and swords. Representatives of the Asante kingdom of present-day Ghana carried a diplomatic staff. The staff was topped by the figure of a hand holding an egg. This image was designed to "convey the warning that neither the king nor his representative should press a matter too hard nor treat it too lightly" (Adjaye 1996:12). Regardless of culture or the period in which they lived, few, if any, diplomats would question the diplomatic message portrayed by the Ashanti staff's image.

Another similarity with current diplomatic practices was the observance of diplomatic protocol and etiquette. It was not uncommon for African diplomats to enjoy diplomatic immunity (freedom from political harassment or persecution by local authorities). This practice was also an extension of the traditional African custom of warmly welcoming African strangers in their midst. Another example of diplomatic protocol and etiquette was the tendency of African kings "to converse only indirectly with their visitors and subjects" (Adjaye 1996:14). What was intended as a sign of respect and courtesy inevitably ensured a prominent role for diplomatic intermediaries, especially those who were knowledgeable about foreign languages and practices.

A final example of diplomacy that resonates with the contemporary era revolves around the "deliberate" and "tortuous" pace of diplomatic negotiations (Adjaye 1996:16). Extensive public flattery and gift giving, most notably intricately woven cloths, were integral aspects of such negotiations. One custom, still popular in West Africa, is the tradition of beginning or ending negotiations with the mutual breaking and eating of kola nuts. Available throughout West Africa, the kola nut is a stimulant that allows discussants to stay awake during extended periods of negotiations that sometimes last throughout the night. The kola nut, a symbol of West African hospitality, is broken into an equivalent number of pieces and shared among the participants attending the meeting.

The diplomatic practices of precolonial African kingdoms were significantly altered due to several international turning points during the past 150 years, beginning with the Berlin Conference of 1884–1885. As a result of this conference, independent Africa except for Ethiopia and Liberia ceased to exist, and African diplomatic relations were controlled by the European colonial powers. A second international event—the extended global conflict of World War II (1935–1945)—heralded the decline of Europe as the most powerful region of the world and the emergence of African nationalist movements intent on achieving independence from colonial rule. This period marked the beginning of the end of colonial rule and the return of control over foreign policy to Africans. The outbreak and intensification of the Cold War (1947–1989) transformed the newly independent African countries into proxy battlefields between the United States and the former Soviet Union, the unparalleled superpowers of the post–World War II era. African conflicts often having little, if anything, to do with the ideological concerns of communism or capitalism threatened to become East-West flashpoints in the face of growing US-Soviet involvement. A fourth international event, the fall of the Berlin Wall in 1989, signaled the end of the Cold War but not the end of international rivalry in Africa. The ideologically based Cold War between the United States and the former Soviet Union was replaced by a Cold Peace (1989–present), in which the great powers struggle for economic supremacy in Africa. The security dimension of this Cold Peace became evident in the aftermath of the September 11, 2001, terrorist attacks against the World Trade Center in New York and the Pentagon in Washington, DC, as the United States sought to enlist its African allies in a global war on terrorism. As African leaders continue to guide their countries during the third decade of the new millennium, they must manage their countries' foreign policies in an international environment marked by the growing competition among the great powers, most notably France, Germany, Japan, the PRC, Russia, and the United States, as well as a number of rising regional powers with interests in Africa, including Brazil, India, Indonesia, Iran, Saudi Arabia, and Turkey.

The classic theme of studies of contemporary African foreign policy is that foreign policy begins and ends with the desires of African presidents (Korany 1986; see also Adar 2015; Cohen 2015; Wright 1998). The primary reason for what has become known as the "big man" syndrome of African foreign policy is that the majority of the first generation of African presidents who took power beginning in the 1950s systematically suppressed and dismantled centers of power capable of challenging the foreign policy supremacy of the presidential mansion. Various efforts undertaken by these leaders included the stifling of a free press, the suspending of constitutions, the banning of opposition parties, the jailing of political opponents, the dismantling of independent judiciaries, and finally the cooptation or jailing of legislative opponents (Schraeder 2004c). In short, the institutional actors typically associated with making their voices heard in the foreign policy making processes of democratic countries were often marginalized in the name of creating single-party regimes capable of promoting unity and development.

The net result of what in essence constituted a highly centralized foreign policy machinery was the promotion of personalized foreign policies derivative of the interests and idiosyncrasies of individual presidents (Jackson and Rosberg 1982). In the Democratic Republic of Congo (DRC), Mobutu Sese Seko assumed power in 1965 through a military coup d'état

Peter J. Schraeder

Presidential mansion in Dakar, Senegal.

supported by the US government, renamed the country Zaire, and gradually concentrated all power around the office of the president (Young and Turner 1989). Often unwilling to listen to his foreign policy experts within the Ministry of Foreign Affairs and having effectively silenced other potential centers of opposition, most notably by disbanding the Zairian National Assembly, Mobutu was known for declaring policies that created international controversy. During a presidential visit to the United States in 1973, Mobutu made a speech before the UN General Assembly in which he announced his decision to rupture all diplomatic ties with Israel. This decision was notable in that it was made without any warning to the Richard M. Nixon White House and effectively derailed State Department efforts to win congressional passage of a Zairian foreign aid bill (Schraeder 1994b:82).

Another outcome associated with the centralization of foreign policy is that the first generation of African presidents often pursued foreign policies strongly tied to those of the former colonial powers. In addition to the variety of formal ties (e.g., military treaties) that bound the newly independent countries to the former colonial powers, the primary reason for what proponents of the dependency school would characterize as "dependent" foreign policies (e.g., Shaw and Aluko 1984) was the shared culture and political values of colonially trained African presidents and their European counterparts. Despite having actively campaigned for political independence, several first-generation presidents benefited from colonial efforts designed to ensure the victory of leaders sympathetic to European concerns. In the case of Senegal, for example, former president Léopold Sédar Senghor, sometimes described by his critics as more French than Senegalese, married a French national, retired to a home in France, and carries the distinction of being the first African to be inducted into France's highly prestigious and selective Académie Française, the national watchdog of French language and culture (see Markovitz 1969).

The most important outcome of the rise to power of the first generation of African presidents is that these leaders would often be more responsive to the foreign policy concerns of their external patrons than to the popular demands of their own peoples. Especially in the case of francophone Africa, the first generation of African presidents signed a variety of defense agreements with France that, rather than ensuring protection from threats from abroad, were designed to ensure their political longevity. Since the 1960s, France has intervened militarily more than thirty times in its former colonies, often at the request of African presidents either under threat from internal opposition movements or seeking to be reinstated in power after being overthrown. Even in cases where pro-French leaders were overthrown by military coups d'état during the decade of the 1960s, the guiding principle of French involvement was the willingness of a particular leader to support French foreign policy objectives. For example, when asked why France did not militarily intervene when David Dacko, a democratically elected president of the Central African Republic, was overthrown in a military coup d'état in 1966, Jacques Foccart, architect of France's policies toward francophone Africa under Presidents Charles de Gaulle and Georges Pompidou, noted in his memoirs that the new leader, Jean-Bédel Bokassa, "after all was a very pro-French military man" (Foccart, with Gaillard 1995:287).

The combination of the Cold War's end and the spread of pro-democracy movements throughout Africa beginning in 1989 has contributed to the democratization of African foreign policies (Adar and Ajulu 2002; Adar and Schraeder 2007). The cornerstone of this democratization trend, especially in countries where multiparty elections have been held, is the alternation of power between long-entrenched (often authoritarian) elites and democratic successors who have very different visions of how best to restructure their domestic political systems. An example of this process was the replacement in 1990 of Namibia's local version of South Africa's apartheid system with a multiparty democracy led by elites associated with the South West Africa People's Organization (SWAPO), most notably former guerrilla leader Sam Nujoma, who served as the country's first democratically elected president from 1990 to 2005. The foreign policy implication of the alternation of power is that new, democratically elected elites may not necessarily share the foreign policy goals and interests of their authoritarian predecessors. The emergence of such new elites should also provide the basis for a realignment in foreign policy, in terms of both the substance of foreign policy and preferred foreign policy relationships, especially in those cases in which a previously unpopular elite was able to illegally maintain itself in power at least partially due to the interventionist practices of the former colonial or another great power. In Namibia, Nujoma's 1990 election under the SWAPO banner signaled the beginning of a restructuring of Namibian foreign policy, most notably the downgrading of foreign policy ties with countries allied to apartheid South Africa, which had served as Namibia's de facto colonial power after Namibia was placed under South African trusteeship at the end of World War I.

The democratization process has also altered the centralized foreign policy structures in several African countries (Schraeder 2001b; Schraeder, with Gaye 1997). In some cases, democratization has been accompanied by policies designed to decrease both the size of the military establishment and its involvement in governmental affairs, including in the realm of foreign policy (Barany 2012, 2019; Kieh and Agbese 2004). In South Africa during the 1980s, the military strongly argued in favor of the Afrikaner regime's decision to undertake destabilization policies against its immediate neighbors (Grundy 1986). In the wake of the country's first multiparty elections in 1994, therefore, the new government headed by Nelson Mandela undertook a series of reforms designed to restore greater civilian control over a military force that had become too prominent in both domestic and foreign policies (Bischoff and Southall 1999). Although civilian control of the military has endured in South Africa, other transitional democracies have not had the same level of success. A case in point is Egypt's transition to democracy in 2011 as marked by the democratic election of President Mohamed Morsi, which was followed by a military coup in 2013 and a return to military rule.

The democratization process has also led to the strengthening of institutional actors, most notably increasingly independent and vocal national legislatures, capable of challenging the presidency in the foreign policy realm (Barkan 2009; Salih 2005). The primary reason behind this newfound legislative role is the creation of democratic political systems that embody the concept of separation of powers between the various branches of government. In the aftermath of Benin's transition to democracy, the democratically elected National Assembly in December 1995 refused to ratify highly unpopular legislation that would have permitted the launching of a third structural adjustment program (SAP) promoted by both the administration of President Nicéphore Soglo (1991–1996) and the IMF and the World Bank. President Soglo's subsequent attempts to break the political stalemate between the legislative and executive branches of government (he announced his intention to launch the SAP through the "exceptional power" granted to the executive under Article 68 of the Constitution) were one of the critical factors that strengthened popular discontent to such a degree that he lost the 1996 presidential elections to his autocratic predecessor, President Mathieu Kérékou (Adjovi 1998:107–139). Soglo had severely underestimated the power of his legislative opponents and their ability to translate deep-seated popular resentment of foreign-imposed SAPs into electoral defeat at the ballot box. For perhaps the first time in African political history, a democratically elected parliament played a critical role in ensuring the defeat of a previously popular and democratically elected president.

The democratization process also portends greater popular input into the foreign policy making process as the policies of a new generation of African leaders are increasingly held accountable to public opinion (see, e.g., Bratton, Mattes, and Gyimah-Boadi 2005). Even during the Cold War era, public opinion played an influential, albeit intermittent, role in African foreign policies. For example, it has been argued that public opinion, fueled primarily by radio broadcasts by Radio France Internationale, was the primary factor that led to bloody clashes between Senegal and Mauritania in 1989 (Parker 1991; see also Pazzanita 1992). Despite the fact that this conflict was neither desired nor promoted by President Diouf of Senegal or President Ould Taya of Mauritania, and despite their best efforts to contain public passions, both of these leaders were confronted by violent clashes that spiraled out of control. In a sense, both leaders, as well as the foreign policies of their respective countries, became prisoners of public opinion.

Peter J. Schraeder

Tunisian parliament in Tunis, Tunisia.

Numerous nonstate actors potentially play important foreign policy roles. In Senegal, for example, Islamic leaders known as *marabouts* constitute an integral part of the domestic political system and play both informal and formal roles in the making of foreign policy (Villalón 1995). They especially played a critical role in reducing tensions between Senegal and Mauritania in the aftermath of the 1989 border conflict by shuttling back and forth across the river that separates the two countries. An equally dramatic case occurred in the mid-1980s, when the Diouf administration was forced to withdraw an invitation to Pope John Paul II to visit the country due to the threats of leading *marabouts* to call upon their *taalibe* (disciples) to occupy the runways at the international airport. Although the pope was subsequently reinvited and visited Senegal several years later in 1991, to the wide acclaim of both Muslims and Christians, the *marabouts* had clearly served notice that sensitive issues needed to be raised with them in advance if the president wished to avoid embarrassing public confrontations. In short, if one wants to completely understand the formulation and implementation of Senegal's foreign policy, as well as that of other African countries, one must take into account the role of religious actors. These can include religious actors within Islam, Christianity, and other religious traditions (e.g., Judaism), not to mention traditional African religions.

(See Chapter 13 for more on the roles of Islam, Christianity, and traditional African religions in contemporary Africa.)

A vast literature focuses on the emergence of violent nonstate actors, most notably African insurgent groups and terrorist organizations, and their influence on African foreign policy (Varin and Abubakar 2017). The emergence of these actors has been at least partially fueled by the traditional foreign policy dilemmas of porous national borders and expanses of ungoverned territory that are common to all African countries. "The fundamental problem facing state-builders in Africa—be they colonial kings, colonial governors, or presidents in the independence era," explains Herbst (2000:11), "has been to project authority over inhospitable territories that contain relatively low densities of people." The classic violent nonstate actor involves insurgent groups that undertake military attacks against the central government (Bøås and Dunn 2007, 2017; Clapham 1998). In some cases, they even create parallel diplomatic networks to promote their guerrilla causes. Such networks are typically limited to neighboring countries that provide economic and military support and that serve as the bases of military operations. The most extensive diplomatic network maintained by an African guerrilla insurgency was that of the African National Congress. From 1960, the year that the ANC was banned by South Africa's apartheid regime, to 1994, the year that Nelson Mandela emerged victorious in South Africa's first multiracial, multiparty democratic elections, the ANC established and maintained over forty diplomatic missions in Africa, Asia, Europe, and the Western Hemisphere (Pfister 2003). A more recent example involves the Polisario Front, which seeks to create an independent Sahrawi Arab Democratic Republic (SADR) from territory claimed and controlled by Morocco. As of 2020, the SADR was recognized by over forty countries, several of which host SADR embassies. The SADR also enjoys observer status at the African Union.

Pan-Africanism and the African Union

African nationalists were inspired by the anticolonial activities of peoples of African descent living in North America and the West Indies during the nineteenth and twentieth centuries. As a result, these nationalists sought to promote a unified African front against colonial rule. What subsequently became known as the pan-African ideal was most forcefully enunciated for the first time at the 1945 meeting of the Pan-African Congress held in Manchester, England. At the conference, participants adopted a Declaration to the Colonial Peoples that affirmed the rights of all colonized peoples to be "free from foreign imperialist control, whether political or economic" and "to elect their own governments, without restrictions from foreign powers" (Ajala 1988:36). In a separate Declaration to the Colonial Powers, participants underscored that if the colonial powers were "still determined to rule mankind by force, then Africans, as a last resort, may have to appeal to force in the effort to achieve freedom" (Ajala 1988:36).

The pan-African ideal gained momentum during the heady independence era of the late 1950s and early 1960s. In an opening address to the first gathering of independent African nations on African soil, held in 1958 in Accra, Ghana, President Kwame Nkrumah proclaimed, "Never before has it been possible for so representative a gathering of African Freedom Fighters to assemble in a free independent African state for the purpose of planning for a final assault upon imperialism and colonialism" (Ajala 1988:39). According to Nkrumah, the realization of the pan-African ideal required a commitment between African leaders and their peoples to guide their countries through four stages: (1) "the attainment of freedom and independence"; (2) "the consolidation of that independence and freedom"; (3) "the creation of unity and community between the African states"; and (4) "the economic and social reconstruction of Africa" (Ajala 1988:30).

Despite overwhelming agreement among African leaders that pan-Africanism constituted a worthy foreign policy goal, disagreement existed over the proper path to ensure such unity. One group of primarily francophone countries known as the Brazzaville Group (named after the capital of the Republic of Congo) sought a minimalist approach: the coordination of national economic policies through standard diplomatic practices. Little consideration was given to the possibility of creating continent-wide institutions. In contrast, Nkrumah and other leaders, who belonged to what became known as the Casablanca Group (named after the Moroccan city), argued instead that the success of pan-Africanism required a political union of all independent African countries, patterned after the federal model of the United States. In speech after speech, Nkrumah promoted two themes that became the hallmark of this international vision: "Africa must unite!" and "Seek ye first the political kingdom!" (Rooney 1988).

A third group of African leaders, who belonged to what became known as the Monrovia Group (named after the capital of Liberia), rejected the idea of political union as both undesirable and unfeasible, primarily due to the assumption that African leaders would jealously guard their countries' newfound independence. They nonetheless sought a greater degree of cooperation than that espoused by the Brazzaville Group. Led by Alhaji Abubakar Tafawa Balewa, prime minister of Nigeria, the Monrovia Group called for the creation of a looser organization of African states. According to this vision of African international relations, African countries would guard their independence but promote growing cooperation in a variety of functional areas, most notably economic, scientific, educational, and social development. An important component of the Monrovia Group approach was a desire to create continent-wide institutions that would oversee and strengthen policy harmonization.

In May 1963, thirty-one African heads of state largely embraced the Monrovia vision of African international relations by launching the Organization of African Unity (OAU), the first pan-African, intergovernmental organization of independent African countries based on African soil. Addis Ababa, Ethiopia, was chosen as the site for the OAU headquarters, and all major decisions and resolutions were formally discussed at the annual Assembly of Heads of State and Government. The sovereign equality of all member states was an important guiding principle of the organization, which differed significantly from the great power domination of the UN, given the special powers conferred upon the five permanent members of the UN Security Council: France, the PRC, Russia, the United Kingdom, and the United States.

The OAU was particularly vocal in its unswerving opposition to colonialism and white minority rule, most notably minority white–ruled regimes in Namibia, South Africa, Zimbabwe, and the former Portuguese-controlled territories of Angola, Mozambique, Guinea-Bissau, and São Tomé and Príncipe. The OAU established a Liberation Committee based in Dar es Salaam, Tanzania, to aid liberation movements with both economic and military assistance (Akindele 1988a). Although disagreements often arose over which tactics would best ensure transitions to majority-ruled governments (e.g., should one support dialogue with a white regime or fund a guerrilla insurgency?), every OAU member expressed public opposition to the continued existence of minority white–ruled regimes. The work of the Liberation Committee largely came to an end in 1994, when South Africa transitioned to a multiracial, multiparty democracy.

The OAU's thirty-nine-year existence is correctly described as a "victory for pan-Africanism" (Olusanya 1988:67). Both critics and sympathetic observers nonetheless questioned the organization's ability to play an effective role in African international relations (Amate 1986; El-Ayouty 1994). In a special issue of the *Nigerian Journal of International Affairs,* which assessed the OAU's continued relevance on the "Silver Jubilee" (twenty-five-year) anniversary of the organization's creation, one Nigerian scholar expressed sadness over the fact that, despite the best of intentions, the OAU had failed to live up to the expectations of its original framers (Olusanya 1988:70).

In July 2002, more than forty African heads of state convened in Durban, South Africa, to launch the AU as the pan-African successor organization to the OAU. Like its OAU predecessor, the AU is headquartered in Addis Ababa, Ethiopia, is based on the sovereign equality of all member states, holds an annual Summit of Heads of State and Government, adopts official positions on a wide array of diplomatic topics affecting the African continent, and counts on a number of offices and institutions designed to strengthen African cooperation—most notably a Pan-African Parliament headquartered in Midrand, South Africa, that is comprised of 235 elected members from AU member states (African Union 2011).

The AU is led by a ten-member executive body—the African Commission—that is composed of a chairperson, deputy chairperson, and eight commissioners who are responsible for the following eight portfolios:

- *Political Affairs,* such as democratic elections and human rights
- *Peace and Security,* most notably efforts devoted to conflict resolution
- *Economic Affairs,* inclusive of promoting regional integration
- *Infrastructure and Energy,* such as the development of the transportation and telecommunications sectors
- *Social Affairs,* ranging from sports and migration to health issues and antidrug efforts
- *Human Resources, Science, and Technology*, such as education and new information technologies
- *Trade and Industry,* most notably efforts devoted to trade and investment
- *Rural Economy and Agriculture,* inclusive of food security and protection of the environment

The impacts of the AU and its predecessor OAU on African international relations are highlighted by the evolution of three sets of international principles, each of which holds important implications for the dependency-decolonization debate. The first principle—the inviolability of frontiers inherited from the colonial era—served as one of the cornerstones of the OAU Charter. Due to the multiethnic nature of most African countries, African leaders were concerned that changing even one boundary would open a Pandora's box of ethnically based secessionist movements and lead to the further Balkanization of the African continent into ever smaller economic and political units (Davidson 1992). In the Nigerian civil war (1967–1970), the OAU not only refused to permit the provision of aid to Biafra (the secessionist southeastern portion of the country) but voted a series of resolutions that underscored official support for the Nigerian federal government (Bukarambe 1988:98). This decision upset international human rights activists, as well as several African countries aiding the secessionist government, because the military-dominated Nigerian government was using starvation methods designed to bring the Biafrans to their knees (Gordon 2003:141–142; Stremlau 1977). As ethnic tensions and separatist movements intensified in the post–Cold War era, African leaders remained firmly committed to maintaining borders inherited from the colonial era. Although the OAU recognized the sovereignty of Eritrea in 1993, after a UN-sponsored referendum in that country resulted in overwhelming popular support for independence, African leaders subsequently noted that this process did not question the hallowed concept of the inviolability of frontiers.

Unlike most African countries, Eritrea was federated to Ethiopia after independence from colonial rule and, therefore, enjoyed the legal right to withdraw from that voluntary union (Iyob 1995).

In contrast, the AU decided not to include a statement in the Constitutive Act establishing the organization that recognizes the inviolability of frontiers inherited from the colonial era, providing the new organization with greater political flexibility. It is thus not surprising that the AU embraced the Southern Sudanese decision achieved via referendum in January 2011 to secede from the Republic of Sudan and create a separate and sovereign Republic of South Sudan. South Sudan's independence was recognized by the AU in 2011, which permitted the country to join the organization that same year. The AU nonetheless remains heavily inclined toward maintaining the territorial integrity of member states, as witnessed by its continued refusal to recognize the independence of the Somaliland Republic, despite the fact that this territory has enjoyed de facto independence since the collapse of the Republic of Somalia in 1991. Somaliland submitted a bid for membership to the African Union in 2005, which prompted the organization to send a fact-finding mission to the territory that same year. Although the final report of the fact-finding mission concluded that the African Union "should find a special method of dealing with this outstanding case," no further progress has been made (ICG 2006).

A second principle embedded in the OAU Charter but rejected by the AU is noninterference in the internal affairs of member states. In the early years of the OAU, African leaders debated whether to allow military leaders who had illegally deposed their civilian counterparts to maintain their OAU seats. This debate was resolved in favor of recognizing whatever group controlled the reins of power in a particular country (Akindele 1988b:82–85). More significant was the silence among African leaders concerning human rights abuses in OAU member states. "Increased repression, denial of political choice, restrictions on the freedom of association, and like events occurred, with rare murmurs of dissent," explains Claude Welch Jr., a specialist on human rights in Africa. "The OAU seemed to function as a club of presidents, engaged in a tacit policy of not inquiring into each other's practices" (Welch 1991:537). During the 1970s, for example, Ugandan dictator Idi Amin was elected OAU chair despite his personal involvement in "politically sanctioned repression and murders" in Uganda (Welch 1991:538).

Although still reluctant to criticize their counterparts, African leaders began to accept a growing role for the OAU in addressing human rights abuses at the beginning of the 1980s. In 1981, the annual Assembly of Heads of State and Government held in Banjul, Gambia, adopted the African Charter on Human and People's Rights (popularly called the Banjul Charter). Despite the ratification of this charter, the OAU's response to events in Nigeria during 1995 demonstrated the organization's reluctance to translate human rights rhetoric into policy action. In response to disturbances among the Ogoni ethnic group in southeastern Nigeria, which began in 1990 over control of that region's vast oil resources, Nigeria's military regime unleashed a brutal campaign of repression that included the November 1995 execution of Nobel Peace Prize candidate Ken Saro-Wiwa and eight other Ogoni activists on trumped-up murder charges (French 1995:E3; see also Osaghae 1995). Although OAU secretary-general Salim Ahmed Salim expressed "disappointment" over the fact that the Nigerian generals failed to "respond positively" to OAU appeals for clemency, the organization did not adopt concrete, comprehensive measures to punish or to internationally isolate the Nigerian regime (quoted in French 1995:E3).

The AU has clearly rejected the OAU principle of noninterference in the domestic affairs of member countries. In fact, Article 4(h) of the Constitutive Act affirms "the right of the Union to intervene in a Member State pursuant to a decision of the Assembly in respect of grave circumstances, namely war crimes, genocide and crimes against humanity," and Article 4(j) underscores "the right of Member States to request intervention from the Union in order to restore peace and security" (Murithi 2007:16–17). "With the adoption of these legal provisions, for the first time in the history of Africa, the continental organization [the AU], working through an appointed group of states, has the authority to intervene in internal situations in any state that may lead to atrocities against minority groups or communities at risk," explains Tim Murithi (2007:17). "In other words, the AU has the right and the responsibility to act." The AU has also adopted the 2007 African Charter on Democracy, Elections, and Governance, thereby committing member states to strengthening democratic practices, most notably holding free and fair elections and ensuring freedom of expression. It is precisely for this reason that the AU has strongly denounced military coups that have overturned constitutionally elected governments, including suspending Mauritania's AU membership in the aftermath of an August 2008 military coup d'état.

A third and final principle—the peaceful settlement of all disputes by negotiation, mediation, conciliation, or arbitration—was adopted by both the OAU and the AU. However, the OAU's embrace of support for the previous two principles of territorial integrity and noninterference in the internal affairs of member states historically impeded that body's ability to mediate either internal conflicts or conflicts between two or more member states. In the 1967–1970 Nigerian civil war, almost reflexive support for the territorial integrity of Nigeria seriously called into doubt the OAU's ability to serve as an impartial negotiator, at least from the viewpoint of the secessionist Igbos. For this reason, the OAU Commission of Mediation, Arbitration, and Conciliation was "stillborn" (Zartman 1995b) and most African-initiated arbitration efforts were carried out on an ad hoc basis by African presidents. For example, Djiboutian president Hassan Gouled Aptidon used his country's stature as the headquarters for the Intergovernmental Authority on Development to mediate the conflict between Ethiopia and Somalia. According to Zartman (1995a:241), a specialist of conflict resolution, such efforts led to success in only 33 percent of roughly twenty-four cases, and this success was often only temporary in nature as warring parties returned to the battlefield.

The ability to dispatch peacekeeping or peacemaking forces once a conflict has broken out is a critical aspect of conflict resolution. The OAU founding fathers attempted to prepare for this eventuality by planning the creation of an African High Command, a multinational military force comprised of military contingents from OAU member states. The African High Command never made it beyond the planning stage, leading once again to a variety of ad hoc measures. In 1981, the OAU sponsored the creation of a short-term, all-African military force designed to resolve an expanding civil war in Chad. Composed of approximately 4,800 troops from Zaire, Nigeria, and Senegal, the OAU force "failed to achieve any concrete solution" due to financial, logistical, and political difficulties and within a few months was "forced to withdraw" (Gambari 1995:225).

The AU has sought to undertake a more robust and leading role in conflict resolution through the establishment of an "ambitious and complex" African Peace and Security Structure, including the creation in 2003 of a Peace and Security Council. This body is made up of fifteen member states that can authorize the imposition of economic sanctions against regimes that have assumed power due to unconstitutional changes (e.g., military coups d'état), or the deployment of military missions under the AU banner. Another component includes an African Standby Force that will enable the AU to react more quickly to security threats, but that remains a work in progress (Engel 2017:263, 269–270). In this regard, the AU has been more aggressive than its predecessor. Its first peacekeeping mission was in Burundi in 2003, followed by a deployment to Darfur, Sudan, in 2004, which was handed off in 2007 to the UN. The most extensive and long-running deployment, the African Union Mission in Somalia (AMISOM), has been in southern Somalia, since 2007 under a mandate from the UN Security Council. The primary goal has been to support the UN-recognized government in Mogadishu against Islamist forces known as al-Shabaab. The peacekeeping mission in Somalia has been controversial due to the deaths of numerous AU soldiers; disputes between AU member states (e.g., Eritrea historically was opposed to AMISOM's intervention); internationalization of the conflict (e.g., Turkey has deployed military forces to the region); the continued weakness of the Mogadishu federal government, which controls very little territory outside of Mogadishu (and would likely fall without foreign support); and the continued strength of al-Shabaab in the rural areas. Despite a greater commitment to conflict resolution, the AU, like the OAU, has been unable to create a permanent African force capable of responding to African conflicts.

The combination of Africa's unstable nation-state system and the basic weakness of the OAU and AU in military affairs has led to a variety of military interventions by individual countries and intergovernmental organizations (Gegout 2017; Schmidt 2013, 2018; Tang Abomo 2019). Four sets of actors periodically have intervened in African conflicts: (1) the UN, as demonstrated by its approval of more than twenty peacekeeping missions in Africa since 1989, not to mention the UN Security Council's authorization for the North Atlantic Treaty Organization (NATO) to undertake military operations in Libya during spring 2011 that led to the overthrow of the regime of Muammar Qaddafi; (2) African regional organizations, such as the decision of the Economic Community of West African States to sponsor a military intervention in Gambia in 2017 to force dictator Yahya Jammeh to cede the presidency to his democratically elected successor, Adama Barrow; (3) foreign powers, most notably France, the United States, and to a lesser degree the United Kingdom, as witnessed by French military intervention in Mali in 2013 to prevent separatists in northern Mali from declaring an independent country of Azawad; and (4) African powers, as demonstrated by Ethiopian and Kenyan military interventions in southern Somalia against the Islamist forces of al-Shabaab.

The tendency of African countries to militarily intervene in neighboring countries has become increasingly prominent in the post–Cold War era (Reno 2011; Thom 2010). The most extreme example of this trend was the expansion of civil conflict in the DRC into what foreign observers now commonly call Africa's First World War. At its height in 2002, this conflict was marked by the introduction of massive numbers of ground troops by at least five African countries: Angola, Namibia, and Zimbabwe—which were fighting on the side of the DRC's government—and Rwanda and Uganda, which were seeking to topple that government. Although the individual stakes of the African countries that contributed troops to this conflict were varied (Clark 2002), together they underscored an emerging reality of African international relations at the dawn of a new millennium: the rising importance of African regional military balances of power and the political-military and economic interests of African regional actors. Africa, having provided a battlefield for superpower interests during the Cold War, provides another for rising African powers intent on dominating the international relations of their respective regions, most notably South Africa in Southern Africa and Nigeria in West Africa. Other regional powers that have attempted to use their size, economic power, and military capabilities to affect their regions include Algeria and Egypt in North Africa, Sudan and Ethiopia in East Africa, the DRC in Central Africa, and Senegal in West

Africa. Moreover, from the perspective of pan-Africanists, such ad hoc interventions are ultimately undesirable, regardless of whether undertaken by foreign or local African powers; rather than representing an African consensus opinion, such interventions are ultimately driven by the self-interests of the intervening country.

Regional Economic Cooperation and Integration

Inspired by the success of the European Union and encouraged by the UN-sponsored Economic Commission for Africa (ECA), based in Addis Ababa, Ethiopia, the first generation of African leaders sought to create regional entities capable of promoting regional cooperation and integration. This vision of African international relations was best captured by the OAU's publication in 1981 of a document, *Lagos Plan of Action for the Economic Development of Africa, 1980–2000,* which proposed the establishment of a continent-wide African Economic Community that would be based on an African Common Market. The guiding logic of the Lagos Plan of Action was that the creation of intergovernmental economic organizations in each of Africa's five major regions—North, East, West, Southern, and Central Africa—would serve as the building blocks for a continent-wide free trade zone.

The flourishing of experiments in regional cooperation and integration throughout the contemporary independence era demonstrates the firm commitment of African leaders to the economic dimension of the pan-African ideal. By the end of the 1980s, it was estimated that at least 160 intergovernmental economic groupings existed on the African continent, with thirty-two such organizations in West Africa alone (Seidman and Anang 1992:73). Among the most notable and far-reaching economic groupings that currently exist in each of Africa's major regions (including dates of launching) are the East African Community (EAC), which was originally launched in 1967 only to collapse in 1977, followed by its revival in 2000; the Economic Community of West African States (ECOWAS, 1975); the Arab Maghreb Union (AMU, 1989); the Southern African Development Community (SADC, 1992), which was originally launched in 1980 as the Southern African Development Coordination Conference (SADCC); the Economic Community of Central African States (ECCAS, 1983); and the Intergovernmental Authority on Development (IGAD, 1996) in Northeast Africa, which was originally launched in 1986 as the Intergovernmental Authority on Drought and Development (IGADD). These regional organizations are complemented by even larger groupings that transcend individual regions, including the Community of Sahel-Saharan States (CEN-SAD, 1998), the Common Market for Eastern and Southern Africa (COMESA, 1981), and the continent-wide African Continental Free Trade Area (AfCFTA, 2018).

African leaders offer several rationales for seeking regional cooperation and integration. The simplest reason is the firm belief that there is strength in numbers. In order to effectively compete within a competitive international economic system dominated by economic superpowers (e.g., the United States and China) and powerful regional economic entities (e.g., the European Union and the North American Free Trade Agreement [NAFTA] zone), African countries must band together and pool their respective resources. African leaders desire to promote self-sustaining economic development and particularly the industrialization of the African continent. Struggling with the reality that many of their countries are economically impoverished and lack the tools for the creation of advanced industries, African leaders believe that they can build upon the individual strengths of their neighbors to forge integrated and self-sustaining regional economies.

Most important, regional economic schemes are perceived as the best means of creating self-reliant development, thereby reducing and ultimately ridding the African continent of the ties of dependency inherited from the colonial era (Asante, with Chanaiwa 1993:741–743). For example, African leaders are rightfully concerned that national control over the evolution of their respective economies is constrained by Africa's continued trade dependency on Europe, at the expense of intraregional trade links with African countries. For this reason, one of the primary objectives of regional economic schemes is to promote intraregional trade with neighbors who theoretically share a common set of development objectives—either due to special geographic features, historical ties, or a shared religion such as Islam in North Africa (see, e.g., Grundy 1985). By strengthening these ties with like-minded neighbors, a stronger African economic entity is expected to emerge that will be capable of reducing foreign influence and strengthening Africa's collective ability to bargain with non-African powers on a more equal basis.

Early optimism began to wane in the aftermath of the launching of several regional integration efforts, which included the creation of supranational authorities and formal economic unions designed to promote intraregional trade and investment. In the case of the initial version (1967–1977) of the EAC, the 1967 decision of Kenya, Tanzania, and Uganda to create a common market with common services, coordinated by a supranational governing body, collapsed ten years later and was followed in 1978–1979 by Tanzania's military intervention in member state Uganda to overthrow the dictatorial regime of Idi Amin (Potholm and Fredland 1980). As explained by Olatunde Ojo (1985), a specialist of regional cooperation and integration in Africa, several factors that contributed to the EAC's decline clarify why other similar efforts, from the 1960s to the present, have either failed, demonstrated minimal progress, or remained aspirational.

An initial problem was the polarization of national development and the perception of unequal gains (Ojo 1985:159–161). As typically occurred in other cases in Africa where the creation of a common market served as the cornerstone of the regional grouping, the most industrialized country (Kenya) usually reaped the benefits of economic integration at the expense of its partners (Uganda and Tanzania). For example, Kenya's share of intra-community trade increased from 63 percent in 1968 to 77 percent in 1974, whereas Uganda's share decreased from 26 percent to 6 percent during the same period. In addition, despite the fashioning of a common policy toward the establishment of new operations by multinational corporations (MNCs), the majority of these firms decided to locate their bases of operations in Kenya due to its more advanced economy and workforce as well as its extensive infrastructural network of roads, railroads, ports, and airports.

The EAC also foundered due to the inadequacy of compensatory and corrective measures (Ojo 1985:161–166). In every integration scheme, some countries inevitably benefit more than others. As a result, policymakers can implement measures, such as the creation of regional development banks or the disproportionate sharing of customs revenue, to correct the imbalance and compensate those countries expected to lose out in the short term. In the case of the EAC, a regional development bank was created to disburse funds in the following manner to the three members: Kenya (22 percent), Tanzania (38 percent), and Uganda (40 percent). However, in this and other cases of integration in Africa, even the richest members are usually incapable of subsidizing bank operations. The actual finances provided to the neediest members, therefore, never even begin to approach true development needs or completely compensate for losses incurred.

Another stumbling block to successful regional integration of the EAC was ideological differences and the rise of economic nationalism (Ojo 1985:168–169). Simply put, ideological differences often ensure a radically different approach to development projects, which in turn can significantly hinder regional integration. In the case of Kenya, a pro-West capitalist regime was very open to private enterprise and foreign investment, particularly the opening of local offices of MNCs. The socialist-oriented regime of Tanzania, however, opted for a self-help strategy known as *ujamaa* (the Kiswahili term for "brotherhood"), which not only denounced private enterprise as exploitative but also restricted the flow of foreign investment and strongly controlled the MNCs. When combined with the growing public perception of unequal gains between the two countries, these ideological differences led to often acrimonious public debate between President Jomo Kenyatta of Kenya and President Julius Nyerere of Tanzania and to the rise of economic nationalism in both countries.

A final element that contributed to the EAC's decline was the impact of foreign influences (Ojo 1985:169–171). Whereas Kenya developed close relationships with the Western bloc nations (e.g., the United States and Britain), Tanzania pursued close links with the socialist bloc (particularly the PRC) and Uganda sought links with the former Soviet Union and the Arab world. These links ensured that the EAC became embroiled in the Cold War rivalry of the 1960s and the 1970s and contributed to the creation of an outwardly directed "strategic image" that prompted EAC member states to look outward toward their foreign patrons rather than inward toward their natural regional partners (Ojo 1985).

Beginning in the 1980s, the failure and stagnation of classic integration schemes prompted African leaders to undertake looser forms of regional economic cooperation in a variety of functionally specific areas such as transportation infrastructure (e.g., regional rail links), energy (e.g., hydroelectric projects on common rivers), and telecommunications (see Aly 1994; Lavergne 1997; Onwuka and Sesay 1985; Oyejide, Elbadawi, and Collier 1997). The logic behind pursuing this form of regionalism is that it does not require the creation of supranational authorities, nor does it require policymakers to sacrifice national control over the sensitive areas of foreign trade and investment. This looser form of economic cooperation has gathered strength in the post–Cold War era, particularly as democratically elected elites increasingly assume power and seek to promote economic cooperation with other democracies in their regions. Indeed, it is this logic that undergirds all six of the current regional economic schemes in Africa.

The 1992 transformation of SADCC into SADC in Southern Africa is a good example of this trend in African regional relations (Oostuizen 2006; Peters 2010). Originally conceived as a vehicle for reducing the economic dependence of the Front-Line States on South Africa during the apartheid era, the transformed SADC now counts South Africa among its members and is seeking to enhance traditional cooperation in a variety of functional realms, most notably transportation (Khadiagala 1994; see also Love 2005). The new SADC is at "the threshold of a new era," according to several reports published by the African Development Bank in conjunction with the World Bank and the Development Bank of South Africa. "Although its effects and the inequities it has embedded will linger for a long time to come, the demise of apartheid opens up prospects unimaginable even a few years ago," explains one report. "New opportunities have emerged in every sector of economic activity for expanded trade and mutually beneficial exchanges of all kinds among the countries of southern Africa" (Morna 1995:65).

Several factors are essential to understanding the optimism surrounding SADC's status as a model for economic cooperation in Africa, particularly in terms of reducing Southern Africa's dependence on foreign economic interests and creating the basis for self-sustaining development in the post–Cold War era (see Blumenfeld 1992; see also Gibb 1998). First, the inclusion of a highly industrialized South Africa provides SADC with an engine for economic growth that will potentially reinvigorate the entire region. In this regard, South Africa is playing a leadership role similar to that enjoyed by Germany in the EU, the United States in NAFTA, and Nigeria in ECOWAS. Second, the majority of SADC members also share a common British colonial heritage. Although a shared colonial past is not a precondition for effective regional cooperation, it facilitates such technical matters as which language should serve as the official language of communication (in the case of SADC, English). A third facilitating factor is the decline in ideological differences between SADC member states that accompanied the end of the Cold War. Angola, Mozambique, and Zimbabwe have discarded in varying degrees their adherence to Marxist principles of development; South Africa has officially renounced its apartheid system; and Tanzania and Zambia have dismantled significant portions of their formerly socialist economies. In essence, there is a growing consensus among SADC member states that effective regional economic cooperation must be based on a shared commitment to some variant of the liberal capitalist model of development.

A final facilitating factor is SADC's commitment to conflict resolution and to the promotion of shared democratic values (Ohlson and Stedman, with Davies 1994). The Cold War's end and the rise of democratization movements have led to the end of civil wars and the holding of democratic elections in many SADC countries, making SADC the most democratic of Africa's six regional integration schemes. Indeed, one of the most important lessons of regional integration theory, which draws upon the success of the EU, is that the existence of elites with a shared commitment to democracy is the foundation of long-term economic cooperation and development. For this reason, the 1992 Windhoek Treaty (named after the capital of Namibia), which consecrated the launching of SADC, underscored the political dimension of regional relationships and its critical role in the continued expansion of economic cooperation. A fully democratic SADC nonetheless remains aspirational. According to Freedom House, which annually ranks each country of the world according to its level of political rights and civil liberties, six SADC countries as of 2020 are ranked as "free" (Botswana, Comoros, Mauritius, Namibia, South Africa, and Seychelles), seven are ranked as "partly free" (Lesotho, Madagascar, Malawi, Mozambique, Tanzania, Zambia, and Zimbabwe), and three are ranked as "unfree" (Angola, Democratic Republic of Congo, and Eswatini).

One cannot underestimate especially the role of national and regional conflicts in hindering regional economic schemes. One of the primary stumbling blocks to regional unity in North Africa's AMU involves the continuing diplomatic impasse between Algeria and Morocco over the fate of the former Spanish Sahara (Worrall 2017). Whereas Morocco has annexed this territory as part of what it considers to be the sovereign territory of the

Peter J. Schraeder

Monument in Hargeisa dedicated to northern Somalia's declaration of independence in 1991 as the Somaliland Republic, which as of 2020 has yet to be recognized by any other country. The monument is built with a plane from the former dictatorship of Mohamed Siad Barre (Republic of Somalia) that was used against the north during the civil war.

Moroccan kingdom, Algeria instead supports independence as an independent country, the Sahrawi Arab Democratic Republic. The fact that the Algerian government continues to give political-military and socioeconomic support to the Polisario Front, which is the guerrilla organization seeking to end Morocco's control and win independence, is not surprisingly denounced by Moroccan authorities. This can be added to the ongoing civil conflict and the lack of an effective government in Libya since the overthrow in 2011 of the dictatorship of Muammar Qaddafi. IGAD in Northeast Africa is similarly stymied by ongoing civil conflict between Somalia's weak central government in Mogadishu and the al-Shabaab insurgency, which has spilled over into neighboring countries and invited international intervention (Adetula, Bereketeab, and Jaiyebo 2016). Moreover, an international diplomatic standoff remains between Mogadishu and the breakaway Republic of Somaliland, which in 1991 declared independence but as of 2020 has yet to be recognized by any country in the world. In short, conflict resolution constitutes an important precondition for the pursuit of meaningful regional economic cooperation.

Role of Foreign Powers in African International Relations

Many important policies affecting contemporary Africa are heavily influenced in the capitals of three sets of countries—the seven former colonial powers, four additional great powers, and several regional powers—that are significantly involved in Africa. Of the former colonial powers, France alone has continued to maintain and even expand extensive political-military and socioeconomic relationships throughout Africa, most notably in francophone Africa (Daguzan 2002; Kroslak 2004; Yates 2018). This is especially true in the more than twenty colonies where French serves as one of the official languages of administration and/or education. An important tool of French foreign policy toward Africa since 1973 is regularly holding a Franco-African Summit that is attended by the presidents of France and Africa. This summit is usually held every two years and rotates between France and a country in francophone Africa.

In contrast, the United Kingdom's official interest in maintaining privileged colonial ties, once rivaled only by those of France, dramatically waned during the contemporary independence era (Bangura 1983; Gallagher 2013; Styan 1996; Vines 2018; Williams 2004). Economic decline prompted British policymakers to make difficult decisions as to where limited economic resources would contribute the most to British foreign policy interests, ultimately prompting Britain's gradual disengagement from Africa. The United Kingdom nonetheless has undertaken sporadic military interventions in its former colonies, as witnessed by its leadership role in dispatching peacekeeping troops to Sierra Leone in West Africa in 2000 (Porteous 2008). The United Kingdom's most noteworthy ongoing involvement with its former African colonies takes place in the context of the Commonwealth of Nations, a loose association of former British colonies throughout the globe that holds an annual summit meeting of heads of state.

There is a range of activity in Africa among the other former colonial powers. At one extreme is Spain, which was never an important diplomatic player due to controlling the smallest number of colonial holdings, but which continues to maintain the only two remaining territorial vestiges of European colonial rule: the small enclaves of Ceuta and Melilla along the Moroccan coast (García and de Larramendi 2002; Naylor 1987; Segal 1989). At the other extreme is Germany, which lost its colonies as a result of World War I but is now one of the globe's great powers. Germany especially focuses on the economic realm, serving as an important source of trade, aid, and investment (Brune, Betz, and Kuhne 1994; Engel 2002; Engel and Kappel 2002; Hofmeier 1994; Schulz and Hansen 1984). The general trend, however, is for the former colonial powers to demonstrate sporadic attention to their former colonies, usually during times of crisis or instability in Africa. This was the case for Italy in Somalia during the 1990s or Belgium in the DRC during the 2000s (Ercolessi 1994; Negash, Papa, and Taddia 2003; Venturi 2018). There is also a cultural element that binds former colonial powers and former colonies. For example, Portugal in the 1990s exhibited a renewed interest in strengthening cultural ties with its former Portuguese-speaking colonies and played an important role in promoting the resolution of civil wars in Angola and Mozambique (Carvalho 2018; MacQueen 1985; Penvenne 2003). One African issue that has galvanized all of the former colonial powers, but especially those with borders on the Mediterranean Sea (France, Italy, and Spain), has been the immigration crisis that emerged in the aftermath of the Tunisian Revolution of 2011 and the broader Arab Spring (Nascimbene and Di Pascale 2011). Although North Africa during the last few decades has served as a transit point for growing numbers of refugees and economic migrants from sub-Saharan and North Africa seeking a better life in Europe, these numbers significantly expanded as a result of the socioeconomic and political-military instability generated by the Arab Spring.

At the level of the great powers, the United States emerged in the 1950s as an influential political-military actor. As discussed further below, whereas anticommunism served as Washington's guiding foreign policy principle during the Cold War, counterterrorism became the central goal in the aftermath of the terrorist attacks of September 11, 2001. In both cases, the United States courted anticommunist and anti-terrorist African allies willing to support Washington's larger foreign policy goals. The former Soviet Union was also a formidable political-military actor during the Cold War but dramatically reduced its African presence after the fall of the Soviet regime in 1991 and the subsequent breakup of the country into fifteen sovereign nations (Andrés 2006; Matusevich 2007). It would only be in the latter half of the 2010s that Russia began to reassert itself in Africa as part of President Vladimir Putin's desire to restore Russia's great power status (Arkhangelskaya and Dodd 2016; Daniel and Shubin 2018; Fidan and Aras 2010). An important symbol of Russia's return to Africa was the convening in 2019 in Sochi, Russia, of the first ever Russia-Africa Summit, which was attended by more than 3,000 Russian and African delegates from all fifty-four African countries, including more than forty African heads of state and President Putin (Standish 2019).

Asian great powers are also playing a crucial role in African international relations. Japan emerged during the 1980s as a rising economic power and serves as an important source of economic aid and trade for individual African countries (Cornelissen 2004; Cornelissen and Mine 2018; Lehman 2010; Lumumba-Kasongo 2010; Morikawa 1997, 2005; Nester 1992; Sato 2005). Japan's arrival in African international relations was marked by the hosting in 1993 of the Tokyo International Conference on African Development (TICAD). Additional TICADs have been held every three to four years, and they are attended by the majority of African leaders. The most influential Asian great power is the PRC. As discussed in Chapter 2, China's Ming Dynasty established substantial contacts with East Africa during the first half of the fifteenth century, before turning inward (Snow 1988; Xinfeng 2017). The same was true of communist China's foray into Africa during the 1960s as part of the Cold War struggle, ultimately reducing its presence after the Cold War's end (Larkin 1971; Xuetong 1988). One dimension of China's Africa policy during this and later periods was a diplomatic battle with Taiwan as to which capital—Beijing or Taipei—was recognized by African governments as the official seat of the Chinese government (Hsiaopong 2009; Taylor 2002). By the beginning of the twenty-first century, the burgeoning demand of the PRC's massive and growing economy for primary resources, strategic minerals, and trade outlets had fueled a dramatic expansion of Chinese-African relations (French 2014; Liu 2018; Lumumba-Kasongo 2011; Taylor 2006). This led to growing discussions among US policymakers about the potential dangers that such activities posed for Western, especially US, interests in Africa (e.g., Council on Foreign Relations 2005). China's determination to play a leading role in Africa is captured by the Forum on China-Africa Cooperation, the first of which was held in Beijing in 2000. Held every three years, this has become the signature event for PRC-Africa relations.

Several regional powers also play influential roles. India is recognized as a rising economic power in Africa (Cheru and Obi 2010; Dubey 1990; Karnik 1988; Taylor 2012; Virk 2018). Indonesia's smaller role in Africa is also driven by economic interests (Tarrósy 2016). Canada and the Nordic countries, most notably Sweden, demonstrate a strong humanitarian interest. Specific issues of foreign policy interest include famine relief, conflict resolution, and women's rights (e.g., Stokke 1989). During the height of the Arab-Israeli conflict, Israel pursued a proactive policy that exchanged Israeli technical aid for continued or renewed diplomatic recognition of the state of Israel (Butime 2014; Decalo 1997; Dussey 2017; Levey 2008; Oded 2010; Peters 1992). Other Middle Eastern regional powers, such as Iran (Lefebvre 2012; McFarland 2010), Saudi Arabia (Creed and Menkhaus 1986), and Turkey (Korkut and Civelekoglu 2012; Ozkan 2014, 2016), pursue Islamic-inspired policies in the predominantly Muslim countries of North and East Africa. In 2020, for example, the Turkish parliament approved President Recep Tayyip Erdoğan's request to send Turkish troops to Libya to bolster the UN-supported government in Tripoli in an expanding civil conflict. Finally, Brazil is the leading Latin American country that has pursued economic links with Africa (Abdenur 2018; Collins 1985; De Castro 2014; He 2012; Seibert and Visentini 2019).

The specific impact of foreign powers on African international relations is illuminated by the evolution of US foreign policy toward Africa. During the Cold War era, US policymakers were principally guided by the ideological interest of containing the former Soviet Union and its communist allies (Schraeder 1994b). A variety of presidential doctrines, beginning with the Truman Doctrine in 1947 and culminating in the Reagan Doctrine of the 1980s, declared Washington's right to intervene against communist advances throughout the world, including in Africa. As a result, pro-West administrations, such as Senegal under President Abdou Diouf, were treated as potential US allies deserving of foreign aid, whereas Marxist administrations, such as Madagascar under Didier Ratsiraka, were isolated. US policymakers also sought special relationships with strategically important regional actors, such as Morocco in North Africa, Ethiopia in the Horn of Africa, and South Africa in Southern Africa, that offered special military access rights or maintained important US technical facilities (e.g., telecommunications stations) deemed critical to containment policies in Africa (Lefebvre 1991). The United States nonetheless expected France and the other European allies to take the lead in their former African colonial territories. As stated by George Ball (1968), undersecretary of state in the Kennedy administration, the United States saw Africa as a special European responsibility, just as European nations were expected to recognize US responsibility in Latin America. According to US policymakers, France emerged as the only European power with both the long-term political will and the requisite military force capable of thwarting communist powers from exploiting instability (Goldsborough 1978; Lellouche and Moisi 1979; see also Hoffman 1967).

The Cold War's end meant the decline of Washington's ideologically based policies in favor of the pursuit of trade and investment (Schraeder 1998). In 1996, the administration of President William J. Clinton unveiled the first formal US trade policy for pursuing new markets throughout Africa (US Department of Commerce 1996). The centerpiece of this economic strategy was congressional legislation, the African Growth and Opportunity Act (AGOA), passed by both houses of Congress under the prodding of the Clinton White House during its second term in office. Africa's enhanced economic standing in Washington was perhaps best captured by President Clinton's decision to make a twelve-day presidential visit to Africa in 1998, which included stops in Botswana, Ghana, Rwanda, Senegal, South Africa, and Uganda. For the first time in US history, a sitting US president had led an extended diplomatic mission to Africa, intent on improving US-African ties and promoting US trade and investment on the African continent.[1]

The response of the administration of President George W. Bush to the terrorist attacks of September 11, 2001, demonstrated the durability of strategic interests in great power involvement in Africa (Schraeder 2001a). These attacks profoundly influenced US foreign policy as the Bush administration announced a global war on terrorism, including pledges to aid countries threatened by terrorism that harkened back to the initial stages of the Cold War, when the Harry S. Truman administration underscored the need to aid countries threatened by communism. In the case of Africa, the Bush administration focused its efforts on North and East Africa. The microstate of Djibouti, for example, emerged in 2003 as the site for the Defense Department's Combined Joint Task Force–Horn of Africa (CJTF-HOA), the primary responsibility of which is to maintain surveillance over the movement of potential terrorist groups in the "Greater Horn of Africa." The US-Djiboutian agreement includes the hosting of a US military base in Djibouti that enables the United States to conduct military operations against terrorist groups in the region. Additional counterterrorism programs launched by the Bush administration included the Trans-Saharan Counter-Terrorism Initiative (TSCTI) and the East Africa Counter-Terrorism Initiative (EACTI), the latter of which is now known as the East African Regional Strategic Initiative (EARSI). Together these programs are indicative of the strengthening of US security ties with African countries deemed important to the US global war on terrorism (Davis 2007).

Barack Obama's election in 2008 as the first African American president of the United States raised "great expectations" concerning the future of US foreign policy toward Africa (Schraeder 2011a). He is the product of the African diaspora and had published two well-received books in which Africa was referenced: *Dreams of My Father: A Story of Race and Inheritance* (1995) and *The Audacity of Hope: Thoughts on Reclaiming the American Dream* (2006). Obama was also the first sitting president to have visited the African continent prior to taking office, including traveling to his father's country of Kenya for five weeks in 1998 before starting Harvard Law School, and to Chad, Djibouti, Kenya, and South Africa for two weeks in 2006 while serving in the US Senate. Africa nonetheless remained marginalized in an Obama White House that by necessity focused on domestic issues and other regions of perceived greater importance, most notably daunting challenges associated with resolving an inherited financial crisis in the US economy that reached its height as Obama entered office and inheriting two wars in Afghanistan and Iraq.

One of President Obama's most controversial Africa-related decisions was to support military intervention in Libya. This decision constituted an exception to his otherwise cautious approach, and ironically had the impact of making his administration even more reticent about becoming involved in Africa. Specifically, the administration was confronted with growing international calls to prevent the regime of Muammar Qaddafi from unleashing genocide in the eastern portion of Libya. Although the White House was initially divided over the proper course of US action, Samantha Power, who served on the White House National Security Council as special assistant to the president and senior director for multilateral affairs and human rights, and Hillary Clinton, who served as secretary of state, prevailed in internal bureaucratic debates in favor of a more aggressive US approach. The White House decided in favor of a US-supported and NATO-led military campaign under the banner of the international human rights norm of the Responsibility to Protect (R2P) that ultimately led to the overthrow of the Qaddafi regime. However, the United States and the Western powers did little in the period following Qaddafi's overthrow as the country descended into civil conflict, calling into question the administration's true commitment to R2P (Tang Abomo 2019). Indeed, Obama was quoted in a retrospective on his administration's foreign policy as noting that he considered the Libyan intervention as the "biggest mistake" of his presidency (Goldberg 2016).

Donald J. Trump's election in 2016 under the campaign theme of "Make America Great Again" also raised expectations, but of a different kind. It was hoped especially among Africans that a successful businessman who was the coauthor of a popular book, *Trump: The Art of the Deal*, would usher in a new era of US trade and investment in Africa's rising economies (Schraeder 2018). Yet the reality of US-African relations under the Trump administration has been a period of continued White House neglect, intensified by unfilled Africa-related posts throughout the national security bureaucracies. The White House has instead pursued a military-based, counterterrorism approach originally set in place by the Bush administration and largely continued under the Obama administration. Other broad foreign policies, especially those related to reducing immigration flows and renegotiating trade agreements, have had negative repercussions on the African continent. The so-called Muslim ban affected travel to the United States from predominantly Muslim countries, including three in Africa (Libya, Somalia, and Sudan). Africanists have been particularly dismayed by racist, Africa-related statements, by President Trump. For example, the president was attributed as having said, "Why are we having all these people from s***hole countries come here?" as part of a White House discussion related to African, Haitian, and other immigrants of color. The reaction on the part of Africans not surprisingly was swift and highly negative.

The common thread in US foreign policy from the Truman to the Trump administrations is that presidents traditionally have devoted less attention to Africa compared to other regions of perceived greater concern. At the top of the foreign policy hierarchy is Europe, including Russia and the other countries that were once part of the Soviet Union and that were central to the Cold War struggle, and more recently the Middle East and South Asia in the aftermath of the attacks of September 11, 2001, and the emergence of a global war on terrorism. Subsequent foreign policy priorities include Asia (most notably how to counter a rising China) and Latin America, with Africa being last. The neglect of Africa at the highest reaches of the US policymaking establishment is the direct result of a wide array of factors: a president's typical lack of knowledge and, therefore, the absence of a deep-felt interest in a region that historically enjoyed few enduring political links with the United States as compared to the former European colonial powers; a tendency to view Africa as the responsibility of those same European colonial powers, especially France, whose leaders were often willing to take the lead in crisis situations; the impracticality of having one person monitor relations with 195 countries worldwide, including 54 in Africa, and, therefore, the necessity of delegating responsibility for handling foreign policy for those regions considered marginal to the White House; and the necessity of balancing domestic priorities with foreign affairs necessities, especially during a first term in office when the ultimate priority of all presidents is to assure reelection, with simple electoral logic typically suggesting that Africa is not a priority for the vast majority of the voting public. Even President Obama, who had deeper connections to Africa than any previous president before entering office, relegated Africa to the region of least importance in US foreign policy during his administration.

The net result of White House neglect of Africa is that US foreign policy toward Africa, perhaps more so than that toward any other region of the world, remains largely delegated to the high-level bureaucrats and political appointees within the bureaucracies of the executive branch. Exceptions exist, as demonstrated by the willingness of the White House to pressure Sudan's government in 2004 to seek a peaceful resolution of civil conflict in the southern portion of the country, but these are rare occurrences typically due to pressures from grassroots constituencies that have the ear of the president and that most importantly are considered crucial to reelection. In the case of Sudan, for example, an array of Christian groups deemed essential to Republican victories in 2004 effectively lobbied the Bush White House to "do something" to stop what they perceived as a genocidal policy that a northern-based Islamic regime was carrying out against a southern-based, predominantly Christian population, including the practice of southern Christians being sold as slaves in northern Sudan.

In order to fully understand US foreign policy toward Africa, one must, therefore, focus on the policies and interactions of the African affairs bureaus of the traditional national security bureaucracies, such as the State Department, the Pentagon, and the Central Intelligence Agency, as well as their counterparts within the increasingly important economic realm, most notably the Department of Commerce. To be sure, the White House sets the overall parameters of US foreign policy, which impacts all regions of the world, including Africa. But the unique nature of the US policymaking system ensures that specific policy initiatives related to Africa often emerge from and are coordinated by the national security bureaucracies with little White House input. The net result of what can be referred to as bureaucratic influence in the policymaking process is the continuation of established policies toward individual African countries, even when an administration with different beliefs than its predecessor takes office, such as in the shift from the Obama to the Trump administration (Schraeder 1994a).

It is noteworthy that the Cold War's end had raised expectations that the great powers would coordinate with each other to address a host of challenges confronting the African continent, most notably the resolution of regional conflicts and the promotion of regional economic development (Gromyko and Whitaker 1990). Expectations of great power cooperation nonetheless were dampened by what Jeffrey E. Garten (1993) refers to as the emergence of a Cold Peace, in which the great powers compete for markets and influence in all regions of the world, including Africa. The defining characteristic of the Cold Peace, which harkens back to the "scramble for Africa" during the colonial era, is the emergence of a highly competitive and sometimes conflicting system in which great power policies are driven by the same factor: economic self-interest. This conceptualization of international politics does not preclude the existence of countervailing elements, most notably the emergence of a more cosmopolitan international regime—as marked by the 1997 Ottawa Treaty banning antipersonnel landmines, the establishment of international tribunals to deal with crimes of humanity in Rwanda and the former Yugoslavia, and the creation of an International Criminal Court (ICC). Nor does it ignore the durability of strategic interests in great power involvement in Africa, as witnessed by the Bush administration's search for allies in North and East Africa in the aftermath of the terrorist attacks of September 11, 2001. The simple point is that economic interests are key to understanding contemporary great power competition and conflict in Africa.

Great power competition has particularly emerged in the highly lucrative fossil fuel, strategic minerals, telecommunications, and transport industries, leading to strained great power ties. In the case of France, for example, policymakers viewed the penetration by US and other Western companies as an intrusion or even as aggression into France's sphere of influence in francophone Africa. The seriousness with which this issue was treated at the highest levels of the French policymaking establishment was demonstrated by the public admission of Minister of Cooperation Michel Roussin that a series of meetings had been held on how best to defend French interests, including those within the economic realm, against those of the United States (Glaser and Smith 1994; see also Védrine and Moïsi 2000).

The stakes involved were clearly demonstrated by competition between Elf-Aquitaine (a French oil company) and the Occidental Petroleum Corporation or "Oxy" (a US oil company) in the Republic of Congo. Desperately in need of nearly $200 million to pay government salaries before legislative elections, newly elected president Pascal Lissouba turned for help to Elf-Aquitaine (which controls 80 percent of the country's oil production). When its French manager refused to approve either a $300 million loan or a $300 million mortgage on the future production of three promising new offshore oil deposits, Lissouba initiated secret negotiations with the US-based Oxy. An agreement was signed but renounced eight months later by the Lissouba administration due to intense pressure from the French (Schraeder 2000). US-French competition in the lucrative petroleum industry is not limited to the Republic of Congo, nor is it unique in terms of great power relations. It is rather indicative of a more competitive foreign policy environment between the Western powers, a rising China, a resurgent Russia, and a host of emerging regional powers in which Africa has become an increasingly important source of fossil fuels, strategic minerals, and other primary resources (e.g., see Ellis 2003; Klare and Volman 2004).

Rising great power competition holds important implications for the dependency-decolonization debate. From the viewpoint of a new generation of African leaders, rising economic competition among the great powers provides an opportunity to lessen previously privileged ties of dependence and to pursue special relationships and especially economic contracts with countries willing to provide the best offer. Although the ultimate resolution of the "oil war" in the Republic of Congo in favor of France suggests that the ties of dependency were not automatically broken by the Cold War's end, the Lissouba government nonetheless was able to obtain a better agreement from the French as a result of "playing the American card." In other cases, such as the decision of President Patrice Talon of Benin (elected in 2016) to offer a lucrative pipeline contract to China's National Petroleum Corporation at the expense of previously privileged ties with the French oil industry, a new generation of African leaders is successfully utilizing their increased independence within the international system to acquire the best deals for their respective countries.

The United Nations and International Financial Institutions

The relationship of African countries to the UN and to a host of international financial institutions is important to understanding the relevance of the decolonization-dependency debate (Warner and Shaw 2018). During the initial decades of the contemporary independence era, a variety of factors suggested that membership in the UN was facilitating the ability of the first generation of African leaders to assume greater control over the international relations of their respective countries (Jonah 2018). In addition to serving as a concrete symbol of African independence, UN membership also provided African leaders with an important international forum for promoting African views on a variety of international issues such as unequivocal support for the complete decolonization of the African continent, opposition to apartheid in South Africa, the promotion of socioeconomic development, and the need for disarmament and attention to regional security. Most important, the UN provides a unique forum for diplomatic negotiations. Financially unable to maintain embassies throughout the world, let alone throughout the African continent, African diplomats take advantage of the fact that almost all countries maintain a permanent mission in New York to carry out the day-to-day business of diplomacy (Mathews 1988).

In an era in which it has become fashionable for many Westerners, particularly those in the United States, to criticize their countries' involvement in the UN as providing few if any tangible economic or political benefits, it is important to recognize that UN agencies often play substantial administrative and development roles in many African countries. In several African capital cities, there are a variety of UN offices whose budgets and staffs sometimes approach those of their counterparts within the host government. In Dakar, the capital of Senegal, for example, offices represent a variety of UN agencies, including the United Nations Development Programme (UNDP), the United Nations Children's Fund (UNICEF), the United Nations High Commissioner for Refugees (UNHCR), the World Health Organization (WHO), the International Labour Organization (ILO), and the United Nations Educational, Scientific and Cultural Organization (UNESCO). Capturing the sentiment of African policymakers during the 1960s, a Senegalese diplomat noted that "these agencies were perceived as critical to the fulfillment of African development goals during the initial independence era, and provided a source of hope especially for those impoverished countries lacking both the resources and the expertise to implement the studies and programs pursued by each of these agencies."[2]

In the aftermath of the Cold War, however, a vocal segment of African leaders and intellectuals has been apt to associate the UN with foreign intervention and the imposition of Western values. This position has been partially fueled by the replacement of the classic international norms of sovereignty and nonintervention in the affairs of UN member states with a new set of norms that focus on human rights protection and humanitarian intervention, particularly to save refugees and other peoples threatened by civil conflict and starvation (Deng et al. 1996:5; see also Prendergast 1996). As aptly noted by former UN Secretary-General Boutros Boutros-Ghali (1992:9), "The time of absolute and exclusive sovereignty . . . has passed; its theory was never matched by reality." Indeed, the UN has undertaken more than twenty peacekeeping missions in Africa, with the large majority taking place during the post–Cold War era (Adebajo 2011).

The series of UN-sponsored military interventions in Somalia from 1992 to 1995 serves as one of the most notable examples of the UN's increasingly interventionist role in contemporary Africa. At its height, the UN military operation included over 38,000 troops from twenty countries and led to the effective occupation of southern and central Somalia. The intervention was launched in the absence of any official invitation from a legal Somali authority (which, in any case, did not exist) and in direct opposition to heavily armed militia groups who shared a historical mistrust of UN intentions and operations dating back to the colonial era (Hirsch and Oakley 1995).[3] From the perspective of the UN, the collapse of the Somali state and the intensification of a brutal civil war demanded UN intervention; the conflict was not only spilling over into the neighboring territories of Kenya, Ethiopia, and Djibouti, but it had contributed to the creation of a humanitarian crisis in which approximately 330,000 Somalis were at "imminent risk of death" (Lyons and Samatar 1995:24). According to this logic, the UN could justify international intervention, even in the absence of an official invitation by a legally constituted authority, on the grounds of "abatement" of a threat to international peace (Joyner 1992:229–246).

The Somali case is part of a growing international trend of prompting even internationally recognized governments to accept UN-sponsored humanitarian intervention (Deng 1993; see also Prendergast 1996). In Sudan, for example, a combination of civil war and drought-induced famine, which has led to the deaths of over 500,000 civilians since 1986, prompted the UN Office of Emergency Operations in Africa (OEOA) to undertake a humanitarian intervention in 1989 known as Operation Lifeline Sudan (Deng and Minear 1992). Constituting one of the largest peacetime humanitarian interventions undertaken in UN history, Operation Lifeline Sudan was made possible only by mounting international pressure on the Sudanese regime to recognize the scope of the problem and to accept UN-sponsored intervention. Ultimate acceptance, however, did not ensure ultimate happiness on the part of the Sudanese regime. "Even when the initial issues of involvement are resolved, relations between the donors and the recipient country or population are never entirely harmonious," explains a group of specialists on conflict resolution, led by Francis Deng, a Sudanese national who served as Special Representative of the UN Secretary-General for internally displaced persons. "The dichotomy expressed between 'us' and 'them' becomes inevitable as the nationals feel their pride injured by their own failure and dependency, while the donors and relief workers resent the lack of gratitude and appreciation" (Deng et al. 1996:11).

African perceptions of eroding sovereignty have been reinforced by the rising influence of international financial institutions in African economies (Mkandawire and Olukoshi 1995). By the beginning of the 1980s, African leaders were struggling to respond to the effects of a continent-wide economic crisis that combined internal economic decline with mounting international debt. In order to obtain necessary international capital, most African leaders had little choice but to turn to two international financial institutions: the IMF, which issues short-term stabilization loans to ensure economic solvency, and the World Bank, which issues long-term loans to promote economic development (Jinadu 2018). Unlike typical loans that simply require the recipient to make regular scheduled payments over a specific period of time, IMF and World Bank loans have a series of externally imposed demands, typically referred to as "conditionalities," designed to restructure African economies and political systems in the image of the northern industrialized democracies (Callaghy and Ravenhill 1993a).

The emergence of economic conditionalities was signaled by the 1981 publication of a World Bank study, *Accelerated Development in Sub-Saharan Africa: An Agenda for Action.* The conclusion of this report was that misguided decisions of the first generation of African leaders were responsible for the mounting economic crisis. To resolve this crisis, the World Bank and the IMF proposed linking all future flows of Western financial capital to the willingness of African leaders to sign and implement structural adjustment programs (SAPs): economic blueprints designed to radically restructure African economies. Four sets of private sector reforms are characteristic of SAPs: (1) the termination of food subsidies that kept food prices artificially low, effectively discouraging farmers from planting food crops; (2) the devaluation of national currencies to stimulate exports and the domestic production of manufactured products; (3) the trimming of government bureaucracies; and (4) the privatization of parastatals (state-owned corporations). In short, the SAPs embodied the liberal economic consensus of the northern industrialized democracies that Africa's future economic success depended on the pursuit of an export-oriented strategy of economic growth that systematically dismantled all forms of governmental intervention in national economies (Campbell and Loxley 1989; Commins 1988).

A second World Bank report published in 1989, *Sub-Saharan Africa: From Crisis to Sustainable Growth: A Long-Term Perspective Study,* heralded the emergence of political conditionalities in IMF- and World Bank–sponsored SAPs. In addition to claiming that African countries that followed IMF and World Bank economic prescriptions were performing better than those that were not, the 1989 report went beyond previous studies by underscoring that the success of economic reforms was dependent on the promotion of "good governance," the creation of transparent, accountable, and efficient political systems patterned after those of the northern industrialized democracies. Simply put, the 1989 report signaled an emerging consensus in favor of making all flows of Western financial capital contingent on the willingness of African leaders to promote the liberalization of their respective political systems (World Bank 1989).

The economic and political conditionalities imposed by the IMF and the World Bank have been challenged by African policymakers and academics. During the 1980s, SAPs were criticized for their complete disregard for the political realities African leaders confront. IMF and World Bank economists failed to consider that cutting off government subsidies, one of the above-noted four pillars of private sector reform always included in SAPs, could lead to often violent urban riots. In Sudan, for example, the launching of an SAP in 1985 sparked an urban insurrection that contributed to the overthrow of the regime of Gaafar Mohammed Nimeiri (Harsch 1989). The implementation of the three remaining pillars of private sector reform also entailed serious political risks, due to their tendency to reinforce short-term economic hardships. The devaluation of the national currency meant an immediate decline in the already marginal buying power of the average citizen, and the trimming of government bureaucracies and the privatization of parastatals triggered significant increases in already high levels of national unemployment. In retrospect, the lack of political sensitivity was a result of the fact that SAPs were usually formulated by international economists with little (if any) political training or firsthand knowledge of the individual African countries their programs were supposed to serve.

SAPs were also challenged by African policymakers and academics during the 1990s despite the fact that both the IMF and the World Bank had engaged in efforts to assess and, when possible, incorporate African sentiments into policy planning documents. Africans were particularly critical of

The international aid community is heavily represented in Africa's conflict zones. Photo captures a row of international aid vehicles, led by Médecins Sans Frontières (Doctors Without Borders), at the town of Goma, in the eastern portion of the Democratic Republic of Congo.

the consensus of IMF and World Bank economists that economic and political conditionalities were mutually reinforcing and, therefore, could be pursued simultaneously (Sandbrook 1993). As demonstrated by Africa's experiments with democratization after the fall of the Berlin Wall in 1989, the creation of democratic political systems complete with institutional checks and balances has hindered the implementation of SAPs. Indeed, democratically elected African presidents and parliamentary representatives often hesitate to enact legislation that will place significant economic burdens on already impoverished populations and thereby potentially contribute to their political demise the next time elections are held.

The end of the Cold War has had a dramatic effect on the role of conditionalities in the African continent's international economic relations. The terms of the debate have shifted away from such Cold War–inspired questions as whether Marxism or an African variant of socialism is favorable to capitalism, or whether single-party or multiparty regimes can better promote the welfare of their respective peoples. Instead, the IMF and the World Bank now consider how to best facilitate the creation of capitalist, multiparty political systems throughout Africa.

The critical dilemma confronting Africa's newly elected democratic leaders is the extent to which they will attempt to work with international financial institutions. If they wholeheartedly embrace SAPs for the future economic health of their societies, they are bound to alienate important actors within their political systems and, therefore, run the risk of losing subsequent democratic elections. In the case of Benin, for example, the democratically elected government of President Soglo was rejected in the 1996 presidential elections after only one term of office, at least partially as a result of his administration's strong support for externally inspired SAPs. In contrast, if democratically elected African leaders refuse to embrace SAPs, they run the risk of losing access to international capital and contributing to the further decline of their economies.

Cautiously optimistic interpretations suggest that reform-minded African leaders and external supporters of change must adopt "realistic, hardheaded" analyses of Africa's economic plight that avoid both the Afro-pessimism of critics of change and the overly optimistic cheerleading stance of those who believe that change can be implemented quickly, smoothly, and relatively free of pain (Callaghy and Ravenhill 1993b). According to this viewpoint, although even the best-intentioned and most reform-minded African leaders may find themselves "hemmed in" by a variety of international constraints that restrict policy choices, they are capable of pursuing paths that may lead to economic success over the long term (Callaghy and Ravenhill 1993b). More pessimistic interpretations from the dependency tradition suggest that African countries "desperate for access to international capital" are "uniquely vulnerable" to the demands of the IMF and the World Bank.

"While dependency analysts long argued that international capitalist structures provided the context within which development in Africa occurred," explains William Reed (1992:85), "it was only as Africa approached the 1990s that international financial institutions—controlled by the leading capitalist powers and designed to bolster the international capitalist economy—were able to impose policy prescriptions directly upon African governments."

African leaders have sought to curb the impact of economic and political conditionalities by formulating alternative frameworks for development. One of the earliest attempts was the adoption of the Lagos Plan of Action (LPA) at the 1980 OAU Assembly of Heads of State and Government held in Freetown, Sierra Leone. The LPA was not taken seriously in international financial circles due to its contradictory assumption that Western governments and financial institutions would finance the pursuit of self-reliant economic development designed to delink the African continent from the international economic system. In 1989, the Economic Commission for Africa published a document, *African Alternative Framework to Structural Adjustment Programmes for Socioeconomic Recovery and Transformation (AAF-SAP),* that drew at least the grudging acceptance of IMF and World Bank economists. Acknowledging that African leaders were partially responsible for Africa's economic crisis and that some form of economic restructuring was necessary, the 1989 report nonetheless castigated the IMF and the World Bank for ignoring the social and political impacts of SAPs. The report specifically called on international donor agencies to promote "structural adjustment with a human face": to plan for and respond to the short-term negative social impacts (e.g., rising unemployment) that inevitably accompany the good-faith efforts on the part of African leaders to implement SAPs (UNECA 1989).

One far-reaching alternative framework for development advanced by African leaders and placed under the guidance of the AU was the New Economic Partnership for Africa's Development (NEPAD) (Ikome 2007). The essence of NEPAD was a recognition by African countries that they needed to undertake economic and political reforms if they wished to attract the foreign capital deemed necessary for Africa's development from the northern industrialized democracies (Hope 2002). Specifically, African leaders sought increases in grant aid (as opposed to loans that must be paid back), foreign investment, and trade from the northern industrialized democracies. In return, they agreed to participate in a two-stage African Peer Review Mechanism to assess the degree to which they were undertaking promised economic and political reforms. Whereas stage one involved undertaking a self-assessment, stage two involved submitting the assessment for review by a group of eminent Africans. The process was significantly flawed, in that authoritarian regimes, such as the dictatorship of Paul Kagame in Rwanda, not surprisingly gave themselves glowing self-reviews, which were then essentially rubber-stamped by the panel of eminent Africans. In essence, the peer review process and NEPAD more generally were "doing little more than legitimizing authoritarian governments in the eyes of donors by providing them with a regional stamp of approval" (Whitaker and Clark 2018:141). Although ultimately unsuccessful, the NEPAD "goal of having a selective international organization with clear criteria for membership and a rigorous process of peer review remained intriguing to observers," including to Africans who wish to emulate similar (and successful) structures and processes within the European Union (Whitaker and Clark 2018:141).

A second alternative framework for development involves the applicability to Africa of the so-called Asian model of development: the rapid, export-oriented growth that led to the economic success of the "Asian tigers" of Hong Kong, South Korea, Singapore, and Taiwan (World Bank 1993). The example of South Korea is especially noteworthy. Success in this case was largely due to authoritarian policies that directly contradict the political conditionalities imposed on African leaders. In South Korea, a military leadership intent on ending corruption and promoting economic development illegally took power in a 1961 military coup d'état and significantly curtailed political pluralism and participation (Callaghy and Ravenhill 1993b:546). The implications of this lesson (i.e., that the successful implementation of highly unpopular SAPs requires an enlightened form of authoritarianism) were reinforced by Ghana's implementation of SAPs during the 1980s under the authoritarian leadership of Flt. Lt. Jerry Rawlings. Often cited by IMF and World Bank studies as a model for other African countries, the Rawlings regime was able to impose draconian initiatives due to its iron-fisted control over the political system. The authoritarian nature of the Rawlings regime enabled it to impose SAPs that discriminated against the urban population, particularly workers, while preventing the strikes and urban unrest that derailed similar programs in other African countries (Herbst 1993).

The potential significance of authoritarianism in Ghana's successful economic transformation and the Asian success story of another dictatorship—the PRC—has not been lost on authoritarian African leaders seeking to transform their economies and international relations while at the same time maintaining their hold over political power. Although Ghana has ultimately emerged as one of the most democratic countries in contemporary Africa, Chinese leaders proudly proclaim (and demonstrate) that the PRC model of economic growth and development can be achieved without political liberalization. Not surprisingly, China's phenomenal economic growth, which in recent decades has allowed the country to flex its socioeconomic and political-military muscle in international relations, has been noticed by African leaders. Moreover, the PRC is increasingly offering an alternative source of loans and financing to African leaders, dictators and democrats alike, who chafe at the political demands for reform from the northern industrialized democracies.

A resurgent, authoritarian Russia appears to be joining China in promoting such an authoritarian model of development. Together, these two powers provide a powerful pole of support for African leaders in search of alternatives to the neoliberal model of open economies, SAPs, and democratic multiparty political systems. At the very minimum, the rise of these two authoritarian great powers contributes to a more pluralistic international environment in which African leaders are increasingly able to play one great power against another so as to achieve the best deals for their countries.

Toward the Future

The end of the Cold War and the rise of democratization movements served as transformative events in the evolution of the international relations of the African continent. These events in turn allow us to draw some tentative conclusions about the dependency-decolonization debate. Although neither approach was completely supported or rejected by the analysis, three trends—the democratization of African foreign policies, rising competition among the great powers, and the rising assertiveness of African regional powers—suggest that African leaders are exerting greater control over the international relations of their respective countries. Yet proponents of the dependency approach can point to the increasingly pervasive nature of intervention on the part of the UN and international financial institutions as supportive of their vision of international relations. Moreover, despite some promising developments related to SADC and ongoing efforts within the AU to promote democracy and regional security, neither the AU's pursuit of pan-Africanism nor regional experiments in economic cooperation and integration offer compelling evidence to resolve the dependency-decolonization debate. A common element in all five of the topics that I have discussed, however, is the potential importance of the democratization process and its impact on the rise of a new generation of African leaders committed to democratic principles. Although it is perhaps too early to tell, one can hypothesize that, if democratization becomes more deeply embedded in Africa, it will facilitate the peeling away of another layer of dependency and allow a new generation of African leaders to assume greater control over the international relations of their respective countries.

Notes

1. The only exceptions to this trend include President George H. W. Bush's one-day visit to Somalia in 1993 while in transit to the Middle East, and President Jimmy Carter's March 29–April 2, 1978, visit to Nigeria.
2. Senegalese diplomat, interviewed by the author, Dakar, Senegal, January 1995.
3. Somali distrust of the UN stems from the decision of that international body to support the reimposition in 1950 of Italian colonial rule over what is currently known as the Republic of Somalia.

7

Population and Urbanization

Jeffrey W. Paller

African societies are experiencing a rapid urban transformation. Whereas only 33 million Africans lived in cities in 1950, the UN's population division estimates that 472 million Africans currently live in cities, with the number increasing each day. The region's 3.5 percent urbanization rate is the fastest in the world today with twenty-one of the thirty fastest-growing cities now in Africa. Sixty-five cities have more than 1 million people. This urbanization is taking place amid a broader demographic boom on the African continent. The population has doubled in the last three decades and is expected to triple by the end of the century. Between 2020 and 2100, Africa's population will likely grow from 1.3 billion to 4.3 billion. Some countries are particularly affected. For example, Nigeria is expected to reach 400 million people by 2150 (some estimates are larger), making it the third-largest country in the world. In addition, the population boom is young: 60 percent of Africans are under twenty-five years of age. Improved healthcare and increasing life expectancy are fueling the population boom.

The demographic boom and rapid urbanization are bringing new challenges. Nearly half of all urban Africans live in slum-like conditions (Tusting et al. 2019), lacking access to clean water, sanitation, tenure security (protection against forced eviction), durable housing, and sufficient living space. Water-borne diseases like cholera are threatening city life, while heart disease and diabetes are emerging health issues. Desertification, coastal erosion, and other environmental threats are worsened by population growth and urbanization. Job creation and infrastructural development are wildly insufficient. The African Development Bank estimates that more than 10 million jobs will need to be created each year, and that $130 billion needs to be spent on infrastructure, including $66 billion on universal access to water and sanitation. In addition, 700 million units of housing are needed to house the growing population. The implications are particularly severe for political development. Urban expansion and the proliferation of slums place demands on city and national governments while providing new opportunities for leaders to build political followings. Party machines establish dense organizational networks, reshaping social ties and power structures. Migrant communities make claims to land that often put them at odds with host populations in struggles over valuable urban space. Governments and wealthy landowners justify forced evictions and demolitions as necessary for urban development, but also use them as part of their strategies of social control.

Urban growth also provides significant opportunities for human development, economic growth, and political liberalization. Urban residents have better access to educational opportunities and quality healthcare than rural dwellers. Women often have more rights and autonomy in cities, especially with respect to employment and property rights. Food insecurity and absolute poverty are lower in Africa's urban centers. Cities accommodate industrialization and agglomeration, and the emerging middle class attracts a thriving retail sector. Foreign direct investment is flooding into cities, fueling a construction boom. Cities are also often at the forefront of political change. Democratic revolutions that spread across the continent in the early 1990s emerged in cities. Urbanites are often more cosmopolitan, less beholden to ethnic identities, and more likely to demand responsiveness and accountability from their leaders. Cities are typically more politically liberal and open than rural areas.

The remainder of this chapter, which is divided into seven sections, examines how Africa's rapid urbanization and population boom take place in a longer historical and political context. Section one explains how Africa's urbanization is a contentious political process. It explores how struggles over power and decisionmaking will determine whether urbanization will be sustainable and inclusive or foster inequality and deepen poverty, which will become more entrenched. Sections two through four explain, respectively, the historical context of African urban growth, the different economic and political constraints that African megacities face, and the institutional features underlying Africa's secondary cities. The next two sections explore two pressing urban challenges: namely, the rebuilding of African cities after war and confronting climate change. A final section offers thoughts on the future of urban Africa.

The Contentious Politics of African Urbanization

Africa's urbanization is different than the experiences of other regions of the world. Urbanization in Africa is often caricatured as "fast, late, and poor" (Cartwright et al. 2018). Although industrialization and manufacturing attracted people from the countryside in Europe, Asia, and the Americas, Africa is urbanizing without large-scale industrialization. It is also the last region to experience widespread urban expansion. In many cities, colonialism contributed to an early wave of urbanization, and Africans settled in "native areas" that lacked formal urban planning. Cities where colonialists governed affairs became economic and political powerhouses that would persist after independence. The 1980s sparked a new wave of urbanization as war, failing agricultural policies, and state failure pushed residents from the countryside to the city. Today, natural population increase and improved healthcare are the leading contributors to urban growth. Nonetheless, residents now find themselves in cities that do not have the capacity to provide sufficient services or jobs, leading to the growth of a vibrant informal sector that provides economic opportunities and livelihoods, and the proliferation of informal settlements.

In this way, four characteristics make the process of African urbanization unique. First, urbanization is occurring without industrialization. Second, political and economic informality—norms and procedures outside of official sanctioning—dominate urban life. Third, colonialism shaped specific legacies, most notably the economic and political primacy of single cities, usually capitals. Fourth, ambiguous property rights and land governance undermine inclusive development across the continent, creating opportunities of accumulation for political elites.

These characteristics of African urbanization call into question the dominant paradigms in social science that treat urbanization as a linear process associated with economic modernization and bureaucratization. This linear understanding is disentangled from politics. Instead, urbanization is a contentious political process whereby population growth leads to competing and often conflicting claims on a city (Paller 2017). Throughout Africa's past, cities experienced skewed land allocation, invasions and squatting, immigrant and population expulsions, demolitions, exclusive urban planning, and the formation of parallel governance structures. But Africa's urban history is also one of creativity, cooperation, and political dialogues and debates.

Migration and the growth of nonindigenous populations in cities can also contribute to new social conflict, either in the formation of new identities or the politicization of ethnic and indigenous identities. Raleigh (2015:91) argues, "Modern African political and institutional transitions to democracy have effectively led to urban disenfranchisement and poor governance; this resulted in the continued reproduction and exacerbation of spatial inequalities," triggering new forms of urban violence. But liberalization and urbanization have also led to the formation of cosmopolitan neighborhoods and new claims of citizenship by previously marginalized populations

(Paller 2019). As urban expansion continues, there is new pressure on land, leading to multiple claimants of property, which creates winners and losers. Land rights are weak and ambiguous, especially for the urban poor.

This has important implications for policy. Sustainable urban development requires overcoming the legacies of colonialism that led to the underinvestment of native areas (Fox 2014), urban planning that privileged a settler elite and promoted marginalization of Africans (Njoh 2013), and the institutionalization of primate cities in which single settlements are disproportionately larger than those in the rest of the country. Relatedly, it requires upgrading "slum" neighborhoods by investing in infrastructure and integrating leadership structures into municipal government. This requires that municipal governments work with national governments through initiatives of multilevel governance, especially with respect to allocation of resources, capacity of authorities, and legitimacy of institutions (Haas and Wani 2019). Stated simply, urbanization is contentious, and cities are the arena of vibrant politics.

Historical Legacies of Settlement and Belonging

Africa's population boom and rapid urbanization do not happen in a historical vacuum. Instead, the political, economic, and social roots of Africa's cities date back centuries. Early settlement patterns placed cities on certain paths that still shape development outcomes today. In particular, cities' urban origins can affect how populations make political claims to the city.

Bill Freund's *The African City: A History* provides a useful template to understand the different time periods when African cities formed. Freund distinguishes between three types of cities: precolonial African kingdoms; trading centers, or cities that emerged from long-distance exchange and trade with foreigners prior to colonialism; and colonial creations that were formed during the colonial era by imperial powers, labeled here colonial creations. Another type of city developed in the postcolonial era (e.g., Abuja and Yamoussoukro), as new leaders attempted to distribute population and power across their countries in new ways. While there is significant variation within each type of city, this framework provides a helpful summary of the different kinds of cities across the continent, which can help explain the different practices of politics and strategies of governance that emerge.

Precolonial African Kingdoms

African societies were slow to urbanize. The slow pace compared to other world regions can be partially explained by challenges of physical geography. Political scientist Jeffrey Herbst observed that "relatively low population densities in Africa have automatically meant that it always has been more expensive for states to exert control over a given number of people compared to Europe and other densely settled areas" (2000:11). Herbst argues that the cost of expanding the domestic power infrastructure over sparsely populated people undermined state power, including the lack of centralization of people in consolidated spaces.

Unlike European states, African countries did not establish cities to collect taxes for making war, instead facing "the luxury of escaping the brutal history of continued war that so mars the barbaric European experience in the twentieth century" (Herbst 2000:112). This created a state system whereby weak states existed without coercive power over their territories. This had significant implications for urban formation: few cities developed strong infrastructure and official plans because communities prioritized mobility over controlling territory, and they did not rely on taxation to win wars. It is also a partial explanation as to why so many African cities are governed informally: formal tax collection, transport, and economic activity contribute to only a small portion of urban development.

But this does not mean that precolonial states—with functioning cities—did not exist. Political centralization occurred in places with agriculturally productive environments that were part of larger regional trade networks (Monroe 2013:21). It also occurred on coasts that could tap into global trading networks. Populations settled in spatially concentrated spaces and built towns and cities in these productive spaces. Most of these cities were under the control of a kingdom, empire, or local ethnic group prior to European powers' arriving in the city. Some were military bases of those groups, inhabiting politically advantageous locations. While they were free from being birthed by colonial violence, interethnic wars, battles, and conquests by kings and leaders often contributed to the political development of the city.

Cities that emerged from precolonial kingdoms have a long history of integrating outsiders. This cosmopolitanism is represented in the design and structure of urban spaces that were developed without originating from coercively authoritative, European-style state entities. Instead, first-comers to these precolonial cities often made strong indigenous claims, contributing to urban cores that centered around palaces of kings or chiefs. Conflict often revolved around struggles for land, control, and authority between traditional authorities—chiefs, kings, or other royals. Chieftaincy disputes are one manifestation of urban claims-making today. Politically, indigenous populations often claim authority and control municipal government, contributing to possible disputes between central government and municipal authorities.

Trading Centers

Some cities emerged before colonial rule because of economic interaction with foreign traders, including Europeans, Arabs, Indians, and other African groups. Many of these cities emerged along the coast, and most of these towns and cities formed between the sixteenth and nineteenth centuries (e.g., Accra, Kampala, Lagos, and Luanda). Cities like Mombasa and Zanzibar have an Islamic imprint, while others emerged as boomtowns surrounding natural resource endowments (e.g., Kimberley). One of the most important types of trade was in slavery, which demanded population hubs. Other trading post cities were on popular caravan routes where traders brought goods before the construction of railroads.

Although these urban centers share features with precolonial kingdoms, they are notable because of the emergence of a legal and merchant class that served as intermediaries between indigenous groups and foreign traders and explorers. The emergence of this elite class is politically important: the new elite extended beyond traditional authorities and served as an important buffer to imperial powers once they took control of these cities. In some cases, this class became the urban bourgeoisie, creating a new cleavage in society between elites and commoners. They benefited from missionary education, trading opportunities with foreigners, and travel prospects. But they also became an important source of resistance to colonial powers, especially with respect to land tenure, evictions, and demolitions. Their role is paradoxical: they accumulated a considerable amount of land and capital and called for progress and modernization, but they also viewed themselves as protectors of African ways of life.

Garth A. Myers

Many countries in Africa are rapidly urbanizing, and cities like Dar es Salaam, Tanzania, are growing more rapidly than any other cities on earth.

Today, descendants from these families are leaders across Africa, holding executive positions in government, political parties, and businesses. This class is especially influential in the growth of cities. This urban elite played an important role in resisting colonialism in many states while also resisting forced evictions and slum demolitions. At the same time, the accumulation of property by outsiders and by this entrenched economic and political elite has contributed to a counterreaction by traditional elites, leading to conflicts between traditional authorities and government technocrats. We observe this by way of tensions between competing informal and formal institutions. Today, real estate development contributes to land disputes between private businesses, government bodies, and traditional authorities, and claims take the form of private property, eminent domain, and customary tenure, respectively.

Colonialism had a major impact on cities as well as on how the city fits into the broader structure of the African state. But the emergence of a merchant elite *prior* to colonialism makes these cities different from colonial creations, giving the indigenous population certain claims to land and urban space that did not develop until independence in the next type of city.

Colonial Creations

Some cities are colonial creations (e.g., Conakry, Harare, Lusaka, and Nairobi). These cities did not exist as large urban clusters before colonialism. The imperial powers created the cities so that they could serve as settler outposts for administrators, workers, and foreigners. These cities constituted blatantly racist urban plans: settlers built well-planned and modern neighborhoods for themselves, while slums and informal settlements proliferated for native populations. Sometimes these slums were designated as their own city, so as not to be associated with the bigger urban and often economic hub nearby. When these neighborhoods constituted a public health threat—bubonic plague, cholera, and other disease outbreaks were common—colonial authorities resorted to forced evictions and slum demolitions. Dating back to colonial rule, slums and informal settlements housed the laboring poor—a population of poor workers who served the colonial regime as different forms of servants.

Today, many of these neighborhoods continue to house the working-class poor, but they are heavily politicized as politicians and slumlords use informality as a tool to extract rents and votes. The development of a racialized city has important implications for ethnic relations: claims to urban space are embedded in broader struggles over citizenship. Colonial urban planning set the precedent for belonging in the city, and politicians and leaders use this language to exclude minority groups and marginalized populations today. In some cases, tensions take the form of xenophobic attacks and antiforeigner business and homeownership policies. Xenophobia has been particularly problematic in South African cities, whose urban structures emerged out of apartheid-era state policies.

Finally, many colonial cities developed around "enclave economies" (Leonard and Straus 2003), or those that depended on the extraction of primary commodities. For example, Lubumbashi (called Elisabethville during colonial rule) was the copper mining capital of the modern-day Democratic Republic of Congo and remains the heart of its extractive industries. Infrastructure development continues to serve extractive purposes rather than those based on investments in human capital and industrialization. Today, claims to urban space emerge from this template—private developments serving the interests of an extremely rich elite and foreign-based expatriate population. This contributes to high incidences of land grabbing, part of a process that Marxist scholars call accumulation by dispossession (Harvey 2008).

These processes of urban development are ideal types, and not all cities within each category developed in the same way. But this typology provides a general overview of the historical diversity in urban formation across the continent.

The Impact of Colonialism

Africa's urbanization is not driven by industrialization as it was in the West. Africa's historically distinct urbanization dynamics appear to have emerged out of late colonialism (Myers 2003, 2011) amid global capitalism. Colonial infrastructure investment was designed for export of raw materials, land appropriation and speculation, and resource extraction, with industrial activity actively discouraged until near-independence for many countries (Davis 2006; Fox 2012). But the imprint of colonialism has left a lasting legacy on African cities.

Urban planner Ambe Njoh (2013:113) argues that Western urban planning has been institutionalized across Africa and has been used as a "tool of acculturation" or assimilation to a dominant culture. "Western-imposed urban centres," he writes, "were externally conditioned and sought to serve the needs of colonial master nations." Colonial administrators prioritized the "rules of civility in urban space" based on reason, order, and science. Indigenous and migrant African communities were kept out of city planning and largely left unregulated (Njoh 2006). Africans lived in communities that were not regulated formally, and they developed in an unplanned nature. Public services were not provided, contributing to the development of nonstate providers of services and vibrant associational life.

Colonial authorities used zoning laws and building codes in the attempt to control urban development and strengthen social control over indigenous populations (Njoh 2009). Urban development that deviated from colonial codes and laws was considered illegal and was not condoned (Ocheje

2007). Colonial urban policy left an important legacy: "The norm of city planning consisted of slum clearance, relocation and redevelopment," explains Ocheje (2007:183). "For this reason, planners in Africa refuse to accept the notion that unauthorized settlements, no matter how they came about, should be 'regularized,' as that would be to condone illegality."

Governments use the threat of forced eviction and forceful demolitions to counter the authorities' fear of poor urban populations. They also do so to counter short-term urban problems like flooding without tackling larger structural problems that contribute to large-scale urban growth (Obeng-Odoom 2010). In this way, the roots of state-neighborhood community tensions date to colonial times and early periods of African urban development (Fox 2014). Today, most cities maintain the legacies of inequality that emerged out of colonialism. Municipal governments and urban planners have yet to establish policies to counter these deep injustices so as to prioritize the needs of the urban poor.

Urban Settlement in Benin City, Douala, and Harare

Benin City, Douala, and Harare represent the diversity of Africa's urban past. These cities formed at very different times, contributing to distinct governance and development challenges today. Benin City, Nigeria, was the powerful capital of the Benin Empire, which was one of West Africa's largest empires from the thirteenth to the sixteenth centuries. Its origin is traced to the twelfth century. It is now the capital of Edo State and is known for the ancient city's walls and planning, which impressed even its colonial settlers when they arrived. Most of these walls do not exist today, and the historical architecture is not preserved. The city revolves around the *oba*'s (king's) palace. The *oba*, with assistance from the *odionwere* (community leader), controls the access to and use of land. Typical of most precolonial Nigerian cities, the palace, religious site, and open-air market formed the center of the city (Ozo 2009).

The city developed around a series of moats and walls (Ozo 2009). The structures were built to keep out enemies who would harass residents of the city. Surrounding towns and villages copied this model and developed in concentric rings around the *oba*'s palace. They would later be integrated into the city (Connah 1967). The king of 1686 is credited with the general layout of the city. Customary law dictated that all members of the community held shrines, markets, and sacred groves in public trust. The city became a provincial capital in 1897 under the British colonial regime. But the British set the city ablaze in 1897 after capturing it, burning down many of the traditional structures. Cement structures replaced dirt buildings, but the "traditional character of the city remained virtually intact" (Ozo 2009:496).

Like many secondary cities, which will be discussed later in the chapter, Benin City benefited from its designation as the regional capital of the

Mid-Western Region after independence in 1963 (which became Bendel State in 1976, and the state capital of Edo State in 1991). Since then, the city has grown from 100,000 to 800,000 people. The rapid growth drastically changed the physical imprint as banks and financial services flooded the city, middle-class civil servants moved in, and car ownership and usage skyrocketed. Politically, the influx of outsiders threatened local control of the city. This was particularly evident with the redevelopment of a bank building that would threaten traditional ways of life. Ozo writes, "age-old custom . . . forbids outsiders, including palace chiefs whose access is limited to certain sections, from seeing interior sections of the palace. The proposed tall building in that location was potentially a threat to the custom in view of the open courtyard (ugha) structure of the palace" (2009:499). Conflicts like these were common.

Tensions between traditional authorities and the municipal government became heated, contributing to protests and social conflict. Central government conservation efforts conflicted with the desires of local authorities. Although Benin City adopted a master plan in 1970, the plan does not shape urban development in practice because it does not consider social conflict, especially the role of traditional authorities, in everyday governance and in matters of land.

Douala, on the other hand, emerged as the economic center of what is today Cameroon because of precolonial trade, thus originating as a trading center. The inhabitants of the area, the Duala, became important merchants in expanding trade, especially of ivory and palm oil. The expansion of the transatlantic slave trade strengthened their position as middlemen as they established themselves as important links with foreign traders and interior populations (Austen 1983). Austen writes, "The Duala advantage was their domination of canoe navigation on the Cameroon Littoral rivers and their direct monopoly of direct access to European merchants" (1983:3). The development of the city as a trading post attracted the German administration, and it became their headquarters in 1884. The French seized control of Douala in 1914 and replaced German rule in the territory in 1916 (the French ruled alongside the British). The city boomed thereafter as exports increased and activity in the port intensified.

The Duala people became the elite of the region, as they established links with colonial authorities, became entrenched in the Protestant missions, took advantage of Western education, sold land to the German and French, and became prosperous merchants. The German administration's redesign of the city in 1914, in which it established the immigrant quarters of New Bell, created new divisions among the Duala and other migrant groups and a distinct cleavage between groups that became institutionalized over time (Schler 2008). While segregated living spaces emerged before German colonial rule, new urban plans and zoning formally institutionalized the host-stranger dichotomy. In addition, the new plans for Douala undermined the authority of the Duala because it separated them from the laboring population, cutting into their economic livelihoods as well as preventing them from serving as their landlords. Schler goes so far as to show that the Duala "claimed the proposed removal to New Bell would result in nothing short of 'cultural ruin'" (2008:26).

As is the case in many trading post cities, the Duala emerged as an urban elite that established itself prior to colonialism. Therefore, their role was contradictory: they benefited from Western education and missionary activity but at the same time were threatened by German and then French colonial rule. For these reasons, they became leading voices in the anticolonial and nationalist movement. They also involved themselves in politics. For example, they collaborated with the French in 1957 to block the Douala municipality from becoming a local government area because immigrant groups would be able to dominate due to their rising numbers, hampering

Peter J. Schraeder

Urban art in Douala, Cameroon.

Duala authority in their home area (Austen 1983:21). For these reasons, urban governance is embedded in historical and social structures that can hinder sustainable development, raising more questions about who has the right to the city and whom development should benefit.

Finally, Harare is a classic example of a colonial creation, or a city that imperial powers built to serve as an extractive outpost and settler colony. The city was founded in 1890 by a small military force of the British South Africa Company and was called Salisbury until the new independence government changed its name to Harare in 1982. The settlement became a municipality in 1897 and grew and developed with the building of the railroad in 1899 that connected the city with Beira. The city became a thriving market and mining center. From its origins Harare was a planned city with tree-lined boulevards, well-demarcated zoning, and formal transport routes.

Settlers planned Salisbury to segregate British residents and colonial administrators from the indigenous populations, contributing to deeply entrenched racial segregation and creating lasting legacies as buildings and settlements that did not subscribe to formal plans were demolished and prevented from further development. This kept the city well-ordered until the 1980s and 1990s, when the country experienced a massive economic crisis. Thousands of people flooded the city and were forced to settle in backyard shacks and informal settlements. By 2003, the majority of the population in Harare was poor.

In 2005, the city carried out Operation Murambatsvina ("Restore Order"), an exercise meant to "clean up the city" by demolishing illegal structures, clearing the roadways of informal vendors, and improving the image of the city (Potts 2006). The government used formal planning laws and regulations as justification to carry out the exercise. But many attribute the government's motivation to politics, as it punished poor, urban voters who supported the opposition Movement for Democratic Change. The governing Zimbabwe African National Union–Popular Front (ZANU-PF) party could then rebuild support by distributing targeted patronage goods in the context of crisis.

Demolition and eviction had significant political consequences. In a survey among Harare residents, Bratton and Masunungure (2006) report that the major victims were poor, unemployed families. It did not have the intended effects of forcing them back to their hometowns but instead led to increasing political polarization, as well as more distrust in state institutions. While the government responded to contemporary political and economic situations, evictions and demolitions were possible due to the inherited legal and institutional frameworks that emerged at the origins of Harare's urban development. In the next section I explain how these historical factors continue to impact urban policy today.

Global Goals and Local Tensions in Megacities

Africa has some of the fastest growing cities in the world. Cairo, Kinshasa, and Lagos already rank among the fifty largest cities in the world, and their strengthening ties to foreign governments and international capital firmly embed them in the global economy. It is only a matter of time before Accra, Dar es Salaam, Johannesburg, and Nairobi join the ranks of the world's largest cities. The desire to be a world-class city is at the forefront of city governments and planners, who aim to attract massive investment in mega sports facilities for international events or a high-rise financial district (Cheeseman and de Gramont 2017; Myambo 2017), gated communities, and entire new cities (Grant 2009; Sims 2010; Watson 2014). China's aggressive investments in infrastructure contribute to this rapid growth and development.

Megacities are urban centers with more than 10 million residents. According to the World Urbanization Prospects, Abidjan and Nairobi will surpass this threshold by 2040, and by 2050 Addis Ababa, Bamako, Dakar, Ibadan, Kano, and Ouagadougou will join the ranks. Africa is projected to have fourteen megacities in the next thirty years. These cities offer incredible opportunities for investment, land speculation, and construction contracts. African cities are promoted as the new frontier for global capital flows (Steel, Van Noorloos, and Otsuki 2019). Tech hubs have expanded across many of these cities as they are the sites of Africa's rapidly growing middle and upper classes.

This has contributed to what some scholars call "urban land grabs" (Steel, Van Noorloos, and Otsuki 2019; Zoomers et al. 2017). Zoomers et al. explain, "The global land rush . . . is partly a consequence of increasing urban demand and the restructuring of value chains. . . . Moreover, cities themselves act as major 'land grabbers,' as they expand due to population growth, the spread of middle class lifestyles and suburbanisation, speculation, and new city development" (2017:245). The growth of these cities has encouraged infrastructure developments, new construction booms, and urban renewal in city centers.

Many African leaders have high modernist goals where shiny skyscrapers, massive highways, and gated communities provide a vision of a new future (Sims 2010; Watson 2014). Watson (2014) labels these "urban fantasies," based on "speculative urbanism" (Goldman 2011). These fantasies take the form of urban renewal, urban extension, or entirely new satellite cities. Birnin Zana ("the Golden City"), the fictional city of Wakanda in the Hollywood blockbuster *Black Panther,* is even being peddled as a vision of the future African city. These new cities encourage a vision of escape, social segregation, and exclusion (Klopp and Paller 2019). Many African leaders are looking to Dubai, Singapore, and Chinese cities as models of high modernism that do not require democratizing the political system. Largely absent from these plans are the urban poor, as they espouse a vision of a "city without slums" (Huchzermeyer 2011). Examples of these projects include Tatu City and Konza Techno City in Nairobi, Hope City in Accra, Kigamboni in Dar es Salaam, Eko Atlantic in Lagos, and Cité le Fleuve in Kinshasa (Watson 2014; see Van Noorloos and Kloosterboer 2018 for an extended list).

To make way for these high-end developments, cities engage in what some scholars have called "urban cleaning," where government forces, including the police and military, destroy "illegal" slum settlements (Raleigh 2015). Evictions and displacements have occurred in Zimbabwe (2005, 2007), Angola (2007), Kenya (2008, 2009, 2010), Nigeria (2000, 2009), Sudan (2005), South Africa (2010), Ethiopia (2011, 2017), Uganda (2011), and many other countries. For different groups and individuals, the struggle for urban space is a battle for a higher economic position (Macharia 2007).

State coercion and social control are particularly evident in instances of forced evictions, where state governments use demolitions as a way to make urban slums intelligible (Ghertner 2010). Demolitions in Kenya were used to curb popular dissent and as a way to punish opponents and reward loyal followers (Klopp 2008). While justified as responses to "public nuisances" or public health crises, demolitions serve powerful political interests by attaching the problem facing cities to these "illegal spaces" that are morally objectionable (Ghertner 2008; Macharia 1992).

Africa's megacities are also attracting the attention of the diaspora. Many people in the diaspora whose families fled war, economic turmoil, or authoritarian governments from the 1970s to the 1990s are returning home. They often settle on the outskirts of large cities in gated communities and posh developments. For example, many Ghanaians returned to the country in 2000 when President John Kufuor won the presidency and the country experienced a turnover of power after the two-decade tenure of Jerry Rawlings. The returning diaspora brought financial resources, professional skills, and global connections. They invested in new businesses and embedded themselves in politics. The youth frequented malls and fancy bars, changing the entertainment options in the city. This is represented in the TV show *An African City*, which demonstrates the changing culture and society of African urban life. Even if members of the diaspora do not return to their home country, they send money home and invest in property, providing a source of funding that far exceeds foreign aid. (See Chapter 14 for further discussion.)

Africa's city dwellers confront their changing and rapidly growing cities in numerous ways. Citizens must confront livelihood and land-use changes, spatial alteration and social segregation, or physical displacement (Steel, Van Noorloos, and Otsuki 2019). Most new development projects in megacities are tailored to fit the needs of the elite. For example, new highways are built to cater to those with cars. To do so, structures are often demolished and street hawkers are relocated. Many residents who lose their homes because modern housing developments are built cannot afford the new accommodations and are forced to relocate. Urban construction provides politicians numerous opportunities to engage in corruption and rent seeking, undermining the public welfare. Traditional authorities, especially those who claim ownership or custodianship of urban property, flex their muscles and profit from skyrocketing land prices. The urban poor are typically the losers in the process.

Lagos Becomes a Global City

Lagos is constantly changing and growing. The city is characterized by its hustle, with people on the move—or stuck in traffic. Author Chimamanda Ngozi Adichie (2019) provides this apt description:

> A city in a state of shifting impermanence. A place still becoming. In newer Lagos, houses sprout up on land reclaimed from the sea, and in older Lagos, buildings are knocked down so that ambitious new ones might live. A street last seen six months ago is different today, sometimes imperceptibly so—a tiny store has appeared at a corner—and sometimes baldly so, with a structure gone, or shuttered, or expanded. Shops come and go. Today, a boutique's slender mannequin in a tightly pinned dress; tomorrow, a home accessories shop with gilt-edged furniture on display.

The population is estimated at 23.5 million people and grows by 85 people each hour. It is the eighth fastest growing city in Africa but likely to be its largest for the next century. It is the financial powerhouse of West Africa and the cultural heart that produces cutting-edge art houses and birthed Nollywood (the Nigerian Hollywood). For many years, it had a reputation as a place for thieves, corruption, anarchy, and internet scams. It is now celebrated for quality regional government, enhanced tax collection, and the development of a social contract between citizens and Lagos State. It has become a model city in West Africa (Kaplan 2014).

The transformation of Lagos has come with serious costs. Rising inequality and crime persist, and the traffic can bring life to a standstill. The urban poor feel the brunt of the urban transformation the hardest. Many have been displaced from their neighborhoods as their homes are demolished. The nonprofit organization Justice and Empowerment Initiatives (JEI) documents forty-two waterfront communities that are under threat of forced eviction with very little legal recourse because they do not have secure land rights. Forced evictions and demolitions are now a normal part of urban development strategies in Lagos and across the continent. For example, in November 2016, approximately 30,000 residents of the Otodo Gbame slum in Lagos were forcibly evicted from their homes (Paller 2017). Otodo Gbame is an ancestral fishing village located on the valuable waterfront. The Elegushi family of local chiefs claims ownership and custodianship over the land by customary law. Politicians and developers maintain close ties to the family. They use these land claims to advance their own agendas.

As cities grow, property values rise. Informal settlements, like Otodo Gbame, often sit on valuable property. To complicate matters, indigenous families and customary authorities have traditional standing as custodians of the land. Real estate deals are often not documented in the official record; property rights and land titles remain ambiguous and insecure. In this case, community members suspect that the Elegushi family plans to sell the land beneath Otodo Gbame to developers who will build homes for wealthy people. The family allegedly hired thugs to evict the slum dwellers, set fire to their homes, and demolished them with the backing of the police. When residents tried to put out the fires, the police reportedly fired tear gas and bullets, driving them into the Lagos Lagoon, where several drowned.

The action directly violated a recent court injunction that ordered a halt to the planned demolition of waterfront structures by the Lagos State government. While the slum dwellers appeared to have the court ruling on their side, the state government nonetheless moved forward with the demolition. The Nigerian Slum and Informal Settlement Federation, an advocacy group, sent a letter to the judge urging the importance of human rights, as well as emphasizing the residents' "right to the city." The group argued, "We belong to the city and we have a right to the city as well as a right to shelter and livelihood. Forceful eviction is not only unlawful, it is also ineffective."

The situation was quickly politicized. Officials offered their support for the demolition despite the fact that most residents supported the ruling party. The governor was slow to issue a statement, and the local government did not strongly defend the community. The residents protested and received backing from internationally funded human rights organizations such as Justice and Empowerment Initiatives. Amnesty International issued a statement declaring, "The authorities involved in this destruction are in flagrant violation of the law." In November 2016, a Lagos State High Court ordered the state government to consult with residents and provide relocation options before taking further action. The court found that the recent demolition was "inhuman and degrading."

Residents still do not have legal ownership of their homes. In March 2017, Lagos State authorities allegedly violated the court ruling and demolished some 4,700 structures in Otodo Gbame without proper notice. They were forced to move to other waterfront communities. The rest of the waterfront communities continue to face the threat of imminent demolition. In rapidly growing megacities like Lagos, the interests and goals of the political and economic elite brush up against the needs and desires of the poor. High-end development projects like Eko Atlantic—a six-square-mile filled-in island modeled after Singapore and Dubai—prioritize the needs of a small slice of the population, leaving behind millions of Nigerians who reside in the city.

Urban development results in winners and losers. These outcomes are the results of politics. In the case of Otodo Gbame, the lack of political representation or connections with traditional authorities or the state government left them without strong advocates to pursue their cause. As megacities grow and enter the global economy—a process that Adichie calls "still becoming"—more groups make claims on the city, privileging the strong and powerful over the rest.

Institutions and Development in Secondary Cities

Africa's megacities like Johannesburg, Kinshasa, and Lagos attract the bulk of scholarly and popular attention. But most of the population growth is actually happening in Africa's smaller cities. More than half of African cities have populations below 500,000 people, and cities with populations below 300,000 will house the majority of African urban dwellers in the next few decades (UN DESA 2015). The term "secondary cities" is used to designate those that have 30 percent or less of the largest city's population (Roberts 2014:124). These cities can be crucial for poverty alleviation because many households that exit out of absolute poverty do so by first transitioning into the nonfarm economy in growing towns, not by migrating to big cities (Christiaensen, De Weerdt, and Todo 2013). The UN even points to secondary cities as a crucial ingredient to drive inclusive growth across the continent (Habitat III 2016).

Secondary cities face an especially difficult challenge because of their narrow economic base, low levels of human capital, and insufficient local government revenues. Poverty in most African countries is characterized as a rural phenomenon, partially due to the lack of accurate and specific data on urban poverty. The use of the "poverty line" continues to be the dominant approach to estimate poverty, and this metric's reliance on household income masks clearly deplorable living conditions in many of the continent's cities, including overcrowding, poor sanitation, exposure to disease outbreaks like cholera, high unemployment rates, and vulnerability to natural disasters such as floods (Ghana Statistical Service 2013). In addition, these cities often struggle with local political tensions while being embedded in national institutional structures that undermine their potential for development. Four factors are especially important in enabling or constraining development in Africa's secondary cities: political and administrative institutions, chieftaincy affairs, natural resource endowments, and electoral competition.

Political and Administrative Institutions

Constitutional structure and decentralization policies greatly impact the urban development of secondary cities. The decision of a country to adopt a federal or unitary system of government affects state-city relationships as well as local control and the ability to generate revenue. In federal systems, there are typically three arenas of authority, including the municipality; regional, state, or county; and national governments. In addition, some countries that have adopted federal systems, like Ethiopia and Nigeria, allocate local citizenship rights that privilege indigenous populations, impacting the host-migrant relationships that develop over time. For example, Ethiopia's federation includes nine states that are "structured on the basis of settlement patterns, language, identity and consent of the people." Nigeria also has affirmative action policies for indigenes.

In contrast, unitary systems typically restrict decisionmaking to the local municipality. The autonomy that the unit has vis-à-vis the national government shapes urban development patterns. The administrative rules that determine decisionmaking, such as whether a mayor is elected or appointed, or which funds are available for development, can greatly impact the development of a city. The structure of unitary governments, and how they incorporate decentralization, varies widely. Ghana, for example, has 254 metropolitan/municipal/district assemblies. Population size is supposed to shape district creation, but political maneuverings and gerrymandering end up determining allocation. In addition, the president appoints the mayors (called metropolitan/municipal/district chief executives), giving the cen-

Lagos, Nigeria, will soon be one of the most populous cities in the world.

tral government immense power over local communities. Grossman and Lewis (2014) find that in Uganda, a unitary state with a history of decentralization reforms, administrative unit proliferation occurs where there is a confluence of interests between the national executive and local citizens and elites. This finding illuminates the importance of politics in the implementation of decentralization policies and the creation of administrative units.

Kenya's 2010 constitution restructured its state in a process of devolution, where forty-seven counties gained local autonomy and control over resources. County capitals, most of which are secondary cities, were significantly impacted, as local entrepreneurs and politicians were newly empowered, and a flood of public and private investment came to many of these cities. The status of cities as district, regional, or county capitals also impacts the development trajectory of secondary cities. But decentralization is not a silver bullet, and it can replace central government corruption with elite capture of local governments (Bardhan and Mookherjee 2006).

Chieftaincy Affairs

Urbanization often takes place in a context of already ambiguous land ownership. Urban growth places even more pressure on land and increases property values in towns and cities. This can spark new claims to land and territory by local elites. In many parts of the continent, traditional authorities control access to land, providing the basis of public authority (Lentz 2013; Lund 2016). But in many places, traditional authority is not clearly demarcated, and there are conflicts over legitimacy and power. Local conflicts over traditional authority can greatly impede urban development.

Traditional authorities often inhabit the position of chiefs. But the chieftaincy is not a static institution. Rather, politicians often infuse themselves in chieftaincy affairs, using their power to gain influence. They make linkages with chiefs to expropriate land for development or for their personal profits. Chiefs also establish ties to politicians to expand their own influence and extend their power at the grassroots (Paller 2014). The relationship between traditional authorities and African states is part of a complicated history; the British governed through indirect rule by empowering some traditional authorities at the expense of others (Mamdani 1996). The legacy of direct rule by the French also contributed to a politics of exclusion, where citizenship rights were restricted to certain groups (often the indigenous groups or "sons-of-the-soil") at the expense of migrants. This fueled civil conflict across the continent, including in Côte d'Ivoire, Cameroon, Nigeria, and elsewhere.

The colonial legacies are still felt today. For example, the roots of conflict in Ghana, including the Konkomba-Dagomba War (also called the Guinea Fowl War), the Bawku Conflict, and the Ga Mashie Chieftaincy Dispute all have deep historical origins. The major political parties have aligned with particular groups, exacerbating and deepening the conflicts. These competitions over territory and sons-of-the-soil conflicts cannot be separated from the underlying chieftaincy institutions that govern land at the grassroots. Where chieftaincy disputes exist, political divisions are more likely to undermine sustainable urban development. This is because divided cities are politically polarized cities, making residents less able to come together to advocate for policies that are in the best interests of the broader population (Trounstine 2016).

Natural Resource Endowments

Secondary cities often develop because they are the sites of natural resource endowments. They start as boomtowns, or settlements that undergo rapid population and economic growth because of the discovery of a precious natural resource. Mining and extraction have long played a central role in African economies, and early accounts of African urbanization placed the mining town at the center of analysis. Most of these studies examine southern African states like Zambia, Zimbabwe, and South Africa, but the boomtown phenomenon extends north and west to countries as diverse as Democratic Republic of Congo, Ghana, Guinea, and Nigeria.

Political economists have coined the "resource curse," suggesting that the discovery of natural resources undermines prospects for economic growth and democratic development (Ross 2015; Leonard and Straus 2003). A dominant view suggests that resource extraction without formal, private property rights contributes to socioeconomic underdevelopment and potential displacement (Barbier, Damania, and Léonard 2005). It can contribute to social dispossession, erode indigenous ways of life, and exacerbate patronage politics.

Resource extraction also shapes the development of cities. Kirshner and Power (2015) examine the impact of mining on Tete in Mozambique. They coined the term "extractive urbanism" to show how resource economies benefit some groups while displacing and dispossessing others. While the authors document significant infrastructure upgrades (especially with respect to road networks), they suggest that the urbanization process transforms "labor geographies" and contributes to new conflicts over land ownership. Franklin Obeng-Odoom (2014) examines the new "oil city" of Sekondi-Takoradi in Ghana. He finds that the oil boom provides new avenues of accumulation and an influx of foreign investment, but also cases of displacement and dispossession. Deborah Bryceson (2011) analyzes the growth of Katoro, Tanzania, and discusses how residents of the growing market town took control of the urbanization process and created a thriving center of trade and exchange.

These studies, and many others, highlight the importance of land ownership, underscore the potential for urban land grabs, and highlight speculative investments by outsiders (Goldman 2011; Sheppard et al. 2015). It is for these reasons that Zoomers et al. (2017:250) call for a "socially inclusive urbanization" that envisions "new tools for addressing the urban land rush that pay sufficient attention to the connectivity between rural and urban spheres as they evolve in the face of investment flows and land conversions." Cities with a recently discovered precious natural resource sometimes experience higher likelihoods of political tensions between host populations and migrant communities as well. Specifically, because these cities experience a large increase in speculative investments, existing land and legal institutions cannot adjudicate property ownership. Boomtowns then become politically polarized cities, contributing to the rise of conflict along partisan and ethnic lines.

Electoral Competition

The third wave of democratization that is discussed in great detail in Chapter 4 brought multiparty competition to most countries across Africa. Even in countries that have experienced democratic backsliding like Rwanda, Tanzania, and Uganda, electoral competition continues to be vibrant in its cities. Controlling cities provides a valuable source of mobilization power, making it easier to distribute patronage to well-established "machines" in urban areas. Cities that are opposition strongholds, however, often find it hard to demand resources from the central government and can be marginalized from a nation's economic development. Cities that support the ruling party might receive disproportionate shares of development expenditures, while those known to have voted for opposition parties might be discriminated against.

Recent evidence points to the tendency of central governments to sabotage opposition-controlled municipal areas in terms of the distribution of public resources. Resnick (2014) has shown how this phenomenon—what she calls vertically divided authority—contributes to undermining the delivery of urban services in Senegal, South Africa, and Uganda. In addition, Crook (2017) has found that "the dominance of clientelist forms of politics undermines the legitimacy of local taxation; where voters expect their representatives to provide specific pay-backs to themselves or their communities in return for support and payment of tax." He concludes, "It is extremely difficult to establish a 'collective interest' for the local government area." This can undermine municipal governance because the central government is often unwilling to support the distribution of resources to an area that is not under its political control (Parnell and Simon 2014). As cities become more important to national politics (e.g., Beall, Goodfellow, and Rodgers 2013), central governments establish new modes of control in growing cities.

The governance of African cities, therefore, is a "deeply political exercise" where the tension between national and urban governments shapes the prospects for urban development (Gore 2015:209). In particular, the question of whom governance is for shapes development processes but is largely left out of technocratic approaches to urban governance (Gore 2019). In addition, collaborations between governments and civil society organizations play an important role in African cities (Gore 2019:198), especially as international financing is increasingly necessary for infrastructural projects and development initiatives.

A focus on secondary cities demonstrates how important national-level institutions and countrywide economic policies are to urban development. Secondary cities are very susceptible to regional dynamics as well as to shifts in national government priorities. They are much more dependent on forces outside of their control than megacities, which can tap into a bigger tax base, global networks, and a well-established urban economy.

Secondary Cities in Northern Ghana

Most African countries have significant spatial inequalities of development. Due to the historical factors discussed earlier in this chapter, much of the growth and development occurred in primate cities and urban centers that received significant investments during the colonial era. Colonial regimes also privileged certain groups over others as a divide-and-rule strategy to maintain control. Most of these groups occupied coastal lands or southern territories. These development trajectories typically continued after independence. Ghana is illustrative of this north-south divide, where its northern regions have lagged behind in development since independence. The World Bank went so far as to say that twenty years of rapid economic development in Ghana "has done nothing to reduce the historical North–South divide in standards of living" (2011:28). Abdul-Gafaru Abdulai's research (e.g., Abdulai 2017; Abdulai and Hickey 2016) uncovers the political factors that deepen these spatial inequalities. He argues that northern politicians are underrepresented in government, especially in positions that make funding decisions. This has serious distributional consequences: more development funding, especially with respect to education, is allocated to the south than it is to the north.

It is in this political-economic context that secondary cities in northern Ghana are developing today. Rural residents are migrating to cities like Bolgatanga and Tamale in huge numbers, but the infrastructure and service provision cannot keep up with the growth. Across Ghana, the proportion of residents in large metropolitan areas with access to piped water experienced a downward trend during the 2000s. An increasing number of urban residents across all city classes do not have access to any toilet facilities, including private facilities, public toilets, and pit latrines. Between 2000 and 2010, there was an increase in the proportion of households without any toilet facility in all city size groups in Ghana. Yet secondary cities were hit the hardest: "The worst decline was witnessed in smaller urban centres, followed by smaller municipalities" (Molini and Paci 2015:19). To make matters worse, northern cities are dependent on the central government for financial transfers.

These cities are part of a broader network of urban agglomerations. Northern cities share a marginalized history, colonial legacies, cultural similarities, economic opportunities, and transport infrastructure. Tamale is the largest city in northern Ghana (with more than 900,000 people) and is one of the fastest growing cities in West Africa. It has become a hub for international nongovernmental organizations (NGOs) working in the region. The opening of the international airport in 2008 greatly increased accessibility. Like Bolgatanga (the capital of Upper East region), Tamale has benefited from its status as a regional capital of the Northern Region. Investments in the municipal hospital, university, and mosques have also sparked urban growth. As the city has grown, it has also become a refuge for those fleeing ethnic conflict in Bawku and violence surrounding chieftaincy disputes in Bolgatanga and Yendi. Many northerners who moved to southern cities like Kumasi and Accra are moving back to Tamale, or at the very least investing in homes in the city. Land speculation is now a prosperous business.

The regional capital status of Tamale helped it overtake Yendi as the largest city in the region. Tamale's central location, as well as its location on economic trade routes, spurred its population growth. Historically, Yendi was very powerful because it housed the palace of the *yaa naa*, the king of the Dagbon people. Today, Yendi is hampered by a serious chieftaincy conflict that has split the Dagbon people since 2002. The historical origins of the dispute are much deeper and have been politicized throughout Ghana's recent past.

Urbanization in Bolgatanga and Tamale is raising land values, contributing to land tensions between various families and chiefs. In turn, this has increased the authority of chiefs. In Bolgatanga, this has reignited a chieftaincy dispute, which has been politicized by local leaders and politicians. This constrains urban development because it causes a politically polarized city, undermining the potential for collective decisionmaking. It could have far larger consequences if the conflict escalates, as residents might flee to Tamale or other cities in the region. The urban development trajectories of these secondary cities in northern Ghana demonstrate how much of urban growth depends on regional dynamics, as well as the institutions and economic prospects that are shaped by national government.

Rebuilding Cities After War

Africa was the site of some of the most brutal wars and conflicts in the world during the 1980s and the 1990s. But as Scott Straus (2012) proclaimed in an *African Affairs* article entitled "Wars Do End!" the end of these wars has important implications for urban development: cities became the center of postconflict reconstruction. During the wars, cities were places of refuge, where villagers fled fighting and sought escape. But cities also became new sites of conflict. Cities in postconflict Africa are crucial sites of rebuilding the state (often from scratch), as well as places where ex-combatants and civilians have to reimagine a new future together.

Angola, Côte d'Ivoire, Liberia, Mozambique, Sierra Leone, and Somalia fought deadly civil wars between the 1970s and the 2000s. Their cities of Abidjan, Beira, Freetown, Hargeisa, Luanda, Maputo, Mogadishu, and Monrovia became sites for experiments in statebuilding once fighting ended. One of the first tasks is demilitarization and disarmament, especially among ex-combatants. Many warlords have already resettled in slum areas that are largely outside of state control. In Hargeisa, the government set up vocational training programs in the effort to reintegrate ex-combatants so that they could gain necessary skills for formal employment (Jhazbhay 2008). Similarly, Freetown tried a disarmament, demobilization, and reintegration (DDR) initiative in the early 2000s, to relatively successful results. Rebuilding the police and security forces, as well as finding new dispute resolution techniques, remains a serious challenge.

A second task is to integrate internally displaced persons (IDPs) into local society and the national polity. Many of these groups fought on different sides during the war, making peaceful coexistence a significant challenge. Land governance and allocation is one of the most highly contested issues after war, with groups making competing claims to the same land. In addition, politicians and policymakers are rebuilding the state and writing new constitutions, attempting to secure their interests in the new nation. These political struggles often play out at the neighborhood level. In addition, cities become the base for humanitarian aid and expatriate life. This can lead to the proliferation of private security forces, gated communities, and extremely expensive goods and services. This problem is particularly pronounced in cities like Luanda in Angola, and Juba in South Sudan.

The city is also where citizens and excombatants alike attempt to imagine a new future. Identities form, urban citizenships are created, and alliances emerge. But residents are also stuck with the legacies of the war, which are shaped by the built environment (Hoffman 2017). The rebuilding of Mogadishu represents the challenges of postconflict urban reconstruction, as its redevelopment is occurring amid serious security challenges. The city remains a target of al-Shabaab terrorist attacks. In many ways, the city is rebuilding without a national political settlement. Journalist Andrew Harding characterizes Mogadishu as "a city of grudges, score-settling, and fiercely whispered judgments" (2016:xv). Clan alliances structure politics in the city, playing a far more important role in governance and daily affairs than formal institutions. Dating back to the Siad

Barre regime before the war, the control of Mogadishu is synonymous with control of the Somali state.

In post-independence Somalia, clan leaders and politicians have captured state resources to empower their own clans and communities. Today, the city is divided into three unequal parts: North Mogadishu, South Mogadishu, and the Medina (Marchal 2006). The "Green Line" separated the north from the south, marking a distinct boundary between different political interest groups. While the Green Line does not currently exist in reality, "it remains in people's minds because of the violent crisis among the Abgal [a subclan of the Hawiye] that is playing out in North Mogadishu as well as the Abgal's collective attitude towards factions in South Mogadishu who, they contest, do not have a right to live as equals in the capital city" (Marchal 2006:215). Struggles over who owns Mogadishu continue to structure daily affairs and divide the population. But at the same time, remittances flow into the country, raising property values. Residents of the diaspora return home, creating new divisions between people who stayed in the country during the war and those who fled to Kenya, the United Kingdom, or the United States. The rebuilding of Mogadishu is clearly a contentious political process.

Confronting Climate Change

Africa's rapid urbanization is also taking place in the context of climate change. Africa's cities are already feeling the impact. Droughts inland push migrants to cities, while rising sea levels threaten inhabited coastlines. Ninety-eight percent of African cities experienced an increase in temperatures between 1990 and 2015 (Atlas of the Human Planet 2018). Scholars predict that African countries will be especially hit hard by climate change. Parnell and Walawege (2011) sound the alarm: "Africa's rapidly expanding and very fragile urban areas (many of them coastal) are likely to be the major locus of the impact of GEC [global environmental change] over the next thirty to fifty years because of their fast rate of population growth and weak state capacity to manage GEC induced urbanisation and GEC at the city scale."

Cities across the continent are feeling the pressure from climate change. Zimbabwean cities Bulawayo and Harare are rationing water because of a water crisis a year after Cape Town, South Africa, narrowly avoided Day Zero (the day on which there would be no more potable water). Water is in short supply in Maputo (Mozambique), Buake (Côte d'Ivoire), and Accra (Ghana). Mudslides in Freetown, Sierra Leone, killed at least 400 people in August 2017. Hundreds of people are displaced in Saint Louis, Senegal, as sea levels rise and fisherfolk lose their livelihoods. Coastal areas generate 56 percent of West Africa's GDP (World Bank 2019), and these are some of the areas most affected by climate change.

Governments approach climate change in a very different way than ordinary people. Governments often blame the urban poor, and scapegoat squatters and residents living in extralegal and informal settlements. For example, after flooding in Dar es Salaam (Schofield and Gubbels 2019), Lagos, and Accra (Paller 2019), authorities quickly identified homes along waterways they deemed a threat and marked them with an X. They swiftly demolished the structures. Rwanda has proposed a $5 billion "green city" in Kigali that it plans to replicate across the country if successful. International financial institutions are partnering with national and municipal governments to help make African cities resilient and sustainable. Accra, Addis Ababa, Cape Town, Dakar, Durban, Kigali, Lagos, Nairobi, and Paynesville were all part of the Rockefeller Foundation's 100 Resilient Cities initiative. This project supported cities as they developed a road map to respond to shocks like earthquakes, fires, and floods but also to prepare for the daily environmental stresses that affect urban life.

It is becoming increasingly clear that resilient cities require the strength and cooperation of local communities, many of which settle in informal areas. This approach requires "climate change adaptation," or moving beyond technocratic approaches to development, and instead harnessing the creative potential of citizens. Climate change adaptation requires "a competent, capable local government that is able and willing to work with the inhabitants of the settlements most at risk" (Dodman, Bicknell, and Satterthwaite 2012:362).

Cape Town's experience confronting its water crisis provides some important lessons (Alexander 2019). The city warned its residents that Day Zero was on the horizon. The national government reallocated water from surrounding agricultural regions to Cape Town. The municipal government enforced tariffs and enforcement prohibitions on heavy users. Swimming pools and lawn care were prohibited. The city also implemented a new pressure system. The city relied on behavioral nudges to change behavior, relying on shaming and honor mechanisms to limit water usage. In turn, residents did change their behavior, especially after a widespread drought-awareness campaign. They discussed the issue at community meetings, and the water crisis became a central issue in civic engagement campaigns. The case of Cape Town illustrates the importance of government-community partnerships in combating climate change. National governments, municipalities, and local communities need to work together to coproduce solutions that are in the best interests of all residents (Ostrom 1996).

Coastal populations, especially fisherfolk, are feeling the pressures of climate change. Rising sea levels, in addition to increased activity of foreign trawlers from countries like China, are undermining indigenous fishing practices and destroying livelihoods. This is a huge problem on the Gulf of Guinea in West Africa, where Gambian, Ghanaian, Nigerian, and Senegalese fisherfolk are unable to catch enough fish to support themselves. Already, thousands of coastal residents have been displaced, and more climate refugees are projected in the coming decades. Coastal communities are likely to be hit the hardest.

There is now a vibrant debate about how to plan for climate change in African cities. Vanesa Castán Broto sums up the challenge: "Climate change only exacerbates the mismatch between planners' sketches of the city and its actual dynamics" (2014:5). Leading urbanist Susan Parnell suggests that cities are now front and center in the international community's policies of sustainable development and will be instrumental to how African countries confront climate change in the future (Parnell and Walawege 2011).

Combating Climate Change in Beira, Mozambique

On March 13, 2019, Cyclone Idai tore through Beira, one of Mozambique's largest cities. The Buzi and Pungue Rivers that flow through the city flooded. The Red Cross declared that more than 90 percent of the 500,000-person city was destroyed. Electricity was cut off while city streets lay under more than six feet of water. More than 146,000 people were displaced from their homes, and at least 500 people were killed. More than 1,000 people contracted cholera in the aftermath of the disaster. Rescue workers struggled to reach areas devastated by the storm, and it was declared the worst natural disaster to hit southern Africa in the past two decades. The storm spread inland, affecting communities across Malawi and Zimbabwe as well. Former first lady of Mozambique, Graca Machel, provided this straightforward assessment: "[Beira] will go down in history as having been the first city to be completely devastated by climate change."

Climate experts suggest that climate change is driving sea-level rise and extreme temperatures, contributing to more rainfall, stronger storm surges, and heavier wind. Beira's mayor Daviz Simango explains, "We have never seen this before. Our infrastructures were prepared to handle winds up to 120 kilometres (75 miles) per hour, but this time we were subjected to winds of 240 kph" (150 miles) per hour (Nhamirre and Gumede 2019). Mozambique is the country third most vulnerable to climate change in Africa (behind Somalia and Madagascar) due to its long coastline, extreme poverty, and poor infrastructure.

Beira has been preparing for climate change for many years. It has long been considered one of Africa's climate-vulnerable cities due to coastal erosion and urban flooding. To tackle the challenge, the city secured foreign investment and aid to improve water, drainage, and sanitation infrastructure, as well as to rehabilitate river flow and develop green spaces. Environmental sustainability protocols and procedures have guided real estate development, transport improvements, coastal protection, and port dredging. The Arab Bank for Economic Development in Africa, the World Bank, the European Union, the KfW Development Bank, the German Society for International Cooperation (GIZ), the Department for International Development (DFID), and the Chinese government all invested in the modernization of the city. The Netherlands is perhaps the most influential development partner (Shannon et al. 2018); it helped craft a master plan for the city and institutionalized the Beira Partnership. This partnership resulted in the public-private partnership called the Land Development Company, which was tasked with generating revenues from urban expansion.

Murtah Shannon's research (2019a, 2019b) does an excellent job of uncovering the important political factors that shape Beira's development. Most notably, Beira is a stronghold of the Mozambican National Resistance (RENAMO) opposition political party. Because of this, the city has been marginalized and neglected by the central government because of residents' lack of support for the governing Mozambican Liberation Front (FRELIMO) party. These political parties have a violent past, as clashes between their supporters led to a bloody civil war between 1977 and 1992. Beira has long been of regional strategic importance because of its port, dating back to its founding in 1887 as a concession to the Mozambique Company to meet the demands of an "effective occupation" put forth by the Berlin Conference. In the 1970s, Rhodesia supported RENAMO. Zimbabwe later sent foreign troops into the city so that it could access the port during the civil war. The foreign intervention contributed to enhanced security, making it a refuge for many people fleeing the conflict (Sidaway 1993). Beira has always been seen as a gateway to the world and the global economy.

The city became a powerful node in the "Beira corridor," a strategic region in central Mozambique that experienced natural gas finds off the coast that led to rapid economic growth in the early 2000s. During this period, the mayor of Beira split from RENAMO and established his own opposition party, the Democratic Movement of Mozambique (MDM). He won the 2008, 2013, and 2018 elections. The political factionalism—what Resnick (2014) terms vertically divided authority—has frustrated urban development, and the threat of FRELIMO interference is a constant worry for the municipal government. This has forced the municipality to go it alone and bypass the central government in search of international donors.

Beira's climate change vulnerability, as well as its marginalization by the central state, made it almost entirely dependent on international aid. In the 1980s, Mozambique privatized the port with support from Western lenders. The Netherlands has focused its attention on the city, seeking public-private partnerships to advance Dutch interests (Shannon et al. 2018). These massive infrastructural investments have not come without challenges, particularly around land. Development projects have displaced local communities from their land, and ambiguity around land security and title continues to sow divisions in local neighborhoods. Urban farmers are especially affected because there are no laws that protect their rights in urban areas (Shannon et al. 2018). This suggests how urban resilience depends on the coordination between local communities, municipal governments, central authorities, and international donors.

The challenges in Beira will intensify. The population is projected to double in ten or fifteen years, placing more pressure on infrastructure and land access. The World Bank has approved a $90 million grant to support Mozambique's disaster management plan, as well as an additional $545 million to Malawi and Mozambique to rebuild infrastructure and improve the water supply. The Netherlands continues to support projects in line with the city's master plan. But perhaps most importantly, struggles over power and decisionmaking can erode these efforts, demonstrating how the contentious politics of African urbanization shapes the continent's efforts to combat climate change.

The Future of Urban Africa

Cities are forced to build more housing, provide jobs, and construct infrastructure for their growing populations. These challenges are difficult enough, but cities are also confronting climate change and the need to reconstruct their societies and polities after civil wars. They are beset by entrenched political and institutional legacies that constrain sustainable development. In these ways, Africa's rapid urbanization is creating contradictory outcomes. It is enabling the emergence of a growing middle class that is transforming the continent. Rapid population growth, new forms of urban planning, and massive infrastructure development provide an incredible opportunity for development. Megacities will sprawl and smaller cities and towns will grow into economic powerhouses. Foreign companies and governments are moving fast into these new markets, shifting the geopolitics of the world.

But inequalities between social classes and ethnic groups are deepening, which in turn polarizes political divisions. Cities are politically contentious. The "right to the city" is negotiated by host populations and new migrants, political parties competing for votes, community leaders seeking to extend their own power over urban space, and property developers hoping to make a quick profit. Like all processes of urbanization across the globe, the future of African cities will be a political struggle over ownership, control, and belonging in the city.

8

Public Health

Amy S. Patterson

The World Health Organization (WHO) defines health as not merely the absence of disease but as "a state of complete physical, mental and social well-being" (WHO 1948). In many ways, Africa has made significant progress on health: life expectancy increased from thirty-five years in 1960 to sixty-one years in 2015; measles deaths declined by 50 percent between 1999 and 2014; smallpox was eradicated in 1979; and polio, trachoma, and river blindness have almost been eradicated (World in Data 2019; WHO 2014). Yet Africa still lags behind other regions on many health indicators: life expectancy; morbidity (sickness) and disability from neglected tropical diseases like schistosomiasis; infant and child mortality; maternal mortality; deaths from road traffic accidents, acquired immunodeficiency syndrome (AIDS), tuberculosis (TB), and malaria; and premature deaths from cancers (GBD 2018). These indicators show that the human right to health—what the International Covenant on Economic, Social and Cultural Rights describes as the "right of everyone to the enjoyment of the highest attainable standard of physical and mental health"—remains aspirational (Davies 2010:63).

The primary purpose of this chapter, which is divided into five sections, is to explore the unique aspects of healthcare on the African continent. The first section examines health governance, or the large number of institutions and organizations, competing approaches, and multiple issue sectors involved in health. Coordinating health responses among multiple players presents challenges that affect achieving the right to health. The next two sections examine communicable diseases, most notably malaria, AIDS, TB, and Ebola (section two), and noncommunicable diseases, such as cancers, diabetes, cardiovascular diseases, chronic respiratory diseases, and mental health disorders (section three). These two sections show how, unlike high-income countries such as the United States, most African countries face a "double disease burden": both communicable diseases and noncommunicable diseases cause high levels of mortality, morbidity, and disability (Agyepong et al. 2017). Section four explores why health remains a low political priority for donors, African governments, and the public. A concluding section outlines future African health challenges.

Governing Health: Multiple Actors, Competing Approaches, and Different Sectors

African health governance includes intergovernmental organizations (e.g., the WHO), multilateral donors such as the World Bank, bilateral donors (e.g., the United States), private foundations such as the Gates Foundation, national governments, nongovernmental organizations, community-based organizations, faith-based organizations, and advocates. This large number of actors makes coordination, communication, and accountability difficult (Fidler 2010).

In 2015, donors provided $36.4 billion for health globally with over one-third of this money going to Africa (IHME 2015). While a sizable amount, donors finance only 9 percent of total healthcare expenditures in Africa. Because they focus on big ticket items like malaria control, AIDS, and immunizations, and because of their expertise and professional staff, donors have significant influence (Ogbuoji et al. 2019). For example, even though it spends less on global health than the US government, the Gates Foundation, or the World Bank (IHME 2015), the WHO can shape global health priorities. It capitalizes on its long history since 1948, its placement in the UN system, and its membership of 194 countries. However, because it depends on UN member states for funding and because it is structured into six autonomous regional offices, the WHO's influence is tenuous. At the country level, it must support national priorities (Patterson and Gill 2019; Youde 2012).

Since the 1990s, the World Bank, the Global Fund to Fight AIDS, Tuberculosis and Malaria (Global Fund), the Gates Foundation, and Gavi (the Vaccine Alliance) have overtaken the WHO's influence. A multilateral lending agency established in 1946, the World Bank has provided significant funding for health since the 1990s, including support for African AIDS programs in the early 2000s. Since the 1990s, it has focused on market-based solutions for health-system strengthening (Youde 2012). Established in 2002, the Global Fund provides grants to low- and middle-income countries to address AIDS, TB, and malaria. It is innovative because countries must establish a country coordinating mechanism—a committee of officials from government, civil society, the private sector, and donor agencies—that applies for and administers country grants. This structure facilitates broad participation and country ownership, but it can make decisionmaking inefficient (Patterson 2018). The Global Fund is also innovative because even though it receives donations from countries (the United States is the largest contributor), foundations, and corporations, it funds projects based solely on their technical merit. Each year it disburses roughly $4 billion to projects in almost one hundred countries (Global Fund 2019).

The Gates Foundation spent $2.6 billion on health in 2015 (IHME 2015). In Africa, it finances programs for polio eradication, malaria prevention, child and maternal health, reproductive health, and new health technologies. It is also the second biggest donor to the WHO (Huet and Paun 2017). The foundation illustrates how private entities (which provided 25 percent of global health funding in 2015) can drive innovation because they are not beholden to donors or national governments (Bendavid et al. 2017). Critics counter that the size of the Gates Foundation allows it to set the global health agenda. For example, in 2000, the foundation helped to establish Gavi, a collaboration that has increased immunization rates for childhood diseases across Africa. Overseen by a board of officials from donor and developing countries, the Gates Foundation, the vaccine industry, the WHO, the World Bank, the United Nations Children's Fund (UNICEF), and civil society groups, Gavi provides funds to UNICEF to purchase and distribute vaccines in low-income countries while NGOs and host-country governments oversee service delivery and vaccine education. Gavi incentivizes vaccine research, production, and distribution by guaranteeing a market for products (Clinton and Sridhar 2018).

Bilateral donors also shape African health programs, and over half of bilateral health funds go to the continent. In 2016, the United States was the largest donor for global health, providing 42 percent (over $10 billion) of all donor funds. The next largest bilateral donors were the United Kingdom ($2.4 billion), Germany ($1.2 billion), France ($971 million), and Japan ($871 million) (Donor Tracker 2017). In 2019, the United States spent over 50 percent of its health funds on AIDS. Other issues with significant US funding included maternal and child health (11 percent of funds), malaria (9 percent), and family planning and reproductive health (6 percent) (KFF 2019b). In general, European countries fund basic health programs, like child nutrition and maternal, neonatal, and child health. China is a rising donor in Africa, providing over $5 billion between 2000 and 2013, primarily for health infrastructure and malaria control. It focuses health aid on countries with which it has strong export relations (Shajalal et al. 2017).

All these global actors collaborate with African governments, which fund 44 percent of healthcare expenditures (Ogbuoji et al. 2019). Yet even though it may seem that donors can dictate health priorities, the picture is more complicated. State sovereignty means that governments must approve policies and programs, and the donors' need to achieve project results means they cannot ignore government objectives (Whitfield 2009). Even in a country like Malawi where 90 percent of the government's health budget comes from donors, government officials illustrate agency in policymaking and implementation (Anderson and Patterson 2017). Some officials selectively use health data to emphasize particular problems, make dramatic media pleas for donor support, and establish national health committees to lock in donor funding (Barnes, Brown, and Harman 2015). Some countries also seek private funding sources to help them advance their interests. For example, in 2018, the Gates Foundation agreed to pay $76 million that Nigeria owed Japan for its polio campaign because Nigeria had reached the benchmark of 80 percent polio immunization coverage "in at least one round each year in very high risk areas across 80 percent of the country's local government areas" (Kazeem 2018). The payment helped the government's budget deficit and the foundation's goal of polio eradication.

Outside the realm of government, NGOs, faith-based organizations, community-based organizations, and advocates are crucial health actors. International NGOs like Africare or local NGOs like the Zambian Cancer Society receive grants from donors to implement programs on issues ranging from maternal health to cancer prevention. Religiously based health centers, many of which were established by the colonial-era missionaries, provide roughly 40 percent of health care in Africa (Patterson 2011). Religious leaders and institutions also educate millions about health topics, including AIDS, malaria prevention, and, increasingly, noncommunicable diseases such as hypertension (high blood pressure) and diabetes (Abanilla et al. 2011). Community groups provide countless hours of labor caring for people with AIDS, transporting the sick, and supporting people with mental health disorders. At times, these caregiving activities are socially isolating, physically exhausting, and economically devastating (Maes 2014). For some people, caregiving is an action associated with citizenship. Caregivers' love of country and belief that governments must be accountable for public health motivate their activities (Patterson 2019). Health advocacy organizations like the Treatment Action Campaign and the Tanzanian Tobacco Control Forum try to influence national health policies, although they often lack resources and access to politicians. For example, the Treatment Action Campaign successfully used mass mobilization to lobby the South African government to distribute life-extending antiretroviral therapy to people living with HIV, the virus that causes AIDS (Mbali 2013).

Competing approaches to health also complicate governance. One tension is between disease-specific (vertical) programs like the US President's Emergency Plan for AIDS Relief (PEPFAR) and comprehensive approaches like the WHO's promotion of universal health coverage. Although highly efficient, vertical programs may ignore the complexity of health and distract policymakers from improving health systems (Storeng 2014). In contrast, universal health coverage, as agreed to by UN member states in 2015 as part of the seventeen Sustainable Development Goals, seeks to ensure that all people receive comprehensive prevention, treatment, rehabilitation, and palliative care without incurring financial hardship (WHO 2019c). In low-income countries, primary healthcare workers, such as nurses and community health workers, often provide this coverage. These individuals educate about health issues, help with management of chronic conditions such as diabetes, and follow up on patients with mental health disorders.

A second tension revolves around public-private partnerships and their use of performance-based financing. Promoted by the World Bank to foster efficiency in service delivery, public-private partnerships like Gavi include governments, NGOs, foundations, and private companies. Opponents criticize their focus on measurable results, inclusion of businesses that profit from the partnership, and the use of simplistic, technical health solutions (Storeng 2014). They are also criticized for utilizing performance-based financing, which requires that the recipient (e.g., Ministry of Health) achieve a particular target (e.g., a specific number of people tested for HIV) in order to get the next installment of project funding. Achieving targets can be challenging for health systems that stress primary healthcare because providers must manage long-term health conditions and address overall patient well-being (Low-Beer et al. 2007). Finally, public-private partnerships may erode health equity, if their focus on efficiency prevents them from serving hard-to-reach populations or embracing expensive treatments (Buse and Waxman 2001). Yet Gavi's success shows that public-private partnerships can achieve positive outcomes.

Overall, critics of vertical programs and public-private partnerships argue that promoting health requires collaboration across sectors to treat diseases and to address their underlying causes. Maternal mortality, or the death of about 200,000 African women annually during pregnancy or childbirth, provides an example (WHO 2014). Narrow, health-focused solutions include training more skilled birth attendants to assist women in pregnancy and childbirth and providing medications to stop bleeding in labor. A multisectoral approach would include the provision of transportation from rural areas to health clinics, and the enforcement of laws against child marriage, since teen marriage leads to pregnancy among adolescents, who face higher risks of birth complications. A multisectoral approach also would provide reproductive technologies to prevent unwanted pregnancies; promote economic opportunities so households do not resort to marrying their girls (and sometimes boys) before eighteen years of age; increase access to education to prevent early marriage and teen pregnancy; and educate communities about the potential risks of home-based births (Garenne 2015; Misunas, Gastón, and Cappa 2019). A multisectoral approach demands cooperation, coordination, and leadership from the global to local levels, factors lacking in health governance.

Communicable Diseases

Caused by a virus, bacteria, fungus, or parasite, communicable diseases spread from one individual to another through respiration, saliva, fecal-oral transmission, blood, sexual transmission, and/or vertical transmission from mother to child during pregnancy, childbirth, or breastfeeding (DeLaet and DeLaet 2012:51–52). Malaria, AIDS, and TB constitute much of this burden, although the Ebola outbreaks in West Africa and the Democratic Republic of Congo have raised global attention to communicable diseases and highlighted how weak health infrastructure and public distrust of governments can undermine health.

Malaria, AIDS, and TB

Even though malaria deaths globally fell 50 percent between 2000 and 2014 and deaths among African children under five years old declined 58 percent (WHO 2014), malaria remains a significant health challenge in Africa, particularly for children, pregnant women, and those with the HIV virus. Spread via the female *Anopheles* mosquito, the parasite kills almost 1 million people annually (mostly children), decreases worker productivity, and depletes household resources. Severe malaria (cerebral malaria) during childhood can lead to brain injury and the onset of epilepsy, making the long-term health and education costs of malaria infection for those children and their families significant (Christensen and Eslick 2015). Since 1998, the Roll Back Malaria Partnership, a consortium of 500 governments, donors, and NGOs, has promoted the use of insecticide-treated bed nets, rapid malaria diagnostic testing, and artemisinin-based combination therapies. As of 2019, these WHO-approved therapies, which are made from a compound extracted from the plant *Artemisia annua*, could successfully treat all strains of malaria present globally (RBM 2019). In 2019, Ghana, Kenya, and Malawi launched a pilot vaccine with only a 40 percent efficacy rate in hopes of driving down the number of cases of cerebral malaria and child deaths (Masina 2019).

While malaria disproportionately affects children, AIDS, a disease with no cure, affects people in their most productive years. HIV transmission can occur through intravenous drug use and homosexual relations, but most HIV infections in Africa have occurred through heterosexual relations. Africans comprise two-thirds of the world's 36 million people living with HIV. Southern Africa has two-thirds of the world's children living with HIV, with almost all infected vertically. AIDS remains a leading cause of death among African women of reproductive age (KFF 2019a:2), and over 25 million Africans

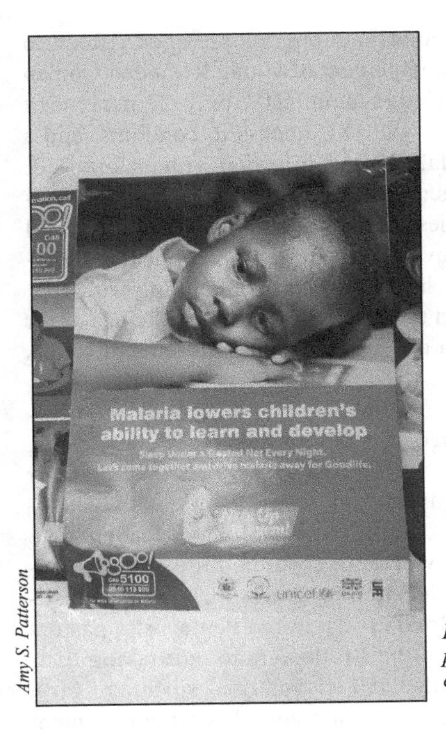

Amy S. Patterson

Health education poster on malaria prevention in a rural community health center in Eastern Region, Ghana.

were living with HIV in 2017 (UNAIDS 2018:20). HIV prevalence, or the percentage of people aged fifteen to forty-nine estimated to be living with HIV, varies across Africa, from 27 percent in Eswatini to 0.4 percent in Senegal (*Economist* 2018; KFF 2019a). Southern Africa has the highest HIV prevalence because of widespread, long-term male migration that contributed to multiple sexual partners (Campbell 2003). However, political inaction in the 1980s and 1990s in most African countries exacerbated the epidemic, as officials downplayed the risk and denied cases. In an extreme example, in 2000 then South African president Thabo Mbeki questioned the link between HIV and AIDS; refused to provide nevirapine, a medicine that prevents mother-to-child transmission of HIV; and discouraged use of antiretroviral therapy. The president's actions led some people to avoid HIV testing and delayed the provision of antiretroviral therapy to millions. Over 300,000 people died prematurely because of the government's unwillingness to provide medications (Chigwedere and Essex 2010; Fassin 2007).

HIV prevention methods include sexual abstinence, avoiding sexual relations with partners whose HIV status is unknown, and condom use, although individuals need knowledge and empowerment to use these tools.

HIV knowledge is incomplete, particularly among people aged fifteen to twenty-four years. For example, while 65 percent of young Rwandan women had correct and comprehensive knowledge about HIV, only 23 percent of young South African men did (UNAIDS 2018). Access to condoms, and a willingness to use them, is also low. Malnutrition, infection with malaria, TB, and sexually transmitted infections increase vulnerability to HIV (Stillwaggon 2006). Poverty may exacerbate these health conditions, although not all people living with HIV are living in poverty. Poverty also complicates adherence to antiretroviral therapy, because impoverished people living with HIV may be unable to pay for transportation to clinics to get their medicines or for the food needed to prevent the nausea and weakness that these medications can cause (Kalofonos 2010).

Religious leaders and institutions have played a multifaceted and complex role in AIDS. Some have hampered effective responses. In some cases, this is by saying that AIDS results from "sinful behaviors" like adultery or prostitution, pronouncements that stigmatize and blame people with the disease and cause people to avoid HIV testing. Some religious leaders also affect HIV prevention policies for the worse. In Uganda, for example, Pentecostal pastors designed youth HIV education programs that stressed abstinence and condemned condom use (Boyd 2015). Some Pentecostal pastors and traditional healers have even urged their followers to quit taking their antiretroviral medications, asserting that if believers had sufficient faith then God would heal them. Not surprisingly, following this pronouncement has led to deaths in some cases (van Djik et al. 2014).

Other religious leaders and institutions are at the forefront of leading effective AIDS responses. Religious leaders led anti-stigma and HIV education campaigns in Ghana and Senegal (Patterson 2011). The Catholic Church in Zambia began the first home-based care program for people dying from AIDS in southern Africa (Iliffe 1995). In 1998, religious leaders formed the African Network for Religious Leaders Living with or Personally Affected by HIV and AIDS to provide comprehensive HIV education in churches. Some even included discussions of condom use. Many religious leaders say that antiretroviral therapy is a "gift from God" and urge their followers to take their medications as prescribed (Patterson 2011).

Gender affects HIV prevention and treatment. Women comprise 56 percent of Africans living with HIV (UNAIDS 2018). On average, African women have fewer economic opportunities, less education, and lower incomes than men do, making them more likely to depend on male partners (Anderson 2015). This dependence, as well as the societal emphasis on marriage and motherhood, makes it hard for a woman to deny sexual relations with a male partner (Baylies and Bujra 2000). Intimate partner violence, a practice that affects 25 percent of Zambian women, also makes abstinence or demanding condom use difficult (UNAIDS 2018). Young women may forge sexual relationships with older men ("sugar daddies" or "blessers") in return for money for school fees, food, or housing (Fallon 2018). Because older men usually have had previous sexual partners, the practice increases young women's HIV risk. Indeed, 25 percent of new HIV infections in Africa are among young women. Gender roles also affect HIV testing and treatment. Because testing often occurs in antenatal clinics, more women than men know their HIV status and can access antiretroviral therapy (UNAIDS 2018). As a result, more men living with HIV than women living with HIV die from AIDS. Social constructions of masculinity cause men to delay seeking treatment or to deny their HIV status. Men often perceive AIDS clinics to be "women's spaces," where healthcare workers blame them for AIDS. As breadwinners, men also say they cannot spend hours in clinic lines to seek care (Skovdal et al. 2011).

HIV infection makes a person twenty to thirty times more likely to develop active TB, which is the top killer of people living with HIV. In 2018, TB infected over 10 million people worldwide (WHO 2018). Spread through sneezing and coughing, the TB bacteria thrives in overcrowded environments with poor healthcare and low access to TB testing and treatment. In South Africa, a country with an 18 percent HIV prevalence, over 300,000 people became infected with TB and almost 80,000 died in 2017 (TBFacts.org 2019; UNAIDS 2018). Even though TB cases have declined globally, cases of multidrug-resistant TB and extensively drug-resistant TB have increased. TB is treatable with antimicrobial drugs, but because the treatment lasts six to nine months, adherence is difficult. Treatment for multidrug-resistant TB and extensively drug-resistant TB has been less effective, requiring at least eighteen months and causing serious side effects (WHO 2018). In early 2020, results from a study of a new six-month therapy showed a 90 percent success rate, significantly advancing treatment for drug-resistant forms of TB (Emery 2020). People with TB face stigma and isolation, factors that undermine testing and treatment (*Frontline* 2014).

AIDS, TB, and malaria are costly. Malaria reduces a country's gross national product by 5–6 percent for countries with a high disease burden. In 2014, for example, Ghanaian businesses lost $6.5 million due to malaria (Nonvignon et al. 2016). Because they primarily affect productive adults, AIDS and TB cause families to divert productive labor and household funds to care for the sick. When breadwinners die, households can become destitute. AIDS has caused businesses to pay sizable sums to train new workers, and it has orphaned millions of children (Hunter 2003). These outcomes caused experts in the late 1990s to predict that AIDS would destroy African economies, render African militaries ineffective, and foster political instability (Price-Smith 2009). In 2000, the UN Security Council held a special session to discuss AIDS as a threat to national and international security (Patterson 2006; Rushton 2011).

Many of these dire predictions did not materialize (O'Keefe 2012), primarily because of the global AIDS response. Donor mobilization reflected global AIDS activism and post-9/11 concerns that AIDS would destabilize countries. In addition to World Bank efforts and the establishment of the Global Fund (see above), US president George W. Bush, under pressure from evangelical Christians, set up PEPFAR in 2003 (Kapstein and Busby 2013; Patterson 2006). By 2019, PEPFAR had contributed over $90 billion to AIDS programs globally (KFF 2019c). Most funding is channeled through US NGOs (e.g., Catholic Relief Services), government agencies (e.g., Centers for Disease Control and Prevention), and universities (e.g., Johns Hopkins School of Public Health). PEPFAR has focused on prevention of HIV transmission (most recently among girls fifteen to twenty-four years old), prevention of mother-to-child transmission, care programs for AIDS orphans and vulnerable children, livelihood support for people living with HIV, and distribution of antiretroviral therapy (US Department of State 2018). During its first five years, one-third of prevention funds went to programs that emphasized abstinence and monogamy in relationships. After the removal of this requirement in 2008, PEPFAR has gradually decreased funding for these programs, primarily because large-scale studies show that they have little effect on sexual behavior (Stanford Medicine 2016). By late 2018, PEPFAR had supported over 15 million voluntary medical male circumcisions, because studies show circumcision, a rare practice in Southern and East Africa, reduces the rate of HIV transmission to men by roughly 60 percent (US Department of State 2018; Wamai et al. 2015). Through promoting HIV testing, the AIDS response has increased the number of people who can prevent HIV transmission and access treatment (Kharsany and Karim 2016).

Before 2003, only about 50,000 Africans could access the treatment they needed. The medications, which had been available in the West since 1996, cost over $10,000 per person per year, a price that reflected the fact that the pharmaceutical companies had patent protection through the World Trade Organization's TRIPs Agreement. TRIPs (Trade Related Intellectual Property Rights) gives the creator the sole right to make and sell the product for twenty years. Although some countries like Brazil, India, and Thailand produced generic AIDS medications, these were not available in Africa. Through activism and new funding sources, this situation changed (Kapstein and Busby 2013). PEPFAR and the Global Fund now purchase generic AIDS medications, and in 2017, 70 percent of Africans in need of antiretroviral therapy could access it (Nash, Yotebieng, and Sohn 2018). Because consistent adherence to antiretroviral therapy reduces by 96 percent the likelihood that a person with HIV will sexually transmit the virus to another person (Cohen et al. 2011), the WHO recommends that individuals begin treatment as soon as they test positive. Access to this therapy led to a 39 percent decline in AIDS deaths and an increase in life expectancy in Southern and East Africa between 2005 and 2013 (KFF 2019a).

Because of its significant funding and institutionalization, the AIDS response has shaped health and development in Africa. Donors have prioritized AIDS, even in contexts with low HIV prevalence where local people desire other health initiatives (Benton 2015; Dionne 2017). Although supporters of vertical programs like PEPFAR say that these efforts create positive spillover effects for health, the evidence to support this outcome is unclear (Shiffman, Berlan, and Hafner 2009). The significant infusion of AIDS money has led some African NGOs to focus on AIDS, not issues like food security or education (Morfit 2011). All countries but South Africa depend on donors to provide their citizens with antiretroviral therapy, and these medications must be taken for life. For example, in 2014, PEPFAR covered 69 percent of the cost of antiretroviral therapy in Kenya and 75 percent in Mozambique, while the Global Fund covered 78 percent in Malawi and 87 percent in Ghana (KFF 2019a:9). Dependence is worrisome since all donors except the United States decreased funding for AIDS between 2010 and 2018. The decline occurred after the unprecedented increase from $1.2 billion in 2002 to $7.8 billion in 2008 (KFF 2019a:7; Kates, Wexler, and Lief 2019).

The sixth Sustainable Development Goal seeks an end to AIDS by 2030. Doing so will require the response to reach some of the most vulnerable and stigmatized people in Africa, including men who have sex with men, people who inject drugs, and sex workers. Studies show high HIV prevalence among these groups, although data are sparse. In most African countries, discrimination in healthcare facilities and employment as well as laws against homosexuality, sex work, and drug use make it difficult to provide HIV testing, education, and antiretroviral therapy to these populations (UNAIDS 2018). Addressing these gaps necessitates recognizing the right to health for all people.

The Ebola Outbreaks in West Africa and the Democratic Republic of Congo

During 2014–2015, the hemorrhagic disease Ebola infected over 28,000 people primarily in Guinea, Liberia, and Sierra Leone and led to over 11,000 deaths. In summer 2018, Ebola again appeared, first in the northwest part of the Democratic Republic of Congo (DRC) and then in the eastern part of the country (North Kivu and Ituri provinces). As of December 2019, there were 3,222 confirmed infections, 2,207 deaths, and 1,088 survivors (WHO 2019a). A virus spread through bodily fluids, Ebola causes fever, fatigue, headache, vomiting, diarrhea, and in some cases internal and external bleeding. Both outbreaks showed that inattention to health structures, distrust, and international approaches that vacillate between neglect and crisis undermine the right to health. They also illustrate that while donors and governments delay action, local people often devise their own culturally appropriate responses. In West Africa, for example, priests educated their followers about the disease; communities organized safe burials; and pastors and imams set up food distribution for quarantined communities (Patterson 2018; Richards 2016).

In West Africa, the first Ebola case occurred in December 2013 in Guinea. The virus spread quickly because of significant trade and migration between and within Guinea, Liberia, and Sierra Leone (Alexander et al. 2015:12). When the first cases occurred in clinics, workers lacked protective equipment like gloves or knowledge about Ebola, often mistaking it for malaria. As a result, healthcare workers were twenty-one times more likely than the general population to be infected (Evans, Goldstein, and Popova 2015). Fearing infection in clinics, people did not seek care for non-Ebola conditions like malaria, pregnancy complications, and TB, a pattern that increased mortality from those conditions (Decroo, Fitzpatrick, and Amone 2017).

Both Ebola outbreaks show that underfunded healthcare services, corruption, and distrust of governments prevent health institutions from delivering the highest standard of care (Karan, Katz, and Jha 2018; Wilkinson and Leach 2015). In West Africa, years of economic reforms that cut healthcare budgets and capped workers' salaries meant healthcare infrastructure was weak (Benton and Dionne 2015). Corruption had undermined healthcare spending in both countries and led to widespread distrust of government officials. In Liberia, for example, people thought that government officials had "invented" Ebola in order to get foreign aid (Patterson 2018). Only 2 percent of people in the eastern part of the DRC trusted the national government, a fact that may have led one-fourth to say that Ebola was not real (Larson 2019). The Congolese government's decision to postpone voting in the December 2018 presidential elections in the opposition-controlled region exacerbated distrust. Distrusting healthcare workers and government information, people during both outbreaks blamed spiritual causes, avoided clinics, and sought traditional cures and religious healing (Richards 2016).

The global response to both outbreaks moved from neglect to crisis. Global leaders sought to portray each as a security threat to galvanize attention. In West Africa, there was little action during the outbreak's first eight months because the WHO assumed its protocols from prior Ebola outbreaks would be adequate and because its decentralized structure hampered decisionmaking (Kamradt-Scott 2016). Neglect fit within the conventional narrative of Africa as the site of infectious diseases (Nunes 2016). Although the WHO had workers on the ground early in the outbreak in the DRC, by July 2019 donors had provided only half of the needed $100 million for the response. Fieldworkers reported being overworked and undersupplied (Grady 2019). The WHO also declined three times to classify the 2019 outbreak as a "public health emergency of international concern," a label used to designate a highly unusual outbreak that has the potential to spread across borders and affect travel and trade (Youde 2012).

In the West African outbreak, the international community switched into crisis mode in August 2014 as a result of two events: the Liberian Eric Duncan traveled to Texas and died from Ebola in a Dallas hospital, and two US healthcare workers contracted Ebola in Liberia and returned to the United States. Western populations became fearful, and the international NGO Médecins Sans Frontières (Doctors Without Borders) and the Centers for Disease Control and Prevention, the US federal government agency charged with protecting public health, stoked the fear with their dire predictions of millions of Ebola deaths (Kamradt-Scott 2016). In August 2014, the WHO finally declared a public health emergency of international concern. In the Congolese outbreak, the crisis point happened in July 2019 with the first case of Ebola in Goma, an urban center near Rwanda. Shortly thereafter, the WHO also declared a public health emergency of international concern (Grady 2019). It renewed that statement of concern in October 2019 (UN News 2019).

Viewing these outbreaks as a crisis helped leaders to frame them in security terms, although the target of the security risk differed for each. When President Barack Obama and UN Security Council members discussed Ebola in West Africa as a "threat to international peace and security," they turned the target of the security risk into the global community, not solely West Africans. This narrative played into the idea that disease threats to the West originate among "others" in the global South (Wald 2008). Securitization of the issue generated resources. In September 2014, President Obama asked the US Congress for $6 billion for the response, and he deployed 3,000 US troops to Liberia to transport supplies and build Ebola treatment units. UN Security Council Resolution 2177 then established the first ever military mission to address a health crisis (Garrett 2015). Although securitization brought money, supplies, and personnel, it also turned the Ebola response into a "war" as opposed to a humanitarian action, and the language of human rights (e.g., the right to access, nondiscrimination, and privacy) was notably absent (Eba 2014; Hofman and Au 2017). Public health officials used coercive security tactics like checkpoints, roadblocks, states of emergency, and curfews, actions that local people resented and at times evaded. For example, when the Liberian government quarantined the West Point community outside Monrovia, riots erupted because residents needed to leave the area to earn money for food, and security forces killed a young man. Securitization also meant that after the threat to the West was gone, there was no pressing need for continued investments (Patterson 2018). Thus, even though the WHO set up the Pandemic Emergency Finance Facility to respond to future outbreaks, this body remained underfunded and understaffed (Moon et al. 2017).

Officials also discussed the outbreak in the DRC using security terms, but the threatened target was not the West or the international community. Instead, they portrayed Ebola as one more danger in a region that has suffered years of low-level, localized conflict, with over 100 militia groups vying for land and minerals. Militias and government troops have targeted local populations, leading to thousands of displaced persons. Rural instability, shifting power dynamics, and mobile populations problematized care provision, contact tracing (i.e., finding the people who have interacted with an infected person and thus may be infected themselves), and administration of a new, highly effective Ebola vaccine (Karan, Katz, and Jha 2018). Insecurity exacerbated the Ebola danger to local populations and healthcare workers. Out of fear and misunderstanding, some local populations killed vaccination team members, and rebel groups that thought the government was using the response as a ploy then attacked Ebola treatment units (Goldstein 2019). By December 2019, there had been 386 attacks during the outbreak, with seven responders killed and seventy-seven injured (Branswell 2019). The Congolese case illustrates how conflict undermines health not only because it injures and kills people, but also because it disrupts healthcare services and

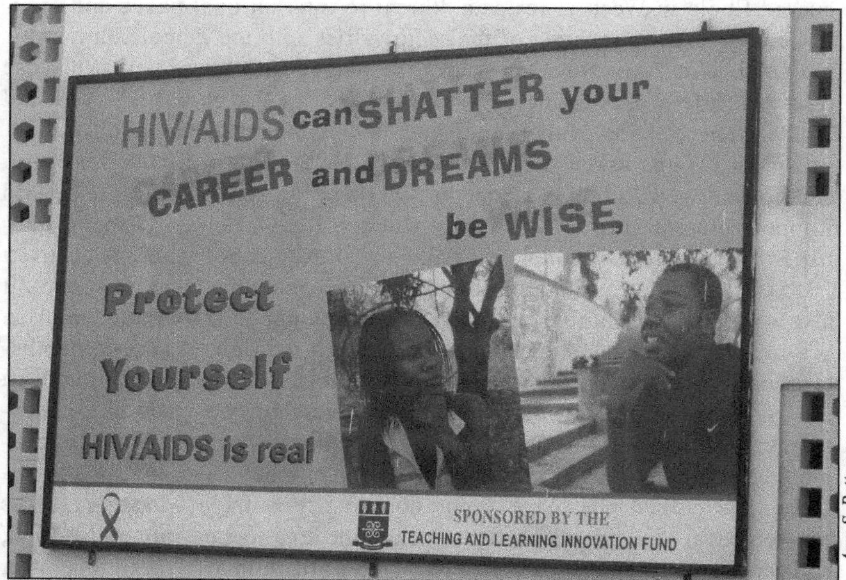

HIV/AIDS education poster, University of Ghana.

the spread of health information (Price-Smith 2009). The case also shows that the securitization of outbreaks may not generate resources and attention, particularly if the threat is distant and tied to a conflict that is perceived to be intractable. These processes undermine the right to health for all.

Noncommunicable Diseases and Mental Health Disorders

In 2017, noncommunicable diseases caused 71 percent of all global deaths, with 80 percent of those occurring in low- and middle-income countries. Although data are incomplete, experts assert that these diseases are rapidly increasing in Africa (WHO AFRO 2019). Because of late diagnosis and inadequate treatment, noncommunicable diseases often lead to premature death in Africa. For example, many women with breast cancer are diagnosed only after tumors are sizable, resulting in poor prognosis (Confortini and Krong 2015). Noncommunicable diseases also cause long-term disabilities, recurring sickness, and lost worker productivity, all of which drive down economic output and increase health costs (Patterson 2018).

Several factors contribute to the rise of noncommunicable diseases. First, fewer childhood deaths mean more people are living to adulthood, and noncommunicable diseases are more likely to occur with age. Second, urbanization leads to exposure to pollutants that contribute to cancers and respiratory diseases. Most African cities also lack spaces for exercise, and physical inactivity is a risk factor for noncommunicable diseases. Third, rising household incomes and Africa's trade liberalization have increased exposure to commercial determinants of health like processed foods, tobacco, and alcohol, all of which increase the risk of noncommunicable diseases (WHO 2013a). Of these, tobacco is the biggest health threat. Although the percentage of adults using tobacco varies from 4.5 percent in Ethiopia to 27 percent in Lesotho, tobacco use has increased in Africa. Since the 1990s, transnational tobacco companies such as Philip Morris International have purchased African cigarette manufacturers, increased production, and marketed tobacco to a growing urban middle class (Drope 2011; Lee, Ling, and Glanz 2012; Warner and Mackay 2006). The food and alcohol industries engage in similar practices, and their products have led to increased obesity and hypertension (Hofman and Parry 2017; Searcy and Richtel 2017).

Mental health disorders such as depression, anxiety, schizophrenia, suicide, and substance abuse present a growing "silent epidemic" in Africa (Monteiro 2015:79; Sankoh, Servalie, and Weston 2018). Data on mental health disorders in Africa are limited because of low levels of diagnosis and treatment. Experts estimate that 18 to 36 percent of populations globally will experience a mental disorder in their lifetime (Ambikile and Iseselo 2017). Mental health disorders cause 14 percent of deaths and one-third of the global burden of disability (Vigo et al. 2019; WHO 2017). Poverty, food insecurity, unemployment, conflict and displacement, gender discrimination, intimate partner violence, and the stigma of living with HIV contribute to mental health disorders (Akyeampong, Hill, and Kleinman 2015; Gibbs, Govender, and Jewkes 2018; Kelland 2019). In turn, mental health disorders exacerbate these challenges and undermine physical health (Lund 2018).

Several factors have hampered the response to mental health disorders in Africa. First, there are only 1.4 mental health workers per 100,000 people in Africa versus the global average of 9 per 100,000 people (Sankoh, Servalie, and Weston 2018). Ethiopia, a country of almost 100 million people, had only one child psychiatrist in 2017. Mali, a country of almost 17 million, had only twenty-eight mental health workers (WHO 2017). The lack of mental healthcare workers contributes to a significant treatment gap. In Sierra Leone, for example, 98.8 percent of people who needed mental healthcare in 2017 could not access it (Sankoh, Servalie, and Weston 2018). Second, mental health disorders are highly stigmatized, causing people to suffer silently and hide their conditions. Stigma undermines advocacy campaigns and public education. Because of their complex causes, mental health disorders may be attributed to curses or witchcraft (Akyeampong, Hill, and Kleinman 2015). The spiritual emphasis, as well as the lack of access to and availability of biomedical treatment, leads individuals to seek help from traditional healers and religious leaders. Although some of these leaders collaborate with health centers to identify patients (Osafo 2016), this does not always occur and treatment may be delayed (Schierenbeck et al. 2013). Some families take their affected relatives to Pentecostal pastors for prayer, fasting, and exorcism, even though some pastors may deny patients food, beat them, or chain them to trees (Arias et al. 2016; Carey 2015). Few countries have laws to protect the human rights of these individuals. For those countries with laws, they are often not enforced.

Even though the third Sustainable Development Goal aims to combat noncommunicable diseases and promote mental health, donors and African governments have done little beyond tobacco control. In 2005, the World Health Assembly agreed to the Framework Convention on Tobacco Control, a treaty that requires signatories to ban advertising, establish smoke-free environments, levy tobacco taxes, require warning labels on packaging, and develop public education and cessation programs. Many African countries lobbied for the treaty and then quickly signed and ratified it. As of 2019, Eritrea, Malawi, Morocco, Somalia, and South Sudan were the exceptions (Patterson and Gill 2019). Yet implementation has been slow because governments lack capacity and because the industry has effectively lobbied national legislatures and maneuvered around regulations. Thus, while most African countries have adopted advertising bans and warning labels, few have levied the taxes needed to deter tobacco use, particularly among youth and low-income people (Drope 2011; Goldman 2016).

Although the WHO unveiled action plans for noncommunicable diseases and mental health in 2013 (WHO 2013a, 2013b), donor activities remain limited. PEPFAR supports cervical and breast cancer screening in some HIV testing sites, and Gavi distributes the vaccine against the human papillomavirus in some countries. (Human papillomavirus—HPV—causes cervical cancer, a cancer highly prevalent among women with HIV.) In November 2019, Norway became the first donor country to launch a program to combat noncommunicable diseases in low-income countries, pledging over $20 million for 2020 (Fletcher 2019). The United Kingdom has established programs on postpartum depression as part of maternal health in some countries, and the World Bank has a small mental health initiative. Yet, as of 2019, only 0.3 percent of donor assistance for health was for mental health (Liese, Gribble, and Wickremsinhe 2019), and just over 1 percent was for noncommunicable diseases (Fletcher 2019).

Similarly, few African governments have established and/or implemented national alcohol and nutrition policies, and few have increased their budgets for noncommunicable diseases (WHO 2013a). In the words of one Tanzanian health expert, governments have "no strategy, no funding, no plans" (Patterson 2018:137), and most government programs on noncommunicable diseases are woefully understaffed. The public perceptions that communicable diseases pose the greatest health danger, are too costly to address, and result from individual lifestyle choices contribute to inaction (Parkhurst and Vulimiri 2013; Patterson 2018). The situation is even worse for mental health, with African governments allocating only about 1 percent of their health budgets to the issue. Most funding goes for mental institutions that tend to house people with extreme cases of psychosis and schizophrenia, not to community healthcare workers who address common mental disorders like depression. Training for primary healthcare workers, facilities that provide care, and availability of pharmaceuticals are limited (Schierenbeck et al. 2013).

Inaction remains even though studies increasingly show that mental healthcare and prevention of noncommunicable diseases can occur at low cost in resource-poor settings (see Bollyky 2012; Nuwer 2018). Educating populations about the risk factors for noncommunicable diseases, implementing taxes on tobacco, training community-based mental health workers, screening for some cancers, and managing hypertension are possible. Studies also show that mental health promotes physical health, by fostering adherence to medications, such as antiretroviral therapy for people living with HIV, and urging health-promoting behaviors, such as limiting alcohol intake (see Nakimuli-Mpungu et al. 2012). By not recognizing how communicable diseases, noncommunicable diseases, and mental health intertwine, donors, governments, and NGOs undermine the right to health (Patel et al. 2018).

Political Prioritization of Health

Health has received relatively low priority in Africa, despite the human right to health and the contribution that good health makes to economic growth (Bloom, Canning, and Sevilla 2004). Good health increases labor productivity and enables people to invest in other goods and services, including education (Sharma 2018). Good health for women correlates with increased household assets, savings, income, school enrollment, performance in education, and job performance (Onarheim, Iversen, and Bloom 2016). In contrast, poor child health reduces educational attainment and the potential for financial earnings when children become adults (Currie 2009).

The low prioritization of health is evident in inadequate donor funding, as well as misguided vertical health programs. Although donors spend billions of dollars annually on health, this funding is insufficient even for high-profile issues like AIDS (UNAIDS 2018). At times, donors address health issues that local populations do not prioritize (Dionne 2017), while the health issues that affect millions get little attention. For example, even though TB was the top infectious killer globally in 2019, it received only 3 percent of US global health funds (KFF 2019b). As mentioned above, donors often prefer to support vertical, disease-specific health programs rather than comprehensive healthcare through primary healthcare services. Vertical programs with their use of performance-based financing reflect donors' emphasis on neoliberal economic policies that have cut investments in public health infrastructure, capped workers' salaries, and privatized care. These policies hollowed out public health infrastructure and fostered a growing divide between those who can pay for private care and those who must use inadequate public systems (Benton and Dionne 2015).

Low prioritization of health also is apparent in inadequate national government health budgets. In the 2001 Abuja Declaration, African leaders promised to spend 15 percent of their government budgets on health by 2015. Tanzania was the only country to meet this goal, and eleven countries actually cut spending during the fourteen-year period (Ogbuoji et al. 2019). Low public spending has contributed to an estimated 23,000 healthcare workers' migrating annually, because of low pay, long hours, and inadequate working conditions. High-income countries provide an enticement when their hospitals recruit African doctors and nurses to meet their own personnel shortages and care demands from aging populations (Cooper et al. 2013:6). Africa faces dire shortages of doctors, nurses, and pharmacists. In 2016, there was not even one physician per 10,000 people in Burkina Faso, Chad, or Sierra Leone, and even the middle-income country of South Africa had just nine doctors per 10,000 people. In contrast, Sweden had fifty-three, Germany forty-two, and the United States twenty-five (WHO 2019b). Staff shortages erode service delivery, foster corruption (as people pay "fees" to see a doctor), and undermine health.

Inadequate funding for health also results in poor implementation of existing national health policies. Two examples illustrate. First, many African countries have passed laws to control tobacco use. Yet ministries of health lack the resources to enforce the regulations against advertising, public smoking, and tobacco sales included in those laws. It is often the case that there is only one person in the Ministry of Health who works on tobacco control or, more broadly, noncommunicable diseases (Patterson 2018). Second, inadequate funding, as well as poor planning and weak oversight, can lead to drug shortages, even if a country has a policy to provide medications at no cost at public health facilities. Such "stock-outs" endanger patients' health because patients may forego treatments if they must pay to travel to other facilities to get medications or purchase them at private pharmacies (Wales et al. 2014).

There are several reasons why health is a low policy priority. First, in most African countries, the Ministry of Health is politically weak. Since most African states centralize power in the executive (see Chapter 6), presidents may use ministry positions to reward political allies (Bleck and van de Walle 2019). If those political appointees then gain an independent power base, presidents may transfer them or remove them. This practice undermines policy implementation, ministry-parliament connections, ministry-donor relationships, and accountability. Low-level ministry officials tend to be overworked and under-resourced technocrats, most of whom lack the political connections to affect policy. These political dynamics mean ministry officials cannot effectively lobby for additional resources. In addition, corruption scandals in some countries have further undermined health officials' political clout. For example, in 2010 an audit revealed that the Ministry of Health in Zambia had allegedly mismanaged $14 million from the Global Fund. The scandal undermined the ministry's influence and its relations with donors (Usher 2010).

A second factor contributing to low prioritization of health is public opinion. A 2012 survey found that only 5 percent of people said health should be the government's top priority versus 20 percent who said employment should be (Afrobarometer 2012). These numbers reflect the region's high levels of poverty, food insecurity, and unemployment, despite economic growth over the last decade. Yet, Africans should have an incentive to care about health, since 37 percent of Africa's health expenditures are paid out of pocket (compared to 10 percent in the United States), and 11 percent of Africans annually spend so much on health that their household financial stability is threatened (Ogbuoji et al. 2019).

Third, except for the AIDS issue, health advocacy has been limited in Africa. Unlike in the United States where organizations like the American Cancer Society raise significant funds and lobby for national and state policies, African health advocacy groups tend to be underfunded, confined to the capital city, and led by educated, middle-class individuals who often do not represent most Africans. Although they strive to advocate on health, these groups' reach can be limited and their dependence on external funding high (Patterson and Gill 2019). Additionally, the stigma associated with some health issues like AIDS, breast and cervical cancers, and mental health disorders problematizes how advocates frame these issues to generate interest among policymakers. Finally, some health issues like AIDS, mental health disorders, malaria, TB, maternal mortality, and neglected tropical diseases (such as schistosomiasis or rabies) disproportionately affect women, migrants, the poor, rural farmers, and/or children. Historically, it has been easier for politicians to ignore these politically marginalized groups, thereby undermining the right to health (Patterson 2018).

Future African Health Challenges

This chapter has investigated the challenges of promoting a right to health in Africa. Health governance, with its multiple actors, sectors, and approaches, makes reaching consensus on health responses difficult. Africa's double burden of communicable and noncommunicable diseases challenges the region's limited financial and human resources. Despite the fact that good health has positive spillover effects for socioeconomic development, health receives inadequate policy attention and financing. Political dynamics, limited public interest, weak advocacy groups, and the fact that marginalized people suffer the most from poor health services contribute to health being a low policy priority.

The limited prioritization of health meant the continent was ill prepared for the COVID-19 pandemic that had infected over 7 million people and killed roughly 425,000 worldwide by June 2020. Caused by a novel coronavirus that first appeared in China in December 2019 and then spread to South Korea, Western Europe, Iran, and the United States, the disease can cause death through acute respiratory distress, particularly for the elderly and people with underlying health conditions such as diabetes. Because most African countries cancelled flights to China in January 2020, the continent experienced no cases during early 2020. However, by mid-March several African countries confirmed infections and COVID-19 deaths (WHO 2020). Health officials predicted that underinvestment in health-care systems (which leads to inadequate supplies of masks, gloves, oxygen, hospital beds, respirators, and a lack of health-care personnel) would make it difficult to provide adequate care for individuals who might become seriously ill. Even confirming cases was problematic, since WHO-provided test kits were only available in forty countries and since many people with mild cases may avoid health-care centers (Nordling 2020). WHO-prescribed prevention methods such as "social distancing" (sometimes termed "physical distancing," that is, staying six feet away from other people) seemed impossible in crowded communities. For example, Nairobi's informal settlement of Kibera has over 300,000 people per square kilometer (Merelli 2020). Underinvestment and corruption in health services also meant populations distrusted government health-messages (Patterson 2020), as rumors about the virus and the ways to prevent it spread. In addition, xenophobic attitudes toward Chinese and Europeans increased (*Africanews* 2020; Coffey 2020).

To address the increase in cases, governments adopted stringent policies, though not without some cost to human rights and economic output. One day after it confirmed its first COVID-19 case, for example, the Tanzanian government shuttered all schools for a month; it then closed universities (*Citizen* 2020). Although high-income countries had adopted a similar action, online coursework often replaced in-person instruction. This method was more difficult in low-income countries with less internet access. These actions raised concerns about how out-of-school youth might occupy their time. For example, teenage pregnancy rates, rape, and sexual violence increased in West Africa when governments closed schools during the Ebola outbreak (Yasmin 2016). When people reacted to a state-imposed curfew in Kenya, dozens suffered police brutality (Muraya 2020). With seventeen cases, Rwanda became the first African country to impose a complete lockdown, closing borders, shops, markets, and workplaces and empowering local "security organs" to enforce regulations (*Deutche Welle* 2020). As airlines cut flights, trade declined, and tourists cancelled trips, a predicted resulting economic downturn could deepen health challenges, including the spread of other communicable diseases and mental health disorders (Lee 2020; BBC News 2020). Future studies should assess the impacts of a COVID-19 related rise in unemployment, poverty, and food insecurity for public health.

COVID-19 illustrates how health and globalization intertwine, creating complex health challenges that require innovative responses. Similarly, the continent's emerging health challenges that result from its youthful population and climate change will require multisectoral approaches. An estimated 65 percent of the total population of Africa falls within what many scholars define as the "youth" category of eighteen to thirty-five years (Mpungose and Monyae 2018). Donors, governments, and NGOs must pay more attention to young people and support their efforts on health education and advocacy, as well as their education and employment. HIV infections are growing most rapidly among young women; substance abuse among young men fuels the rise in mental health disorders; early marriage corresponds with maternal mortality; and the prevention of an epidemic of noncommunicable diseases will partly depend on young people's establishing positive health behaviors and, more broadly, on their socioeconomic situation. In addition, climate change already has affected health, and its impacts will most likely become more severe. It has led to malnutrition from drought-destroyed crops, new patterns in vector-borne diseases like malaria, outbreaks of water-borne infections like cholera due to flooding, and destruction of healthcare facilities (McMichael 2013). One study in South Africa indicated that health systems have yet to train healthcare workers and plan for weather-related disasters such as flooding or droughts (Chersich and Wright 2019).

To address these problems, donors, governments, NGOs, and populations will have to commit to overcoming the obstacles to health governance that prevent collaboration and limit policy prioritization. Doing so will require not only leadership but also an approach to health that is people-centered, appreciates the complexity of the human experience, and embraces a holistic view of health (Agyepong et al. 2017:2803). In short, health as a basic human right must become not merely an aspiration but a reality.

9

Environmental Challenges

Garth A. Myers

The African continent undeniably faces numerous environmental challenges. It must be underlined from the beginning in any assessment of Africa's environmental challenges that the continent is huge, diverse, and complex. These three factors are as true of Africa's physical environments as they are for its human geography. As Chapter 2 shows, Africa has many vast plateaus; five major basins; long stretches of fertile volcanic mountains not far from desolate wastelands below sea level; lakes that are among the world's largest (Lake Victoria), deepest (Lake Tanganyika), and most rapidly shrinking (Lake Chad); and an array of features famous for their similarly dramatic contrasts. With its great variations in longitude and topography, Africa is both the most tropical continent and one with extraordinarily diverse and complex climates and life forms. Thus any sentence that contains the phrase, "Africa is . . ." ought to automatically be given an asterisk. One cannot boil "Africa" down to some simple uniformity (Adams, Goudie, and Orme 1999; Grant 2015; Myers 2009).

This is also quite true for Africa's environmental challenges. Because of the diversity and complexity of this vast continent's environments (among other factors), its environmental issues are also diverse and complicated (Adams 1992; Adams, Goudie, and Orme 1999; Lewis and Berry 1988). Parts of the continent face cyclical droughts and the threat of desert expansion while others face severe flooding from inundating rains. Some countries have had successful programs for wildlife management in conditions of tremendous species richness, whereas others have endemic species facing extinction or lack significant species richness. While global climate change is impacting the entire continent, neither the impacts nor their severity are uniform. I have concentrated on a broad overview in this chapter, but with a few case examples for analyzing environmental challenges and as much of a balance between specificity and general themes as is possible. It is also worth noting that Africa's diversity and complexity mean it is nigh on impossible to offer comprehensive coverage for all environmental challenges for this vast continent.

The remainder of this chapter is divided into eight sections. The first explores the applicability of a political ecology perspective to environmental issues in Africa. The next two sections examine the broadest themes possible in relation to these issues: global climate change and the environmental questions surrounding economic development. The next four sections focus on parks and wildlife; population, health, and environment; piracy; and urban environments. A final section offers general conclusions.

Political Ecology and Africa's Environmental Challenges

I note from the outset that this chapter surveys Africa's environmental challenges from a political ecology perspective. Political ecology offers an interdisciplinary approach that recognizes that one cannot see environmental problems strictly as natural phenomena. Nearly a half century of research in Africa has provided ample evidence that, regardless of the environmental issue being discussed, the causes of the challenges must be understood in their historical, cultural, political, and economic dimensions alongside the biophysical factors. Forty years ago, the Swedish anthropologist Gudrun Dahl (1979:12) laid out the purpose of a political ecology in her book *Suffering Grass*, about Kenya's Isiolo Boran livestock-raising culture. She argued that a natural science "ecology can only provide partial answers to our questions. There is already considerable evidence that it is not so much ecological change in itself that causes crisis . . . but that political and economic changes frequently express themselves in ecological effects."

For one example to illustrate the importance of a political-ecological view on Africa's environmental challenges, let us consider soil erosion, which is a particularly serious issue in a number of mountainous regions of eastern Africa, including parts of Ethiopia, Rwanda, Burundi, Kenya, Tanzania, and Uganda. Physical geography and climatology are certainly part of the story, because steeper slopes and the orographic effect (which brings higher rainfall totals to the windward side of mountains as moist air masses are forced to rise and thus precipitate) generally lead to greater volume and velocity of runoff that can take topsoil with it (Adams, Goudie, and Orme 1999; Lewis and Berry 1988). But these highland areas are also the most fertile agricultural lands in East Africa, and the principle of island biogeography means that many mountains, as if they are islands in seas of savannas and steppes, are rich in biodiversity and endemic species. Under colonial regimes, highland areas in the region were seized by white settlers or demarcated as national parks and conservation areas, leaving them off-limits for African farmers or herders (Neumann 1998). This in turn crowded African herders and farmers into other, often less productive lands, which then frequently led to increasing conflicts, overuse, and much higher farm densities exceeding ecological carrying capacities (Derman, Odgaard, and Sjaastad 2007).

Beyond colonial histories, one would also need to consider the politics and governance regimes of the postcolonial era in searching for the causes of East African soil erosion, and the politicization of cultural differences in several of these states. Postcolonial Kenya, for instance, has experienced what is locally termed *majimboism* (regionalism) and, for many years, the manipulation of local land clashes and resource grievances by political leaders, often based around ethnic identities. Uganda's politics have similarly seen severe regionalism, which has played out in natural resource management. And, of course, Rwanda and Burundi have experienced extreme genocidal violence shaped by politicized cultural identities in the postcolonial era. Most East African countries experienced severe debt crises that forced them to sign up for structural adjustment programs (SAPs) in the 1980s and 1990s that demanded an emphasis on developing sources of foreign exchange. SAPs inevitably required countries to intensify natural resource extraction and expand agricultural exports, since industrialization was minuscule in the region prior to independence. Were a scholar to study only soil erosion rates in any of these countries' highland agricultural zones and, potentially, conclude that local farming practices were causing soil erosion, this would seriously miss the broader historical, political, economic, and cultural context behind the erosion. Therefore, in this chapter, I take the broader political-ecological map and narrative as the baseline for understanding the environmental challenges of the continent, inspired by works such as Adams (1992), Bassett and Crummey (2003), Leach and Mearns (1996), and Schroeder (1999), among many others.

Global Climate Change

A second broad point that is essential for understanding Africa's environmental challenges is that global climate change constitutes perhaps the most urgent arena of development planning and environmental policy. Naomi Klein, in *This Changes Everything* (2014:107), points to the fivefold increase in extreme climate events in the world in the last thirty years as an obvious marker of the need for entirely rethinking—as her title put it—"everything." Yet the knowledge bases and policy frameworks for dealing with climate change are often as wrongly skewed as the map of projected impacts. Addaney and Cobbinah (2019:7) note that "Africa's contribution to global climate change is comparably negligible" yet "it remains the most affected region." It is also under-researched in both rural and urban studies in Africa; their book is the first comprehensive survey for the region's cities, and no such survey exists for rural Africa. Simon and Leck (2014:613) show that what they more broadly refer to as global environmental change research is much more developed for the global North than for the global South. Parallel to concerns on climate change issues, Du Toit et al. (2018) found that only 38 percent of African countries have had any research conducted for which publications exist on green infrastructure that would be a part of climate change adaptation and mitigation strategies.

African actors and agents have had less of a voice in developing and implementing global climate change adaptation and mitigation policy frameworks. Policies imposed from hegemonic global North actors often undermine local actions to combat climate change, "privileging international actors and financial markets" (Ernstson and Swyngedouw 2019:15; Silver 2019). "Are we not left," Swyngedouw and Ernstson (2019:37) ask, "with the gnawing feeling that, despite the elevation of the ecological condition to the dignity of a global public concern, the socio-ecological parameters keep eroding further?" This erosion, along with the gap between the global North and South, extends to more general or popular literature on climate change. Klein's provocative book is nonetheless substantially skewed toward North American and European understandings, as in her critique of the "lifestyle decisions of earnest urbanites who like going to farmers' markets on Saturday afternoons and wearing upcycled clothing" (2014:91) or her advocacy for public money that "should go to the kinds of ambitious emission-reducing projects . . . the smart grids, the light rail, the citywide composting systems, the building retrofits, the visionary transit systems, the urban redesigns" (108). She does acknowledge that "these types of improvements are of course in far greater demand in developing countries like the Philippines, Kenya and Bangladesh that are already facing some of the most severe climate impacts," but there is little nuance in her reference to these diverse global South contexts, or appreciation for how wildly inappropriate the dashed-off list of policy solutions here may be outside of the northern contexts that form her priority focus (Klein 2014:108). Klein (2014:459) does use Frantz Fanon (1996:55) to argue that "the issue which blocks the horizon . . . is the need for a redistribution of wealth," in claiming that the "unfinished business of liberation" requires policies to address climate change that also combat inequality. But too often this sort of critique of Western-dominated capitalism as it intersects with the "planetary ecological crisis and global political insecurity" somehow "feels compelled to rely on Dickensian metaphors to describe contemporary urban processes in the non-West [and especially Africa] that are structurally different from that of nineteenth-century Europe" (Chattopadhyay 2012:75).

Simon and Leck (2014:613) contend that "diversity within the [global] south" on policies for mitigation of or adaptation to change is "so profound on all variables, that comparable historical colonial legacies are no longer adequate markers of post-colonial identities and senses of shared futures" on a dramatically transformed planet. Addaney and Cobbinah's (2019:4) ground-breaking edited volume forges past the potentially debilitating realization such diversity might engender for Africa alone, even while acknowledging that "adaptation to . . . climatic variations has become a daunting task for governments, city authorities and residents." Their research showed the diversity within Ghana, between impacts in northern towns like Tamale and coastal cities like Accra—even Accra's many low-lying settlements face greater threat than the comparably higher elevation but still-coastal circumstances of most settlement areas in Cape Coast.

Addaney (2019:482) notes that even in Africa, the urban vulnerabilities "are well-documented," but "less attention has been paid to how the city government plans to adapt to climate change and enhance the resilience of the local population." On the ground in many poorer cities and rural towns in Africa, ordinary residents have demonstrated direct awareness of climate change realities. Okaka and Odhiambo (2018) found that over 90 percent of their 290 research subjects in Mombasa were aware of climate change and could trace its primary causes. When the rainy season began early in Cape Coast in March 2019 just as a catastrophic cyclone devastated Beira, Mozambique, "global warming" was a consistent exclamation, from the clerks in the guesthouse where I was staying, to drivers, to street hawkers. While policies and implementations are different matters than such cursory awareness, Africans are not always hopelessly "behind." African governments and nongovernmental organizations play important roles, for example, in the Sustainable Urban Development Network (SUD-Net) out of UN Habitat in Nairobi, which launched its Cities and Climate Change Initiative (CCCI) in 2008.

Climate extremes and biome diversity have to be the starting point for any attempts to classify Africa's environments' vulnerability to climate change. At the same time, there are some generally common patterns in terms of physical settings. For many scientists, scholars, and planners, perhaps the largest overarching theme for these physical settings would be *risk*. Water is one of the most complicated sources of risk in African environments, perhaps especially in cities. Half of all African cities with more than 750,000 people are within fifty miles of the coast, and many others (including some of the region's largest urban areas, such as Brazzaville, Khartoum, and Kinshasa) are predominantly located in low-lying riverine settings. Coastal cities or near-coastal cities are likewise also often on river mouths, estuaries, or deltas. UN Habitat considers fourteen big cities (those with more than 1 million people), six intermediate cities (500,000 to 1 million residents), and thirty-seven small cities (100,000–500,000 people) in Africa to be at risk due to rising sea levels. A great many cities in Africa face other significant flood risks. These are often most severe in poor, informal settlements. Even in cities at relatively high average elevations, poorer areas and informal settlements are typically at lower elevations in zones subject to seasonal flooding. Dakar, Dar es Salaam, Khartoum, Maputo, Mogadishu, and many other major urban areas have experienced severe flooding in the last few years alone (Myers 2016).

Vulnerabilities from climate change do not stop with sea-level risk and flooding, however. Many of Africa's urban and rural settlements outside of the low elevation coastal zone are in arid and semiarid areas facing increased water stress and declining agricultural yields—meaning potential food and water shortages in these cities and in the countryside. Still others are in steeply sloped settings prone to increased erosion, discussed above, which also threatens food security or leads to greater flood risks. Some regions of Africa face all of these risks, and more. According to the latest projections of the Intergovernmental Panel on Climate Change, Africa faces growing freshwater shortages; increased water-borne disease threats (including the spread of malaria into East African highlands that were previously malaria-free); and dramatic decreases in agricultural yields, especially from rain-fed agriculture, leading to widespread food shortages. The most severe threats of freshwater shortages, unsurprisingly, appear to be in arid and semiarid areas such as the Sahel. But even tropical cities with plentiful precipitation have failed to keep pace with the rise of consumer water demand under conditions of rapid urbanization. In combining the whole range of risks, the Climate Change Vulnerability Index (CCVI) for 2014 mapped many African areas among the most vulnerable places on the planet. According to the CCVI 2014, the Democratic Republic of Congo, Ethiopia, Guinea-Bissau, Nigeria, Sierra Leone, and South Sudan comprise six of the ten most vulnerable countries, with extreme risk (Myers 2016).

Yet assessing these climate change issues merely through the lens of *risk* would miss also seeing them as wellsprings of opportunities. After all, so many settlements in Africa are on coasts or navigable rivers precisely because of trade opportunities that continue to rise. Africans have a long history of producing solutions to environmental crises—otherwise *Homo sapiens sapiens*, which began in Africa, would not have lasted very long. Contemporary global climate change is arguably one of the most daunting challenges in that very long history. But do not count Africans out when it comes to innovations aimed at mitigation and adaptation.

The remainder of this chapter examines more specific environmental challenges rather than the overarching concern with climate change. As we turn to these challenges, though, bearing in mind the political-ecological approach, it is worth underscoring that it is often the case that outsiders approach Africa's environments as though Africans are helpless victims or, worse, knowing culprits in environmental destruction. In contrast, the reality is that much work is being done, often successfully, by African regional, national, and local and community agencies of environmental management, whether in wildlife conservation, environmental management in general, or sustainable development programs and policies.

Environmental Challenges of Economic Development

Nearly every environmental challenge on the continent has connections with processes of economic development (Moss 2011). In part this is due to the continued heavy reliance of a majority of African economies on the primary sector (agriculture, fishing, forestry, and mining), and specifically the direct extraction of natural resources and their export as primary (unprocessed) goods. Even where secondary sector (manufacturing) activities are significant in Africa, environmental challenges arise. Among the directly development-related environmental challenges on the continent, one finds air pollution, water pollution, solid waste and toxic waste management, land degradation and scarcity, and deforestation. Less direct links to development are present for desertification, flooding, and other challenges.

The most valuable and largest-scale mining, gas, and petroleum extraction operations are of course heavily capitalized and dominated by major corporations. But there are significant avenues for the involvement of small-scale, low-technology, and often informal miners. Many African governments

World Bank

Commercial logging, as in Gabon, is one factor leading to a rapid loss of forests, including rainforests, in Africa and elsewhere in the developing world.

sign away huge stretches of their oceans to international "factory" fishing ships, but there are still a large number of fisherfolk dependent on small-scale, low-technology, near-shore fish catches. And, in forestry, for every forest parcel cut down by massive companies under huge contracts, there are many more people engaged in the small-scale, low-technology harvesting of trees. Thus the contrasts of environments across the region are reflected in the contrasts of social exploitation strategies for them.

As Africa remains a continent with a rural, agricultural majority, I begin with rural, agricultural environments. Just as Africa has a tremendous diversity of environments, human societies utilize these environments to produce diverse livelihoods. The region remains the world's most rural and agricultural region, but within the broad rubric of agriculture, one finds communities that utilize the environment in very different ways. Several countries (Botswana, Burundi, the DRC, Kenya, Rwanda, and Tanzania) still have small percentages of their populations whose livelihoods revolve around hunting and gathering. Great differentiations exist between and within agricultural societies—between larger-scale, private, profit-oriented farming, commercial plantations, and so-called smallholder farming (because the farms they hold are small). There are some areas that are heavily reliant on high technology, mechanization, and large-scale irrigation where many smallholders utilize animals for plowing or perform all labor by hand. Parts of the region benefit from warm and hot year-round temperatures as well as two rainy seasons, enabling two (and in a few areas even three) harvests per year. Other farming systems are extremely precarious and reliant on unpredictable and seasonal rainfall. And, overall, it is crucial to remember that all of these rural and agricultural farming systems and societies are undergoing constant change: it is a complete fallacy to think of rural peoples as timeless and unchanging. For one example, while colonial Kenya was heavily reliant on large-scale, white-owned tea and coffee plantations, and these two commodities still dominate Kenya's export earnings, both tea and coffee production have now become smallholder-dominated. One of the best symbolic representations of this era of vast changes came in a recent billboard advertisement by a South African cell phone company in Tanzania, picturing a Maasai herder, dressed in traditional clothing, tending his herd, but while on his cell phone. The ad's tag line? "A Lion's Worst Nightmare." And in fact, Maasai and other low-technology rural herders in East Africa bank by phone and check meat or milk prices in Nairobi on the internet.

Thus in contemplating environmental issues in African agriculture, diversity and complexity must be front and center. High population density, low-technology labor-intensive peasant production yields much different environmental challenges than high-technology, export-oriented agriculture or monoculture plantation systems. It is important to focus on the specific farming systems' environmental impacts in devising policies to meet the resultant challenges.

Land grabbing, where large-scale deals are made for sales of land in the region, presents one scenario at the grander level. Land grabbing is certainly happening in the twenty-first century across Africa, at another intersection of society and environment that has political-economic overtones. The online, open-access Land Matrix database maintained by the Land Portal Foundation reported millions of hectares of land had been sold in deals by 2014 across Africa, and by 2017 it had documented 558 land deals, more than half of which happened in East Africa. This included more than 10 million hectares in the Republic of Congo; more than 3 million hectares in DRC, Ethiopia, Mozambique, South Sudan, and Sudan; and at least a million hectares of Ghana, Guinea, Liberia, Mali, Nigeria, Sierra Leone, Tanzania, and Zambia, alongside lesser but still important proportions of most other countries' territories.

But alarmist rhetoric has obscured a more complex reality. Large-scale investments are touted by some observers as a needed jolt in the arm for economies in the region or as a means for pushing out unsustainable and unproductive peasant production. For others, most of these investments amount to mere speculation that do little beyond further marginalizing such farmers. Lorenzo Cotula's (2013:7) extensive research on the topic of land grabbing led him to argue for "both positive and negative outcomes" but more negativity surrounding the largest deals. What is more, he found evidence that local elites were front and center in major land deals, and if foreign investors were involved, they were more likely to be South Africans rather than the expected Chinese investors and speculators (Carmody 2011). While "Chinese operators have been active players in the global land rush," there is very little "hard evidence of a key role played by China in the rush for Africa's land" (Cotula 2013:61–62).

Investors from the United States and Western Europe have become active as well in land grabbing. Investments and "grabs" vary substantially, from completely transparent, legal transactions that involve few uncompensated dispossessions to thoroughly corrupt, illegal sales that require widespread forced removal of African residents. Investors and governments often take advantage of weak legislation or enforcement of existing land laws to profit from the grabbing. And, in general terms, land grabbing on a large scale seems to have the potential for significant negative environmental consequences. It will lead to increased landlessness and also to intensification of production on already overcrowded small-scale farmlands. Deforestation, soil erosion, land degradation, and, in some areas, desertification can all be directly or indirectly bound up with land grabbing.

For another example of how development and environmental challenges in largely rural agricultural settings are inseparable when examined from a political-ecological perspective, let us consider West Africa's massive role in the production of chocolate. In an average year, roughly two-thirds of the world's cocoa beans are produced in West Africa, with Côte d'Ivoire and Ghana as the main suppliers. Globally, chocolate and cocoa products are worth more than $75 billion. Most of West Africa's cocoa (about 80 percent) is exported as raw material that is the primary ingredient of chocolate produced by European or US companies, and the overwhelming majority of chocolate consumers are in Europe and North America. West Africa's cocoa farmers' profits comprise about 4 percent of the total annual value of the chocolate market, and almost none of the world's chocolate bars are produced in West Africa. Cocoa farming's labor conditions are generally quite poor, and the industry's socioeconomic benefits to West Africa, while they vary by cocoa-producing country, are minimal by comparison to the immense value to corporations that sell chocolate. Its impacts on the environment, particularly across the vast farming regions where monoculture cocoa plantations have depleted biodiversity, are generally negative—and, unlike other forms of agriculture, it is extremely difficult and time-, labor-, and resource-consuming to rotate crops or transform production regimes since cocoa is a tree crop that often takes years to become productive. How did this development-environment conundrum happen?

The beginning of the answer is intimately linked with European colonialism in West Africa. Cocoa comes from the cacao tree (*Theobroma cacao*), which is native to tropical rainforests of Central and South America. At the end of the nineteenth century, very few cacao trees grew outside of their region of origin. But between 1895 and 1925, as the United Kingdom secured its control over Gold Coast colony (today's Ghana), a massive cocoa boom took hold of the colony. While some cocoa farmers rapidly became the core of Ghana's eventual elite class and others held on to the stable middle economically, they had no control over global markets and no capital for the establishment of cocoa processing or chocolate factories. As with nearly every economic relationship of Africa's colonial era, the controlling interests resided in Europe—in this case with British chocolate makers like Cadbury's (Amin 1972). A similar story pertains to France with Côte d'Ivoire, and other European countries gained industrial might through connections to the British and French colonies of West Africa. Hence the world consumes famous Dutch-processed cocoa, Swiss chocolate bars, or Hershey's Kisses, when a cacao tree cannot grow at all in Holland, Switzerland, or Hershey, Pennsylvania.

By the time West African cocoa-producing countries gained independence in the 1950s and 1960s, any real chance of transforming the terms of trade or global shape of the market to be more beneficial to West Africa already seemed remote. With globalization has come corporate consolidation. Orla Ryan (2011:127) calculated that even by 2005 some 57 percent of the European chocolate market was controlled by five European companies

(Lindt, Nestlé, Cadbury [now owned by US-based Mondelez International], Godiva [now owned by Yildiz, a Turkish firm], and Ferrero). Most of the rest belonged to the US-based multinational producers of Hershey and Mars.

At the same time, Ryan (2011) thoroughly details the dynamics and histories internal to Ghana and Côte d'Ivoire that have played into the narrative of how so few development gains and so many environmental and social costs have accrued to the main producers of—and workers in the fields harvesting—the basic ingredient. One factor has been the failure of the major cocoa-producing states to band together to gain power in decisionmaking in the global marketplace in the way that the Organization of Petroleum Exporting Countries (OPEC) was able to do. Political interference in cocoa marketing and political instability in the region have further eroded the capacity for these countries to become the key players that their status as "Chocolate Nations" ought to be able to secure. For various reasons, including plant disease, West African producers have been slow to pick up on the potentially lucrative and more environmentally friendly organic and fair-trade markets that have been growing in Europe and North America—even Ghanaian cocoa farmers' greatest success in this fancy, high-end arena, the expensive Divine chocolate bar produced exclusively from a Ghanaian fair-trade cooperative, is marked *Made in Germany*. Even with these factors internal to West Africa playing an important role, though, the saga of the journey from West African cocoa bean to the European and North American chocolate sweets that so many people enjoy is a bitter one that quite graphically continues to evidence the detrimental political-ecological legacies of colonialism and imperialism for African development and environmental challenges in the age of globalization.

Many of Africa's wealthier economies are those where mining and oil production are the dominant industries. These extractive industries often present massive environmental challenges to countries with poor capacity for addressing them (Campbell 2009). Colonial and global economic narratives often play central roles in making environmental challenges more vexing there. Let us take the example of the Copperbelt of Zambia to see how complex and intertwined development and environmental challenges can be in Africa. The Copperbelt is the heart of Zambia's economy, wherein copper is typically responsible for most of the gross domestic product (GDP). Yet there is little escaping the idea of the Copperbelt as a poisoned place. The Copperbelt's air quality places it among the world's worst areas, in large part due to copper mining, processing, and smelting (Vitková et al. 2011). Its soils are toxic, particularly in unforested (cleared) areas accessible for farming (Ettler et al. 2014). Its surface waters and groundwater contain heavy metals and carcinogens well above standard levels for human consumption. Its plant life is "rich" in arsenic, cobalt, and copper contamination. The animals are not immune from this uptake. Farms in its Kafue River valley that utilize leaking sewage pipes for irrigation show how this toxicity finds its way into the human food supply. People's bodies ingest the arsenic, zinc, copper, cobalt, and manganese of the fire, air, earth, and water.

We could take that last paragraph as a depiction of the Copperbelt today as a carcinogenic landscape and stop there. But the historical geography and metabolic conceptualization of political ecology demand the tracing of this ecological poisoning backward in time and outward in geographical space. Why does the Copperbelt exist? Certainly there was some trade in its copper resources before the twentieth century. Indeed, from as early as the seventh century, there is evidence of copper mining there (Roberts 1976). But the large-scale exploitation of its resources is inseparable from the imperial project of the British South Africa Company (BSAC) and its founder, Cecil Rhodes.

Present-day Zambia drew the attention of Rhodes and the BSAC for its apparent mineral wealth, but major copper mining did not begin until the 1920s. While the Great Depression of the 1930s interrupted its development somewhat, the Copperbelt attracted a range of international mining investments. By the 1940s and 1950s it had become a zone of rapid industrialization and urbanization. It even became a globally significant region for science and especially social science research into the impacts of industrialization and urbanization on African society (Epstein 1958; Mitchell 1956; Powdermaker 1962). Although sociology and cultural anthropology were at the forefront of these colonial-era studies, environmental issues occasionally surfaced—notably in Audrey Richards's research into the region's *citimene* agricultural system and impacts of labor migration to the Copperbelt on rural deforestation (Moore and Vaughan 1994). And the new Copperbelt towns (Chililabombwe, Chingola, Kitwe, Luanshya, Mufulira, and Ndola), each associated with different copper mines, smelters, or both, grew to have their own separate "garden cities" (really, leafy suburbs) for their white residents (Padfield 2011).

Colonial Zambia (then known as Northern Rhodesia) was heavily reliant on copper mining for its economic survival, and independent Zambia continued this dependence. For most of the contemporary independence era, more than 90 percent of Zambia's foreign exchange has come from copper, a significant amount of which is exported as raw ore. Having gone through the post-independence nationalization of the mines and the steady decline of global copper prices, the Copperbelt today is experiencing an unsteady boom (Fraser and Larmer 2010) and an expansion of copper mining farther west into what is being called the New Copperbelt (Hampwaye and Rogerson 2010; Negi 2014). The region's boom-and-bust cycles, heavy external dependence, and serious environmental costs stretch back to the beginning of colonial-era exploitation. It is impossible to see the current patterns—even if they involve Chinese, Indian, and South African capital—outside of the long sweep of that history (Negi 2013). It is also hard to see the Copperbelt outside of its rural surroundings—especially with its "wavering urban character" and frequent recourse to return migration to those rural areas or to cyclical migration between them and the Copperbelt towns (Mususa 2012; Potts 2005). It was, in the first place, an environment created by colonialism to be nakedly exploited; it remains one. Its colonial environment did much to shape its contemporary challenges.

African Parks and Wildlife

Africa's environments are substantive parts of the stereotypical image of Africa in the world (Ferguson 2006). Many outsiders associate "Africa" with large land mammals, wildlife conservation television shows, and tropical rainforests and savannas. Like the wildlife shows that so often come around near their conclusions to the endangered status of their featured species, the stereotypical view, when considering the region's environments, links them to a series of problems and crises: desertification, deforestation, soil erosion, wildlife extinction, and so on. It is not so much that none of these images reflect any of the region's realities. Indeed, three African countries (the DRC, Madagascar, and Tanzania) are among the top ten countries in the world in species richness, meaning the number of different species of any kind found there, and two of these (the DRC and Madagascar) are in the top ten in the world for rates of endemism, or the proportions of those species that are found nowhere else. Deserts do seem to be expanding in several countries, as tropical moist forests are decreasing. Topsoil erosion rates in several countries in the region (Ethiopia, Madagascar, and Rwanda, for example) are estimated to be very high, and soil fertility is declining there, with agricultural yields along with them. Major endemic species, and not just the famous large land mammals, do face the threat of extinction. One might, therefore, look to expand conservation areas and preservation programs, and urgently.

The problems are many, though, with this line of thinking on the environment. Too much of the time, African environments are taken as natural only when they are pristine—when they look, as the geographer Roderick Neumann (1998) pointedly put it, "the way Africa is supposed to look": without people. This notion of Africa's natural environments as devoid of humans is as far from reality as possible, since human history in the very environments Neumann was writing about (northern Tanzania) is the oldest human history on the planet. And, as he helped to show, human activities over thousands of years actually shaped—for one glaring example—the ecology of the Serengeti plains that epitomize "the way Africa is supposed to look." The crisis points around parks and preserves are seldom simply natural environmental problems, either. Political economy and cultural history are always present in the dynamics, often well beyond the mere physical-environmental processes (Schroeder 2012). The worst period of deforestation in Madagascar's history was the period of French colonial conquest and exploitation, not the current era—more than half of the "pristine" forest was lost before independence to French plantations, logging, and military campaigns of pacification (Harcourt et al. 1992). The fact that so much of the best dry-season pasture lands were taken by formerly white-only ranching or dairy farming areas, or alienated away into national parks and wildlife reserves, has had a great deal to do with soil erosion and desertification all across Kenya, as noted earlier.

Too little note is taken of African agency in countering these environmental problem areas. While parks and preserves often have indirect, negative impacts, one can also use the geography of parks to recognize that African countries are far ahead of many other states around the world in the effort to preserve biodiversity, at least geographically speaking. Many countries have pioneered new, participatory forms of wildlife conservation meant to benefit local people, such as Zimbabwe's CAMPFIRE (Communal Areas Management Program for Indigenous Resources). The late Wangari Maathai, the first African woman to be awarded the Nobel Peace Prize, founded and ran the hugely influential Greenbelt Movement (which began in Kenya) for environmental protection and women's empowerment (Maathai 2006). The CILSS (a French acronym for the Comité Permanent Inter-états de la lutte contre la secheresse dans le Sahel, the Permanent Interstate Committee for the Struggle Against the Drought in the Sahel) works across the Sahel at the grassroots to combat desertification and solidify rural livelihoods. Even where these organizations are stifled or stymied by political obstacles, there is no doubt that their activism has made a real difference in building local environmentalist consciousness and changing the dynamics (Shinn 2014).

Population, Health, and the Environment

Population is a sore spot for Africans and Africanists in relation to the development-environment nexus. Stereotypical received wisdom counts Africa as overpopulated and this overpopulation as the main cause for deforestation, desertification, land degradation, and other environmental crises. Yet much of Africa remains sparsely populated. Tracing this backward for a few hundred years, we must note that the slave trade's effects left many cultures without large segments of their able-bodied people, and fertility declines were widespread. Many African societies responded by developing religious and spiritual systems built around enhancing fertility, but the colonial era still began with what colonial regimes identified as widespread labor shortages. To many African people, the twentieth century (particularly after the end of World War I) represented an opportunity for recovery from centuries of genocide.

The common trope of the early contemporary independence period touted by naysayers (often labeled Afro-pessimists) to trumpet the region's

World Bank

Desertification threatens many areas of Africa, especially the Sahel.

"overpopulation" must be seen in that light. One thinks of tiny Mauritius, an island that gained independence in 1968 when 61 percent of its land surface was covered in sugar cane plantations begun under colonial rule. Doomsayers invoked the specter of Thomas Malthus to claim the country was headed for a famine due to overpopulation, with its inability to feed itself tied to finite land resources and rapid population growth. More than a half century later, those claims look rather laughable for a country with crude birth and death rates comparable to the United States and one of the most diversified, high-income industrial bases in Africa. A fair amount of the island is still covered with sugar cane fields—the waste from which joins the rest of the island's organic garbage in becoming the fuel that produces most of Mauritius's electricity to run its plentiful garment factories and call centers (Bowman 1991).

The complete reversal of fortunes for Mauritius in population terms suggests that there is little besides false geographic determinism behind worries that Africa is overpopulated. One can only claim that Niamey, Niger, for instance, is overpopulated, but Las Vegas, Nevada (in the middle of the desert, whereas Sahelian Niamey is on one of the world's major rivers), somehow, is not, if one ignores the fundamental question of the distribution of resources. Las Vegas is one of the most rapidly growing US cities despite its seemingly inhospitable setting because US society has enough wealth to move enough water and food to Las Vegas to help its population of more than a million people to thrive. Overpopulation is, at its core, a false term. The real concern must be about the geographic distribution of resources and access to development inputs (agricultural land, banking and credit for farmers, birth control, education, and many more). To be sure, high population growth rates across the continent play a role in environmental challenges. The more people, the more resources are needed, and when economies are not expanding rapidly enough to absorb the new population into the workforce as it comes of age or high rates of inequality skew the distribution of resources, increased exploitation of the environment emerges.

Severe rural land concentration and landlessness, along with violent conflict, have helped fuel another population dynamic with substantive socioenvironmental challenges in the region: migration. As of 2009, nearly 9 million Africans were considered "people of concern" by the United Nations High Commissioner for Refugees (UNHCR), comprising almost 40 percent of the global total. By 2017 that number had crossed the 20 million mark in sub-Saharan Africa alone. This population can be further divided into the 6 million classed as refugees—because they have crossed an international border—and the 14.5 million who are considered internally displaced persons (IDPs). Two-thirds of the region's refugees and IDPs come from—and reside in—four countries: the DRC, Somalia, South Sudan, and Sudan. Over 5 million refugees, IDPs, or other people of concern for UNHCR originated from or resided in the DRC alone in 2017. The Central African Republic was not far behind.

It is no coincidence that the top five producers of IDPs in the region are among the world's five most fragile states. Because of the fluid nature of both African boundaries and African national identities, it is plausible to conceive of many IDPs as occupying transnational spaces, too. Along with refugees, IDPs often find themselves in border-area camps; seven out of ten African refugees and IDPs are found in camp environments. The more intractable and long-lasting African conflicts, such as those in the Central African Republic, eastern DRC, Somalia, and both South Sudan and Sudan, produce an increasing array of programs for refugee settlement in hosting countries, through which such camps are designed to be transformed into agricultural settlements. These settlements are especially notable in hosting countries that border conflict zones, where the host countries do not currently contribute many domestic refugees, such as from Chad, Ethiopia, Kenya, Tanzania, and Uganda. Some 3 million African refugees have succeeded in claiming asylum and resettling outside of camps in those neighboring countries, and—for instance in the case of Mozambique since 1992—millions more have been repatriated back home at the cessation of conflict. But severe, protracted conflicts have led to semi-permanent camp cities in transient netherworlds that are, in effect, between states, and these can be highly damaging to fragile environments.

Perhaps the most notable of these spaces is Kenya's Dadaab camp complex, near its highly porous northern border with Somalia. Dadaab is actually comprised of five separate camps, with a combined population of 350,000 people at the peak of the conflict (the 2019 population is officially 211,000). Founded in 1991, Dadaab has been home to many Somalis for a quarter century. The camp city contains an entire generation born and raised there. In May 2015, Kenya ordered the closure of Dadaab in response to an attack by armed Islamist militants on a university in the nearby town of Garissa, because the terrorists who carried out the attack allegedly had ties back to Dadaab. In reality, this forced closure proved difficult to accomplish, given the fact that Dadaab's residents are in effect already resettled in Kenya. Only Somalia's peace and stability, which would facilitate the repatriation of Dadaab's people, would permanently end the need for Dadaab to exist. In the meantime, spaces like Dadaab around the region continue to have substantial impacts on local and national environments, given the resource expenditures necessary to maintain them and the limited capacity for food production in desert and semidesert conditions (Rawlence 2016).

Afro-pessimist doom scenarios regarding African environments often include alarmist accounts of health crises. The 2014 Ebola outbreak in Guinea, Liberia, and Sierra Leone provides an example. I had intelligent professor colleagues of mine worrying over my safety in traveling to Cape Town, South Africa, very far from the Ebola outbreak, because the Ebola outbreak had struck "Africa" and not just three small Atlantic West African states. Little effort was made in the media to highlight that when Ebola victims showed up in Mali, Nigeria, or Senegal (and in the latter two examples, in Dakar and Lagos, the primate or largest cities in an urban hierarchy of those countries), it did not spread. Strict public health actions and community engagement eliminated the threat. What is more, the virus did not appear in Côte d'Ivoire, Benin, Gambia, Ghana, or Togo—all of which have cross-border population movements in normal times on a daily basis with the impacted countries. Again, effective measures and strict enforcement ruled the day, even in countries recently emerging from war, such as Côte d'Ivoire. This is not to claim that African countries do not face severe health crises with grave potential for environmental damage or that healthcare provision is sufficient across the continent, but more clear-eyed assessments of crises are consistently in short supply (see Chapter 8 for a more extensive discussion).

The HIV/AIDS pandemic is a similar case, given its association with all of Africa in the public imagination. To be sure, HIV/AIDS has had a severe impact in Africa, but (1) many countries' rates of HIV infection and especially of mortality and new infections have gone down significantly in the last decade with the availability of antiretroviral (ARV) drugs to fight it, and (2) it is highly geographical, even within countries with higher rates. Zambia is an example for both (1) and (2). While the overall national rate of HIV infection among adults over age fifteen has remained steady in Zambia at or near 15 percent (still one of the highest rates in the region), with ARV treatment the rate of new infections has been halved since 2001, and the mortality rate had declined to below 1 percent by 2014. Solid declines are evident among young women, pregnant women, young men, and infants infected by transmission in utero. In fact, the overall percentage remains steady largely because so many HIV patients are *not* dying, so they remain a part of the national population count. Rates of infection vary substantially within Zambia, too, so that the overall rate of 15 percent hides the disparities between urban Lusaka and the Central and Copperbelt provinces (where HIV positive rates overall were near 20 percent in 2007), and rural Zambia, with an overall HIV infection rate of 10 percent. In other words, urban Zambians are twice as likely to contract the virus. And yet, given the higher access to healthcare in urban Zambia, Lusaka and Copperbelt residents were more than twice as likely to have access to ARV treatment that can prevent the development of HIV into full-blown AIDS. What the Zambian case suggests in relation to HIV/AIDS is that there is a distinct geography to and great diversity within healthcare systems and capabilities in the region. This then plays out in facing environmental challenges. Most significantly, a healthier rural workforce reduces labor shortages at harvest time, increasing the productivity of yields and thereby positively impacting the food supply.

Piracy and the Environment

How marine piracy off the coast of Somalia is viewed depends quite a bit on how one understands the political ecology and geopolitics of the situation. Somalia has had no effective national government across the extent of the territory world maps identify as Somalia since 1991. With the collapse of that government came the collapse of environmental protection agencies and the coast guard. In the wake of the collapsed coast guard, international fishing fleets quite literally took advantage of the lawlessness on the high seas to fish indiscriminately off Somalia's coast. These were really the first pirates off of that coast. Local Somalis, including unemployed former members of the old coast guard, took to the ocean to defend the country's territorial waters and to demand payment from these international fishing fleets. The ease with which supposed ransom payments came, however, turned the operation into a much more criminal enterprise, and Somali pirates began to seize international ships of many shapes and sizes to demand ransom payments. Eventually, many major powers of the world economy, including China, Japan, the United States, and Western Europe, sailed into Somalia's seas to combat piracy because the pirates appeared to threaten the flows of petroleum, in particular, out of the Persian/Arabian gulf as tankers neared the Horn of Africa on the way to those countries. The interests of these powers, however, remain far from the realm of concern that initiated the piracy in the first place: the pillaging of Somalia's marine resources (Gilmer 2014; Samatar, Lindberg, and Mahayni 2010).

This sort of piracy is not as uncommon on land across the region as one might be led to believe. For example, the corruption and shady dealings that surround Nigeria's oil industry, diamond mining in Angola or Sierra Leone, or almost any natural resource industry in the DRC are all forms of piracy. One of the more egregious cases involves the extraction of a rare-earth mineral from the eastern Congo called coltan (for its conglomeration of columbite and tantalite). Coltan is crucial as a stabilizing element in cell phones, and its abundance in the eastern DRC contrasts with its absence almost anywhere else on earth. Most outsider analysis of the corruption in coltan mining places the blame squarely with the leading combatants in the decades-long civil war in this part of the DRC. Yet every human being on earth with a cell phone in her or his hand is indirectly complicit in the perpetuation of the war, as is most obviously every manufacturer of cell phones, since they turn a blind eye at best to the situation from which they are profiting (although it must be added that manufacturers have increasingly sought alternative coltan sources to avoid the poor imagery of profiting from the war zone). The coltan case is a prime example of why the common stereotypes of African corruption (most notoriously in environments and natural resources) are so often flawed: they neglect the fact that any corruption in Africa depends upon corrupt practices in the markets for African natural resources, whether in Asia, Europe, or the Americas. This extends to the global sale of ivory obtained through poaching of elephant tusks, hippopotamus teeth, or rhino horn. African piracy depends upon piracy elsewhere.

Urban Environmental Challenges in Africa

I have already hinted at several environmental challenges in urban areas, and I have suggested that it is often difficult to tease out urban from rural challenges. Be that as it may, there are still several areas of concern that are more prominent in cities and suburbs, given their densities of population, built environments, infrastructures, and industrial production (see Chapter 7 for a more detailed discussion of urban Africa in all of its aspects). In urban-environmental perspectives found in planning and policy realms, the concerns tend toward solid waste management, flooding, sanitation, air and water pollution, land degradation, haphazard construction, and the impacts of climate change, to name a few of the main issues (Myers 2005). The Economist Intelligence Unit's (2011) *African Green Cities Index* focused on energy and carbon dioxide, water, sanitation, transport, waste, land use, air quality, and environmental governance as urban environmental challenges, for example.

When one reads the scholarly literature on urban environments in Africa, one can easily reach this basic conclusion: African cities are a mess. Environmental calamities abound. Environmental settings and governance structures leave cities highly vulnerable to the negative effects of climate change. The soils are septic from so much overflowing human waste. The surface waters are putrid, left standing because what few drains there are get clogged with solid waste that does not get collected. The water infrastructure that does function brings only polluted water to the small percentage of residents with access. Road infrastructures are so poor and traffic so bad that air pollution chokes the multitudinous pedestrian passersby. Indoor air pollution from charcoal cooking in poorly ventilated small domestic spaces leads to as much toxicity inside as out. Earth, air, water, fire, solid, liquid, gaseous—no matter the element or state, it is in bad shape. Or so it would seem (Myers 2016).

To be certain, there are major points of crisis in African urban environments, such as with solid waste management (Adama 2007; Myers 2005; Salim 2010). But even with garbage, there are multiple means for interpreting the crisis, and actors at all levels from national to state and grassroots are actively seeking to meet the challenges. This is evident, for instance, in the sweeping policy shift over the last few years to ban single-use plastic bags—a shift where many African cities (like Kigali, Nairobi, or Zanzibar) have been several years ahead of US cities, for example. And, helpfully, there is an increasing tendency to investigate the nuances behind such calamitous portraits of urban Africa. UN Habitat's *State of African Cities* reports, though they are not uniformly insightful, have offered the most sweeping recalibrations of Afro-pessimism's urban story. The 2014 report, in particular, brought to the fore new ways of seeing urban environmental challenges in Africa. The report's vision of what the urban environmental problems are on the continent included the following key concerns: water scarcity, flooding (and sometimes, paradoxically, urban Africa experiences both of these first two at once), water pollution, poor waste management, health and sanitation, and recurring environmental disasters. The main causal factors cited are environmental change and climate change, weak governance, and poor management. But from these largely familiar causes, the report's authors take off in fairly new and intriguing directions. First, the effort to tie urban and rural dynamics together brings the authors to effectively attend to issues of (urban and rural) food security (for example, the geographic networks across the region that impact urban food security), energy security (for instance in cogent analysis of links between lower rainfall totals and reduced electricity supply in many countries highly dependent on hydroelectricity, such as Tanzania), and droughts (increasing with climate change in certain areas, further impacting urban food and energy security).

Second, the report is highly critical of the way urban planning has performed across the continent, not for stereotyped reasons (corruption in Africa, say) but instead due to the heavy influence of "the normative orientations of urban planning in the Global North" (UN Habitat 2014:11). These orientations lead planners to obsessions with master planning, building regulation, and control (of buildings and people). And, when planners do turn to the environment, "expensive green technofixes" divert attention "from needful communities to provide elite green enclaves that entrench inequalities" (UN Habitat 2014:37). This led the authors to boldly declare that "Africa and the world community need to rethink what constitutes a city since the Western concept is no longer the sole legitimate template for its application in Africa" (UN Habitat 2014:37). They thus call for "a radical re-imagination of African approaches to urbanism" (UN Habitat 2014:7). This call was, at times, rather vague. Yet at other times, there were detailed or specific recommendations that might be workable, like the call for a "radical decentralization of powers" to foster "community self-organization" that could happen with a "devolution of controls over revenue collection" in a "bottom-up system of government" (UN Habitat 2014:11). One can even see, for instance in Nairobi's notorious informal settlement of Kibera, examples of what community self-organization and bottom-up governance might lead to in urban environments (Odbert and Mulligan 2015). This political critique, indeed, potentially applies equally to urban and rural environmental governance on the continent.

In fact, great debates have arisen and endured in African studies regarding the development-environment interactions of rural and urban areas. A dominant voice within these debates has held that urban areas extract resources from the countryside and exploit rural environments in a parasitic fashion. Whatever validity one might find to such claims, the fact remains that African cities are among the leading cities in the world for the practice of urban agriculture. Parks, preserves, forested areas, and natural open spaces are also widespread in Africa's cities, despite stereotypes of African cities as "cities of slums." Centers of higher learning across the continent tend to be urban, as do higher literacy rates, and the curricula in many countries feature environmental education lessons from primary levels onward that are improving popular knowledge of healthy and efficient environmental management. Environmental awareness-raising programs and environmental activism are on the rise across the continent, especially in urban areas, and water issues are often central to this activism. In the peri-urban slum of Pikine outside Dakar, hip-hop artists, other musicians, graffiti artists, and Senegalese professional wrestlers have played major roles in environmental activism in recent years, including work in flood relief and prevention (Fredericks 2018; Myers 2016).

Water provisioning can also be an important entrepreneurial arena of environmental management from the grassroots in urban Africa, particularly in informal settlements. A Nigerien-American geography research team has highlighted the policy implications of the ignorance of officials about the struggles of poor Niamey residents to obtain water, and the crucial role of entrepreneurial water vendors in providing this most basic need (Bontianti et al. 2014). Water and sanitation activists in Nairobi also built a highly successful business, Ikotoilet, from environmentally efficient toilets (Njeru, Johnston-Anumonwo, and Owuor 2014). Innovation and creativity abound in the provision of urban environmental services, proving that one must be cautious about only seeing the environment as a source of problems in Africa's cities.

Conclusion

Although there are many environmental challenges in Africa, there are also many agents and activists rising to meet these challenges. Nairobi, for example, hosts both the UN Environment Program and UN Habitat but also is home to a lively civil society with environmental activism at its heart. African regional organizations, such as the Southern African Development Community (SADC) or the East African Community (EAC), are often very involved in addressing environmental issues and have been for at least thirty years (SARDC 1994). Within most African countries, both national and grassroots environmental organizations exist, and sometimes these gain substantive power. Developmentalist states are not always the enemy of environmental management, and grassroots groups are not always the champions of progressive causes to combat environmental crises (Moore 1993). And it is vital to avoid seeing Africa's environmental challenges, or regional and local efforts to confront them, in isolation from the world. From Nairobi's Mathare Valley Sports Club's powerful presence at the Rio de Janeiro Earth Summit of 1992 through Johannesburg's hosting of the World Summit on Sustainable Development in 2002, and the millions of African youth participants in the "Fridays for Future" student climate strikes of 2018–2019, Africans are lively participants in the world's environmental dynamics.

Some issues are beyond the command of the continent, demanding planetary solutions. The position of most African states in the global economy further undermines the continent's efforts to seek the famed "African solutions to African problems" in the environment. But a lifetime of studying environmental issues in Africa has continually reminded me that unpredictable outcomes emerge where least expected—people power triumphing against dictatorships in Burkina Faso or Sudan in recent years comes to mind. The colonialist "way Africa is supposed to look" and the received wisdom on African environments have been challenged for a half century now by scholars focusing on the continent's environmental issues.

The size, diversity, and complexity of the continent make for parallel diversity and complexity in addressing or assessing environmental challenges. At the broadest level, though, we can see the frequency with which outsized roles for colonialism, and then global capitalism and national states aligned with it, are at work in producing environmental challenges. I have shown this for cases as varied as land grabbing, cocoa farming, copper mining, and wildlife management. Just as commonly, though, we find that the agency of Africans, whether in local or national states or local NGOs, in addressing these environmental challenges too often has been underappreciated. A political-ecological approach can help to reorient our understanding toward that agency.

10

Family and Kinship

Barbara G. Hoffman

Everyone everywhere knows what a family is, right? Then why has it been so difficult for Western scholars to form consensus on definitions of kinship and family in Africa? In her article "Household and Community in African Studies," published in 1981, anthropologist Jane Guyer refused to attempt to define "family" in the African context, finding it less than useful as an analytical concept (1981:105). At that point in the late twentieth century, many scholars had thrown up their hands at trying to pin down what family means in African contexts, not because the word is meaningless, but because it has such a wide range of types, forms, purposes, modes of operation, and intersections with the economic, religious, reproductive, and sexual domains of daily life that vary so extensively from culture to culture. There is no one-size-fits-all definition.

Africa, like the United States, has nuclear families, extended families, blended families, adoptive families, and matrifocal families. But in Africa there are also matrilineages, patrilineages, clans, age-sets, and other ways of grouping people through kinship and its extensions (Shapiro 2018). In some societies, people may foster other people's children or be given children through adoption, sometimes permanently, sometimes temporarily (Alber 2004; Howle 2009). Kin relations are organized using kin terms such as mother, father, son, daughter, husband, wife, and co-wife. In many, if not all, African societies, these kinship terms can also be applied to a number of other persons not related by blood or marriage as a way of growing one's network and cultivating "wealth" in people using an idiom everyone understands. This is often referred to as fictive kinship. Nevertheless, addressing an unrelated person as mother or father, or brother or sister, situates the relationship within the frame of kinship and helps to structure both attitudes and actions. The high salience of familial networks in everyday life distinguishes African families from the typical North American or European family principally because of the rights kin have in each other and the seriousness with which their mutual obligations are taken. In most African cultures, nothing is more important than family.

Where I live in the United States, family has the connotation of "people I am related to by blood or adoption and by marriage," so that it includes my mother, father, their siblings, my siblings, my parents' siblings' children, my siblings' children, my grandparents on both sides, the husbands and wives of my siblings and of my parents' siblings, but not the brothers or sisters of those husbands and wives. As we will see, in many African societies, multiple members of the above list would be left out of some kin inventories. The patterns of how families have been structured and restructured over time in African cultures have been the subject of a rather large body of mostly anthropological scholarly work for about a century, but in this chapter we will draw primarily on the studies of the past four decades to explore the shapes and functions of African families today.

The remainder of this chapter is divided into three broad sections. The first section provides an overview of the ways in which kinship is structured in most African societies. Section two focuses on how concepts of family impact decisions about who can marry whom and how marriages are made. It also discusses how the rules of kinship and marriage affect the lives of parents and children throughout life, as well as after death. This section also examines how the type and structure of societies play a role in shaping families, leading to differences in kinship practices. I provide an ethnographic analysis of three specific cultures. Finally, section three explores the impacts of globalization and urbanization on family and kinship.

Types and Terms of Kinship

The most basic family unit in Africa is the mother and child(ren). There is no kin relationship more important in an African person's life than that with their mother. In many African societies, such as Kenya, Mali, and South Africa, where the men can marry more than one woman, what we call polygyny, the next level of family unit consists of the husband, his wives, and their children. In places where the members of polygynous families all live together in one household or compound, every child may consider each of the father's wives to be a mother, and each of the children of the other wives of their father to be their brother or sister. In Mali, for example, there is no word in Mande languages for "stepbrother" or "half sister." Instead, being a sister of a different mother is just being a sister! Things get more complicated when wives and husbands live separately, but that will be discussed later in the chapter.

One characteristic of African families that distinguishes them from most North American families is the privileging of the line of descent through either the father or the mother. Most commonly, certain members of the family share a status called a patrilineage, membership in which flows from one generation to the next only through men. There are also matrilineal societies where membership in the lineage is passed down through women, but these are fewer and decreasing in number. One way to think about this is to imagine that you are related to your father, his siblings, and his father in a way that you are not related to your mother, her siblings, or her mother. This is very different from the bilateral kinship most common in the United States, where children are equally related to their mother and father. Where this type of kinship flows through only one parental line, the society is unilineal.

These unilineal groupings of kin endow upon their members not only a particular identity or status within the family, but also some control over resources or property. In such cases, the lineage is also a descent group, meaning that only the members of the lineage should inherit rights in that property. We might think of this kind of lineage as a type of corporation that owns property and produces wealth. Just as individuals are hired into and fired from corporations without affecting the status of the corporation or the conduct of its business, so people are born into a lineage and leave it behind at death without altering the existence or the business of the lineage.

When charting kin relations, we need a starting point, so anthropologists designate one person as "Ego" and map out the rest of the relations from there. We use symbols to represent blood relations. For example, being the child of two people is represented by vertical lines, and being a brother or sister is represented by an inverted horizontal bracket that extends vertical lines to each sibling. In Figure 10.1, we see a man (our Ego), his brother and sister, their mother and father, his brother's wife and son, his own son and two daughters, a daughter-in-law and son-in-law, and the grandchildren and one great-grandchild. On Ego's wife's side, we see her sister, her brother, and their parents. Only a subset of all of these people are members of the patrilineage: Ego, his father (but not his mother), his children (but not his wife), his brother and sister, his brother's children (but not his sister's children, if she had any), and his son's children (but not his daughter's).

The general rule in such a society is that every child belongs to their father's lineage. Ego, his father, and his children of both sexes are all members of his patrilineage. Among his grandchildren, however, only his son's children belong to the patrilineage, not his daughter's. They belong to *their* father's lineage. His wife also is not a member of his lineage; she belongs to *her* father's lineage. The members of the patrilineage are depicted here in dark gray; those in other lineages are white. All of the people in this family represented by the dark gray nodes share a special kinship bond that the others are excluded from: membership in the patrilineage. For a matrilineal society, the line of descent would be the reverse: a woman would be Ego, and her son's and grandson's children would not be members of the lineage; only those of daughters, granddaughters, and so forth.

Figure 10.1 Charting Kin Relations

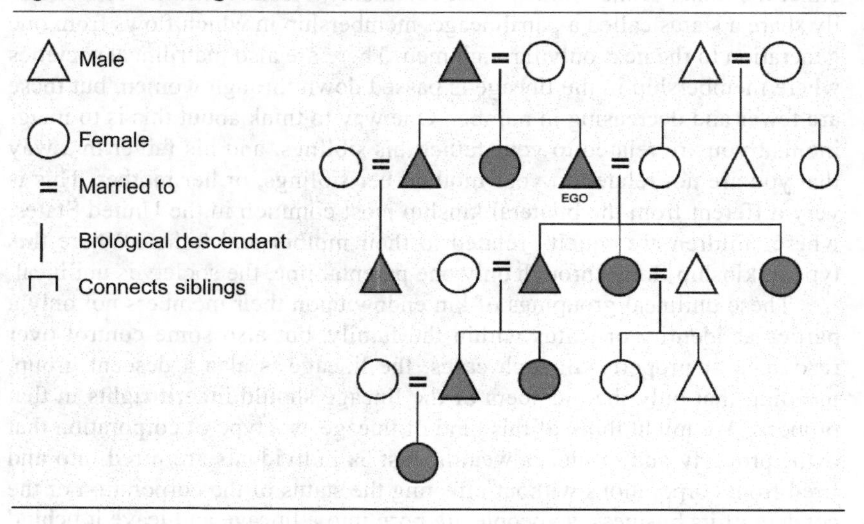

Equally important, lineage membership directly impacts what relatives call each other, their kinship terminology, and also who can marry whom. The most common type of kinship terminology used in unilineal societies around the world, not just in Africa, is one that uses the same terms for both father and father's brother as well as for mother and mother's sister, so only father's sister is "aunt" and only mother's brother is "uncle." Anthropologists call this bifurcate merging kin terminology since it splits the kin universe into two parts but then allows them to blend. How they do so is the fascinating part (see Figure 10.2).

When one calls someone "mother" or "father," what does one call that person's son or daughter? Why, brother or sister, of course. And the son or daughter of an aunt or uncle is a cousin, right? So, in a unilineal society with this kinship terminology system, an important distinction is made between the children of father's brother (also called father) and the children of father's sister (aunt). The former are called brothers and sisters, also known to anthropologists as parallel cousins (children of two siblings of the same sex). The latter are called cousins, also known as cross-cousins (children of two siblings of opposite sex).

Why this difference? It determines lineage membership. In a patrilineage, the children of two brothers belong to the same descent group. That degree of relatedness is conveyed through the use of the kin terms they all use: all will call both brothers father.[1] In turn, they will call each other brother or sister rather than cousin.

Figure 10.2 Bifurcate Merging Kin Terminology

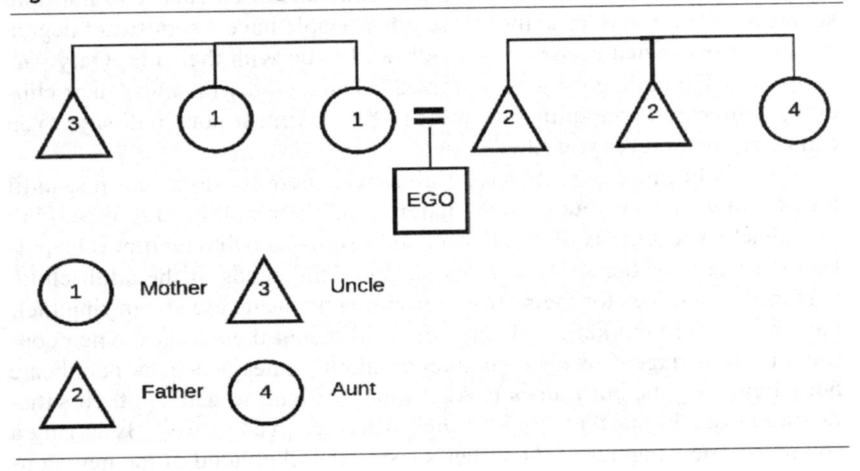

In addition to lineage membership, distinguishing biological cousins this way also affects marriage practices. In many such societies, the preferred marriage alliance has long been between two cross-cousins. The advantages are several. As we have seen, in a patrilineal society, children belong to their father's lineage. So, if a man's son marries the man's sister's daughter, the children she bears will belong to their father's lineage. If, however, she marries a man from a different lineage, both the daughter and her children are "lost" to her mother's patrilineage. Chances are that she will go to live near the relatives of her husband's lineage, thus depriving her family of origin of her companionship and labor and also of those of her children.

Marriages in Africa unite entire families, not just the individuals involved. This broader union is symbolized in the exchanges that are negotiated between families prior to marriage and fulfilled either before or during the marriage, known variously as bridewealth or bride service. Bridewealth is a form of material recognition of the consequences of marriage for the woman and her family: the loss to her lineage of her person, companionship, labor, and children is symbolically assuaged with gifts that may include money, clothing, household items, furnishings, animals, land, and even houses, appliances, or cars for the very wealthy. Bride service denotes an agreed-upon number of years that the groom will spend working for the bride's father and typically living near the bride's family. Bride service might include working in the father's fields or taking care of his animals in a rural setting or some equivalent thereof in an urban context, such as working in the father's shop.

To better appreciate these practices and their implications, we also need to examine the concept of "rights in persons." Understandings of individual rights and liberties differ greatly in African contexts, but a general rule applies:

everyone goes through life answering to someone else, usually to multiple someone elses, in the sense that those other people have a significant degree of control over what each person is allowed to do with their life. Only parents who have undergone a Westernized socialization will say to their children, "You can do anything you want in life!" Almost none will say, "You can marry whomever you like!"

This is because parents have rights over their children, not just until they turn twenty-one, but until the parents and their siblings die. What kind of rights? Expectations of obedience, conformity to behavioral norms, putting the needs of the aging parents ahead of the needs of the adult child, performing services for them (from providing medical care to carrying their bags home from market), and very often following their wishes when contracting a marriage. Losing a daughter to another lineage does not eradicate her parents' rights, but it does make it more difficult to demand their satisfaction as quickly as they could if their daughter lived nearby. By having a son marry the daughter of the father's sister, the likelihood of the new family living with or near the father so that the children can know (and help) the other members of their lineage is quite high.[2] Similar goals can be achieved by having a son marry a mother's brother's daughter. The children of such a union would belong to the husband's lineage.

Where the newlyweds live after the wedding is often related to the type of kinship system in effect. People living in patrilineal societies most often go to live with or near the father of the groom. This is called "patrilocality" or "virilocality." In matrilineal groups, the tendency is to live with or near the bride's mother's kin, often an uncle. This is called "matrilocality," "uxorilocality," or in the case of living near an uncle, "avunculocality." In some situations, a couple in a patrilineal society will live matrilocally for a period of time, perhaps while the groom is performing his bride service or until the first child is born. Also, couples are typically not considered fully married until all the bridewealth has been transferred, bride service completed, or children successfully born.

Once the marriage is established, there are significant pressures to keep the bonds of kinship thus created in place, no matter the circumstances. Where bridewealth has been exchanged, it must be replaced in cases of divorce. Bride service is especially complicated to "reimburse." Where lineages are involved in providing bridewealth, divorce costs both lineages and entails difficult and sometimes protracted negotiations. Divorce also affects the status of women more than it does men. In Mali, for example, most women will agree to a polygynous marriage contract to avoid the shame of being a divorced woman once the husband develops a serious relationship with another woman and wants to marry her (Hoffman and Keita 2017; Whitehouse 2017). In cultures where ownership of herds is tied up with kinship, such as the Nuer and Atuot of South Sudan, ensuring the maintenance of the marital kin unit can extend beyond the death of one partner (Burton 1978; McKinnon 2000).

In many societies the kinship bonds will be continued through practices known as the "levirate" or the "sororate." When a man marries his deceased brother's wife and takes in her children, that is the levirate. When he marries his deceased wife's sister to serve as mother to his children, that is the sororate. Less commonly, some groups such as the Nuer and Atuot even arrange "ghost" marriages so that if an adult man dies without fathering a son first, his lineage may arrange a marriage of the widow with another man to stand in and father children in the name of the deceased. Among the Nuer, the daughter of a man who dies without a son has the duty to marry a wife in her father's name. For these societies, the levirate, woman-woman marriage, and ghost marriage serve to keep the transmission of ownership of cattle moving from one generation to the next within the male line (Burton 1978:403; Verdon 1982:575). In other societies, such as the Nnobi, an Igbo clan in Nigeria, men without sons could appoint a daughter to serve as a son to inherit land, what Ifi Amadiume calls "male daughters." And, daughters whose mothers died without sons could marry a "female husband" to inherit the land in the case of the father's death and maintain the lineage intact (Amadiume 1987:34).

In urban areas, the marriage and family practices explored thus far are indeed changing as discussed below. They nonetheless remain the most common types of marriage and kinship systems in Africa today, despite the growing tendency to opt for companionate marriage where the partners choose each other on the basis of mutual affection and establish nuclear families consisting of father, mother, and children (Cole and Thomas 2009; Whitehouse 2016). In addition, there are other kinds of marriage and kinship systems in African cultures. For example, many North African groups allow parallel cousin marriage and use terminology systems that designate each relative on the parental generation with a different term. There are also documented instances of polyandry, the marriage of one woman with more than one man, but mostly in certain parts of Nigeria (Chalifoux 1980; Levine and Sangree 1980; Muller 1980). The societies that practice polyandry are today extremely rare in comparison with those where polygyny is the norm.

Family and Social Organization

There are over 2,000 ethnolinguistic groups in Africa, all operating within social contexts that have historical roots in particular types of social organization. Over time, most of these groups have changed in structure, culture, and even location. Nonetheless, the nature of the society at large is often reflected in the type of families it fosters. It will be useful to discuss a range of contemporary family structures in a selection of types of social organization that are still in existence as of 2020.

World Bank

Although African societies are changing, the role of families in passing on valuable skills to their children remains important. In urban Zambia, a self-employed father is teaching his young son to make charcoal burners.

Foraging Bands

The least complex type of social structure in Africa is the small group of relatives and friends who roam from place to place gathering plant foods and hunting animals for meat. These groups are commonly referred to as hunter-gatherer bands, but we will use the term "foragers" to indicate people who acquire most of their nutritional needs from nature, without planting food crops or domesticating animals. This is the oldest known form of human social organization and presumably the only one operative on the planet until the advent of horticulture and animal domestication some 10,000 years ago. In Africa, foragers dominated the continent until farmers and herders began to claim the use of the land around the start of the common era (CE).

Over the past two millennia, most foragers in Africa became sedentary and took up farming or adopted a nomadic or seminomadic herding lifestyle. However, even today there are hundreds of thousands of Africans who are foragers or recently former foragers in East, Central, and Southern Africa (Lee and Hitchcock 2001:258; Marlowe 2005:55). Some, such as the Baka and Mbuti, live in the forests of Central Africa. Multiple groups can be found in the Rift Valley from Ethiopia to Tanzania. The Hadza of Tanzania are the most persistent foragers, resistant to sedentarization or incorporation into food-producing communities, according to anthropologist Frank Marlowe (2005, 2010), who has worked with the Hadza for over two decades. Perhaps the best known are the San/Bushmen/Ju/'hoansi of Southern Africa who live mostly in the Kalahari regions of Angola, Botswana, Namibia, South Africa, and Zambia. Anthropologist Marjorie Shostak's (1981) longitudinal ethnography of the life of a !Kung San woman named Nisa and ethnographic filmmaker John Marshall's five-decade series on the Ju/'hoansi have given us great insight into the workings of the forager band and the families within it.

Foragers typically live in small groups consisting of family, friends, and visitors. Marriages tend to be serially monogamous, but polygynous unions are not unheard of. Among the groups that periodically move to find food resources, houses tend to be small and impermanent and material belongings few. Domestic life takes place outdoors, in the common areas shared by all the members of the group. Although most hunting of large game is done by men, women also hunt small animals such as hares. Women do the vast share of the gathering of plant foods, but men also participate on the days they are not hunting. In foraging groups where the contribution to sustenance is shared between women and men, gender relations tend to be rather egalitarian (Leacock 1981). Among the San of southern Africa, first marriages may be arranged by the parents, but subsequent marriages are made by choice. It is rare for a woman to choose to be married to a man who already has a wife (Shostak 1981). Among the Hadza of Tanzania, marriage is not arranged, and parents are consulted but not necessarily obeyed if they object to their children's choice (Marlowe 2010:151). In both groups, men who are good hunters are most highly sought after for husbands, though women provide the bulk of the caloric needs of the couple and their children.

Nisa: An Ethnographic Vignette of Family Life in a Foraging Band

Marjorie Shostak lived with Nisa's band in the 1970s and then visited again in the 1990s. At first, the foragers lived in semipermanent camps of ten to thirty individuals with each nuclear family (wife, husband, and children) occupying a small house made from locally available natural materials whose door faced the center of a tight cluster of homes. Family life transpired in the public space; indoors was for sleeping only. While membership in the band could change frequently as friends and relatives came and went, a "stable core of closely related older people who have proved successful in living and working together" held the group together in an area of land acknowledged to "belong" to the male or female descendant of the "original" inhabitants (Shostak 1981:9–10). The resources, including the water source, are available to all members, not just to the owner. Leadership is not gendered. Both women and men can be acknowledged leaders of a band once they have acquired the knowledge and experience to earn the respect of the group. Since both women and men contribute to the caloric needs of the whole group, theirs is a fairly egalitarian society. Women contribute 60–80 percent by weight of the food, while men primarily contribute meat from the animals they hunt. Even though meat is celebrated more than the plant foods, eggs, and small animals that women supply, it is harder to come by; only 25 percent of the hunts are successful, and the meat must be equitably shared with the other members of the band. As a result, excellent hunters do not necessarily acquire power (Shostak 1981:9–17).

Learning how to hunt successfully is a requirement for marriage, and so forager husbands are often quite a bit older than their wives. A girl may be eligible for marriage even before she begins to menstruate, but a boy must be old enough to hunt, kill, and slaughter before he can take a wife. Among Nisa's people, sexual play was a vital part of childhood for girls and boys, and could be homosexual as well as heterosexual, all part of the learning experience. But eventually, people marry the opposite sex and, when the young woman is sexually mature, begin to have children. Parents arrange the first marriage to ensure that the appropriate kin distance is respected (no cousins, and no one with the same name as one's mother, father, or sibling). If the girl is still preadolescent, the young husband may join her in her parents' camp where he can perform bride service by hunting for the group. If the man enjoys life with his wife's kin (uxorilocality) enough, he may opt to stay there for years, or even forever. However, if the girl does not like the man, she can end the marriage. Second and subsequent marriages are a matter of choice—hers and his, not just the parents'. Older men sometimes take a second wife, and learning how to "do co-wives" was part of Nisa's upbringing (Shostak 1981:127–131).

Among Nisa's people, children spend the first three years of their life in constant contact with their mothers so they can nurse at will, night or day. Bed-sharing is the rule, and babies ride on their mothers' hips during the day, parting briefly only to spend time with the father, siblings, or other relatives or family friends. Sometime during the second year, the child initiates separation to play with other children but returns to the mother to nurse. Fathers, according to Shostak, have intense attachments to their children and are very loving, but the time they spend with babies and the work they do for them is much less than that of mothers. Weaning happens after three years, and if the mother gets pregnant again, sooner. This is a traumatic time for both parent and child, reducing the intensity of physical closeness that has bonded mother and child, though mothers continue to carry the child in a sling. Around the age of four, that too must come to an end when the child is expected to walk on his or her own in preparation for the arrival of a younger sibling. Fathers and other relatives may try to spend more time with the child to distract them from the emotional stress of separating from the mother and have been known to tolerate their children's anger and abuse without affront, because the child is considered a senseless being who has not yet developed intelligence. Corporal punishment is not spared, however, when the child's willfulness puts them or others in danger (Shostak 1981:45–50). When she was a small, rebellious girl, just after her little brother was born and she was no longer being breastfed, Nisa began to steal food. She recounts one incident:

> Another time, I took some *klaru* and kept the bulbs beside me, eating them very slowly. That's when mother came back and caught me. She grabbed me and hit me, "Nisa, stop stealing! Are you the only one who wants to eat *klaru*?" . . . Later, I climbed the tree where they had left a pouch hanging, full of *klaru*, and stole the bulbs. . . . They came back, "Nisa, you ate the *klaru*! What do you have to say for yourself?" I said, "Uhn, uhn, I didn't take them." My mother said, "So, you're afraid of your skin hurting, afraid of being hit?" I said, "Uhn, uhn, I didn't eat those *klaru*." She said, "You ate them. You certainly did. Now, don't do that again! What's making you keep on stealing?" . . . Mother broke off a branch and hit me, "Don't steal! Can't you understand? I tell you, but you don't listen. Don't your ears hear when I talk to you?" (Shostak 1981:60–61)

Wedding is a matter of taking up residence together, not marked by great ceremony among either the San or the Hadza. Hadza women simply build a new house that the pair then sleep in regularly. Afterward, they are considered married and are referred to as husband and wife. Shostak reports that among the San she studied, marriages were arranged by the parents, and care was taken to ascertain the eligibility of a potential husband. He had to be a skilled hunter, not elderly compared to the daughter, preferably not yet married, and not too closely related to her, not even a first cousin. Shostak describes the ensuing events this way:

> A hut is built for the couple by members of both families, and is set apart from the rest of the village. As sunset approaches, friends bring the couple to the hut. The bride, with head covered, is carried and laid down inside; the groom, walking, is led to the hut and sits beside the door. Coals from the fires of both families are brought to start the new fire in front of the marriage hut. Their friends stay with them, singing, playing, and joking. The couple stay apart from each other, maintaining a respectful reserve, and do not join in the festivities. After everyone leaves, they spend their first night together in the hut. The next morning, oil is ceremonially rubbed on both of them—each by the other's mother. (Shostak 1981:130)

Parents space their children by avoiding full intercourse as long as a child is nursing, which can last two to three years, until the child can walk. Among the Hadza, the average is 3.4 years between children (Marlowe 2010:151). Both Hadza and San avail themselves of the levirate when a husband dies, but only the San practice the sororate in the case of a wife's death, and sometimes sister marriage, in rare cases of polygyny. For the most part, husbands and wives enjoy egalitarian freedoms, rights, and responsibilities, the more so as they get older and their age differences become less important.

This is much less often the case in societies where men and women contribute substantially different amounts to the caloric intake and other needs of the family, where the division of labor of producing food places men in the position of primary provider. Among pastoralists where men have responsibility for caring for the large animals of the herd and among horticulturalists and agriculturalists where men own the land and produce the major food crops, relations between the sexes tend to be male-dominated rather than egalitarian.

Families in a Tribal Society

Few social sciences other than anthropology continue to talk about "tribes" in Africa, opting instead for what has become the less politically charged term, "ethnic groups." However, recently both anthropologists and at least one political scientist have argued against using ethnicity to substitute for tribe (Moritz 2008; Sangmpam 2017). Others in the same fields just continue to use the term without feeling the need to justify it (Mahmud 1996; Marcus 1985). In fact, there are many clear cases of groups in Africa that correspond to an anthropological definition of tribe: a group comprising multiple lineages and/or clans that produces food principally through agriculture, horticulture, and/or pastoralism; that occupies a territory conventionally recognized by others as theirs even though it lies within the borders of one or more nation-states; and that shares a social history, religion, language, and other ways of life, which may include traditional foods and dress. Anthropologist Aidan Southall adds "political autonomy" to the list of tribal characteristics as part of his argument in favor of abandoning the term (1997:38), but scholarship on the Maasai of Kenya has shown that they have managed to continue most of their tribal organization and lifeways despite having no more political autonomy than any other group living in a sovereign country. Maasai speak of themselves as a tribe (*enkabila*) that crosses international boundaries since Maasailand, their geographical territory, spans the border between Kenya and Tanzania.

Divided into fifteen geographical "sections" (*iloshon*), and joined into five clans (*ilgilat*), the Maasai of both Kenya and Tanzania speak a common language (Maa), believe in the same god (Enkai), wear similar patterns of traditional clothing and jewelry, and share a history of age-sets that can be traced back to 1755 and that continue to be formed today. They also share a strictly gendered division of labor in which the work of men is highly privileged while that of women, although more extensive than that of men, is not. It is valued but does not earn women any particular prestige or power.

The Maasai have been pastoralists for most of their history, with men having full control over their herds, which they are able to sell, trade, or slaughter without consulting anyone else. However, women have only "usage rights" to animals granted to them through marriage. Even today, Maasai men with enough cattle or other means can marry as many women as they like.[3] In her ethnographic film series, *Diary of a Maasai Village*, anthropologist Melissa Lewellyn-Davies documented a period in the lives of one family in the Loita section in southwest Kenya where the patriarch had thirteen wives and over sixty children in 1984. Wives and children are considered a man's property and also his wealth; a man with so many is referred to as "wealthy one" (*olkarsis*).

In these films, the interviewed women freely admit they are not the equals of their husbands, that they are ruled by them, and that they do not want to be their equals. At the same time, Maasai co-wives are not jealous of each other as a rule. Each has her own house, which she herself builds, and her own allocation of animals to milk. There is much mutual aid with childbirth and childcare. In the recent past, and today in some more remote areas, married women were free to take lovers from among their husbands' age-set. Forbidden love was mostly accepted as well. Maasai rules of respect (*enkanyit*) authorize newly initiated young men to have sexual liaisons with uncircumcised girls but forbid sexual unions with circumcised women. When I was filming in a Maasai community in the Keekonyokie section in 2004, I accidentally captured the voices of two elder women discussing the lifelong relationship of one with her warrior boyfriend from her early years as a wife. In his 1986 autobiography, Dr. Tepilit Ole Saitoti, a Maasai from a section in Tanzania, recounts his joy at finding a married woman to have sex with shortly after he healed from circumcision.

Saitoti: An Ethnographic Vignette of Becoming an Adult in Maasai Tribal Society

Saitoti recounts the tale of his initiation into warriorhood, just a step on the way to full adulthood in the Maasai life cycle, and how his father put the fear of shaming the family into him to prepare him for the genital cutting he would undergo. "You must not budge; don't move a muscle or even blink. You can face only one direction until the operation is completed. The slightest movement on your part will mean you are a coward, incompetent and unworthy to be a Maasai man" (Saitoti 1986:66). His brothers mostly tried to reassure him that he would make it through the surgery, but one had his doubts and asked,

> "Are you *orkirekenyi*?" . . . I quickly replied no, and there was laughter. *Orkirekenyi* is a person who has transgressed sexually. For you must not

> have sexual intercourse with any circumcised woman before you yourself are circumcised. . . . If you have not waited, you will be fined. Your father, mother, and the circumciser will take a cow from you as punishment. (Saitoti 1986:66)

Just before the operation, the initiate must walk over the knife that will be used to cut him, being careful not to accidentally kick it because that would indicate he had lied about not having sex. This ordeal is used to divine who is being honest and who is not. Saitoti passed the test, and the operation proceeded.

Saitoti does not detail it in his account, but Maasai male circumcision consists of four incisions: one to open the lower side of the foreskin at the tip, a second to open the upper side, another on the skin at the top of the penis so the glans will protrude through it, and a fourth to cut away and shape the remaining foreskin, which hangs as an appendage to the underside of the glans. Throughout this painful operation, Saitoti kept quiet and did not move. His courage was rewarded with gifts of animals, eight in all. After two weeks, he had healed enough to join the other members of his age-set and begin to enjoy the benefits of his ordeal. Once everyone's wounds were sufficiently healed, their heads were shaved and they were declared to be warriors. Soon enough, Saitoti had worked up the courage to take a lover from among the married women:

> When I entered the house of my *esiankiki*, I called for the woman of the house, and as luck would have it, my lady responded.[4] She was waiting for me. I felt better, and I proceeded to talk to her like a professional. After much talking back and forth, I joined her in bed. . . . The following day when the initiation rites had ended, I decided to return home. I had offended my father by staying away from home without his consent, so I prepared myself for whatever punishment he might inflict on me. (Saitoti 1986:70)

With sexual rules that allow multiple partners other than the spouse, there must be a way to deal with the inevitable children that will come from "outside" relations. In this culture, any child a married woman bears is considered the legitimate child of her husband, sometimes even after he dies. I knew a family where the elderly patriarch had married a sixteen-year-old shortly before he passed away. Two years later, I saw her at the blessing ceremony for the new home the family was moving to as required after a death in the family. She was carrying her newborn son to be blessed with the rest of the family at the outset of the ceremonies. She had moved to the household of her deceased husband's younger brother, levirate style, but I was told her new husband was not the father of the child. It did not matter; the baby was still considered her first husband's offspring and inheritor along with the sons born while he was alive.

The Legacy of an Empire

The forms of social organization established during the Mali Empire (1230–1600 CE) divided people into complementary endogamous castes. Marriage with someone of a different caste was proscribed. This kinship ideology is part of the extensive Mande culture area that developed from the Mali Empire, covering most of the Sahel region west of Niger (see Map 10.1). It extends even farther than the boundaries shown in the map since Mande traders known as Jula penetrated southward long after the empire dissolved and carried the culture with them. In the heartland in Mali, the Mande caste system is evident today in the legacy of the complex societies that developed. Four castes comprise this society: the *hɔrɔn* do most of the farming and governing; the *numu* are responsible for ironworking and pottery; the *jeli* perform at traditional ceremonies and track genealogical relations; and the *garanke* transform animal skins into useful leather objects, where the descendants of slaves continue to carry their status and claim their rewards at life-cycle ceremonies (Hoffman 2001). Caste systems of this model function in a wide range of ethnicities across West Africa (see Tamari 1997 for the most thorough exposition, but also discussions in Johnson 1986 and McNaughton 1988).

Within this caste system, marriage is both lineage-exogamous (meaning one must marry from a different lineage) and caste-endogamous (meaning

Map 10.1 Mali Empire, 1350 CE

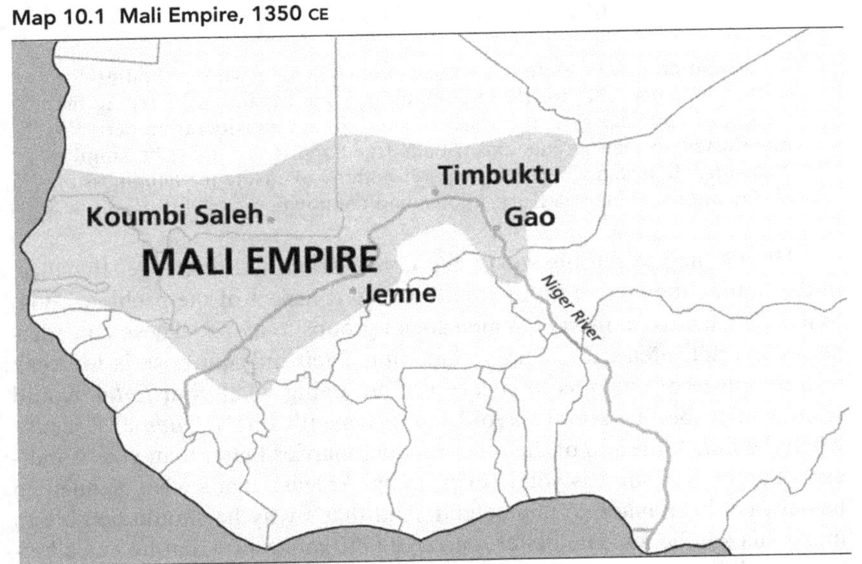

Credit: Wikimedia Commons

one should marry someone from the same caste) within the patrilineal and mostly virilocal Mande societies. It is the *jeli*'s job to keep track of who is related to whom and how to ensure that incest rules are not violated when cross-cousins marry. *Jeli* genealogists are consulted during prenuptial negotiations, especially if there is any question after several generations of cross-cousins have married. Children belong, of course, to their father's lineage, so in the formerly rare cases of marriage across castes, the children would belong to their father's caste as well. Shortly after its founding, the Mali Empire was ruled by a series of Muslim kings or emperors.[5] Over time, the majority of the population converted to Islam as well, so the number of wives one man could marry became limited to four. Although there is no Mande word for "step" or "half" sister, as mentioned above, two important concepts convey Mande notions of differences between siblings of the same mother and those of the same father but different mothers: *badenya* refers to sharing a mother and connotes harmony, unity, and solidarity; *fadenya* evokes sharing a father but not a mother and suggests rivalry, competition, and jealousy. Both words are used in ordinary speech about matters much larger than the family, such as community conflicts and even wars (Bird and Kendall 1980; Hoffman 2001). As long as polygynous families exist, there will be a dynamic tension between being siblings of the breast and being siblings of the semen.

Ethnographic Vignette: Fadenya and Caste in the Mande

Malian anthropologist and novelist Fatoumata Keita writes of the considerations given to such issues when selecting a wife for one's son in her ethnographic novel, *When the Cauris Go Silent*:

> What mattered was to find a "good woman"; one who embodies the virtues indispensable to life in community; one capable of carrying the weight of self-sacrifice, the spirit of sharing and consideration actively manifested so that parents and friends live happily. That she be simply, Nandaman hoped, a woman who spares nothing to ensure the happiness of all the family of his son Kary, known and unknown.

He just had to put his son in the bonds of a good marriage. Because, in the Mande they pay a lot of attention to this aspect of the problem. Who to marry, who not to marry? Which social groups to avoid? These considerations are not intended to imply contempt. Their only purpose is to sneak into the maze of customs to succeed in not being what your *faden* would want you to be. To simply avoid being beneath one's *fadenw*. Because when the *faden*, the son of the other mother, marries better than you, it indicates that he will surpass you in everything. At least, that's what Nandaman has always been made to understand. And that's why he should be able to marry his son better. The better marriage is to make sure that he has a better wife than his brothers. Not in beauty or opulence. Not in elegance or in person. But a wife who, by her behavior, discretion, and control of her person, will protect her husband from humiliation, will protect him from those who want to harm him, and who will support him in any trial. That's how he himself had stayed ahead of his *fadenw*, Nandaman thought.

> *Fadenya*, this double competition of constant rivalry between sons of the same father, is a kind of emulation that implies a perpetual competition among brothers. Competition that can sometimes lead to complicated relationships. However, according to Nandaman, it depends on how *fadenw* manage their *fadenya*, but also on what their mothers whisper in their ears. Because, in Kary's father's opinion, if the child belongs to everyone in Mande society, his two ears belong only to his mother. So, according to what their mothers tell them, the *fadenw* may or may not have harmony in their relationship. To succeed in living together, they can decide, guided by the good sense of the mothers, to let certain things go, to turn a blind eye on others, to consider themselves simply brothers. (Keita 2017:33–34, translation mine)

In the casted societies of the Mande culture area, one role of the *jeli* is to be the mediator in situations of conflict, potential or actual. Later in the book, Keita portrays the agonizing conversation between a *jeli* and a young wife married for five years without giving birth whose husband has decided to marry another woman.

> "Titi, in this world, nothing is new. Anything you live or do, other people have already experienced, or done before you. We are not the first, nor will we be the last in our adventures or in our misadventures. Well, that said, a woman does not say, 'I will not accept that my husband does this or that to me!' Otherwise, the beautiful days will find you elsewhere than in your home."
>
> Djelikê had stopped for a while, to breathe deeply before dropping, "Lucky wife! May God's will be your will, your husband charges us to come and announce the arrival of your sister scheduled for next Thursday."
>
> "My sister? But what sister are you talking about?"
>
> "Your co-wife! The one who will come to help you."
>
> Djelikê's mouth had suddenly grown huge in Titi's eyes. "Support me? Help me! But who did I ask for help?"
>
> "Do not say that, woman. Everyone needs help. Sufficiency or uniqueness befits only God, the One. And it's God who wants the man to marry a woman, two, three, or even four. That's why you, Titi, you will have a sister who would allow you to rest a little."[6]
>
> "Rest! Who did I tell that I am tired of fulfilling my responsibilities as a wife? Do not come and offer me what I did not ask for!"
>
> "No! Lucky woman! The arrival of this new wife could trigger positive waves that would allow you to quench your desire to be a mother!" (Keita 2017:119–120, translation mine)

The situation Keita is depicting is one that happened to one of her family members just a few years ago. Only a *jeli* has the moral and social authority to convey such a message to a young, educated wife. A wife married under a polygynous contract has no say in the matter. The division of Mande societies into casted groups remains an integral part of the culture, and their impacts on the family are many, even as life in the city becomes the norm for an increasing percentage of the population.

Impacts of Globalization and Urbanization on Family and Kinship

Africa is home to a number of the fastest growing cities on the planet, and it has experienced some of the most rapid cultural change under the influences of globalizing flows of religious belief systems, media, and new urban cosmopolitan styles (Appadurai 1996; Ferguson 1999, 2006). Africa's participation in global culture started long ago, however, through the trade of both material goods and ideas. This section draws on my field experience in Kenya and Mali to make some observations about how globalization and urbanization are affecting family and kinship in two African societies.

Imported Religions

The general evolution of Christianity and Islam as imported religions is extensively discussed in Chapter 13. The general trend, at least concerning Christianity, is that although it was practiced as early as the first century CE in the northeast part of the African continent (Egypt and Ethiopia), subsequently spreading throughout North Africa during the Roman Empire, it did not spread to sub-Saharan Africa until the sixteenth century with the arrival of European missionaries. My own field research among the Maasai clearly demonstrates that it was only in the twentieth century that the numbers of foreign missionaries recruiting converts to every variety of Christian church approached invasion levels. In the small Kenyan Maasai community where I worked, Kisamis, with a population of roughly 10,000, the number of churches went from one in 1993 to six in 2002. The greatest number of parishioners were from the ranks of junior elders, those in their twenties at the time who had been initiated and begun having children. In a 2004 interview with a mixed group of church leaders at the Kisamis Presbyterian Church of East Africa, I asked what role their church was playing in evaluating Maasai cultural practices and which, in particular, the church was striving to change. In this community that was just beginning to experience the devastating effects of HIV/AIDS, that church's top priority was to stop arranged marriages so that marital partners would choose to remain faithful to each other alone, and no additional spouses would be brought into the family. In parts of Southern Africa, HIV/AIDS has orphaned so many children that there are now entire villages inhabited only by AIDS orphans (Dilger 2008; Zagheni 2011), and many other Africans from Mozambique

Peter J. Schraeder

Smaller families, such as this Senegalese family in Dakar, Senegal, are becoming more popular in African urban areas.

to Somalia have lost their mothers, fathers, brothers, and sisters (see Chapter 8 for a complete discussion of HIV/AIDS).

Islam is another imported religion that has had a great impact on family roles and kinship systems in many parts of Africa, but primarily in the predominantly Muslim countries of North, East, and West Africa. Islamic rules weigh heavily in considerations of how a marriage is legally conducted in that both the man and the woman must publicly consent to it. It limits the number of wives a husband may marry to a maximum of four and constrains how husbands and wives should behave toward one another. Although they both have rights in each other, the husband has forms of authority over the wife that she does not have over him. In Mali, for example, he has the final say on where the family will live. Islam also governs how children will inherit once their father has passed away: sons divide the inheritance equally, while daughters inherit only two-thirds of the male share.

Roles of the Media

When I arrived in Mali to conduct doctoral research in 1984, local broadcast television had been in existence less than six months. Although some African countries were producing television before independence, most did not acquire the technology until after independence in the 1950s. By the end of the twentieth century, most countries boasted private as well as national stations and were beginning to access satellite and cable services. In the 1980s and early 1990s, the local productions in Mali focused on traditional art forms, such as the music of the *jeli*, and the news. Television was broadcast for a few hours each evening and only in the capital city until the early twenty-first century when 24/7 satellite services such as Africable and Multicanal became both available and affordable for the average middle-class household in every part of the country. The small screen brought images of very different and enticing kinds of homes, lifestyles, families, and behaviors between husbands and wives into Malian homes through *telenovelas*, soap operas, and films from Brazil, France, India, and Mexico. Aspirations changed dramatically. In 1984, a popular saying held that every young city woman sought a husband who could provide the "five Vs": *voiture*, *villa*, *video*, *vacances*, and *virement* (car, house, videocassette recorder, vacations abroad, and salary paid directly into the bank). Such a saying today would surely include *ordinateur, parabole, et portable* (computer, satellite dish, and cell phone).

In recent years, Malian local television and film producers have turned their cameras on issues of changing norms of marriage and sexuality, boldly exploring the problems in the lives of the women and children in a polygynous household in the series *Dou, la Famille* and the urban trend of increasing tolerance of homosexual unions in *Le Grin*. In my research on these two television series, I found that responses to these portrayals of ordinary life in Bamako fell predictably along generational lines: people fifty years of age and older were highly critical of both series, perceiving *Dou* as a critique of a style of family life corrupted by wealth and selfishness, and *Le Grin* as a depiction of the moral degradation of contemporary urban Malian life. The twenty- to twenty-nine-year-old cohort was enthusiastic about both shows. Only 12 percent of this younger generation considered *Dou* to be a critique of Malian family life, and 86 percent were staunch fans of the principal homosexual character in *Le Grin*. In just over two decades, the span of a generation, attitudes about family among those soon to establish their own families had radically changed (Hoffman 2014).

Changing Urban Habitat Styles

During the last forty years, three developments in Mali's economy significantly contributed to altered perceptions of family. First, large numbers of Malian expatriates, mostly youth who had left to find work in Europe or North America in the late 1980s and early 1990s, were able to send home substantial sums of money in the form of remittances. Second, the privatization of banks in the 1990s under the first democratically elected government and in response to the demands of externally supported structural adjustment programs made access to mortgages much more widely available to those with a steady salary. Finally, access to land, which had been completely owned and controlled by the government, was opened to private companies in order to create several new neighborhoods. These companies developed the sanitary and power infrastructure in the entire neighborhood, then sold plots to individuals on which to build new homes. As a result, Bamako has doubled in area in the past twenty years.

The homes that have been built in these new neighborhoods are for the most part very different from the homes their owners grew up in. In older parts of the city where compound-style households dominated, the patriarch would have his own quarters or even his own separate house, while each wife and her children would share a one- or two-room unit, either in a large structure where all lived under one roof or in separate small buildings. Meal preparation was done in a communal kitchen area of the compound, with each wife taking turns being responsible for cooking for the entire family and then spending the night in the husband's bed. This is the style of habitation in which all the man's children consider all of his wives as their mothers and all of his children as brothers and sisters.

This pattern is being replicated in a few parts of the new neighborhoods, but a novel configuration has also emerged. Mali is by default a "separation of property" country where husbands and wives almost never share ownership of anything, from cars to houses.[7] Those women who acquire city plots and build houses for themselves and their children are in a position to refuse to allow another co-wife to take up residence there, creating pressure on the husband to find a different lodging for each of his wives if they have not already built their own. In 2008, I interviewed a man in his late sixties who had three wives, all of them living in different parts of the city in houses they themselves had paid to have built on land they owned. The husband has no home of his own, but instead travels from one wife's house to the other, spending two nights in each home in sequence. Each wife has children who live with her. The children do not consider the other wives to be their mothers, and only address them by their first names. They also do not consider the children of the other wives to be their brothers and sisters. In this new style of Malian urban family, each child has just one mother even when their father has several wives. This is not an isolated case. The former model of polygyny is beginning to resemble Western ideas of what bigamy looks like (Hoffman and Keita 2017). It remains to be seen what kinds of legal issues will be encountered by the heirs of men with multiple wives and children who live apart in this manner, in Mali in particular, but also elsewhere in Africa where women increasingly are gaining rights to own property.

Conclusion

Changes like those I have personally witnessed in Kenya and Mali are occurring all over the continent. Although polygyny is legal today in twenty-six of Africa's fifty-four countries, it is increasingly rare in practice, especially in urban areas where the cost of living works against men's abilities to support, even minimally, more than one wife. Cross-cousin marriage is on the decrease mostly because unmarried people today generally want to choose their own spouses and the legal systems in place support their doing so.[8] The institutional pressures against marriage outside of one's caste are also weakening as urban populations become increasingly multicultural and multiethnic and as older generations die out. The pressures to marry outside one's own lineage to avoid incest continue. However, lineage control of jointly owned property has waned to the point that what most lineages confer on their members now is an identity. Having been codified in postcolonial legal systems, individual property rights today generally outweigh those of the family, lineage, or community in the courts, except in unique contractual arrangements such as the group ranches of some Maasai in western Kenya (Fox 2018).

Ideas about families and kinship are rapidly changing under multiple influences, both external and internal. As more members of the remaining foraging groups settle and take up horticulture and pastoralism, their egalitarian marital practices and child-spacing habits are transforming. Soon, the majority of the members of the Maasai tribe will have adopted Christianity, and Maasai women's sexual freedoms will be a thing of the past. The forms of kinship and social stratification rooted in the Mali Empire that were practiced in so many countries in West Africa for so long are becoming more fluid and adaptable to altered circumstances. It takes but one generation to wipe out a small language; all that is necessary is to stop teaching it to the children. The same is true of cultural change. Those aspects of tradition that are not passed on will eventually die out, and new practices will rise in their place, even regarding the rules of family life.

Notes

The research for this chapter was partially funded by Cleveland State University's Faculty Scholarship Initiative.

1. Typically, the languages distinguish between older and younger brothers of one's father by designating them something akin to "little/younger father" or "big/older father."

2. Most students react to the thought of marriage between what we would consider first cousins to be dangerous to the children born to such a union. This myth has been succinctly debunked in a study by anthropologist Martin Ottenheimer, *Forbidden Relatives: The American Myth of Cousin Marriage*, as well as in a number of more recent genetic studies.

3. The latest national law, enacted in 2014, declares that any Kenyan man can marry as many women as he likes without seeking prior approval of the previous wife/wives.

4. *Esiankiki* is the term for young, beautiful, circumcised women. Calling for the "woman of the house" means greeting the woman who built it and owns it, as only wives can do.

5. The Mande word *mansa* applies to both.

6. Since polygynous husbands rotate their time with their wives, on the nights he is with one, the other can "rest."

7. If a couple wants to opt for joint property, they must declare it in their marriage contract.

8. A recent evolutionary study indicates cross-cousin marriage has positive health consequences that may keep it alive in parts of Africa where certain pathogens are prevalent (Hoben, Buunk, and Fisher 2015:103).

11

Roles of Women

Gretchen Bauer

African women lead the world in women's representation in national legislatures today and have done so since the early 2000s. In Rwanda, for example, there are more women than men in the Chamber of Deputies and a greater percentage of women than in any national legislature anywhere else in the world. More than a dozen African countries have 30 percent women or more in their single or lower houses of parliament, while countries like the United States trail behind with only 20 or 25 percent women in their houses of Congress. Four African countries—Ethiopia, Rwanda, Seychelles, and South Africa—are among the handful of countries worldwide with gender parity cabinets in which an equal number of female and male cabinet ministers serve in the executive. In Ghana, Sophia Akuffo is chief justice of the Supreme Court. In Ethiopia, Meaza Ashenafi is president of the Federal Supreme Court. African women writers like Chimamanda Adichie from Nigeria, Aminatta Forna from Sierra Leone, Taiye Selasi from Ghana, NoViolet Bulawayo from Zimbabwe, and Kopana Matlwa from South Africa are contributing award-winning fiction while carrying on the work of their foremothers like Ama Ata Aidoo from Ghana, Mariama Ba from Senegal, Buchi Emecheta from Nigeria, and Nadine Gordimer from South Africa. Meanwhile, African feminists and their organizations like Pepperdem Ministries from Ghana and Sister Namibia from Namibia are challenging the patriarchy every day; they and women politicians and women writers are exploding myths about agentless African women. At the same time, African women by and large still trail African men in terms of socioeconomic indicators like education and literacy (although this gap is closing and even being surmounted in some countries); access to healthcare, energy, land, and sanitation; and overall assets (i.e., income and wealth). African women also trail women worldwide, except perhaps South Asian women, in many of these indicators.

As throughout this book, it will be a challenge to generalize the experiences of African women. Just over half the population of Africa, women are dispersed across fifty-four countries; inhabit the tremendously varied geographies of the continent; reside in urban, peri-urban, and rural settings or migrate or commute among them; belong to all of the 2,000 ethnic groups (and languages); practice Christianity, Islam, traditional religions, and their various mixes; may be the market traders, business leaders, or emerging entrepreneurs in their countries; or may be eking out an existence on a subsistence plot far from the capital city. This chapter will attempt to provide a narrative of the experiences of African women over the decades, based on the existing secondary literature. In the main, the narrative will focus on the political roles that African women have played from before the onset of European colonialism to the present moment when globalization has reached all corners of the continent.

The remainder of this chapter is divided into six sections. The first three examine the roles of African women in precolonial Africa, colonial Africa, and during the first decades of the contemporary independence era. The next three sections explore the roles of African women in political transitions, including women's movements and LGBTIQ rights movements, women's political leadership in Africa today, and African feminism.

Women in Precolonial Africa

Across much of Africa, formal rule by the European colonial powers was established from the 1880s onward, with the Berlin Conference of 1884–1885 often given as an official starting point. Many scholars have argued that European colonialism diminished African women's political and other roles, at least vis-à-vis African men (Berger and White 1999; Parpart 1988; Staudt 1987). For example, Jane Parpart has written that "for most African women (with the exception of some urban women) the colonial period was characterized by significant losses in both power and authority. . . . New opportunities eventually appeared for [men], while women's economic and political rights often diminished. Colonial officials ignored potential female candidates for chiefships, scholarships and other benefits. Many female institutions were destroyed" (1988:210).

Iris Berger (2016:3–4) describes the historical and cultural contexts of the precolonial period: indigenous political, economic, and religious systems that were "complex and varied, ranging from centralized kingdoms with strong rulers and clear patterns of social hierarchy to smaller-scale communities based around extended families and clans," with societies that depended on farming, herding, or trade. While "most of Africa was rural, towns along the oceans and the coasts of the desert fringe developed distinctive patterns of indigenous urban culture, economics and architecture." She adds that "in most societies men were politically and economically dominant." For women, greater freedom and authority came with age, once they had passed their childbearing years.

What were some of those political and other roles held by women in precolonial Africa? In her history of African women, Kathleen Sheldon (2017) describes three epochs in precolonial Africa during which women held notable leadership roles. First, for the period before 1700, despite the relative absence of historical resources from which to learn more about women in Africa at the time, Sheldon notes that the evidence that does exist "points toward women's central roles in their societies and their leadership potential, especially in communities that followed matrilineal lines of succession" (2017:1). Matrilineal descent systems are those that privilege "the mother's family, with the mother's brother playing an important role in the lives of his sister's children. Matrilineal societies embodied an idea of community organization that 'favours the personal and social power of women'" (Sheldon 2017:14). Sheldon observes that Africa is the "most noted" of world regions for having a high incidence of matrilineal descent systems, in particular in parts of West, Central, and Southern Africa (2017:14). Patrilineal descent systems, by contrast, are those in which descent is traced through the father's family or lineage. The inheritance or conferral of property (including land), rights, names, and titles is affected by the descent system. Sheldon further observes about the period before 1700 that "women were involved in the economy from the earliest times, particularly through their work cultivating crops and participating in local and long-distance trade networks. They were also likely responsible for essential items to community well-being, such as making cooking pots and introducing food preparation methods" (2017:1). Despite these contributions, Sheldon states that African women in this period rarely held any form of public power or position though they may have acted in advisory roles and occasionally acted as chiefs (most likely as regents).

For the next period, during the seventeenth and eighteenth centuries, Sheldon again observes that it is difficult to accurately portray African women's roles and experiences given that the historical evidence was likely to be "inconsistent"—sources often reflected "the biases of observers" as those observers largely were (male) European merchants, missionaries, and explorers (2017:36). What the sources do reveal about this period includes that women were already active and accomplished market traders with significant trade networks by the time that Europeans first arrived along the West Africa coast at the end of the fifteenth century. By the mid- to late seventeenth century, according to Sheldon (2017:37), market women along the coast had "emerged as key figures in the growing international trade networks." Well into the eighteenth century, African women traders played "a visible role mediating trade between African and European merchants and communities" (Sheldon 2017:39). In Sierra Leone, successful women traders included African women who had returned to Africa from the Americas or Europe, where they had once been enslaved, to settle in coastal communities. Indeed, the overseas slave trade, primarily to the Americas, was a grim fact of life in communities all along Africa's west and central coasts at the time. While African women were estimated to only be about 40 percent of those taken to the Americas, they were more likely to be enslaved within Africa, albeit with a very different experience of slavery (Sheldon 2017:44). At the same time, during these centuries some women across the continent held positions of political authority. These included serving as soldiers, guards, and queen mothers in Dahomey; as "Iyadole" mediating conflicts and determining the position of markets among the Yoruba in Nigeria; as members of secret societies overseeing girls' initiation and other rites of passage in Sierra Leone; and as royal women acting as regents in Ethiopia, among others (Sheldon 2017:44–56).

In the last of three precolonial epochs, in the nineteenth century, according to Sheldon (2017), religion (in particular Islam and Christianity) and slavery impacted African women's lives and experiences in notable ways. African religions were deeply embedded in African polities and societies long before the arrival of Islam in the seventh century and Christianity more broadly in the nineteenth century (not to discount the presence of Christianity in Egypt already in the first century) and influenced all aspects of life. Female deities and goddesses often held powerful sway. For women, the introduction of Islam brought contradictory impacts. In some parts of West Africa, according to Sheldon (2017:65), "strict interpretations of Islamic beliefs and practices encouraged greater limitations on women's public presence." So, whereas women may once have served as political leaders or participated actively in markets, the adoption of Islam may have led to seclusion in the home, certain forms of more modest dress, and so on. But in other instances, such as in Senegal, such an impact was not common. Rather, Sheldon writes, "for Wolof women in Senegal, Islam provided a set of legal rights that protected them from some aspects of overt subordination. For instance, as Muslim women they had the right to inherit property from their fathers" (Sheldon 2017:66). Other rights included being able to keep money earned, rights to their own children, and the expectation of maintenance for children from fathers. Again, the vast diversity of Africa made for a diversity of Islam in Africa as well.

The arrival of Christianity in Africa south of the Sahara largely coincided with the arrival of the first Europeans to Africa, among them Catholic and Protestant missionaries, from the sixteenth century onward but with the greatest presence from the nineteenth century (Sheldon 2017:72–73). Missionaries, who were mostly male and initially more interested in attracting African men, built mission stations from which to evangelize and eventually offer education (Sheldon 2017:73). Women missionaries served mostly as teachers at mission schools and as nurses. Christian missionaries in Africa focused heavily on those practices that they considered "pagan and uncivilized, and these were frequently centered on marriage and family concerns that directly concerned women, such as mission disapproval of polygyny, bridewealth and initiation rites" (Sheldon 2017:73). For these reasons many Africans at least initially rejected Christianity while others sought to modify it within their own independent churches. But the church and education were also one and the same. As Oyeronke Oyewumi (1997:128) notes, "the school was the church and the church was the school." Mission schools were part and parcel of the colonial endeavor and also initially geared toward men and boys. Oyewumi (1997:128) suggests that "the initial disadvantage of females in the [colonial] educational system is arguably the main determinant of women's inferiority and lack of access to resources in the colonial period and indeed in the contemporary period." Sheldon agrees that early in the nineteenth century, missionary efforts were more likely to be focused on African men, though argues that by half a century later, some African women were "seeking refuge" at mission stations. At mission schools the students were far more likely to be boys than girls, at least in the early years, and the curriculum for girls had a decidedly domestic focus (Sheldon 2017:73). Heather Switzer (2018) conveys the aspirations and provocations of Maasai schoolgirls in one part of Kenya in the early twenty-first century and how, decades after the first mission schools were established, a secondary school education now allows young Maasai girls to delay and even decide their own marriages and to (in their own words) contemplate a future different than that of their mothers.

Finally, the nineteenth century was one of continued slaving from African shores (and interiors) to the Americas, despite the British and French directives to end the trade (but not the institution) in 1807. By the nineteenth century African women were more vulnerable than men to being captured and enslaved as part of the transatlantic slave trade, even though a few women were slave owners and slave traders themselves (Sheldon 2017:77). And while it took a century for the transatlantic slave trade to come to an end, internal slavery in Africa was not immediately affected (Sheldon 2017:77). Indeed, in some parts of Africa, domestic slavery continued to exist into the twenty-first century, or still exists today, albeit of a very different nature than the chattel slavery of the Americas that lasted well into the nineteenth century. Harmony O'Rourke (2017) tells the story of Hadija, a Muslim Hausa immigrant whose husband passed away in the Cameroon Grassfields, and who in the middle of the twentieth century had to assert and defend herself as a wife and not a slave-concubine in order to inherit from her deceased husband. Even when slavery has been abolished, as in Mauritania in 1981, its legacy can live on in the lives of former slaves and their descendants, though it is also the case, as Katherine A. Wiley (2018) writes, that even women descended from slaves may be able to use attributes such as wealth, respect, and distance from slavery to enhance their economic activity and lives overall.

Women in Colonial Africa

How did African women fare under colonialism? Once again it is less easy to know how African women fared under colonialism because as Oyewumi (1997:121) reminds us, "the histories of both the colonized and the colonizer have been written from the male point of view—women are peripheral if they appear at all." And when African women have appeared in the histories of colonialism, it has often been as the "hapless victims" of colonialism rather than as historical subjects. In their edited volume on African women in colonial histories, Jean Allman, Susan Geiger, and Nakanyike Musisi (2002:1) seek to reveal how African women negotiated the range of political, economic, and social forces of colonialism. They ultimately undermine "any image of African women as hapless victims." African women, they emphasize, "were active agents in the making of the colonial world." Furthermore, not all African women lived a single "homogeneous African women's experience."

Under apartheid in South Africa, African women were described as suffering a "triple oppression" based on race, gender, and class identities as Africans, as women, and as the impoverished. In writing about Guinea-Bissau, Urdang (1975) described the challenge for women of fighting "two colonialisms": struggling against the Portuguese colonials as well as standing up to their male comrades in the anticolonial liberation movement. But Oyewumi (1997:122) queries the notion of a double colonization—"one from European domination and another from indigenous tradition imposed by men"—wondering "what is being doubled." Rather, she suggests that "both manifestations of oppression are rooted in the hierarchical race/gender relations of the colonial situation"; African women "were dominated, exploited, and inferiorized as Africans together with African men and then separately inferiorized and marginalized as African women." Allman, Geiger, and Musisi (2002:3) describe "a reconfigured patriarchy rooted in indigenous and colonial ideologies" under colonialism, against which African women struggled. Their book goes on to provide a number of examples, which are previewed in the introductory chapter.

In one essay in the Allman, Geiger, and Musisi volume, *Women in African Colonial Histories*, based on the autobiography of an African midwife (Aoua Keita) in French West Africa, Jane Turrittin shows "how a colonially trained midwife's resistance to her Eurocentric training" led her to become socially and politically radicalized (2002:8). In another essay focusing on the Buganda from Uganda, Holly Hanson shows how the queen mother once "had autonomous authority, grounded in land ownership, which she used to check the excesses of the king and safeguard the interests of the nation," but her position was gradually diminished by long-distance trade and the trade in slaves that "enriched and empowered provincial chiefs while weakening centralized authority" (9). In another essay, focused on the Asante in Ghana, Victoria Tashjian and Jean Allman show that "it was not only women of high rank and status whose positions were undermined by colonial rule and the dramatic economic change which often preceded it," but also common women, for example, who suffered greater demands upon their labor with the introduction of cash crops and the monetization of the economy (9). In one of the final essays, Misty Bastian focuses on women's collective action under colonialism, in particular the well-known Women's War of 1929 in Nigeria, and highlights "the continuities between women's pre-war forms of collective action, especially song and dance, and their verbal rhetoric and nonverbal displays during the war" (9).

But it has also been argued that the onset of colonialism in Africa may have opened up some opportunities for women. For example, in her study of Yoruba women in nineteenth-century and colonial Nigeria, Marjorie K. McIntosh (2009:24) focuses on how Yoruba women "responded to the changing world around them, and how they created new opportunities in the interstices between traditional practice and colonial policies." She describes how under colonial rule, Yoruba women shifted to the production of palm oil and kernels for sale rather than only home consumption in response to increasing British demand, or how Yoruba women "flocked into the courts to end unhappy marriages and legitimize new ones" when the British introduced laws that authorized divorce. Or when Yoruba women "converted the domestic skills they had learned in Western schools, intended to make them better housewives, into methods of earning money for themselves and their families" (McIntosh 2009:24). Still, this is not to discount the range of negative impacts that Oyewumi (1997) has indicated and that McIntosh (2009:23) recounts, such as "European patriarchal ideas embodied within colonial policies; Christianity's denigration of women's roles in traditional Yoruba religious practices; sex discrimination in favor of males in colonial education and waged employment; the commercialization of land and women's exclusion from private ownership; and the legal marginalization of women through the process whereby flexible traditional rules were encoded into legal principles now defined as customary law."

For decades now, feminist scholars especially have sought to undo the ways in which African women were made invisible under colonialism. They

Feminine Star Africa Photos

Beatrice and Mavis are apprentice seamstresses with the Feminine Star Skills Training Project in Hohoe, Volta Region, Ghana.

rather sought to write "women into African colonial histories" (Allman, Geiger, and Musisi 2002:3; O'Barr 1975). In some such early essays in the late 1980s and 1990s, Susan Geiger (1987, 1990, 1996) wrote about the need to restore African women to African historiography, in particular to the history of nationalist movements that arose during the twentieth century to lead the struggles for national independence. She documents the neglect of women manifest in those histories, ostensibly stemming from a lack of written records, the predominance of men in national-level political leadership, and an understanding of gender as a category relevant at the domestic or community level but not at the national or global level. For example, Geiger (1987) used life history research and a feminist theoretical perspective to write about women activists, like Bibi Titi Mohammed in Tanganyika (present-day Tanzania) and her pivotal role in the nationalist efforts of the Tanganyika African National Union (TANU). Among other things, Mohammed and other women activists like her were responsible for building the membership ranks of TANU by enrolling more than 5,000 card-carrying women as members, mostly informal sector urban Muslim women, such that within a year or two of its founding, the majority of TANU members were women. Similarly, Elizabeth Schmidt (2005:22) writes about the role of women organizers in colonial Guinea who mobilized mass support among women for the nationalist movement, acting as sloganeers and using sexually charged lyrics to mock and shame those not sufficiently engaged in the nationalist struggle in Guinea. Cheryl Johnson (1982) shows how Nigerian women chose to form their own organizations (rather than join men's organizations) to protest colonial policies that threatened their social status and to contribute to the nationalist struggle in Nigeria. They mobilized from the 1920s onward in organizations such as the Lagos Market Women's Association, the Nigerian Women's Party, and the Abeokuta Women's Union. Allman (2009) writes about Hannah Kudjoe in Ghana and the important role she played as propaganda secretary in the nationalist Convention People's Party, only to have her "disappear" after independence, with her contributions unrecognized by the independence government beginning in 1957. Also writing about Ghana, Naaborko Sackeyfio-Lenoch (2018:27) describes how women activists, in particular Evelyn Amarteifio, and one of their organizations, the National Federation of Gold Coast Women, "created a new form of internationalism that merged the nation-building strategies of Kwame Nkrumah and the Convention People's Party with women's efforts elsewhere in Africa and the wider Diaspora," in the process moving beyond more conventional nationalist narratives of the time.

Women in the First Decades of Independence

African women were neither hapless victims of colonialism, nor did they stand by idly during the fight for independence. Rather, they mobilized the masses to join and support nationalist movements and political parties across the continent. Mostly in Southern Africa, where armed struggle was required to attain independence and black majority rule, women fought alongside men in armed liberation struggles, usually from camps in exile. African women, who were the majority of the subsistence farmers across the continent and, like all Africans, primarily rural dwellers, joined in the early gains of independence in the early 1960s. These included a new sense of nationhood among people who were no longer subjects but citizens who were able to bask in the restoration of African heritages; expanded infrastructure, including communication, transportation, and agricultural extension services, leading to modest gains in economic growth and per capita income; social upliftment in terms of the building and expansion of health centers, hospitals, schools, and universities, leading to increased literacy, school enrollment, and life expectancy rates and decreasing infant and maternal mortality rates; and the expansion of urban centers with their greater services, higher standards of living, and, it was hoped, industrialization and wage employment.

By and large, however, political independence beginning in the 1950s did not necessarily restore women's rights and institutions, or their power and authority. Rather, in many African countries there was a quick turn (within the first decade of independence) to single-party or military rule (a return to the authoritarian rule of the colonial period), during which political power was highly centralized in the executive and constitutions were abandoned, legislatures dissolved, judiciaries ignored, political parties proscribed, and independent organizations and associations outlawed.

Elections were seldom held, so no women or men were being elected to political office. But this is not to say that military regimes eschewed the participation of women. On the contrary, when they were not scapegoating and abusing market traders and other successful women, authoritarian military regimes such as those in Nigeria in the 1980s and 1990s, according to Amina Mama (1998:4), improvised a banal game of gender politics that became a key mechanism through which militarism was extended, legitimized, and consolidated. Mama (1995:41) referred to this as "femocracy": an antidemocratic female power structure that claims to exist for the advancement of ordinary women but is unable to do so because it is dominated by a small clique of women, primarily first ladies, whose authority derives from being married to powerful men. Jibrin Ibrahim (2004) has shown how the "first lady syndrome" manifested itself in Ghana in the 1980s in the form of the 31st December Women's Movement under the leadership of Nana Konadu Agyemang Rawlings, wife of military leader Jerry Rawlings, and in Nigeria during the 1990s under the guise of the Maryam Abacha Foundation led by the military dictator Sani Abacha's wife.

Despite the proliferation of single-party and military regimes in the first decades of independence, many African governments joined the global trend of adopting national gender machineries (i.e., those government institutions that would promote gender equality and women's empowerment). As in many countries, the first national gender machineries emerged in Africa in the late 1970s in the aftermath of the 1975 Mexico City United Nations Conference on Women, the first of a few United Nations conferences on women held over the span of two decades. By 1980, forty-one African countries had established the first national gender machineries for women, including gender ministries. By 1985, when the third United Nations Conference on Women was held in Nairobi, fifty-one countries had done so (Tripp et al. 2009:138). The importance of national gender machineries was reaffirmed at the fourth United Nations Conference on Women held in Beijing in 1995. National gender machineries were meant to address gender relations in a comprehensive way and often involved the establishment of ministries of women's affairs or similar departments within existing ministries.

Despite global recognition of the importance of national gender machineries, some scholars have argued that they have been largely ineffectual for a number of reasons. In some cases, the gender machineries were created by illegitimate governments like single-party or military regimes in order to appease the international community rather than to embrace gender equality. In other cases, the national gender machineries were poorly funded; one assessment suggested that donor countries might be offering "lip service and peanuts" in their contributions to national gender machineries (Tsikata 2000, 2001). In many African countries, bilateral and multilateral donors have contributed the funding for the national gender machineries. As a

Gretchen Bauer

Novelists Bisi Adjapon and Maria Kwami participate in the PaGya Literary Festival in Accra, Ghana, sponsored by the Writers Project of Ghana.

result, their agendas have been donor-driven rather than locally determined. Moreover, national gender machineries have been undermined by the above-described femocracy and first lady syndrome, both of which are strongly associated with military regimes.

Women in Political Transitions

By the end of the 1980s, African economies and political systems were in crisis. Many have referred to the 1980s as a "lost decade" for Africa or even to Africa itself as a "lost continent" at that time. (More recently in the 2000s that narrative has been replaced by one of "Africa rising" and Africa as the "hopeful continent.") Across the continent, but especially in West Africa, dozens of military coups beginning in the first decade after independence had produced years of brutal military rule interrupted by the occasional civilian regime. Despite the suggestion that militaries—with their discipline and technological prowess—might be better at economic development than their civilian counterparts, this proved to be the case nowhere. In other parts of the continent, national liberation movements were still engaged in the struggle for independence or found themselves challenged by rebel movements as soon as they attained that independence. In others, civil wars and other political instability also followed independence, again wreaking havoc with economies. Oil price increases during the 1970s and the world recession that followed led to falling demand and prices for many of Africa's commodities, forcing many countries into overwhelming debt. It also led them to embrace the structural adjustment programs (SAPs) of the international financial institutions that were aimed at restructuring failing economies. SAPs, however, included harsh austerity measures, to which women and children were most vulnerable (Emeagwali 1995). African women bore the brunt of the crises of their states, and the negative impact was manifest in myriad socioeconomic indicators (in many of which women still trail men across the continent).

African women responded in divergent ways to this post-independence trajectory. In the rural areas, for example, many women embraced a survival strategy of organizing at the grassroots level; such organizing eventually took on political mandates, and the organizations evolved into mobilized national women's movements. Wangari Maathai's Greenbelt Movement is one such example of an organization originally formed to meet the income needs of rural women that eventually pushed for a transition to democracy in Kenya, but not before she was imprisoned and abused by government authorities (Maathai 2003, 2006). In the urban areas, by contrast, educated elite women pursued a gender equality approach to ameliorate economic and political problems. They sought, among other things, to address their subordinate positions in politics and decisionmaking, leading to greater numbers of women who sought public office. As democratic political transitions unfolded across the continent beginning in the late 1980s and early 1990s, both responses were apparent. In both cases, women's movements emerged and played a pivotal role in bringing about political transitions from the early 1990s onward.

African Women's Movements

Since the 1980s, a plethora of women's organizations and movements have emerged across Africa. They were distinct from those nascent women's organizations that contributed to national independence and liberation movements in the years before independence, and from the first lady–led, state-sanctioned women's associations and party wings of the first few decades of independence. The third United Nations Conference on Women, held in Nairobi in 1985, was widely considered a turning point. It provided an impetus for the formation of women's organizations and the emergence of national women's movements across the continent. The groups had disparate origins and a range of goals. Some emerged from the grassroots as attempts to ameliorate difficult economic conditions, but over time they became much more political in their focus—ultimately seeking regime change. In Kenya, for example, the Greenbelt Movement began as a way to replace trees and provide income to rural women farmers. It ended up deeply involved in the effort to democratize the country. Women also came together in many places to help end conflicts. The most well-known example of this was the group of Muslim and Christian Liberian women who "prayed the devil [Charles Taylor] back to hell," ultimately helping to bring an end to two decades of civil conflict in that country (Gbowee 2011).

Indeed, African women and their organizations played pivotal roles in the democratic transitions that commenced in Africa in the early 1990s (see Chapter 4 for a broader analysis of this trend). According to Aili Mari Tripp (2001b:142), "Like student organizations, labor unions, and human rights activists, women's organizations openly opposed corrupt and repressive regimes through public demonstrations and other militant actions." In many instances, women's organizations and movements joined forces with other civil society organizations to topple undemocratic regimes. Once political transitions were under way, women and their organizations and movements took advantage of the early political openings "to make bolder strides in the political arena" (Tripp 2001b:143). Among other things, women consolidated independent women's organizations; demanded women's expanded participation in politics, through affirmative action policies if necessary; and even formed their own political parties in countries as diverse as Kenya, Lesotho, Zambia, and Zimbabwe (Tripp 2001b). African women leaders like Wangari Maathai in 2004 and Leymah Gbowee and Ellen Johnson Sirleaf in 2011 were recognized for their contributions to bringing about peace and democracy in Africa by being awarded with Nobel Peace Prizes.

Not all women's movements in Africa participated significantly in political transitions in their countries. In Botswana, where the same political party has been democratically reelected and hence in power since independence, the 1980s and 1990s were years of heightened women's mobilization focused initially on laws that discriminated against women and the need for legal reform, before shifting to political education and women's political empowerment. In 1994, the women's group Emang Basadi issued Africa's first "Women's Manifesto," hoping to prompt the inclusion of their concerns into the manifestos of political parties competing in national elections (Bauer 2011; Leslie 2006). Across the continent, coalitions of women's groups issued manifestos in the following decade. Ghana's manifesto, issued in 2004 with a second edition in 2016, seeks to influence electoral outcomes, among other things, and was authored by a coalition of women's organizations that emerged in strength in the years after Ghana's transition from decades of military rule in the early 1990s (Fallon 2008; Prah 2007). Prominent among the issues driving women's mobilization in Ghana has been the need for legislation to address domestic violence (they were successful in seeing the passage of a domestic violence bill in 2007) and the lack of women in political office, especially in parliament (an affirmative action bill that would address this has languished for years). In Niger, too, Alice Kang (2015) identified the important role of women activists (working together with allies in government) in mobilizing for successful women's rights reforms. In countries like Rwanda, South Africa, Tanzania, and Uganda, women's organizations exerted pressure on political parties and the government to adopt electoral gender quotas and other affirmative measures to bring more women into political office, often relying on commitments made by their governments in national, regional, and international protocols and conventions (Bauer and Britton 2006). On the whole, "associational autonomy" from the state and dominant party has proved to be a critical feature for success for women's movements, with associational autonomy defined as a movement able "to set its own far-reaching agenda and freely select its own leaders" (Tripp 2001a:101).

African LGBTIQ Rights

In more recent years, African women have also mobilized around the rights of lesbians and other sexual minorities, typically in the face of very negative attitudes and strong counter mobilization. (See Chapter 12 for a more complete discussion of the pursuit of LGBTIQ rights in Africa.) Elizabeth Baisley (2015) has shown how attempts by Ghana's LGBTIQ rights movements to use decolonization and human rights frames to advance their claims have been appropriated, challenged, and dominated by opponents of LGBTIQ rights in the country. In a move that is common across Africa, opponents of LGBTIQ human rights claims invoke accusations of cultural imperialism, pointing to, among other things, assistance and support from international LGBTIQ organizations in seeking to discredit LGBTIQ rights movements. Abadir Ibrahim (2015:263) warns that this "Africanisation of homophobia is based on false premises," given that much of the anti-LGBTIQ sentiment across Africa stems from colonial "religious and legal norms that policed sexuality and gender" and more recently has been aided and abetted if not fomented by Christian evangelical churches from the United States. Still, in general, LGBTIQ Africans exist in societies in which homophobia is rife among the population at large and among African heads of state and other leaders who deride and, in many instances, persecute sexual minorities.

In Namibia and South Africa, which have relatively strong LGBTIQ rights movements, lesbian activists have used visibility and invisibility strategies selectively to improve their access to citizenship rights, using the latter in particular during recurring periods of political hostility or internal crisis (Currier 2012a). In other words, depending on the national political climate, they may be vocal and visible in their advocacy on their own behalf, while at other times they may seek to advocate much more quietly and behind the scenes. Ashley Currier (2012b:441) suggests that LGBTIQ rights movements in some African countries embody even larger goals in that "organized gender and sexual dissidents, including women's, feminist, and LGBTIQ activists, are part of a growing trend of decolonization movements that have emerged in post-independence nations in the South to challenge the direction and goals" of decolonization—that is, the ways national liberation movements that became ruling parties (e.g., Namibia or South Africa) have handled democratization in the post-transition period. These movements have also served, Currier (2012b:442) contends, as reminders that the process of decolonization continues long after black majority rule or independence have been won.

Abla Dzifa Gomashie

Poster for a candidate running in a National Democratic Congress (NDC) party primary election in 2019.

Women's Political Leadership in Africa Today

As noted at the outset of this chapter, some African countries are world leaders in terms of women's representation in a single or lower house of parliament, and a few African countries are in the lead in terms of gender parity in cabinets and women-led judiciaries. Those countries with the highest representation of women in parliament all use some form of electoral gender quota, the type of which depends on the type of electoral system the country uses to elect its members of parliament. Tripp and Kang (2008), among others, argue that electoral gender quotas, together with certain types of electoral systems, offer the most explanatory power for women's increased representation around the world today.

Scholars use the concept of descriptive representation to describe the composition of a national legislature, but it can also be broadened to describe the attributes of those who are elected, in addition to how many are elected from different groups. In Africa, female parliamentarians, like their male counterparts, tend to be more educated and more affluent than their constituents. They are also more likely than their constituents to be in one of a few high-status professions such as education, finance, law, or medicine. Existing portraits of African women parliamentarians show them often to be seasoned politicians and educated professionals, though their origins may well have been from the rural areas. Women parliamentarians might be human rights campaigners, women's rights activists, scholars and researchers, attorneys, teachers, farmers, and from any other number of professions.

In seeking to assess the impact of women's political leadership around the world, scholars have deployed two concepts—the substantive representation of women's interests and the symbolic representation of women's interests—to try to gauge the extent to which it makes a difference to have more women in political office. Substantive representation refers to advancing women's interests through the policymaking process, whether publicly or behind the scenes. This may be measured, for example, in terms of promoting or accomplishing certain policy agendas or legislative items. Of course, passing laws is only the first step in a long process of implementation and enforcement. Symbolic representation refers to altering gendered ideas about the roles of women and men in politics, raising awareness of what women can achieve, legitimating women as political actors, and encouraging women to become more involved in politics as voters, activists, candidates, and leaders (Franceschet, Krook, and Piscopo 2012:15–18). In many ways, symbolic representation effects may be the most transformative, taking place as they do outside of national legislatures. By educating people about women's leadership capabilities, they may also help to bring more women into parliaments. Moreover, it is through symbolic representation effects that cultural changes are most likely to occur.

A review of the scholarship on the substantive representation impacts of having more women in parliament suggests that many such impacts may be identified (Bauer 2019). For example, Peace Medie (2013) has described how the women's movement in Liberia has been successful in training the police to enforce the new rape law, resulting in a lower rate of withdrawal of cases. She argues that women's groups have been bolstered in doing this by a favorable political context. Across the continent scholars have shown that in those countries with more women in parliament for longer periods of time, such as Rwanda, South Africa, Tanzania, and Uganda, new laws have been passed in the areas of gender-based violence, family law, and land rights that address women's interests (Bauer 2019).

Examples of symbolic representation effects of more women in parliament exist as well. For example, I found that in Botswana, early role models—women ministers and women members of parliament—inspired other women to believe that they too, like men, could be chiefs, positions that traditionally had never been available to women, except as regents (Bauer 2016). Jennie Burnet (2011:320–321) found in Rwanda that with the dramatic increases in women's presence in government, women had "won respect" in their families and communities. Burnet (2011:317–319) observes that quotas had a widespread impact in changing ordinary Rwandans' perceptions of women as political leaders, increasing the political and social agency of women (e.g., women speaking out more at meetings), and leading to increased autonomy for women as "economic subjects" and vis-à-vis domestic resources.

While the number of women in African legislatures is growing significantly, it is also the case that many obstacles stand in the way of more women being elected, with differences in those obstacles depending on the type of electoral system used. Outside the national legislature, for example in the executive branch, are many political offices to which citizens are appointed rather than elected. Melinda Adams, John Scherpereel, and Suraj Jacob (2016) note that countries with higher levels of women's representation in parliament do not necessarily have higher levels of women in cabinets, and that countries with fewer women in parliament may have more women in cabinets. While parliamentarians must stand in elections for parliament, ministers are appointed to office. Thus, the possibility also exists, as has happened recently in four countries (Ethiopia, Rwanda, Seychelles, and South Africa), that gender parity or 50/50 female/male cabinets may be appointed by a president or prime minister.

Judiciaries present yet another frontier for African women, on a continent where multiple systems of law coexist, including customary, civil, common, and Islamic. In a number of African countries today, women serve as chief justices of supreme courts or as presidents of constitutional courts (Bauer and Dawuni 2016), with a tremendous amount of variation across countries and across courts. African women are also being appointed in record numbers as magistrates and judges to the lower courts. Some countries like Rwanda and Tanzania, with government-wide commitments to including more women in politics and decisionmaking, also have more women in their judicial branch. As law schools help to fulfill pipelines to judicial appointments, more and more African women will take their place in the third branch of government.

African Feminism

This chapter concludes with a consideration of African contributions to feminism. From early on, African feminists have made significant contributions to global feminism, including an African feminist research methodology (Mama 2011). One notable African feminist, Oyeronke Oyewumi (2004), pointed out that among the Yoruba of Nigeria, age was the more important hierarchy than gender, and that an older woman could be more powerful than a man. She also reminded readers that in the Yoruba language there is no word for he or she, rather one word is used for both, as is also the case in many other African languages (for example, Twi and Swahili, among others), meaning that some distinctions that English speakers (and others) take for granted may be absent. She suggests that the US or European feminism born of the oppression of the nuclear family, in which women are first and foremost wives, has little resonance in Africa where people have historically lived in extended families in which a woman's role as mother was much more significant. Another notable African feminist, Amina Mama (1995), distilled how one of the most predominant forms of rule, the military regime, especially in 1970s and 1980s Africa, utilized the rhetoric of gender and development to mobilize women for the regime, in particular through the deployment of state-sanctioned and -led women's movements typically headed by the first lady of the country. Decker and Baderoon (2018:219) cite Sierra Leonean scholar Filomena Steady, who observed in the early 1980s that African women were the original feminists. In general, African feminists led the response—that is, correction—to the white, middle-class, first and second wave feminism that emanated from the United States. Across the continent, many leading African feminists have been scholar-activists, including Josephine Beoku-Betts from Sierra Leone; Akosua Adomako Ampofo, Takyiwah Manuh, and Dzodzi Tsikata from Ghana; Amina Mama from Nigeria; Josephine Ahikire, Sylvia Tamale, and Winnie Byanyima from Uganda; and Amanda Gouws, Pregs Govender, Shireen Hassim, Sheila Meintjes, and the late Elaine Salo from South Africa. Since 2002, the African Gender Institute at the University of Cape Town in South Africa has published the cutting-edge online academic journal *Feminist Africa*. African and Africanist scholar feminists in the United States have founded the African Feminist Initiative to provide a scholarly virtual meeting place for African feminism (Decker and Baderoon 2018).

Today, as Akosua Darkwah (forthcoming) observes, "African feminism has come of age." Most recently, African feminists have been at the forefront of using social media to change public discourses and bring their messages to other Africans and the world. In Ghana, women have been reclaiming the term feminist and mainstreaming it. In their social media posts on Twitter and Facebook and other platforms, they critique the male-dominated societies in which they live and expose the contradictions of patriarchy (Asiedu 2019). In its early days, one feminist organization in Ghana, Pepperdem Ministries, constantly "flipped the script" on their Facebook page, switching the genders in typical narratives for all to see the hypocrisy inherent in the differential expectations of male and female behaviors and roles. Another group, Our Collective Vagina, has a closed Facebook page providing a safe space for Ghanaian feminists to share information as well as humor and satire. While it is true that most of those with access to data and the internet are the more educated and more affluent, feminist social media sites are providing an opportunity and the platforms for especially younger African feminists to spread their message and to serve as role models to others of their generations (Asiedu 2019).

In South Africa, a 2019 gathering of scholars, women's movement and community-based activists, politicians, political party members, commissioners for gender equality, and others sought to evaluate the trajectory of the national gender machinery in that country in the first twenty-five years since the 1994 transition to black majority rule. In a summary, Amanda Gouws (2019) laments that there is little left in South Africa of the original feminist agenda put forward by women activists at the time of the 1994 transition. Herself a feminist scholar practitioner, she recounts how feminist activists and feminist academics were able to accomplish an enormous amount in the early days of the political transition, including the establishment of the architecture for the National Gender Machinery: Office of the Status of Women, a Women's Empowerment Unit, a Joint Monitoring Committee on the Quality of Life and the Status of Women, a multiparty gender caucus, gender desks in all state departments, and a Commission for Gender Equality. During the first parliament (1994–1999) feminists were able to see a number of laws passed around domestic violence, maintenance, customary marriage, and termination of pregnancy (Britton 2005). But by the end of twenty-five years, as Gouws notes, corruption, a "hollowing out of the state," and women's lack of access to the patronage networks on which politics thrive in South Africa have meant that many of the early gains have been lost or erased. In many other countries across Africa, the struggle continues as women follow in the footsteps of their foremothers and mobilize in numbers in organizations, contest for legislative offices, and fill executive or judicial assignments, all with the goal of improving the lives of Africans across the continent.

12

LGBTIQ Rights

Marc Epprecht, S. N. Nyeck, and S. M. Rodriguez

We have three objectives in this chapter. The first is to provide the cultural context and a basic historical narrative of the struggles to achieve and defend lesbian, gay, bisexual, transgender, intersex, and queer (LGBTIQ) rights in Africa.[1] We understand very well that Africa is not a country, but for the purposes of a chapter that introduces the issues for the first time in this volume, we find sufficient commonalities and shared trends to warrant some careful general observations across regions and even across the Sahara. As our second objective, we summarize the state of the art of critical theory that is guiding research and activism on a topic that necessarily broaches sexuality, gender, race, colonialism, religion, and the many other fraught intersectional factors at play. And third, we provide a case study of the interplay of local and global activisms, with suggested lessons for what's next, strategically and tactically, in pursuit of the rights, dignity, health, and belonging of all citizens, irrespective of their sexual orientation or gender identity and expression.

Historical and Cultural Context

The rights and dignity of people who do not conform to heterosexual gender and sexuality norms were rarely an issue in Africa prior to very recent times. Such people existed in traditional cultures throughout the continent from time immemorial, although obviously without the modern identities that people today attach to them (homosexual, queer, kuchu, sexual minorities, LGBTIQ, and so on). Their variance from social norms (notably, refusal to marry or insistence on marriage to a person of the same sex) would typically be explained and accommodated uncontroversially within traditional belief systems and the prevailing heteronormative paradigm. Traditional belief systems, it should be stressed, did not draw the kind of hard lines that define individuals distinctly from communities or that separate the living, the dead, and the unborn as neatly as the modern, Western worldview does. For example, a woman who would or *could* not marry a man but instead lived a life of celibacy or in a union with another woman or girl might be understood as the embodiment of a long-dead masculine spirit who had played a leadership role for the whole community. How could a revered masculine spirit allow its temporary corporeal home (the woman's body) to have sex with a corporeal man? That would be very queer indeed, and maybe even dangerous (see Nkabinde 2008 for a contemporary reflection upon the phenomenon).

Numerous cases in the ethnography reveal such female-embodied masculine spirits have played an important role in the ritual life of the people. They were intermediaries between the living world and powerful male ancestors. Female-female ritual and marriages have also been noted, and while these were usually explained as fictive or placeholder relationships that maintained the heteropatriarchal kinship system, the possibility of an erotic element between women has also, appropriately, been acknowledged (Herskovits 1967 [1938]:340; see Dankwa 2013 for a contemporary manifestation of this in Ghana). Many cases have also been attested in which men had sex with men or boys for quite specific ritual purposes that in no way impinged upon their masculine role as a virile progenitor. On the contrary, because of certain taboos or ideas of "pollution" around female sexuality, there could be times when sex with a male might actually enhance a man's heterosexual masculinity. Of course there could also be instances where the violation of norms was so flagrant that it could only be explained by evil or sorcery, in which case remedies would need to be carefully considered (Epprecht 2006).

Historical studies of Islam in Africa south of the Sahara suggest that it tended to accommodate many traditional beliefs and mores, including spirit possession and flexible gender/sexuality systems. The *bori* cult among the Hausa, and the *zar* cult in Sudan, for example, typically involved cases of unhappy women who acted out sexual frustration in ways that shamed their husbands to be more attentive. Islamic reformers from the eighteenth century who denounced such practices sometimes revealed other sexual issues in dispute. One, on his way from the Senegal region to perform the *hajj* (pilgrimage) to Mecca in the early nineteenth century, was particularly scandalized by the same-sex relationships he witnessed among female African slaves expressed in the name of Islam within the *bori* cult (Montana 2004). Many Muslim societies meanwhile had a caste of male-bodied people whom we might today describe as transgender. They played an important and respected role in elite hospitality (see Gaudio 2009 on the *yan daudu* among the Hausa, and Mbaye 2018 on the *gor djiguen* among the Wolof, for example).

Europeans, Persians, Turks, and Arabs all encountered gender and sexual practices in their travels in Africa that sometimes surprised or shocked them (Bleys 1995). In the slave trade era, this included men who had been sold into captivity then caught practicing the "nefarious sin," as the Portuguese called male-male anal intercourse. There were as well isolated scandals in the colonial age that arose from conflict between African traditions and the expectations of Christian morality that supposedly underlie European rule. The latter included new laws that criminalized not just homosexual acts but many other aspects of African gender and sexual mores. In Belgian-ruled Burundi, for example, the state in 1930 forced the king to abdicate due to his persistent homosexual indiscretions (Epprecht 2013). Scandal also occasionally arose from new African sexual arrangements and practices that emerged in the colonial context but were seen to endanger the colonial reputation and/or political economy. As an example, in 1906 and 1907 the colonial state in Transvaal (South Africa) conducted two commissions of inquiry into allegations of widespread male-male sex among migrant laborers working in the gold mines. The allegations—shown to be largely true in the case of African men—threatened to disturb the delicate balance between the harsh exploitation of African labor and the conceit of a colonial civilizing mission (Edwards and Epprecht 2020).

For the most part, however, colonial states and ideologues buttressed the authority of the most conservative chiefs and imams while abetting the rise of a small "respectable" class of Christian and Muslim compradors who could carry out the middling tasks of governance. These men, who often bristled at the racism and hypocrisy of white colonialists, had every reason to suppress the appearance, and even the suggestion, of moral laxity among their people. As Evans-Pritchard's informants told him in the 1930s, the old ways that allowed for some flexibility in sexual arrangements (and even talking about them) had largely died out since the missionaries came (Evans-Pritchard 1970; see also Epprecht 2008).

The origins of what we would today call a homosexual identity or self-awareness lay in the early twentieth century among Europeans in the colonies who were attuned to emerging theories of psychosocial development back in Europe (Karsch-Haack, Sigmund Freud, Jung, and so forth). Stephanie Newell (2006) has documented such a case in British-ruled Igboland (Nigeria). John Moray Stuart-Young was an English author, palm oil trader, and self-described "Uranist" who fled England to escape homophobic prejudice (among other things) to live in Onitsha in the 1910s–1930s. A Uranist was a man who loved young men platonically. Whether that was true or not, what makes Stuart-Young interesting is that he was outspokenly critical of British colonialism and, for all his sexual eccentricity, was accorded a hero's funeral by the Igbo whom he defended against racial injustice.

Men like Stuart-Young were generally despised by the dominant colonial culture (there are no known cases of European women in Africa in this period who identified as "Sapphists" or lesbians, but we can safely assume that they too would have been despised or pitied). It was only after World War II that the idea of homosexuality as a natural state of being deserving of respect began to cohere in a nascent way in colonial culture. This was, in part, a response to the liberating aspects of the war against fascism and to white South Africans' greater engagement with global cultural and intellectual trends. We can discern glimmerings of it in the writing of Mary Renault, an Englishwoman who relocated to Durban in 1948, where she built a career as a writer of historical fiction that normalized loving homosexual relations (Sweetman 1993).[2]

While Renault never came out as lesbian herself, she was a leader in the continent's first gay rights movement. This arose in response to a police raid on a private party in a posh suburb of Johannesburg in 1966, an event that has been termed Africa's Stonewall (Gevisser and Cameron 1994). The South African government at that time portrayed itself as a guardian both of Christian morality and of the supremacy of the white race. White men dressing in women's clothes and kissing each other, as revealed by the raid, were regarded as an affront to both goals. The government thus sought to crack down on white men's homosexual transgressions. The self-styled Law Reform Movement (LRM) was an attempt by mostly middle-class white men and women to resist the proposed repression with scientific and legal arguments. The LRM ultimately failed in that effort, but by challenging the moralist side of the debate, it probably alerted the police to the impossibility of enforcing the enhanced repressive laws. Effectively turning a blind eye, police thereafter de facto tolerated the emergence of discreet gay scenes in and around health clubs and bars in major urban centers like Hillbrow (Johannesburg) and Sea Point (Cape Town). Similar scenes, or milieux, developed in the late 1970s and early 1980s in other relatively cosmopolitan African capitals like Abidjan, Dakar, Harare, and Kampala often connected through expatriate networks to the West.

South Africa again led the way on the continent with the formation of groups specifically dedicated to advancing gay rights in the manner then beginning to demonstrate some successes in the West. The Gay Association of South Africa (GASA) was the first (1982), followed by an alphabet soup of others advancing different identity and racial politics.[3] Another first was the coming out of a prominent black anti-apartheid activist, Simon Nkoli, in 1986, who later established an organization to reach out to blacks beyond the color- and class-privileged confines of the earlier activism. In 1987, yet another first came when the then deputy president of the African National

Congress, the leading anti-apartheid movement/political party, explicitly acknowledged that gay rights would be integral to a future democratic society (Hoad, Martin, and Reid 2005). This became a fact in 1996 when all the major political parties voted to include sexual orientation among the many aspects of identity that were protected from discrimination in the new national constitution. LGBTIQ groups subsequently successfully challenged a host of discriminatory laws through the courts, culminating in winning equality in the right to marriage, one of the first countries in the world to achieve this (2006).

After South Africa, Zimbabwe was the next country to see a gay rights association emerge with a public voice. Gays and Lesbians of Zimbabwe (GALZ) was established in 1990 by a small group of middle-class whites, but fairly quickly attracted a membership more in line with the majority African population (Epprecht and Clark forthcoming 2020). GALZ was subsequently active in supporting a like-minded association in Botswana, followed by Namibia, "affinity groups" in smaller cities and townships

Memory in Action, Johannesburg (South Africa)

Poster announcing the Second Annual Lesbian and Gay Pride March in Johannesburg, South Africa.

around Zimbabwe, and a nascent continental network. The first significant pan-African initiative appeared in 1998 in the form of an online news digest, *Behind the Mask.* Through the early 2000s, new groups appeared in one country after the other, including the first in francophone Africa (Senegal and Cameroon). At the time of writing, there are LGBTIQ groups in virtually every country on the continent, and quite robust regional associations, such as the Coalition of African Lesbians and African Men's Sexual Health and Rights (AMSHeR).

Different groups embrace different constituencies and strategies. Many, for example, eschew direct challenges to the state on human rights grounds, fearing (with good reason) that this would only invite intensified repression. They opt instead for an indirect approach with the same ultimate goal in view. Using public health or harm-reduction arguments and sometimes highly euphemistic language or inscrutable acronyms, this form of activism implies human rights without necessarily naming them or making them known beyond bureaucratic or subnational levels (hence avoiding political attention). Friends in the West have learned to support this strategy. The World Bank, for example, came out with an analysis that put a price tag on different levels of discrimination (Beyrer et al. 2011), and the United Nations Development Programme has linked the achievement of several of the Sustainable Development Goals for the presumed heterosexual majority to the removal of discriminatory laws and stigmatizing attitudes toward sexual minorities (O'Malley and Holzinger 2018).

Support from the West has played a key role in these developments, morally (anti-apartheid activists boycotted GASA for its failure to speak out about racial oppression), financially (*Behind the Mask* was primarily funded by HIVOS and Atlantic Philanthropies, among many groups and initiatives that could not have survived without the help), and politically (with sometimes direct and sometimes behind-the-scenes diplomatic pressure, as in the fight against Uganda's Anti-Homosexuality Bill, discussed below). Western solidarity, however, has been a double-edged sword in many cases, making it easy for opponents of sexual minority rights to cry "Western imperialism" and to link homophobia to patriotism. In other cases, donors have engendered dependency, propagated alienating language, and led to class divisions or mistrust within receiving organizations (Theron, McAllister, and Armisen 2016). In Joseph Massad's (2002) provocative analysis, Western solidarity groups' insistence that Egyptians come out in recognizably Western form tragically resulted in greater repression than before.

Along with the political struggle, African artists have engaged in the fight against homophobia in the cultural sphere. As early as the 1980s, proudly gay Nigerian photographer Rotimi Fani-Kayode published erotic photos of African men, albeit from the safety of London. Sympathetic depictions of gay characters started to appear in African literature, plays, and films in the 1990s. The coming out of prize-winning Kenyan author Binyavanga Wainanaina in 2004 was another cultural milestone. Even Nollywood, notorious for its conservative gender politics, created a lesbian character in a leading role in the feature film *Emotional Crack*. She dies, of course, but not without some pathos (GALZ 2008).

Greater visibility attracted growing, unwanted attention, as GALZ discovered when it tried to get a stand at the Zimbabwe International Book Fair in 1995. Despite the fair's theme of human rights, GALZ was effectively banned and then repeatedly denounced in evocative language by no less than Robert Mugabe, then president of the country. Mugabe went on to make opposition to gay rights a theme in his presidential campaign, equating it to resistance to Western imperialism. Many other African political and religious leaders followed suit to create a situation where vigilantism, extortion, and mob violence against suspected homosexuals and their allies drove many activists back into the closet or to seek refugee asylum in the West. Perhaps the most notorious instance of political homophobia was in Uganda, where an Anti-Homosexuality Bill proposed by parliament in 2008 originally included the death penalty for "aggravated homosexuality" and up to three years' imprisonment for failing to report suspected homosexual behavior. But even in South Africa, with all its constitutional protections, hateful rhetoric and entrenched stigma fueled acts of violence, including the practice of so-called corrective rape.

Notwithstanding pervasive homo- and transphobia and the problematic assistance of Western donors, LGBTIQ activists, artists, and intellectuals have survived and even thrived in Africa in the past decade. Several African countries have moved to accept key demands to end discrimination in the workplace and over adoption rights, respect privacy, end forced anal examinations, and much more. In the next section, we examine how activists in particular have been learning from such successes (and other frustrations) to improve the effectiveness and the targeting of their work.

Themes and Theories

Two broad themes emerged from the cultural context and historical narratives surrounding the existence of LGBTIQ persons in Africa that also informed critical theorizing through research and human rights activism from the early 2000s onward. The first theme was how the traditional cultural context explained and accommodated diverse genders and sexualities, mainly through ritualized spaces and language. Basically, this research established that same-sex sexuality was not a Western import to Africa.

The second theme, comprising the more direct challenge to critical theory seeking to inform activism for LGBTIQ rights, was to discern implications of the above for a democratic vision of Africa, and to offer perspectives on accommodating these rights within the state. As of the 2000s, all of Africa had been divided into independent nation-states, with sovereign powers to reform domestic policy. This means that the postcolonial African state had effectively replaced disparate traditional structures of governance as prime regulators of citizenship and morality even if traditional spaces continued to be recognized in most countries albeit as subjects of the state.

The official stances of African postcolonial states on homosexuality reflect social sentiments primarily influenced by the colonial theologies of two major Abrahamic religions: Christianity and Islam. It is important to note that while Christian and Islamic theologies are not static, the broad context in which they were imported to Africa was fraught with contempt for indigenous African bodies, deities, cultures, and institutions. Because theology, or the body of knowledge about God, primarily operates at the level of imagination, it was a lot easier for the Africans to overthrow the political institutions of colonialism than to get rid of the empire of the mind. Consequently, African postcolonial states maintained colonial laws that criminalized same-sex desires and practices. This retention evidences the fact that nuanced understandings of homosexuality and gender diversity in traditional settings were never taken into account during the transition into independent states. As one scholar laments, "traditional African societies understood the impossibility, if not the danger, of attempting to regulate sexuality fully by ingraining it into the language and practices of ritualized space. . . . [Today] the ritualized legal power of African postcolonial states seems to make no provision for that which—because it has not been thoroughly researched in Africa—might be considered 'things yet to be understood'" (Nyeck 2014:79). Because the two major Abrahamic religions are monotheistic (they believe in one God above all other gods), the colonial context that sustained their spread in Africa reinforced their exclusionary and hegemonic proclivities. Colonial views about homosexuality then were treated as sacrosanct, unchallengeable, and as the only truth that reflected the ideal of human behavior and aspiration. This theological framework gave cultural reason to the African postcolonial state to subdue its indigenous perspectives on human sexualities through the adoption of criminalizing laws as the final and uncontroversial affirmation of newly acquired legal entitlements as a sovereign entity.

In the early 2000s, critical scholarship and activism then emerged to interrogate and confront political and social conventions related to gender and sexual diversity in order to retrieve LGBTIQ humanity from different systems of oppression in Africa. Thus, at the onset of the second millennium, activism in particular was heavily state-centered and leveraged human rights discourse to present LGBTIQ persons as citizens endowed with inalienable rights. Critical activism emerging in this period documented the physical and mental abuses of LGBTIQ persons across Africa as tantamount to denial of citizenship and full belonging. The problem that most activists and thinkers encountered, however, was that the Universal Declaration of Human Rights[4] adopted in 1948, though intended to cover everybody, had not worked well in practice for LGBTIQ persons whose demand for rights required an acknowledgment of both their general and their specific realities. Without a specific international language and principles for protection, LGBTIQ persons were treated as a misnomer in international law.

In 2006, a group of international human rights experts drafted the Yogyakarta Principles as additional specifications on state obligation and for the application of international human rights law in sexual orientation and gender identity cases.[5] This development had an impact in Africa because it provided in 2007 a point of entry for continental activism for the protection of LGBTIQ persons at the African Commission on Human and Peoples' Rights[6] (henceforth the Commission), an independent organ of the African Union created in 1986. The Commission is a space for dialogue between African states and civil society organizations on issues pertaining to human and peoples' rights[7] based on the idea of limited state sovereignty with regard to human rights abuses. Its resolutions are nonbinding on African states but carry high symbolic value in public policy and agenda setting at the continental level. To complement the Commission's mandate, the African Court on Human and Peoples' Rights (henceforth the Court)[8] was created in 1998 and came into effect in 2004. Its decisions are final and binding on its protocol signatory states. This makes it theoretically possible for citizens to take their own governments to a higher court for violations of their rights.[9]

Since the ratification of the Commission's charter in 1981, concerns about gender identity and sexual orientation went strangely missing in its reports and resolutions. To rectify this oversight, the Coalition of African Lesbians (CAL) lobbied the Commission with allies to recognize the existence of LGBTIQ persons as endowed with rights.[10] The evidence presented of human rights abuses that CAL encountered in more than a decade of activism and engagement (Ndashe 2011) alarmed the Commission and led to the adoption of resolution ACHPR/Res.275(LV) in 2014. This acknowledged the universal rights prohibiting discrimination and violence against persons on the basis of "their real or imputed sexual orientation or gender identity."[11] In this resolution, the Commission strongly urged African states to put an end to all sorts of violence including rape based on sexual orientation or gender identity and to protect human rights defenders. In early 2015, CAL was granted observer status with the Commission. Among other prerogatives, an observer status grants an NGO standing to bring cases to the Court. This decision was, by far, the biggest victory for critical continental LGBTIQ activism.

Although not legally binding on African states, the resolution nevertheless put the human rights concerns of LGBTIQ persons at the highest level of policymaking in a way that could not be ignored. For one, the prerogative of an observer status provided CAL with a real opportunity to bring cases of LGBTIQ rights abuses in Burkina Faso, Ghana, Malawi, Mali, and Tanzania to Court (the only states that then recognized the competence of the Court to receive cases from an NGO). The real possibility that some states might be compelled to respond to LGBTIQ claims at the highest human rights court in Africa raised a lot of anxiety among policymakers.

CAL's victory was hard won as the feminist Bev Ditsie demonstrates in the documentary video *The Commission: From Silence to Resistance*: "When sexual orientation came up the first time, it really shook [up] the system," as some political influencers perceived homosexuality as a "new virus" and rejected any discussion on the issue as un-African, unethical, and ungodly. A formal backlash unfolded over the following years (2015–2016), first from the Executive Council of the African Union. Primarily composed of the ministers of foreign affairs, the Executive Council rebuked the Commission in not so subtle language through decisions EX.CL/Dec.887(XXVII) and EX.CL/Dec.902(XXVIII) Rev.1. It urged the Commission to

> take into account the fundamental African values, identity and good traditions, and to withdraw the observer status granted to NGOs who may attempt to impose values contrary to the African values; in this regard, requests the ACHPR to review its criteria for granting Observer Status to NGOs and to withdraw the observer status granted to the Organization called CAL, in line with those African Values.[12]

The Commission passed resolution ACHPR/Res.361(LIX)[13] by November 2016, amending its criteria for granting observer status to NGOs, and withdrew CAL's status based on the idea that African values were fundamentally in opposition to LGBTIQ rights. And on such grounds alone, the debate was closed at the African Union's level, at least for some time. For CAL, however, the Commission's decision shows it is not an independent body and "exemplifies the backlash that women and LGBTIQ movements are facing on the continent . . . persistent attacks on their rights to freedom of expression and association."[14] Hence, as critical activism explicates LGBTIQ existence in Africa on the basis of human rights discourse, institutional accommodation at the highest level of continental ritualized political power remains fuzzy. The African Union's Executive Council's reaction to CAL's observer status assumes there is something fundamental about African identity and "good traditions" that forecloses LGBTIQ existence and participation in the mechanisms of governance. The problem is that no politician to date has been able to specify and demonstrate what these so-called immutable foundational good traditions and values are and how they work for the betterment of Africa's life. The point is that this kind of rebuke of LGBTIQ activism is easy and popular and works as a real empire of the mind.

Nonetheless, at the state level, critical LGBTIQ activism has registered important victories, and several countries decriminalized homosexuality at the beginning of the new millennium: Cape Verde (2004), Lesotho (2012), São Tomé and Príncipe (2012), Mozambique (2015), Seychelles (2016), Angola (2019), and Botswana (2019).[15] These countries joined South Africa and the eleven nations where homosexuality has never been criminalized—Benin, Burkina Faso, Côte d'Ivoire, DRC, Djibouti, Equatorial Guinea, Gabon, Madagascar, Mali, Niger, and Rwanda. Thus one notes that critical LGBTIQ activism in Africa has effectively penetrated the imagination of political citizenship; the postcolonial state is responding and changing, albeit unsteadily.

Given the now cliché critique of LGBTIQ activism as irrelevant to postcolonial cultural imagination, activists have sought but found it hard to adopt a more conscious intersectional approach to human rights. LGBTIQ activism in Africa has always embedded some forms of intersectional strategy in building critical alliances with public health initiatives to combat HIV, and with the women's/feminist movement to frame issues in a way that supports mutually beneficial funding schemes. (An example of how this is done in practice will be shown later in discussing the strategies of CAL.) Strategic partnerships with public health initiatives are perhaps the oldest since HIV became a prioritized area of policy intervention in the mid-1990s in Africa. Although public health strategies have mostly benefited gay men, leaving lesbian women behind (Matebeni et al. 2013), they have nevertheless contributed to raising awareness about stigma and discrimination as impediments to successful implementation of national health plans (Makofane et al. 2013; Makofane, Spire, and Mtetwa 2018).

The general idea here is that LGBTIQ lives intersect with other types of vulnerabilities. The implication is that solidarity starts at a meeting point of vulnerability. A more conscious approach that fully integrates intersectionality (Crenshaw 1991) as a framework for mobilizing has been harder to implement without controversy in part because it demands that other types of systemic oppressions in Africa and their root causes be integrated in demands for justice. The implication is that sometimes these root causes may, by the very fact of their ramifications, prohibit or galvanize action or inaction, support or resistance, visibility and invisibility. Awareness of the root causes forces the LGBTIQ movement in Africa to grapple with power inequality within its ranks and with its international partners, not just with diverse constituencies within African countries.

To illustrate, in 2016 while the United Nations was considering the appointment of a Special Rapporteur, or Independent Expert on Sexual Orientation and Gender Identity with a worldwide mission, CAL objected to the creation of this office or any "special mechanism" in "isolation from broader issues related to gender and sexuality."[16] One would have expected, given its bid at the Commission, that CAL would welcome such a reporting

Memory in Action, Johannesburg (South Africa)

Poster announcing a conference sponsored by the Coalition for African Lesbians (CAL), a continent-wide organization based in South Africa.

mechanism at the United Nations and offer its support as did other LGBTIQ NGOs in Africa, but it did not. This dissent was the first public and high-level disagreement on the meaning of intersectionality among prominent LGBTIQ NGOs in Africa and revealed the strategic challenges that exclusionary activism may pose. CAL at the time argued that the establishment of a Special Rapporteur on Sexual Orientation and Gender Identity made it harder to establish another mandate for a Special Rapporteur on Sexuality and Gender. Simply put, the objection maintained, "We do not want special rights. We are not asking for and demanding special rights and do not want to be associated with LGBT exceptionalism. . . . Sexuality and gender are much more than sexual orientation and gender identity."[17] While CAL's objections were primarily addressed to an international audience, similar calls for internal critical reflections on LGBTIQ activism in Africa were heard. Theron, McAllister, and Armisen (2016) lamented about the hyper-professionalization of activism, suggesting that the managerial style of LGBTIQ organizing has shifted incentives away from base-building and broader coalition building. Ultimately, the form of activism may not reach the grassroots as it should and may rely on and recreate the class biases that disproportionately affect LGBTIQ people.

Through its ability to shift political positions that led to the decriminalization of homosexuality in several states, its documentation of human rights abuses, and its persistent challenge to discriminatory institutions, LGBTIQ activism contributes to broadening the scope of human rights across African regions. As it encounters unequal power relations internally and internationally, activism is self-critical of some of its strategies, and there is no consensus on whether it helps or hurts to adopt an exclusionary stance on rights versus an inclusive approach aimed at broadening a coalition of support. Just as accommodating the demands of LGBTIQ rights is differentially appreciated among the African states, so is self-critique of queer strategies and impact among the activists.

Critical scholarship has taken many directions but has undoubtedly sought to respond to the accusation that LGBTIQ life is a foreign liability. In some ways, this accusation is misguided because since the early 2000s, scholarly production about LGBTIQ issues in Africa has been on the rise. But, as Matebeni notes, to date, "no academic institution in the continent ha[s] a dedicated queer studies program" (2019:1334), and without institutional support, academic production on the continent undergoes similar struggles as political activism. That the bulk of scholarly writings on LGBTIQ issues in Africa is done by scholars who live outside of the continent demonstrates the expanding global interest in gender and sexuality studies. It also demonstrates the insignificant impact that such an interest has on institutions of higher education in Africa. Notwithstanding this fact, recent (2019) contributions to the *Global Encyclopedia of Lesbian, Gay, Bisexual, Transgender, and Queer History* show Africa gets disproportionate attention as a region—roughly 180,000 words in ninety entries, mostly by Africans and African-based scholars, the majority of whom are female authors. Thus, intellectual contributions from scholars living and working in Africa are engaged and embedded in the practice of resistance and critique through the kinds of perspectives they offer. Focus here is on the ways in which African scholars holistically interrogate dominating assumptions about what is African and what is not, and the techniques they deploy to ground critical perspectives in Africa within and beyond sexuality.

Take for instance the African Union's previous high-level argument that "fundamental African values, identity and good traditions" are opposed to LGBTIQ ways of life. Whereas this belief describes attributes of Africans that bear a certain kind of aesthetics needing protection, it also inspires activist strategies and responses that seek to "rescue" LGBTIQ persons as a single category from verbal abuse. Critical scholarship from Africa consistently challenges political statements intended to isolate and divide by emphasizing inclusive perspectives. To illustrate, writing on beauty and queerness, Matebeni asserts that it is not so much the description of the thing that matters but its relational potency. Beauty is beauty not because it is beautiful, but because it has been prioritized as such and limited to the perception of those who see the world in binary logics. Consequently, keeping objections based on fundamental values in mind, a "queer" perspective helps one understand not just what is said about beauty, but more importantly, that "ugliness" is relational rather than natural. Ugliness is located in the social assumptions about beauty, "for if beauty remains this fixed, then it can be argued that beauty has been made ugly" (Matebeni 2016:32). By extension, this queer framework allows us to circumvent the oppositional logic embedded in calls for equality between African and LGBTIQ values, and rather focus on the disidentification and self-debasement that regards certain African people (queer people) as the ugly within.

All this is to say that critical scholarship complements activism in Africa by resisting the oversimplification of LGBTIQ experiences. Thus, where political pundits and conservative agents see unreconcilable opposition between African values and LGBTIQ identities, critical scholarship maintains that the fate of LGBTIQ and Africa is intertwined. Minorities and (presumed) majorities are similarly situated within global networks of powerful scripts that flow primarily from the global North to Africa and that tend to entrench cultural and economic inequalities (Matebeni 2014; Wainaina 2005; Nyeck 2019). Furthermore, critical scholarship has recognized multiple and complex queer experiences in need of interpretative work that averts reifying identities and claims rooted in labels (such as LGBTIQ or "heterosexual") derived from the history of thought and activism in the West. The uncritical assertion of such labels, ungrounded in the specificities of local experience, may suggest the same fixity that activists decry in homophobic political statements (Bennett 2018; Higginbotham 2018).

Where does all of this lead us? For one, LGBTIQ activism is real and alive in Africa, and countries have been shifting their positions by decriminalizing homosexuality. The arduous work of changing social attitudes is under way though extremely difficult for at least two reasons. First, Africa's marginalization in the world's social order causes people to view international incursions, even with a human rights leaning, with suspicion. Power imbalance in the world and in the realm of ideas, the monopoly of channels of communications (social media, print media, transnational television networks), and economic policies make cultural imagination a fertile ground for resisting perceived and real Western dominance in Africa. As formal laws are changing, a lot more work is needed to change social attitudes and minds. Second, unlike in Europe and North America, religion plays an important role in African peoples' lives. Expanding the boundaries of inclusion with and for LGBTIQ persons in Africa further calls for a critical reappraisal of the specific roles that culture and religion play in shaping perception. The case of Uganda in recent years is informative about the critical need for queering Christian theology in Africa and of the real threat that conservative ideology presents to human rights on the continent.

A Case Study of Homophobia and Resistance: Uganda, 1999–Present

In Kampala, Uganda, in 1999, Anglican priest Reverend Erich Kasirye noticed a segment of his parishioners struggling spiritually with isolation and anxiety. Upon realizing that the common struggle revolved around sexuality and gender, the religious leader decided to organize a support unit for the gay and bisexual men. In this unit, members found the much-desired camaraderie around their identity struggles with semiregular meetings, conversations, and celebration.[18] In 2001, joined by Bishop Christopher Senyonjo, the grouping became Integrity Uganda, a transnational affiliate of the Episcopal organization called Integrity USA. In that same year, this group ceased to be a lone organization for LGBTIQ people in Uganda. It was joined by the newly formed Gay and Lesbian Alliance (GALA).

Within the next ten years, this collectivizing would mushroom to feature roughly two dozen organizations. Two particularly renowned groups included Freedom and Roam Uganda (FARUG), which formed in 2003 to support lesbian women, and Sexual Minorities Uganda (SMUG), which formed in 2004 for the entire community. The two organizations became the most active and tactically diverse LGBTIQ groups in Uganda. All of the organizations experienced shifts in their represented constituencies: GALA morphed to focus on bisexuals; FARUG for all lesbians, bisexuals, and trans people; and SMUG grew to coalesce organizations rather than individuals. However, these early organizations ultimately cohered in a way that ensured cooperative strategizing in the early years. The missions of such activism expanded from the desire to form affinity groups to appeals to decriminalize colonial-era sodomy legislation, enjoy fully open social inclusion, and have rights to family formation.

In 2009, LGBTIQ organizing in Uganda suffered a devastating fracture due to the Anti-Homosexuality Bill (AHB), a piece of legislation drafted for goals that colonial-era sodomy laws were imagined not to achieve. The British colonial laws retained by the Ugandan Penal Code of 1950 defined sodomy vaguely as an "unnatural offence" committed when a man had "carnal knowledge" of another against the order of nature. Implied was that the other party was a man, severing the connection of the law from a particular action (of anal sex, which could occur between any two people) and instead adhering it to a gendered interaction (presumed unnatural, between two men). The definition was revised in 2000, when the Gender References Act introduced gender-neutral language to the offense and changed the law to read as "any person" who gains carnal knowledge of any person. This effectively criminalized lesbian or female same-sex sexual interactions for the first time in the country. However, concerned by the simultaneous presence of LGBTIQ organizations and absence of sodomy convictions, parliamentarians called for a stronger law, better able to quell the disquieting growth of the rights movement. These anti-queer rumblings began in 2003 but became a fixed conversation in parliament by 2009 (Rodriguez 2018). In that year, parliamentarian David Bahati introduced the bill that would come to be widely known as the "Kill the Gays Bill."

The AHB sought to achieve three major goals for the nation. The bill would legally define homosexuality for the first time, stripping away the ambiguity of the former language of the "unnatural offence." Homosexuality, in the second clause of Part I, very specifically includes acts of oral, anal, and vaginal penetration by physical body part or "sexual contraption." Innova-

Memory in Action, Johannesburg (South Africa)

Poster announcing the "Gay Men's Health Forum" as part of a township AIDS project in Johannesburg, South Africa.

tively, the mere intention of committing homosexuality while touching another person constitutes the offense of homosexuality. This language creates a loophole through which one can be tried for homosexuality without ever actually having sex. The law then inscribes identity and interaction in ways that were only implied in earlier sodomy legislation. Second, the imagined law would strengthen anti-sodomy enforcement mechanisms by establishing an extradition clause that allows for the forced return and sentencing of Ugandan "offenders" who are traveling or living abroad. It would also officially require anyone aware of another who identifies as LGBTIQ to report them to the police, and criminalize the "promotion" of homosexuality. Although largely treated as a new and strange concept, the idea of promotion also has firm British ties, as British prime minister Margaret Thatcher's regime also passed legislation barring such promotion in the 1980s. Although historically, promoting homosexuality describes the various actions that lead to its normalization (sexual health education, forming advocacy groups), the promotion of homosexuality as written into the Anti-Homosexuality Bill also included specific language on funding and marketing events, publishing pornographic material, and recording seminars or activities via electronic devices (AHB 2009, Part I, Clause 13). As a final major development, the bill would punish repeat offenders and treat the allegedly most egregious forms of same-sex sexual assault with the death penalty.[19]

Therefore, parallel to the development of organizing for queer social and political citizenship grew the oppositional political activity to silence, repress, and erase LGBTIQ (or *kuchu*) Ugandans from the cultural imaginary. Although thoroughly contested by both research (Epprecht 2006; Murray and Roscoe 1998) and common knowledge, many predominant, anti-gay logics (Currier 2018) continue to circulate, increasing the anti-queer animus in the region (Thoreson 2014). The particularly resonant anti-LGBTIQ frames in Uganda include that homosexuality is un-African, fueled by imperialist interests, and represents a moral decay from which the nation cannot afford to suffer. Interestingly, this logic was supported by US missionary Scott Lively, who visited Uganda shortly before the proposal of the Anti-Homosexuality Bill to proselytize against the harms of the "gay agenda" of the United States. Lively's position highlighted that the United States had been corrupted by such an agenda and that Uganda must engage proactively to ensure that the gay agenda did not take over the otherwise moral country.

Another resonant anti-gay logic in Uganda is that homosexuality runs contrary to communal values by supporting individual, mercenary-like gains. In fact, economic tensions underlie much of the political fears of LGBTIQ activism, as the efforts to politicize and criminalize sexuality aligned with claims to combat cultural imperialism and spiked when international governance bodies threatened to sanction the country for its support of the anti-homosexuality legislation (Rodriguez 2018). While international concerns included Uganda's economic mismanagement and deteriorating human rights record, the apparent focus on gay rights inflamed domestic tensions around the internationalized identities that form the LGBTIQ community. The fear that the normalization of LGBTIQ identities signaled a cultural shift away from communalism and African values pervaded and was exacerbated by various economic concerns of the moment.

Six years of national debate around these issues propagated increasingly strong religious narratives that sought to exclude and eliminate LGBTIQ Africans, in high contrast with the previous Kasirye- and Ssenyonjo-styled religious aspirations. Many of these narratives relied on a historical imagining of a precolonial culture absent of sexual and gender diversity, as well as religious claims-making that excluded homosexuality from Christianity and Islam. Uganda, however, has had a significant public history concerning religion and sexuality, particularly following the royal courts of Buganda[20] and their relationships to gender (Nannyonga-Tamusuza 2002, 2009) and same-sex sexual practices (Rao 2015).

Many critical African-studies scholars, queer theorists, and Queer African studies scholars regard the gender binary as an invention and colonial import. While scholars do not propose that a gender binary did not exist in any African society, it has been made abundantly clear that many societal approaches to gender—and, therefore, labor divisions and sexual unions—were much more varied in historical customs than in current recognized institutions. Nannyonga-Tamusuza's (2002, 2009) historical review of precolonial gender in Buganda highlights that although gender indeed structured society, it was situational, fluid, and second to hierarchical status (royalty or commoner). Nannyonga-Tamusuza (2009:144) explains the following:

> The historical construction of gender is dependent on whether one belongs to royalty or the commoners' class. The gender socialization within the palace assigns both the princes and princesses a man gender, and the commoners—both male and female—a woman gender. However the woman gender assigned to the commoner males is only situational. They retain a man gender outside the palace contexts.

The fluidity of gender in the context of status in precolonial Buganda directly contrasts its fixed nature in the Western, colonial era and what is now witnessed in contemporary (postcolonial) Uganda. Various positionalities may structure one's gender identities, behaviors, and sense of self. In this context, the sense of self forms in community and in relation to another, rather than individually, due solely to genitalia. A relational gender reveals more about the power structure in society than what is essential to biology and, therefore, may permit a more expansive set of acceptable behaviors. Relatedly, there exists a rich vocabulary of gender-fluid descriptors in several regions, as described by Adrian Jjuuko (2019). These include "kyakulassajja (male-like woman) or nakawanga (she-cock) for women who behaved like men, and ekikazikazi (womanly male) for men who behaved like women" in Buganda. Jjuuko (2019) also reviews a number of scholars whose research focuses on historical gender diversity within the Basigu (La Fontaine 1959), Banyoro (Needham 1973), Iteso (Lawrence 1957), and Lango (Driberg 1923).

Claims to a historical culture devoid of sexual and gender diversity in Uganda have been used to devalue LGBTIQ movement-making but have largely relied on bias-motivated sentiments and erroneous summaries of local history. This is particularly striking in Uganda, where one of the largest holidays in the country—Ugandan Martyrs Day—commemorates a historical moment when same-sex sexual desire instituted in the monarchy collided with the newfound Christian movement in Uganda. When the *kabaka* (king) Mwanga II called for the previously normalized sexual interactions shared between king and pages, the pages, newly converted to Christianity, defied the order (Rao 2015). This denial occurred multitudinous times between 1885 and 1888, a period when Muslim traders—some of whom purportedly were also inclined to have sex with boys—were seeking to establish their influence over Mwanga and Buganda. Rather than suffer the indignity of continued defiance by those ordered to serve, the *kabaka* had between thirty and forty-five rebellious pages killed. This act prompted British military intervention and the establishment of colonial rule.

Once colonized, the British Protectorate of Uganda began to commemorate this historical event, reimagining it as a triumph of the British Empire's modern Christianity over African traditionalist and Muslim sexual depravity (Apter 1960). Contemporarily, the event gathers thousands of pilgrims from around the country, who continue to recognize the martyrs as a reflection of the strength and righteousness of Christian morals in the culture. Depending on the light under which the popular holiday is viewed, the event can reflect the entrenchment of colonial political motivations, the currency of Christianity over other religious beliefs in every corner of the country, or the cultural memory of resistance that Ugandans appreciate. However, what cannot be disputed or changed is that same-sex sexual practices and desires certainly predate colonialism. This reality, however, suffers overshadowing by the narrative that such desires are "un-African."

While religion may help some frame their homophobia, religion itself is not the cause of politicized homophobia. To say that it is disregards the efforts of religious leaders to nurture the well-being of LGBTIQ people. It also undermines the reality of the coexistence of homosexuality and religious practice. That is to say that, at least according to movement leaders (Barigye 2016), the majority of LGBTIQ Ugandans retain identities as Christians or Muslims, just as the rest of the citizens of the majority-Abrahamic country.[21]

Instead, religion supports the largely preconceived biases of some political actors, who then apply many far-reaching efforts to spread the beliefs among the country.

While the threat of violence has undoubtedly harmed and disrupted activists, it has not ended the movement for LGBTIQ rights in Uganda. Instead, kuchu activists have reorganized the social movement to inquire, "How can we imagine LGBTIQ rights in Africa?" What efforts should Ugandan groups strive toward—when, why, and how? While the different methods of answering this question have led to factionalization of the movement (Rodriguez 2018:80–85), they also have exposed tactical and philosophical diversity that should be considered.

A first effort can be witnessed as organizations campaign against the anti-queer logic that LGBTIQ identities are imported by Western imperial powers. In order to address this, activists and activist-researchers have thoroughly dispelled the idea through (auto)ethnographic and interview data (Nyanzi 2013; SMUG 2014; Tamale 2007). This effort imagines a "right to indigeneity and cultural/national belonging." The borders of Uganda formed around the queer bodies present in the region. As such, one must fight to have sexual and gender diversity recognized as indigenous rather than foreign. The label "kuchu" results from such an effort. Kuchu, in fact, is a "localized label" (Nyanzi 2013) denoting the status of being a sexual minority and/or gender nonconforming person. It is commonly used in Kampala and encapsulates all LGBTIQ labels and identities (Tamale 2003), including other variations and terms that do not exist outside of Uganda, such as "311 gay" (Minor 2014) or "chapati" (Nyanzi 2013). Kampala-based activists began to circulate the term in the early 2000s (Minor 2014) and it has since become quite popular, despite the simultaneous currency of globalized identity labels such as gay, bisexual, or transgender. *Call Me Kuchu* (Zouhali-Worrall and Fairfax Wright 2012) became a feature documentary following activist David Kato before and just after his murder in 2011. The title pays homage to the act of self-determination in naming oneself and one's group in a globalized and neo-imperial era. Another way that this effort has been made is to assert the truth of the number of kuchu people who have "never had any form of interaction with whites" (Tamale 2007:2). This is, ironically, a reality asserted even by the president of Uganda, Yoweri Museveni in 1999, who publicly confessed that homosexuals of his village were referred to as *ebitingwa* and not persecuted (Rodriguez 2018).[22]

Kuchu activists asserted this belonging by pushing back against cultural outsiders who instigated the anti-gay fears that propelled violence and support for the Anti-Homosexuality Bill. Teaming up with the Center for Constitutional Rights (New York City, USA), SMUG and other activists mobilized the rarely used Alien Tort Statute in a federal court to counter Scott

Lively's anti-gay mission in Uganda (*SMUG v. Scott Lively* 2013). Through the lawsuit, they alleged that Scott Lively and his contemporaries aided and abetted the crime against humanity of persecution in Uganda as they roused the antagonism and fear that led to the Anti-Homosexuality Bill in its "Kill the Gays" iteration. The activists traveled from Kampala, Uganda, to Massachusetts to expose the role of US missionaries in spreading hate violence and cultural anxieties. In doing so, they were able to reframe the us-versus-them contention that so often excludes kuchus from indigenous belonging. While the lawsuit did not end in official charges against Scott Lively, activists crossed borders in order to redefine their boundaries and send a message that US actors would be held accountable for the "moral" interventions that perpetuate harm.

In addition, and very much in relation to the effort to assert belonging and indigeneity, activists also rally for the right to work and organize in service to their communities. While the Anti-Homosexuality Bill was the most notable anti-gay effort on the national level, the lesser-known Non-Governmental Organizations (NGO) Act passed in parliament in November 2015 and became law shortly after, in March 2016. The NGO Act ensured much stricter rules explicitly monitoring and dissolving "subversive activities" like LGBTIQ organizing. This thereby criminalizes unregistered organizations and those who work for them. While many kuchus combine work and activism, in terms of being professional activists, many others undertake various entrepreneurial efforts to serve both kuchu and non-kuchu communities (Rodriguez 2018:64–66). They imagine that contributing to the wider society through general, nonactivist labor would do more to produce compassion from straight citizens. Similarly, activists have attempted farming initiatives that would provide sustainable food and job security. Such an effort has been imagined as a complement to the short-term solutions proposed by international LGBTIQ and human rights organizations that have largely sought to remove kuchus from Uganda for their safety (Rodriguez 2018:73–75). While this has become an important initiative for outed kuchus and certain activists, the efforts fail to secure a future for queer life in the country and for those who want to stay.

The threat of violence, however, does not come only from random, homophobic vigilantes hoping to curb the "crime"; emotional, psychological, sexual, and otherwise physical violence occurs regularly at the hands of the police. This violence has been institutionalized in police interactions, especially during raids and arrests. Similar to the initiation of an LGBTIQ movement in the United States, with the riots at Compton's Cafeteria in San Francisco (1966) and Stonewall Inn in New York City (1969), LGBTIQ rights in Uganda have been imagined as the right to live free of police violence. This crucial imagining comes on the tail of countless reports of abuse and violence by the police, as addressed by SMUG and partner organizations. As such, SMUG has initiated meetings and trainings with the police to sensitize and deinstitutionalize the sexual violence that occurs during strip searches and booking and in custody. Additionally, the organization prioritizes documenting police violence so as to aid the process of rights-based claims-making on a transnational level.

Lastly, freedom of expression—both creative and protest—has proven a key imagining of rights for kuchu activists. Within Ugandan activism has emerged a truly impressive array of creative media: news outlets such as *Kuchutimes*, the magazine *Bombastic*, the musical group Talented Ugandan Kuchus, anonymized published erotica, and more. These initiatives have been wholly created and produced by local actors. These "artivists" have also participated in and collaborated with many transnational, largely European- and US-based creatives to produce works such as the films *Call Me Kuchu* (Zouhali-Worrall and Fairfax Wright 2012), *God Loves Uganda* (Williams 2013), and *The Pearl of Africa* (Von Wallström 2016). Altogether, the efforts have offered the small country's movement a tremendous amount of exposure and have mobilized a message of resilience, power, and communal love.

Conclusion

The negotiation of sexual identities and of the rights of LGBTIQ people in Africa to claim citizenship was until very recently widely considered a minor footnote, if not frivolous or completely irrelevant to Africans' wider struggles for independence, development, and dignity on the world stage. The fact that this negotiation—which has been ongoing in explicit terms for many decades now—has come to warrant a chapter in the sixth edition of this book is, therefore, a much-welcomed development. We have argued that LGBTIQ struggles involve transnational and local actors who are both deeply engaged in and have an impact on the wider struggles for independence, development, and dignity on the world stage. Theorizing, strategizing, representing, and acting—all of these aspects of the struggle for social justice for sexual minorities unfold in complex ways in relation to culture, language, political economy, and global interventions. Notwithstanding powerful and sometimes unanticipated obstacles, transnational, national, and local networks have emerged throughout the continent that suggest strong potential for belonging in the future.

Notes

1. Terminology is debated in the scholarship and by sexual minority activists themselves. The imputed meanings of various terms are highly contingent upon context; one may be derogatory in one place and time, but not in another. We have thus decided simply to stick with three of the currently most commonly used and least controversial terms (LGBTIQ, gay, and homosexual). We understand that other letters could be added or removed from the first to reflect evolving

debates and consciousness, and that others have wide currency in certain areas (for example, sexual orientation and gender diversity [SOGIE], or men who have sex with men [MSM]), but we simply wish to acknowledge diversity within a very broadly shared political project. For discussion, see Matebeni, Monro, and Reddy 2018; Jayawardene 2019; and Matebeni 2019.

2. Another pioneer in this respect was Renée Liddicoat, whose work as a psychologist broke the ice in the academic sphere in Africa to make the case for nondiscrimination against homosexuals (Liddicoat 1962).

3. Most notably the Rand Gay Organization (RGA) for blacks who broke from GASA, the Organization for Lesbian and Gay Activists (OLGA) for whites, and the Gay and Lesbian Organization of the Witwatersrand (GLOW), for all who embraced antiracism as a cornerstone of the struggle for sexual liberation.

4. See the Universal Declaration of Human Rights, https://bit.ly/2HJaXAj (accessed July 2019).

5. The Yogyakarta Principles, https://bit.ly/2Ycf3xB (accessed July 2019).

6. In considering rights, the Commission divides them into two categories: the rights of the individual and the rights of groups. Emphasis is put not just on rights but also on duties and obligations as a framework for rights.

7. For more information see the African Commission on Human and Peoples' Rights, https://bit.ly/2YcYLEE (accessed July 2019). The former Organization of African Union's treaty prohibited African states from intervening in the domestic affairs of other African countries. Human rights struggles were viewed as "domestic issues" before the formation of the African Union, the mandate of which is less restrictive.

8. For more information see the African Court on Human and Peoples' Rights, https://bit.ly/2ZjOyTd (accessed July 2019).

9. Ibid. The competency of the Court to do such a thing is in fact based on two criteria. First is its founding protocol, and second is individual state recognition of its mandate. This means that an NGO working on human rights cannot bring up to the Court a case that happened in a country that has not ratified the founding protocol of the Court. As of 2018, only nine (out of fifty-four) countries had accepted the Court's competency in this regard: Benin, Burkina Faso, Côte d'Ivoire, Gambia, Ghana, Malawi, Mali, Tanzania, and Tunisia. See http://www.african-court.org/en/index.php/news/press-releases/item/257-the-gambia-becomes-the-ninth-country-to-allow-ngos-and-individuals-to-access-the-african-court-directly (accessed December18, 2019).

10. CAL is a network of fourteen organizations in ten African countries, headquartered in Johannesburg. Some of its international allies include the Women Human Rights Defenders International Coalition (www.defendingwomen-defendingrights.org), the Sexual Rights Initiative (www.sexualrightsinitiative.com), the Association of Women's Rights in Development (www.awid.org), and Sexuality Policy Watch (www.sxpolitics.org). See https://www.cal.org.za/ (accessed July 2019). See also Ndashe (2011) on this case, and more generally on the potential of the Court to advance LGBTIQ rights.

11. See document at https://bit.ly/2OlHPY3 (accessed July 2019).

12. See document at https://bit.ly/2ZgNjo7 (accessed July 2019).

13. CAL, "Women and Sexual Minorities Denied a Seat at the Table by the African Commission on Human and Peoples' Rights," August 17, 2018, https://bit.ly/2NulSkL.

14. Ibid.

15. Guinea-Bissau decriminalized same-sex relations in 1993.

16. See CAL, "Coalition of African Lesbians Says NO to a Special Rapporteur on Sexual Orientation, Gender Identity," May 29, 2016, https://bit.ly/2YeAY7l.

17. Ibid.

18. Account shared by Christopher Senteza in 2003, at the Lesbian and Gay Christian Movement (LGCM) Conference.

19. These forms of assault included adult-child same-sex sexual engagement; drugging a person for the purpose of sexual assault; having sex while HIV-positive; and engaging with someone unable to consent due to disability.

20. Buganda is a large kingdom that was combined with others in East Africa to form the nation-state now called Uganda. The name Uganda, although representing a collection of five kingdoms, actually derives from this particular one.

21. According to the 2014 National Census, 85 percent of the country adheres to Christianity, while 14 percent adheres to Islam.

22. This was also a key finding of a scientific study commissioned by the president (i.e., that homosexuality is a natural phenomenon that was present in Africa among humans and animals "way before the coming of the white man" [Uganda Ministry of Health 2014]). Ironically, the president chose to ignore this finding in favor of other opinions expressed in the scientific statement that provided political cover for signing the AHB into law (Paszat forthcoming).

13

Religion

Ambrose Moyo and
Peter J. Schraeder

The importance of religion in any attempt to understand African life in all its social, economic, and political aspects cannot be overemphasized. John S. Mbiti's (1969:1) observation that Africans are "notoriously religious," consciously or unconsciously, is still true of a large majority of people, urban or rural, educated or less educated, male or female, rich or poor. Even those who claim to be atheist, agnostic, or antireligion, of whom there are a growing number, often have no option but to participate in extended family activities, some of which require the invocation of supernatural powers. Religion permeates all aspects of African traditional societies. It is a way of life in which the whole community is involved, and as such it is identical with life itself. Even antireligious persons still have to be involved in the lives of their religious communities because, in terms of African thought, life can be meaningful only in community, not in isolation. Indeed, as aptly captured in Laura S. Grillo, Adriaan van Klinken, and Hassan J. Ndzovu's book, *Religions in Contemporary Africa: An Introduction*, which was published fifty years after Mbiti's 1969 volume, "Religion is so much a part and parcel of African life that we even dare to say that one cannot understand African politics, media, popular culture and so on without engaging with religious thought and practice" (2019:5).

The primary purpose of this chapter is to provide an overview of the major religious trends in Africa. We do so by placing the "religious" within the broader context of societal, political, and international forces at play. We by necessity must draw on a variety of disciplines, such as international studies, political science, religious studies, and theology, to accomplish this goal. We begin in section one by setting out the numbers of African believers associated with various religious faiths and their geographical distribution throughout the African continent. These numbers demonstrate that Africans adhere to an array of religious faiths that are representative of the globe's major religions. The majority of the chapter is devoted to exploring the three principal religious traditions that enjoy the largest number of believers in Africa: (1) African indigenous religious beliefs and practices that together can be referred to as African traditional religions; (2) Christianity, including its expressions in African indigenous Christian movements; and (3) Islam, most notably Islamic reform movements. In each of these cases, we concentrate on the basic, common elements of each broad religious tradition and point out some of the significant differences as we go along. A final section offers general conclusions.

A comment is in order regarding the theological sources for understanding the three principal faiths of the African continent. The study of Christian and Islamic traditions poses no insurmountable difficulties with regard to our sources of information. Both have their sacred texts, namely, the Old Testament and the New Testament for Christianity and the Quran for Islam (also written as Qur'an or Koran). The founders of these two traditions, their primary sources, and their geographical origins remain the same for all adherents of these faiths regardless of the different interpretations. African traditional religions have no sacred texts, their beginnings cannot be pinpointed, and each of the many traditions is typically practiced by one African group with no reference whatsoever to the religion practiced by other groups. Each African group exists as a complete social, economic, religious, and political entity with no missionary designs. With the many basic, common elements, there are also some differences in religious beliefs and practices that speak against generalizations. As unrelated and independent as African groups may appear, they nonetheless share some basic religious beliefs and practices. These shared features suggest a common background or origin. As a result, African traditional religions are often treated as a single religious tradition, just as Christianity and Islam have many denominations or sects but continue to be treated as single entities (Martey 2009; see also Mbiti 2015; Olupona and Nyang 2103).

Adherence to Religious Faiths in Africa

The African continent is home to an assortment of faith traditions that vary widely in terms of the numbers and geographical dispersion of believers. We are able to obtain a snapshot of what these numbers looked like as of 2015, the most recent year for which data are available through the World Christian Database (WCD) (Johnson and Zurlo 2020). Despite its title, the WCD provides a statistical breakdown by country of the number of adherents to all of the world's major religions. In the case of Africa, these estimates are based on a total population of nearly 1.2 billion Africans (see Table 13.1).

Table 13.1 Religious Beliefs in Africa

	Africa Total		North Africa		East Africa		Southern Africa		Central Africa		West Africa	
	Total	Percent	Total	Percent	Total	Percent	Total	Percent	Total	Percent	Total	Percent
Traditional beliefs	101,360,799	8.50	477	0.00	32,351,876	9.58	19,847,182	11.76	9,211,063	6.24	39,950,201	11.33
Christians	580,248,408	48.65	9,237,752	4.97	186,954,291	55.36	133,520,998	79.13	121,586,163	82.31	128,949,204	36.57
Muslims	496,274,163	41.61	175,409,475	94.33	114,513,223	33.91	8,833,079	5.23	15,307,096	10.36	182,211,290	51.68
Agnostics	7,493,228	0.63	1,114,024	0.60	993,985	0.29	3,608,799	2.14	745,722	0.50	1,030,698	0.29
Atheists	672,603	0.06	101,800	0.05	145,017	0.04	258,803	0.15	90,861	0.06	76,122	0.02
Hindus	3,242,348	0.27	7,018	0.00	1,612,295	0.48	1,453,365	0.86	124,031	0.08	45,639	0.01
Baha'is	2,429,469	0.20	44,374	0.02	853,730	0.25	712,228	0.42	584,634	0.40	234,503	0.07
Buddhists	334,733	0.03	23,066	0.01	28,020	0.01	241,924	0.14	7,040	0.00	34,683	0.01
Chinese folk	215,970	0.02	16,630	0.01	67,241	0.02	119,763	0.07	5,710	0.00	6,626	0.00
Jains	109,172	0.01	0	0.00	106,960	0.03	2,212	0.00	0	0.00	0	0.00
Sikhs	84,346	0.01	2,245	0.00	64,154	0.02	13,188	0.01	0	0.00	4,759	0.00
New religion	136,968	0.01	0	0.00	718	0.00	22,345	0.01	49,467	0.03	64,438	0.02
Jews	96,717	0.01	4,778	0.00	18,830	0.01	70,985	0.04	456	0.00	1,668	0.00
Other	37,360	0.25	0	0.00	951	0.00	36,409	0.02	0	0.00	0	0.00
Total	1,192,736,284	100.00	185,961,639	100.00	337,711,291	100.00	168,741,280	100.00	147,712,243	100.00	352,609,831	100.00

Source: Johnson and Zurlo (2020).

An opening point is that up until 1900, the vast majority of Africans followed African traditional religions, which are described in greater detail in section two of this chapter. More than a century later, the percentage of Africans who could be classified as "principally" adhering to a traditional African faith had decreased to 8.5 percent or 101 million Africans. Although this large number still ensures that African traditional religions remain one of the top three forms of religious expression in contemporary Africa, it nonetheless is indicative of the dramatic rise of two other religious traditions during the last century: Christianity, with over 580 million African followers (49 percent of the continental total), and Islam, with over 496 million African followers (42 percent of the continental total).

Two aspects of this trend are important. First, there is tremendous regional variation among the three dominant religions. Whereas North Africa is the region with the highest concentration of Muslims (94 percent), Southern Africa is home to the smallest percentage (only 5 percent). The remaining regions are 52 percent Muslim (West Africa), 34 percent Muslim (East Africa), and 10 percent Muslim (Central Africa). The dynamics are different for Christianity. Central Africa has the highest concentration of Christians (82 percent), followed by Southern Africa (79 percent), East Africa (55 percent), West Africa (37 percent), and North Africa (5 percent). The dynamics are different still for traditional African religions: Southern Africa has the highest concentration (12 percent), followed by West Africa (11 percent), East Africa (10 percent), Central Africa (6 percent), and North Africa (0 percent). In short, region matters.

Second, we underscore the word "principally" in our above description, in that many Africans embody a "syncretic" belief system in which adherence to a new faith such as Christianity or Islam nonetheless incorporates many aspects of their traditional African religions, such as spirits and witchcraft, in which they still believe (Ashforth 2005; Geschiere 2013; Moore and Sanders 2001). As a result, statistics must be taken with a grain of salt. African adherence to traditional African religions in the contemporary independence era is arguably much higher than indicated by statistics, which are based on what one believes to be one's "primary" religious affiliation. This is due to the fact that many Africans embody a mix of religious beliefs that join their traditional African religious beliefs with any one of the globe's other religious faiths. As once explained to Peter J. Schraeder, one of the coauthors of this chapter, by a university-educated Senegalese citizen who self-identified as Catholic, the reality of his belief system was according to him perhaps 80 percent based on the teachings and scriptures of the Catholic church and 20 percent based on traditional African religious beliefs that were still prevalent in his life. For example, he believed in the mystical powers of his local *marabout* (a traditional religious leader), with whom he periodically consulted when he needed support at various points in his life, such as taking the national exam that determined what college he potentially could attend. One is rarely truly one or the other (i.e., either a complete and total adherent to African traditional religious belief or to one of the global religious traditions).

Table 13.1 provides additional insights into the kaleidoscope of contemporary religious life in Africa. First, agnostics and atheists together comprise more than 8 million African adherents (less than three-quarters of 1 percent of the continental total). Whereas agnostics are defined by the WCD as "persons who claim no religion or claim that it is not possible to know if God, gods, or the supernatural exist," atheists are defined as "persons who deny the existence of God, gods, or the supernatural." Such beliefs can be found in all African countries in all African regions (Johnson and Zurlo 2020).

All of the remaining religious faiths with followers on the African continent can be classified as "minority religions." Two of these—Hinduism and Baha'i—nonetheless exceed a million adherents each, placing these religions in the top tier of minority faiths in Africa. India is the spiritual home of the more than 1 billion Hindus in the world, including over 3.2 million in Africa, who are the followers of the core Hindu traditions of Vaishnavism, Shaivism, and Shaktism, as well as of various neo-Hindi sects and reform movements (e.g., see Gopalan 2014; Hiralal 2014; see also Atiemo 2017; Wuaku 2009). Hindus are principally concentrated in the former British colonies of South Africa (1,318,494), Mauritius (556,798), Tanzania (466,179), Uganda (322,524), and Kenya (236,028). This religious reality is due to the fact that the United Kingdom brought large numbers of their subjects from British colonial India to serve in a variety of capacities in their African empire. Mauritius is unique within this post-British colonial context in that it is the only African country where a religion other than Christianity or Islam (in this case, Hinduism) is the largest religion (roughly 44 percent of the population).

Baha'ism is the second-largest minority faith in Africa. Founded in 1844 by Baha'u'llah in Persia (contemporary Iran), it enjoys over 2.4 million adherents in all fifty-four African countries (Lee 2011). Baha'i communities are governed by the Universal House of Justice, a nine-member body located on Mount Caramel in Haifi, Israel, that is elected every five years by the members of national Baha'i assemblies. Followers are bound by Baha'u'llah's book of laws, known as the Kitab-i-Aqdas. The largest concentrations of Baha'is are found in Kenya (431,312), the DRC (326,670), Zambia (297,006), South Africa (262,898), and Tanzania (229,324).

The remainder of Africa's minority religions claim less than 350,000 adherents each. They nonetheless play important roles within their individual societies or regions. Originating in India and spreading throughout Asia, the Buddhist faith brings together at least three broad traditions of followers of the Buddha, including Mahayana ("The Great Vehicle"), Theravada

("The School of the Elders"), and Tibetan Lamaists, or followers of the Dalai Lama, the spiritual leader who lives in exile in India. Buddhists number 334,733 in Africa, and are largely concentrated in South Africa (230,805, or 69 percent of the African total), followed by Libya (16,086), Tanzania (12,204), Côte d'Ivoire (11,554), Guinea (10,882), and Nigeria (9,673) (Clasquin and Krueger 1999; see also Parker 2009; Clasquin 2004). Africa is also home to 215,970 Chinese folk-religionists (followers of indigenous religions of China), 109,172 Jains (followers of the Svetambara and Digambara reform movements from Hinduism), and 84,346 Sikhs (also originating in India, and including the Akali, Khalsa, Nanapanthi, Nirmali, Sewapanthi, and Udasi traditions of Sikhism). In all three cases, the vast majority of adherents are found not surprisingly in East and Southern Africa, due to the greater contacts of these regions with Asia over the centuries. One should avoid mere geographical determinism, however. The statistics also show that "new religionists," which number 136,968, and which the WCD defines as followers of the "so-called New Religions of Asia" inclusive of "new syncretist religions combining Christianity with Eastern religions," are principally found in West Africa (30,116 in Ghana and 18,905 in Nigeria) and Central Africa (19,310 in the DRC, 12,984 in Cameroon, and 10,703 in Gabon) as well as South Africa (19,628).

Finally, the African continent is home to 96,717 adherents to the Jewish faith who consider Israel as the historical and contemporary cradle of Judaism and the Torah as their sacred text (Chitando 2005; Friedman 2000; Hull 2009; Key 2014; Simon, Laskier, and Reguer 2003; see also Mark and da Silva Horta 2013). The majority (96 percent) of African Jews are split among six countries: South Africa (69,534), Ethiopia (15,880), Morocco (2,603), Uganda (2,007), Tunisia (1,897), and Nigeria (1,207). These numbers are striking in that they represent but a portion of what historically used to be a larger Jewish population in Africa. In the mid-nineteenth century, Ethiopia alone was home to between 200,000 and 350,000 "Beta Israel" or Ethiopian Jews who are also referred to as Falasha Jews. Many were resettled in Israel as part of a series of airlifts during the 1980s known as Operation Falasha, which took place after the advent of the 1974 Ethiopian Revolution and the emergence of a dictatorial African-Marxist regime under the leadership of Mengistu Haile Mariam. North Africa in particular was historically the home of hundreds of thousands of Jews, who progressively left after the beginning of the contemporary independence era in 1951, against the backdrop of rising tensions between the contemporary State of Israel that was founded in 1948 and the predominantly Arab states of North Africa and the Middle East, most notably the Six-Day War in 1967 (Gottreich and Schroeter 2011; Simon, Laskier, and Reguer 2003). In Tunisia, for example, the Jewish population numbered more than 100,000 adherents in 1948. The vast majority emigrated to either France or Israel following Tunisia's independence in 1956. A small but vibrant Jewish community remains on the island of Djerba in southeastern Tunisia, which is home to the El-Ghriba synagogue, one of the few remaining, still-functioning synagogues in North Africa, and one of the oldest synagogues in the world.

The religious symbolism associated with Tunisia's El-Ghriba synagogue demonstrates how even one of Africa's smallest minority religious communities can become the centerpiece of African politics and international relations. Specifically, the synagogue was the site of an attack perpetrated in 2002 by the al-Qaeda terrorist group that resulted in the deaths of fourteen German tourists and three Tunisian and two French citizens. There is no doubt that anti-Semitism was an impetus behind the attack. The international shock waves created by this attack led to a dramatic decline in tourism to Tunisia, an important source of jobs and revenue for the Tunisian government and society. As such, it also captured the anti-Western impetus of the attack (i.e., a desire to stem the negative influences of Western culture by stopping tourism from members of those societies). The dictatorship of Zine el-Abidine Ben Ali nonetheless refused to acknowledge the terrorist, anti-Semitic, and anti-Western roots of this attack, preferring instead to sweep the event and the devastation wrought on the local Jewish community under the rug. Indeed, when Schraeder visited the site with his family in fall 2002 while serving as a Fulbright lecturer in Tunisia, they were told by local police guarding the synagogue that what happened was a mere traffic accident; the driver of a gasoline truck had simply lost control of his vehicle, which exploded outside of the exterior wall of the synagogue. It would only be after the Tunisian Revolution of 2011 and the transition to democracy in Tunisia, that Jewish groups from the island of Djerba were able to pressure the transitional government to not only commemorate the victims of the attack but provide pledges to protect the local Jewish community. On April 11, 2012, President Moncef Marzouki met with the families of the victims of the attack and delivered a speech expressing the government's support for and determination to protect the local Jewish community.

Although extremely small in size, Tunisia's Jewish community reminds us that minority religions play important roles in Africa. Having noted that point, the analysis now turns to exploring in greater detail the three largest religious traditions on the African continent: African traditional religions, Christianity, and Islam.

African Traditional Religions

The term "African traditional religions" incorporates the indigenous religious beliefs and customs that are practiced throughout the African continent. Although African traditional religions have no sacred books or definitive creeds, they nonetheless embody five sets of theological beliefs: (1) belief in

Peter J. Schraeder

Instructions upon entry to the El-Ghriba Synagogue on the island of Djerba, Tunisia. This is one of the oldest, still-functioning synagogues in North Africa.

a Supreme Being; (2) belief in spirits/divinities; (3) belief in life after death; (4) religious personnel and sacred places; and (5) witchcraft and magic practices. We explore these beliefs by drawing on examples that we have personally experienced throughout our careers in Africa. We especially draw on examples from Moyo's life as a citizen of Zimbabwe and as a member of that country's Shona people, which like all ethnic groups maintains a rich culture of traditional religious beliefs and practices.

Belief in a Supreme Being

The African perception of the universe is centered on the belief in a Supreme Being who is the creator and sustainer of the universe. God, as far as the African traditionalist is concerned, is the ground of all being. Humanity is inseparably bound together with all of God's creation since both derive their lives from God, the source of all life. This strong belief in God appears to be universal in traditional societies. The question to be asked is, How is this God perceived?

Names in African societies tell a whole story about the family—its history, relationships, hopes, and aspirations. African societies have many names for the Supreme Being. These names are expressions of the different forms in which God relates to creation. In other words, God in African traditional thought can only be known in the different relationships as expressed in God's names. For example, among the Shona people of Zimbabwe, God is *Musikavanhu* (creator of humankind) and *Musiki/uMdali* (creator), which affirms that God is the originator of all there is. But *Musikavanhu* goes beyond the idea of creator to the notion of the parenthood of God. Hence, God is also designated *Mudzimu Mukuru* (the Great Ancestor). As parent, God is also the sustainer of creation. God's creativity is continuous and is celebrated with every new birth, and each rite of passage is an expression of gratitude to God for having sustained the individual and the community that far. These names also affirm the belief in the continuous creativity of God. Similarly, in the names *Chidziva Chepo* or *Dzinaguru,* God is perceived as the giver and the source of water. Each time it rains, God is sustaining creation in a visible way. This explains, in ceremonies relating to drought, why people appeal directly to God. So also the name *Samasimba* (owner of power/almighty) affirms God not only as the most powerful being but also as the source and owner of all power.

The African traditionalist does not perceive God as some Supreme Being in merely speculative terms. That which is real has to be experienced in real-life situations, directly or indirectly. God can, therefore, be real only insofar as God has been experienced in concrete life situations in different relationships with people and the rest of creation. In other words, African traditional thought cannot conceive of God in abstract terms as some being who exists as an idea mysteriously related to this world—distant, unconcerned, uninterested in what goes on here below. Consequently, Africans' view of God arises out of concrete and practical relationships as God meets their needs. In that way, they experience God's love and power (see Mbiti 1970; McVeigh 1974).

In terms of African thought, there can be only one Supreme Being. Interestingly enough, before the encounter with Christianity, some African societies already had some concept of the Trinity. This seems to have been the case in some African societies, as demonstrated by Emmanuel K. Twesigye in his research into his people's traditional religions in southern and western Uganda. In an interview with an old traditionalist, Antyeri Bintukwanga, Twesigye uncovered the following information:

> Before the Europeans came to Uganda and before the white Christian missionaries came to our land of Enkole or your homeland of Kigezi, we had our own religion and we knew God well. We knew God so well that the missionaries added to us little. . . . We even knew God to be some kind of externally existing triplets: *Nyamuhanga* being the first one and being also

> the creator of everything, *Kazooba Nyamuhanga* being his second brother who gives light to all human beings so that they should not stumble either on the path or even in their lives. . . . *Kazooba's* light penetrates the hearts of people and God sees the contents of the human hearts by *Kazooba*'s eternal light. . . . The third brother in the group is *Rugaba Rwa Nyamuhanga*, who takes what *Nyamuhanga* has created and gives it to the people as he wishes. . . . You see! We had it all before the missionaries came, and all they did teach us was that *Nyamuhanga* is God the Father, *Kazooba* Jesus Christ his son and not his brother as we thought, and that *Rugaba* as the divine giver is the Holy Spirit. (Twesigye 1987:93)

In traditional societies God is believed to be eternal, loving, and just, the creator and sustainer of the universe. God's existence is simply taken for granted, hence the absence of arguments for or against the existence of God. Atheism is foreign to African thought. The most widely used name for God among the Shona people of Zimbabwe is *Mwari,* which means literally "the one who is."

Belief in Divinities and Spirits

The Supreme Being is believed to be surrounded by a host of supernatural or spiritual powers of different types and functions. Their nature, number, and functions vary from region to region, and they may be either male or female, just as God in many African traditions is perceived as being both male and female. The numerous divinities, called *orisha* among the Yoruba in Nigeria or *bosom* among the Akan of Ghana (and sometimes referred to as "lesser divinities" in order not to confuse them with the Supreme Being), are found in most West African traditions but generally not in East and Southern African traditions. These *orisha* are subordinate to the Supreme Being. They are believed to be servants or messengers of *Olodumare* (God). God has assigned to each one of them specific areas of responsibility. For example, the divinity *Orunmila* is responsible for all forms of knowledge and is, therefore, associated with divination and the oracle at Ile-Ife in Nigeria. The *orisha* are believed either to have emanated from the Supreme Being or to be deified human beings. Some of the divinities are associated with the sky, earth, stars, moon, trees, mountains, rivers, and other natural elements (see Idowu 1962).

Perhaps more universal among African traditionalists is the belief in ancestor spirits, called *vadzimu* among the Shona people of Zimbabwe or *amadhozi* among the Zulu/Ndebele traditions. These are spirits of the deceased mothers and fathers who are recognized in a special ceremony, usually held a year after they have died. This ceremony is called *umbuyiso* (the bringing-home ceremony) in Zulu/Ndebele or *kurova guva* by the Zezuru. From that moment, the deceased person becomes an active "living dead" member of the community and is empowered to function as a guardian spirit and to mediate with God and other ancestors on behalf of his or her descendants. Among the Shona people of Zimbabwe, it is to these spirits that most prayers and sacrifices are made, but often the prayers are concluded by instructing the ancestors to take the prayers and offerings to *Musikavanhu* (creator of humankind) or *Nyadenga* (the owner of the sky/heavens).

The significance of ancestors among Africans has led to the common misconception that these spirits are worshiped. Traditionalists categorically deny that they worship their ancestor spirits, but rather worship God through them. Ancestor spirits are departed elders. African peoples in general have a very high respect for elders. If, for example, one has grievously wronged his or her parents, it would be utterly disrespectful and unacceptable to go directly to those same parents and ask for forgiveness. One would have to go through some respectable elderly person to whom one would give some token of repentance to take to the parent. Similarly, when a young man and his fiancée decide to get married, the prospective father-in-law will have to be approached by the young man's parents through a carefully chosen and respectable mediator. In the same spirit, a person cannot approach a chief or king directly but must have his or her case taken to the chief through a subchief. Even more so, God—the transcendent, the greatest and most powerful being, the Great Ancestor and creator of all—must be approached through intermediaries. The ancestor spirits are believed to be closest both to their living descendants and to the Supreme Being and are thus most qualified to function as intermediaries.

Ancestor spirits are not the objects of worship. They are guardian spirits and intermediaries. They are believed to be responsible to God for all their actions. As family elders they must be respected and if not, just like the living elders, they can get angry and demand that they be appeased. Quite often, the name of the Supreme Being is not mentioned in petitions. Still, it is believed that God is the ultimate recipient of all prayer and sacrifices. Although not worshiped, the ancestors in some traditions are closely associated with the Supreme Being, so much so that it becomes difficult to determine in some of the prayers whether the address is to God or to the ancestor. Take, for example, the following prayer of the Shilluk, who rarely address God directly. Nyikang is the founding ancestor of the Shilluk.

> There is no one above you, O God [Juok]. You became the grandfather of Nyikang; it is you Nyikang who walk with God, you became the grandfather of man. If famine comes, is it not given by you? . . . We praise you, you who are God. Protect us, we are in your hands, and protect us, save me. You and Nyikang, you are the ones who created. . . . The cow for sacrifice is here for you, and the blood will go to God and you. (Parrinder 1969:69)

As far as the Shona people of Zimbabwe are concerned, God and the ancestors are one; an address to one is an address to the other. This means that, even if at times one does not hear the name of God mentioned, it does not mean the people do not worship God. God and ancestors are closely associated and work very closely with each other. For example, they believe that children are a gift of *Mwari* (God) and the *vadzimu* (ancestors). So, frequently one will hear the people say *kana Mwari nevadzimu vachida* ("if God and the ancestors are willing"). When faced with misfortune, they will say *Ko Mwari wati ndaita sei?* ("What crime does God accuse me of?"), or they will say *mudzimu yafuratira* ("the ancestors have turned their backs"; that is, on the individual or family, hence the misfortune) (Moyo 1987).

There are different categories of ancestor spirits. There are family ancestors, with family being understood in its extended sense. These have responsibility only over the members of their families, and it is only to them (i.e., family ancestor spirits) that the members can bring their petitions, never to the ancestors of other families. Then, there are ancestors whose responsibilities extend over the larger ethnic group or people and not just over their own immediate families. These relate to the founders of the ethnic group or people and are represented by the royal house. They play an active role in matters that affect the entire community, such as drought or some epidemic. They are called *Mhondoros* (lion spirits) among the Shona people. Most significantly, ancestor spirits serve as intermediaries.

Belief in Life After Death

Death is believed to have come into the world as an intrusion. Human beings were originally meant to live forever through rejuvenation or some form of resurrection. So, most African peoples have myths that intend to explain the origin of death. There are, for example, some myths that depict death as having come in because some mischievous animal cut the rope or removed the ladder linking heaven, the abode of the Supreme Being, and the earth, the abode of humankind. Such a rope or ladder allowed people to ascend to and descend from heaven for rejuvenation. Other myths see death as punishment from God for human disobedience.

Despite the loss of the original state of bliss and the intervention of death, it is generally believed that there is still life beyond the grave, that life may take several forms. In some traditions, the dead may be reincarnated in the form of an animal such as a lion, a rabbit, or a snake. In that form one cannot be killed, and, if reborn as a lion, one can protect one's descendants from the danger of other animals. Or the person may be reincarnated in one of his or her descendants. In general, people believe there is a world of the ancestors and, when one dies, one goes on a long journey to get to that world. The world of the ancestors is conceived of in terms of this world; hence, people are buried with some of their utensils and implements. That world is also thought of as overlapping with this world, and ancestors are believed to be a part of the community of the living. The terms "living dead" or "the shades" are approximately accurate English renderings of those invisible members of the community (see Berglund 1976; Mbiti 1969).

That there is life after death is also affirmed in the belief that a dead person can return to punish those who have wronged him or her while still alive. One of the most feared spirits among the Shona of Zimbabwe is the *ngozi,* a vengeful spirit that will kill members of the family of the person who wronged the individual while still alive until payment or retribution has been made.

In general, people believe they are surrounded by a cloud of ancestors with whom they must share everything they have, including their joys and frustrations. Their expectation of the hereafter is thought of in terms of what people already know and have experienced. People know there is a future life because they interact with their departed ancestors through spirit mediums.

Religious Leadership and Sacred Places

There are different types of religious leaders in African traditional religions. These can be either male or female. Where the tradition has regular shrines for specific deities, there will be some resident cultic officials. At the shrine at Matongeni in Zimbabwe, for example, the priestly community is made up of both males and females, with roles clearly defined. The Yoruba of Nigeria and the Akan of Ghana have regular cultic officials presiding at the shrines of their divinities. They offer sacrifices and petitions on behalf of their clients. Among most of the Bantu-speaking peoples, heads of families also carry out priestly functions on matters that relate to their families.

Another category of religious leadership, perhaps the most powerful, is that of spirit mediums. These are individual members of the family or clan through whom the spirit of an ancestor communicates with its descendants. They can be either male or female, but most are female. Among these are family spirit mediums and territorial spirit mediums that rule over an entire people or geographical region, such as *Mbuya* (grandmother) Nehanda in Zimbabwe. The territorial spirits wield a great deal of power and, to use the example of Zimbabwe, they played a significant political role in mobilizing people in their struggles for liberation from colonialism. The "first war of liberation" in Zimbabwe (then Southern Rhodesia) against European colonial rule was led by *Mbuya* Nehanda, a spirit medium who was eventually hanged by the colonial regime. During the time of the "second war of liberation" against a minority, white-ruled regime, her mediums as well as other spirit mediums worked very closely with the freedom fighters by mobilizing the people and sanctioning the war. The freedom fighters, most of whom claimed to be Marxist-Leninist, soon discovered that they could not wage a successful war without the support of the spirit mediums (Ranger 1985:175–222; Lan 1985). Thus, the mediums have political as well as religious roles to play. Through these mediums, people discern the will of the ancestors, get an explanation for the causes of whatever calamities they may be enduring, or obtain advice on what the family or the tribe should do in order to avert similar danger. Mediums are highly respected members of the community from whom people seek advice of any nature.

The other important category of religious leaders is that of the diviner. Again, diviners may be either male or female. Communication with the spirit world is vital for African traditional religions. Through divination, people are able to communicate with their ancestral spirits and the divinities. These are consulted in the event of some misfortune, sickness, death, or calamity. They communicate with the spirit world to determine the cause of the problem and to seek possible solutions. There are different methods of divining, using, for example, palm nuts, bones, a bowl of water, wooden dice carved with animals and reptiles, cowries (seashells), or pieces of ivory. Divination would normally be conducted at some location set aside for that purpose. In Yorubaland, Ifa divination centered at Ile-Ife is the most famous. The system is very elaborate and uses palm nuts (Awulalu 1979; Bascom 1969).

Finally, since religion permeates all aspects of life, the kings and the chiefs also carry out some leadership roles. Where the whole nation is involved, it is the responsibility of the head of the community to take the necessary action to consult the national or territorial spirits. It is also their duty to ensure that all the religious functions and observances are carried out by the responsible authorities.

With regard to sacred places, reference has already been made to shrines that serve particular divinities such as those among the Yoruba of Nigeria or the Akan of Ghana. Among the Zulu people of South Africa, there is a room in each homestead with an elevated portion (*umsamu*) where rituals to the ancestor spirits are performed. The cattle kraal is also associated with ancestors and is, therefore, an important place for ritual action. Sacred mountains and caves are almost universal among African peoples. They are often associated with ancestors or any of the divinities. Religious officials will ascend these mountains or go into those caves only on special occasions. Such mountains are also often associated with the abode of the Supreme Being. In Zimbabwe, there are several such mountains that serve as venues for prayer and sacrifice, particularly in connection with prayers for rain in cases of severe drought.

Witchcraft and Magic

To complete the portrayal of African traditional religions, it is also necessary to look at the negative forces in these religious traditions. African traditionalists believe that God is the source of all power, which God shares with other beings. The power of the divinities and ancestors, or that derived from medicine, is primarily viewed as positive power to be used for constructive purposes. However, that same power can also be used for destructive purposes, in which case it becomes evil power. Witches and sorcerers represent those elements within African societies that use power for the purpose of destroying life. (In general, witches are female and sorcerers are male.)

Witchcraft beliefs are widespread in contemporary Africa even among educated Christians and Muslims, typically as a response to the insecurities of modern life (see Ashforth 2005; Geschiere 2013; Moore and Sanders 2001). Even children are being accused and in rising numbers, according to UNICEF (2010) in a report on West and Central Africa. It is generally believed that witches can fly by night, can become invisible, delight in eating human flesh, and use familiar animals such as hyenas or baboons as their means of transport. Witches are believed to be wicked and malicious human beings whose intention is simply to kill, which they do by poisoning or cursing their victims. Witches, sorcerers, and angry ancestor spirits are usually identified as the major causes of misfortune or death in a family.

Magic has two aspects: to protect or to harm. Magic can be used to protect the members of the family, as well as their homestead, cattle, and other property, from witches and other enemies of the family or the individual. Yet magic can also be used through spells and curses to harm or to kill. Beliefs related to magic and witchcraft clearly belong to the category of superstition. They represent ways in which people try to explain the causes of misfortune or social disorders. Misfortune, sickness, or death may also be explained as an expression of one's ancestors' displeasure regarding the behavior of their descendants (see Evans-Pritchard 1937).

In sum, it must be stated that African traditional religions continue to influence the lives of many people today, including some of the highly educated as well as many of those who self-identify as African Christians and African Muslims. It must also be pointed out that African religions are not static. Contacts with Christian and Islamic traditions have brought about transformations and syncretism in all three. As Paul Bohannan and Philip Curtin (1995:124) remark, "There is an amazingly close overlap between the basic ideas of Islam and Christianity, and of the African religions. Neither Islam nor Christianity is foreign in its essence to African religious ideas." The reverse is also true. Although Christianity and Islam have added distinct elements to African religions, each has been and continues to be adapted to and shaped by Africa's indigenous religious heritage, as we demonstrate in the following sections.

Christianity in Africa

Christianity brings together "the followers of Jesus Christ of all traditions and confessions," including but not limited to Anglicans, Catholics,

Protestants, and Orthodox (Johnson and Zurlo 2020). It has experienced phenomenal growth on the African continent during the twentieth and twenty-first centuries. It bears repeating from the previous section that 580 million Africans (or 49 percent of all Africans) are Christian, making it one of the three largest religious traditions on the African continent. Stated another way, nearly five of every ten Africans are Christians. Since so much has been written on Christianity as a broad religious tradition, it is not necessary for our purposes to deal with its specific beliefs (see Adogame, Gerloff, and Hock 2008; Oduyoye 2009; Sanneh and Carpenter 2005; Sundkler and Steed 2000). We instead focus on the historical development of the religion on the African continent. Special attention is paid to those aspects that give African Christianity its own identity.

Early Christianity in North Africa and Ethiopia

Christianity in Africa dates back to Egypt in the first century. According to the ancient historian Eusebius, writing in approximately 311 CE, the Christian church in Egypt was founded by Saint Mark, author of the second gospel and a companion of Paul, a tradition still maintained by the Egyptian Coptic church. By the end of the first century, Christianity had penetrated into rural Egypt and had become the religion of the majority of the people. This continued during the rule of the Roman Empire, during which period Alexandria became one of the most important Roman cities outside of Rome. Egypt has one of the oldest Christian churches, surpassed perhaps only by Rome in terms of longevity of tradition and continuity in the same locality (King 1971:1).

The discovery of Christian and non-Christian documents at the Nag Hammadi caves in Egypt shows that quite early in the history of Christianity, Egypt had become a center for many different and even conflicting Christian groups and a center for theological reflection and debate (Robinson 1982). The city of Alexandria was the home of outstanding theologians, such as Origen, Cyprian, and Clement of Alexandria, whose writings on the different aspects of the Christian faith have influenced the church throughout the ages. The great "heretic" Arius (died 336 CE), originally from the region that is present-day Libya, provoked a controversy that rocked the church for several decades when he taught that Christ was only a human being. The controversy produced two creeds, namely, the Nicene and the Athanasian Creeds, which are used together with the Apostles' Creed as definitive statements of the Christian faith throughout Christendom. The two creeds were formulated at the two great councils of Nicaea in 325 CE and of Alexandria in 362 CE. The Athanasian Creed was named after Athanasius, the bishop of Alexandria, who championed the case against Arius.

The discoveries from Nag Hammadi also demonstrate that Egyptian Christians were very open-minded as they searched for an African Christian identity. They welcomed and accommodated new ideas in their search for indigenous expressions of their Christian faith. For example, in its search for an authentic Christian life devoid of all fleshly desires and serving God through a life of self-denial, prayer, and worship, Egypt was the mother of monasticism (in which believers renounce worldly pursuits in favor of devoting themselves solely to spiritual work). The many caves and the nearby desert provided most ideal locations for such ascetic pursuits. Christianity became and remained the dominant religious tradition until Egypt was conquered by Muslim forces beginning in the seventh century, after which Islam emerged as the dominant religion. Christianity has survived, although it has been reduced to the status of a minority religion (Robinson 1982). According to the WCD, Christians number just over 9 million or 9.6 percent of the Egyptian population (Johnson and Zurlo 2020).

Christianity subsequently spread southeast to Ethiopia. The apostle Philip is reported in the Acts of the Apostles to have baptized an Ethiopian eunuch, who returned to his home country to share his newfound faith with his people. Independent evidence dates the coming of Christianity to Ethiopia to the fourth century. With the conversion of the emperor, church and state became united. The Ethiopian Orthodox church, which is one of the most thoroughly African churches in its ethos (Oduyoye 1986:30), has continued to the present and has maintained close links with the Coptic church. As of 2020, Christianity represented the dominant faith of nearly 59 million Christians or 59 percent of the Ethiopian population (Erlikh 2010; Johnson and Zurlo 2020).

Christianity also achieved a strong following as early as the second century across the remainder of North Africa during the period of Roman rule (Decret 2009). The centerpiece of this influence was the Roman province of Africa Proconsularis and its capital city of Carthage, which incorporated the western portion of present-day Libya, most of present-day Tunisia, and the eastern portion of present-day Algeria. Farther west were the Roman North African provinces of Mauritania Caesariensis and Mauritania Tingitania (present-day Algeria and Morocco), and farther east were the Roman provinces of Cyrenaica (present-day Libya) and of course Aegyptus (present-day Egypt), the latter of which already has been discussed. Roman North Africa produced influential theological thinkers and writers such as Tertullian of Carthage, who was the first person to use the word "Trinity" in his description of the Godhead, and Saint Augustine, the bishop of Hippo, whose ideas on such issues as grace, original sin, and the kingdom of God shaped both Western Catholicism and the Protestant Reformation. As in the case of Egypt, Christianity in the remainder of North Africa did not survive the Arab conquests. It currently claims only 223,165 adherents across Algeria, Libya, Morocco, and Tunisia (Johnson and Zurlo 2020).

The Spread of Christianity South of the Sahara

There is no evidence of attempts by the African churches in Ethiopia, Egypt, or the remainder of Roman North Africa to spread Christianity south of the Sahara. The earliest such efforts to Christianize the rest of Africa were those of the Portuguese missionaries of the Jesuit and Dominican orders in the fifteenth century who followed Portuguese traders traveling around the coast of Africa on their way to Asia, often going into the hinterland of Africa to trade in gold and ivory. In West Africa, Roman Catholic missionaries established Christian communities in the Congo and Angola beginning in 1490, but these disintegrated after two centuries, in part because of the slave trade. Missionary work was also started in Southern Africa at Sofala (present-day Mozambique). It was from there that Father Gonzalo da Silveira led a group of Portuguese Jesuit missionaries in 1560 to the people of the vast empire of Mwanamutapa in what is now Zimbabwe. On his way to the capital of the empire, he claims to have baptized 450 persons among the Tonga people. His mission, however, ended with his execution by the emperor, whom he had converted and baptized Christian. This was apparently the result of pressure from the emperor's Arab trading partners, who feared Christian missionaries would open the door for Portuguese traders to threaten their monopoly. Subsequent Portuguese missionary efforts to the empire by both the Jesuits and the Dominicans were also unsuccessful. Their missionary efforts in East Africa suffered a similar fate.

A new phase in the evangelization of Africa was introduced by the rise of the antislavery movement in Europe and the United States in the early nineteenth century. The result was that the United Kingdom decided to send freed slaves to Sierra Leone (whose capital city was named Freetown to celebrate this reality), France sent freed slaves to Gabon (which similarly named its capital city Libreville, or Freetown in French), and the United States sent freed slaves to Liberia (the capital city of which was named Monrovia because the initiative was started under President Monroe). In each case, the freed people who had become Christians in their captivity overseas now spread Christianity within their new African communities. Famous among these was Samuel Adjai Crowther, who was missionary to his own people in Nigeria and later became the first African Anglican bishop. The evangelical movement culminated in a "missionary scramble for Africa" (akin to the later, more politically motivated scramble for Africa discussed in Chapters 4 and 6) that involved all major denominations in Europe and North America. Famous characters in this process included David Livingstone, a missionary who is nonetheless better known for his exploits as an explorer, and Robert Moffat (Livingstone's father-in-law), who was the first to translate the Bible into Setswana (one of the national languages of Botswana). Many Africans were also involved in these missionary efforts after their conversions, crossing borders in the company of white missionaries or by themselves. As a result of the efforts of such people, Christianity was firmly established in most of sub-Saharan Africa by the beginning of the twentieth century (Sanneh 1983).

The nineteenth-century missionary activities in Africa were a resounding success, in which almost all major Christian denominations were involved. These activities were facilitated by the support and protection that missionaries received from colonial administrators. Indeed, the Christianization of Africa went hand in hand with its colonization. The missionaries arrived in most countries before the colonialists and learned the language of the local people. They helped the colonialists negotiate and draft the agreements that cheated African chiefs out of their land and its resources. To African nationalists, missionaries appeared to have collaborated with the forces of imperialism. In what is now a famous aphorism, the role of Christian missionaries in the colonization of Africa was described by Kenyan nationalist leader (and Kenya's first president) Jomo Kenyatta: "When the missionaries came the Africans had the land and the Christians had the Bible. They taught us to pray with our eyes closed. When we opened them they had the land and we had the Bible" (quoted in Mazrui 1986:149–150). (See the discussions in Chapters 3 and 4 for more information on colonialism.)

Despite its association with colonialism, missionary Christianity had a significant political impact on contemporary Africa. Wherever the missionaries went, they built schools, where a large majority of the first generation

Peter J. Schraeder

Many Christian churches, such as Our Lady of Africa, a Roman Catholic basilica in Algiers, Algeria, were built during the colonial era.

of African leaders were educated (see Mazrui 1986:285–286). These institutions helped create awareness among oppressed Africans that they were of equal value with their white oppressors before God, and this inspired many to rise up in defense of their freedom or to liberate themselves. The education that Africans received from mission schools gave them a sense of pride and value that the colonial regimes were not interested in creating. Many of the missionaries also stood up for some of the rights of Africans.

The Rise of African Independent Churches During the Contemporary Independence Era

The contemporary independence era (1951–present) was marked by the rise of *African independent churches*, a broad umbrella term for African churches and denominations that separated from the European-dominated churches, assumed new and distinctly African forms that were sometimes radically different in their doctrines and general ethos from their Western parent churches, and thus served as authentic African expressions of the Christian faith. One of the earliest documented examples of these churches involved a Congolese woman named Donna Beatrice, who as early as 1700 claimed to have been possessed by the spirit of Saint Anthony. Giving up all her belongings to the poor, she proclaimed a message of the coming judgment of God. She proclaimed that Christ and his apostles were black and that they lived in São Salvador (present-day Angola). Beatrice's proclamations served as a poignant expression of the "yearning for a Christ who would identify with the despised African" (Daneel 1987:46). The basic question Beatrice raised and that many of the new African Christian churches have been asking is, "How could the white Christ of the Portuguese images, the Christ of the exploiters—how could he ever help the suffering African, pining for liberty?" (Daneel 1987:46). By the 1960s, there were at least 6,000 new African independent churches spread throughout most of Africa, including Islamic Africa (Barrett 1968:18–36).

The emergence of African independent churches was driven by several factors (Daneel 1987:68–101; Barrett 1982; Fashole-Luke et al. 1978; Hastings 1976). First, the African Christians did not find much of an African ethos in the missionary-founded churches. Indeed, the missionaries typically discouraged African traditional practices of faith healing, prophecy, and speaking in tongues, and disapproved of polygyny, ancestor veneration, witches, and traditional medicine. Africans wanted churches in which they could express their Christian faith in African symbols and images, churches where they could feel at home, so to speak. Christianity as proclaimed by the missionaries was for them not comprehensive enough to meet their spiritual needs. As a result, many people even today secretly continue to participate in African traditional rituals. There was no serious attempt on the part of the historical churches to understand African traditional spirituality and culture. Instead, many traditional beliefs and practices were simply labeled "heathen" or "superstitious" and were thus forbidden.

Second, as far as most Africans were concerned, the missionaries and the colonialists were birds of a feather. After all, they shared a common worldview and a common racist perception of Africans. The missionaries tolerated and even practiced racial discrimination to the extent of providing separate entries and sections in sanctuaries, and "by so doing [the church] preached against itself and violated human rights" (Plangger 1988:446). Such contradictions in what people heard missionaries preach and what they practiced contributed significantly to the formation of some of the independent churches. This was especially true of the refusal or slowness on the part of missionaries to relinquish church leadership to the indigenous people.

A third reason for the emergence of African independent churches was the translation of the Bible into African languages. African Christians could now read and interpret the Bible for themselves. They soon discovered, for example, that biblical paragons of faith such as Abraham and David were polygamists. They also learned that the Fifth Commandment demands that parents be honored, and that it is the only commandment that comes with a promise, namely, "that your days may be long on earth." For African peoples the "parents" include the ancestor spirits. The translation of the Bible into African languages is thus one of the major contributions by the missionaries to the development of indigenous African Christian spirituality and to the development of African Christian theologies. In the African independent churches, the Bible plays a central role; in some churches, one service may have as many as five or six sermons, all of which are biblically based. The tendency in these churches is to be fundamentalist in interpreting the Bible.

Finally, some indigenous churches headed by women were a reaction to the male dominance found in Western Christian churches and in African society in general. For example, spirit possession cults in East Africa are dominated by women. They are considered to be the female counterpart of male veneration of lineage ancestors. Again, folk Catholicism in Zimbabwe is a largely feminine popular religion, with an emphasis on devotion to the Virgin Mary, mother of Jesus (Ranger 1986:42, 52, 58). Women have also been leaders in such movements as Alice Lichina in Kenya, the Nyabingi of Kenya/Uganda, and Magoi's healing/possession movement in Mozambique (Mikell 1997:26). In Southern Africa, women play important roles as healers and diviners, often mixing indigenous beliefs and practices with Christianity. For example, they often rely on "prophecy, speaking in tongues, ecstatic dancing, and laying on of hands rather than herbs to heal" (Gort 1997:300–301).

African independent churches, and their evolution, can be divided into three broad groups (Daneel 1987:43–67; see also Grillo, van Klinken, and Ndzovu 2019). First, there are what can be referred to as the Ethiopian-style churches, which appeared at the end of the nineteenth century. The term "Ethiopian" captures how these churches were inspired by the fact that Ethiopia was never colonized, thereby serving as an inspiration for political, economic, and religious movements seeking an independent African voice. These were essentially protest movements that broke away from the white-dominated missionary churches that tended to align themselves with oppressive colonial regimes. They identified themselves with the aspirations of oppressed Africans and sought to give theological expression and spiritual support to the struggle for liberation. The references to Ethiopia in texts such as Psalm 68:31 were, as observed by Daneel (1987:38), "interpreted as a sign that the oppressed Black people have a specially appointed place in God's plan of salvation." The Ethiopian-style churches tended to maintain the same doctrines and even hymnbooks as the church from which they broke away. They nonetheless had African religious leaders.

The second type of African independent churches is the spirit-type churches, which appeared at the beginning of the twentieth century. These are often referred to as Zionist churches because the name Zion often appears in the self-designations of these movements. They are prophetic in character and place a great deal of emphasis on the work of the Holy Spirit, which manifests itself in speaking in tongues, healing, prophecy, dreams, and visions and which helps to identify witches and cast out evil spirits. Their worship services include drums and dancing. They are more concerned with the practical benefits that religion can provide in this world than with otherworldly salvation. At the same time, they have a tendency to forbid their members from adhering to various aspects of traditional African religion, such as divination (Morrison, Mitchell, and Paden 1989:76). Zionist churches include the Aladura or "praying" churches in Nigeria and the Harris churches in Côte d'Ivoire (Ranger 1986:3). An excellent example is the Kimbanguist church in the DRC, which was started during the colonial era by Simon Kimbangu, a great healer and prophet. Since his activities were not acceptable to the missionary church, he was arrested shortly after the start of his ministry and tried for subversive activities by the Belgian colonial authorities. He was sentenced to death, but the sentence was later commuted to life imprisonment; he died in 1951. Today, the Kimbanguist church, officially known as the Eglise de Jésus Christ par le Prophète Simon Kimbangu (Church of Jesus Christ According to the Prophet Simon Kimbangu), is reported to be one of the largest African independent churches with most of its followers in the DRC and other countries in Central Africa (see Mazrui 1986:152–156).

The spirit-type churches represent a serious attempt to Africanize the Christian faith by responding concretely to the needs and aspirations of the African people. These movements take the Africans' worldview seriously. For example, if salvation is to be real, it must include liberation from evil spirits, sickness, and disease. For it to be meaningful and relevant, Christianity must offer protection against black magic, sorcery, and witchcraft, all of which are issues of vital concern to African societies (Kiernan 1995b:23–25). The spirit-type churches are nonetheless against participation in traditional African religious rites and substitute specifically Christian rites to fill the vacuum. The prophet who is inspired by the Holy Spirit, for example, takes the place and assumes the functions of the traditional diviners and spirit mediums. Similarly, requests for rain are made directly to God through the mediation of Christian leaders rather than through spirits mediated by traditional religious leaders.

Pentecostal-charismatic churches are a third form of African independent churches. These appeared at the beginning of the twentieth century and were associated with Western mission churches of the Pentecostal variety, such as the Assemblies of God, coming from the United States. The essence of this type of African independent church is captured by the two words in its title. Whereas the "word 'Pentecostal' originates from the biblical story about Pentecost (Book of Acts), according to which the Holy Spirit was poured out over the followers of Jesus after his ascension," the "word 'charismatic' has its origins in the Greek word charismata, which is used in the New Testament for the gifts of the Holy Spirit, such as prophecy, speaking in tongues and healing" (Grillo, van Klinken, and Ndzovu 2019:77). The primary difference between the spirit-type and Pentecostal-charismatic churches lies in their origins: whereas the origins of the former are primarily African, those of the latter are primarily from the West, most notably the United States.

The severe economic crisis experienced by most African countries during the 1980s contributed to the rise of what religious scholars refer to as neo-Pentecostal churches, which have continued to expand and increasingly dominate the Christian religious landscape during the last fifty years (Grillo, van Klinken, and Ndzovu 2019; see also Gifford 2004). These churches are typically based on two theological elements: (1) a "prosperity gospel" promising wealth, health, and happiness to believers; and (2) an ability to heal the physically sick and mentally ill, including deliverance from evil demons, witchcraft, and the spirit world more generally speaking (Kiernan 1995a, 1995b, 1995c; see also Asamoah-Gyadu 2004, 2014; Corten and Marshall-Fratani 2001). In both cases, the promised results are associated with the here and now (i.e., the believer's current life on earth) rather than on a more abstract and in any case future afterlife. In terms of spreading the gospel, these churches follow the model of television evangelists in the United States who lead megachurches. As explained by Birgit Meyer (quoted in Grillo, van Klinken, and Ndzovu 2019:79), they often include "flamboyant leaders" who "dress in the latest (African) fashion, drive nothing less than a Mercedes Benz, participate in the global Pentecostal jet set," and broadcast their religious message through "flashy TV and radio programs."

Gifford (1998) portrays these new churches as a response to the failure of the modernization and development agenda in Africa. With conditions of life so problematic for many Africans, and opportunities for advancement in the public or private sectors often limited, religion is seen by many as the best avenue for improving their lives. Not surprisingly, the neo-Pentecostal churches appeal to many ambitious, better-educated, younger Africans in urban areas who want to get rich. It also appeals to ambitious, noneducated, younger Africans in the rural areas who see few opportunities, and like their urban counterparts, wish to become rich (Gifford 1998; Khumalo 2008:4; Simone 2010:219). Indeed, churches such as the neo-Pentecostal churches with external, often international links may have access to jobs, incomes, and other resources unavailable elsewhere. Moreover, many of these churches, especially the faith gospel churches, legitimate the accumulation of wealth as "God's will," thus lessening the risk of the accusation of witchcraft from envious relatives or neighbors.

Nonetheless, without major economic and political transformation, belief in faith and personal endeavor alone as the means to riches or reliance on deliverance from witches as the cure for social problems is unlikely to work for most of Africa's suffering people. As Terence O. Ranger (2003:117) argues, "prosperity Christianity" is more about survival than rising to the heights of entrepreneurial success. Magic is often substituted for thrift, and rewards are received for non-economic reasons. Yet among Africa's impoverished masses, the gospel of prosperity sustains a belief that God will not allow the faithful to perish. An especially poignant example of this need for faith in the midst of human misery is found in Abdoumaliq Simone's (2010:134) description of Kinshasa, the capital of the DRC, where residents are increasingly "dedicated to religion with endless prayer services and financial obligations to the church." In essence, the poorest of the poor in the city believe that God will "show a way even in the belly of the beast." The entrepreneurism such faith encourages under the context in which so many Africans live is mainly "penny capitalism"—that is, informal sector activities among the young and women that prevent starvation.

Many of the new neo-Pentecostal churches are founded by a charismatic leader who claims to have a mystical experience and is regarded as a prophet by his or her followers (Haynes 1996:174). The churches are often millenarian, that is, expecting the imminent end of the world, at which time only believers will be saved. Critical or rational thought is discouraged, and dissent from what the evangelist says is viewed as opposing God (Gifford 1998:178). Such views can give rise to extremist religious movements with tragic results, as occurred in Uganda. Early in 2000, leaders of the Movement for the Restoration of the Ten Commandments of God killed over 900 members of their church, one of the worst cult killings in modern history. Cult leader Joseph Kibwetere, a former teacher, public official, businessman, and devout Catholic, came under the sway of Credonia Mwerinde (allegedly "the real power"). She claimed that the Virgin Mary appeared to her and told her the end of the world was coming. The motive for the mass murder is unclear, but apparently members of the cult became disillusioned and questioned the leaders' authority (and appropriation of members' financial assets) (see Maykuth 2000).

The Political Roles of Christian Churches During the Contemporary Independence Era

One of the realities of the initial decades of the contemporary independence era is that Christian churches often remained silent and at worst were compliant when confronted with the growing authoritarianism of their respective governments, as single-party regimes replaced multiparty regimes and military dictators replaced their civilian counterparts in military coups d'état. For example, many independent churches in Kenya supported President Daniel arap Moi despite his record of antidemocratic and corrupt rule (Gifford 2009). In Liberia before the 1990 civil war, Pentecostal churches backed any government, however oppressive, that promoted evangelism. One of the most atrocious examples was the complicity and direct involvement of Catholic clergy and lay persons in the 1994 genocide against the

April A. Gordon

Evangelical Christian churches such as this one in South Africa are surging in popularity in many African countries.

Tutsis and moderate Hutu in Rwanda. Church leaders were mostly Hutu and closely tied to the Hutu-dominated government (see Gifford 1998:51–55; Longman 1998; Ranger 2003:116).

African Christians have also been involved in violent political movements seeking the overthrow of secular African governments. Earlier in this chapter, we discussed the Movement for the Restoration of the Ten Commandments of God in Uganda. Another group in Uganda is the Lord's Resistance Army (LRA) under the leadership of Joseph Kony, who considers himself a prophet. The LRA has been at war with the Ugandan government since 1986. Its goal is to replace the government with one based on Moses's Ten Commandments. Thousands of people, especially children, have been forcibly conscripted to fight for the LRA. Thousands also have been killed and subjected to sexual violence, not only in Uganda but in the neighboring countries of the Central African Republic, DRC, and South Sudan, where the LRA is also active (Oloya 2013). Obviously, any religion in the wrong hands and under circumstances favorable to it has the potential for extremism and violence.

Africa's wave of democratization that began with the fall of the Berlin Wall in 1989 altered the church-state relationship (i.e., the role of Christian actors within Africa's political systems). For example, Christian religious actors, like other actors within civil society, became increasingly willing to both support and promote democratic change. These ranged from individual priests and pastors who took part in protests at the local level to more senior Christian leaders who were part of a national religious hierarchy who directly confronted the leadership of an authoritarian regime. This shift is clearly demonstrated by the evolving role of the Catholic Church in DRC politics during the era of Mobutu Sese Seko's dictatorship. In 1965, when Mobutu took power in a military coup d'état, the Catholic archbishop of Kinshasa (the country's capital city), Joseph Malula, sent a letter pledging the support of the Catholic church. "Mr. President, the Church recognizes your authority, because authority comes from God. We will loyally apply the laws you establish. You can count on us in your work of restoring the peace toward which all so ardently aspire" (quoted in Boyle 1992:49). Twenty-seven years later in 1990, Catholic bishops in the DRC signed the first of several letters calling for political change, including presenting themselves as "honest brokers" between the Mobutu dictatorship and pro-democracy elements of civil society (Boyle 1992:62–66). "Certainly other groups and particular individuals have played a more prominent role than the bishops in formal political opposition to the Mobutu regime," explains Patrick Boyle (1992:64). "The publication of the letters from the bishops, however, opened wider the floodgates of public opposition not only because it tapped a deep seated contempt for the Mobutu regime, a sentiment that was confirmed when Mobutu decided to set the bishops' letter aside, but also because the church, a traditionally conservative institution and at times closely associated with the regime, took the risk of strong public confrontation after years of perceived inaction" (see also Schraeder 2016; Schuck and Crowley-Buck 2016). This case is not unique but rather indicative of the growing role of Christian churches in Africa's wave of democratization (Gifford 1995; Phiri 2001).

It is important to remember, however, that the above trend is neither universal (i.e., it does not affect all Christian churches equally, in all African countries) nor unidirectional (i.e., the trend is not automatically moving toward greater church support for democratization). In Zambia, for example, the antidemocratic and corrupt practices of the democratically elected administration of President Frederick Chiluba were frequently downplayed or overlooked because Chiluba was an outspoken, born-again Christian who put potentially critical Christian leaders in positions of influence in the government (Gifford 1998:51, 204–205, 216–217). Moreover, church leaders, like other members of civil society, are susceptible to the financial benefits and prestige that government leaders can bestow on them and their churches (Gifford 1998:87–88), and those who have benefited from political arrangements (both clergy and lay persons) use the churches to organize opposition to reform (Anderson 2006:74–79). In Eswatini, for example, King Mswati III fended off a democratization movement with the help of fundamentalist Christian leaders, who used the Bible to support monarchy as divinely ordained (Hall 2003).

Regardless of whether they support or oppose political change, and regardless of their specific Christian denomination, Christian churches are increasingly embedded in what can be referred to as the "Pentecostalization of the public sphere" (Grillo, van Klinken, and Ndzovu 2019:85; Lindhardt 2015:20; Ranger 2008). Specifically, rather than adhering to the classic religious maxim attributed to Jesus, "Render unto Caesar the things that are Caesar's, and unto God the things that are God's," in essence underscoring the separation of church and state, the Pentecostalization of the public sphere instead captures the growing involvement of the "religious" within the political sphere. This political reality is directly connected to the rise and prominence of neo-Pentecostal churches, which coincided with the African wave of democratization. For at least three decades, "neo-Pentecostal churches appear to have abandoned the idea that the church should not be involved in 'worldly affairs' such as politics, and they have developed new forms of political engagement and political language, often in an explicitly religious guise," explain Grillo, van Klinken, and Ndzovu (2019:87). "Thus, Pentecostal rhetoric is very much concerned, not just with winning individual souls, but with 'claiming the land for Christ' and dedicating the nation to God." One of the best examples of this trend was President Chiluba's declaration upon his inauguration in 1991 that Zambia is a

"Christian nation," followed by the inclusion in 1996 of this same statement in the Zambian Constitution. By the same token, politicians at all levels cooperate with church personnel and use the churches to increase their power and seek legitimacy (Longman 1998:68; Ranger 2003:116).

Islam in Africa

Islam, which means "submission to God," was founded in the seventh century on the Arabian Peninsula by the Prophet Muhammad. Influenced by Judaism and Christianity, Islam established monotheism (belief in one God above all other gods) and a scripturally based religion among Arabs around the towns of Mecca and Medina. Allah (God) revealed to Muhammad how he wanted his followers to live and structure their communities. This revelation is found in the Quran and is believed to be the literal word of God. Muslims, like Jews, believe they are descendants of Abraham, and they respect the Old Testament and the Prophets. Muslims also revere the New Testament and regard Jesus as a prophet. Muhammad, however, is the last and greatest of the prophets, and the Quran is God's supreme revelation. Unlike Judaism, both Christianity and Islam are missionary religions. As such, both Christianity and Islam have been the major contenders for the religious allegiance of Africans.

Islam has experienced phenomenal growth on the African continent during the twentieth and twenty-first centuries. It bears repeating from the first section of this chapter that over 496 million Africans (or 42 percent of all Africans) are Muslim, making it one of the three largest religious traditions on the African continent. Stated another way, over four of every ten Africans are Muslims. Since so much has been written about Islam as a broad religious tradition, it is not necessary for our purposes to deal with its specific beliefs. We instead focus on the historical development of the religion on the African continent. Special attention is paid to those aspects that give African Islam its own identity.

The Early Spread of Islam

Soon after the death of Muhammad in 632 CE, his followers embarked on wars of conquest, first among Arabs on the Arabian Peninsula and then among non-Arabs, most notably in North Africa. Most of Egypt was under the control of Arab Muslims by 640 CE. By then, Egypt's rulers supported the Byzantine Orthodox church while many Egyptians were Coptic Christians who did not accept the Orthodox church's teachings or authority. Many welcomed Arab rule as less oppressive than they had experienced under the Byzantines. The Arabs established themselves initially as a ruling and powerful minority, but Christians were treated as "protected people" (*dhimmi*) who were allowed to practice their faith and regulate their affairs through their own leaders. Still, Christians were second-class citizens required to pay a special tax (*jizya*) in lieu of military service. Nonetheless, educated Christians often held prominent positions in the new Muslim state. Conversion to Islam was gradual. There was some localized persecution and pressure to convert, but most did so for other reasons, including attraction to Islamic tenets, commercial advantage, and a desire to avoid the *jizya* and second-class status. By the end of the eleventh century, Christianity in Egypt had become a minority religion (Mostyn 1988:190).

After Egypt, the Arabs moved on to Roman North Africa where they defeated the Christians, who were primarily based in the towns, and the Berbers, who had remained largely untouched by Christianity in the rural areas. J. S. Trimingham observes that

> the North African Church died rather than was eliminated by Islam, since it never rooted itself in the life of the country. Although considerations such as the prestige of Islam derived from its position as the religion of the ruling minority and the special taxation imposed on Christians encouraged change, the primary reasons for their rapid conversion were the less obvious ones deriving from weaknesses within the Christian communities. Among these were Christianity's failure to claim the Berber soul and its bitter sectarian divisions. (1962:18)

The conversion of the Berbers of North Africa was a slow process. After their initial military conquests, Arabs located in the towns. They gradually intermarried with the Berbers, who became increasingly Islamized and Arabized. Many Berbers were incorporated into Arab armies. This period of conquest of North Africa is reported by the great Arab historian Ibn Khaldun (quoted in Trimingham 1962:18):

> After the formation of the Islamic community the Arabs burst out to propagate their religion among other nations. Their armies penetrated into the Maghrib [Maghreb—the countries of Algeria, Morocco, and Tunisia] and captured all its cantonments and cities. They endured a great deal in their struggles with the Berbers who, as Abu Yazid has told us, apostatized twelve times before Islam gained a firm hold over them.

The Islamization and Arabization of North Africa fostered a series of Arab/Islamic empires across North Africa. In the territory known as present-day Tunisia, control was established by local dynasties within the context of larger Arab empires, including by the Aghlabids (800–909 CE), the Fatimids (909–1148 CE), the Almohads (1159–1229 CE), and the Hafsids (1207–1574 CE). This was followed by a period of rule by the Ottoman Empire (1574–1704 CE), which was followed by a Tunisian dynasty known as the Husaynids (1704–1883 CE). All of these dynasties and empires spawned important cities and centers of higher learning, most notably the inland city of Kairouan. This city is home to the Great Mosque of Kairouan, which was established in 670 CE, making it one of the oldest centers of worship within the Islamic world. Tunis, the capital of present-day Tunisia, is also home to the Al-Zitouna Mosque, which was built in 734 CE out of columns from the ruined city of Carthage. It hosted one of the earliest and most prestigious universities in the Islamic world.

The Spread of Islam South of the Sahara

Whereas Islam spread to North Africa in the aftermath of conquest, the initial spread of Islam south of the Sahara was primarily the result of peaceful, informal missionary efforts (Insoll 2003; Levtzion and Pouwels 2000). For example, Arabized Berber merchants traded manufactured goods from Mediterranean lands in exchange for raw materials that they obtained from sub-Saharan Africa, such as gold, ivory, gum, and slaves. They followed the established trans-Saharan trade routes that connected North Africa with West and Central Africa, many of which had existed long before the rise of Islam. Wherever they went, Muslims established commercial and religious centers near the capital cities. The Nile River provided access to Nubia, Ethiopia, and Sudan. From Sudan, some of the traders went across to West Africa. The introduction of the camel also made it possible to cross the desert from North Africa and establish contacts with West and Central Africa (Lewis 1980:15–16; Voll 1982:80).

Muslim communities were established fairly early in several states in West Africa. In Ghana, for example, by 1076 CE there was an established Muslim center where several mosques almost competed with each other (King 1971:18). By the fifteenth and sixteenth centuries, Islam was the religion of the rulers and elites of many large African states, such as the Songhai Empire (Voll 1982:14). Islam appealed to African elites for several reasons. One was its association with Arab-Muslim civilization and its cosmopolitanism. Islam was also compatible with or at least tolerant of African religious and cultural practices such as ancestor veneration, polygyny, circumcision, magic, and beliefs in spirits and other divinities. In fact, most African believers were barely Islamized, perhaps observing the Five Pillars of the faith—belief in one God and that Muhammad is his prophet, providing alms (*zakat*) to the needy, praying five times a day, fasting during the month of Ramadan, and making the pilgrimage (*hadj*) to Mecca—but often ignoring elements of sharia (Islamic) law or other Islamic practices (e.g., veiling women), which they found incompatible with local custom (Lewis 1980:33–34, 60–62; Callaway and Creevey 1994).

In East Africa, Islam was spread by Persian and Arab merchants beginning in the late seventh century. These merchants established coastal trading towns with local Africans all the way down to Southern Africa. Through intermarriage and commercial contacts, a unique Swahili language and culture developed. There was little movement of traders or Islam into the interior until the late tenth century, however, because there were few centralized kingdoms to attract them (Lewis 1980:7) (see Chapter 3 for additional information on this period).

Islamic civilization contributed much to Africa's own cultural development, affecting all spheres of human activity (e.g., see Hanson 2017; Robinson 2004). It emphasizes literacy and scholarship, traditions that Islam promoted in previously nonliterate African societies. Islam's stress on the community of believers (*umma*) demands the subordination of regional and ethnic loyalties that often separated Africans and impeded the growth of larger political units. Sharia, as the framework for community life, along with Islamic-Arab administrative and political structures, provided models for Africa's statebuilders and gave built-in religious legitimacy to the claims of rulers over the ruled (see Davidson 1991:28–29; Lewis 1980:37; Mazrui 1986:136–137).

By the eighteenth century in West Africa, Islamic consciousness was spreading from the upper classes to the masses. This new wave of Islamization was being carried by African Muslims through militant mass movements under the religious banner of jihad (literally "to struggle," but often translated as "holy war"). The desire of pious Muslim leaders such as Uthman dan Fodio in northern Nigeria (early nineteenth century) was for social, moral, and political reform. The imposition of more rigorous, Islamic states on lax African believers and non-Islamic peoples was the goal. Jihad thus became a religious justification for wars of conquest and political centralization (Mazrui 1986:184–185; Voll 1982:80–81).

The new wave of Islamization was not solely the result of militant movements. Various Sufi (mystical) religious orders or brotherhoods (*tariqas*) dedicated to a more faithful adherence to Islam were at work. One of the earlier ones (sixteenth century) was the Qadiriyya, introduced to the great Muslim center of learning Timbuktu by an Arab sheikh (leader) (Lewis 1980:18–19). In the nineteenth century, the Tijaniyya from Fez, Morocco, gained many followers. The Qadiriyya greatly influenced Uthman dan Fodio, whose jihad movement led to the founding of the Muslim caliphate at Sokoto (Voll 1982:80–81) (see Chapter 3).

Sufi brotherhoods under the inspiration of their religious leaders (*marabouts*) were able to mobilize large numbers of people for political and economic as well as purely religious ends. Among these ends was resistance to European imperialism in the nineteenth century. Using the ideas of jihad and the brotherhood of all believers, Muslims were able to organize resistance on a wider scale than African political units or ethnicity would allow (Mazrui 1986:284). In Senegal, the Mourides transformed jihad into economic enterprise as *marabouts* organized their followers to produce peanuts on brotherhood land. (Peanuts are a source of peanut oil, which is used for a variety of purposes, most notably cooking.) Even today, the

Mourides are a major political and economic force in Senegal. They attract many followers for practical reasons but also because of their liberalism in enforcing Islamic law (Voll 1982:249–250).

In East Africa, Mahdism galvanized mass opposition to European imperialism in Sudan. The Mahdi in Islam is a messianic figure sent by God to save the believers during times of crisis. The Mahdi Muhammad Ahmed and his followers defeated the British at Khartoum in 1885, although the Mahdist forces were eventually defeated (Mazrui 1986:151–152).

European colonialism and missionary Christianity did not halt the spread of Islam in Africa. In West Africa, colonial rulers made peace with Muslim leaders by protecting their conservative rule over their people and prohibiting Christian proselytizing or mission schools in Muslim areas (Voll 1982:247). Muslims won many new converts for a variety of reasons. The racism and segregation policies of the Europeans contrasted sharply with the Muslim belief in the equality of believers. Also, in many cases, Muslim army officers under the British and the French treated Africans kindly, dealing with their grievances. They were tolerant in helping fellow Africans adjust African customary law to Islamic law (Zakaria 1988:203). Indirectly, colonialism promoted Islamic expansion through the introduction of improved communications and rapid social change (Voll 1982:245). Islam proved able to adjust and change as well as to meet new needs and conditions.

April A. Gordon

The Great Mosque in the town of Touba is the center of devotion for Senegal's Mouride brotherhood. Amadou Bamba, the founder of the Mourides, is buried here.

Islam During the Contemporary Independence Era

Islamic organizations and practices have undergone remarkable changes in order to cope with Western influences, including Christianity (Loimeier 2016). In some cases the process has involved accommodation and new interpretations of Islam. In other instances, Christianity and Westernization are seen as enemies of Islam and failed experiments, unable to solve Africa's many problems. Such views have spawned a growing number of fundamentalist movements.

Initially after independence, conservative nineteenth-century organizations either died out or transformed themselves. In Sudan, the followers of the Mahdi formed a modern political party that competed in national elections. In Nigeria, also, conservative and reformist Muslims formed political parties, partly in competition with Christians in non-Muslim sections of the country. Few of these political parties, however, were explicitly Islamic. The Mourides of Senegal reorganized and assumed modern economic and political roles to maintain their influence (Voll 1982:145–250).

The spirit of jihad and forced conversion were largely replaced by a respect for religious pluralism. This was undoubtedly a result of the long history of mutual accommodation between African traditional religions and Islam in the past as well as contact with Christianity. In most sub-Saharan African states, Muslims are a minority, or at least not the only religious community, a fact that tends to reinforce Muslim support for secular states. Muslim leaders readily accepted non-Muslim leaders, such as Léopold Senghor (a Catholic), who was president of Senegal for many years. Pluralism is also promoted by the fact that family and ethnic loyalties still take precedence over religious ties for most Africans (Zakaria 1988:204–205) (see Chapter 10 for more on the centrality of the family in Africa).

For the masses of Muslim Africans, African traditional beliefs and practices have continued, although with some adaptations to conform to similar practices in Islam. In writing about the Wolof of Senegal, John S. Mbiti concludes:

> In spite of the impact of Islam, there is still a much deeper layer of pagan belief and observances. . . . Men and women are loaded with amulets, round the waist, neck, arms, legs, both for protection against all sorts of possible evil, and to help them achieve certain desires. Most frequently these contain a paper on which a religious teacher has written a passage from the Koran, or a diagram from a book on Arabic mysticism, which is then enveloped in paper, glued down and covered with leather, but sometimes they enclose a piece of bone or wood, a powder, or an animal claw. (1969:245)

These are basically African elements, not Islamic, and are practiced by many African groups.

A survey of African indigenous Islamic communities in other parts of Africa also reveals the persistence of African-based practices. As is true of many Christians, ancestor veneration, the wearing of amulets to ward off misfortune and to protect cattle and homesteads, and beliefs in magic, witchcraft, and sorcery have continued. New elements include the use of charms. Also, as Mbiti (1969:249) observes, "In addition to treating human complaints," traditional healers "perform exorcisms, sometimes using Koranic quotations as magical formulae."

African Muslims, as well as African Christians, are seeking to redefine or modify their religion and religious identity in response to modern needs and challenges. For many Muslims, this means finding a way to incorporate more orthodox Islamic practices and beliefs into those of their pre-Islamic African religious and cultural heritage. Moreover, many African Muslims are seeking new religious responses to meet the political, economic, and social challenges they are facing. This has led a small minority of Muslims to seek a fundamentalist reaffirmation of Islam, sometimes influenced by fundamentalist movements promoted by external powers, such as Iran (Brenner 1993; Hunwick 1995; Ilesanmi 1995; Voll 1982:250, 337). However, as the Pew Forum (2010) has found, although most Muslims and Christians are deeply religious, both mostly believe that people of other religions should be free to practice their faith. Yet it is also true, as we discuss below, that Muslims find aspects of modern life in Africa to be of concern to them and see religion as a proper response.

Among those adapting to contemporary concerns, Sufi brotherhoods have been at the forefront in providing accommodation between the demands of Islam and popular aspirations, both religious and secular. One such movement is Hamallism, a branch of the Tijaniyya. Hamallism is a social and religious reform movement that stresses the full equality of all people and the liberation of women. It opposes the materialism and corruption of conservative Islamic leaders. Before the contemporary independence era, Hamallists opposed those Muslim leaders who cooperated with French colonialism. Hamallism influenced political leaders like Modibo Keita, former president of Mali, and Diori Hamani, former president of Niger (Voll 1982:254). On the other hand, anti-Sufi movements such as the Izala in Nigeria and Niger (Movement for Suppressing Innovations and Restoring the Sunna) have attracted many from the urban merchant class with their opposition to *marabouts* and an emphasis on individualism and putting wealth into investments (Grégoire 1993).

In Sudan, Islamic fundamentalists gained dominant influence over the government. Their efforts to impose sharia on the entire country, including the non-Muslim south, led to a secessionist struggle that ended with South Sudan's independence in 2011 (O'Fahey 1993). The fundamentalists obliterated previous nonsectarian, modernist Islamic movements such as the

Republican Brothers, founded by Mahmoud Mohammed Taha. The Brothers sought a reform of Islam in light of modern realities, including advocating the equality of men and women. Taha was executed in 1985 for "heresy" (Al-Karsani 1993).

Elsewhere, and similar to the new Christian churches that are searching for a more African Christianity, some Muslims are promoting controversial new forms of Africanized Islam. In East and West Africa, the peaceful Ahmadiyya movement (originally from India) owes its success to its vigorous missionary efforts. The Ahmadiyya translated the Quran into Swahili and other local languages (the first to do so) since most African Muslims do not know Arabic. It is estimated that there are nearly 9.6 million Ahmadiyya believers in Africa. Members are often prominent in government and business circles and more secular. They have made significant efforts to promote the status of women. For example, women are allowed to pray in the mosque with men. The Ahmadiyya are seen as heretical by more orthodox believers (Haynes 1996:195). Much more controversial and violent was the Maitatsine movement centered in northern Nigeria. In the 1960s and 1970s, Cameroonian Mahammadu Marwa claimed to be a new prophet of Islam. Marwa was killed along with 100 other people when his followers sparked a violent confrontation with police in the city of Kano in 1980. Rioting by his followers in 1990 left 5,000 people dead. A successor to the Maitatsine movement was the Kalo Kato sect, whose members were involved in an uprising in Kano in 1980 and in Yola in 1992 in which thousands of people died (Haynes 1996:188–191). The name Kalo Kato literally means "a man says" in the local Hausa language, and is a reference to the sayings or hadiths that have been posthumously attributed to the Prophet Muhammad. According to Kalo Kato, only the Quran can serve as the authoritative guidance of God.

The Political Roles of Islam During the Contemporary Independence Era

Muslim religious actors, like their Christian counterparts, were either compliant or silenced as their political leaders created authoritarian regimes during the early decades of the contemporary independence era. This was especially true in North Africa, where an authoritarian security apparatus known as the *mukhabarat* particularly suppressed Islamic groups that were perceived as threatening the secular, authoritarian political order. In Egypt, the Muslim Brotherhood, which is the country's leading politico-religious actor, has been persecuted and repressed by a series of military regimes led by Gamal Abdul Nasser (1954–1970), Anwar Sadat (1970–1981), Hosni Mubarak (1981–2011), and Abdel Fattah el-Sisi (2013–present). The Muslim Brotherhood's only respite from repression was the brief period during which their party ruled Egypt under the presidency of Mohamed Morsi

(2012–2013), who was nonetheless overthrown in a military coup d'état (see also Hansen and Mesøy 2009).

Critics of the role of Islamic actors within politics sometimes raise the myth of "Islamic exceptionalism," or the idea that Islam is incompatible with democracy and, therefore, that different political rules have to be applied to predominantly Muslim countries. For example, some argue that Islamic parties will abuse their power and improperly use their election opportunity to create an Islamic authoritarian regime (i.e., they will not follow the same rules that brought them power, once they are in power). It was precisely this argument that the Algerian military used to suspend the Algerian elections of 1991. They argued that the Islamic Salvation Front, which had won more than 50 percent of the vote in the 1990 local government elections and was on the verge of winning the 1991 parliamentary elections, could not be trusted to maintain democracy if they indeed took office. The real reason, of course, was that the Algerian military did not want to yield power to an Islamist political party. The decision to suspend the electoral process ushered in a period of brutal civil war, which led to tens of thousands of deaths from 1991 to 2002.

The myth of Islamic exceptionalism remains a potent belief in the United States and the other northern industrialized democracies, which was reinforced by the terrorist attacks of September 11, 2001, and later attacks in Europe, such as the 2015 attack that took place in France's national theater. This perception was captured by an exchange between one of the leading US experts on Islam, John Esposito, and an immigration officer in the United Kingdom. The immigration officer is reported to have asked Esposito, "What will you be doing in Edinburgh?" To which Esposito responded that he was going to give a keynote address on the relationship between Islam and democracy. The immigration officer smiled, stamped his passport, and then said, "Well, that is going to be a very brief speech" (quoted in Esposito and Mogahed 2007:29).

The idea of Muslim exceptionalism is belied by the fact that a majority of the globe's Muslims live under democratically elected governments. This includes the two majority-Muslim countries with the largest Muslim populations: Indonesia (the world's most populous Muslim country with more than 200 million Muslim citizens) and Bangladesh (with more than 135 million Muslim citizens). It is also refuted by the existence of Muslim-majority democracies in Africa, such as Senegal, which has become increasingly democratic since independence in 1960, and Tunisia, which in 2011 transitioned to democratic rule. Indeed, despite a variety of challenges associated with this transition, including terrorist attacks, guerrilla insurgencies on its borders with Algeria and Libya, and a precarious economy, Muslim-majority Tunisia has emerged as the most democratic country in the Arab world and one of the most democratic countries on the African continent.

The African wave of democratization that began in 1989, including its North African variant that emerged in 2011 in Tunisia as part of the Arab Spring, significantly affected mosque-state relations (i.e., the role of Muslim actors within Africa's political systems). First, this period of democratization was accompanied by the rise of al-Qaeda and other internationally oriented terrorist groups, such as the Islamic State of Iraq and Syria (ISIS), leading to mounting local and international concerns about global Islamic extremists' gaining ground in the predominantly Muslim regions of Africa. In August 2011, for example, al-Qaeda's North African branch—al-Qaeda in the Islamic Maghreb (AQIM)—released a two-part video that called for Muslims from all Arab Spring countries to join their organization as an avenue for fighting against their oppressive governments (de Montesquiou 2011). Counterterrorism experts especially note the impact of ISIS in the predominantly Muslim countries of North and East Africa, which expanded following the June 2014 announcement of a new "worldwide caliphate" with a capital in Raqqa, Syria (e.g., see Yourish, Watkins, and Giratikanon 2016). For example, the Algerian terrorist group formerly known as Jund al-Khilafah fi Ard al-Jazair transformed itself into a branch of ISIS, titled the Islamic State of Iraq and the Levant–Algeria Province (ISIL-AP). Such recruitment efforts had dramatic impacts, and the predominantly Muslim countries of North Africa served as one of the leading sources of foreign fighters to ISIS during the Syrian civil war, including 6,000 from Tunisia, 1,500 from Morocco, 600 each from Egypt and Libya, and 170 from Algeria (Schumacher and Schraeder 2019: 696). Foreign fighters are individuals who leave their home countries to fight in a conflict on foreign soil (in this case, the Syrian civil war).

The African wave of democratization also has been accompanied by the rise of several homegrown, violent, Islamic-inspired movements that seek to overthrow secular African governments. In Somalia, for example, al-Shabaab (which means "The Youth") since 2006 has been waging a guerrilla insurgency against the UN-backed government based in Mogadishu (the capital city) in a quest to impose a theocratic form of governance based on Islam and sharia law (Hansen 2013; see also De Waal 2004). This guerrilla insurgency and the wider Somali civil war have led to several foreign interventions, ranging from the US-led Operation Restore Hope in 1991 to the more recent (2007–present) African Union–authorized military intervention known as AMISOM. This guerrilla insurgency is taking place against the backdrop of Somalia's "failed state," which has been unable to form an effective central government since the overthrow in 1991 of a brutal dictatorship led by Mohamed Siad Barre.

Another example of a homegrown, violent, Islamic-inspired movement is Boko Haram (which means "Western education is forbidden"). Since 2009, Boko Haram has been waging a brutal guerrilla and terrorist campaign against the Nigerian government in its quest to transform Nigeria into a theocracy governed by Islam and sharia law. It has resorted to a variety of tactics, such as the internationally reported kidnapping and enslaving of 276 schoolgirls from a secondary school in the town of Chibok in northern Nigeria in April 2014 (Comolli 2015; MacEachern 2018; Thurston 2017). It is important to remember, however, that the emergence of these and other radical Islamic movements is not indicative of violence that is somehow inherent in Islam. Rather, Islam, like Christianity and any other religion in the wrong hands and under circumstances favorable to it, has the potential for extremism and violence.

An important reality of Africa's wave of democratization is that the majority of African Muslims, as is the case with Muslims throughout the world, prefer democratic forms of governance, albeit influenced by their religious faith. The evolving contours of what can be referred to as "Muslim democracy" were captured in a book, *Who Speaks for Islam? What a Billion Muslims Really Think* (Esposito and Mogahed 2007; see also McCauley and Gyimah-Boadi 2009). The book is based on a series of Gallup Polls that were undertaken between 2001 and 2007 in thirty-five countries that are predominantly Muslim or that have substantial Muslim populations, including on the African continent. According to the results, whereas approximately 20 percent of Muslims favor the creation of secular democracies, based on the strict separation of mosque and state in which sharia plays no role within law and legislation, another 20 percent of Muslims support instead the creation of a theocratic political system, in which mosque and state are one and sharia serves as the sole source of law and legislation. In between these two extremes, the vast majority of the globe's Muslims, or 60 percent, favor the creation of a democratic system in which sharia serves as *one source* of law and legislation, but *not the only source*. In short, these polling results clearly demonstrate that the vast majority of the predominantly Muslim world, including African Muslims, prefers a model of Muslim democracy that embraces religious values and that involves religion as one but not the only source of governance (e.g., see Ndzovu 2014).

Finally, the African wave of democratization has fostered the rise of religiously based Islamist parties that seek to change peacefully the domestic and foreign policies of their countries (Villalón 2012). There are dozens of Islamist parties, ranging from more extreme Salafist parties that argue in favor of creating theocratic regimes to more moderate Islamist parties that accept the democratic rules of the game but nonetheless wish to make sharia law more prominent in their respective societies (Storm 2013). This was one of the reasons behind the introduction of sharia law by twelve northern states in Nigeria beginning in 1999. The foreign policy impacts of moderate Islamist parties have particularly attracted the attention of foreign policy specialists, in that these parties won elections, took office, and affected foreign policy in three African cases, all of which are located in North Africa:

Tunisia's Ennahda party, which won a plurality of votes and led a coalition government known as the troika from 2011 to 2014, when it was forced to relinquish power; Egypt's Freedom and Justice Party (FJP), which in 2012 captured a majority of parliamentary seats and the presidency in the country's first democratic elections, only to be overthrown in 2013 as a result of a military coup d'état; and Morocco's Justice and Development (PJD) party, which won a leading share of parliamentary seats in the 2011 elections and has since led Morocco's government. "While sharing many similarities with non-Islamist parties," explains Mecham (2019:640), "these parties brought unique ideological and identity preferences to both domestic and foreign policy."

The foreign policy impacts of moderate Islamist parties' taking power have included prioritizing preferential foreign policy links with other predominantly Muslim countries; pursuing foreign policy interests outside of traditional foreign policy channels due to the fact that Islamist parties often face powerful, institutionalized political rivals (e.g., the military); tending to seek indigenous, more regionally based foreign policy solutions as a result of perceived "colonial intrigues"; and having "a willingness to fight for 'just causes' at the expense of strategic relationships or traditional alliances" (Mecham 2019:649–656; see also Adraoui 2018). For example, the PJD minister of foreign affairs, Saad-Eddine el-Othmani, ignored domestic criticism over his priority to improve Moroccan-Algerian relations, historically fraught due to Algeria's rejection of Morocco's sovereignty claim over the former Western Sahara, as witnessed by being the first Moroccan minister of foreign affairs to visit Algiers in over a decade. "This may have been the result of the PJD's pan-Islamic worldview, which emphasized commonalities between the religious interests of Moroccans and Algerians over historical differences in nationalism and between the republican and monarchical institutions of the two countries" (Mecham 2019:655). As is the case with political parties everywhere, however, a variety of domestic and international constraints have moderated the foreign policy impacts of Islamist party leaders. "As the North African experience has shown," concludes Mecham, "Islamist parties in government find that they must inevitably walk the line between ideology and pragmatism as they try to translate the ideals that served them well in political opposition to the realities of the global stage" (2019:658).

Religions of Tolerance or Intolerance?

Although it is not possible to do justice to so broad a topic as African religions within the space of a chapter, we hope this survey has illustrated the breadth of the continent's religious traditions and current trends. Africans, like people everywhere, embrace religions they feel speak to their experience and their need for identity and meaning—religions that promise some kind of justice and redress of their existential problems. In Africa, a meaningful religion is one oriented toward promotion of human interests in good health, economic well-being, and human development, as well as managing social relations and easing conflict (Kiernan 1995b:25). After decades of misrule and economic and political decline from 1951 to 1989, followed by the political openings associated with the African wave of democratization (1989–present), Africans are seeking solutions to, or at least relief from, suffering, uncertainty, and disruptive socioeconomic and political changes. In this regard, although vast majorities of African Muslims and African Christians are tolerant of each other's faiths and have positive views of each other, an unfortunate by-product of Africa's ongoing socioeconomic and political challenges has been growing tensions and animosities, especially between the more fundamentalist elements of each religion. Muslims from Saudi Arabia and the Gulf states are pouring money into Africa to expand conservative Islam, which conflicts with the more tolerant Islam espoused by most African Muslims. At the same time, Christian missionaries, mostly from the United States, are pouring money and missionaries into Africa to promote conservative Christianity, which conflicts with the more tolerant Christianity followed by most African Christians (Rice 2004). Extremism can be found in both religious traditions. The question in Africa, as well as in many other areas of the world, is whether tolerant, emancipatory religions of peace, rather than religions of intolerance, repression, and violence, will be embraced as Africans seek to meet their worldly and spiritual needs.

14

Looking Ahead

Peter J. Schraeder

The African Union ratified and published in 2015 a forward-thinking document, "Agenda 2063: The Africa We Want," to serve as an aspirational plan or blueprint for the future evolution of the African continent (AU Commission 2015). The target year of 2063 was chosen because that year will mark the hundredth anniversary of the founding of the Organization of African Unity, which served as the AU's precursor. Africa's future, according to this document, is based on two pillars: pan-Africanism, which has served as the guiding principle of both the AU and the OAU since the latter's founding in 1963; and the African renaissance (rebirth), which is a recognition of the dramatic socioeconomic and political-military opportunities and challenges that have occurred on the African continent since 1989. "We echo the Pan-African call that Africa must unite in order to realize its Renaissance," explain the signatories, further noting that Agenda 2063 serves as a "robust framework" for pursuing the goal of making the twenty-first century "the African Century" (AU Commission 2015:1). The aspirational goals set out by this document range from the political-military priorities of promoting a "peaceful and secure Africa" that is marked by "good governance, democracy, respect for human rights, justice and the rule of law," to the socioeconomic objectives of ensuring a "prosperous Africa" based on "inclusive growth" and "sustainable development" that are "people-driven, relying on the potential of African people, especially its women and youth" (AU Commission 2015:2).

The primary purpose of this chapter is also to look ahead by setting out some points of reflection regarding future trends and prospects. These are not meant to be a comprehensive review of all socioeconomic and political-military developments affecting the African continent that have been treated in the previous chapters. They are simply intended as a selection of important topics to provide food for thought as you continue with your exploration of contemporary Africa in the future.

Points of Reflection

Strengthening Democracy in Africa

One of the recurring themes of this book is that democracy and democratic practices have become more prominent on the African continent as a result of the African wave of democratization that was sparked in 1989 by the fall of the Berlin Wall and the collapse of single-party communist regimes in Eastern Europe and the former Soviet Union. A powerful, recent example of this trend was Tunisia's Jasmine or Dignity Revolution of 2011. This revolutionary watershed not only toppled the dictatorship of Zine el-Abidine Ben Ali and replaced it with one of Africa's strongest democracies, but it also triggered a domino effect in North Africa and neighboring regions as prodemocracy demonstrators confronted dictatorships and demanded socioeconomic and political-military reforms, collectively referred to as the Arab Spring. Together these trends—often referred to as Africa's second independence, second liberation, or renaissance—represent a new chapter in the evolution of African history as presented in Chapter 3 by Thomas O'Toole and Kirstie Lynn Dobbs.

The political impacts of this new historical era are twofold. First, the universe of African democracies has significantly expanded from 1988 (the year preceding the beginning of the African wave of democratization) to the present. As Peter J. Schraeder explains in Chapter 4, whereas only four countries (8 percent of the continental total) in 1988 could be characterized as leaning democratic, very democratic, or highly democratic, the total has increased to seventeen countries (31 percent of the continental total) as of this writing. As also discussed in Chapter 4, the African wave of democratization has contributed to the gradual decline of personal rule in which power is ultimately vested in individual African leaders, in favor of the expansion of legally based institutions that are capable of constraining the actions of those same African leaders. Whereas an extraordinary 88 percent of all African countries in 1988 embodied political systems with high, very high, or extremely high degrees of personal rule, the total has declined to 28 percent of the continental total as of this writing. In short, democracy has become more widespread and deeply engrained throughout Africa during the last three decades.

Democratization of African Policymaking Establishments

A second impact is that Africa since 1989 has witnessed the democratization of African policymaking establishments. This entails the emergence and strengthening of power centers outside of African presidential mansions that are increasingly capable of challenging the policymaking supremacy of African leaders regarding both domestic and foreign policies. At the level of the state, these power centers include the constitution, the national parliament, the judiciary (most notably the supreme court), and the various bureaucracies that comprise the executive branch, such as the ministry of foreign affairs, the economic affairs bureaucracies (especially the ministries of trade and finance), the ministry of defense, and the security affairs bureaucracies (especially the ministries of interior and intelligence). The democratization of African policymaking establishments also fosters the involvement and influence of numerous nonstate actors, such as the media, public opinion, and political parties. The increased number, autonomy, and influence of these actors has contributed to the enlargement of the policymaking space in African countries. "To be sure, many leaders still look for ways to hamper or manipulate constraints on their authority," explains Peter M. Lewis (2019:80), director of the African studies program at Johns Hopkins University, "yet the great majority of rulers in Africa today face counter-vailing influences that did not exist a generation ago." At the bare minimum, resurgent and newly emergent state and nonstate actors are questioning and shaping the domestic and foreign policy initiatives of their executives.

The gradual democratization of African policymaking establishments has enabled African governments to more effectively respond to a variety of challenges, although much still remains to be done. In Chapter 5, for example, Michael Kevane provides an overall "optimistic forecast for African economic development," citing a variety of positive economic developments during the last three decades, including the dramatic decline in mortality and morbidity and greater access to schooling and to information. However, he cautions—to cite but one concern—that the agricultural sector, which "remains the principal source of livelihoods for about half of African populations" is "increasingly vulnerable to regional ecological degradation and global climate change." Garth A. Myers picks up on this latter point in his discussion in Chapter 9 of the environmental challenges confronted by African leaders. He adopts a "political ecology" perspective (i.e., that one cannot view Africa's environmental challenges as strictly natural phenomena) that recognizes the growing agency of a variety of African organizations in the environmental realm. He cites, for example, Wangari Maathai, who was the first African woman to win a Nobel Peace Prize for, among other actions, creating the globally influential Greenbelt Movement, which began in Kenya. Indeed, in Chapter 7, Jeffrey W. Paller explores "how struggles over power and decisionmaking will determine whether urbanization will be sustainable and inclusive or foster inequality and deepen poverty, which will become more entrenched." The enormity of this policymaking challenge according to Paller is demonstrated by the fact that nearly half of all urban Africans live in slum-like conditions. Finally, Amy S. Patterson in Chapter 8 explains how the last three decades have witnessed the proliferation of public health actors, including intergovernmental organizations, multilateral and bilateral donors, private foundations, individual African governments, nongovernmental organizations, community and faith-based organizations, and local advocacy groups. Although a welcome development, Patterson nonetheless cautions that this large and growing number of state and nonstate actors "makes coordination, communication, and accountability difficult."

An example of a nonstate actor that has become increasingly important in terms of translating popular wishes into actual government policies is African public opinion, or the beliefs of a country's citizens at any given point in time. Public opinion polling was only sporadically conducted during the 1950s and the 1960s, virtually disappearing as African regimes became increasingly authoritarian. A core dilemma for researchers was that the first generation of African leaders "thought that they knew best what 'the people' wanted" and "therefore discouraged or prohibited public opinion surveys, which threatened to reveal that ordinary people were less than fully content with the strategy and performance of the governments of the day" (Bratton, Mattes, and Gyimah-Boadi 2005:50). The turning point for public opinion surveys was the African wave of democratization and the opening up of political regimes, in which a variety of regime types but especially democracies embraced the importance of understanding what their publics believed and desired. Surveys in growing numbers have been carried out by African governments, international organizations, and academic research groups and foundations, including the World Values Survey, the Pew Global Attitudes Project, and the Afrobarometer, the latter of which constitutes the most extensive public opinion initiative on the African continent.

Several conclusions can be drawn from the Afrobarometer about the evolving relationship between African public opinion and African policy, including both domestic and foreign policies. At the most basic level, African citizens, like their counterparts throughout the globe, clearly favor democracy over dictatorship. According to Gyimah-Boadi, "ordinary Africans have been consistent in expressing a clear desire for democratic governance," which they have repeated in "multiple Afrobarometer surveys involving more than a quarter-million interviews conducted in all corners of the region over two decades" (2019:87). Second, continental trends coexist with policy preferences that are unique to a specific African subregion or subset of countries. The predominantly Arab-Muslim populations of North Africa typically have exhibited support for an independent Palestinian state and opposition to Israel at higher levels than populations in other African regions (Jamal and Tessler 2008). A third conclusion is that African public opinion plays a greater policymaking role on a more regular basis in countries that are more democratic. "This is due to the simple fact that African populations in African democracies are freer to publicly state and advance their positions," explains Korwa Gombe Adar, a Kenyan specialist of African politics and foreign policy. "It is also due to the growing belief among African executives that popular support, even within illiberal African democracies, is necessary to win elections."[1] Finally, African public opinion is most often mobilized by issues that have a direct impact on the daily lives of average Africans. This includes, for example, how changes in the national economy affect local bread and butter issues (i.e., local perceptions of economic safety). A classic foreign policy example involved growing public opposition to the adoption of structural adjustment programs during the 1980s and the 1990s, which led several African countries to change course (Bratton, Mattes, and Gyimah-Boadi 2005:97–129). These issues also include how perceptions of local physical safety are affected by guerrilla insurgencies, terrorist activities, human trafficking, or drug trafficking.

Growing Web of Ties That Strengthens and Empowers African Civil Society

African civil society is defined as voluntary organizations that seek access to the formal institutions of state power, such as the presidency and the

Peter J. Schraeder

Addis Ababa's Bole International Airport comes to a halt as workers, who embodied public opinion in Ethiopia, line up to get a glimpse of the arrival of Eritrean President Isaias Afwerki in July 2018 as part of a historic peace accord with Ethiopia.

parliament, with the objective of influencing both domestic and foreign policies. This broad umbrella category includes student groups, women's organizations, labor unions, human rights organizations, and religious groups. The activities of these organizations were crucial to opening up authoritarian regimes beginning in the 1980s. Equally important, their growing coordination during the last three decades with like-minded organizations in their region, across the African continent, and internationally has made it more difficult for authoritarian regimes to suppress their activities. Indeed, the regional and international ties enjoyed by African civil society organizations are clearly deeper and more extensive than they were three decades ago, thereby fostering a more vocal and self-sustaining role for African civil society within the policymaking establishment.

The growing web of ties created by African labor organizations is illustrative. In the aftermath of the Arab Spring, fifteen independent Arab trade unions in 2011 created the Arab Democratic Trade Union (ADTUF) in Amman, Jordan, which seeks "to promote the fundamental values of democratic and independent trade unionism and to increase regional union solidarity and unity" (ITUC 2011). Six independent trade unions from the North African subregion were part of ADTUF's original signatories, including Tunisia's General Union of Tunisian Workers, the Egyptian Federation of Independent Trade Unions, the Free Libyan Workers Federation, and three groups from Morocco: the Moroccan Workers' Union, the Democratic Confederation of Labour, and the General Union of Moroccan Workers (ITUC 2011). African labor organizations have also fostered ties at the continental level. The core pan-African labor grouping is the African Regional Organization of the International Trade Union Confederation (ITUC-Africa), which is one of three regional union organizations under the broader ITUC umbrella. It was launched in 2007 through a merger of the International Confederation of Free Trade Unions–African Regional Organization and the Democratic Organization of African Workers' Trade Union. ITUC-Africa is based in Lome, Togo, and represents roughly 16 million union members and more than 100 trade union centers in fifty-one African countries.

African unions have also nurtured ties with like-minded labor groups at the international level. These can be with the national trade organizations of other countries, such as the American Federation of Labor and Congress of Industrial Organizations (AFL-CIO) in the United States, as well as with their affiliates. The AFL-CIO enjoys an alliance with the Washington, DC–based Solidarity Center, a nonprofit devoted to strengthening the global labor movement that in turn maintains regional offices in Kenya and Nigeria, as well as country offices in South Africa and Zimbabwe. Ties are also sought with international organizations, most notably the International Labour Organization (ILO) of the UN. As of 2020, the ILO maintains Decent Work Technical Support Team offices in Cameroon, Egypt, Senegal, and South Africa, and country offices in Algeria, the DRC, Ethiopia, Madagascar, Nigeria, Tanzania, Zambia, and Zimbabwe (ILO 2020). These and other international linkages provide knowledge, training, and financial support that strengthen African unions as policy actors.

Tunisia's General Union of Tunisian Workers provides food for thought. It was one of four civil society actors known as the Quartet that in 2015 were jointly awarded the Nobel Peace Prize. The other three civil society actors were the Tunisian Confederation of Industry, Trade, and Handicrafts; the Tunisian Order of Lawyers; and the Tunisian Human Rights League. In the award statement, the Nobel Peace Prize Committee credited the Quartet with leading a national dialogue that brought Tunisia back from the brink of civil war, thereby preventing the potential collapse of Tunisia's transition to democracy. "It was thus instrumental in enabling Tunisia, in the space of a few years, to establish a constitutional system of government guaranteeing fundamental rights for the entire population, irrespective of gender, political conviction or religious belief" (Nobel Peace Prize Committee 2015).

Self-Determination of Peoples and Secessionist Movements

Jeffrey W. Neff and Adam Hii conclude their Chapter 2 on African geography by highlighting the limited success of many African governments in extending their power over the geographic expanses of their territories during the contemporary independence era. One recurring outcome associated with this political-geographic reality has been the rise of a variety of guerrilla insurgencies, most notably secessionist movements that seek the self-determination of their peoples within individual African countries. It is an open question whether these efforts, which serve as a fourth trend, will evolve into a new, secessionist wave of independence that will continue to alter the geographical boundaries inherited from the Conference of Berlin (1884–1885) and the colonial era more broadly speaking. Indeed, several African countries in all regions of the African continent are beset by political movements and/or guerrilla insurgencies that ultimately seek international recognition of their territories as independent countries within the international system (Bereketeab 2014; de Vries, Englebert, and Schomerus 2019; Thomas and Falola 2020). Examples include northern Somalia's secession as the Somaliland Republic from the Republic of Somalia in East Africa; the Polisario Front's struggle to create an independent Sahrawi Arab Democratic Republic from territory claimed and controlled by Morocco in North Africa; the Southern Cameroons Ambazonia Consortium United Front's declaration of independence for the anglophone portion of Cameroon (former Southern Cameroons) as the Republic of Ambazonia in Central Africa; a guerrilla insurgency led by the Movement of Democratic Forces of Casamance in southern Senegal to create a Republic of Casamance in West Africa; and the pursuit by the Baroste Royal Establishment in southwestern Zambia to create an independent country of Barotseland in Southern Africa. As of 2020, only two countries have emerged from secessionist movements: Eritrea, which was recognized on May 24, 1993, as Africa's fifty-third sovereign country after a brutal civil war against an Ethiopian dictatorship; and South Sudan, which was recognized on July 9, 2011, as Africa's fifty-fourth sovereign country after an equally brutal civil war against a Sudanese dictatorship.

The case of Somaliland, which declared its independence from the Republic of Somalia on May 18, 1991, with Hargeisa as its capital, provides a fascinating case study. According to Saad Ali Shire, minister of foreign affairs and international cooperation with whom I met while conducting research in Hargeisa in 2018, two broad sets of reasons are key as to why Somaliland deserves to be recognized as Africa's fifty-fifth African country[2] (see also Bradbury 2008; Hoehne 2015; Renders 2012). At the most basic level, he argues that, after achieving independence from British colonial rule on June 26, 1960, Somaliland was duly recognized as a sovereign entity by the UN and thirty-five countries, including the United States. Several days later, on July 1, the independent country of Somaliland voluntarily joined with its newly independent southern counterpart (the former UN Trust Territory of Somalia that was a former Italian colony) to create the Republic of Somalia. The basic point is that Somaliland voluntarily joined a union after independence, and that under international law it should (and does) have the right to abrogate that union, as it did in 1991. As a result, recognizing Somaliland's independence would not call into question the inherited boundaries of the colonial era.

The political basis for Somaliland's claim is that the voluntary union of 1960 was derailed in 1969 by a military coup d'état in Mogadishu that ushered in more than two decades of brutal military rule under the dictatorship of General Mohamed Siad Barre. According to this argument, Barre destroyed the foundations of the north-south democratic compact by unleashing a murderous campaign against northern civilians that resulted in more than 50,000 deaths and over 500,000 refugees as part of a widening civil war during the 1980s. Even after Barre was overthrown in 1991 by a coalition of guerrilla armies, including the northern-based Somali National Movement, northern expectations of a government of national unity were dashed when southern guerrilla movements reneged on an earlier agreement and unilaterally named a southerner president, which in turn was followed by the intensification of inter- and intraclan conflict in the south. Nearly thirty years of unfulfilled promises and authoritarian policies ripped the fabric of the already fragile north-south political compact. A point of no return had been reached for Somalilanders intent on reasserting their country's independence. A popular mandate was added when a resounding number of ballots cast (97 percent) in a national Somaliland referendum favored the adoption of a new constitution that explicitly underscored Somaliland's independence.

Although the merits of this and other secessionist cases are left to the reader to decide, the Somaliland case embodies one additional important reality: international recognition would provide the de jure (legal) basis for a de facto reality that already exists throughout the territory. Specifically, 70 percent of Somalilanders are under the age of thirty and, therefore, have known nothing but Somaliland. For this segment of Somaliland society, which grows larger with each year, the Republic of Somalia is simply a neighboring country that at best is learned about only in history books. There is no personal connection, and thus no going back. The response offered by a twenty-eight-year-old worker in a grocery store in Hargeisa is illustrative. When I asked him what he personally knew about the Republic of Somalia, he laughed, and responded, "Only what I see on YouTube." When I further asked him about how he felt about the possibility of Somaliland rejoining the Republic of Somalia, he responded, "Why would we do that? We have no connection to Somalia. I love my country, which is the only country I have known. It is my motherland, where I was born."[3]

African Violence: From Armed Conflicts to Riots, Protests, and Social Violence

Secessionist movements serve as but one aspect of a broader universe of political violence that has affected the African continent during the African wave of democratization. The specific contours of this violence, which serves as a fifth point of reflection, have been studied by an array of policy think tanks and research institutes. One of the leading African voices in this regard is the South Africa–based Institute for Security Studies (ISS), which also maintains regional offices in Kenya, Ethiopia, and Senegal. International partners, which have focused on the development of quantitative datasets on African conflicts, include the Armed Conflict Location and Event Data Project, which is a US-based nonprofit; the Uppsala Conflict Data Program hosted at Uppsala University in Sweden; and the Heidelberg (Germany) Institute for International Conflict Research. The primary purpose of these and other organizations is to develop empirical, data-driven understandings of African conflicts that can inform policymakers at the local, national, and international levels who are intent on resolving those conflicts.

Two broad findings emerge from these data-driven projects. The first is that there were fewer "high-intensity conflicts and wars" in Africa "where over 500 people are killed" in the 2010s than there were in the 1990s (Aucoin 2017). It was during the 1990s, for example, that the DRC, formerly known as Zaire, became the focal point of what many have referred to as Africa's First World War (Prunier 2009; see also Clark 2002). The roots of this conflict, according to Kevin Dunn and Pierre Englebert, can be traced back to the Rwandan genocide of 1994, "when some 2 million Rwandans—a mix of civilians, Interahamwe (the militia largely held responsible for the genocide), and members of the defeated Rwandan military (the Forces Armees Rwandaises [FAR])—sought refuge in then-Zaire" (Dunn and Englebert 2019:302). These forces, most notably their cross-border attacks against the new, post-genocide government in Rwanda, served as the lightning rod of an intensifying conflict that ultimately transformed the DRC into a battlefield between the armies of at least six countries: Angola, Namibia, and Zimbabwe, which were fighting on behalf of the DRC's government; and Rwanda and Uganda, which were fighting against that government. According to Dunn and Englebert (2019:303), "Over 5 million people were killed in the conflicts between 1994 and 2003 [when a tentative peace agreement was signed and foreign troops were removed], mostly from disease, starvation, and other conflict-related causes, making it the deadliest war since World War II." Although the African continent, including the DRC in its eastern provinces, continues to be confronted by a series of conflicts in the 2020s, these do not reach the scale or intensity of those experienced during the 1990s.

A second broad finding is that "violence in Africa has been moving away from armed conflicts to higher levels of riots, protests, and social violence" (Aucoin 2017). Recent research demonstrates that countries that are experiencing various forms of political unrest, such as the five North African countries since the beginning of the Arab Spring in 2011, will exhibit greater levels of violence by violent nonstate actors, including insurgent groups, terrorist organizations, and foreign fighters (Schumacher and Schraeder 2019; see also Varin and Abubakar 2017). This development is puzzling, in that observers generally anticipated that the Arab Spring would result in the transformation of North African societies for the better, contributing to a decrease in violence. The opposite has occurred, as witnessed by the fact that terrorist attacks in North Africa dramatically increased from 102 attacks in 2010 (the year preceding the beginning of the Arab Spring) to a peak of 1,158 terrorist attacks in 2015 (Schumacher and Schraeder 2019:690). These results are indicative of the fact that a decline in regime control that often (but usually temporarily) accompanies political transitions, including to more democratic forms of governance, permits disenchanted, violence-prone actors to move more freely and to perpetrate violent attacks within a given country or geographical region. The wider lesson for the African continent is that whereas democracies are ultimately better at achieving the peaceful resolution of conflicts, the transition process itself may temporarily lead to political instability and hence greater forms of conflict by violent nonstate actors.

Ethiopia's recent history is illustrative of the opportunities and challenges that confront leaders who undertake transitions from authoritarianism to democracy as part of an overall desire to resolve domestic and international conflicts (Temin and Badwaza 2019). The leader in question is Abiy Ahmed who in 2018 became prime minister of Ethiopia's dictatorship after his predecessor resigned. To the surprise of Ethiopians and the international community, Abiy speedily launched a series of reforms designed to transform Ethiopia into a democracy. The highlights included releasing over 48,000 political prisoners, appointing members of the opposition to prominent government positions, promoting passage of a new law that allows civil society to freely organize, and promising to hold democratic elections (Temin and Badwaza 2019:143–145). From an international conflict perspective, Abiy's most noteworthy achievement has been promoting the peaceful resolution of the Ethiopian-Eritrean conflict, which descended into military warfare between the two countries from 1998 to 2000. Abiy promoted peace by accepting the Algiers (Peace) Agreement of 2000 and the decision of a UN-sponsored Ethiopia-Eritrean Boundary Commission that awarded disputed territory to Eritrea. These actions resulted in the dramatic July 2018 visit to Addis Ababa by Eritrean president Isaias Afwerki that is pictured in this chapter. They also prompted Abiy's selection in 2019 for the 100th Nobel Peace Prize. However, the unexpected and unintended consequences of Abiy opening up Ethiopia's political space has been the eruption of often violent ethnic conflicts throughout this multiethnic country. According to the International Crisis Group, violent ethnic clashes as of May 2019 had "claimed thousands of lives and displaced more than 2.9 million people from their homes" (quoted in Temin and Badwaza 2019:145).

Importance of the Sociocultural Dimension

Ethnic conflict in Ethiopia serves as but one dimension of a broader pattern of intensifying sociocultural influences that together serve as a sixth point of reflection for understanding the future of the African continent. In Chapter 11, for example, Gretchen Bauer demonstrated the impressive gains that African women have achieved in the political realm, especially during Africa's wave of democratization. She nonetheless concludes that "the struggle continues as women follow in the footsteps of their foremothers and mobilize in numbers in organizations, contest for legislative offices, and fill executive or judicial assignments, all with the goal of improving the lives of Africans across the continent."

Additional sociocultural elements include the roles of sexual identity and religion. In Chapter 12, for example, Marc Epprecht, S. N. Nyeck, and S. M. Rodriguez explore the efforts of Africa's lesbian, gay, bisexual, transgender, intersex, and queer (LGBTIQ) communities to pursue their political rights amid the homophobia and outright repression by African governments, as witnessed by Uganda's 2009 passage of an Anti-Homosexuality Bill. They underscore the importance of the 2000s as a watershed period during which LGBTIQ groups "appeared in one country after the other." As of 2020, LGBTIQ rights groups can be found in almost every African country, and they are supported by regional associations, such as the Coalition of African Lesbians and African Men's Sexual Health and Rights.

The important and growing role of religion during the African wave of democratization is subsequently treated by Ambrose Moyo and Peter J. Schraeder in Chapter 13. In the case of Islam, for example, this ranges from the positive impacts of moderate Islamist parties that influenced the foreign policies of Egypt, Morocco, and Tunisia after peacefully entering power through democratic elections, to more radical Islamist guerrilla movements (al-Shabaab in Somalia, Boko Haram in Nigeria, and al-Qaeda in the Islamic Maghreb in Algeria) that seek the overthrow of their respective governments through the force of arms. This duality of positive and negative influences is not limited to Islam, but is instead characteristic of all African religions as their believers attempt to navigate an increasingly globalized world. Indeed, as discussed by Barbara G. Hoffman in Chapter 10, what it means to be an African family and concepts of kinship are gradually being altered by the twin forces of urbanization and globalization.

The African diaspora, defined as Africans who have emigrated to live in another country on a temporary or permanent basis, serves as an increasingly important component of Africa's sociocultural fabric (Mangala 2017; see also Brand 2006; Varadarajan 2010). Emigration may entail resettling in another, often neighboring African country or in a different region of the world, most often Europe and North America, but also including Asia, Latin America, and the Middle East. It is estimated that more than 30 million Africans comprise the contemporary African diaspora. The growing importance of this actor was marked by the AU's official recognition in 2003 of the African diaspora as the "sixth region" of the African continent (in addition to North, East, Central, Southern, and West Africa), followed by the AU's creation of a Citizens and Diaspora Directorate that in turn held a Global African Diaspora Summit in 2012.

The impacts of the African diaspora are multiple. At the most basic level, the African diaspora sends remittances home to family to help with daily necessities such as paying for food, utilities, and medical care and longer-term family investments such as children's education and home construction. One official estimate from 2016 is that these remittances were as high as $40 billion annually (IFAD 2016). According to Mangala, however, nearly 75 percent of all remittances are transferred informally and are not captured by official estimates. He argues that the true remittance figure is three to four times higher, or $120–$160 billion (2017:xii). This is an enormous financial infusion that directly affects approximately 120 million family members in Africa, dwarfing annual official development assistance from the northern industrialized democracies. It also has significant impli-

National Museum of African American History and Culture, Washington, DC, which opened in September 2016.

cations for African foreign policy. Not surprisingly, African governments increasingly have courted their overseas communities through a variety of foreign policy activities. These include refocusing existing foreign affairs bureaucracies to underscore the importance of the diaspora, as in the case of Senegal's renamed Ministry of Foreign Affairs and Senegalese Abroad; creating new diaspora bureaus within government (e.g., Ghana's Bureau of Diaspora Affairs); holding diaspora summits at home and abroad, as witnessed by the 2019 Diaspora Celebration and Homecoming Summit held in Accra, Ghana; and sending high-profile official delegations to meet with the diaspora, as demonstrated by a 2010 speech that President Ellen Johnson Sirleaf gave to the Liberian diaspora in Staten Island, New York, as Africa's first democratically elected female head of state. Indeed, one of the most visible and recent symbols of the African diaspora in the United States was the opening in 2016 in Washington, DC, of the National Museum of African American History and Culture.

The African diaspora also plays an important development role, especially in African countries emerging from conflict (Laakso and Hautaniemi 2014; Mohamoud 2006). According to Mangala, the African diaspora has an estimated savings of $53 billion (Mangala 2017:xii). Attracting even a small percentage of this amount—5 percent or $2.65 billion—potentially would have a tremendous financial impact on government-sponsored investment projects. This possibility has not been lost on African governments that in turn have crafted foreign economic policies designed to attract diaspora engagement in long-term development projects. The lack of official diplomatic recognition—no country has yet recognized Somaliland's independence—means that the Somaliland government has no access to international credit through the global financial infrastructure of the IMF and the World Bank, nor is it able to directly receive foreign aid from foreign governments. As a result, Somaliland's government has been forced to pursue a development strategy based on self-reliance that is heavily dependent on capital investments from the Somaliland diaspora (Hoehne and Ibrahim 2014; see also Abdile 2014). The net result has been the central role of diaspora investments in constructing and launching businesses (e.g., the Maansoor Hotel in Hargeisa), hospitals (e.g., the Edna Adan Maternity Hospital in Hargeisa), and institutions of higher learning (e.g., Nugaal University in Lasanod). The case of Somaliland is not unique, but rather indicative of how African diasporas are playing a greater role in African foreign economic diplomacy. This is part and parcel of globalization and the ability of the diaspora to more easily and effectively reconnect with their homelands in Africa.

Growing Competition Among Regional and Great Powers

A seventh recurring theme of this book is that African international relations have been marked by the growing competition between an increasing number of foreign powers since the fall of the Berlin Wall and the Cold War's end in 1989. As Peter J. Schraeder explains in Chapter 6 on African international relations, these foreign powers can be divided into three major groups. First, there are the seven former colonial powers. The most active of these is France, which maintains an extensive African presence, followed by Germany and the United Kingdom. The four remaining former colonial powers—Belgium, Italy, Portugal, and Spain—play important but sporadic roles. A second group of countries includes the great powers, most notably Japan, the PRC, Russia, and the United States. Competition is clearly intensifying between these four powers, as witnessed by Washington's pronouncement in January 2020 that it is "alarmed" by a rising China and a resurgent Russia on the African continent (Schmitt and Gibbons-Neff 2020). The third and newest addition to African international relations includes the rising regional powers from other regions of the world, most notably India and Indonesia from Asia; Brazil from South America; and Iran, Saudi Arabia, and Turkey from the Middle East. The rising influence of these regional powers should not be underestimated.

The fundamental question is whether the growing competition among these foreign powers constitutes an inherently positive or negative development for the African continent. As discussed in Chapter 6, one perspective is that rising competition among foreign powers theoretically should provide African leaders with the ability to achieve the best deals for their countries by playing these powers against each other. One of the examples discussed from francophone Africa was Pascal Lissouba's successfully "playing the American card" (i.e., cozying up to Washington) to persuade France, the former colonial power, to sign a financial agreement that was more favorable to the Republic of Congo. A more recent example from francophone Africa was the decision of President Patrice Talon of Benin to offer a lucrative pipeline deal to China's National Petroleum Corporation at the expense of previously close ties with the French oil industry.

Foreign involvement in Libya's civil war, which at its most basic level constitutes a military contest between the eastern-based military forces of General Khalifa Hiftar and the UN-backed government in Tripoli, nonetheless provides pause. As of March 2020, the number of foreign actors is not only expanding but includes new players. Specifically, at least five countries are providing military support to General Hiftar's military drive on Tripoli as part of a quest to become the next leader of a unified Libya. These countries include Egypt, France, Jordan, Russia, and the United Arab Emirates (UAE). Russia and the UAE have been particularly involved: Russia has funded hundreds of Russian mercenaries, and the UAE has provided fighter aircraft and pilots. The primary military backer of the UN-sponsored government in Tripoli is Turkey under the administration of President Recep Tayyip Erdoğan. The civil war potentially represents a watershed in Turkish intervention in Africa, as witnessed by the Turkish parliament's vote on January 1, 2020, to authorize the sending of Turkish troops to Libya if deemed necessary by the Erdoğan government (Gall 2020). There is no question that the Libyan civil war has been further internationalized as a result of intervention by foreign powers (Walsh 2020). As a result, any comprehensive understanding of contemporary Africa must by necessity include an analysis of the international dimension.

"All God's Children Need Traveling Shoes"

This chapter's final theme is actually more of a challenge than a trend as you potentially continue your exploration of contemporary Africa in the future. I have always been inspired by my favorite poet and author, Maya Angelou (1928–2014), whose writings provide a number of universal messages. My personal favorite is her 1986 book, *All God's Children Need Traveling Shoes*, which is but one installment of a multivolume series of autobiographical essays setting out the evolution of her life. In this particular volume, Maya Angelou describes her life as someone who, during the early 1960s, moved to Africa along with her son, Guy, to live and experience African life, culture, and politics, first in Cairo, Egypt, and subsequently in Accra, Ghana.

She offers in candid prose both the ups and downs of this period of her life, which ended in 1964 when she moved back to the United States. The metaphorical beauty of this book, and the challenge that it poses, is wonderfully captured in its title. Specifically, if someone wants to better understand another culture, country, or region of the world, they must put on their "traveling shoes" and engage on a personal level. This can entail any number of activities related to the African continent, ranging from exploring books devoted to Africa or enrolling in African studies courses, to working in a job that regularly connects you to Africa, or traveling to the African continent to experience African life in one African community. The key, of course, is not the type of engagement, but simply the fact that you remain engaged.

Notes

1. Author interview with Korwa Gombe Adar, Nairobi, Kenya, July 24, 2018.
2. Author interview with Saad Ali Shire, Hargeisa, Somaliland, July 29, 2018.
3. Author interview, Hargeisa, Somaliland, July 27, 2018.

Acronyms

ACLED	Armed Conflict Location and Event Data Project
ADTUF	Arab Democratic Trade Union
AEGIS	Africa-Europe Group for Interdisciplinary Studies
AfCFTA	African Continental Free Trade Area
AFL-CIO	American Federation of Labor and Congress of Industrial Organizations
AFRICOM	United States Africa Command
AGOA	African Growth and Opportunity Act
AHB	Anti-Homosexuality Bill
AIDS	acquired immunodeficiency syndrome
AMISOM	African Union Mission in Somalia
AMSHeR	Coalition of African Lesbians and African Men's Sexual Health and Rights
AMU	Arab Maghreb Union
ANC	African National Congress (South Africa)
AOF	Afrique Occidentale Française (French West Africa)
AQIM	al-Qaeda in the Islamic Maghreb
ARV	antiretroviral
ASA	African Studies Association
ATM	automated teller machine
AU	African Union
BCE	before common era
BDP	Botswana Democratic Party
BSAC	British South Africa Company
CAL	Coalition of African Lesbians

CAMPFIRE	Communal Areas Management Program for Indigenous Resources
CCCI	Cities and Climate Change Initiative
CCM	Chama Cha Mapinduzi (Tanzania)
CCVI	Climate Change Vulnerability Index
CE	common era
CEN-SAD	Community of Sahel-Saharan States
CENTCOM	United States Central Command
CIA	Central Intelligence Agency
CILSS	Permanent Interstate Committee for the Struggle Against the Drought in the Sahel
CJTF-HOA	Combined Joint Task Force–Horn of Africa
COMESA	Common Market for Eastern and Southern Africa
CPDM	Cameroon People's Democratic Movement
DDR	disarmament, demobilization, and reintegration
DFID	Department for International Development
DHS	Demographic and Health Surveys
DRC	Democratic Republic of Congo
EAC	East African Community
EACTI	East Africa Counter-Terrorism Initiative
EARSI	East African Regional Strategic Initiative
ECA	Economic Commission for Africa
ECCAS	Economic Community of Central African States
ECOWAS	Economic Community of West African States
EPRDF	Ethiopian People's Revolutionary Democratic Front
EU	European Union
FARUG	Freedom and Roam Uganda
FJP	Freedom and Justice Party (Egypt)
FRELIMO	Mozambican Liberation Front
GALA	Gay and Lesbian Alliance
GALZ	Gays and Lesbians of Zimbabwe
GASA	Gay Association of South Africa
GDP	gross domestic product
GIZ	German Society for International Cooperation
GLOW	Gay and Lesbian Organization of the Witwatersrand
GNI	gross national income
GNP	gross national product
HIV	human immunodeficiency virus
ICC	International Criminal Court
IDP	internally displaced persons
IEA	International Energy Agency
IFP	Inkatha Freedom Party (South Africa)
IGAD	Intergovernmental Authority on Development

IGADD	Intergovernmental Authority on Drought and Development
IHME	Institute for Health Metrics and Evaluation
ILO	International Labour Organization
IMF	International Monetary Fund
IPCC	Intergovernmental Panel on Climate Change
ISIL-AP	Islamic State of Iraq and the Levant–Algeria Province
ISIS	Islamic State of Iraq and Syria
ISS	Institute for Security Studies (South Africa)
ITCZ	Intertropical Convergence Zone
ITUC	International Trade Union Confederation
ITUC-Africa	African Regional Organization of the International Trade Union Confederation
JEI	Justice and Empowerment Initiatives
KANU	Kenya African National Union
KFF	Kaiser Family Foundation
LGBTIQ	lesbian, gay, bisexual, transgender, intersex, and queer
LGCM	Lesbian and Gay Christian Movement
LPA	Lagos Plan of Action
LRA	Lord's Resistance Army
LRM	Law Reform Movement (South Africa)
MDM	Democratic Movement of Mozambique
MMD	Movement for Multiparty Democracy (Zambia)
MNC	multinational corporation
MSM	men who have sex with men
NAFTA	North American Free Trade Agreement
NATO	North Atlantic Treaty Organization
NDC	National Democratic Congress (Ghana)
NDI	National Democratic Institute
NEPAD	New Economic Partnership for Africa's Development
NGO	nongovernmental organization
NP	National Party
NPP	New Patriotic Party (Ghana)
NRC	National Resource Center
OAU	Organization of African Unity
OEOA	Office of Emergency Operations in Africa
OLGA	Organization for Lesbian and Gay Activists
OPEC	Organization of Petroleum Exporting Countries
PAC	Pan-African Congress
PEPFAR	President's Emergency Plan for AIDS Relief
PJD	Justice and Development Party (Morocco)
PNDC	Provisional National Defense Council (Ghana)
PRC	People's Republic of China
PRPB	People's Revolutionary Party of Benin

R2P	responsibility to protect
RENAMO	Mozambican National Resistance
RGA	Rand Gay Organization
SADC	Southern African Development Community
SADCC	Southern African Development Coordination Conference
SADR	Sahrawi Arab Democratic Republic (Western Sahara)
SAP	structural adjustment program
SDF	Social Democratic Front (Cameroon)
SMUG	Sexual Minorities Uganda
SNF	Somali National Front (Somalia)
SNM	Somali National Movement (Somalia)
SOGIE	sexual orientation and gender diversity
SPM	Somali Patriotic Movement (Somalia)
SUD-Net	Sustainable Urban Development Network
SWAPO	South West Africa People's Organization (Namibia)
TANU	Tanganyika African National Union (Tanzania)
TB	tuberculosis
TICAD	Tokyo International Conference on African Development
TPLF	Tigray People's Liberation Front (Ethiopia)
TRIPS	Trade-Related Intellectual Property Rights
TSCTI	Trans-Saharan Counter-Terrorism Initiative
UAE	United Arab Emirates
UN	United Nations
UNAIDS	Joint United Nations Program on HIV/AIDS
UNDP	United Nations Development Programme
UNESCO	United Nations Educational, Scientific and Cultural Organization
UNHCR	United Nations High Commissioner for Refugees
UNICEF	United Nations Children's Fund
UNIP	United National Independence Party (Zambia)
USC	United Somali Congress (Somalia)
USGS	US Geological Survey
WCD	World Christian Database
WHO	World Health Organization
WPE	Workers' Party of Ethiopia
ZANU-PF	Zimbabwe African National Union–Popular Front

Basic Political Data

Algeria

Official Name People's Democratic Republic of Algeria
Capital City Algiers
Date of Independence July 3, 1962
Colonizing Country France
Colonial and Earlier Independence Names French Algeria; Algeria
Official Language Arabic, Tamazight (Berber)
Area (square miles/square kilometers) 919,595/2,381,741
Population 41,318,000
Gross National Income (GNI) $167,870,000,000
GNI Per Capita $3,960
Literacy 75%
Life Expectancy 76

Angola

Official Name Republic of Angola
Capital City Luanda
Date of Independence November 11, 1975
Colonizing Country Portugal
Colonial and Earlier Independence Names Angola
Official Language Portuguese
Area (square miles/square kilometers) 481,354/1,246,700
Population 29,784,000
Gross National Income (GNI) $117,793,000,000
GNI Per Capita $3,330
Literacy 66%
Life Expectancy 62

Benin

Official Name Republic of Benin
Capital City Porto-Novo
Date of Independence August 1, 1960
Colonizing Country France
Colonial and Earlier Independence Names French Dahomey; Dahomey (1960–1975)
Official Language French
Area (square miles/square kilometers) 43,484/112,622
Population 11,176,000
Gross National Income (GNI) $9,261,000,000
GNI Per Capita $800
Literacy 33%
Life Expectancy 61

Botswana

Official Name Republic of Botswana
Capital City Gaborone
Date of Independence September 30, 1966
Colonizing Country United Kingdom
Colonial and Earlier Independence Names Bechuanaland Protectorate
Official Language English
Area (square miles/square kilometers) 224,606/581,726
Population 2,292,000
Gross National Income (GNI) $17,041,000,000
GNI Per Capita $6,820
Literacy 81%
Life Expectancy 67

Burkina Faso

Official Name Burkina Faso
Capital City Ouagadougou
Date of Independence August 5, 1960
Colonizing Country France
Colonial and Earlier Independence Names Partitioned during colonial era among Côte d'Ivoire, French Sudan, and Niger (1932–1947); Upper Volta (1960–1984)
Official Language French
Area (square miles/square kilometers) 105,792/274,000
Population 19,193,000
Gross National Income (GNI) $12,471,000,000
GNI Per Capita $610
Literacy 35%
Life Expectancy 60

Burundi

Official Name Republic of Burundi
Capital City Bujumbura
Date of Independence July 1, 1962
Colonizing Country Germany, subsequently Belgium
Colonial and Earlier Independence Names During colonial era part of Ruanda-Urundi
Official Language French
Area (square miles/square kilometers) 10,745/27,830
Population 10,864,000
Gross National Income (GNI) $3,474,000,000
GNI Per Capita $290
Literacy 62%
Life Expectancy 57

Cameroon

Official Name Republic of Cameroon
Capital City Yaoundé
Date of Independence January 1, 1960
Colonizing Country Germany, subsequently France and the United Kingdom
Colonial and Earlier Independence Names Kamerun; Cameroun (French trusteeship territory that became independent in 1960); Northern Cameroons (British trusteeship territory that opted through a United Nations–sponsored plebiscite in 1961 to federate with Nigeria); Southern Cameroons (British trusteeship territory that opted through a United Nations–sponsored plebiscite in 1961 to federate with Cameroun); in 1961, new federation became known as Federal Republic of Cameroon (1961–1972); United Republic of Cameroon (1972–1984)
Official Language English, French
Area (square miles/square kilometers) 183,569/475,442
Population 25,054,000
Gross National Income (GNI) $34,299,000,000
GNI Per Capita $1,360
Literacy 71%
Life Expectancy 58

Cape Verde

Official Name Republic of Cape Verde
Capital City Praia
Date of Independence July 5, 1975
Colonizing Country Portugal
Colonial and Earlier Independence Names Cape Verde; federation with Guinea-Bissau (1975–1981)
Official Language Portuguese

Area (square miles/square kilometers) 1,557/4,033
Population 546,000
Gross National Income (GNI) $1,688,000,000
GNI Per Capita $2,990
Literacy 63%
Life Expectancy 73

Central African Republic

Official Name Central African Republic
Capital City Bangui
Date of Independence August 13, 1960
Colonizing Country France
Colonial and Earlier Independence Names Ubangui-Shari; Central African Empire (1976–1979)
Official Language French
Area (square miles/square kilometers) 240,535/622,984
Population 4,659,000
Gross National Income (GNI) $1,954,000,000
GNI Per Capita $390
Literacy 37%
Life Expectancy 52

Chad

Official Name Republic of Chad
Capital City N'Djamena
Date of Independence August 11, 1960
Colonizing Country France
Colonial and Earlier Independence Names Chad
Official Language French
Area (square miles/square kilometers) 495,755/1,284,000
Population 14,900,000
Gross National Income (GNI) $9,851,000,000
GNI Per Capita $630
Literacy 22%
Life Expectancy 53

Comoros

Official Name Union of the Comoros
Capital City Moroni
Date of Independence July 6, 1975
Colonizing Country France
Colonial and Earlier Independence Names Comoros
Official Language Arabic, Comorian, French

Area (square miles/square kilometers) 863/2,235
Population 814,000
Gross National Income (GNI) $655,000,000
GNI Per Capita $760
Literacy 49%
Life Expectancy 64

Congo, Democratic Republic of

Official Name Democratic Republic of Congo
Capital City Kinshasa
Date of Independence June 30, 1960
Colonizing Country Belgium
Colonial and Earlier Independence Names Congo Free State (1885–1908); Belgian Congo (1908–1960); Republic of Congo (1960–1965); Zaire (1971–1997); commonly referred to as Congo-Kinshasa
Official Language French
Area (square miles/square kilometers) 905,355/2,344,858
Population 81,340,000
Gross National Income (GNI) $36,500,000,000
GNI Per Capita $450
Literacy 77%
Life Expectancy 60

Congo, Republic of

Official Name Republic of Congo
Capital City Brazzaville
Date of Independence August 15, 1960
Colonizing Country France
Colonial and Earlier Independence Names Congo; People's Republic of Congo (1970–1991); commonly referred to as Congo-Brazzaville
Official Language French
Area (square miles/square kilometers) 132,047/342,000
Population 5,261,000
Gross National Income (GNI) $7,939,000,000
GNI Per Capita $1,360
Literacy 79%
Life Expectancy 65

Côte d'Ivoire

Official Name Côte d'Ivoire
Capital City Yamoussoukro
Date of Independence August 7, 1960
Colonizing Country France

Colonial and Earlier Independence Names Côte d'Ivoire; Ivory Coast
Official Language French
Area (square miles/square kilometers) 124,503/322,460
Population 24,295,000
Gross National Income (GNI) $39,040,000,000
GNI Per Capita $1,540
Literacy 44%
Life Expectancy 54

Djibouti

Official Name Republic of Djibouti
Capital City Djibouti
Date of Independence June 27, 1977
Colonizing Country France
Colonial and Earlier Independence Names French Somali Coast (prior to 1967); French Somaliland; French Territory of the Afars and the Issas (1967–1977)
Official Language Arabic, French
Area (square miles/square kilometers) 8,958/23,200
Population 957,000
Gross National Income (GNI) $1,829,000,000
GNI Per Capita $1,880
Life Expectancy 62

Egypt

Official Name Arab Republic of Egypt
Capital City Cairo
Date of Independence February 28, 1922
Colonizing Country United Kingdom
Colonial and Earlier Independence Names United Arab Republic (federation with Syria, 1958–1961)
Official Language Arabic
Area (square miles/square kilometers) 386,662/1,001,449
Population 97,553,000
Gross National Income (GNI) $230,946,000,000
GNI Per Capita 3,010
Literacy 75%
Life Expectancy 71

Equatorial Guinea

Official Name Republic of Equatorial Guinea
Capital City Malabo
Date of Independence October 12, 1968

Colonizing Country Spain
Colonial and Earlier Independence Names Spanish Guinea
Official Language Spanish, French, Portuguese
Area (square miles/square kilometers) 10,831/28,051
Population 1,268,000
Gross National Income (GNI) $9,752,000,000
GNI Per Capita $7,060
Literacy 88%
Life Expectancy 58

Eritrea
Official Name State of Eritrea
Capital City Asmara
Date of Independence May 24, 1993
Colonizing Country Italy, subsequently the United Kingdom and Ethiopia
Colonial and Earlier Independence Names Eritrea
Official Language Tigrinya, Arabic, English
Area (square miles/square kilometers) 45,406/117,600
Population 4,475,000
Gross National Income (GNI) $2,584,000,000
GNI Per Capita $520
Literacy 65%
Life Expectancy 65

Eswatini
Official Name Kingdom of Eswatini
Capital City Mbabane
Date of Independence September 6, 1968
Colonizing Country Boer Republic, subsequently the United Kingdom
Colonial and Earlier Independence Names Kingdom of Swaziland; Swaziland Protectorate; Swaziland
Official Languages English, SiSwati
Area (square miles/square kilometers) 6,704/17,364
Population 1,367,000
Gross National Income (GNI) $4,422,000,000
GNI Per Capita $2,960
Literacy 83%
Life Expectancy 58

Ethiopia
Official Name Federal Democratic Republic of Ethiopia
Capital City Addis Ababa
Colonizing Country Never colonized

Colonial and Earlier Independence Names Abyssinia (prior to 1974); People's Republic of Ethiopia (1974–1991)
Official Language Amharic
Area (square miles) 426,373/1,104,300
Population 104,957,000
Gross National Income (GNI) $80,064,000,000
GNI Per Capita $740
Literacy 39%
Life Expectancy 65

Gabon

Official Name Gabonese Republic
Capital City Libreville
Date of Independence August 17, 1960
Colonizing Country France
Colonial and Earlier Independence Names Gabon
Official Language French
Area (square miles/square kilometers) 103,347/267,668
Population 2,025,000
Gross National Income (GNI) $13,681,000,000
GNI Per Capita $6,610
Literacy 82%
Life Expectancy 66

Gambia

Official Name Republic of Gambia
Capital City Banjul
Date of Independence February 18, 1965
Colonizing Country United Kingdom
Colonial and Earlier Independence Names Gambia; federated with Senegal 1982–1989 as Confederation of Senegambia
Official Language English
Area (square miles/square kilometers) 4,008/10,380
Population 2,101,000
Gross National Income (GNI) $987,000,000
GNI Per Capita $450
Literacy 42%
Life Expectancy 61

Ghana

Official Name Republic of Ghana
Capital City Accra
Date of Independence March 6, 1957

Colonizing Country United Kingdom, Germany for Togoland portion
Colonial and Earlier Independence Names Gold Coast
Official Language English
Area (square miles/square kilometers) 92,098/238,534
Population 28,834,000
Gross National Income (GNI) $45,764,000,000
GNI Per Capita $1,490
Literacy 72%
Life Expectancy 63

Guinea

Official Name Republic of Guinea
Capital City Conakry
Date of Independence October 2, 1958
Colonizing Country France
Colonial and Earlier Independence Names French Guinea
Official Language French
Area (square miles/square kilometers) 94,926/245,857
Population 12,717,000
Gross National Income (GNI) $10,441,000,000
GNI Per Capita $800
Literacy 32%
Life Expectancy 60

Guinea-Bissau

Official Name Republic of Guinea-Bissau
Capital City Bissau
Date of Independence September 10, 1974
Colonizing Country Portugal
Colonial and Earlier Independence Names Portuguese Guinea
Official Language Portuguese
Area (square miles/square kilometers) 13,948/36,125
Population 1,861,000
Gross National Income (GNI) $1,350,000,000
GNI Per Capita $660
Literacy 46%
Life Expectancy 57

Kenya

Official Name Republic of Kenya
Capital City Nairobi
Date of Independence December 12, 1963
Colonizing Country United Kingdom

Colonial and Earlier Independence Names Kenya
Official Language English
Area (square miles/square kilometers) 224,081/580,367
Population 49,700,000
Gross National Income (GNI) $74,118,000,000
GNI Per Capita $1,440
Literacy 79%
Life Expectancy 67

Lesotho
Official Name Kingdom of Lesotho
Capital City Maseru
Date of Independence October 4, 1966
Colonizing Country United Kingdom
Colonial and Earlier Independence Names Basutoland Protectorate
Official Language English, Sesoto
Area (square miles/square kilometers) 11,720/30,355
Population 2,233,000
Gross National Income (GNI) $2,957,000,000
GNI Per Capita $1,280
Literacy 77%
Life Expectancy 54

Liberia
Official Name Republic of Liberia
Capital City Monrovia
Date of Independence July 26, 1847
Colonizing Country Assessment ranges from never officially colonized to quasi-American colony that was established in 1817 by the American Colonization Society.
Colonial and Earlier Independence Names Liberia
Official Language English
Area (square miles/square kilometers) 43,000/111,369
Population 4,732,000
Gross National Income (GNI) $1,855,000,000
GNI Per Capita $380
Literacy 43%
Life Expectancy 63

Libya
Official Name State of Libya
Capital City Tripoli
Date of Independence December 24, 1951

Colonizing Country Italy, subsequently the United Kingdom military administration
Colonial and Earlier Independence Names Two separate Italian colonies, Italian Tripolitania and Italian Cyrenaica, were unified in 1934 as the colony of Italian Libya; after 1947 British Military Administration of Italy; Socialist People's Libyan Arab Jamahiriya (1977–2011); Libya
Official Language Arabic
Area (square miles/square kilometers) 679,362/1,759,540
Population 6,375,000
Gross National Income (GNI) $51,793,000,000
GNI Per Capita $6,540
Literacy 60%
Life Expectancy 72

Madagascar

Official Name Democratic Republic of Madagascar
Capital City Antananarivo
Date of Independence June 26, 1960
Colonizing Country France
Colonial and Earlier Independence Names Madagascar; Malagasy Republic (1965–1990)
Official Language French, Malagasy
Area (square miles/square kilometers) 226,658/587,041
Population 25,571,000
Gross National Income (GNI) $11,146,000,000
GNI Per Capita $400
Literacy 72%
Life Expectancy 66

Malawi

Official Name Republic of Malawi
Capital City Lilongwe
Date of Independence July 6, 1964
Colonizing Country United Kingdom
Colonial and Earlier Independence Names Nyasaland
Official Language Chichewa, English
Area (square miles/square kilometers) 45,747/118,484
Population 18,622,000
Gross National Income (GNI) $6,161,000,000
GNI Per Capita $320
Literacy 62%
Life Expectancy 63

Mali

Official Name Republic of Mali
Capital City Bamako
Date of Independence September 22, 1960
Colonizing Country France
Colonial and Earlier Independence Names French Sudan; Mali Federation (short-lived, 1959–1960, federation of two former French colonies of Mali and Senegal)
Official Language French
Area (square miles/square kilometers) 478,841/1,240,192
Population 18,542,000
Gross National Income (GNI) $14,916,000,000
GNI Per Capita $770
Literacy 33%
Life Expectancy 58

Mauritania

Official Name Islamic Republic of Mauritania
Capital City Nouakchott
Date of Independence November 28, 1960
Colonizing Country France
Colonial and Earlier Independence Names Mauritania
Official Language Arabic, French
Area (square miles/square kilometers) 397,955/1,030,700
Population 4,420,000
Gross National Income (GNI) $4,967,000,000
GNI Per Capita $1,100
Literacy 46%
Life Expectancy 63

Mauritius

Official Name Republic of Mauritius
Capital City Port Louis
Date of Independence March 12, 1968
Colonizing Country France, subsequently the United Kingdom
Colonial and Earlier Independence Names Île-de-France, Mauritius; Ile Maurice, Mauritius
Official Language English
Area (square miles/square kilometers) 788/2,040
Population 1,265,000
Gross National Income (GNI) $13,510,000,000
GNI Per Capita $10,140

Literacy 93%
Life Expectancy 74

Morocco
Official Name Kingdom of Morocco
Capital City Rabat
Date of Independence March 2, 1956
Colonizing Country France
Colonial and Earlier Independence Names Morocco
Official Language Arabic, Tamazight (Berber)
Area (square miles/square kilometers) 274,461/710,850
Population 35,740,000
Gross National Income (GNI) $107,083,000,000
GNI Per Capita $2,860
Literacy 69%
Life Expectancy 76

Mozambique
Official Name Republic of Mozambique
Capital City Maputo
Date of Independence June 25, 1975
Colonizing Country Portugal
Colonial and Earlier Independence Names Mozambique; People's Republic of Mozambique (1975–1990)
Official Language Portuguese
Area (square miles/square kilometers) 309,496/801,590
Population 29,669,000
Gross National Income (GNI) $11,914,000,000
GNI Per Capita $420
Literacy 51%
Life Expectancy 58

Namibia
Official Name Republic of Namibia
Capital City Windhoek
Date of Independence March 21, 1990
Colonizing Country Germany, subsequently South Africa
Colonial and Earlier Independence Names South West Africa (1915–1990)
Official Language English
Area (square miles/square kilometers) 318,696/825,418
Population 2,534,000
Gross National Income (GNI) $13,052,000,000

GNI Per Capita $4,600
Literacy 88%
Life Expectancy 64

Niger

Official Name Republic of Niger
Capital City Niamey
Date of Independence August 3, 1960
Colonizing Country France
Colonial and Earlier Independence Names Niger
Official Language French
Area (square mile/square kilometers) 489,191/1,267,000
Population 21,477,000
Gross National Income (GNI) $7,942,000,000
GNI Per Capita $360
Literacy 15%
Life Expectancy 60

Nigeria

Official Name Federal Republic of Nigeria
Capital City Abuja
Date of Independence October 1, 1960
Colonizing Country United Kingdom
Colonial and Earlier Independence Names Nigeria
Official Language English
Area (square miles/square kilometers) 356,669/923,768
Population 190,886,000
Gross National Income (GNI) $364,278,000,000
GNI Per Capita $2,080
Literacy 51%
Life Expectancy 53

Rwanda

Official Name Republic of Rwanda
Capital City Kigali
Date of Independence July 1, 1962
Colonizing Country Germany, subsequently Belgium
Colonial and Earlier Independence Names During colonial era part of Ruanda-Urundi; Rwanda
Official Language English, French, Kinyarwanda
Area (square miles/square kilometers) 10,347/26,798
Population 12,208,000
Gross National Income (GNI) $8,936,000,000

GNI Per Capita $720
Literacy 68%
Life Expectancy 67

São Tomé and Príncipe
Official Name Democratic Republic of São Tomé and Príncipe
Capital City São Tomé
Date of Independence July 12, 1975
Colonizing Country Portugal
Colonial and Earlier Independence Names São Tomé and Príncipe
Official Language Portuguese
Area (square miles/square kilometers) 372/964
Population 204,000
Gross National Income (GNI) $393,000,000
GNI Per Capita $1,770
Literacy 90%
Life Expectancy 67

Senegal
Official Name Republic of Senegal
Capital City Dakar
Date of Independence August 20, 1960
Colonizing Country France
Colonial and Earlier Independence Names Senegal; Mali Federation (short-lived, 1959–1960, federation of two former French colonies of Mali and Senegal); federated with Gambia 1982–1989 as Confederation of Senegambia
Official Language French
Area (square miles/square kilometers) 75,955/196,723
Population 15,851,000
Gross National Income (GNI) $15,805,000,000
GNI Per Capita $950
Literacy 43%
Life Expectancy 67

Seychelles
Official Name Republic of Seychelles
Capital City Victoria
Date of Independence June 29, 1976
Colonizing Country United Kingdom
Colonial and Earlier Independence Names Seychelles
Official Language Creole, English
Area (square miles/square kilometers) 174/451
Population 96,000

Gross National Income (GNI) $1,378,000,000
GNI Per Capita $14,180
Literacy 94%
Life Expectancy 74

Sierra Leone

Official Name Republic of Sierra Leone
Capital City Freetown
Date of Independence April 27, 1961
Colonizing Country United Kingdom
Colonial and Earlier Independence Names Sierra Leone
Official Language English
Area (square mile/square kilometers) 27,699/71,740
Population 7,557,000
Gross National Income (GNI) $3,663,000,000
GNI Per Capita $510
Literacy 32%
Life Expectancy 52

Somalia

Official Name Republic of Somalia
Capital City Mogadishu
Date of Independence July 1, 1960
Colonizing Country Italy (former southern portion known as Italian Somaliland) and the United Kingdom (former northern portion known as British Somaliland)
Colonial and Earlier Independence Names Former northern portion known as British Somaliland gained independence on June 26, 1960, as the Republic of Somaliland; former southern portion known as Italian Somaliland and subsequently as the Trust Territory of Somalia under Italian Administration gained independence five days later on July 1, 1960; on July 1, 1960, the two independent, sovereign Somali territories voluntarily federated to create the Republic of Somalia (1960–1969), which was later known as the Somali Democratic Republic (1969–1980). The northern portion seceded and declared independence as the Republic of Somaliland on May 18, 1991, with Hargeisa as the capital city. As of 2020, no other country has recognized Somaliland's independence.
Official Language Arabic, Somali
Area (square miles/square kilometers) 246,201/637,657
Population 14,743,000
Gross National Income (GNI) $7,337,000,000
Life Expectancy 56

South Africa

Official Name Republic of South Africa
Capital City Although Pretoria serves as the administrative capital and, therefore, is the capital city typically listed on maps, Cape Town is the legislative capital and Bloemfontein is the judicial capital.
Date of Independence May 31, 1961
Date of Transition to Black Majority Rule May 10, 1994, inauguration day of Nelson Mandela as the country's first democratically elected president after the transition to black majority rule
Colonizing Country Netherlands, subsequently the United Kingdom
Colonial and Earlier Independence Names Cape, Natal, Transvaal, and Orange Colonies; Union of South Africa (1910–1961)
Official Language Afrikaans, English, IsiNdebele, IsiSwati, IsiXhosa, IsiZulu, Sepedi Sesotho, Setswana, Tshivenda, Xitsonga
Area (square miles/square kilometers) 471,445/1,221,037
Population 56,717,000
Gross National Income (GNI) $338,936,000,000
GNI Per Capita $5,430
Literacy 94%
Life Expectancy 63

South Sudan

Official Name Republic of South Sudan
Capital City Juba
Date of Independence July 9, 2011
Colonizing Country Sudan, United Kingdom
Colonial and Earlier Independence Names Sudan (formerly part of the Republic of Sudan)
Official Language English
Area (square miles/square kilometers) 248,777/644,329
Population 12,576,000
Gross National Income (GNI) $2,466,000,000
GNI Per Capita $390
Life Expectancy 57

Sudan

Official Name Republic of Sudan
Capital City Khartoum
Date of Independence January 1, 1956
Colonizing Country Egypt, subsequently the United Kingdom
Colonial and Earlier Independence Names Sudan
Official Language Arabic, English

Area (square miles/square kilometers) 718,723/1,861,484
Population 40,533,000
Gross National Income (GNI) $107,384,000,000
GNI Per Capita $2,380
Literacy 54%
Life Expectancy 64

Tanzania
Official Name United Republic of Tanzania
Capital City Dodoma
Date of Independence December 9, 1961
Colonizing Country Germany, subsequently the United Kingdom
Colonial and Earlier Independence Names Tanganyika; Island of Zanzibar achieved independence on December 10, 1963, as the People's Republic of Zanzibar and Pemba; Tanganyika and Zanzibar joined together in April 1964 to form the United Republic of Tanganyika and Zanzibar; Tanzania
Official Language English, Swahili
Area (square miles/square kilometers) 364,945/945,203
Population 57,310,000
Gross National Income (GNI) $51,569,000,000
GNI Per Capita $910
Literacy 78%
Life Expectancy 66

Togo
Official Name Togo (Togolese Republic)
Capital City Lomé
Date of Independence April 27, 1960
Colonizing Country Germany, subsequently France
Colonial and Earlier Independence Names German Togoland; Togo; Togolese Republic
Official Language French
Area (square miles/square kilometers) 21,925/56,785
Population 7,798,000
Gross National Income (GNI) $4,979,000,000
GNI Per Capita $610
Literacy 64%
Life Expectancy 60

Tunisia
Official Name Republic of Tunisia
Capital City Tunis
Date of Independence March 20, 1956

Colonizing Country France
Colonial and Earlier Independence Names Tunisia
Official Language Arabic, French
Area (square mile/square kilometers) 63,170/163,610
Population 11,532,000
Gross National Income (GNI) $38,850,000,000
GNI Per Capita $3,500
Literacy 79%
Life Expectancy 76

Uganda

Official Name Republic of Uganda
Capital City Kampala
Date of Independence October 9, 1962
Colonizing Country United Kingdom
Colonial and Earlier Independence Names Uganda
Official Language English
Area (square miles/square kilometers) 91,136/236,040
Population 42,863,000
Gross National Income (GNI) $25,281,000,000
GNI Per Capita $600
Literacy 70%
Life Expectancy 60

Zambia

Official Name Republic of Zambia
Capital City Lusaka
Date of Independence October 24, 1964
Colonizing Country United Kingdom
Colonial and Earlier Independence Names Northern Rhodesia; Barotseland Protectorate (Western Province)
Official Language Bemba, Nyanja, Tonga, Lozi, Lunda, Kaonde, Luvale, English
Area (square miles/square kilometers) 290,586/752,614
Population 17,094,000
Gross National Income (GNI) $25,003,000,000
GNI Per Capita $1,300
Literacy 83%
Life Expectancy 62

Zimbabwe

Official Name Republic of Zimbabwe
Capital City Harare

Date of Independence April 18, 1980
Colonizing Country United Kingdom
Colonial and Earlier Independence Names Southern Rhodesia; Rhodesia
Official Language English
Area (square miles/square kilometers) 150,872/390,757
Population 16,530,000
Gross National Income (GNI) $15,794,000,000
GNI Per Capita $910
Literacy 89%
Life Expectancy 61

Sources: The data on capital city, date of independence, colonizing country, official language, and area (square miles/square kilometers) are from a dataset on African foreign policy maintained by the editor (see Schraeder 2020). The data on population, gross national income, GNI per capita, literacy, and life expectancy are also included in the Schraeder (2020) dataset but are originally from the OECD (2018).

References

Abanilla, Patricia, Ken-Yen Huang, Daniel Shinners, Andrea Levy, Kojo Ayernor, Ama de-Graft Aikin, and Olugbenga Ogedegbe. 2011. "Cardiovascular Disease in Ghana: Feasibility of a Faith-Based Organizational Approach." *Bulletin of World Health Organization* 89(9) (December): 648–656.

Abdenur, Adriana Erthal. 2018. "Brazil-Africa Relations: From Boom to Bust?" In Dawn Nagar and Charles Mutasa (eds.), *Africa and the World: Bilateral and Multilateral International Diplomacy*. Basingstoke: Palgrave Macmillan, 189–208.

Abdile, Mahdi. 2014. "The Somali Diaspora in Conflict and Peacebuilding: The Peace Initiative Programme." In Liisa Laakso and Petri Hautaniemi (eds.), *Diasporas, Development and Peacemaking in the Horn of Africa*. London: Zed Books, 77–97.

Abdulai, Abdul-Gafaru. 2017. "Rethinking Spatial Inequality in Development: The Primacy of Power Relations." *Journal of International Development* 29(3) (December): 386–403.

Abdulai, Abdul-Gafaru, and Sam Hickey. 2016. "The Politics of Development Under Competitive Clientelism: Insights from Ghana's Education Sector." *African Affairs* 115(458) (January): 44–72.

ACLED (Armed Conflict Location and Event Data Project). 2019. "Data Export Tool (dataset)." https://www.acleddata.com/data/.

Adama, Onyanta. 2007. *Governing from Above: Solid Waste Management in Nigeria's New Capital City of Abuja*. Stockholm: Stockholm University Press.

Adams, Melinda, John Scherpereel, and Suraj Jacob. 2016. "The Representation of Women in African Legislatures and Cabinets: An Examination with Reference to Ghana." *Journal of Women, Politics and Policy* 37(2) (April): 145–167.

Adams, William M. 1992. *Wasting the Rain: Rivers, People and Planning in Africa*. Minneapolis: University of Minnesota Press.

Adams, William M., Andrew Goudie, and Anthony Orme. 1999. *The Physical Geography of Africa*. New York: Oxford University Press.

Adar, Korwa. 2015. "Foreign Policy Processes in African States." In Klaus Brummer and Valerie M. Hudson (eds.), *Foreign Policy Analysis Beyond North America*. Boulder: Lynne Rienner, 101–120.

Adar, Korwa G., and Rok Ajulu (eds.). 2002. *Globalization and Emerging Trends in African States' Foreign Policy–Making Process: A Comparative Perspective of Southern Africa*. Aldershot: Ashgate.

Adar, Korwa, and Peter J. Schraeder (eds.). 2007. *Globalization and Emerging Trends in African Foreign Policy: A Comparative Perspective of Eastern Africa*. Lanham: Rowman and Littlefield.

Addaney, Michael. 2019. "Adaptation Governance and Building Resilience in the Face of Climate Change in African Cities: Policy Responses and Emerging Practices from Accra." In P. B. Cobbinah and M. Addaney (eds.), *The Geography of Climate Change Adaptation in Urban Africa*. New York: Palgrave Macmillan, 479–498.

Addaney, Michael, and P. B. Cobbinah. 2019. "Climate Change, Urban Planning and Sustainable Development in Africa: The Difference Worth Appreciating." In P. B. Cobbinah and M. Addaney (eds.), *The Geography of Climate Change Adaptation in Urban Africa*. New York: Palgrave Macmillan, 3–26.

Adebajo, Adekeye. 2011. *UN Peacekeeping in Africa: From the Suez Crisis to the Sudan Conflicts*. Boulder: Lynne Rienner.

Adetula, Victor A. O., Redie Bereketeab, and Olugbemi Jaiyebo. 2016. *Regional Economic Communities and Peacebuilding in Africa: The Experiences of ECOWAS and IGAD*. Uppsala, Sweden: Nordiska Afrikainstitutet.

Adichie, Chimamanda Ngozi. 2019. "Still Becoming: At Home in Lagos with Chimamanda Ngozi Adichie." *Esquire*, April 29. https://www.esquire.com/uk/culture/a27283913/still-becoming-at-home-in-lagos-with-chimamanda-ngozi-adichie/.

Adjaye, Joseph K. 1996. *Diplomacy and Diplomats in Nineteenth Century Asante*. Trenton: Africa World Press.

Adjovi, Emmanuel V. 1998. *Une élection libre en Afrique: La présidentielle du Bénin (1996)*. Paris: Karthala.

Adogame, Afe, Roswith Gerloff, and Klaus Hock (eds.). 2008. *Christianity in Africa and the African Diaspora: The Appropriation of a Scattered Heritage*. New York: A&C Black.

Adraoui, Mohamed-Ali (ed.). 2018. *The Foreign Policy of Islamist Political Parties: Ideology in Practice*. New York: Oxford University Press.

Africanews. 2020. "On COVID-19, Africa Must 'Prepare for the Worst Now'—WHO Says." *Africanews*, March 19, 2020. https://www.africanews.com/2020/03/19/on-covid-19-africa-must-prepare-for-the-worst-now-who-says/.

African Union. 2011. "African Union: A United and Strong Africa." www.au.int/en/.

Afrobarometer. 2012. "Afrobarometer Round 5 (2010–2012)." https://www.afrobarometer-online-analysis.com/aj/AJBrowserAB.jsp.

Agyepong, Irene, Nelson Sewankambo, Agnes Binagwah, Awa Marie Coll-Seck, Tumani Corrah, Alex Ezeh et al. 2017. "The Path to Longer and Healthier Lives for All Africans by 2030: The *Lancet* Commission on the Future of Health in Sub-Saharan Africa." *Lancet* 390(10114) (December): 2803–2859.

AHB (Anti-Homosexuality Bill) (Uganda). 2009. Retrieved via www.wthrockmorton.com, December 2009.

Ahluwalia, Pal. 2012. *Politics and Post-Colonial Theory: African Inflections*. London: Routledge.

Ahmed, Dirdeiry A. 2015. *Boundaries and Secession in Africa and International Law: Challenging Uti Possidetis*. Cambridge: Cambridge University Press.

Ajala, Adekunle. 1988. "Background to the Establishment, Nature and Structure of the Organization of African Unity." *Nigerian Journal of International Affairs* 14(1): 35–66.

Ajayi, J. F. Ade, Lameck K. H. Goma, and G. Ampah Johnson. 1996. *The African Experience with Higher Education*. Accra: Association of African Universities.

Ajefu, Joseph Boniface. 2018. "Migrant Remittances and Assets Accumulation Among Nigerian Households." *Migration and Development* 7(1) (January): 72–84.

Ake, Claude. 1981. *A Political Economy of Africa*. London: Longman.

———. 1995. *Democracy and Development in Africa*. Washington, DC: Brookings Institution.

Aker, Jenny C., and Joshua E. Blumenstock. 2015. "The Economic Impacts of New Technologies in Africa." In C. Monga and J. Y. Lin (eds.), *The Oxford Handbook of Africa and Economics*. Oxford: Oxford University Press, 354–371.

Aker, Jenny C., Rachid Boumnijel, Amanda McClelland, and Niall Tierney. 2016. "Payment Mechanisms and Antipoverty Programs: Evidence from a Mobile Money Cash Transfer Experiment in Niger." *Economic Development and Cultural Change* 65(1) (October): 1–37.

Akindele, R. A. 1985. "Africa and the Great Powers: With Particular Reference to the United States, the Soviet Union and China." *Africa Spectrum* 20(2): 125–151.

———. 1988a. "The Organization of African Unity and the Conflict Situation in Southern Africa." *Nigerian Journal of International Affairs* 14(1): 124–154.

———. 1988b. "The Organization of African Unity: Four Grand Debates Among African Leaders Revisited." *Nigerian Journal of International Affairs* 14(1): 73–94.

Akyeampong, Emmanuel, Allan Hill, and Arthur Kleinman (eds.). 2015. *The Culture of Mental Illness and Psychiatric Practice in Africa*. Bloomington: Indiana University Press.

Alber, Erdmute. 2004. "Grandparents as Foster-Parents: Transformations in Foster Relations Between Grandparents and Grandchildren in Northern Benin." *Journal of the International African Institute* 74(1) (February): 28–46.

Alexander, Christian. 2019. "Cape Town's 'Day Zero' Water Crisis, One Year Later." *Citylab*, April 12. https://www.citylab.com/environment/2019/04/cape-town-water-conservation-south-africa-drought/587011/.

Alexander, Kathleen, Claire E. Sanderson, Madav Marathe, Bryan L. Lewis, Caitlin M. Rivers, Jeffrey Shaman, John Drake et al. 2015. "What Factors Might Have Led to the Emergence of Ebola in West Africa?" *PLoS Neglected Tropical Diseases* 9(6) (June): e0003652.

Ali, Rubaba, A. Federico Barra, Claudia Berg, Richard Damania, John Nash, and Jason Russ. 2015. *Highways to Success or Byways to Waste: Estimating the Economic Benefits of Roads in Africa*. Washington, DC: World Bank.

Al-Karsani, Awad Al-Sid. 1993. "Beyond Sufism: The Case of Millennial Islam in Sudan." In Louis Brenner (ed.), *Muslim Identity and Social Change in Sub-Saharan Africa*. Bloomington: Indiana University Press, 135–153.

Allman, Jean. 2009. "The Disappearing of Hannah Kudjoe: Nationalism, Feminism and the Tyrannies of History." *Journal of Women's History* 21(3) (Fall): 13–35.

Allman, Jean, Susan Geiger, and Nakanyike Musisi (eds.). 2002. *Women in African Colonial Histories*. Bloomington: Indiana University Press.

Alpers, Edward. 1975. *Ivory and Slaves in East Central Africa*. London: Heinemann.

Altinok, Nadir, Noam Angrist, and Harry Anthony Patrinos. 2018. *Global Data Set on Education Quality (1965–2015)*. Washington, DC: World Bank.

Aluko, Olajide (ed.). 1987. *Africa and the Great Powers in the 1980s*. Lanham: University Press of America.

Aly, Ahmad A. H. M. 1994. *Economic Cooperation in Africa: In Search of Direction*. Boulder: Lynne Rienner.

Amadiume, Ifi. 1987. *Male Daughters, Female Husbands: Gender and Sex in an African Society*. London: Zed Books.

Amate, C. O. C. 1986. *Inside the OAU: Pan-Africanism in Practice*. New York: St. Martin's Press.

Ambikile, Joel Seme, and Masunga Iseselo. 2017. "Mental Health Care and Delivery System at Temeke Hospital in Dar es Salaam." *BMC Psychiatry* 17(109) (March).

Amin, Samir. 1972. "Underdevelopment and Dependence in Black Africa—Origins and Contemporary Forms." *Journal of Modern African Studies* 10(4) (December): 503–524.

———. 1973. *Neo-Colonialism in West Africa*. Harmondsworth, England: Penguin.

Amirah-Fernandez, Haizam. 2008. "Spain's Policy Towards Morocco and Algeria: Balancing Relations with Southern Neighbors." In Yahia Zoubir and Haizam Amirah-Fernandez (eds.), *North Africa: Politics, Region, and the Limits of Transformation*. London: Routledge, 348–364.

Anderson, Emma-Louise. 2015. *Gender, Risk and HIV: Navigating Structural Violence*. New York: Palgrave Macmillan.

Anderson, Emma-Louise, and Amy S. Patterson. 2017. *Dependent Agency in the Global Health Regime: Local African Responses to Donor AIDS Efforts*. New York: Palgrave Macmillan.

Anderson, John. 2006. *Religion, Democracy, and Democratization*. New York: Routledge.

Andrés, Antonio Sánchez. 2006. "Political-Economic Relations Between Russia and North Africa." Working Paper 22/2006. Madrid: Real Instituto Elcano. http://www.realinstitutoelcano.org/wps/portal/rielcano_en/contenido?WCM_GLOBAL_CONTEXT=/elcano/elcano_in/zonas_in/dt22-2006.

Anglin, Douglas. 1990. "Southern African Responses to Eastern European Developments." *Journal of Modern African Studies* 28(3) (September): 431–455.

Anyaso, Claudia E. (ed.). 2011. *Fifty Years of U.S. Africa Policy: Reflections of Assistant Secretaries for African Affairs and U.S. Embassy Officials*. Memoirs and Occasional Papers Series. Washington, DC: Association for Diplomatic Studies and Training.

Appadurai, Arjun. 1996. *Modernity at Large: Cultural Dimensions of Globalization*. Minneapolis: University of Minnesota Press.
Apter, D. E. 1960. "The Role of Traditionalism in the Political Modernization of Ghana and Uganda." *World Politics* 13(1) (October): 45–68.
Arias, Daniel, Lauren Taylor, Angela Ofori-Atta, and Elizabeth Bradley. 2016. "Prayer Camps and Biomedical Care in Ghana: Is Collaboration with Mental Health Care Possible?" *PLOS ONE* 11(9) (September).
Arkhangelskaya, Alexandra, and Nicole Dodd. 2016. "Guns and Poseurs: Russia Returns to Africa." In Justin van der Merwe, Ian Taylor, and Alexandra Arkhangelskaya (eds.), *Emerging Powers in Africa: A New Wave in the Relationship?* Basingstoke, UK: Palgrave Macmillan, 159–175.
Arriola, Leonardo R. 2018. "Financial Institutions: Economic Liberalisation, Credit and Opposition Party Success." In Nic Cheeseman (ed.), *Institutions and Democracy in Africa: How the Rules of the Game Shape Political Developments*. New York: Cambridge University Press, 92–114.
Asabere, Paul K., Carl B. McGowan Jr., and Sang Mook Lee. 2016. "A Study into the Links Between Mortgage Financing and Economic Development in Africa." *International Journal of Housing Markets and Analysis* 9(1) (March): 2–19.
Asamoah-Gyadu, J. Kwabena 2004. *African Charismatics: Current Developments Within Independent Indigenous Pentecostalism in Ghana*. Leiden: Brill.
———. 2014. "Foreword." In Clifton R. Clarke (ed.), *Pentecostal Theology in Africa*. Eugene, OR: Wipf and Stock.
Asante, S. K. B., with David Chanaiwa. 1993. "Pan-Africanism and Regional Integration." In Ali A. Mazrui (ed.), *General History of Africa,* Vol. 8: *Africa Since 1935*. Berkeley: University of California Press, 724–743.
Ashforth, Adam. 2005. *Witchcraft, Violence, and Democracy in South Africa*. Chicago: University of Chicago Press.
Ashour, Maha, Daniel Orth Gilligan, Jessica Blumer Hoel, and Naureen Iqbal Karachiwalla. 2019. "Do Beliefs About Herbicide Quality Correspond with Actual Quality in Local Markets? Evidence from Uganda." *Journal of Development Studies* 55(6): 1285–1306.
Asiedu, Kwasi Gyamfi. 2019. "Clicktivism: Ghanaian Feminists Are Using Social Media to Change Public Discourse." Development and Cooperation, August 14. https://www.dandc.eu/en/article/ghanaian-feminists-are-using-social-media-change-public-discourse.
Asongu, Simplice A. 2013. "How Has Mobile Phone Penetration Stimulated Financial Development in Africa?" *Journal of African Business* 14(1) (April): 7–18.
Asongu, Simplice A., and Jacinta C. Nwachukwu. 2017. "Conclusion: An Argument for a Development Paradigm in Africa That Reconciles the Washington Consensus with the Beijing Model." In Y.-C. Kim (ed.), *China and Africa*. Cham, Switzerland: Palgrave Macmillan, 263–283.
Atiemo, Abamfo Ofori. 2017. "'Returning to Our Spiritual Roots': African Hindus in Ghana Negotiating Religious Space and Identity." *Journal of Religion in Africa* 47(3–4) (July): 405–437.
Atlas of the Human Planet. 2018. EU Science Hub. https://ec.europa.eu/jrc/en/publication/eur-scientific-and-technical-research-reports/atlas-human-planet-2018.
AU Commission. 2015. "Agenda 2063: The Africa We Want." https://au.int/sites/default/files/documents/36204-doc-agenda2063_popular_version_en.pdf.
Aucoin, Ciara. 2017. "Less Armed Conflict but More Political Violence in Africa." Institute for Security Studies, April 12. https://issafrica.org/iss-today/less-armed-conflict-but-more-political-violence-in-africa.
Austen, Ralph A. 1983. "The Metamorphoses of Middlemen: The Duala, Europeans, and the Cameroon Hinterland, ca. 1800–ca. 1960." *International Journal of African Historical Studies* 16(1): 1–24.
———. 2010. *Trans-Saharan Africa in World History*. New York: Oxford University Press.
Awojobi, Omotola, and Glenn P. Jenkins. 2015. "Were the Hydro Dams Financed by the World Bank from 1976 to 2005 Worthwhile?" *Energy Policy* 86 (November): 222–232.

Awulalu, J. Omosade. 1979. *Yoruba Beliefs and Sacrificial Rites.* Burnt Mill, Harlow (Essex): Longman.

Azevedo, Mario. 1993. "European Exploration and Conquest." In Mario Azevedo (ed.), *Africana Studies.* Durham: Carolina Academic Press, 103–116.

Bah, M. Alpha. 1993. "Legitimate Trade, Diplomacy, and the Slave Trade." In Mario Azevedo (ed.), *Africana Studies.* Durham: Carolina Academic Press, 65–85.

Baisley, Elizabeth. 2015. "Framing the Ghanaian LGBT Rights Debate: Competing Decolonization and Human Rights Frames." *Canadian Journal of African Studies* 49(2): 383–402.

Ball, George. 1968. *The Disciples of Power.* Boston: Little, Brown.

Bangura, Yusuf. 1983. *Britain and Commonwealth Africa: The Politics of Economic Relations, 1951–1975.* Manchester: Manchester University Press.

Barany, Zoltan. 2012. *The Soldier and the Changing State: Building Democratic Armies in Africa, Asia, Europe, and the Americas.* Princeton: Princeton University Press.

———. 2019. "Military Influence in Foreign Policy–Making: Changing Dynamics in North African Regimes." *Journal of North African Studies* 24(4) (July): 579–598.

Barbier, Edward B., Richard Damania, and Daniel Léonard. 2005. "Corruption, Trade and Resource Conversion." *Journal of Environmental Economics and Management* 50(2) (September): 276–299.

Bardhan, Pranab, and Dilip Mookherjee. 2006. "Decentralisation and Accountability in Infrastructure Delivery in Developing Countries." *Economic Journal* 116(508) (January): 101–127.

Barigye, A. 2016. "Uganda's LGBT Faith Leaders Say God's Love Is Unconditional." Religion News Service, November 29. https://religionnews.com/2016/11/29/ugandas-lgbt-faith-leaders-say-gods-love-is-unconditional/.

Barkan, Joel D. (ed.). 2009. *Legislative Power in Emerging African Democracies.* Boulder: Lynne Rienner.

Barnes, Amy, Garrett Brown, and Sophie Harman. 2015. *Global Politics of Health Reform in Africa.* New York: Palgrave Macmillan.

Barrett, Christopher B., Luc Christiaensen, Megan Sheahan, and Abebe Shimeles. 2017. *On the Structural Transformation of Rural Africa.* Washington, DC: World Bank.

Barrett, David B. 1968. *Schism and Renewal in Africa.* Nairobi: Oxford University Press.

———. 1982. *World Christian Encyclopedia: A Comparative Survey of Churches and Religions in the Modern World 1900–2000.* Nairobi: Oxford University Press.

Barrientos, Armando, and Juan Miguel Villa. 2015. "Evaluating Antipoverty Transfer Programmes in Latin America and Sub-Saharan Africa: Better Policies? Better Politics?" *Journal of Globalization and Development* 6(1) (May): 147–179.

Bartsch, Sarah M., Katrin Gorham, and Bruce Y. Lee. 2015. "The Cost of an Ebola Case." *Pathogens and Global Health* 109(1) (February): 4–9.

Bascom, William. 1969. *Ifa Divination: Communication Between Gods and Men in West Africa.* Bloomington: Indiana University Press.

Bassett, Thomas, and Donald Crummey (eds.). 2003. *African Savannas: Global Narratives and Local Knowledge of Environmental Change.* Oxford: James Currey.

Bastagli, Francesca, Jessica Hagen-Zanker, Luke Harman, Valentina Barca, Georgina Sturge, Tanja Schmidt, and Lucca Pellerano. 2016. *Cash Transfers: What Does the Evidence Say? A Rigorous Review of Programme Impact and the Role of Design and Implementation Features.* London: Overseas Development Institute.

Bates, Robert. 1981. *Markets and States in Tropical Africa.* Los Angeles: University of California Press.

Bates, Robert H., V. Y. Mudimbe, and Jean O'Barr (eds.). 1993. *Africa and the Disciplines: The Contributions of Research in Africa to the Social Sciences and Humanities.* Chicago: University of Chicago Press.

Bauer, Gretchen. 2011. "Update on the Women's Movement in Botswana: Have Women Stopped Talking?" *African Studies Review* 54(2) (September): 23–46.

———. 2016. "'What's Wrong with a Woman Being Chief?': Women Chiefs and Symbolic and Substantive Representation in Botswana." *Journal of Asian and African Studies* 51(2) (April): 222–237.

———. 2019. "Women in African Parliaments: Progress and Prospects." In Olajumoke Yacob-Haliso and Toyin Falola (eds.), *The Palgrave Handbook of African Women's Studies*. New York: Palgrave Macmillan.

Bauer, Gretchen, and Hannah E. Britton (eds.). 2006. *Women in African Parliaments*. Boulder: Lynne Rienner.

Bauer, Gretchen, and Josephine Dawuni (eds.). 2016. *Gender and the Judiciary in Africa: From Obscurity to Parity?* New York: Routledge.

Bayart, Jean-François. 2000. "Africa in the World: A History of Extraversion." *African Affairs* 99(395) (April): 217–267.

Baylies, Carolyn, and Janet Bujra (eds.). 2000. *AIDS, Sexuality and Gender in Africa: Collective Strategies and Struggles in Tanzania and Zambia*. New York: Routledge.

BBC News. 2020. "Coronavirus: How Will Covid-19 Affect African Economies?" March 21. https://www.bbc.com/news/av/world-africa-51980430/coronavirus-how-will-covid-19-affect-african-economies.

BBC News Africa. 2012. "Somalia's al-Shabab Join al-Qaeda." February 10. https://www.bbc.com/news/world-africa-16979440.

Beall, Jo, Tom Goodfellow, and Dennis Rodgers. 2013. "Cities and Conflict in Fragile States in the Developing World." *Urban Studies* 50(15) (November): 3065–3083.

Beck, Linda J. 2008. *Brokering Democracy in Africa: The Rise of Clientelist Democracy in Senegal*. New York: Palgrave Macmillan.

Behuria, Pritish, and Tom Goodfellow. 2019. "Leapfrogging Manufacturing? Rwanda's Attempt to Build a Services-Led 'Developmental State.'" *European Journal of Development Research* 31 (October): 1–23.

Bendavid, Eran, Trygve Ottersen, Liu Peilong, Rachel Nugent, Nancy Padian, John-Arne Rottingen et al. 2017. "Development Assistance for Health." In D. T. Jamison, H. Gelband, S. Horton, P. Jha, R. Laxminarayan, C. N. Mock et al. (eds.), *Disease Control Priorities: Improving Health and Reducing Poverty*. Washington, DC: World Bank, 299–314.

Benjaminsen, Tor A., and Boubacar Ba. 2019. "Why Do Pastoralists in Mali Join Jihadist Groups? A Political Ecological Explanation." *Journal of Peasant Studies* 46(1): 1–20.

Bennett, Jane. 2018. "Queer/White South Africa: A Troubling Oxymoron?" In Zethu Matebeni, Surya Monro, and Vasu Reddy (eds.), *Queer in Africa: LGTIQI Identities, Citizenship and Activism*. New York: Routledge, 99–113.

Benton, Adia. 2015. *HIV Exceptionalism: Development Through Disease in Sierra Leone*. Minneapolis: University of Minnesota Press.

Benton, Adia, and Kim Yi Dionne. 2015. "International Political Economy and the 2014 West Africa Ebola Outbreak." *African Studies Review* 58(1) (April): 223–236.

Bereketeab, Redie (ed.). 2014. *Self-Determination and Secession in Africa: The Post-Colonial State*. London: Routledge.

Berg, Claudia N., Brian Blankespoor, and Harris Selod. 2018. "Roads and Rural Development in Sub-Saharan Africa." *Journal of Development Studies* 54(5): 856–874.

Berger, Iris. 2016. *Women in Twentieth-Century Africa*. Cambridge: Cambridge University Press.

Berger, Iris, and E. Francis White. 1999. *Women in Sub-Saharan Africa: Restoring Women to History*. Bloomington: Indiana University Press.

Berglund, Axel-Ivar. 1976. *Zulu Thought Patterns and Symbolism*. London: C. Hurst.

Bergner, Daniel. 2006. "The Call." *New York Times Magazine*, January 29, 40–47.

Betts, Raymond F. 1972. *The Scramble for Africa: Causes and Dimensions of Empire*. Lexington: D. C. Heath.

Beyrer, Chris, Andrea Wirtz, Damian Walker, Benjamin Johns, Frangiscos Sifakis, and Stephan D. Baral. 2011. *The Global HIV Epidemics Among Men Who Have Sex with Men*. Washington, DC: World Bank.

Bird, Charles S., and Martha B. Kendall. 1980. "The Mande Hero: Text and Context." In Ivan Karp and Charles S. Bird (eds.), *Explorations in African Systems of Thought*. Bloomington: Indiana University Press, 13–26.

Bischoff, Paul-Henri, and Roger Southall. 1999. "The Early Foreign Policy of the Democratic South Africa." In Stephen Wright (ed.), *African Foreign Policies*. Boulder, CO: Westview Press, 154–181.

Bjornlund, Eric, Michael Bratton, and Clark Gibson. 1992. "Observing Multiparty Elections in Africa: Lessons from Zambia." *African Affairs* 91(364) (July): 405–431.

Black, David. 2004. "Canada and Africa: Activist Aspirations in Straitened Circumstances." In Ian Taylor and Paul Williams (eds.), *Africa in International Politics*. London: Routledge, 136–154.

———. 2015. *Canada and Africa in the New Millennium: The Politics of Consistent Inconsistency*. Waterloo: Wilfrid Laurier University Press.

Bleck, Jaimie, and Nicolas van de Walle. 2019. *Electoral Politics in Africa Since 1990: Continuity in Change*. New York: Cambridge University Press.

Bleys, Rudi C. 1995. *The Geography of Perversion: Male-Male Sexual Behavior Outside the West and the Ethnographic Imagination, 1750–1918*. New York: New York University Press.

Blondy, Alain. 2018. *Le Monde Mediterraneen: 15,000 ans d'histoire*. Paris: Perrin.

Bloom, David, David Canning, and Jaypee Sevilla. 2004. "The Effect of Health on Economic Growth." *World Development* 32(1) (January): 1–13.

Blumenfeld, Jesmond. 1992. *Economic Interdependence in Southern Africa: From Conflict to Cooperation?* New York: St. Martin's Press.

Bøås, Morten, and Kevin C. Dunn (eds.). 2007. *African Guerrillas: Raging Against the Machine*. Boulder: Lynne Rienner.

——— (eds.). 2017. *Africa's Insurgents: Navigating an Evolving Landscape*. Boulder: Lynne Rienner.

Bohannan, Paul, and Philip Curtin. 1995. *Africa and Africans*. 4th ed. Prospect Heights: Waveland Press.

Boko, Michel, Isabelle Niang, Anthony Nyong, and Coleen Vogel. 2007. "Africa." In Martin Parry, Osvaldo Canziani, Jean Palutikof, Paul van der Linden, and Clair Hanson (eds.), *Climate Change 2007: Impacts, Adaptation, and Vulnerability: Contribution of Working Group II to the Fourth Assessment Report of the Intergovernmental Panel on Climate Change*. Cambridge: Cambridge University Press, 433–467.

Bollyky, Thomas. 2012. "Developing Symptoms: Noncommunicable Diseases Go Global." *Foreign Affairs* 91(3) (May/June): 134–144.

Bontianti, A., H. Hungerford, H. Younsa, and A. Nouma. 2014. "Fluid Experiences: Comparing Local Adaptations to Water Inaccessibility in Two Disadvantaged Neighborhoods in Niamey, Niger." *Habitat International* 43 (July): 283–292.

Boone, Catherine. 2003. *Political Topographies of the African State: Territorial Authority and Institutional Choice*. Cambridge: Cambridge University Press.

Boutayeb, Abdesslam, and Saber Boutayeb. 2005. "The Burden of Non Communicable Diseases in Developing Countries." *International Journal of Equity in Health* 4(2) (January): 1–8.

Boutros-Ghali, Boutros. 1992. *An Agenda for Peace: Preventative Diplomacy, Peace-Making, and Peace-Keeping*. New York: United Nations.

Bowman, Larry. 1991. *Mauritius: Democracy and Development in the Indian Ocean*. Boulder: Westview Press.

Boyd, Lydia. 2015. *Preaching Prevention: Born-Again Christianity and the Moral Politics of AIDS in Uganda*. Athens: Ohio University Press.

Boyle, Patrick M. 1992. "Beyond Self-Protection to Prophecy: The Catholic Church and Political Change in Zaire." *Africa Today* 39(3): 49–66.

Bradbury, Mark. 2008. *Becoming Somaliland*. London: Progressio.

Brand, Laurie A. 2006. *Citizens Abroad: Emigration and the State in the Middle East and North Africa*. New York: Cambridge University Press.

Brann, Conrad Max Benedict. 1993. "Democratization of Language Use in Public Domains in Nigeria." *Journal of Modern African Studies* 31(4) (December): 644–645.

Branswell, Helen. 2019. "Four Ebola Response Workers Killed in Attacks, Forcing Withdrawal from Critical DRC Region." *STAT News*, November 28. https://www.statnews.com/2019/11/28/four-ebola-response-workers-killed-in-attacks-drc.

Bratton, Michael. 1998. "After Mandela's Miracle in South Africa." *Current History* 97(619) (May): 214–219.

Bratton, Michael, and Eldred Masunungure. 2006. "Popular Reactions to State Repression: Operation Murambatsvina in Zimbabwe." *African Affairs* 106(422) (January): 21–45.

Bratton, Michael, Robert Mattes, and E. Gyimah-Boadi. 2005. *Public Opinion, Democracy, and Market Reform in Africa.* Cambridge: Cambridge University Press.

Bratton, Michael, and Nicolas van de Walle. 1997. *Democratic Experiments in Africa: Regime Transitions in Comparative Perspective.* Cambridge: Cambridge University Press.

Brautigam, Deborah. 2009. *The Dragon's Gift: The Real Story of China in Africa.* Oxford: Oxford University Press.

Brenner, Louis (ed.). 1993. *Muslim Identity and Social Change in Sub-Saharan Africa.* Bloomington: Indiana University Press.

Britton, Hannah E. 2005. *Women in the South African Parliament: From Resistance to Governance.* Chicago: University of Illinois Press.

Brooks, George. 2003. *Eurafricans in Western Africa: Commerce, Social Status, Gender, and Religious Observance from the Sixteenth to the Eighteenth Century.* Athens: Ohio University Press.

Broto, Vanesa. 2014. "Planning for Climate Change in the African City." *International Development Planning Review* 36(3) (January): 257–264.

Brown, Sally, Abiy S. Kebede, and Robert J. Nicholls. 2009. *Sea-Level Rise and Impacts in Africa, 2000 to 2100.* Southampton: University of Southampton.

Brummer, Klaus, and Valerie M. Hudson (eds.). 2015. *Foreign Policy Analysis Beyond North America.* Boulder: Lynne Rienner.

Brune, Stefan, Joachim Betz, and Winrich Kuhne (eds.). 1994. *Africa and Europe: Relations of Two Continents in Transition.* Münster: Lit Verlag.

Bryceson, Deborah Fahy. 2011. "Birth of a Market Town in Tanzania: Towards Narrative Studies of Urban Africa." *Journal of Eastern African Studies* 5(2) (May): 274–293.

Buijtenhuijs, Rob, and Céline Thiriot. 1995. *Democratization in Sub-Saharan Africa, 1992–1995: An Overview in Literature.* Leiden: African Studies Centre.

Bukarambe, Bukar. 1988. "Regional Order and Local Disorder: The OAU and Civil Wars in Africa." *Nigerian Journal of International Relations* 14(1): 95–111.

Burnet, Jennie. 2011. "Women Have Found Respect: Gender Quotas, Symbolic Representation, and Female Empowerment in Rwanda." *Politics and Gender* 7(3) (September): 303–334.

Burton, John W. 1978. "Ghost Marriage and the Cattle Trade Among the Atuot of the Southern Sudan." *Africa: Journal of the International African Institute* 48(4): 398–405.

Buse, Ken, and Amalia Waxman. 2001. "Public-Private Health Partnerships: A Strategy for WHO." *Bulletin of the World Health Organization* 79(8) (October): 748–754.

Butime, Herman. 2014. "Shifts in Israel-Africa Relations." *Strategic Assessment* 17(3): 81–91.

Calderón, César, and Luis Servén. 2004. "The Effects of Infrastructure Development on Growth and Income Distribution." Working Paper no. 3400. Washington, DC: World Bank. https://openknowledge.worldbank.org/handle/10986/14136.

Caldwell, J. C. 1977. "Demographic Aspects of Drought: An Examination of the African Drought of 1970–1974." In D. Dalby, R. J. H. Church, and F. Bezzaz (eds.), *Drought in Africa.* London: International African Institute, 93–99.

Callaghy, Thomas M. 1984. *The State-Society Struggle: Zaire in Comparative Perspective.* New York: Columbia University Press.

———. 1987. "The State as Lame Leviathan: The Patrimonial Administrative State in Africa." In Zaki Ergas (ed.), *The African Sate in Transition.* Basingstoke: Macmillan, 87–116.

———. 2000. "Africa and the World Economy: Caught Between a Rock and a Hard Place." In John W. Harbeson and Donald Rothchild (eds.), *Africa in World Politics: The African State System in Flux.* Boulder: Westview Press, 43–82.

Callaghy, Thomas M., and John Ravenhill (eds.). 1993a. *Hemmed In: Responses to Africa's Economic Decline.* New York: Columbia University Press.

———. 1993b. "How Hemmed In? Lessons and Prospects of Africa's Responses to Decline." In Thomas M. Callaghy and John Ravenhill (eds.), *Hemmed In: Responses to Africa's Decline.* New York: Columbia University Press, 520–563.

Callaway, Barbara, and Lucy Creevey. 1994. *The Heritage of Islam: Women, Religion, and Politics in West Africa.* Boulder: Lynne Rienner.

Camau, Michael, and Stephen Geisser. 2003. *Syndrome Autoritaire: Politique en Tunisise de Bourguiba a Ben Ali.* Paris: de Sciences Po.

Campbell, Bonnie (ed.). 2009. *Mining in Africa: Regulation and Development.* London: Pluto.

Campbell, Bonnie K., and John Loxley (eds.). 1989. *Structural Adjustment in Africa*. New York: St. Martin's Press.
Campbell, Catherine. 2003. *"Letting Them Die": Why HIV/AIDS Prevention Programmes Fail*. Bloomington: Indiana University Press.
Carey, Benedict. 2015. "The Chains of Mental Illness in West Africa." *New York Times*, October 11.
Carmody, Padraig. 2011. *The New Scramble for Africa*. Malden: Polity.
Carothers, Christopher. 2018. "The Surprising Instability of Competitive Authoritarianism." *Journal of Democracy* 29(4) (October): 129–135.
Cartwright, Anton, Ian Palmer, Anna Taylor, Edgar Pieterse, Susan Parnell, and Sarah Colenbrander. 2018. "Developing Prosperous and Inclusive Cities in Africa—National Urban Policies to the Rescue." Working Paper. London: Coalition for Urban Transitions.
Carvalho, Clara. 2018. "Africa and Portugal." In Dawn Nagar and Charles Mutasa (eds.), *Africa and the World: Bilateral and Multilateral International Diplomacy*. Basingstoke: Palgrave Macmillan, 143–166.
Castillo-Chavez, Carlos, Roy Curtiss, Peter Daszak, Simon A. Levin, Oscar Patterson-Lomba, Charles Perrings et al. 2015. "Beyond Ebola: Lessons to Mitigate Future Pandemics." *Lancet Global Health* 3(7) (July): e354–e355.
Cavatorta, Francesco, and Vincent Durac. 2011. *Civil Society and Democratization in the Arab World: The Dynamics of Activism*. New York: Routledge.
Chalifoux, Jean-Jacques. 1980. "Secondary Marriage and Levels of Seniority Among the Abisi (PITI), Nigeria." *Journal of Comparative Family Studies* 11(3) (Summer): 325–343.
Charbonneau, Bruno. 2019. "Intervention as Counter-Insurgency Politics." *Conflict, Security and Development* 19(3) (June): 309–314.
Charles, Joseph O. 2005. "Social Relations and the 'Trinity' in Ibibio Kinship: The Case of Ibibio Immigrants in Akpabuyo (Efikland), Nigeria." *Journal of Anthropological Research* 61(3) (Autumn): 337–356.
Charlton, Roger. 1993. "The Politics of Elections in Botswana." *Africa: Journal of the International African Institute* 63(3) (July): 330–371.
Chattopadhyay, Swati. 2012. "Urbanism, Colonialism and Subalternity." In T. Edensor and M. Jayne (eds.), *Urban Theory Beyond the West: A World of Cities*. London: Routledge, 75–92.
Chazan, Naomi. 1989. "Planning Democracy in Africa: A Comparative Perspective of Nigeria and Ghana." *Policy Sciences* 22(2/3) (October): 325–357.
——— (ed.). 1991. *Irredentism and International Politics*. Boulder: Lynne Rienner.
Cheeseman, Nic. 2015. *Democracy in Africa: Success, Failures, and the Struggle for Political Reform*. Cambridge: Cambridge University Press.
———. 2018. *Institutions and Democracy in Africa: How the Rules of the Game Shape Political Developments*. Cambridge: Cambridge University Press.
Cheeseman, Nic, and Diane de Gramont. 2017. "Managing a Mega-City: Learning the Lessons from Lagos." *Oxford Review of Economic Policy* 33(3) (Autumn): 457–477.
Chege, Michael. 1995. "The Military in the Transition to Democracy in Africa: Some Preliminary Observations." *CODESRIA Bulletin* 3(13): 7–9.
Chen, Yunnan, Irene Yuan Sun, Rex Uzonna Ukaejiofo, Tang Xiaoyang, and Deborah Bräutigam. 2016. *Learning from China? Manufacturing, Investment, and Technology Transfer in Nigeria*. Washington, DC: International Food Policy Research Institute.
Cheney, Kristen. 2012. "Locating Neocolonialism, 'Tradition,' and Human Rights in Uganda's 'Gay Death Penalty.'" *African Studies Review* 55(2) (September): 77–95.
Chersich, Matthew, and Caradee Wright. 2019. "Climate Change Adaptation in South Africa: A Case Study on the Role of the Health Sector." *Globalization and Health* 15(22) (March): 1–16.
Cheru, Fantu, and Cyril Obi (eds.). 2010. *The Rise of China and India in Africa: Challenges, Opportunities and Critical Interventions*. London: Zed.
Chigwedere, P., and M. Essex. 2010. "AIDS Denialism and Public Health Practice." *AIDS Behavior* 14(2) (April): 237–247.
Chitando, Ezra. 2005. "Studying African Judaism: Some Methodological Challenges." *Journal for the Study of Religion* 18(2): 55–74.

Christensen, S. S., and G. D. Eslick. 2015. "Cerebral Malaria as a Risk Factor for the Development of Epilepsy and Other Long-Term Neurological Conditions: A Meta-Analysis." *Transactions of the Royal Society of Tropical Medicine and Hygiene* 109(4) (April): 233–238.

Christensen, Steen. 2002. "Denmark and Africa—Past and Present Relations." In Lennart Wohlegemuth (ed.), *The Nordic Countries and Africa: Old and New Relations*. Uppsala: Nordic Africa Institute, 5–28.

Christiaensen, Luc, Joachim De Weerdt, and Yasuyuki Todo. 2013. *Urbanization and Poverty Reduction: The Role of Rural Diversification and Secondary Towns*. Washington, DC: World Bank.

Christian Century. 1995. "Churches Seek 'Critical Distance.'" April 19.

Church, R. J. Harrison. 1967. *Africa and the Islands*. New York: John Wiley.

Citizen. 2020. "Tanzania Extends School Closure to Universities Due to Virus." March 18. https://www.thecitizen.co.tz/news/-Tanzania-extends-school-closure-to-universities-due-to-virus-/1840340-5495352-qgiccoz/index.html.

Clapham, Christopher (ed.). 1998. *African Guerrillas*. Bloomington: Indiana University Press.

Clark, John F. 1998. "Zaire: The Bankruptcy of the Extractive State." In Leonardo A. Villalón and Phillip E. Huxtable (eds.), *The African State at a Critical Juncture: Between Disintegration and Reconfiguration*. Boulder: Lynne Rienner, 109–125.

———. 2002. *The African Stakes of the Congo War.* New York: Palgrave.

———. 2007. "The Decline of the African Military Coup." *Journal of Democracy* 18(3) (July): 141–155.

Clark, John F., and David Gardinier (eds.). 1997. *Political Reform in Francophone Africa*. Boulder: Westview Press.

Clark, Shelley, and Sarah Brauner-Otto. 2015. "Divorce in Sub-Saharan Africa: Are Unions Becoming Less Stable?" *Population and Development Review* 41(4) (December): 583–605.

Clarke, Walter, and Jeffrey Herbst (eds.). 1997. *Learning from Somalia: The Lessons of Armed Humanitarian Intervention*. Boulder: Westview Press.

Clasquin, Michel. 2004. "Ixopo: The Evolution of a South African Buddhist Centre." *Journal for the Study of Religion* 17(1): 45–65.

Clasquin, Michel, and Jacobus S. Krueger. 1999. *Buddhism and Africa*. Pretoria: Unisa Press.

Clinton, Chelsea, and Devi Sridhar. 2018. *Governing Global Health: Who Runs the World and Why?* New York: Oxford University Press.

Cocks, Tim. 2003. "Spirited Away in the Night by the Lord's Army." *Mail and Guardian,* February 25. https://mg.co.za/article/2003-02-25-spirited-away-in-the-night-by-lords-army.

———. 2007. "Pentecostals Buckle Up Africa's Bible Belt." *Mail and Guardian*, June 27. https://mg.co.za/article/2007-06-27-pentecostals-buckle-up-africas-bible-belt.

Coffey, David. 2020. "Foreigners Feel the Heat of Kenya's Coronavirus Fears." RFI (Radio France Internationale), March 20. http://www.rfi.fr/en/international/20200319-foreigners-feel-the-heat-of-kenya-s-coronavirus-fears-nairobi-covid-19-xenophobia-european-mzungu.

Cohen, Herman J. 2015. *The Mind of the African Strongman: Conversations with Dictators, Statesmen, and Father Figures*. Washington, DC: New Academia Publishing.

Cohen, Myron, Ying Chen, Marybeth McCauley, Theresa Gamble, Mina Hosseinipour, Nagalingeswaran Kumarasamy, James Hakim, et al. 2011. "Prevention of HIV-1 Infection with Early Antiretroviral Therapy." *New England Journal of Medicine* 365(6) (August): 493–505.

Cole, Jennifer. 2005. "Foreword: Collective Memory and the Politics of Reproduction in Africa." *Africa* 75(1) (February): 1–9.

Cole, Jennifer, and Lynn M. Thomas (eds). 2009. *Love in Africa*. Chicago: University of Chicago Press.

Collier, Ruth Berins. 1982. *Regimes in Tropical Africa: Changing Forms of Supremacy, 1945–75*. Berkeley: University of California Press.

Collins, Paul D. 1985. "Brazil in Africa: Perspectives on Economic Cooperation Among Developing Countries." *Development Policy Review* 3(1) (May): 21–48.

Collord, Michaela. 2018. "The Legislature: Institutional Strengthening in Dominant-Party States." In Nic Cheeseman (ed.), *Institutions and Democracy in Africa: How the Rules of the Game Shape Political Developments.* New York: Cambridge University Press, 281–303.

Commins, Stephen K. (ed.). 1988. *Africa's Development Challenges and the World Bank: Hard Questions, Costly Choices*. Boulder: Lynne Rienner.
Comolli, Virginia. 2015. *Boko Haram: Nigeria's Islamist Insurgency*. London: C. Hurst.
Compagnon, Daniel. 1990. "The Somali Opposition Fronts: Some Comments and Questions." *Horn of Africa* 13(1–2) (January): 29–54.
Confortini, Catia, and Briana Krong. 2015. "Breast Cancer in the Global South and the Limitations of a Biomedical Framing: A Critical Review of the Literature." *Health Policy and Planning* 30(1) (December): 1350–1361.
Connah, Graham. 1967. "New Light on the Benin City Walls." *Journal of the Historical Society of Nigeria* 3(4) (June): 593–609.
———. 1987. *African Civilizations*. Cambridge: Cambridge University Press.
Cooper, Andrew, John Kirton, Franklyn List, and Hany Besada (eds.). 2013. *Africa's Health Challenges: Sovereignty, Mobility of People and Healthcare Governance*. Aldershot: Ashgate.
Coquery-Vidrovitch, Catherine. Translated by David Maisel. 1988. *Africa: Endurance and Change South of the Sahara*. Berkeley: University of California Press.
———. Translated by Beth Gillian Raps. 1997. *African Women*. Boulder: Westview Press.
Cornelissen, Scarlett. 2004. "Japan-Africa Relations: Patterns and Prospects." In Ian Taylor and Paul Williams (eds.), *Africa in International Politics*. London: Routledge, 116–135.
Cornelissen, Scarlett, and Yoichi Mine. 2018. "Africa-Japan Relations in the Post–Cold War Era." In Dawn Nagar and Charles Mutasa (eds.), *Africa and the World: Bilateral and Multilateral International Diplomacy*. Basingstoke: Palgrave Macmillan, 269–286.
Corten, André, and Ruth Marshall-Fratani. 2001. *Between Babel and Pentecost: Transnational Pentecostalism in Africa and Latin America*. Bloomington: Indiana University Press.
Cotula, Lorenzo. 2013. *The Great African Land Grab? Agricultural Investments and the Global Food System*. London: Zed Books.
Council on Foreign Relations. 2005. "More Than Humanitarianism: A Strategic U.S. Approach Toward Africa." Task Force Report no. 56. New York: Council on Foreign Relations.
Creed, John, and Kenneth Menkhaus. 1986. "The Rise of Saudi Regional Power and the Foreign Policies of Northeast African States." *Northeast African Studies* 8(2–3): 1–22.
Crenshaw, Kimberly. 1991. "Mapping the Margins: Intersectionality, Identity Politics, and Violence Against Women of Color." *Stanford Law Review* 43(6) (July): 1241–1299.
Crook, Richard C. 2017. "Democratic Decentralisation, Clientelism and Local Taxation in Ghana." *IDS Bulletin* 28(2) (March).
Currie, Janet. 2009. "Healthy, Wealthy, and Wise: Socioeconomic Status, Poor Health in Childhood, and Human Capital Development." *Journal of Economic Literature* 47(1) (March): 87–122.
Currier, Ashley, 2012b. "The Aftermath of Decolonization: Gender and Sexual Dissidence in Postindependence Namibia." *Signs* 73(2) (January): 441–467.
———. 2012a. *Out in Africa: LGBT Organizing in Namibia and South Africa*. Minneapolis: University of Minnesota Press.
———. 2018. *Politicizing Sex in Contemporary Africa: Homophobia in Malawi*. Cambridge: Cambridge University Press.
Daguzan, Jean-François. 2002. "France, Democratization and North Africa." *Democratization* 9(1) (March): 135–148.
Dahl, Gudrun. 1979. *Suffering Grass: Subsistence and Society of Waso Borana*. Stockholm: Stockholm Studies in Social Anthropology, University of Stockholm.
Daneel, M. L. 1987. *The Quest for Belonging: Introduction to a Study of African Independent Churches*. Gweru: Mambo.
Daniel, Rosaline, and Vladimir Shubin. 2018. "Africa and Russia: The Pursuit of Strengthened Relations in the Post–Cold War Era." In Dawn Nagar and Charles Mutasa (eds.), *Africa and the World: Bilateral and Multilateral International Diplomacy*. Basingstoke, UK: Palgrave Macmillan, 51–70.
Dankwa, Serena. 2013. "'The One Who First Says I Love You': Female Same-Sex Relations and Relational Masculinity in Postcolonial Ghana." In S. N. Nyeck and Marc Epprecht (eds.), *Sexual Diversity in Africa: Politics, Theory, Citizenship*. Montreal: McGill-Queen's University Press, 170–187.

Danladi, Iliya Bauchi, Basiru Mohammed Kore, and Murat Gül. 2017. "Vulnerability of the Nigerian Coast: An Insight into Sea Level Rise Owing to Climate Change and Anthropogenic Activities." *Journal of African Earth Sciences* 134 (July): 493–503.

Darkwah, Akosua. Forthcoming. "Internet Activism Ghanaian Feminist Style." In Josephine Beoku Betts and Akosua Adomako Ampofo (eds.), *Producing Inclusive Feminist Knowledge: Positionalities and Discourses in the Global South*. Bingley: Emerald.

Davenport, Thomas, and Christopher Saunders. 2000. *South Africa: A Modern History*. Basingstoke: Macmillan.

Davidson, Basil. 1989. *Modern Africa: A Social and Political History.* London: Longman.

———. 1991. *African Civilization Revisited.* Trenton: Africa World Press.

———. 1992. *The Black Man's Burden: Africa and the Curse of the Nation-State.* London: James Currey.

Davies, Sara. 2010. *Global Politics of Health*. Malden: Polity.

Davis, Benjamin, Sudhanshu Handa, Nicola Hypher, Natalia Winder Rossi, Paul Winters, and Jennifer Yablonski. 2016. *From Evidence to Action: The Story of Cash Transfers and Impact Evaluation in Sub-Saharan Africa*. New York: FAO and UNICEF.

Davis, John (ed.). 2007. *Africa and the War on Terrorism*. Aldershot: Ashgate.

Davis, Mike. 2006. *Planet of Slums*. New York: Verso.

De Castro, Carolina Milhorance. 2014. "Brazil's Cooperation with Sub-Saharan Africa in the Rural Sector: The International Circulation of Instruments of Public Policy." *Latin American Perspectives* 41(5) (December): 75–93.

De Montesquiou, Alfred. 2011. "Al-Qaeda in North Africa Seeks Arab Spring Jihad." *CBS News*, August 15. https://www.cbsnews.com/news/al-qaeda-in-north-africa-seeks-arab-spring-jihad/.

De Villiers, Marq, and Sheila Hirtle. 2002. *Sahara: A Natural History*. New York: Walker and Co.

De Vries, Lotje, Pierre Englebert, and Mareike Schomerus (eds.). 2019. *Secessionism in African Politics: Aspiration, Grievance, Performance, Disenchantment*. London: Palgrave Macmillan.

De Waal, Alexander. 2004. *Islamism and Its Enemies in the Horn of Africa.* Bloomington: Indiana University Press.

deBlij, Harm J., and Peter O. Muller. 2010. *Geography: Realms, Regions, and Concepts*. New York: John Wiley and Sons.

Decalo, Samuel. 1976. *Coups and Army Rule in Africa: Studies in Military Style.* New Haven: Yale University Press.

———. 1992. "The Process, Prospects, and Constraints of Democratization in Africa. *African Affairs* 91(362) (January): 7–35.

———. 1997. *Israel and Africa: Forty Years, 1956–1996.* Gainesville: Florida Academic Press.

Decker, Alicia, and Gabeba Baderoon. 2018. "African Feminisms: Cartographies for the Twenty-First Century." *Meridians: Feminism, Race, Transnationalism* 17(2) (November): 219–231.

Decret, François. 2009. *Early Christianity in North Africa*. Eugene: Wipf and Stock.

Decroo, Tom, Gabriel Fitzpatrick, and Jackson Amone. 2017. "What Was the Effect of the West African Ebola Outbreak on Health Programme Performance, and Did Programmes Recover?" *Public Health Action* 7(Suppl. 1) (June): S1–S2.

DeLaet, Debra, and David DeLaet. 2012. *Global Health in the 21st Century: The Globalization of Disease and Wellness*. Boulder: Paradigm.

Delehanty, James. 2014. "Africa: A Geographic Frame." In Maria Grosz-Ngate, John H. Hanson, and Patrick O'Meara (eds.), *Africa*. 4th ed. Bloomington: Indiana University Press, 7–31.

Delprato, Marcos, Kwame Akyeampong, and Máiréad Dunne. 2017. "Intergenerational Education Effects of Early Marriage in Sub-Saharan Africa." *World Development* 91 (March): 173–192.

Deng, Francis M. 1993. *Protecting the Dispossessed: A Challenge for the International Community.* Washington, DC: Brookings Institution.

Deng, Francis M., Sadikiel Kimaro, Terrence Lyons, Donald Rothchild, and I. William Zartman. 1996. *Sovereignty as Responsibility: Conflict Management in Africa.* Washington, DC: Brookings Institution.

Deng, Francis M., and Larry Minear. 1992. *The Challenges of Famine Relief: Emergency Operations in the Sudan.* Washington, DC: Brookings Institution.

Derman, B., R. Odgaard, and E. Sjaastad (eds.). 2007. *Conflicts over Land and Water in Africa*. Oxford: James Currey.
Devarajan, Shantayanan, William R. Easterly, and Howard Pack. 2003. "Low Investment Is Not the Constraint on African Development." *Economic Development and Cultural Change* 51(3) (April): 547–571.
Diamond, Larry. 1989. "Beyond Authoritarianism and Totalitarianism: Strategies for Democratization." *Washington Quarterly* 12(1) (Winter): 141–163.
———. 1995. "Nigeria: The Uncivic Society and the Descent into Praetorianism." In Larry Diamond, Juan J. Linz, and Seymour Martin Lipset (eds.), *Politics in Developing Countries: Comparing Experiences with Democracy*. Boulder: Lynne Rienner, 417–491.
———. 1999. "Introduction." In Larry Diamond and Marc F. Plattner (eds.), *Democratization in Africa*. Baltimore: Johns Hopkins University Press, ix–xxvii.
Dilger, Hansjörg. 2008. "'We Are All Going to Die': Kinship, Belonging, and the Morality of HIV/AIDS-Related Illnesses and Deaths in Rural Tanzania." *Anthropological Quarterly* 81(1) (December): 207–232.
Dionne, Kim Yi. 2017. *Doomed Interventions: The Failure of Global Responses to AIDS in Africa*. New York: Cambridge University Press.
Ditsie, Bev Palesa (dir.). 2017. *The Commission: From Silence to Resistance* [film]. https://bit.ly/2YEeCaI.
Dobbs, Kirstie Lynn, and Peter J. Schraeder. 2019. "Evolving Role of North African Civil Society Actors in the Foreign Policymaking Process: Youth, Women's, Labour and Human Rights Organisations." *Journal of North African Studies* 24(4) (July): 661–681.
Dodman, David, Jane Bicknell, and David Satterthwaite (eds.). 2012. *Adapting Cities to Climate Change: Understanding and Addressing the Development Challenges*. Condon: Routledge.
Donor Tracker. 2017. "Global Health: Who Are the Top Donor Countries?" https://donortracker.org/sector/global-health.
Doss, Cheryl, Chiara Kovarik, Amber Peterman, Agnes Quisumbing, and Mara van den Bold. 2015. "Gender Inequalities in Ownership and Control of Land in Africa: Myth and Reality." *Agricultural Economics* 46(3) (May): 403–434.
Dossou, Krystel M. R., and Bernadette Glehouenou-Dossou. 2007. "The Vulnerability to Climate Change of Cotonou (Benin): The Rise in Sea Level." *Environment and Urbanization* 19(1) (April): 65–79.
Driberg, Jack Herbert. 1923. *The Lango: A Nilotic Tribe of Uganda*. London: T. Fisher Unwin.
Drope, Jeffrey (ed.). 2011. *Tobacco Control in Africa: People, Politics and Policies*. New York: Anthem.
Du Toit, M., S. Cilliers, M. Dallimer, M. Goddard, S. Guenat, and J. Cornelius. 2018. "Urban Green Infrastructure and Ecosystem Services in Sub-Saharan Africa." *Landscape and Urban Planning* 180 (December): 328–338.
Dubey, Ajay K. 1990. *Indo-African Relations in the Post-Nehru Era (1965–1985)*. Delhi: Kalinga Publications.
Dunn, Kevin C., and Pierre Englebert. 2019. *Inside African Politics*. Boulder: Lynne Rienner.
Dussey, Robert. 2017. "The State of Israel: A Partner in the Development of the African Continent." *Jewish Political Studies Review* 28(3/4) (Fall): 25–29.
Eba, Patrick. 2014. "Ebola and Human Rights in West Africa." *Lancet* 384(9960) (December): 2091–2093.
Echenberg, Myron. 1991. *Colonial Conscripts: The Tirailleurs Sénégalais in French West Africa, 1857–1960*. Portsmouth: Heinemann.
The Economist. 2003a. "Faithful, but Not Fanatics." June 26.
———. 2003b. "Uganda's Child Rebels: Thou Shalt Not Kill." September 6.
———. 2005a. "An Awkward Friend for America." September 3.
———. 2005. "Bob Geldof and Bono Have Some Unlikely Friends in America." July 2. https://www.economist.com/united-states/2005/06/30/right-on.
———. 2018. "How a Small African Nation Is Beating AIDS." March 1. https://www.economist.com/middle-east-and-africa/2018/03/01/how-a-small-african-nation-is-beating-aids.
Economist Intelligence Unit. 2011. *African Green Cities Index: Assessing the Environmental Performance of Africa's Major Cities*. Munich: Siemens AG.

Edwards, Iain, and Marc Epprecht. 2020. *Rediscovering Working Class Homosexuality in South Africa: Voices from the Archive*. Pretoria: HSRC Press.
Efevbera, Yvette, Jacqueline Bhabha, Paul E. Farmer, and Günther Fink. 2017. "Girl Child Marriage as a Risk Factor for Early Childhood Development and Stunting." *Social Science and Medicine* 185 (July): 91–101.
Ehebrecht, Daniel, Dirk Heinrichs, and Barbara Lenz. 2018. "Motorcycle-Taxis in Sub-Saharan Africa: Current Knowledge, Implications for the Debate on 'Informal' Transport and Research Needs." *Journal of Transport Geography* 69 (May): 242–256.
Ehret, Christopher. 2002. *The Civilizations of Africa: A History to 1800*. Charlottesville: University Press of Virginia.
El-Ayouty, Yassin (ed.). 1994. *The Organization of African Unity After Thirty Years*. New York: Praeger.
Ellis, Jessica, Laura Elledge, and Mary de Chesnay. 2019. "Obstetric Fistula: The Cost to Child Brides." In M. de Chesnay and B. Anderson (eds.), *Caring for the Vulnerable*. Burlington: Jones and Bartlett Learning, 211–218.
Ellis, Stephen. 2003. "Briefing: West Africa and Its Oil." *African Affairs* 102(406) (January): 135–138.
Eltis, David. 2000. *The Rise of African Slavery in the Americas*. Cambridge: Cambridge University Press.
Emeagwali, Gloria (ed.). 1995. *Women Pay the Price: Structural Adjustment in Africa and the Caribbean*. Trenton: Africa World Press.
Emery, Gene. 2020. "New TB Drug Regimen Controls Resistant Disease in 9 of 10 Cases: Study." Reuters, March 4, 2020. https://www.reuters.com/article/us-health-tb-regimen/new-tb-drug-regimen-controls-resistant-disease-in-9-of-10-cases-study-idUSKBN20S02Y.
Engel, Ulf. 2002. "Briefing: Still in Search of a Political Agenda: Germany's Africa Policy Under the Red-Green Government, 1998–99." *African Affairs* 99(394) (January): 113–118.
———. 2017. "The African Union's Peace and Security Architecture—from Aspiration to Operationalization." In John W. Harbeson and Donald Rothchild (eds.), *Africa in World Politics: Constructing Political and Economic Order*. 6th ed. Boulder: Westview Press, 262–282.
Engel, Ulf, and Robert Kappel (eds.). 2002. *Germany's Africa Policy Revisited: Interests, Images and Incrementalism*. Münster: Lit Verlag.
Engelbrecht, Francois, Jimmy Adegoke, Mary-Jane Bopape, Mogesh Naidoo, Rebecca Garland, Marcus Thatcher, John McGregor, Jack Katzfey, Micha Werner, and Charles Ichoku. 2015. "Projections of Rapidly Rising Surface Temperatures over Africa Under Low Mitigation." *Environmental Research Letters* 10(8) (August): 085004.
Englebert, Pierre. 2019. "The DRC's Electoral Sideshow." *Journal of Democracy* 30(3) (July): 124–138.
Entelis, John P. 2005. "The Democratic Imperative vs. Authoritarian Impulse: The Maghrib State Between Transition and Terrorism." *Middle East Journal* 59(4) (Autumn): 537–558.
Epprecht, Marc. 2006. *Hungochani: The History of a Dissident Sexuality in Southern Africa*. Montreal: McGill-Queen's University Press.
———. 2008. *Heterosexual Africa? The History of an Idea from the Age of Exploration to the Age of AIDS*. Athens: Ohio University Press.
———. 2013. *Sexuality and Social Justice in Africa*. London: Zed Books.
Epprecht, Marc, and Bev Clark. Forthcoming 2020. "The Struggle for Sexual Minority Rights in Zimbabwe in Context." In JoAnn McGregor, Miles Tendi, and Jocelyn Alexander (eds.), *Handbook of Zimbabwean Politics*. Oxford: Oxford University Press.
Epstein, A. L. 1958. *Politics in an Urban African Community*. Manchester: Manchester University Press.
Ercolessi, Maria Cristina. 1994. "Italy's Policy in Sub-Saharan Africa." In Stephan Brune, Joachim Betz, and Winrich Kuhne (eds.), *Africa and Europe: Relations of Two Continents in Transition*. Münster: Lit Verlag, 87–108.
Erlikh, Ḥagai. 2010. *Islam and Christianity in the Horn of Africa: Somalia, Ethiopia, Sudan*. Boulder: Lynne Rienner.
Ernstson, Hemrik, and Erik Swyngedouw. 2019. "Politicizing the Environment in the Urban Century." In H. Ernstson and E. Swyngedouw (eds.), *Urban Political Ecology in the Anthropo-Obscene: Interruptions and Possibilities*. New York: Routledge, 3–21.

Esedebe, P. Olisanwuche. 1982. *Pan-Africanism: The Idea and the Movement 1776–1963*. Washington, DC: Howard University Press.
Esposito, John L., and Dalia Mogahed. 2007. *Who Speaks for Islam? What a Billion Muslims Really Think*. New York: Gallup Press.
Ettler, V., L. Konecný, L. Kovárová, M. Mihaljevic, O. Šebek, B. Kríbek, V. Majer et al. 2014. "Surprisingly Contrasting Metal Distribution and Fractionation Patterns in Copper Smelter-Affected Tropical Soils in Forested and Grassland Areas (Mufulira, Zambian Copperbelt)." *Science of the Total Environment* 473–474 (March): 117–124.
Evans, David, Markus Goldstein, and Anna Popova. 2015. "Health-Worker Mortality and the Legacy of the Ebola Epidemic." *Lancet* 3(8) (August): 439–440.
Evans-Pritchard, E. E. 1937. *Witchcraft, Oracles and Magic Among the Azande*. Oxford: Clarendon Press.
———. 1970. "Sexual Inversion Among the Azande." *American Anthropologist* 72(6) (December): 1428–1434.
Evens, T. M. S. 1989. "The Nuer Incest Prohibition and the Nature of Kinship: Alterlogical Reckoning." *Cultural Anthropology* 4(4) (November): 323–346.
Fage, John, and William Tordoff. 2002. *A History of Africa*. 4th ed. New York: Routledge.
Fallon, Amy. 2018. "South Africa Pushed to Combat HIV Among Girls #Blessed by Sugar Daddies." Reuters, March 25. https://www.reuters.com/article/us-safrica-women-aids/south-africa-pushes-to-combat-hiv-among-girls-blessed-by-sugar-daddies-idUSKBN1H2031.
Fallon, Kathleen. 2008. *Democracy and the Rise of Women's Movements in Sub-Saharan Africa*. Baltimore: Johns Hopkins University Press.
Fanon, Frantz. 1996 [1961]. *The Wretched of the Earth*. New York: Grove Press.
Farwell, Byron. 1986. *The Great War in African (1914–1918)*. New York: W. W. Norton.
Fashole-Luke, G., R. Gray, A. Hastings, and G. Tasie (eds.). 1978. *Christianity in Independent Africa*. London: Rex Collins.
Fassin, Didier. 2007. *When Bodies Remember: Experiences and Politics of AIDS in South Africa*. Berkeley: University of California Press.
Fatton, Robert, Jr. 1992. *Predatory Rule: State and Civil Society in Africa*. Boulder: Lynne Rienner.
Faure, Yves. 1993. "Democracy and Realism: Reflections on the Case of Côte d'Ivoire." *Africa: Journal of the International African Institute* 63(3): 313–329.
Feather, Christopher, and Chris K. Meme. 2018. "Consolidating Inclusive Housing Finance Development in Africa: Lessons from Kenyan Savings and Credit Cooperatives." *African Review of Economics and Finance* 10(1): 82–107.
Ferguson, James. 1999. *Expectations of Modernity: Myths and Meanings of Urban Life on the Zambian Copperbelt*. Berkeley: University of California Press.
———. 2006. *Global Shadows: Africa in the Neoliberal World Order*. Durham: Duke University Press.
Fidan, Hakan, and Bülent Aras. 2010. "The Return of Russia-Africa Relations." *Bilig* 52 (December): 47–68.
Fidler, David. 2010. "The Challenges of Global Health Governance." Working Paper. New York: Council on Foreign Relations International Institutions and Global Governance Program. https://www.cfr.org/report/challenges-global-health-governance.
Fletcher, Elaine Ruth. 2019. "Norway Launches the First-Ever Strategy by Major International Donor to Combat Non-Communicable Diseases." *Health Policy Watch*, November 22. https://www.healthpolicy-watch.org/norway-launches-first-ever-strategy-by-major-international-donor-to-combat-non-communicable-diseases.
Foccart, Jacques, with Philippe Gaillard. 1995. *Foccart parle: Entretiens avec Philippe Gaillard* 1. Paris: Fayard/Jeune Afrique.
Fourchard, Laurent. 2011. "Between World History and State Formation: New Perspectives on Africa's Cities." *Journal of African History* 52(2) (July): 223–248.
Fox, Graham R. 2018. "Maasai Group Ranches, Minority Land Owners, and the Political Landscape of Laikipia County, Kenya." *Journal of Eastern African Studies* 12(3): 473–493.
Fox, Sean. 2012. "Urbanization as a Global Historical Process: Theory and Evidence from Sub-Saharan Africa." *Population and Development Review* 38(2) (June): 285–310.

———. 2014. "The Political Economy of Slums: Theory and Evidence from Sub-Saharan Africa." *World Development* 54 (February): 191–203.
Franceschet, Susan, Mona Lena Krook, and Jennifer Piscopo. 2012. "Conceptualizing the Impact of Gender Quotas." In Susan Franceschet, Mona Lena Krook, and Jennifer Piscopo (eds.), *The Impact of Gender Quotas.* Oxford: Oxford University Press, 3–26.
Franklin, Sarah, and Susan McKinnon. 2000. "New Directions in Kinship Study: A Core Concept Revisited." *Current Anthropology* 41(2) (April): 275–279.
Fraser, Alistair, and Miles Larmer (eds.). 2010. *Zambia, Mining, and Neoliberalism: Boom and Bust on the Globalized Copperbelt.* New York: Palgrave Macmillan.
Fredericks, Rosalind. 2018. *Garbage Citizenship: Vital Infrastructures of Labor in Dakar, Senegal.* Durham: Duke University Press.
Freedom House. 2019. "Freedom in the World (dataset)." https://freedomhouse.org/content/freedom-world-data-and-resources.
French, Howard D. 1995. "Nigeria Comes on Too Strong." *New York Times,* November 20.
French, Howard W. 2014. *China's Second Continent: How a Million Migrants Are Building a New Empire in Africa.* New York: Vintage Books.
Freund, Bill. 2007. *The African City: A History.* Cambridge: Cambridge University Press.
———. 2016. *The Making of Contemporary Africa.* 3rd ed. Boulder: Lynne Rienner.
Friedman, Steven. 2000. "Another Voice in Africa: Towards a New Jewish Identity." *Journal for the Study of Religion* 17(1): 151–174.
Friedman, Willa Helterline. 2018. "Antiretroviral Drug Access and Behavior Change." *Journal of Development Economics* 135 (November): 392–411.
Frimpong-Ansah, Jonathan H. 1992. *The Vampire State in Africa: The Political Economy of Decline in Ghana.* Trenton: Africa World Press.
Frontline. 2014. "TB Silent Killer." Aired on PBS, March 25. Season 31, episode 17.
Gall, Carlotta. 2020. "Turkish Parliament Approves Sending Troops to Libya." *New York Times*, January 3, A4.
Gallagher, Julia. 2013. *Britain and Africa Under Blair: In Pursuit of the Good State.* Manchester: Manchester University Press.
GALZ (Gays and Lesbians of Zimbabwe). 2008. *Unspoken Facts: A History of Homosexualities in Africa.* Harare: Gays and Lesbians of Zimbabwe.
Gambari, Ibrahim A. 1995. "The Role of Foreign Intervention in African Reconstruction." In I. William Zartman (ed.), *Collapsed States: The Disintegration and Restoration of Legitimate Authority.* Boulder: Lynne Rienner, 221–233.
García, Bernabé López, and Miguel Hernando de Larramendi. 2002. "Spain and North Africa: Towards a 'Dynamic Stability.'" *Democratization* 9(1) (September): 170–191.
Garenne, Michel. 2015. "Maternal Mortality in Africa: Investigating More, Acting More." *Lancet Global Health* 3(7) (July): 346–347.
Garrett, Laurie. 2015. "Ebola's Lessons: How the WHO Mishandled the Crisis." *Foreign Affairs* 94(5) (September/October): 80–107.
Garten, Jeffrey E. 1993. *A Cold Peace: America, Japan, Germany, and the Struggle for Supremacy.* New York: Three Rivers Press.
Gaudio, Rudolf Pell. 2009. *Allah Made Us: Sexual Outlaws in an Islamic City.* Malden: Wiley-Blackwell.
GBD (Global Burden of Disease). 2018. "Global, Regional, and National Age-Sex-Specific Mortality for 282 Causes of Death in 195 Countries and Territories, 1980–2017: A Systematic Analysis for the Global Burden of Disease Study 2017." *Lancet* 392(10159) (November): 1736–1788.
Gbowee, Leymah. 2011. *Mighty Be Our Powers: How Sisterhood, Prayer and Sex Changed a Nation at War.* New York: Beast Books.
Gebresilasse, Mesay M. 2018. "Rural Roads, Agricultural Extension, and Productivity." Unpublished manuscript.
Gegout, Catherine. 2017. *Why Europe Intervenes in Africa: Security, Prestige, and the Legacy of Colonialism.* New York: Oxford University Press.
Geiger, Susan. 1987. "Women in Nationalist Struggle: TANU Activists in Dar es Salaam." *International Journal of African Historical Studies* 20(1): 1–26.
———. 1990. "Women and African Nationalism." *Journal of Women's History* 2(1) (Spring): 227–244.

———. 1996. "Tanganyikan Nationalism as 'Women's Work': Life Histories, Collective Biography and Changing Historiography." *Journal of African History* 37(3) (November): 465–478.

Gellar, Sheldon. 1995. *Senegal: An African Nation Between Islam and the West*. 2nd ed. Boulder: Westview Press.

Geschiere, Peter. 2013. *Witchcraft, Intimacy, and Trust: Africa in Comparison*. Chicago: University of Chicago Press.

Gevisser, Mark, and Edwin Cameron (eds.). 1994. *Defiant Desire: Gay and Lesbian Lives in South Africa*. Johannesburg: Ravan.

Ghana Statistical Service. 2013. *2010 Population and Housing Census: National Analytical Report*. http://www.statsghana.gov.gh/gssmain/fileUpload/pressrelease/2010_PHC_National_Analytical_Report.pdf.

Ghertner, D. Asher. 2008. "Analysis of New Legal Discourse Behind Delhi's Slum Demolitions." *Economic and Political Weekly* 43(20): 57–66.

———. 2010. "Calculating Without Numbers: Aesthetic Governmentality in Delhi's slums." *Economy and Society* 39(2): 185–217.

Gibb, Richard. 1998. "Southern Africa in Transition: Prospects and Problems Facing Regional Integration." *Journal of Modern African Studies* 36(2) (June): 287–306.

Gibbs, Andy, Kaymarlin Govender, and Rachel Jewkes. 2018. "An Exploratory Analysis of Factors Associated with Depression in a Vulnerable Group of Young People Living in Informal Settlements in South Africa." *Global Public Health* 13(7) (July): 788–803.

Gibson, Richard. 1972. *African Liberation Movements: Contemporary Struggles Against White Minority Rule*. London: Oxford University Press.

Gifford, Paul. 1995. *The Christian Churches and the Democratization of Africa*. Leiden: Brill.

———. 1998. *African Christianity: Its Public Role*. Bloomington: Indiana University Press.

———. 2004. *Ghana's New Christianity: Pentecostalism in a Globalizing African Economy*. Bloomington: Indiana University Press.

———. 2009. *Christianity, Politics, and Public Life in Kenya*. New York: Columbia University Press.

Gifford, Prosser, and Wm. Roger Louis. 1971. *France and Britain in Africa: Imperial Rivalry and Colonial Rule*. New Haven: Yale University Press.

Gilbert, Erik, and Jonathan T. Reynolds. 2008. *Africa in World History*. Upper Saddle River: Pearson Education.

Gilmer, B. 2014. *Political Geographies of Piracy: Constructing Threats and Containing Bodies in Somalia*. New York: Palgrave Macmillan.

Glaser, Antoine, and Stephen Smith. 1994. *L'Afrique sans Africains: Le rêve blanc du continent noir*. Paris: Editions Stock.

Global Fund. 2019. "Background." https://www.theglobalfund.org/en/.

Goemans, Hein, Kristian Skrede Gleditsch, and Giacomo Chiozza. 2016. "Archigos: A Database of Political Leaders (dataset)." https://www.rochester.edu/college/faculty/hgoemans/data.htm.

Goldberg, Jeffrey. 2016. "The Obama Doctrine." *The Atlantic* (April). https://www.theatlantic.com/magazine/archive/2016/04/the-obama-doctrine/471525/.

Goldman, Michael. 2011. "Speculative Urbanism and the Making of the Next World City." *International Journal of Urban and Regional Research* 35(3) (May): 555–581.

Goldman, T. R. 2016. "Tobacco Taxes: Health Policy Brief." *Health Affairs*, September 19. https://www.healthaffairs.org/do/10.1377/hpb20160919.471471/full.

Goldsborough, James O. 1978. "Dateline Paris: Africa's Policeman." *Foreign Policy* 33 (Winter): 174–190.

Goldstein, Joseph. 2019. "Ebola Outbreak Worsens as Doctors Dodge Attacks." *New York Times*, May 20.

Gopalan, Karthigasen. 2014. "Defending Hinduism or Fostering Division? The Decision to Introduce Hindu Religious Instruction in Indian Schools in South Africa During the 1950s." *Journal of Religion in Africa* 44(2) (May): 224–250.

Gordon, April. 2003. *Nigeria's Diverse Peoples: A Reference Sourcebook*. Santa Barbara, CA: ABC-CLIO.

Gore, Christopher. 2015. "Climate Change Adaptation and African Cities: Understanding the Impact of Government and Governance on Future Action." In Craig Johnson, Noah Toly, and Heike Schroeder (eds.), *The Urban Climate Challenge*. New York: Routledge, 215–234.

———. 2019. "Agency and Climate Governance in African Cities." In Jeroen van der Heijden, Harriet Bulkeley, and Chiara Certomà (eds.), *Urban Climate Politics: Agency and Empowerment*. Cambridge: Cambridge University Press, 190–209.

Gort, Enid. 1997. "Swazi Traditional Healers, Role Transformation, and Gender." In Gwendolyn Mikell (ed.), *African Feminism: The Politics of Survival in Sub-Saharan Africa.* Philadelphia: University of Pennsylvania Press, 298–309.

Gottreich, Emily Benichou, and Daniel J. Schroeter (eds.). 2011. *Jewish Culture and Society in North Africa.* Bloomington: Indiana University Press.

Goujon, Emmanuel, and Aminu Abubakar. 2006. "Nigeria's 'Taliban' Plot Comeback from Hide-Outs." *Mail and Guardian,* January 11. https://mg.co.za/article/2006-01-11-nigerias-taliban-plot-comeback-from-hideouts.

Gouws, Amanda. 2019. "Little Is Left of the Feminist Agenda That Swept South Africa 25 Years Ago." The Conversation, August 5. https://theconversation.com/little-is-left-of-the-feminist-agenda-that-swept-south-africa-25-years-ago-121212.

Grady, Denise. 2019. "Ebola Outbreak in Congo Is Declared a Global Health Emergency." *New York Times,* July 17.

Grant, Richard. 2009. *Globalizing City: The Urban and Economic Transformation of Accra, Ghana*. Syracuse: Syracuse University Press.

———. 2015. *Africa: Geographies of Change*. New York: Oxford University Press.

Grégoire, Emmanuel. 1993. "Islam and the Identity of Merchants in Maradi (Niger)." In Louis Brenner (ed.), *Muslim Identity and Social Change in Sub-Saharan Africa.* Bloomington: Indiana University Press, 106–115.

Griffiths, Ieuan L. 2005. *The African Inheritance*. London: Routledge.

Grillo, Laura S., Adriaan van Klinken, and Hassan J. Ndzovu. 2019. *Religions in Contemporary Africa: An Introduction*. London: Routledge.

Gromyko, Anatoly A., and C. S. Whitaker. 1990. *Agenda for Action: African-Soviet-US Cooperation.* Boulder: Lynne Rienner.

Grossman, Guy, and Janet I. Lewis. 2014. "Administrative Unit Proliferation." *American Political Science Review* 108(1) (February): 196–217.

Grosz-Ngate, Maria, John H. Hansen, and Patrick O'Meara (eds.). 2014. *Africa.* 4th ed. Bloomington: Indiana University Press.

Grundy, Kenneth. 1985. "The Impact of Region on Contemporary African Politics." In Gwendolen M. Carter and Patrick O'Meara (eds.), *African Independence: The First Twenty-Five Years.* Bloomington: Indiana University Press, 97–125.

———. 1986. *The Militarization of South African Politics.* Bloomington: Indiana University Press.

Guyer, Jane I. 1981. "Household and Community in African Studies." *African Studies Review* 24(2/3) (September): 87–138.

———. 1996. *African Studies in the United States: A Perspective*. Atlanta: African Studies Association.

Gyimah-Boadi, E. 2019. "Aspirations and Realities in Africa: Democratic Delivery Falls Short." *Journal of Democracy* 30(3) (July): 86–93.

Haas, Astrid R. N., and Shahrukh Wani. 2019. "Urban Governance Institutions: Policy Options for Fast Growing Cities." Cities That Work Paper Series. London: International Growth Centre. https://www.theigc.org/wp-content/uploads/2019/04/CtW_GovernancePolicyPaper.pdf.

Habitat III. 2016. "New Urban Agenda." http://habitat3.org/wp-content/uploads/NUA-English.pdf.

Haggblade, Steven, Melinda Smale, Veronique Thériault, and Amidou Assima. 2017. "Causes and Consequences of Increasing Herbicide Use in Mali." *European Journal of Development Research* 29(3) (June): 648–674.

Hakem, A. 1980. "La civilisation de Napata et de Meroé." In G. Mokhtar (ed.), *Histoire générale de l'Afrique.* Vol. 2. Paris: UNESCO (Jeune Afrique), 315–346.

Hall, James. 2003. "Religion Scores over Democracy." News from Africa (May). http://africa.peacelink.org/newsfromafrica/articles/art_595.html.

Ham, Melinda. 1993. "Zambia: History Repeats Itself." *Africa Report* 38(3): 13–16.

Hammerstad, Anne. 2018. "Africa and the Nordics." In Dawn Nagar and Charles Mutasa (eds.), *Africa and the World: Bilateral and Multilateral International Diplomacy*. Basingstoke, UK: Palgrave Macmillan, 287–314.

Hampwaye, Godfrey, and Chris Rogerson. 2010. "Economic Restructuring in the Zambian Copperbelt: Local Responses in Ndola." *Urban Forum* 21(4) (November): 387–403.
Handa, Sudhanshu, Luisa Natali, David Seidenfeld, Gelson Tembo, Benjamin Davis, and Zambia Cash Transfer Evaluation Study Team. 2018. "Can Unconditional Cash Transfers Raise Long-Term Living Standards? Evidence from Zambia." *Journal of Development Economics* 133 (July): 42–65.
Hansen, Stig Jarle. 2013. *Al-Shabaab in Somalia: The History and Ideology of a Militant Islamist Group, 2005–2012*. Oxford: Oxford University Press.
Hansen, Stig Jarle, and Atle Mesøy. 2009. *The Muslim Brotherhood in the Wider Horn of Africa*. Oslo: Norwegian Institute for Urban and Regional Research.
Hanson, John H. 2017. *The Ahmadiyya in the Gold Coast: Muslim Cosmopolitans in the British Empire*. Bloomington: Indiana University Press.
Hanson, Stephanie. 2010. "Al-Shabab." New York: Council on Foreign Relations. https://www.cfr.org/backgrounder/al-shabab.
Haraguchi, Nobuya, Charles Fang Chin Cheng, and Eveline Smeets. 2017. "The Importance of Manufacturing in Economic Development: Has This Changed?" *World Development* 93 (May): 293–315.
Harbeson, John, Donald Rothchild, and Naomi Chazan (eds.). 1994. *Civil Society and the State in Africa*. Boulder: Lynne Rienner.
Harcourt, C., J. Sayer, M. Collins, and the International Union for the Conservation of Nature (IUCN). 1992. *The Conservation Atlas of Tropical Forests: Africa*. New York: Macmillan.
Harding, Andrew. 2016. *The Mayor of Mogadishu: A Story of Chaos and Redemption in the Ruins of Somalia*. New York: St. Martin's Press.
Hargreaves, John D. 1996. *Decolonization in Africa*. 2nd ed. London: Longman.
Harsch, Ernest. 1989. "After Adjustment." *Africa Report* 34(3) (May/June): 46–50.
Harvey, David. 2008. "The Right to the City." *New Left Review* 53 (September/October): 23–40.
Hassim, Shireen. 2006. *Women's Organizations and Democracy in South Africa: Contesting Authority*. Madison: University of Wisconsin Press.
Hastings, Adrian. 1976. *African Christianity*. New York: Seabury.
Hauge, Jostein, and Ha-Joon Chang. 2019. "The Role of Manufacturing Versus Services in Economic Development." In P. Bianchi, C. R. Durán, and S. Labory (eds.), *Transforming Industrial Policy for the Digital Age*. Northampton: Edward Elgar Publishing, 12–36.
Haushofer, Johannes, and Jeremy Shapiro. 2016. "The Short-Term Impact of Unconditional Cash Transfers to the Poor: Experimental Evidence from Kenya." *Quarterly Journal of Economics* 131(4) (November): 1973–2042.
Haynes, Jeff. 1996. *Religion and Politics in Africa*. London: Zed.
He, Tianhao. 2012. "Back to ABCs: Emerging Partnerships Among Africa, Brazil, and China." *Harvard International Review* 34(1) (Summer): 30–33.
Heilbrunn, John R. 1993. "Social Origins of National Conferences in Benin and Togo." *Journal of Modern African Studies* 31(2) (June): 277–299.
Henderson, J. Vernon, Adam Storeygard, and Uwe Deichmann. 2017. "Has Climate Change Driven Urbanization in Africa?" *Journal of Development Economics* 124 (January): 60–82.
Herbst, Jeffrey. 1993. *The Politics of Reform in Ghana, 1982–1991*. Berkeley: University of California Press.
———. 2000. *States and Power in Africa: Comparative Lessons in Authority and Control*. 2nd ed. Princeton: Princeton University Press.
Herskovits, Melville J. 1967 [1938]. *Dahomey: An Ancient West African Kingdom*. Evanston: Northwestern University Press.
Hess, Robert L. 1966. *Italian Colonialism in Somalia*. Chicago: University of Chicago Press.
Hibou, Beatrice. 2006. *La Force de l'obeissance: Econimie Politique de la Repression en Tunisie*. Paris: La Decouverte.
Higginbotham, Derrick. 2018. "Beyond Identity: Queer Affiliation and the Politics of Solidarity in Gordimer's *None to Accompany Me* and Duiker's *The Quiet Violence of Dreams*." In Zethu Matebeni, Surya Monro, and Vasu Reddy (eds.), *Queer in Africa: LGTIQI Identities Citizenship and Activism*. New York: Routledge, 84–98.
Hine, John, Manu Sasidharan, Mehran Eskandari Torbaghan, Michael Burrow, and Kristianto Usman. 2019. *Evidence of the Impact of Rural Road Investment on Poverty Reduction and*

Economic Development. K4D Helpdesk Report. Brighton, UK: Institute of Development Studies.

Hines, Annie L., and Nicole B. Simpson. 2014. "Migration, Remittances and Human Capital Investment in Kenya." *Economic Notes: Review of Banking, Finance and Monetary Economics* 48(3) (November): e12142.

Hiralal, Kalpana. 2014. "Forging a Gujarati Hindu Identity in South Africa a History of Gujarati Hindu Organisations in South Africa 1900–1983." *Nidān* 26(12) (December): 60–82.

Hirsch, John L., and Robert B. Oakley. 1995. *Somalia and Operation Restore Hope: Reflections on Peacemaking and Peacekeeping*. Washington, DC: US Institute for Peace.

Hjort, Jonas, and Jonas Poulsen. 2019. "The Arrival of Fast Internet and Employment in Africa." *American Economic Review* 109(3) (March): 1032–1079.

Hoad, Neville, Karen Martin, and Graeme Reid (eds.). 2005. *Sex and Politics in South Africa*. Cape Town: Double Story.

Hoben, Ashley D., Abraham P. Buunk, and Maryanne L. Fisher. 2015. "Factors Influencing the Allowance of Cousin Marriages in the Standard Cross Cultural Sample." *Evolutionary Behavioral Sciences* 10(2) (March): 98–108.

Hodgkin, Thomas. 1957. *Nationalism in Colonial Africa*. New York: New York University Press.

Hoehne, Markus Virgil. 2015. *Between Somaliland and Puntland: Marginalization, Militarization and Conflicting Political Visions*. London: Rift Valley Institute.

Hoehne, Markus Virgil, and Mohamed Hassan Ibrahim. 2014. "Rebuilding Somaliland Through Economic and Educational Engagement." In Liisa Laakso and Petri Hautaniemi (eds.), *Diasporas, Development and Peacemaking in the Horn of Africa*. London: Zed Books, 53–76.

Hoffman, Barbara G. 2001. *Griots at War: Conflict, Conciliation, and Caste in Mande*. Bloomington: Indiana University Press.

———. 2014. "Out on Malian Television: Media and Culture Change in an Emerging Cosmopolitan Metropolitan Center." *Mande Studies* 14: 127–148.

Hoffman, Barbara G., and Fatoumata Keita. 2017. "Innovations dans l'Habitat et Transformations Culturelles dans la Ville/Innovations in Habitat and Cultural Transformations in the City." *Proceedings of DAKAR 2016: Innovation, Transformation, and Sustainable Futures in Africa* 1(1) (August): 145–153.

Hoffman, Danny. 2017. *Monrovia Modern: Urban Form and Political Imagination in Liberia*. Raleigh: Duke University Press.

Hoffman, Stanley H. 1967. "Perceptions, Reality and the Franco-American Conflict." *Journal of International Affairs* 21(1): 57–71.

Hofman, Karen, and Charles Parry. 2017. "Big Alcohol Is Poised to Expand into Africa: Why This Is Bad News for Health." The Conversation, May 24. https://theconversation.com/big-alcohol-is-poised-to-expand-into-africa-why-this-is-bad-news-for-health-68383.

Hofman, Michiel, and Sokhieng Au (eds.). 2017. *The Politics of Fear: Médecins Sans Frontières and the West African Ebola Epidemic*. New York: Oxford University Press.

Hofmeier, Rolf. 1994. "German-African Relations: Present and Future." In Stefan Brune, Joachim Betz, and Winrich Kuhne (eds.), *Africa and Europe: Relations of Two Continents in Transition*. Münster: Lit Verlag, 71–86.

Holm, John, and Patrick Molutsi (eds.). 1989. *Democracy in Botswana*. Gaborone: Macmillan Botswana.

Hope, Kempe Ronald, Sr. 2002. "From Crisis to Renewal: Toward a Successful Implementation of the New Partnership for Africa's Development." *African Affairs* 101(404) (July): 387–402.

Hopkins, Tony. 2014. *An Economic History of West Africa*. London: Routledge.

Hornsby, David J. 2014. "Changing Perception into Reality: Canada in Africa." *International Journal* 69(3) (September): 334–352.

Hovhannisyan, Nune, and Wolfgang Keller. 2015. "International Business Travel: An Engine of Innovation?" *Journal of Economic Growth* 20(1) (March): 75–104.

Howle, Signe. 2009. "Adoption of the Unrelated Child: Some Challenges in the Anthropological Study of Kinship." *Annual Reviews of Anthropology* 38: 149–166.

Hsiao-pong, Philip Liu. 2009. "Planting Rice on the Roof of the UN Building: Analysing Taiwan's "Chinese" Techniques in Africa, 1961–Present." *China Quarterly* 198 (June): 381–400.

Hubbard, Mark. 1993. "Cameroon: A Flawed Victory." *Africa Report* 38(1): 41–44.

Huchzermeyer, Marie. 2011. *Cities with "Slums": From Informal Settlement Eradication to a Right to the City in Africa*. Cape Town: University of Cape Town Press.
Huet, Natalie, and Carmen Paun. 2017. "Meet the World's Most Powerful Doctor: Bill Gates." *Politico*, May 4. https://www.politico.eu/article/bill-gates-who-most-powerful-doctor.
Hughes, Melanie, and Aili Mari Tripp. 2015. "Civil War and Trajectories of Change in Women's Political Representation in Africa, 1985–2010." *Social Forces* 93(4) (June): 1513–1540.
Hull, Richard. 2009. *Jews and Judaism in African History*. Princeton: Markus Wiener Publishers.
Hunter, Susan. 2003. *Black Death: AIDS in Africa*. New York: Palgrave Macmillan.
Huntington, Samuel P. 1991. *The Third Wave of Democratization in the Late Twentieth Century*. Norman: University of Oklahoma Press.
Hunwick, John O. 1995. *Religion and National Integration in Africa: Islam, Christianity, and Politics in the Sudan and Nigeria*. Evanston: Northwestern University Press.
Hyden, Goran. 1983. *No Shortcuts to Progress*. Berkeley: University of California Press.
Ibrahim, Abadir. 2015. "LGBT Rights in Africa and the Discursive Role of International Human Rights Law." *African Human Rights Law Journal* 15(2) (January): 263–281.
Ibrahim, Jibrin. 2004. "The First Lady Syndrome and the Marginalisation of Women from Power: Opportunities or Compromises for Gender Equality?" *Feminist Africa* 3 (September): 48–69.
ICG (International Crisis Group). 2006. "Somaliland: Time for African Union Leadership." International Crisis Group Report no. 110. Brussels, Belgium, May 23. https://www.crisisgroup.org/africa/horn-africa/somalia/somaliland-time-african-union-leadership.
Idowu, E. B. 1962. *Olodumare: God in Yoruba Belief*. Ikeja: Longman.
———. 1971. *African Traditional Religion: A Definition*. Maryknoll: Orbis.
IEA (International Energy Agency). 2010. *Energy Essentials: Hydropower*. Paris: Organization for Economic Cooperation and Development/International Energy Agency. www.iea.org/papers/2010/Hydropower_Essentials.pdf.
———. 2019. *Nigeria Energy Outlook: Analysis from Africa Energy Outlook 2019*. https://www.iea.org/articles/nigeria-energy-outlook
IFAD (International Fund for Agricultural Development). 2016. "IFAD Remittances at the Post Office in Africa: Serving the Financial Needs of Migrants and their Families in Rural Areas." Rome, November.
IHME (Institute for Health Metrics and Evaluation). 2015. "Financing Global Health 2015 Brief." http://www.healthdata.org/infographic/financing-global-health-2015-brief.
Ikome, Francis Nguendi. 2007. *From the Lagos Plan of Action to the New Partnership for Africa's Development: The Political Economy of African Regional Initiatives*. Midrand: Institute for Global Dialogue.
Ilesanmi, Simeon O. 1995. "Recent Theories of Religion and Politics in Nigeria." *Journal of Church and State* 37(2) (Spring): 309–327.
Iliffe, John. 1995. *Africans: The History of a Continent*. Cambridge: Cambridge University Press.
———. 2017. *Africans: The History of a Continent*. 3rd ed. Cambridge: Cambridge University Press.
ILO (International Labour Organization). 2019. "Africa: About the Region." https://www.ilo.org/africa/about-us/lang—en/index.htm.
———. 2020. "ILO Offices in Africa." https://www.ilo.org/africa/about-us/offices/lang—en/index.htm.
Insoll, Timothy. 2003. *The Archaeology of Islam in Sub-Saharan Africa*. Cambridge: Cambridge University Press.
ITUC (International Trade Union Confederation). 2011. "A New Arab Democratic Trade Union Forum: For Freedom, Social Justice, and Dignity." September 16. www.ituc-csi.org/a-new-arab-democratic-trade-union.
Iyob, Ruth. 1995. *The Eritrean Struggle for Independence: Domination, Resistance, Nationalism, 1941–1993*. Cambridge: Cambridge University Press.
Izard, M. 1984. "The Peoples and Kingdoms of the Niger Bend and the Volta Basin from the 12th to the 16th Century." In D. T. Niane (ed.), *General History of Africa*. London: Heinemann, 211–237.
Jackson, Robert H., and Carl G. Rosberg. 1982. *Personal Rule in Black Africa: Prince, Autocrat, Prophet, Tyrant*. Berkeley: University of California Press.
Jaffe, Hosea. 2017. *History of Africa*. London: Zed Books.

Jamal, Amaney A., and Mark A. Tessler. 2008. "Attitudes in the Arab World." *Journal of Democracy* 19(1): 97–110.

Jamieson, David, and Scott E. Kellerman. 2016. "The 90 90 90 Strategy to End the HIV Pandemic by 2030: Can the Supply Chain Handle It?" *Journal of the International AIDS Society* 19(1): 20917.

Jayawardene, Sureshi M. 2019. "Language in Africa." In Howard Chiang et al. (eds.), *Global Encyclopedia of Lesbian, Gay, Bisexual, Transgender, and Queer History.* Farmington Hills, MI: Charles Scribner's Sons, 903–909.

Jeffries, Richard. 1989. "Ghana: The Political Economy of Personal Rule." In Donald B. Cruise O'Brien, John Dunn, and Richard Rathbone (eds.), *Contemporary West African States.* Cambridge: Cambridge University Press, 75–98.

Jena, Farai. 2018. "Migrant Remittances and Physical Investment Purchases: Evidence from Kenyan Households." *Journal of Development Studies* 54(2): 312–326.

Jhazbhay, Iqbal. 2008. "Somaliland's Post-War Reconstruction: Rubble to Rebuilding." *International Journal of African Renaissance Studies* 3(1) (October): 59–93.

Jinadu, L. Adele. 2018. "Sub-Saharan Africa: The World Bank and the International Monetary Fund." In Dawn Nagar and Charles Mutasa (eds.), *Africa and the World: Bilateral and Multilateral International Diplomacy*. Basingstoke: Palgrave Macmillan, 475–498.

Jjuuko, A. 2019. "Uganda." In Howard Chiang (ed.), *Global Encyclopedia of Lesbian, Gay, Bisexual, Transgender, and Queer (LGBTQ) History.* New York: Charles Scribner's Sons, 1681–1687.

Johns, Sheridan, and R. Hunt Davis Jr. (eds.). 1991. *Mandela, Tambo, and the African National Congress: The Struggle Against Apartheid, 1948–1990: A Documentary Survey*. New York: New York University Press.

Johnson, Cheryl. 1982. "Grassroots Organizing: Women in Anti-Colonial Activity in Southwestern Nigeria." *African Studies Review* 25(2–3) (September): 137–157.

Johnson, John William. 1986. *The Epic of Son-Jara: A West African Tradition.* Bloomington: Indiana University Press.

Johnson, Todd M., and Gina A. Zurlo (eds.). 2020. "World Christian Database." Leiden: Brill.

Johnson Sirleaf, Ellen. 2009. *This Child Will Be Great: Memoir of a Remarkable Life by Africa's First Woman President*. New York: HarperCollins.

Jonah, James O. C. 2018. "Africa at the United Nations: From Dominance to Weakness." In Dawn Nagar and Charles Mutasa (eds.), *Africa and the World: Bilateral and Multilateral International Diplomacy*. Basingstoke: Palgrave Macmillan, 359–370.

Joseph, Richard. 1993. "Ghana: A Winning Formula." *Africa Report* 38(1): 45–46.

Joyner, Christopher C. 1992. "International Law." In Peter J. Schraeder (ed.), *Intervention into the 1990s: U.S. Foreign Policy in the Third World.* Boulder: Lynne Rienner, 229–246.

July, Robert W. 1998. *A History of the African People*. Chicago: Waveland Press.

Kalofonos, Ippolytos Andreas. 2010. "'All I Eat Is ARVs': The Paradox of AIDS Treatment Interventions in Central Mozambique." *Medical Anthropology Quarterly* 24(3) (September): 363–380.

Kamradt-Scott, Adam. 2016. "WHO's to Blame? The World Health Organization and the 2014 Ebola Outbreak in West Africa." *Third World Quarterly* 37(3) (January): 401–418.

Kang, Alice. 2015. *Bargaining for Women's Rights: Activism in an Aspiring Muslim Democracy*. Minneapolis: University of Minnesota Press.

Kantamaneni, Komali. 2016. "Coastal Infrastructure Vulnerability: An Integrated Assessment Model." *Natural Hazards* 84(1) (July): 139–154.

Kaplan, Seth D. 2014. "What Makes Lagos a Model City." *New York Times,* January 8.

Kapstein, Ethan, and Joshua Busby. 2013. *AIDS Drugs for All: Social Movements and Market Transformations*. New York: Cambridge University Press.

Karan, Abraar, Ingrid Katz, and Ashish Jha. 2018. "Ebola in the DRC Is More About the DRC Than It Is About Ebola." *Health Affairs*, November 16. https://www.healthaffairs.org/do/10.1377/hblog20181115.584389/full/.

Karnik, S. S. 1988. "India-Africa Economic Relations: A Select Bibliography." *Africa Quarterly* 25(3–4): 63–110.

Kates, Jennifer, Adam Wexler, and Eric Lief. 2019. "Donor Government Funding for HIV in Low- and Middle-Income Countries in 2018." Global Health Policy, July 16. https://

www.kff.org/report-section/donor-government-funding-for-hiv-in-low-and-middle-income -countries-in-2018-report.

Kazeem, Yomi. 2018. "Bill and Melinda Gates Foundation Is Paying Off Nigeria's $76 Million Polio Debt." *Quartz Africa,* January 15. https://qz.com/africa/1179881/bill-and-melinda -gates-to-pay-off-nigerias-76-million-polio-japan-debt.

Keim, Curtis, and Carolyn Somerville. 2018. *Mistaking Africa: Curiosities and Inventions of the American Mind.* 4th ed. New York: Westview Press.

Keita, Fatoumata. 2017. *Quand les Cauris se Taisent*. Bamako: La Sahelienne.

Keita, Kalifa. 1998. "Conflict and Conflict Resolution in the Sahel: The Tuareg Insurgency in Mali." *Small Wars and Insurgencies* 9(3): 102–128.

Kelland, Kate. 2019. "Mental Illness Affects a Fifth of People Living in War Zones." Reuters, June 11. https://www.reuters.com/article/us-health-mental-conflict/mental-illness-affects -a-fifth-of-people-living-in-war-zones-idUSKCN1TC2U4.

Kent, S. (ed.). 1997. *Cultural Diversity Among Twentieth-Century Foragers: An African Perspective*. Cambridge: Cambridge University Press.

Kevane, Michael. 2014. *Women and Development in Africa: How Gender Works*. Boulder: Lynne Rienner.

Key, Andre E. 2014. "Toward a Typology of Black Hebrew Religious Thought and Practice." *Journal of Africana Religions* 2(1): 31–66.

KFF (Kaiser Family Foundation). 2019a. "The Global HIV/AIDS Epidemic: Fact Sheet." http://files.kff.org/attachment/Fact-Sheet-The-Global-HIV-AIDS-Epidemic.

———. 2019b. "U.S. Global Health Budget: Overview." https://www.kff.org/global-health -policy/fact-sheet/breaking-down-the-u-s-global-health-budget-by-program-area.

———. 2019c. "The U.S. President's Emergency Plan for AIDS Relief (PEPFAR)." https:// www.kff.org/global-health-policy/fact-sheet/the-u-s-presidents-emergency-plan-for.

Khadiagala, Gilbert M. 1994. *Allies in Adversity: The Frontline States in Southern African Security, 1975–1993.* Athens: Ohio University Press.

Kharsany, Ayesha, and Quarraisha Karim. 2016. "HIV Infection and AIDS in Sub-Saharan Africa: Current Status, Challenges and Opportunities." *Open AIDS Journal* 10 (April): 34–48.

Khumalo, Sibongile. 2008. "Pentecostals Lead Congregations to Financial Benefits." *Business Report,* March 13. https://www.iol.co.za/business-report/economy/pentecostals-lead -congregations-to-financial-benefits-709846.

Kieh, George Klay, Jr., and Pita Ogaba Agbese (eds.). 2004. *The Military and Politics in Africa: From Engagement to Democratic and Constitutional Control.* Aldershot: Ashgate.

Kiernan, Jim. 1995a. "The African Independent Churches." In Martin Prozesky and John de Gruchy (eds.), *Living Faiths in South Africa.* Cape Town: David Philip, 116–128.

———. 1995b. "African Traditional Religions in South Africa." In Martin Prozesky and John de Gruchy (eds.), *Living Faiths in South Africa.* Cape Town: David Philip, 15–27.

———. 1995c. "The Impact of White Settlement on African Traditional Religions." In Martin Prozesky and John de Gruchy (eds.), *Living Faiths in South Africa.* Cape Town: David Philip, 72–82.

Kilson, Martin. 1963. "Authoritarian and Single-Party Tendencies in African Politics." *World Politics* 25(2) (January): 262–294.

King, Noel. 1971. *Christian and Moslem in Africa.* New York: Harper and Row.

King-Akerele, Olubanke. 2012. *Women's Leadership in Post-Conflict Liberia: My Journey.* Accra: Digibooks.

Kirshner, Joshua, and Marcus Power. 2015. "Mining and Extractive Urbanism: Postdevelopment in a Mozambican Boomtown." *Geoforum* 61 (May): 67–78.

Klare, Michael T., and Daniel Volman. 2004. "Africa's Oil and American National Security." *Current History* 103 (May): 226–231.

Klein, Herbert S. 1999. *The Atlantic Slave Trade.* Cambridge: Cambridge University Press.

Klein, Martin. 1977. "Servitude Among the Wolof and Sereer of Senegambia." In Suzanne Miers and Igor Kopytoff (eds.), *Slavery in Africa: Historical and Anthropological Perspectives*. Madison: University of Wisconsin Press, 335–363.

Klein, Naomi. 2014. *This Changes Everything: Capitalism vs. the Climate.* New York: Simon and Schuster.

Klopp, Jacqueline M. 2008. "Remembering the Destruction of Muoroto: Slum Demolitions, Land and Democratisation in Kenya." *African Studies* 67(3) (December): 295–314.

Klopp, Jacqueline M., and Jeffrey W. Paller. 2019. "Slum Politics in Africa." In *Oxford Research Encyclopedia of Politics*. Oxford: Oxford University Press.

Kodongo, Odongo, and Kalu Ojah. 2016. "Does Infrastructure Really Explain Economic Growth in Sub-Saharan Africa?" *Review of Development Finance* 6(2) (December): 105–125.

Korany, Bahgat (ed.). 1986. *How Foreign Policy Decisions Are Made in the Third World: A Comparative Analysis*. Boulder: Westview Press.

Korkut, Umut, and Ilke Civelekoglu. 2012. "Becoming a Regional Power While Pursuing Material Gains: The Case of Turkish Interest in Africa." *International Journal* 68(1) (Winter): 187–203.

Korres, Nicholas E., Nilda R. Burgos, and Stephen O. Duke. 2018. *Weed Control: Sustainability, Hazards, and Risks in Cropping Systems Worldwide*. Boca Raton: CRC Press.

Kroslak, Daniela. 2004. "France's Policy Towards Africa: Continuity or Change?" In Ian Taylor and Paul Williams (eds.), *Africa in International Politics*. London: Routledge, 61–82.

La Fontaine, J. S. 1959. *The Gisu of Uganda*. London: International African Institute.

Laakso, Liisa, and Petri Hautaniemi (eds.). 2014. *Diasporas, Development and Peacemaking in the Horn of Africa*. London: Zed Books.

Laïdi, Zaki. 1990. *The Superpowers and Africa: The Constraints of a Rivalry, 1960–1990*. Chicago: University of Chicago Press.

Laitin, David D., and Said S. Samatar. 1987. *Somalia: Nation in Search of a State*. Boulder: Westview Press.

Lamphear, John, and Toyin Falola. 1995. "Aspects of Early African History." In Phyllis M. Martin and Patrick O'Meara (eds.), *Africa*. 3rd ed. Bloomington: Indiana University Press, 73–96.

Lan, David. 1985. *Guns and Rains: Guerrilla and Spirit Mediums in Zimbabwe*. Harare: Zimbabwe Publishing House.

Lange, D. 1984. "The Kingdoms and Peoples of Chad." In D. T. Niane (ed.), *General History of Africa*. London: Heinemann, 238–265.

Larkin, Bruce D. 1971. *China and Africa, 1949–1970: The Foreign Policy of the People's Republic of China*. Berkeley: University of California Press.

Larson, Krista. 2019. "Study: Many in Ebola Outbreak Don't Believe Virus Is Real." AP, March 28. https://www.apnews.com/3a4260df676f47efb535f6bd5af4ef6f.

Lavergne, Real (ed.). 1997. *Regional Integration and Cooperation in West Africa: A Multidimensional Perspective*. Trenton: Africa World Press.

Lawrence, J. C. D. 1957. *The Iteso: Fifty Years of Change in a Nilo-Hamitic Tribe of Uganda*. London: Oxford University Press.

Leach, Melissa, and Robin Mearns (eds.). 1996. *The Lie of the Land: Challenging Received Wisdom on African Environments*. Oxford: James Currey.

Leacock, Eleanor Burke. 1981. *Myths of Male Dominance: Collected Articles on Women Cross-Culturally*. New York: Monthly Review Press.

Leclant, J. 1980. "L'empire de Koush: Napata et Meroé." In G. Mokhtar (ed.), *Histoire Générale de l'Afrique*. Paris: UNESCO, 295–314.

Lee, Anthony. 2011. *The Baha'I Faith in Africa: Establishing a New Religious Movement, 1952–1962*. Leiden: Brill.

Lee, Liz. 2020. "Condom Shortage Looms After Coronavirus Lockdown Shuts World's Top Producer." Reuters, March 27, 2020. https://www.reuters.com/article/us-health-coronavirus-malaysia-karex/condom-shortage-looms-after-coronavirus-lockdown-shuts-worlds-top-producer-idUSKBN21E1OJ.

Lee, Richard B., and Robert K. Hitchcock. 2001. "African Hunter-Gatherers: Survival, History, and the Politics of Identity." *African Study Monographs* 26 (March): 257–280.

Lee, Richard G. 1993. *The Dobe Ju/'hoansi*. Fort Worth: Harcourt Brace.

Lee, Sungkyu, Pamela Ling, and Stanton Glantz. 2012. "The Vector of the Tobacco Epidemic: Tobacco Industry Practices in Low and Middle-Income Countries." *Cancer Causes and Control* 23(Suppl. 1) (March): 117–129.

Lefebvre, Jeffrey A. 1991. *Arms for the Horn: U.S. Security Policy in Ethiopia and Somalia 1953–1991*. Pittsburgh: University of Pittsburgh Press.

———. 2012. "Iran in the Horn of Africa: Outflanking US Allies." *Middle East Policy* 19(2) (June): 117–133.
Lehman, Howard P. 2010. *Japan and Africa: Globalization and Foreign Aid in the 21st Century*. London: Routledge.
Leithead, Allistair. 2018. "The 'Water War' Brewing over the New Nile River Dam." BBC News, February 24. https://www.bbc.com/news/world-africa-43170408.
Lellouche, Pierre, and Dominique Moisi. 1979. "French Policy in Africa: A Lonely Battle Against Destabilization." *International Security* 3(4) (Spring): 108–133.
Lemarchand, René. 1988. "The State, the Parallel Economy and the Changing Structure of Patronage Systems." In Donald Rothchild and Naomi Chazan (eds.), *The Precarious Balance: State and Society in Africa*. Boulder: Westview Press, 149–170.
Lentz, Carola. 2013. *Land, Mobility, and Belonging in West Africa*. Bloomington: Indiana University Press.
Leonard, David K., and Scott Straus. 2003. *Africa's Stalled Development: International Causes and Cures*. Boulder: Lynne Rienner.
Leslie, Agnes Ngoma. 2006. *Social Movements and Democracy in Africa: The Impact of Women's Struggle for Equal Rights in Botswana*. New York: Routledge.
Levey, Zach. 2008. "Israel's Exit from Africa, 1973: The Road to Diplomatic Isolation." *British Journal of Middle Eastern Studies* 35(2) (December): 205–226.
Levine, David I., Theresa Beltramo, Garrick Blalock, Carolyn Cotterman, and Andrew M. Simons. 2018. "What Impedes Efficient Adoption of Products? Evidence from Randomized Sales Offers for Fuel-Efficient Cookstoves in Uganda." *Journal of the European Economic Association* 16(6) (December): 1850–1880.
Levine, Nancy E. 2008. "Alternative Kinship, Marriage, and Reproduction." *Annual Review of Anthropology* 37(1) (October): 375–389.
Levine, Nancy E., and Walter H. Sangree. 1980. "Conclusion: Asian and African Systems of Polyandry." *Journal of Comparative Family Studies* 11(3) (Summer): 385–410.
Levitsky, Steven, and Lucan A. Way. 2002. "Elections Without Democracy: The Rise of Competitive Authoritarianism." *Journal of Democracy* 13(2) (April): 51–65.
———. 2010. *Competitive Authoritarianism: Hybrid Regimes After the Cold War*. New York: Cambridge University Press.
Levtzion, Nehemia, and Randall Pouwels (eds.). 2000. *The History of Islam in Africa*. Athens: Ohio University Press.
Lewis, I. M. 1980. *Islam in Tropical Africa*. Bloomington: Indiana University Press.
Lewis, Lawrence, and Len Berry. 1988. *African Environments and Resources*. Boston: Unwin and Hyman.
Lewis, Peter M. 2019. "Aspirations and Realities in Africa: Five Reflections." *Journal of Democracy* 30(3) (July): 76–85.
Lewis, Williams, and Robert Gordon. 1954. "Libya After Two Years of Independence." *Middle East Journal* 8(1) (Winter): 41–53.
Li, Richard P. Y., and William R. Thompson. 1975. "The 'Coup Contagion' Hypothesis." *Journal of Conflict Resolution* 19(1) (March): 63–88.
Liddicoat, Renée. 1962. "Homosexuality." *South African Journal of Science* 58(5): 145-149.
Liebenow, Gus J. 1985. "The Military Factor in African Politics: A Twenty-Five-Year Perspective." In Gwendolen M. Carter and Patrick O'Meara (eds.), *African Independence: The First Twenty-Five Years*. Bloomington: Indiana University Press, 126–159.
———. 1986. *African Politics: Crises and Challenges*. Bloomington: Indiana University Press.
Liese, Bernhard, Rebecca Gribble, and Marisha Wickremsinhe. 2019. "International Funding for Mental Health: A Review of the Last Decade." *International Health* 11(5) (September): 361–369.
Lindhardt, Martin. 2015. "Introduction: Presence and Impact of Pentecostal/Charismatic Christianity in Africa." In Martin Lindhardt (ed.), *Pentecostalism in Africa: Presence and Impact of Pneumatic Christianity in Postcolonial Societies*. Leiden: Brill, 1–53.
Little, Kenneth. 1970. *West African Urbanization: A Study of Voluntary Associations in Social Change*. Cambridge: Cambridge University Press.
Liu, Haifang. 2018. "Africa and China: Winding into a Community of Common Destiny." In Dawn Nagar and Charles Mutasa (eds.), *Africa and the World: Bilateral and Multilateral International Diplomacy*. Basingstoke, UK: Palgrave Macmillan, 71–94.

Lofchie, Michael F. 1989. "Reflections on Structural Adjustment in Africa." In Emory University, Governance in Africa Program (ed.), *Beyond Autocracy in Africa*. Atlanta: Carter Center, 121–125.
Loimeier, Roman. 2016. *Islamic Reform in Twentieth-Century Africa*. Edinburgh: Edinburgh University Press.
Longman, Timothy P. 1998. "Empowering the Weak and Protecting the Powerful: The Contradictory Nature of Churches in Central Africa." *African Studies Review* 41(1) (April): 49–72.
Lonsdale, John. 1989. "African Pasts in African Futures." *Canadian Journal of African Studies* 23(1): 126–146.
Love, Janice. 2005. *Southern Africa in World Politics: Local Aspirations and Global Entanglements*. Boulder: Westview Press.
Lovejoy, Paul E. 2011. *Transformations in Slavery: A History of Slavery in Africa*. Cambridge: Cambridge University Press.
Low-Beer, Daniel, Houtan Afkhami, Ryuichi Komatsu, Prerna Banati, Musoke Sempala, Itamar Katz et al. 2007. "Making Performance-Based Funding Work for Health." *PLoS Medicine* 4(8) (August): e219.
Luckham, Robin. 1994. "The Military, Militarization and Democratization in Africa." *African Studies Review* 37(2) (September): 13–75.
Lugard, Sir F. D. 1922. *The Dual Mandate in British Tropical Africa*. Edinburgh: Blackwood.
Luiu, Carlo, Mehran Eskandari Torbaghan, and Michael Burrow. 2018. *Rates of Return for Railway Infrastructure Investments in Africa*. K4D Helpdesk Report. Brighton, UK: Institute of Development Studies.
Lumumba-Kasongo, Tukumbi. 2010. *Japan-Africa Relations*. New York: Palgrave Macmillan.
———. 2011. "China-Africa Relations: A Neo-Imperialism or a Neo-Colonialism? A Reflection." *African and Asian Studies* 10(2–3) (January): 234–266.
Lund, Christian. 2016. "Rule and Rupture: State Formation Through the Production of Property and Citizenship." *Development and Change* 47(6) (November): 1199–1228.
Lund, Crick. 2018. "Why Africa Needs to Start Focusing on the Neglected Issue of Mental Health." The Conversation, February 8. http://theconversation.com/why-africa-needs-to-start-focusing-on-the-neglected-issue-of-mental-health-91406.
Lungu, Gatian F. 1986. "The Church, Labour and the Press in Zambia: The Role of Critical Observers in a One-Party State." *African Affairs* 85(340) (July): 385–410.
Lyons, Terrence. 2019. *The Puzzle of Ethiopian Politics*. Boulder: Lynne Rienner.
Lyons, Terrence, and Ahmed I. Samatar. 1995. *Somalia: State Collapse, Multilateral Intervention, and Strategies for Political Reconstruction*. Washington, DC: Brookings Institution.
Maathai, Wangari. 2003. *The Greenbelt Movement: Sharing the Approach and the Experience*. Herndon: Lantern Books.
———. 2006. *Unbowed: A Memoir*. New York: Anchor Books.
MacEachern, Scott. 2018. *Searching for Boko Haram: A History of Violence in Central Africa*. New York: Oxford University Press.
MacFarquhar, Neil. 2011. "Mali Tackles Al Qaeda and Drug Traffic." *New York Times*, January 1.
MacGaffey, Janet. 1988. "Economic Disengagement and Class Formation in Zaire." In Donald Rothchild and Naomi Chazan (eds.), *The Precarious Balance: State and Society in Africa*. Boulder: Westview Press, 171–188.
———. 1991. *The Real Economy of Zaire: The Contribution of Smuggling and Other Unofficial Activities to National Wealth*. Philadelphia: University of Pennsylvania Press.
Macharia, Kinuthia. 1992. "Slum Clearance and the Informal Economy in Nairobi." *Journal of Modern African Studies* 30(2) (June): 221–236.
———. 2007. "Tensions Created by the Formal and Informal Use of Urban Space: The Case of Nairobi, Kenya." *Journal of Global South Studies* 24(2) (September): 145–162.
MacQueen, Norman. 1985. "Portugal and Africa: The Politics of Re-Engagement." *Journal of Modern African Studies* 23(1) (March): 31–51.
MacQueen, Norrie. 1997. *The Decolonization of Portuguese Africa: Metropolitan Revolution and the Dissolution of Empire*. London: Longman.
Maes, Kenneth. 2014. "'Volunteers Are Not Paid Because They Are Priceless': Community Health Worker Capacities and Values in an AIDS Treatment Intervention in Urban Ethiopia." *Medical Anthropology Quarterly* 29(1) (March): 97–111.

Magnusson, Bruce A. 2005. "Democratic Legitimacy in Benin: Institutions and Identity in Regional Context." In Leonardo A. Villalón and Peter VonDoepp (eds.), *The Fate of Africa's Democratic Experiments: Elites and Institutions*. Bloomington: Indiana University Press, 75–95.

Mahmud El Zain. 1996. "Tribe and Religion in the Sudan." *Review of African Political Economy* 23(70): 523–529.

Mail and Guardian. 2009. "Scores Killed as Militants and Nigeria Security Forces Clash." December 30. https://mg.co.za/article/2009-12-30-scores-killed-as-militants-and-nigeria-security-forces-clash.

———. 2010. "Somali Radio Stations Bow to Islamist Ban on Music." April 14. https://mg.co.za/article/2010-04-14-somali-radio-stations-bow-to-islamist-ban-on-music/.

Makofane, Keletso, Charles Gueboguo, Daniel Lyons, and Theo Sandfort. 2013. "Men Who Have Sex with Men Inadequately Addressed in African Aids National Strategic Plans." *Global Public Health* 8(2): 129–143.

Makofane, Keletso, Bruno Spire, and Phumi Mtetwa. 2018. "Tackling Global Health Inequities in the HIV Response." *Lancet* 392(10144) (July): 263–264.

Mama, Amina. 1995. "Feminism or Femocracy? State Feminism and Democratisation in Nigeria." *Africa Development/Afrique et Développement* 20(1): 37–58.

———. 1998. "Khaki in the Family: Gender Discourses and Militarism in Nigeria." *African Studies Review* 41(2) (September): 1–18.

———. 2011. "What Does It Mean to Do Feminist Research in African Contexts?" *Feminist Review Conference Proceedings*, e4–e20. https://nigs.paginas.ufsc.br/files/2017/08/fr201122a-AMINA-MAMA-Feminist-Research-in-Africa.pdf.

Mamdani, Mahmood. 1996. *Citizen and Subject: Contemporary Africa and the Legacy of Late Colonialism*. Princeton: Princeton University Press.

Mamo, Nemera, Sambit Bhattacharyya, and Alexander Moradi. 2019. "Intensive and Extensive Margins of Mining and Development: Evidence from Sub-Saharan Africa." *Journal of Development Economics* 139 (June): 28–49.

Mandela, Nelson. 1995. *Long Walk to Freedom: The Autobiography of Nelson Mandela*. Boston: Little, Brown.

Mangala, Jack (ed.). 2017. *Africa and Its Global Diaspora: The Policy and Politics of Emigration*. New York: Palgrave Macmillan.

Manning, Patrick. 1990. *Slavery and African Life*. Cambridge: Cambridge University Press.

Marchal, Roland. 2006. "Resilience of a City at War: Territoriality, Civil Order and Economic Exchange in Mogadishu." In Deborah F. Bryceson and Deborah Potts (eds.), *African Urban Economies*. London: Palgrave Macmillan, 207–229.

Marcus, Michael A. 1985. "'The Saint Has Been Stolen': Sanctity and Social Change in a Tribe of Eastern Morocco." *American Ethnologist* 12(3) (August): 455–467.

Mark, Monica. 2012. "Nigeria: 'Sharia or Nothing.'" *Mail and Guardian*, February 3. https://mg.co.za/article/2012-02-03-nigeria-sharia-or-nothing.

Mark, Peter, and José da Silva Horta. 2013. *The Forgotten Diaspora: Jewish Communities in West Africa and the Making of the Atlantic World*. Cambridge: Cambridge University Press.

Markovitz, Irving L. 1969. *Léopold Sédar Senghor and the Politics of Negritude*. New York: Atheneum.

———. 1970. "Bureaucratic Development and Economic Growth," *Journal of Modern African Studies* 14(2) (June): 183–200.

Marlowe, Frank W. 2005. "Hunter-Gatherers and Human Evolution." *Evolutionary Anthropology: Issues, News, and Reviews* 14(2) (April): 54–67.

———. 2010. *The Hadza: Hunter-Gatherers of Tanzania*. Berkeley: University of California Press.

Marr, Ana, Anne Winkel, Marcel van Asseldonk, Robert Lensink, and Erwin Bulte. 2016. "Adoption and Impact of Index-Insurance and Credit for Smallholder Farmers in Developing Countries: A Systematic Review." *Agricultural Finance Review* 76(1) (May): 94–118.

Marshall, John. 2009. *The John Marshall Ju/'hoan Bushman Film and Video Collection 1950–2000*. Washington: Smithsonian Human Studies Film Archives.

Marshall, Monty G., Ted R. Gurr, and Keith Jaggers, 2019. "Polity IV Project: Political Regime Characteristics and Transitions, 1800–2018 (dataset)." Vienna: Center for Systemic Peace. http://www.systemicpeace.org/inscrdata.html.

Martey, Emmanuel. 2009. *African Theology: Inculturation and Liberation*. Eugene: Wipf and Stock.
Martin, Guy. 1993. "Preface: Democratic Transitions in Africa." *Issue: A Quarterly Journal of Opinion* 21(1/2): 6–7.
Masina, Lameck. 2019. "Malawi Rolls Out Africa's First Malaria Vaccine for Children." *VOA News*, April 25. https://www.voanews.com/science-health/malawi-rolls-out-africas-first-malaria-vaccine-children.
Massad, Joseph. 2002. "Re-Orienting Desire: The Gay International and the Arab World." *Public Culture* 14(2) (Spring): 361–385.
Maswikwa, Belinda, Linda Richter, Jay Kaufman, and Arijit Nandi. 2015. "Minimum Marriage Age Laws and the Prevalence of Child Marriage and Adolescent Birth: Evidence from Sub-Saharan Africa." *International Perspectives on Sexual and Reproductive Health* 41(2) (June): 58–68.
Matebeni, Zethu. 2014. "How NOT to Write About Queer South Africa." In Zethu Matebeni (curator), *Reclaiming Afrikan: Queer Perspectives on Sexual and Gender Identities*. Johannesburg: Modjaji, 61–64.
———. 2016. "Contesting Beauty: Black Lesbians on the Stage." *Feminist Africa* 21: 23–36.
———. 2019. "Queer Theory, African." In Howard Chiang (ed.), *Global Encyclopedia of Lesbian, Gay, Bisexual, Transgender, and Queer History*. New York: Charles Scribner's Sons, 1333–1339.
Matebeni, Zethu, Surya Monro, and Vasu Reddy (eds.). 2018. Queer in Africa: LGBTQI Identities, Citizenship, and Activism. New York: Routledge.
Matebeni, Zethu, Vasu Reddy, Theo Sandfort, and Ian Southey-Swartz. 2013. "'I Thought We Are Safe': Southern African Lesbians' Experiences of Living with HIV." *Culture Health and Sexuality* 15(Supp. 1) (April): 34–37.
Mathews, K. 1988. "The African Group at the UN as an Instrument of African Diplomacy." *Nigerian Journal of International Affairs* 14(1): 226–258.
Mathisen, Harald, and Lars Svåsand. 2002. *Funding Political Parties in Emerging African Democracies: What Role for Norway?* Bergen: Chr. Michelsen Institute.
Matusevich, Maxim. 2007. *Africa in Russia, Russia in Africa: Three Centuries of Encounters*. Trenton: Africa World Press.
Maykuth, Andrew. 2000. "Signs of Massacre Went Unheeded." *Christian Science Monitor*, April 2.
Mazrui, Ali A. 1986. *The Africans: A Triple Heritage*. London: BBC Publications.
Mazrui, Ali A., and Michael Tidy. 1984. *Nationalism and New States in Africa from About 1935 to the Present*. London: Heinemann.
Mbali, Mandisa. 2013. *South African AIDS Activism and Global Health Politics*. New York: Palgrave Macmillan.
Mbaye, Aminata Cécile. 2018. *Les discours sur l'homosexualité au Sénégal. Analyse d'une lutte représentationnelle*. München: AVM Edition.
Mbiti, Isaac, and David N. Weil. 2015. "Mobile Banking: The Impact of M-Pesa in Kenya." In Sebastian Edwards, Simon Johnson, and David N. Weil (eds.), *African Successes*, Vol. 3: *Modernization and Development*. Chicago: University of Chicago Press, 247–293.
Mbiti, John S. 1969. *African Religions and Philosophy*. New York: Praeger.
———. 1970. *African Concepts of God*. New York: Praeger.
———. 2015 [1975]. *Introduction to African Religion*. Long Grove, IL: Waveland Press.
McCann, James C. 2009. *Stirring the Pot: A History of African Cuisine*. Athens: University of Ohio Press.
McCauley, John F., and E. Gyimah-Boadi. 2009. "Religious Faith and Democracy: Evidence from the Afrobarometer Surveys." Afrobarometer Working Paper. September. https://afrobarometer.org/publications/wp113-religious-faith-and-democracy-evidence-afrobarometer-surveys.
McCloskey, Brian, Osman Dar, Alimuddin Zumla, and David L Heymann. 2014. "Emerging Infectious Diseases and Pandemic Potential: Status Quo and Reducing Risk of Global Spread." *Lancet Infectious Diseases* 14(10) (October): 1001–1010.
McFarland, Sherri. 2010. "Africa in Retrospect: Russia, Iran and Chinese Arms Supplies to Sudan." *African and Asian Studies* 9(4) (January): 462–480.
McGowan, Patrick J. 2003. "African Military Coups d'État, 1956–2001: Frequency, Trends and Distribution." *Journal of Modern African Studies* 41(3) (September): 339–370.

McGowan, Patrick J., and Thomas H. Johnson. 1984. "African Military Coups d'État and Under-Development: A Quantitative Historical Analysis." *Journal of Modern African Studies* 22(4) (December): 633–666.

———. 1986. "Sixty Coups in Thirty Years: Further Evidence Regarding African Military Coups d'État." *Journal of Modern African Studies* 24(3) (September): 539–546.

McIntosh, Janet. 2015. "Autochthony and 'Family': The Politics of Kinship in White Kenyan Bids to Belong." *Anthropological Quarterly* 88(2) (Spring): 251–280.

McIntosh, Marjorie K. 2009. *Yoruba Women, Work, and Social Change*. Bloomington: Indiana University Press.

McIntosh, Roderick. 2005. *Middle Niger: Urbanism and Self-Organized Landscapes*. Cambridge: Cambridge University Press.

McKinnon, Susan. 2000. "Domestic Exceptions: Evans-Pritchard and the Creation of Nuer Patrilineality and Equality." *Cultural Anthropology* 15(1) (February): 35–83.

McMichael, Anthony. 2013. "Globalization, Climate Change and Human Health." *New England Journal of Medicine* 368(14) (April): 1335–1343.

McNaughton, Patrick. 1988. *The Mande Blacksmiths: Knowledge, Power, and Art in West Africa*. Bloomington: Indiana University Press.

McVeigh, Malcolm J. 1974. *God in Africa: Conceptions of God in African Traditional Religion and Christianity*. Cape Cod: Claude Stark.

Mecham, Quinn. 2019. "Islamist Parties and Foreign Policy in North Africa: Bridging Ideology and Pragmatism." *Journal of North African Studies* 24(4) (July): 640–660.

Médard, Jean-François. 1992. "Le 'Big Man' en Afrique: Esquisse d'analyse du politicien entrepreneur." *L'Année Sociologique* 42: 35–84.

Medie, Peace. 2013. "Fighting Gender-based Violence: The Women's Movement and the Enforcement of Rape Law in Liberia." *African Affairs* 112(448): 377–397.

Meintjes, Sheila, Anu Pillay, and Meredith Turshen (eds.). 2001. *The Aftermath: Women in Post-Conflict Transformations*. London: Zed Books.

Meirs, Suzanne, and Igor Kopytoff (eds.). 1977. *Slavery in Africa*. Madison: University of Wisconsin Press.

Melliti, Hjaled. 2016. *Carthage: Histoire d'une metropole mediterraneenne*. Paris: Perrin.

Mentan, Tatah. 2004. *Dilemmas of Weak States: Africa and Transnational Terrorism in the Twenty-First Century*. Burlington: Ashgate.

———. 2018. *Africa in the Colonial Ages of Empire: Slavery, Capitalism, Racism, Colonialism, Decolonization, Independence as Recolonization*. Mankon: Langaa Research.

Meredith, Martin. 2005. *The Fate of Africa: A History of Fifty Years of Independence*. New York: PublicAffairs.

Merelli, Annalisa. 2020. "For Most of the World, Social Distancing Is an Unimaginable Luxury." *Quartz*, March 27. https://qz.com/1822556/for-most-of-the-world-social-distancing-is-an-unimaginable-luxury/.

Mesa-Lago, Carmelo, and June S. Beikin (eds.). 1982. *Cuba in Africa*. Pittsburgh: University of Pittsburgh Center for Latin American Studies.

Meyer, Birgit. 2004. "Christianity in Africa: From African Independent to Pentecostal-Charismatic Churches." *Annual Review of Anthropology* 33 (October): 447–474.

Mikell, Gwendolyn. 1997. "Introduction." In Gwendolyn Mikell (ed.), *African Feminism: The Politics of Survival in Sub-Saharan Africa*. Philadelphia: University of Pennsylvania Press, 1–50.

Miles, William. 2007. *Political Islam in West Africa: State-Society Relations Transformed*. Boulder: Lynne Rienner.

Miller, Joseph C. 1975. "Nzinga of Matamba in a New Perspective." *Journal of African History* 16(2): 201–216.

Minor (Peters), Melissa. 2014. "Kuchus in the Balance: Queer Lives Under Uganda's Anti-Homosexuality Bill." PhD diss., Northwestern University.

Minter, William. 1986. *King Solomon's Mines Revisited: Western Interests and the Burdened History of Southern Africa*. New York: Basic Books.

Misunas, Christina, Colleen Murray Gastón, and Claudia Cappa. 2019. "Child Marriage Among Boys in High-Prevalence Countries: An Analysis of Sexual and Reproductive Health Outcomes." *BMC International Health and Human Rights* 19(25) (April).

Mitchell, J. Clyde. 1956. *The Kalela Dance: Aspects of Social Relationships Among Urban Africans in Northern Rhodesia.* Manchester: Rhodes-Livingstone Institute.
Mkandawire, Thandika, and Adebayo Olukoshi (eds.). 1995. *Between Liberalisation and Oppression: The Politics of Structural Adjustment in Africa.* Dakar: Council for the Development of Social Science Research in Africa (CODESRIA).
MkNelly, Barbara, and Michael Kevane. 2002. "Improving Design and Performance of Group Lending: Suggestions from Burkina Faso." *World Development* 30(11) (November): 2017–2032.
Mohamoud, Abdullah A. 2006. *African Diaspora and Post-Conflict Reconstruction in Africa.* DIIS Brief. Copenhagen: Danish Institute for International Studies.
Molini, Vasco, and Pierella Paci. 2015. "Poverty Reduction in Ghana—Progress and Challenges" World Bank Report. http://documents.worldbank.org/curated/en/492511467998463046/Poverty-reduction-in-Ghana-progress-and-challenges.
Molutsi, Patrick P., and John D. Holm. 1990. "Developing Democracy When Civil Society Is Weak: The Case of Botswana." *African Affairs* 89(356) (July): 323–340.
Monga, Célestin, and Justin Yifu Lin. 2015. "Africa's Evolving Economic Policy Frameworks." In C. Monga and J. Y. Lin (eds.), *The Oxford Handbook of Africa and Economics.* Oxford: Oxford University Press, 1–22.
Monroe, J. Cameron. 2013. "Power and Agency in Precolonial African States." *Annual Review of Anthropology* 42 (October): 17–35.
Montana, Ismael Musah. 2004. "Aḥmad ibn al-Qāḍī al-Timbukāḍwī on the Bori Ceremonies of Tunis." In P. Lovejoy (ed.), *Slavery on the Frontiers of Islam.* Princeton: Markus Weiner, 173–198.
Monteiro, Nicole. 2015. "Addressing Mental Illness in Africa: Global Health Challenges and Local Opportunities." *Community Psychology in Global Perspective* 1(2) (October): 78–95.
Moon, Suerie, Jennifer Leigh, Liana Woskie, Francesco Checchi, Victor Dzau, Mosoka Fallah, Gabrielle Fitzgerald, et al. 2017. "Post-Ebola Reforms: Ample Analysis, Inadequate Action." *BMJ* 356(j280) (January).
Moore, Donald. 1993. "Contesting Terrain in Zimbabwe's Eastern Highlands: Political Ecology, Ethnography, and Peasant Resource Struggles." *Economic Geography* 69(4): 380–401.
Moore, Henrietta L., and Todd Sanders (eds.). 2001. *Magical Interpretations, Material Realities: Modernity, Witchcraft and the Occult in Postcolonial Africa.* London: Routledge.
Moore, Henrietta, and Megan Vaughan. 1994. *Cutting Down Trees: Gender, Nutrition and Agricultural Change in the Northern Province of Zambia, 1890–1990.* Portsmouth: Heinemann.
Morfit, Simon. 2011. "AIDS Is Money: How Donor Preferences Reconfigure Local Realities." *World Development* 39(1) (January): 64–76.
Morikawa, Jun. 1997. *Japan and Africa: Big Business and Diplomacy.* Trenton: Africa World Press.
———. 2005. "Japan and Africa After the Cold War." *African and Asian Studies* 4(4) (January): 485–508.
Moritz, Mark. 2008. "A Critical Examination of Honor Cultures and Herding Societies in Africa." *African Studies Review* 51(2) (September): 99–117.
Morna, Colleen Lowe. 1995. "Southern Africa: New Era of Cooperation." *Africa Report* 40(3) (May–June): 64–67.
Morrison, Donald G., Robert C. Mitchell, and John N. Paden. 1989. *Understanding Black Africa.* New York: Irvington.
Moseley, William G., Matthew A. Schnurr, and Rachel Bezner-Kerr (eds.). 2017. *Africa's Green Revolution: Critical Perspectives on New Agricultural Technologies and Systems.* New York: Routledge.
Mosier, Dan L., Donald A. Singer, Barry C. Moring, and John P. Galloway. 2012. "Podiform Chromite Deposits Database and Grade and Tonnage Models." *US Geological Survey Scientific Investigations Report, 5157.* https://pubs.usgs.gov/sir/2012/5157/sir2012-5157_text.pdf.
Moss, Todd. 2011. *African Development: Making Sense of the Issues and Actors.* 2nd ed. Boulder: Lynne Rienner.
Mostyn, Trevor. 1988. *The Cambridge Encyclopedia of the Middle East and North Africa.* New York: Cambridge University Press.
Moyo, Ambrose. 1987. "Religion and Politics in Zimbabwe." In Kirsten Holst Peterson (ed.), *Religion, Development and African Identity.* Uppsala: Scandinavian Institute of African Studies, 59–72.

Mpungose, Luanda, and Lennon Monyae. 2018. "Carrying Forward the Momentum of the 2017 African Union Year of Youth." Policy Insights. Johannesburg: Southern African Institute of International Affairs. https://saiia.org.za/research/year-of-youth-carrying-forward-the-momentum/.

Mueller, Lisa. 2018. *Political Protest in Contemporary Africa*. Cambridge: Cambridge University Press.

Muller, Jean-Claude. 1980. "On the Relevance of Having Two Husbands: Contribution to the Study of Polygynous/Polyandrous Marital Forms of the Jos Plateau." *Journal of Comparative Family Studies* 11(3) (Summer): 359–369.

Munslow, Barry. 1983. "Why Has the Westminster Model Failed in Africa?" *Parliamentary Affairs* 36(2) (April): 218–228.

Munyegera, Ggombe Kasim, and Tomoya Matsumoto. 2016. "Mobile Money, Remittances, and Household Welfare: Panel Evidence from Rural Uganda." *World Development* 79 (March): 127–137.

Muraya, Joseph. 2020. "Leaders Call for the End to Police Brutality in Enforcing Night Curfew." *Capital News*, March 28. https://www.capitalfm.co.ke/news/2020/03/leaders-call-for-an-end-to-police-brutality-in-enforcing-night-curfew/.

Murithi, Tim. 2007. "The Responsibility to Protect, as Enshrined in Article 4 of the Constitutive Act of the African Union." *African Security Review* 16(3) (September): 14–24.

Murray, Stephen O., and Will Roscoe (eds). 1998. *Boy-Wives and Female Husbands: Studies in African Homosexualities*. New York: St. Martin's Press.

Mususa, Patience. 2012. "Mining, Welfare and Urbanization: The Wavering Urban Character of Zambia's Copperbelt." *Journal of Contemporary African Studies* 30(4) (October): 571–587.

Myambo, Melissa Tandiwe. 2017. "Africa's Global City? The Hipsterification of Johannesburg." *New Left Review* 108 (November/December): 75–86.

Myers, Garth A. 2003. *Verandahs of Power: Colonialism and Space in Urban Africa*. Syracuse: Syracuse University Press.

———. 2005. *Disposable Cities: Garbage, Governance, and Sustainable Development in Urban Africa*. Aldershot: Ashgate.

———. 2009. "Africa." In R. Kitchin and N. Thrift (eds.), *International Encyclopedia of Human Geography*. Oxford: Elsevier, 25–30.

———. 2011. *African Cities: Alternative Visions of Urban Theory and Practice*. London: Zed.

———. 2016. *Urban Environments in Africa: A Critical Analysis of Environmental Politics*. Bristol: Policy Press.

Nakimuli-Mpungu, E., J. K. Bass, P. Alexandre, E. J. Mills, S. Musisi, M. Ram, E. Katabira, and J. B. Nachega. 2012. "Depression, Alcohol Use and Adherence to Antiretroviral Therapy in Sub-Saharan Africa: A Systematic Review." *AIDS Behavior* 16(8) (November): 2101–2118.

Nannyonga-Tamusuza, Sylvia. 2002. "Gender, Ethnicity and Politics in Kadongo-kamu Music of Uganda: Analysing the Song Kayanda." In Mai Palmberg and Annemette Kirkegaard (eds.), *Playing with Identities in Contemporary Music in Africa*. Uppsala: Nordiska Afrikainstitutet, 134–148.

———. 2009. "Female-Men, Male-Women, and Others: Constructing and Negotiating Gender Among the Baganda of Uganda." *Journal of Eastern African Studies* 3(2): 367–380.

Nascimbene, Bruno, and Alessia Di Pascale. 2011. "The 'Arab Spring' and the Extraordinary Influx of People Who Arrived in Italy from North Africa." *European Journal of Migration and Law* 13(4) (January): 341–360.

Nash, Denis, Marcel Yotebieng, and Annette Sohn. 2018. "Treating All People Living with HIV in Sub-Saharan Africa: A New Era Calling for New Approaches." *Journal of Virus Eradication* 4(Suppl. 2) (November): 1–4.

Naylor, Phillip C. 1987. "Spain and France and the Decolonization of Western Sahara: Parity and Paradox, 1975–87." *Africa Today* 34(3): 7–16.

Naylor, Phillip C. 2015. *Historical Dictionary of Algeria*. New York: Rowman and Littlefield.

Ndashe, Sibongile. 2011. "Seeking the Protection of LGBTI Rights at the African Commission of Human and Peoples' Rights." *Feminist Africa* 15: 17–38.

———. 2019. "African Commission on Human and Peoples' Rights." In Howard Chiang (ed.), *Global Encyclopedia of Lesbian, Gay, Bisexual, Transgender, and Queer History*. New York: Charles Scribner's Sons, 35–37.

Ndulo, Muna. 2018. "Constitutions: The Politics of Constitutional Reform." In Nic Cheeseman (ed.), *Institutions and Democracy in Africa: How the Rules of the Game Shape Political Developments*. New York: Cambridge University Press, 117–136.
Ndzovu, Hassan J. 2014. *Muslims in Kenyan Politics: Political Involvement, Marginalization, and Minority Status*. Evanston: Northwestern University Press.
Needham, Rodney. 1973. "Right and Left in Nyoro: Symbolic Classification." In Rodney Needham (ed.), *Right and Left: Essays on Dual Symbolic Classification*. Chicago: University of Chicago Press, 299–341.
Negash, Tekeste, Massimo Papa, and Irma Taddia. 2003. "The Horn of Africa, Italy, and After." *Northeast African Studies* 10(3): 13–17.
Negi, Rohit. 2013. "'You Cannot Make a Camel Drink Water': Capital, Geo-History and Contestations in the Zambian Copperbelt." *Geoforum* 45 (March): 240–247.
———. 2014. "'Solwezi Mabanga': Ambivalent Developments on Zambia's New Mining Frontier." *Journal of Southern African Studies* 40(5) (August): 999–1013.
Nester, William R. 1992. *Japan and the Third World: Patterns, Power, Prospects*. New York: St. Martin's Press.
Neuberger, Benyamin. 1986. *National Self-Determination in Postcolonial Africa*. Boulder: Lynne Rienner.
Neumann, Roderick. 1998. *Imposing Wilderness*. Berkeley: University of California Press.
Newell, Stephanie. 2006. *The Forger's Tale: The Search for Odeziaku*. Athens: Ohio University Press.
Newman, Carol, and John Page. 2017. "Industrial Clusters: The Case for Special Economic Zones in Africa." Working Paper Series 015. Helsinki: World Institute for Development Economic Research.
Nhamirre, Joaquin, and Michelle Gumede. 2019. "After Cyclone Ruin, Back to Square One for Mozambique's Beira." Phys.org, April 9. https://phys.org/news/2019-04-cyclone-square-mozambique-beira.html.
Niang, Ibudin, and Oliver Ruppel. 2014. "Africa." In Christopher B. Field, Vincente R. Barros, et al. (eds.), *Climate Change 2014: Impacts, Adaptation, and Vulnerability, Part B: Regional Aspects: Contribution of Working Group II to the Fifth Assessment Report of the Intergovernmental Panel on Climate Change*. Cambridge: Cambridge University Press, 1199–1265.
Njeru, J., I. Johnston-Anumonwo, and S. Owuor. 2014. "Gender Equity and Commercialization of Public Toilet Services in Nairobi, Kenya." In A. Oberhauser and I. Johnston-Anumonwo (eds.), *Global Perspectives on Gender and Space*. New York: Routledge, 17–34.
Njoh, Ambe. 2006. *Planning Power: Town Planning and Social Control in Colonial Africa*. London: University College of London Press.
———. 2009. "Urban Planning as a Tool of Power and Social Control in Colonial Africa." *Planning Perspectives* 24(3) (June): 301–317.
———. 2013. "Modernist Urban Planning as a Tool of Acculturation: Implications for Sustainable Human Settlement Development in Cameroon." *City, Culture and Society* 4(2) (June): 111–120.
Nkabinde, Nkunzi Zandile. 2008. *Black Bull, Ancestors and Me: My Life as a Lesbian Sangoma*. Auckland Park: Fanele.
Nkechi, Ofor Theresa, Alagba Ochuko Samuel, and Meshack Shedrack Ifurueze. 2018. "Housing Finance Market and Economic Growth of West Africa Region: A Study of Nigeria, Ghana and Gambia." *Business and Management Review* 9(3) (April): 188–198.
Nkrumah, Kwame. 1957. *Ghana: The Autobiography of Kwame Nkrumah*. London: Thomas Nelson and Sons.
———. 1965. *Neo-Colonialism: The Last Stage of Imperialism*. New York: International Publishers.
Nobel Peace Prize Committee. 2015. https://www.nobelprize.org/prizes/peace/2015/press-release/.
Noman, Akbar, and Joseph E. Stiglitz. 2015. *Industrial Policy and Economic Transformation in Africa*. New York: Columbia University Press.
Nonvignon, Justice, Genevieve Cecilia Aryeetey, Keziah Malm, Samuel Agyei Agyemang, Vivian Aubyn, Nana Yaw Peprah, Constance Bart-Plange, and Moses Aikins. 2016. "Economic Burden of Malaria on Businesses in Ghana: A Case for Private Sector Investment in Malaria Control." *Malaria Journal* 15(454) (September): 1–10.

Nordling, Linda. 2020. "'A Ticking Time Bomb': Scientists Worry About Coronavirus Spread in Africa." *Science*, March 15. https://www.sciencemag.org/news/2020/03/ticking-time-bomb-scientists-worry-about-coronavirus-spread-africa#.
Nossiter, Adam. 2010a. "Killings in Nigeria Are Linked to Islamic Sect." *New York Times*, October 18.
———. 2010b. "Nigerians Recount Night of Their Bloody Revenge." *New York Times*, March 10.
Nowell, Charles E. 1947. "Portugal and the Partition of Africa." *Journal of Modern History* 19(1) (March): 1–17.
Ntewusu, Samuel Aniegye, and Edward Nanbigne. 2015. "So be nya dagna? ('Is someone Injured?'): The Evolution and Use of Tricycles in Tamale, Northern Ghana." In Akinyinka Akinyoade and Jan-Bart Gewald (eds.), *African Roads to Prosperity: People en Route to Socio-Cultural and Economic Transformations*. Leiden: Brill, 197–211.
Nunes, João. 2016. "Ebola and the Production of Neglect in Global Health." *Third World Quarterly* 37(3) (November): 542–556.
Nunn, Nathan, and Leonard Wantchekon. 2011. "The Slave Trade and the Origins of Mistrust in Africa." *American Economic Review* 101(7) (December): 3221–3252.
Nuwer, R. 2018. "Zimbabwe Is Pioneering a Groundbreaking Mental Health Programme with Stunning Results—and the Rest of the World Is Taking Note." BBC News, October 16. http://www.bbc.com/future/story/20181015-how-one-bench-and-a-team-of-grandmothers-can-beat-depression.
Nyambura, Catherine. 2018. "Repoliticising Women's Rights in Development: Young African Feminisms at the Cutting Edge." *Gender and Development* 26(3) (November): 423–437.
Nyanzi, S. 2013. "Dismantling Reified African Culture Through Localized Homosexualities in Uganda." *Culture, Health and Sexuality* 15(8) (June): 952–967.
———. 2014. "Queering Queer Africa." In Zethu Matebeni (curator), *Reclaiming Afrikan: Queer Perspectives on Sexual and Gender Identities*. Johannesburg: Modjaji, 65–70.
Nyeck, S. N. 2014. "Stretching the Margins and Trading Taboos: A Paradoxical Approach to Sexual Rights Advocacy in Africa." In Sonia Corrêa, Rafael de la Dehesa, and Richard Parker (eds.), *Sexuality and Politics: Regional Dialogue from the Global South*. Rio de Janeiro: Sexuality Policy Watch, 63–95.
———. 2019. "Neoliberalism in Africa." In Howard Chiang (ed.), *Global Encyclopedia of Gay, Lesbian, Bisexual, Transgender, and Queer History*. New York: Charles Scribner's Sons, 1132–1137.
Nyerere, Julius K. 1968. *Freedom and Socialism: Uhuru Na Ujamaa*. New York: Oxford University Press.
Nyong'o, Peter Anyang'. 1992. "Africa: The Failure of One-Party Rule." *Journal of Democracy* 3(1) (January): 7–35.
Nzouankeu, Jacques Mariel. 1993. "The Role of the National Conference in the Transition to Democracy in Africa: The Case of Benin and Mali." *Issue: A Quarterly Journal of Opinion* 21(1/2): 44–50.
O'Barr, Jean. 1975. "Making the Visible Invisible: African Women in Politics and Policy." *African Studies Review* 18(3) (December): 19–27.
Obe, Ayo. 2019. "Nigeria's Emerging Two-Party System?" *Journal of Democracy* 30(3) (July): 109–123.
O'Donnell, Guillermo, Phillippe Schmitter, and Laurence Whitehead (eds.). 1986. *Transitions from Authoritarian Rule*. Baltimore: John Hopkins University Press.
O'Fahey, R. S. 1993. "Islamic Hegemonies in the Sudan: Sufism, Mahdism, and Islamism." In Louis Brenner (ed.), *Muslim Identity and Social Change in Sub-Saharan Africa*. Bloomington: Indiana University Press, 21–35.
O'Keefe, Michael. 2012. "Lessons from the Rise and Fall of the Military AIDS Hypothesis: Politics, Evidence and Persuasion." *Contemporary Politics* 18(2) (June): 239–253.
Oloya, Opiyo. 2013. *Child to Soldier: Stories from Joseph Kony's Lord's Resistance Army*. Toronto: University of Toronto Press.
O'Malley, Jeffrey, and Andreas Holzinger. 2018. *Sexual and Gender Minorities and the Sustainable Development Goals*. New York: United Nations Development Programme.
O'Rourke, Harmony. 2017. *Hadija's Story: Diaspora, Gender, and Belonging in the Cameroon Grassfields*. Bloomington: Indiana University Press.

O'Toole, Thomas. 1984. "The 1929–1931 Gbaya Insurrection in Ubangui-Shari: Messianic Movement or Village Self Defense?" *Canadian Journal of African Studies* 18(7) (March): 329–344.
———. 1986. *The Central African Republic: The Continent's Hidden Heart.* Boulder: Westview Press.
Obama, Barack. 1995. *Dreams of My Father: A Story of Race and Inheritance.* New York: Times Books.
———. 2006. *The Audacity of Hope: Thoughts on Reclaiming the American Dream.* New York: Three Rivers Press.
Obeng-Odoom, Franklin. 2010. "An Urban Twist to Politics in Ghana." *Habitat International* 34(4) (October): 392–399.
———. 2014. *Oiling the Urban Economy: Land, Labour, Capital, and the State in Sekondi-Takoradi, Ghana.* Condon: Routledge.
Ocheje, Paul D. 2007. "'In the Public Interest': Forced Evictions, Land Rights and Human Development in Africa." *Journal of African Law* 51(2) (October): 173–214.
Odbert, C., and J. Mulligan. 2015. "The Kibera Public Space Project: Participation, Integration, and Networked Change." In J. Hou, B. Spencer, T. Way, and K. Yocom (eds.), *Now Urbanism: The Future City Is Here.* New York: Routledge, 177–192.
Oded, Arye. 2010. "Africa in Israeli Foreign Policy—Expectations and Disenchantment: Historical and Diplomatic Aspects." *Israel Studies* 15(3) (Fall): 121–142.
Odey, Emmanuel Alepu, Bodjui Olivier Abo, Zifu Li, Xiaoqin Zhou, and Abdulmoseen Segun Giwa. 2018. "Influence of Climate and Environmental Change in Nigeria: A Review on Vulnerability and Adaptation to Climate Change." *Reviews on Environmental Health* 33(4) (December): 441–447.
Oduyoye, Mercy. 1986. *Hearing and Knowing: Theological Reflections on Christianity in Africa.* Maryknoll: Orbis.
———. 2009. *Hearing and Knowing: Theological Reflections on Christianity in Africa.* Eugene: Wipf and Stock.
OECD (Organization for Economic Cooperation and Development). 2018. "GeoBook: Geographic Flows to Developing Countries (dataset)." https://stats.oecd.org/Index.aspx?DataSetCode=DACGEO.
Ofori, Ruby. 1993. "Ghana: The Elections Controversy." *Africa Report* 38(4): 33–35.
Ogbuoji, Osondu, Ipchita Bharali, Natalie Emery, and Kaci Kenney McDade. 2019. "Closing Africa's Health Financing Gap." Brookings Institution blog, March 1. https://www.brookings.edu/blog/future-development/2019/03/01/closing-africas-health-financing-gap.
Ohlson, Thomas, and Stephen John Stedman, with Robert Davies. 1994. *The New Is Not Yet Born: Conflict Resolution in Southern Africa.* Washington, DC: Brookings Institution.
Ojo, Olatunde. 1985. "Regional Co-Operation and Integration." In Olatunde J. C. B. Ojo, D. K. Orwa, and C. M. B. Utete (eds.), *African International Relations.* London: Longman, 142–183.
Okaka, F. O., and B. D. O. Odhiambo. 2018. "Urban Residents' Awareness of Climate Change and Their Autonomous Adaptive Behavior and Mitigation Measures in the Coastal City of Mombasa, Kenya." *South African Geographical Journal* 100(3) (March): 378–393.
Olupona, Jacob K., and Sulayman S. Nyang (eds.). 2013. *Religious Plurality in Africa: Essays in Honour of John S. Mbiti.* Berlin: Walter de Gruyter.
Olusanya, G. O. 1988. "Reflections on the First Twenty-Five Years of the Organization of African Unity." *Nigerian Journal of International Affairs* 14(1): 67–72.
Omer-Cooper, J. B. 1994. *History of Southern Africa.* 2nd ed. Portsmouth: Heinemann.
Onarheim, Kristine, Johanne Iversen, and David Bloom. 2016. "Economic Benefits of Investing in Women's Health: A Systematic Review." *PLoS ONE* 11(3): e0150120.
Onwuka, Ralph I., and Amadu Sesay (eds.). 1985. *The Future of Regionalism in Africa.* New York: St. Martin's Press.
Oostuizen, Gabriel H. 2006. *The Southern African Development Community: The Organisation, Its Policies and Prospects.* Midrand: Institute for Global Dialogue.
Osafo, Joseph. 2016. "Seeking Paths for Collaboration Between Religious Leaders and Mental Health Professionals in Ghana." *Pastoral Psychology* 65(4) (May): 493–508.
Osaghae, Eghosa E. 1995. "The Ogoni Uprising: Oil Politics, Minority Agitation and the Future of the Nigerian State." *African Affairs* 94(376) (July): 325–344.
Osori, Ayisha. 2017. *Love Does Not Win Elections.* Lagos: Narrative Landscape Press.

Ostrom, Elinor. 1996. "Crossing the Great Divide: Coproduction, Synergy, and Development." *World Development* 24(6) (June): 1073–1087.

Otsuka, Keijiro, and Rie Muraoka. 2017. "A Green Revolution for Sub-Saharan Africa: Past Failures and Future Prospects." *Journal of African Economies* 26(1) (August): 73–98.

Ottenheimer, Martin. 1996. *Forbidden Relatives: The American Myth of Cousin Marriage.* Urbana: University of Illinois Press.

Ouma, Shem Alfred, Teresa Maureen Odongo, and Maureen Were. 2017. "Mobile Financial Services and Financial Inclusion: Is It a Boon for Savings Mobilization?" *Review of Development Finance* 7(1) (June): 29–35.

Oyejide, Ademola, Ibrahim Elbadawi, and Paul Collier (eds.). 1997. *Regional Integration and Trade Liberalization in Sub-Saharan Africa.* New York: St. Martin's Press.

Oyewumi, Oyeronke. 1997. *The Invention of Women: Making an African Sense of Western Gender Discourses.* Minneapolis: University of Minnesota Press.

———. 2004. "Conceptualising Gender: Eurocentric Foundations of Feminist Concepts and the Challenge of African Epistemologies." In Signe Arnfred, Bibi Bakare-Yusuf, and Edward Waswa Kisiang'ani (eds.), *African Gender Scholarship: Concepts, Methodologies, and Paradigms.* Dakar: CODESRIA, 1–8.

Ozkan, Mehmet. 2014. "A Post-2014 Vision for Turkey-Africa Relations." *Insight Turkey* 16(4) (Fall): 23–31.

———. 2016. "Turkey's Political-Economic Engagement with Africa." In Justin van der Merwe, Ian Taylor, and Alexandra Arkhangelskaya (eds.), *Emerging Powers in Africa: A New Wave in the Relationship?* Basingstoke: Palgrave Macmillan, 217–231.

Ozo, Andrew O. 2009. "Urban Change and Conflict in the Traditional Character of an African City: The Example of Benin City, Nigeria." *Planning Perspectives* 24(4) (December): 485–507.

Padfield, R. 2011. "Neoliberalism and the Polarizing Water Geographies of the Zambian Copperbelt." *Waterlines* 30(2) (April): 150–164.

Page, John, and Finn Tarp (eds.). 2017. *The Practice of Industrial Policy: Government-Business Coordination in Africa and East Asia.* Oxford: Oxford University Press.

Paller, Jeffrey W. 2014. "Informal Institutions and Personal Rule in Urban Ghana." *African Studies Review* 57(3) (December): 123–142.

———. 2017. "The Contentious Politics of African Urbanization." *Current History* 116(790): 163–169.

———. 2019. *Democracy in Ghana: Everyday Politics in Urban Africa.* New York: Cambridge University Press.

Parker, Glynis. 2009. "The Conversion of South Africans to Buddhism." PhD diss., University of South Africa, Pretoria.

Parker, John, and Richard Rathbone. 2007. *African History: A Very Short Introduction.* Oxford: Oxford University Press.

Parker, Ron. 1991. "The Senegal-Mauritania Conflict of 1989—a Fragile Equilibrium." *Journal of Modern African Studies* 29(1) (March): 155–171.

Parker, Susan W., and Petra E. Todd. 2017. "Conditional Cash Transfers: The Case of Progresa/Oportunidades." *Journal of Economic Literature* 55(3) (September): 866–915.

Parkhurst, Justin, and Madhulika Vulimiri. 2013. "Cervical Cancer and the Global Health Agenda: Insights from Multiple Policy-Analysis Frameworks." *Global Public Health* 8(10) (November): 1093–1108.

Parnell, Susan, and David Simon. 2014. *National Urbanisation and Urban Strategies: Necessary but Absent Policy Instruments in Africa.* Claremont: UCT Press.

Parnell, Susan, and Ruwani Walawege. 2011. "Sub-Saharan African Urbanisation and Global Environmental Change." *Global Environmental Change* 21(Suppl. 1) (December): S12–S20.

Parpart, Jane. 1988. "Women and the State in Africa." In Donald Rothchild and Naomi Chazan (eds.), *The Precarious Balance: State and Society in Africa.* Boulder: Westview Press.

Parrinder, Geoffrey. 1969. *Religion in Africa.* New York: Praeger.

Paszat, Emma. Forthcoming. "Sexuality Politics, Scientific Manipulation, and the Anti-Homosexuality Act, 2014." *Sexualities.*

Patel, V., S. Saxena, C. Lund, G. Thornicroft, F. Baingana, P. Bolton, et al. 2018. "The *Lancet* Commission on Global Mental Health and Sustainable Development." *Lancet* 392(10157) (October): 1553–1598.

Patman, Robert G. 1990. *The Soviet Union and the Horn of Africa: The Diplomacy of Intervention and Disengagement.* Cambridge: Cambridge University Press.

Patterson, Amy S. 2006. *The Politics of AIDS in Africa.* Boulder: Lynne Rienner.

———. 2011. *The Church and AIDS in Africa: The Politics of Ambiguity.* Boulder: FirstForum Press.

———. 2018. *Africa and Global Health Governance: Domestic Politics and International Structures.* Baltimore: Johns Hopkins University Press.

———. 2019. "Carework as Citizenship During Liberia's Ebola Outbreak and Zambia's AIDS Crisis." *Africa Today* 66(2) (Winter): 28–54.

———. 2020. "The Coronavirus Is About to Hit Africa. Here Are the Big Challenges." *Washington Post*, February 18. https://www.washingtonpost.com/politics/2020/02/18/coronavirus-is-about-hit-africa-here-are-big-challenges/.

Patterson, Amy S., and Elizabeth Gill. 2019. "Up in Smoke? Global Tobacco Control Advocacy and Local Mobilization in Africa." *International Affairs* 95(5) (September): 1111–1130.

Pazzanita, Anthony G. 1992. "Mauritania's Foreign Policy: The Search for Protection." *Journal of Modern African Studies* 30(2) (June): 281–304.

Penvenne, Jeanne Marie. 2003. "Special Issue: Colonial Encounters Between Africa and Portugal: An Introduction." *International Journal of African Historical Studies* 36(1): 1–6.

Perkins, Kenneth. 2014. *A History of Modern Tunisia.* Cambridge: Cambridge University Press.

Peters, Joel. 1992. *Israel and Africa: The Problematic Relationship.* New York: St. Martin's Press.

Peters, Wolff-Christian. 2010. *The Quest for an African Economic Community: Regional Integration and Its Role in Achieving African Unity—the Case of SADC* 591. Hamburg: Peter Lang.

Pew Forum. 2010. "Tolerance and Tension: Islam and Christianity in Sub-Saharan Africa." Pew Forum on Religion and Public Life, April 15. https://www.pewforum.org/2010/04/15/executive-summary-islam-and-christianity-in-sub-saharan-africa/.

Pfister, Roger. 2003. "Gateway to International Victory: The Diplomacy of the African National Congress in Africa, 1960–1994." *Journal of Modern African Studies* 41(3) (March): 51–73.

Phiri, Isaac. 2001. *Proclaiming Political Pluralism: Churches and Political Transitions in Africa.* London: Praeger.

Pitcher, M. Anne, and Manuel P. Teodoro. 2018. "The Bureaucracy: Policy Implementation and Reform." In Nic Cheeseman (ed.), *Institutions and Democracy in Africa: How the Rules of the Game Shape Political Developments.* New York: Cambridge University Press, 160–188.

Plangger, Albert. 1988. "Human Rights: A Motive for Mission." In Carl F. Hallencreutz and Ambrose Moyo (eds.), *Church and State in Zimbabwe.* Gweru: Mambo, 441–459.

Porteous, Tom. 2008. *Britain in Africa.* London: Zed Books.

Posner, Daniel. 2005. *Institutions and Ethnic Politics in Africa.* Cambridge: Cambridge University Press.

Potholm, Christian P., and Richard A. Fredland (eds.). 1980. *Integration and Disintegration in East Africa.* Lanham: University Press of America.

Potts, Deborah. 2005. "Counter-Urbanization on the Zambian Copperbelt? Interpretations and Implications." *Urban Studies* 42(4) (April): 583–609.

———. "'Restoring Order'? Operation Murambatsvina and the Urban Crisis in Zimbabwe." *Journal of Southern African Studies* 32(2) (September): 273–291.

Powdermaker, Hortense. 1962. *Copper Town: Changing Africa, the Human Situation on the Rhodesian Copperbelt.* New York: Harper and Row.

Powell, Jonathan M., and Clayton L. Thyne. 2020. "Coups in the World, 1950–Present (dataset)" https://www.jonathanmpowell.com/coup-detat-dataset.html.

Prah, Mansah. 2007. *Ghana's Feminist Movement: Aspirations, Challenges, Achievements.* Accra: IDEG.

Prendergast, John. 1996. *Frontline Diplomacy: Humanitarian Aid and Conflict in Africa.* Boulder: Lynne Rienner.

Price-Smith, Andrew. 2009. *Contagion and Chaos: Disease, Ecology and National Security in the Era of Globalization.* Cambridge: MIT Press.

Prunier, Gerard. 2009. *Africa's World War: Congo, the Rwandan Genocide, and the Making of a Continental Catastrophe.* New York: Oxford University Press.

Quinn, Charlotte A., and Frederick Quinn. 2003. *Pride, Faith, and Fear: Islam in Sub-Saharan Africa*. New York: Oxford University Press.
Radelet, Steven. 2010. "Success Stories from "Emerging Africa." *Journal of Democracy* 21(4) (October): 87–101.
Raleigh, Clionadh. 2015. "Urban Violence Patterns Across African States." *International Studies Review* 17(1) (March): 90–106.
Raleigh, Clionadh, Andrew Linke, Håvard Hegre, and Joakim Karlsen. 2010. "Introducing ACLED—Armed Conflict Location and Event Data." *Journal of Peace Research* 47(5) (September): 651–660.
Ranger, Terence O. 1985. *Peasant Consciousness and Guerrilla War in Zimbabwe: A Comparative Study*. London: James Currey.
———. 1986. "Religious Movements and Politics in Sub-Saharan Africa." *African Studies Review* 29(2) (June): 1–70.
———. 2003. "Evangelical Christianity and Democracy in Africa: A Continental Comparison." *Journal of Religion in Africa* 33(1) (February): 112–117.
——— (ed.). 2008. *Evangelical Christianity and Democracy in Africa*. Oxford: Oxford University Press.
Rao, Rahul. 2015. "Re-membering Mwanga: Same-Sex Intimacy, Memory and Belonging in Postcolonial Uganda." *Journal of Eastern African Studies* 9(1): 1–19.
Ravenhill, John. 1993. "A Second Decade of Adjustment: Greater Complexity, Greater Uncertainty." In Thomas M. Callaghy and John Ravenhill (eds.), *Hemmed In: Response to Africa's Economic Decline*. New York: Columbia University Press, 18–53.
Rawlence, Ben. 2016. *City of Thorns: Nine Lives in the World's Largest Refugee Camp*. New York: Picador.
RBM (Roll Back Malaria) Partnership. 2019. "Overview." https://endmalaria.org/about-us/overview.
Reader, John. 1999. *Africa: A Biography of the Continent*. New York: Vintage Press.
———. 2011. *Missing Links: In Search of Human Origins*. New York: Penguin Press.
Reed, William Cyrus. 1992. "Directions in African International Relations." In Mark W. DeLancey (ed.), *Handbook of Political Science Research on Sub-Saharan Africa: Trends from the 1960s to the 1990s*. Westport, CT: Greenwood Press, 73–103.
Renders, Marleen. 2012. *Consider Somaliland: State-Building with Traditional Leaders and Institutions*. Leiden: Brill.
Reno, William. 1995. *Corruption and State Politics in Sierra Leone*. Cambridge: Cambridge University Press.
———. 1998. *Warlord Politics and African States*. Boulder: Lynne Rienner.
———. 2011. *Warfare in Independent Africa*. Cambridge: Cambridge University Press.
Resnick, Danielle. 2014. "Urban Governance and Service Delivery in African Cities: The Role of Politics and Policies." *Development Policy Review* 32(s1) (July): s3–s17.
Rice, Andrew. 2004. "Evangelicals v. Muslims in Africa: Enemy's Enemy." *New Republic*, August 9.
Richards, Paul. 2016. *Ebola: How a People's Science Helped End an Epidemic*. Chicago: Zed.
Riedl, Rachel Beatty. 2018. "Institutional Legacies: Understanding Multiparty Politics in Historical Perspective." In Nic Cheeseman (ed.), *Institutions and Democracy in Africa: How the Rules of the Game Shape Political Developments*. New York: Cambridge University Press, 41–60.
Riedl, Rachel Beatty, and Ndongo Samba Sylla. 2019. "Senegal's Vigorous but Constrained Election." *Journal of Democracy* 30(3) (July): 86–93.
Rights Monitoring. 2011. "Central Africa: Lord's Resistance Army Exploits State Weakness." Humanitarian News and Analysis, February 17. https://allafrica.com/stories/201102170172.html.
Riley, Emma. 2018. "Mobile Money and Risk Sharing Against Village Shocks." *Journal of Development Economics* 135 (November): 43–58.
Roberts, Andrew. 1976. *A History of Zambia*. New York: Africana Publishing.
Roberts, Brian H. 2014. *Managing Systems of Secondary Cities: Policy Responses in International Development*. Brussels: Cities Alliance.
Robinson, David. 2004. *Muslim Societies in African History*. Cambridge: Cambridge University Press.

Robinson, James M. 1982. *The Nag Hammadi Library.* New York: Harper and Row.
Robinson, Pearl. 1994. "The National Conference Phenomenon in Francophone Africa." *Comparative Studies in Society and History* 36(3) (July): 575–610.
———. 2004. "Area Studies in Search of Africa." In David Szanton (ed.), *The Politics of Knowledge: Area Studies and the Disciplines*. University of California Press, 119–183.
Rodenburg, Jonne, Jean-Martial Johnson, Ibnou Dieng, Kalimuthu Senthilkumar, Elke Vandamme, Cyriaque Akakpo, Moundibaye Dastre Allarangaye, Idriss Baggie, Samuel Oladele Bakare, and Ralph Kwame Bam. 2019. "Status Quo of Chemical Weed Control in Rice in Sub-Saharan Africa." *Food Security* 11(1) (February): 69–92.
Rodney, Walter. 1972. *How Europe Underdeveloped Africa*. London: Bogle-L'Ouverture.
Rodriguez, S. M. 2018. *The Economies of Queer Inclusion: Transnational Organizing for LGBTI Rights in Uganda*. New York: Rowman and Littlefield.
———. 2016. "At the Juncture of Homonationalism and Homophobic Nationalism: Sexual Justice Organizing in Uganda and the Paradox of Transnational Advocacy." PhD diss., Stony Brook University, New York.
Rooney, David. 1988. *Kwame Nkrumah: The Political Kingdom in the Third World.* New York: St. Martin's Press.
Ross, Michael L. 2015. "What Have We Learned About the Resource Curse?" *Annual Review of Political Science* 18 (May): 239–259.
Rothchild, Donald. 1960. "On the Application of the Westminster Model to Ghana." *Centennial Review* 4(4) (Fall): 468–469.
Rothchild, Donald, and Naomi Chazan (eds.). 1988. *The Precarious Balance: State and Society in Africa.* Boulder: Westview Press.
Rushton, Simon. 2011. "Global Health Security: Security for Whom? Security from What?" *Political Studies* 59(4) (November): 779–796.
Ryan, Orla. 2011. *Chocolate Nations: Living and Dying for Cocoa in West Africa*. London: Zed.
Ryckmans, Pierre. 1955. "Belgian 'Colonialsm.'" *Foreign Affairs* 34(1) (October): 89–101.
Sachs, Jeffrey D., Richard Layard, and John F. Helliwell. 2019. *World Happiness Report 2019.* New York: Sustainable Development Solutions Network.
Sackeyfio-Lenoch, Naaborko. 2018. "Women's International Alliances in an Emergent Ghana." *Journal of West African History* 4(1) (Spring): 27–56.
Saitoti, Tepilit Ole. 1986. *The Worlds of a Maasai Warrior*. New York: Random House.
Salih, M. A. Mohamed (ed.). 2005. *African Parliaments: Between Governance and Government.* New York: Palgrave Macmillan.
Salim, C. 2010. "Municipal Solid Waste Management in Dar es Salaam City, Tanzania." *Waste Management* 30(7) (July): 1430–1431.
Samatar, A., M. Lindberg, and B. Mahayni. 2010. "The Dialectics of Piracy in Somalia: The Rich Versus the Poor." *Third World Quarterly* 31(8) (January): 1377–1394.
Sandbrook, Richard. 1985. *The Politics of Africa's Economic Stagnation.* Cambridge: Cambridge University Press.
———. 1993. *The Politics of Africa's Economic Recovery.* Cambridge: Cambridge University Press.
———. 1996. "Transitions Without Consolidation: Democratization in Six African Cases." *Third World Quarterly* 17(1) (March): 69–77.
Sangmpam, S. N. 2017. *Ethnicities and Tribes in Sub-Saharan Africa: Opening Old Wounds.* New York: Palgrave Macmillan.
Sangree, Walter H. 1980. "The Persistence of Polyandry in Irigwe, Nigeria." *Journal of Comparative Family Studies* 11(3) (Summer): 335–343.
Sankoh, Osman, Stephen Sevalie, and Mark Weston. 2018. "Mental Health in Africa." *Lancet* 6(9) (September): 954–955.
Sanneh, Lamin. 1983. *Christianity in West Africa: The Religious Impact.* Maryknoll: Orbis.
———. 1997. *The Crown and the Turban: Muslims and West African Pluralism.* Boulder: Westview Press.
Sanneh, Lamin O., and Joel A. Carpenter (eds.). 2005. *The Changing Face of Christianity: Africa, the West, and the World.* Oxford: Oxford University Press.
SARDC (Southern African Research and Documentation Centre). 1994. *State of the Environment in Southern Africa.* Harare: SARDC.

Sato, Makoto. 2005. "Japanese Aid Diplomacy in Africa: An Historical Analysis." *Ritsumeikan Annual Review of International Studies* 2: 67–85.
Schaffer, Frederic C. 2000. *Democracy in Translation: Understanding Politics in an Unfamiliar Culture*. New York: Cornell University Press.
Schierenbeck, Isabell, Peter Johansson, Lena Andersson, and Dalena van Rooyen. 2013. "Barriers to Accessing and Receiving Mental Health Care in Eastern Cape, South Africa." *Health and Human Rights* 15(2) (December): 110–123.
Schler, Lynn. 2008. *The Strangers of New Bell: Immigration, Public Space and Community in Colonial Douala, Cameroon, 1914–1960*. Pretoria: Unisa Press.
Schmidt, Elizabeth. 2005. "Top Down or Bottom Up? Nationalist Mobilization Reconsidered with Special Reference to Guinea (French West Africa)." *American Historical Review* 110(4) (October): 975–1014.
———. 2013. *Foreign Intervention in Africa: From the Cold War to the War on Terror*. New York: Cambridge University Press.
———. 2018. *Foreign Intervention in Africa After the Cold War: Sovereignty, Responsibility, and the War on Terror*. Athens: Athens University Press.
Schmitt, Eric, and Thomas Gibbons-Neff. 2020. "Russia Projects Increasing Influence in Africa, Worrying the West." *New York Times*, January 20, A9.
Schofield, Daniela, and Femke Gubbels. 2019. "Informing Notions of Climate Change Adaptation: A Case Study of Everyday Gendered Realities of Climate Change Adaptation in an Informal Settlement in Dar es Salaam." *Environment and Urbanization* 31(1) (April): 93–114.
Schraeder, Peter J. 1994a. "Bureaucratic Incrementalism, Crisis and Change in U.S. Foreign Policy Toward Africa." In Jerel A. Rosati, Joe D. Hagan, and Martin W. Sampson III (eds.), *Foreign Policy Restructuring: How Governments Respond to Global Change*. Columbia: University of South Carolina Press, 111–137.
———. 1994b. *United States Foreign Policy Toward Africa: Incrementalism, Crisis, and Change*. Cambridge: Cambridge University Press.
———. 1998. "The Clinton Administration and Africa (1993–1999)." *Issue: A Journal of Opinion* special issue 26(2).
———. 2000. "Cold War to Cold Peace: Explaining U.S.-French Tensions in Francophone Africa." *Political Science Quarterly* 115(3) (Autumn): 395–420.
———. 2001a. "'Forget the Rhetoric and Boost the Geopolitics': Emerging Trends in the Bush Administration's Policy Toward Africa, 2001." *African Affairs* 100(400) (July): 387–404.
———. 2001b. "South Africa's Foreign Policy: From International Pariah to Leader of the African Renaissance." *Round Table: Commonwealth Journal of International Affairs* 90(359): 229–243.
———. 2004a. "Politics and Economics of the Precolonial Independence Era (Before 1884)." In Peter J. Schraeder (ed.), *African Politics and Society: A Mosaic in Transformation*. Boston: Bedford/St. Martin's, 23–48.
———. 2004b. "Political and Economic Impacts of Colonialism (1884–1951)." In Peter J. Schraeder (ed.), *African Politics and Society: A Mosaic in Transformation*. Boston: Bedford/St. Martin's, 49–79.
———. 2004c. *African Politics and Society: A Mosaic in Transformation*. 2nd ed. Belmont: Wadsworth/Thomson Learning.
———. 2011a. "The Obama Administration's Engagements in Africa Within Historical Context: Great Expectations Versus Daunting Challenges." In Ton Dietz, Kjell Havnevik, Mayke Kaag, and Terje Oestigaard (eds.), *African Engagements: Africa Negotiating a Multipolar World*. Leiden: Brill, 300–326.
———. 2011b. "Traditional Conflict Medicine? Lessons for Putting Mali and Other African Countries on the Road to Peace." *Nordic Journal of African Studies* 20(2): 177–202.
———. 2012a. "Tunisia's Jasmine Revolution and the Arab Spring: Implications for International Intervention." *Orbis: A Journal of World Affairs* 56(4) (November): 662–674.
———. 2012b. "Tunisia's Jasmine Revolution, International Intervention, and Popular Sovereignty." *Whitehead Journal of Diplomacy and International Relations* 13(1) (Winter/Spring): 75–88.
———. 2016. "Rendering unto Caesar? State Regulation of Religion and the Role of Catholicism in Democratic Transitions and Consolidation in Predominantly Catholic Countries."

In Michael J. Schuck and John Crowley-Buck (eds.), *Democracy, Culture, Catholicism: Voices from Four Continents.* New York: Fordham University Press, 297–309.

———. 2018. "'Making America Great Again' Against the Backdrop of an 'Africa Rising'? The Trump Administration and Africa's Marginalization Within U.S. Foreign Policy." *Journal of Diplomacy and International Relations* 20(1) (Fall/Winter): 98–117.

———. 2020. "African Foreign Policy Dataset."

Schraeder, Peter J., with Nefertiti Gaye. 1997. "Senegal's Foreign Policy: Challenges of Democratization and Marginalization." *African Affairs* 96(385) (October): 485–508.

Schraeder, Peter J., and Hamadi Redissi. 2011. "The Upheavals in Egypt and Tunisia: Ben Ali's Fall." *Journal of Democracy* 22(3) (July): 5–19.

Schroeder, Richard. 1999. *Shady Practices: Agroforestry and Gender Politics in the Gambia.* Berkeley: University of California Press.

———. 2012. *Africa After Apartheid: South Africa, Race, and Nation in Tanzania.* Bloomington: Indiana University Press.

Schuck, Michael J., and John Crowley-Buck (eds.). 2016. *Democracy, Culture, Catholicism: Voices from Four Continents.* New York: Fordham University Press.

Schulz, Brigitte, and William Hansen. 1984. "Aid or Imperialism? West Germany in Sub-Saharan Africa." *Journal of Modern African Studies* 22(2) (June): 287–313.

Schumacher, Michael J., and Peter J. Schraeder. 2019. "The Evolving Impact of Violent Non-State Actors on North African Foreign Policies During the Arab Spring: Insurgent Groups, Terrorists, and Foreign Fighters." *Journal of North African Studies* 24(4) (July): 682–703.

Searcy, Dionne, and Matt Richtel. 2017. "Obesity Was Rising as Ghana Embraced Fast Food. Then Came KFC." *New York Times,* October 2. https://www.nytimes.com/2017/10/02/health/ghana-kfc-obesity.html.

Segal, Aaron. 1989. "Spain and Africa: The Continuing Problem of Ceuta and Melilla." In Colin Legum and Marion E. Doro (eds.), *Africa Contemporary Record: Annual Survey and Documents 1987–88.* New York: Africana, A71–A77.

Seibert, Gerhard, and Paulo Fagundes Visentini (eds.). 2019. *Brazil-Africa Relations: Historical Dimensions and Contemporary Engagements from the 1960s to the Present.* Rochester: James Currey.

Seidman, Ann, and Frederick Anang (eds.). 1992. *21st Century Africa: Towards a New Vision of Self-Sustainable Development.* Trenton: Africa World Press.

Shajalal, Mohon, Junfang Xu, Jun Jing, Madeleine King, Jie Zhang, Peicheng Wang, Jennifer Bouey, and Fend Cheng. 2017. "China's Engagement with Development Assistance for Health in Africa." *Global Health Research and Policy* 2(24) (August).

Shannon, Murtah. 2019a. "African Urban Development in a Post-Aid Era: The 'Dutch Approach' to Urban Restructuring in Beira City, Mozambique." *Built Environment* 44(4) (January): 397–419.

———. 2019b. "Who Controls the City in the Global Urban Era? Mapping the Dimensions of Urban Geopolitics in Beira City, Mozambique." *Land* 8(2) (February): 37.

Shannon, Murtah, Kei Otsuki, Annelies Zoomers, and Mayke Kaag. 2018. "Sustainable Urbanization on Occupied Land? The Politics of Infrastructure Development and Resettlement in Beira City, Mozambique." *Sustainability* 10(9) (September): 3123.

Shapiro, Warren (ed.). 2018. *Focality and Extension in Kinship: Essays in Memory of Harold W. Scheffler.* Canberra: ANU Press.

Sharma, Rajesh. 2018. "Health and Economic Growth: Evidence from Dynamic Panel Data of 143 Years." *PLoS ONE* 13(10) (October): e0204940.

Shaw, Timothy M. 1991. "Reformism, Revisionism, and Radicalism in African Political Economy During the 1990s." *Journal of Modern African Studies* 29(2) (June): 191–212.

Shaw, Timothy M., and Olajide Aluko (eds.). 1984. *The Political Economy of African Foreign Policy: Comparative Analysis.* New York: St. Martin's Press.

Shaw, Timothy M., and Catherine M. Newbury. 1979. "Dependence or Interdependence: Africa in the Global Political Economy." In Mark W. DeLancey (ed.), *Aspects of International Relations in Africa.* Bloomington: Indiana University Press, 39–89.

Sheldon, Kathleen. 2017. *African Women: Early History to the 21st Century.* Bloomington: Indiana University Press.

Sheppard, Eric, Vinay Gidwani, Michael Goldman, Helga Leitner, Ananya Roy, and Anant Maringanti. 2015. "Introduction: Urban Revolutions in the Age of Global Urbanism." *Urban Studies* 52(11) (August): 1947–1961.

Shiffman, Jeremy, David Berlan, and Tamara Hafner. 2009. "Has Aid for AIDS Raised All Health Funding Boats?" *JAIDS* 52(Suppl. 1) (November): S45–S48.

Shillington, Kevin. 2019. *History of Africa.* 4th ed. New York: Red Globe Press.

Shimoni, Gideon. 2003. *Community and Conscience: The Jews in Apartheid South Africa.* South Africa: Brandeis University Press.

Shinn, David H. 2005. "Islam and Conflict in the Horn of Africa." Africa News Service, January 21.

Shinn, Jamie. 2014. "The Rhetoric and Reality of Community Empowerment in Coastal Conservation: A Case Study from Menai Bay Conservation Area, Tanzania." *African Geographical Review* 34(2): 107–124.

Shostak, Marjorie. 1981. *Nisa, the Life and Words of a !Kung Woman.* Cambridge: Harvard University Press.

———, Estate of. 2000. *Return to Nisa.* Cambridge: Harvard University Press.

Shubin, Vladimir. 2004. "Russia and Africa: Moving in the Right Direction?" In Ian Taylor and Paul Williams (eds.), *Africa in International Politics.* London: Routledge, 102–115.

Sidaway, James D. 1993. "Urban and Regional Planning and Patterns of Uneven Development in Post-independence Mozambique: An Overview." In *Collected Seminar Papers. Institute of Commonwealth Studies* 45(1993): 138–160.

Sidibe, Boubacar (dir.). 2004. *Dou, la famille* [film]. Bamako: ORTM.

Silver, Jon. 2019. "Suffocating Cities: Climate Change as Socio-Ecological Violence." In H. Ernstson and E. Swyngedouw (eds.), *Urban Political Ecology in the Anthropo-Obscene: Interruptions and Possibilities.* New York: Routledge, 129–147.

Simon, D., and H. Leck. 2014. "Urban Dynamics and the Challenges of Global Environmental Change in the South." In S. Parnell and S. Oldfield (eds.), *The Routledge Handbook on Cities of the Global South.* London: Routledge, 613–628.

Simon, David J. 2005. "Democracy Unrealized: Zambia's Third Republic Under Frederick Chiluba." In Leonardo A. Villalón and Peter VonDoepp (eds.), *The Fate of Africa's Democratic Experiments: Elites and Institutions.* Bloomington: Indiana University Press, 199–220.

Simon, Reeva S., Michael M. Laskier, and Sara Reguer (eds.). 2003. *The Jews of the Middle East and North Africa in Modern Times.* New York: Columbia University Press.

Simone, Abdoumaliq. 2010. *City Life from Jakarta to Dakar: Movements at the Crossroads.* New York: Routledge.

Simpson, Joshua P. 2018. "Do Donors Matter Most? An Analysis of Conditional Cash Transfer Adoption in Sub-Saharan Africa." *Global Social Policy* 18(2) (August): 143–168.

Sims, David. 2010. *Understanding Cairo: The Logic of a City Out of Control.* Cairo: American University in Cairo Press.

Skovdal, Morten, Catherine Campbell, Claudius Madanhire, Zivai Mupambireyi, Constance Nyamukapa, and Simon Gregson. 2011. "Masculinity as a Barrier to Men's Use of HIV Services in Zimbabwe." *Globalization and Health* 7(13) (May): 13.

Smith, Robert S. 1976. *Warfare and Diplomacy in Precolonial West Africa.* 2nd ed. Madison: University of Wisconsin Press.

SMUG (Sexual Minorities Uganda). 2014. "Expanded Criminalisation of Homosexuality in Uganda: A Flawed Narrative: Empirical Evidence and Strategic Alternatives from an African Perspective." https://sexualminoritiesuganda.com/wp-content/uploads/2015/07/SMUG-alternative-to-criminalisation.pdf.

Snow, Philip. 1988. *The Star Raft: China's Encounter with Africa.* New York: Weidenfeld and Nicolson.

Sonobe, Tetsushi. 2016. "Emergence and Subsequent Development of Garment Clusters in Bangladesh and Tanzania." In Tomoko Hashino and Keijiro Otsuka (eds.), *Industrial Districts in History and the Developing World.* New York: Springer, 61–79.

Sonobe, Tetsushi, Keijiro Otsuka, and Tomoko Hashino. 2016. "Toward a New Paradigm of the Long-Term Development of Industrial Districts." In Tomoko Hashino and Keijiro Otsuka (eds.), *Industrial Districts in History and the Developing World.* New York: Springer, 13–21.

Southall, Aidan W. 1997. "The Illusion of Tribe." In Roy Richard Grinker and Christopher Burghard (eds.), *Perspectives on Africa*. Steiner. Oxford: Blackwell, 83–94.
Southall, Roger, and Henning Melber (eds.). 2009. *A New Scramble for Africa? Imperialism, Investment and Development.* Scottsville: University of KwaZulu-Natal Press.
Sow, Ousmane (dir.). 2007. *Le Grin*. Bamako: Centre National de Cinématographie.
Standish. Reid. 2019. "Putin Has a Dream of Africa." *Foreign Policy*. https://foreignpolicy.com/2019/10/25/russia-africa-development-soviet-union/
Stanford Medicine News Center. 2016. "Promoting Abstinence, Fidelity for HIV Prevention Is Ineffective." May 2. https://med.stanford.edu/news/all-news/2016/05/promoting-abstinence-fidelity-for-hiv-prevention-is-ineffective.htm.
Staudt, Kathleen. 1987. "Women's Politics, the State and Capitalist Transformation in Africa." In Irving Markovitz (ed.), *Studies in Class and Power in Africa*. New York: Oxford University Press, 193–208.
Steady, Filomina. 2006. *Women and Collective Action in Africa*. New York: Palgrave Macmillan.
Steel, Griet, Femke Van Noorloos, and Kei Otsuki. 2019. "Urban Land Grabs in Africa?" *Built Environment* 44(4) (February): 389–396.
Steinert, Janina I., Juliane Zenker, Ute Filipiak, Ani Movsisyan, Lucie D. Cluver and Yulia Shenderovich. 2018. "Do Saving Promotion Interventions Increase Household Savings, Consumption, and Investments in Sub-Saharan Africa? A Systematic Review and Meta-Analysis." *World Development* 104 (April): 238–256.
Stepan, Alfred. 1986. "Paths Toward Redemocratization: Theoretical and Comparative Considerations." In Guillermo O'Donnell, Phillippe Schmitter, and Laurence Whitehead (eds.), *Transitions from Authoritarian Rule.* Baltimore: Johns Hopkins University Press, 64–84.
Stifel, David, Bart Minten, and Bethlehem Koru. 2016. "Economic Benefits of Rural Feeder Roads: Evidence from Ethiopia." *Journal of Development Studies* 52(9): 1335–1356.
Stillwaggon, Eileen. 2006. *AIDS and the Ecology of Poverty*. New York: Oxford.
Stokke, Olav (ed.). 1989. *Western Middle Powers and Global Poverty: The Determinants of the Aid Policies of Canada, Denmark, the Netherlands, Norway and Sweden.* Uppsala: Scandinavian Institute of African Studies (in cooperation with the Norwegian Institute of International Affairs).
Storeng, Katerini. 2014. "The GAVI Alliance and the 'Gates Approach' to Health System Strengthening." *Global Public Health* 9(8) (August): 865–879.
Storm, Lise. 2013. *Party Politics and the Prospects for Democracy in North Africa.* Boulder: Lynne Rienner.
Strahler, Arthur N., and Alan H. Strahler. 2005. *Physical Geography: Science and Systems of the Human Environment.* Hoboken: John Wiley and Sons.
Straus, Scott. 2012. "Wars Do End! Changing Patterns of Political Violence in Sub-Saharan Africa." *African Affairs* 111(443) (April): 179–201.
Stremlau, John J. 1977. *The International Politics of the Nigerian Civil War, 1967–1970.* Princeton: Princeton University Press.
Styan, David. 1996. "Does Britain Have an Africa Policy?" In CEAN (ed.), *L'Afrique Politique.* Paris: Karthala and CEAN, 261–286.
Sundkler, Bengt, and Christopher Steed. 2000. *A History of the Church in Africa*. Cambridge: Cambridge University Press.
Suret-Canale, Jean. 1964. *Afrique Noire: L'Ere coloniale*, 1900–1945. Paris: Editions Sociales.
———. 1975. *Difficultés du néo-colonialisme français en Afrique tropicale.* Paris: Centre d'Etudes et de Recherches Marxistes.
Svolik, Milan W. 2012. *The Politics of Authoritarian Rule.* New York: Cambridge University Press.
Sweetman, David. 1993. *Mary Renault: A Biography.* London: Chatto and Windus.
Switzer, Heather. 2018. *When the Light Is Fire: Maasai Schoolgirls in Contemporary Kenya.* Champaign: University of Illinois Press.
Swyngedouw, Erik, and Henrik Ernstson. 2019. "O Tempora! O Mores! Interrupting the Anthropo-Obscene." In H. Ernstson and E. Swyngedouw (eds.), *Urban Political Ecology in the Anthropo-Obscene: Interruptions and Possibilities*. New York: Routledge, 25–47.
Sylla, Lanciné. 1977. *Tribalisme et Parti Unique en Afrique Noire*. Paris: Presses de la Foundation Nationale des Science Politiques.

Szanton, David L. (ed.). 2004. *The Politics of Knowledge: Area Studies and the Disciplines*. Berkeley: University of California Press.
Tadesse, Million A., Bekele A. Shiferaw, and Olaf Erenstein. 2015. "Weather Index Insurance for Managing Drought Risk in Smallholder Agriculture: Lessons and Policy Implications for Sub-Saharan Africa." *Agricultural and Food Economics* 3(1) (November): 1–21.
Tamale, S. 2007. "Out of the Closet: Unveiling Sexuality Discourses in Uganda." In C. M. Cole, T. Manuh, and S. F. Miescher (eds.), *Africa After Gender*. Bloomington: Indiana University Press, 17–29.
———. 2007. "Out of the Closet: Unveiling Sexuality Discourses in Uganda." In C. M. Cole, T. Manuh, and S. F. Miescher (eds.), *Africa After Gender*. Bloomington: Indiana University Press, 17–29.
———. 1999. *When Hens Begin to Crow: Gender and Parliamentary Politics in Uganda*. Boulder: Westview Press.
Tamari, Tal. 1997. *Les Castes de l'Afrique Occidentale: Artisans et Musiciens Endogames*. Paris/Nanterre: Societe d'Ethnologie.
Tang Abomo, Paul. 2019. *R2P and the U.S. Intervention in Libya*. London: Palgrave Macmillan.
Tarrósy, István. 2016. "Indonesian Engagements with Africa and the Revitalised 'Spirit of Bandung.'" In Justin van der Merwe, Ian Taylor, and Alexandra Arkhangelskaya (eds.), *Emerging Powers in Africa: A New Wave in the Relationship?* Basingstoke, UK: Palgrave Macmillan, 233–247.
Taylor, Ian. 2002. "Taiwan's Foreign Policy and Africa: The Limitations of Dollar Diplomacy." *Journal of Contemporary China* 11(30): 125–140.
———. 2012. "India's Rise in Africa." *International Affairs* 88(4) (July): 779–798.
———. 2006. *China and Africa: Engagement and Compromise*. London: Routledge.
TBFacts.org. 2019. "TB in South Africa—Burden, Strategic Plan, Key Populations, TAC." https://www.tbfacts.org/tb-south-africa.
Temin, Jon, and Yoseph Badwaza. 2019. "Ethiopia's Quiet Revolution." *Journal of Democracy* 3(3) (July): 139–154.
Theron, Liesl, John McAllister, and Mariam Armisen. 2016. "Where Do We Go from Here? A Call for Critical Reflection on Queer/LGBTIA+ Activism in Africa." *Pambazuka*, May 12. https://bit.ly/2KcMmXy accessed July 2019.
Thom, William G. 1984. "The Sub-Saharan Africa's Changing Military Environment." *Armed Forces and Society* 11(1) (Fall): 34–38.
———. 2010. *African Wars: A Defense Intelligence Perspective*. Calgary: University of Calgary Press.
Thomas, Charles G., and Toyin Falola. 2020. *Secession and Separatist Conflicts in Postcolonial Africa*. Calgary: University of Calgary Press.
Thomas, Lynn L. 1980. "Crow-Type Skewing in Akan Kinship Vocabulary and Its Absence in Minangkabau." *American Ethnologist* 7(3) (August): 549–566.
Thoreson, R. R. 2014. "Troubling the Waters of a 'Wave of Homophobia': Political Economies of Anti-Queer Animus in Sub-Saharan Africa," *Sexualities* 17(1–2) (February): 23–42.
Thornton, John. 1998. *African and Africans in the Making of the Atlantic World, 1400–1880*. 2nd ed. Cambridge: Cambridge University Press.
Thurston, Alexander. 2018. *Boko Haram: The History of an African Jihadist Movement*. Princeton: Princeton University Press.
Torero, Maximo, and Shyamal Chowdhury. 2005. *Increasing Access to Infrastructure for Africa's Rural Poor*. Washington, DC: International Food Policy Research Institute.
Touval, Saadi. 1963. *Somali Nationalism: International Politics and the Drive for Unity in the Horn*. Cambridge: Harvard University Press.
Trimingham, J. S. 1962. *A History of Islam in West Africa*. London: Oxford University Press.
Tripp, Aili Mari. 2001a. "The Politics of Autonomy and Co-optation in Africa: The Ugandan Women's Movement." *Journal of Modern African Studies* 39(1) (March): 101–128.
———. 2001b. "Women and Democracy: The New Political Activism in Africa." *Journal of Democracy* 12(3) (July): 141–155.
———. 2015. *Women and Power in Postconflict Africa*. Cambridge: Cambridge University Press.
Tripp, Aili Mari, Isabel Casimiro, Joy Kwesiga, and Alice Mungwa. 2009. *African Women's Movements: Transforming Political Landscapes*. New York: Cambridge University Press.

Tripp, Aili Mari, and Alice Kang. 2008. "The Global Impact of Quotas: On the Fast Track to Increased Female Legislative Representation." *Comparative Political Studies* 41(3) (July): 338–361.

Trounstine, Jessica. 2016. "Segregation and Inequality in Public Goods." *American Journal of Political Science* 60(3) (July): 709–725.

Tsikata, Dzodzi. 2000. *Lip-Service and Peanuts: The State and National Machinery for Women in Africa*. Accra: Third World Network–Africa.

———. 2001. "National Machineries for the Advancement of Women in Africa: Are They Transforming Gender Relations?" Social Watch. http://www.socialwatch.org/sites/default/files/pdf/en/nationalmachineries2001_eng.pdf.

Turnbull, Colin (ed.). 1973. *Africa and Change*. New York: Alfred A. Knopf.

———. 1983. *The Mbuti Pygmies: Change and Adaptation*. New York: Holt, Rinehart and Winston.

Turshen, Meredeth, and Clotilde Twagiramariya (eds.). 1998. *What Women Do in Wartime: Gender and Conflict in Africa*. London: Zed Books.

Tusting, Lucy S., Donal Bisanzio, Graham Alabaster, and Ewan Cameron. 2019. "Mapping Changes in Housing in Sub-Saharan Africa from 2000 to 2015." *Nature* 568(7752) (March): 391–394.

Twesigye, Emmanuel K. 1987. *Common Ground: Christianity, African Religion and Philosophy*. New York: Peter Lang.

Uganda Ministry of Health. 2014. "Scientific Statement on Homosexuality." http://www.boxturtlebulletin.com/btb/wp-content/uploads/2014/02/UgandaScientificReportOnHomosexuality.pdf.

UN DESA (United Nations Department of Economics and Social Affairs). 2015. "World Urbanization Prospects: The 2014 Revision." New York: UN DESA. https://www.un.org/en/development/desa/publications/2014-revision-world-urbanization-prospects.html.

UN Habitat. 2014. *State of African Cities 2014: Re-Imagining Sustainable Urban Transitions*. Nairobi: UN Habitat.

UN News. 2019. "UN Committee Says Ebola in DR Congo Still an International Public Health Emergency." October 18. https://news.un.org/en/story/2019/10/1049611.

UNAIDS (Joint United Nations Programme on HIV and AIDS). 2018. "UNAIDS Data 2018." https://www.unaids.org/sites/default/files/media_asset/unaids-data-2018_en.pdf.

UNECA (UN Economic Commission for Africa). 1989. *Africa Alternative Framework to Structural Adjustment Programmes for Socio-Economic Recovery and Transformation (AAF-SAP)*. E/ECA/CM. 15/6/Rev.3. Addis Ababa: UNECA.

UNHCR (United Nations High Commissioner for Refugees). 2011. "Lord's Resistance Army Attacks Populated Areas of Northeastern Congo." United Nations Refugee Agency, March 1. https://www.unhcr.org/en-us/news/latest/2011/3/4d6d24e06/lords-resistance-army-attacks-populated-areas-north-eastern-congo.html.

UNICEF (United Nations Children's Fund). 2010. "Cases of Children Accused of 'Witchcraft' Rising in Parts of West and Central Africa." https://www.unicef.org/protection/nigeria_55301.html.

Urdang, Stephanie. 1975. "Fighting Two Colonialisms: The Women's Struggle in Guinea-Bissau." *African Studies Review* 18(3) (December): 29–34.

US Arms Control and Disarmament Agency. 1975. *World Military Expenditures and Arms Trade 1963–1973*. Washington, DC: US Government Printing Office.

US Bureau of the Census. 2010. International Data Base, International Programs Center. Washington, DC. www.census.gov/ipc/www/idb.

US Department of Commerce. 1997. "A Comprehensive Trade and Development Policy for the Countries of Africa." Report Submitted by the President of the United States to the Congress, February 18, 1997.

US Department of State. 2018. "PEPFAR Now Reaches Over 14 Million People Globally with Lifesaving HIV Treatment." News release, May 16. https://www.pepfar.gov/press/releases/282136.htm.

US EIA (US Energy Information Administration). 2019. "Petroleum and Other Liquids." www.eia.gov/dnav/pet/pet_move_impcus_a2_nus_ep00_im0_mbbl_m.htm.

USGS (US Geological Survey). 2018. "Minerals Yearbook." www.minerals.usgs.gov/minerals/pubs/myb.html.

Usher, Ann Danaiya. 2010. "Donors Lose Faith in Zambian Health Ministry." *Lancet* 376(9739) (August): 403–404.
Vaillant, Janet G. 1990. *Black, French, and African: A Life of Léopold Sédar Senghor*. Cambridge: Harvard University Press.
Van de Walle, Nicolas. 2001. *African Economies and the Politics of Permanent Crisis, 1979–1999*. Cambridge: Cambridge University Press.
Van Dijk, Rijk, Hansjörg Dilger, Marian Burchardt, and Thera Rasing (eds.). 2014. *Religion and AIDS Treatment in Africa: Saving Souls, Prolonging Lives*. Aldershot: Ashgate.
Van Ham, Carolien, and Staffan I. Lindberg. 2018. "Elections: The Power of Elections in Multiparty Africa." In Nic Cheeseman (ed.), *Institutions and Democracy in Africa: How the Rules of the Game Shape Political Developments*. New York: Cambridge University Press, 213–237.
Van Noorloos, Femke, and Marjan Kloosterboer. 2018. "Africa's New Cities: The Contested Future of Urbanisation." *Urban Studies* 55(6) (May): 1223–1241.
Van Rooyen, Carina, Ruth Stewart, and Thea De Wet. 2012. "The Impact of Microfinance in Sub-Saharan Africa: A Systematic Review of the Evidence." *World Development* 40(11) (November): 2249–2262.
Varadarajan, Latha. 2010. *The Domestic Abroad: Diasporas in International Relations*. New York: Oxford University Press.
Varin, Caroline, and Dauba Abubakar (eds.). 2017. *Violent Non-State Actors in Africa: Terrorists, Rebels and Warlords*. New York: Palgrave Macmillan.
Védrine, Hubert, and Dominique Moïsi. 2000. *Les Cartes de la France à l'heure de la mondialisation*. Paris: Fayard.
Venturi, Bernardo. 2018. "Africa and Italy's Relations After the Cold War." In Dawn Nagar and Charles Mutasa (eds.), *Africa and the World: Bilateral and Multilateral International Diplomacy*. Basingstoke, UK: Palgrave Macmillan, 169–188.
Verdon, Michel. 1982. "Where Have All Their Lineages Gone? Cattle and Descent Among the Nuer." *American Anthropologist* 84(3) (September): 566–579.
Vigo, D. V., V. Patel, A. Becker, D. Bloom, W. Yip, G. Raviola, S. Saxena, and A. Kleinman. 2019. "A Partnership for Transforming Mental Health Globally." *Lancet* 6(4) (April): 350–356.
Villalón, Leonardo A. 1995. *Islamic Society and State Power in Senegal: Disciples and Citizens in Fatick*. Cambridge: Cambridge University Press.
———. 2012. "Between Democracy and Militancy: Islam in Africa." *Current History* 111(745) (May): 187–193.
Villalón, Leonardo, and Phillip Huxtable (eds.). 1998. *The African State at a Critical Juncture*. Boulder: Lynne Rienner.
Villalón, Leonardo A., and Peter VonDoepp. 2005. "Elites, Institutions, and the Varied Trajectories of Africa's Third Wave Democracies." In Leonardo A. Villalón and Peter VonDoepp (eds.), *The Fate of Africa's Democratic Experiments: Elites and Institutions*. Bloomington: Indiana University Press, 1–26.
Vines, Alex. 2018. "To Brexit and Beyond: Africa and the United Kingdom." In Dawn Nagar and Charles Mutasa (eds.), *Africa and the World: Bilateral and Multilateral International Diplomacy*. Basingstoke: Palgrave Macmillan, 119–142.
Virk, Kudrat. 2018. "Africa and India: Riding the Tail of the Tiger?" In Dawn Nagar and Charles Mutasa (eds.), *Africa and the World: Bilateral and Multilateral International Diplomacy*. Basingstoke: Palgrave Macmillan, 245–268.
Vítková, M., V. Ettler, J. Hyks, T. Astrup, and B. Kríbek. 2011. "Leaching of Metals from Copper Smelter Flue Dust (Mufulira, Zambian Copperbelt)." *Applied Geochemistry* 26 (June): S263–S266.
Voll, John Obert. 1982. *Islam: Continuity and Change in the Modern World*. Boulder, CO: Westview Press.
Von Wallström, Jonny (dir.). 2016. *The Pearl of Africa* [film].
VonDoepp, Peter. 2018. "The Judiciary: Courts, Judges and the Rule of Law." In Nic Cheeseman (ed.), *Institutions and Democracy in Africa: How the Rules of the Game Shape Political Developments*. New York: Cambridge University Press, 304–326.

Wainaina, Binyavanga. 2005. "How to Write About Africa." *Granta*, May 2. https://bit.ly/2crD3Fr.

Wald, Patricia. 2008. *Contagious: Cultures, Carriers, and the Outbreak Narrative*. Durham: Duke University Press.

Wales, Joseph, Julia Tobias, Emmanuel Malangalila, Godfrey Swai, and Leni Wild. 2014. "Stock-Outs of Essential Medicines in Tanzania." London: ODI. https://www.odi.org/publications/8432-stock-outs-essential-medicines-tanzania-political-economy-approach-analysing-problems-and.

Walsh, Declan. 2020. "United Nations Effort to Limit Arms in Libya Is Flouted on All Sides." *New York Times*, February 3, A5.

Wamai, Richard, Brian J. Morris, Robert C. Bailey, Jeffrey D. Klausner, and Mackenzie N. Boedicker. 2015. "Male Circumcision for Protection Against HIV Infection in Sub-Saharan Africa: The Evidence in Favour Justifies the Implementation Now in Progress." *Global Public Health* 10(5–6) (January): 639–666.

Warner, Jason, and Timothy M. Shaw (eds.). 2018. *African Foreign Policies in International Institutions*. New York: Palgrave Macmillan.

Warner, K. E., and J. Mackay. 2006. "The Global Tobacco Disease Pandemic: Nature, Causes and Cures." *Global Public Health* 1(1) (August): 65–86.

Watson, Vanessa. 2014. "African Urban Fantasies: Dreams or Nightmares?" *Environment and Urbanization* 26(1) (April): 215–231.

Weigert, Stephen L. 1996. *Traditional Religion and Guerrilla Warfare in Modern Africa*. New York: St. Martin's Press.

Welch, Claude E., Jr. 1991. "The Organization of African Unity and the Promotion of Human Rights." *Journal of Modern African Studies* 29(4) (December): 535–555.

Whitaker, Beth Elise, and John F. Clark. 2018. *Africa's International Relations: Balancing Domestic & Global Interests*. Boulder: Lynne Rienner.

Whitehouse, Bruce. 2016. "Love, Materialism, and Consensual Marriage in Bamako, Mali." *Africa Todaca Today* 62(3) (March): 30–46.

———. 2017. "The Trouble with Monogamy: Companionate Marriage and Gendered Suspicions in Bamako, Mali." *Mande Studies* 19: 131–149.

Whitfield, Lindsey (ed.). 2009. *The Politics of Aid: African Strategies for Dealing with Donors*. New York: Oxford University Press.

WHO (World Health Organization). 1948. "Constitution of the World Health Organization." http://apps.who.int/gb/bd/PDF/bd48/basic-documents-48th-edition-en.pdf#page=7.

———. 2013a. "Global Action Plan for the Prevention and Control of Non-Communicable Disease 2013–2020." http://apps.who.int/iris/bitstream/10665/94384/1/9789241506236_eng.pdf?ua=1.

———. 2013b. "Mental Health Action Plan 2013–2020." https://apps.who.int/iris/bitstream/handle/10665/89966/9789241506021_eng.pdf?sequence=1.

———. 2014. "The Health of the People: What Works: The African Regional Health Report." https://apps.who.int/iris/bitstream/handle/10665/137377/9789290232612.pdf;jsessionid=A9C58416B58EF4248213B4470C3CD02A?sequence=4.

———. 2017. "Mental Health Atlas—2017 Country Profiles." https://www.who.int/mental_health/evidence/atlas/profiles-2017/en/.

———. 2018. Global Tuberculosis Report: Executive Summary 2018. https://www.who.int/tb/publications/global_report/GraphicExecutiveSummary.pdf?ua=1.

———. 2019a. "Ebola in the Democratic Republic of the Congo: Health Emergency Update." https://www.who.int/emergencies/diseases/ebola/drc-2019.

———. 2019b. "Global Health Observatory Data Repository." http://apps.who.int/gho/data/node.main.HWFGRP_0020?lang=en.

———. 2019c. "Universal Health Coverage." https://www.who.int/en/news-room/fact-sheets/detail/universal-health-coverage-(uhc).

———. 2019d. "World Health Statistics 2019: Monitoring Health for the SDGs." https://www.who.int/gho/publications/world_health_statistics/2019/en/.

———. 2020. "Coronavirus Disease 2019 (COVID-19). Situation Report." Press Release, March 27. https://www.who.int/docs/default-source/coronaviruse/situation-reports/20200327-sitrep-67-covid-19.pdf?sfvrsn=b65f68eb_4.

WHO (World Health Organization) AFRO. 2019. "Noncommunicable Diseases." https://www.afro.who.int/health-topics/noncommunicable-diseases.
Widner, Jennifer A. 1991. "The 1990 Elections in Côte d'Ivoire." *Issue: A Journal of Opinion* 20(1) (Winter): 31–40.
———. 1994. *Economic Change and Political Liberalization in Sub-Saharan Africa*. Baltimore: Johns Hopkins University Press.
———. 2005. "Africa's Democratization: A Work in Progress." *Current History* 104(682) (May): 216–221.
Wiley, Kathrine Ann. 2018. *Work, Social Status and Gender in Post-Slavery Mauritania*. Bloomington: Indiana University Press.
Wilkinson, Annie, and Melissa Leach. 2015. "Briefing: Ebola-Myths, Realities, and Structural Violence." *African Affairs* 114(454) (January): 136–148.
Williams, Paul. 2004. "Britain and Africa After the Cold War: Beyond Damage Limitation?" In Ian Taylor and Paul Williams (eds.), *Africa in International Politics*. London: Routledge, 41–60.
Williams, R. R. (dir). 2013. *God Loves Uganda*. Brooklyn: Full Credit Productions.
Wilson, Henry. 1994. *African Decolonization*. London: Edward Arnold.
Wing, Susanna D. 2008. *Constructing Democracy in Africa: Mali in Transition*. New York: Palgrave Macmillan.
———. 2013. "Mali: Politics of a Crisis." *African Affairs* 112(448) (July): 476–485.
Winrow, Gareth M. 1990. *The Foreign Policy of the GDR in Africa*. Cambridge: Cambridge University Press.
Wiseman, John A. 1977. "Multi-Partyism in Africa: The Case of Botswana." *African Affairs* 76(302) (January): 70–79.
World Bank. 1981. *Accelerated Development in Sub-Saharan Africa: An Agenda for Action*. Washington, DC: World Bank.
———. 1989. *Sub-Saharan Africa: From Crisis to Sustainable Growth: A Long-Term Perspective Study*. Washington, DC: World Bank.
———. 1993. *The East Asian Miracle: Economic Growth and Public Policy*. Washington, DC: World Bank.
———. 2011. "Tackling Poverty in Northern Ghana." http://documents.worldbank.org/curated/en/445681468030627288/Tackling-poverty-in-Northern-Ghana.
———. 2019. "West Africa's Coast: Losing Over $3.8 billion a Year to Erosion, Flooding, and Pollution." https://www.worldbank.org/en/region/afr/publication/west-africas-coast-losing-over-38-billion-a-year-to-erosion-flooding-and-pollution.
———. 2019. World Development Indicators. https://datacatalog.worldbank.org/dataset/world-development-indicators.
World in Data. 2019. "Life Expectancy." https://ourworldindata.org/life-expectancy.
Worrall, James. 2017. *International Institutions of the Middle East: The GCC, Arab League, and Arab Maghreb Union*. London: Routledge.
Wright, Stephen (ed.). 1998. *African Foreign Policies*. Boulder: Westview Press.
WSP International. 2005. *Rebuilding Somaliland: Issues and Possibilities*. Lawrenceville, NJ: Red Sea Press.
Wuaku, Albert Kafui. 2009. "Hinduizing from the Top, Indigenizing from Below: Localizing Krishna Rituals in Southern Ghana." *Journal of Religion in Africa* 39(4) (November): 403–428.
Wunsch, James S., and Dele Olowu. 1990. *The Failure of the Centralized State: Institutions and Self-Governance in Africa*. Boulder: Westview Press.
Xinfeng, Li. Translated by Shelly Bryant. 2017. *China in Africa: In Zheng He's Footsteps*. Cape Town: BestRed.
Xing, Li. 2016. "Conceptualising the Dialectics of China's Presence in Africa." In Justin van der Merwe, Ian Taylor, and Alexandra Arkhangelskaya (eds.), *Emerging Powers in Africa: A New Wave in the Relationship?* Basingstoke: Palgrave Macmillan, 77–106.
Xuetong, Yan. 1988. "Sino-African Relations in the 1990s." *CSIS Africa Notes* 84 (April): 1–5.
Yalew, Amsalu, Georg Hirte, Hermann Lotze-Campen, and Stefan Tscharaktschiew. 2018. "Climate Change, Agriculture, and Economic Development in Ethiopia." *Sustainability* 10(10) (October): 3464.

Yasmin, Seema. 2016. "The Ebola Rape Epidemic No One's Talking About." *Foreign Policy*, February 2. https://foreignpolicy.com/2016/02/02/the-ebola-rape-epidemic-west-africa-teenage-pregnancy/.
Yates, Douglas A. 2018. "France and Africa." In Dawn Nagar and Charles Mutasa (eds.), *Africa and the World: Bilateral and Multilateral International Diplomacy*. Basingstoke, UK: Palgrave Macmillan, 95–118.
Youde, Jeremy. 2012. *Global Health Governance*. Malden: Polity.
Young, Crawford. 1965. *Politics in the Congo: Decolonization and Independence*. Princeton: Princeton University Press.
———. 1994. *The African Colonial State in Comparative Perspective*. New Haven: Yale University Press.
Young, Crawford, and Thomas Turner. 1985. *The Rise and Decline of the Zairian State*. Madison: University of Wisconsin Press.
———. 1989. *The Rise and Decline of the Zairian State*. Madison: University of Wisconsin Press.
Young, John. 1998. "The Tigray People's Liberation Front." In Christopher Clapham (ed.), *African Guerrillas*. Bloomington: Indiana University Press, 36–52.
Yourish, Karen, Derek Watkins, and Tom Giratikanon. 2016. "Where ISIS Has Directed and Inspired Attacks Around the World." *New York Times*, March 22. https://www.nytimes.com/interactive/2015/06/17/world/middleeast/map-isis-attacks-around-the-world.html.
Zaffiro, James J. 1989. "The Press and Political Opposition in an African Democracy: The Case of Botswana." *Journal of Commonwealth and Comparative Politics* 27(1): 51–73.
Zagheni, Emilio. 2011. "The Impact of the HIV/AIDS Epidemic on Kinship Resources for Orphans in Zimbabwe." *Population and Development Review* 37(4) (December): 761–783.
Zakaria, Rafiq. 1988. *The Struggle Within Islam*. London: Penguin.
Zartman, I. William. 1976. "Europe and Africa: Decolonization or Dependency?" *Foreign Affairs* 54 (January): 325–343.
———. 1985. *Ripe for Resolution: Conflict and Intervention in Africa*. New York: Oxford University Press.
——— (ed.). 1995a. *Collapsed States: The Disintegration and Restoration of Legitimate Authority*. Boulder: Lynne Rienner.
———. 1995b. "Inter-African Negotiation." In John W. Harbeson and Donald Rothchild (eds.), *Africa in World Politics: Post–Cold War Challenges*. Boulder: Westview Press, 209–233.
Zoomers, Annelies, Femke van Noorloos, Kei Otsuki, Griet Steel, and Guus Van Westen. 2017. "The Rush for Land in an Urbanizing World: From Land Grabbing Toward Developing Safe, Resilient, and Sustainable Cities and Landscapes." *World Development* 92 (April): 242–252.
Zouhali-Worrall, Malika, and Katherine Fairfax Wright (dirs.). 2012. *Call Me Kuchu* [film]. Los Angeles: Cinedigm Entertainment Group.

The Contributors

Gretchen Bauer is professor in the Department of Political Science and International Relations at the University of Delaware.

Kirstie Lynn Dobbs is a full-time lecturer in the Department of Political Science and Public Policy at Merrimack College.

Marc Epprecht is professor in the Department of Global Development Studies at Queen's University, Canada.

Adam Hii served in the Peace Corps in Botswana and is currently a PhD candidate in the Department of Political Science at Loyola University Chicago.

Barbara G. Hoffman is professor and director of anthropology in the Department of Criminology, Anthropology, and Sociology at Cleveland State University.

Michael Kevane is associate professor in the Department of Economics in the Leavey School of Business at Santa Clara University.

Ambrose Moyo is professor emeritus in the Department of Religious Studies, Classics and Philosophy at the University of Zimbabwe and is currently the executive director of the Ecumenical Church Leaders Forum in Zimbabwe.

Garth A. Myers is professor of urban international studies at Trinity College.

Jeffrey W. Neff is professor emeritus in the Department of Geosciences and Natural Resources Management at Western Carolina University

S. N. Nyeck is a visiting scholar with the Vulnerability and the Human Condition Initiative of the School of Law at Emory University and a research associate with Critical Studies in Higher Education Transformation at Nelson Mandela University in South Africa.

Thomas O'Toole is professor emeritus in the Department of Sociology and Anthropology at St. Cloud State University in Minnesota.

Jeffrey W. Paller is assistant professor in the Department of Politics at the University of San Francisco.

Amy S. Patterson is professor in the Department of Politics at the University of the South.

S. M. Rodriguez is assistant professor in the Department of Sociology at Hofstra University.

Peter J. Schraeder is professor of political science and dean of the College of Arts and Sciences at Loyola University Chicago.

Index

About the Book

The sixth edition of *Understanding Contemporary Africa,* and the first under the editorship of Peter J. Schraeder, combines the historic strengths of the previous editions with coverage of new topics suggested over the years by the many instructors who regularly assign the text in their classes.

Entirely new chapters on the politics of public health, the changing roles of women, LGBTIQ rights, environmental challenges, and population and urbanization, along with new treatments of such classic topics as geography, history, politics, economics, international relations, and more, make for an unparalleled introduction to the complexities of Africa today.

Peter J. Schraeder is professor of political science and dean of the College of Arts and Sciences at Loyola University Chicago.